The Foundations of Communication in CRIMINAL JUSTICE SYSTEMS

The Foundations of Communication in CRIMINAL JUSTICE SYSTEMS

Daniel Adrian Doss
University of West Alabama, Livingston, USA

William H. Glover
Belhaven University

Rebecca A. Goza
University of Central Oklahoma, Edmond, USA

Michael Wigginton, Jr.
University of Mississippi, University, USA

CRC Press
Taylor & Francis Group
Boca Raton London New York

CRC Press is an imprint of the
Taylor & Francis Group, an **informa** business

CRC Press
Taylor & Francis Group
6000 Broken Sound Parkway NW, Suite 300
Boca Raton, FL 33487-2742

First issued in paperback 2020

ISBN-13: 978-1-4822-3657-6 (hbk)
ISBN-13: 978-0-367-66918-8 (pbk)

Library of Congress Cataloging-in-Publication Data

Doss, Daniel Adrian.
The foundations of communication in criminal justice systems / Daniel Adrian Doss, William H. Glover, Jr., Rebecca A. Goza, Michael Wigginton, Jr.
pages cm
Includes bibliographical references and index.
ISBN 978-1-4822-3657-6 (hardcover : alk. paper) 1. Communication in law enforcement. 2. Criminal justice, Administration of. I. Title.

HV7936.C79.D67 2015
364.01'4--dc23 2014033365

Visit the Taylor & Francis Web site at
http://www.taylorandfrancis.com

and the CRC Press Web site at
http://www.crcpress.com

Contents

Preface

The combination of occasional insomnia and late-night movies may lead to the writing of books. During a sleepless night, I experienced a television showing of *Cool Hand Luke* (Internet Movie Database, 1967) during the wee hours. Among this movie's most memorable lines are, "What we've got here is failure to communicate. Some men, you just can't reach. So, you get what we had here last week, which is the way he wants it. Well, he gets it. I don't like it any more than you men" (Internet Movie Database, 1967). This portion of movie script spurred me to search meticulously for law enforcement or criminal justice textbooks that were authored from the perspective of communication. I located relatively few, reviewed their contents, and believed some colleagues and I could offer a new approach regarding the subject matter. The sandman's absence sparked a moment of inspiration that resulted in the crafting of a book outline.

Nearly a year later, after having finished a draft manuscript of this book, I once again found myself awake during the wee hours because of discomforts resulting from hernia surgery and the necessity of proofreading chapters. I again had the joys of late-night television while waiting for the pills from my trusty bottles of Demerol and Phenergan to blissfully quash the pain and soreness, and vastly modify my proofreading abilities. A Clint Eastwood movie marathon was on the tube that night.

Within the movie *Dirty Harry* (Internet Movie Database, 1971), one scene involved Eastwood communicating with a subdued perpetrator, and framing his situation rather directly. Specifically, Eastwood stated, "I know what you're thinking, punk. You're thinking 'Did he fire six shots or only five?' Now, to tell you the truth, I forgot myself in all this excitement. But, being this is a .44 Magnum, the most powerful handgun in the world and will blow your head clean off, you've gotta ask yourself a question: 'Do I feel lucky?' Well, do ya, punk?" (Internet Movie Database, 1971) Although fictitious, such a scene provides some important lessons regarding communication—it is often oral, quick, precise, to the point, and involves a sound, mutual understanding of the intended and inferred messages that are exchanged between senders and receivers. Human memory is imperfect. Therefore, people may be unable to recall completely and communicate accurately the details of an event. Communication also often involves the expressing of statements and the posing of questions that require varying amounts of thoughtfulness.

In reality, law enforcement officers and the personnel within the justice system often encounter various impediments that affect their ability to communicate with others. When law enforcement officers encounter members of the general public, some people may be mute, deaf, blind, or unable to speak English. Other medical conditions may also impede communicating effectively and efficiently. Members of the general public may offer different accounts of a mutually observed event (e.g., an automobile accident, act of crime, or domestic incident), thereby necessitating discretion, investigation, and wariness by the interviewing law enforcement officer. Malfunctioning technologies, such as radios, cellular telephones, and so forth, may also impair the ability to communicate. Therefore, when communicating with the members of society, law enforcement officers and personnel within the justice domain often encounter circumstances that diminish the ability to communicate efficiently and effectively.

Other considerations of communicating are as follows:

- Communicating is approximately 93% nonverbal (CUPW/UPCE-PSAC, 2013).
- One must generally hear something at least three times before the intended message can be effectively remembered (CUPW/UPCE-PSAC, 2013).
- Approximately 83% of adults learn concepts through visual means (CUPW/UPCE-PSAC, 2013).
- Approximately 7% of communicating involves what one says; approximately 38% relates to how one says something; and approximately 55% involves "body movement" (CUPW/UPCE-PSAC, 2013).

These items represent a rather personal view of communication between people. However, many perspectives of communication exist. Communication is a big business upon which law enforcement organizations, corrections facilities, security organizations, and court systems rely on daily to support their functioning. These entities rely on telephone service, fax machines, electronic mail, surface mail, and wireless modalities in varying degrees. These services and products and various aspects of their components are not necessarily innate to the justice system. Instead, they are obtained from outside vendors of goods and services (e.g., AT&T, Comcast, Microsoft, or Motorola) that supply a range of products and services ranging from software to cellular telephones.

Communication represents a method of influencing societal behaviors. Among localities, numerous billboards, television and radio commercials, and newspapers often communicate messages that are intended to modify the behaviors of the local citizenry. Specifically, campaigns against drunk driving may be broadcast to mass audiences as a method of attempting to diminish instances of driving while intoxicated. Another familiar communications initiative is the "Click It or Ticket" campaign in which citizens are told to use their seat belts or face certain consequences if they are caught while driving without using a seat belt.

Communicating with the citizenry to influence behaviors also accommodates messages that influence both adults and children. Certainly, there are the unforgettable messages that are intended to sway behavior involving the McGruff Crime Dog and Smokey Bear. The former encourages people to report crimes, whereas the latter encourages people to ensure that camp fires are watered down before leaving a forest.

Other perspectives of communication involve homeland security and national security. Truck drivers may be conceptualized as the eyes and ears of American roadways throughout the nation (McElreath et al., 2013). If they see something suspicious, then they are encouraged to report it to authorities (McElreath et al., 2013). Furthermore, communication resources are components of critical national infrastructure (McElreath et al., 2013). They must be protected and maintained at all times during periods of both peace and distress (McElreath et al., 2013).

Communication may be considered from an operational perspective. Emergency dispatchers must communicate clearly, concisely, and unemotionally to allocate and direct emergency resources. Depending on departmental policies, law enforcement personnel often use "ten-codes" to communicate efficiently and effectively while simultaneously encrypting portions of their messages to enhance communications security. However, when working with other agencies during an emergency, some efforts may be made by law enforcement entities to abandon "ten-codes" in favor of plain English to improve the effectiveness and efficiency of communicating.

A little imagination and some research will result in many other perspectives of communication that influence the justice system. Communication is an innate aspect of human existence and society. It is ubiquitous and inescapable. Understanding some of its basic principles, hopefully, will improve one's abilities to communicate efficiently and effectively.

It's now almost six weeks after hernia surgery. I'm once again awake during the wee hours at 3:17 a.m. I'm cranking out this preface while hearing the sounds of my ferocious, one-eyed Jack Russell terrier, Sprat, barking heartily at squirrels outside my window. An old rerun of *Gomer Pyle, U.S.M.C.* is on the tube tonight. Despite my best efforts to silence Sprat and to ensure rural tranquility among the hills and hollows of north Mississippi, we're having some communication problems. The dog doesn't speak English or squirrel, and I don't speak terrier. I could care less for talking to squirrels. Although I've performed my best impersonation of Sergeant Carter as a method of attempting to make my little man hush, he just doesn't get it … so, to quote the movie *Cool Hand Luke* (Internet Movie Database, 1967) again, "What we've got here is failure to communicate."

Hopefully, kind reader, my fellow authors and I shall successfully communicate to you various concepts of justice system communication that may assist you in your endeavors. We hope there will be few, if any, communications failures as you read through these materials. We hope that you find this book to be interesting, useful, meaningful, and beneficial. If you experienced this book as an instructor or student, used it within your profession, or read it because of outright curiosity, then we encourage you to communicate with us regarding your feedback.

Thank you for your valuable time, kind attention, and interest in our work.

Daniel Adrian Doss

References

CUPW/UPCE-PSAC. (2013). Communication facts. Special needs—Breaking through barriers for workers who have children with special needs. Retrieved from http://specialneedsproject.ca/resources/useful-tools/330-communication-facts.html (accessed September 16, 2013).

Internet Movie Database. (1967). *Cool Hand Luke. Cool Hand Luke* quotes. Retrieved from http://www.imdb.com/title/tt0061512/quotes (accessed September 22, 2013).

Internet Movie Database. (1971). *Dirty Harry. Dirty Harry* quotes. Retrieved from http://www.imdb.com/title/tt0066999/quotes (accessed September 13, 2013).

McElreath, D., Jensen, C., Wigginton, M., Doss, D., Nations, R., & Van Slyke, J. (2013). *Introduction to homeland security* (2nd ed.). Boca Raton, FL: CRC Press.

Acknowledgments

Thanks to Almighty God for this publication opportunity. Micah 6:8—"He hath shewed thee, O man, what is good; and what doth the Lord require of thee, but to do justly, and to love mercy, and to walk humbly with thy God?"

This work is for my parents—Jerry W. Doss and Margaret S. Doss. When I was little, you always said I should eventually write a book. Well, here's another one!

For my little girl, Caleigh—I love you! Now that Daddy is finished with his "big book thingy," we can watch Mickey Mouse all night!

Thank you to my coauthors, Dr. Bill Glover, Becky Goza, and Dr. Mike Wigginton. Your participation and friendship are greatly appreciated, and I have thoroughly enjoyed this opportunity to collaborate with you.

Thank you to the faculty and staff of the University of West Alabama. Your encouragement was essential in keeping our efforts focused when completing the manuscript.

Thank you to the faculty and staff of the Department of Legal Studies at the University of Mississippi and the Department of Criminal Justice at the University of Massachusetts (Lowell). It was your graduate programs that sparked the idea of blending the topics of business and criminal justice as a research endeavor.

Daniel Adrian Doss

To my dad, who taught me (by example) how to have the drive and courage to succeed, and to my mother, who taught me not to run over people in the process.

William H. Glover, Jr.

This book is for my mom Judy Chadwell, my brother, Cory, and my sister, Emma-Leigh. I live life to its fullest because you can't. Special thank you to my mentors in the doctoral program, Drs. Lee Tyner and Adrian Doss. I appreciate every opportunity you give me and try to follow your every suggestion without fail.

Rebecca A. Goza

To my wife, Lisa, who gave me unwavering support and compassion and who has been by my side through some difficult times. I love you with all my heart.

Michael Wigginton, Jr.

List of Acronyms

AAC	Augmentative and alternative communication
AAR	After-action review
ACLJ	American Center for Law and Justice
ACLU	American Civil Liberties Union
ADA	Americans with Disabilities Act
ANOVA	Analysis of variance
BTS	Bureau of Transportation Statistics
CALEA	Communications Assistance for Law Enforcement Act/Commission on Accreditation for Law Enforcement Agencies
CAP	Common alerting protocol
CBP	Customs and Border Protection
CCA	Corrections Corporation of America
CEO	Chief executive officer
CLP	Common Language Protocol
CMAS	Commercial Mobile Alert System
CNN	Cable News Network
COC	Chain of custody
COPS	Community-Oriented Policing Services
CQT	Control Question Test
DADD	Dads Against Drunk Driving
DHS	Department of Homeland Security
DOJ	Department of Justice
DOL	Department of Labor
DOT	Department of Transportation
DUI	Driving under the influence
EAS	Emergency Alert System
ECPA	Electronic Communications Privacy Act
EMS	Emergency medical services
EPAA	Employee Polygraph Protection Act
EWS	Emergency warning system
FBI	Federal Bureau of Investigation
FCC	Federal Communications Commission
FDOT	Florida Department of Transportation
FEMA	Federal Emergency Management Agency
FHA	Federal Highway Administration
FISA	Foreign Intelligence Surveillance Act
FLSA	Fair Labor and Standards Act
FMLA	Family and Medical Leave Act
f/s	Frames per second

FTA	Federal Transit Administration
GETS	Government Emergency Telecommunications Service
GKT	Guilty Knowledge Test
HHS	Health and Human Services
Hz	Hertz
IC	Incident commander
IPAWS	Integrated Public Alert and Warning System
JIC	Joint Information Center
JIS	Joint Information System
LAC	Local assistance center
LAPD	Los Angeles Police Department
LPR	License plate reader
MADD	Mothers Against Drunk Driving
mph	Miles per hour
m/s	Meters per second
MSDS	Materials safety data sheet
MSPA	Migrant and Seasonal Agricultural Worker Protection Act
NASA	National Aeronautics and Space Administration
NCA	National Communications Association
NCS	National Communications System
NECP	National Emergency Communications Plan
NIH	National Institutes of Health
NIMS	National Incident Management System
NLP	Natural language processing
NMB	National Mediation Board
NOAA	National Oceanic and Atmospheric Administration
NOPD	New Orleans Police Department
NWS	National Weather Service
OPORD	Operations Order
OSHA	Occupational Safety and Health Act
OSU	Ohio State University
PIO	Public information officer
PRSA	Public Relations Society of America
PSA	Public service advertisement
PSC	Public service campaign
PWS	Public warning system
RDP	Route Diversity Program
RFP	Request for proposal
SHARES	Shared Resources High Frequency Radio Program
SSA	State Secrets Act
SWOT	Strengths, weaknesses, opportunities, and threats
TCP	Traffic control point
TSP	Telecommunications Service Priority
UM	University of Michigan
USMS	U.S. Marshal Service
WPS	Wireless Priority Service

Authors

Daniel Adrian Doss, PhD—Dr. Doss's background includes assistant professor, College of Business Administration, University of West Alabama; assistant professor, Belhaven College; adjunct assistant professor, Embry-Riddle Aeronautical University; and chair of Graduate Business and Management, University of Phoenix (Memphis). His professional career consisted of software engineering and analytical positions in both the defense and commercial industries. Corporate entities included full-time and contract positions with Federal Express and uMonitor.com, and contract positions, via Data Management Consultants, with Loral Corporation (formerly IBM Federal Systems) and Lockheed-Martin. Additional credentials include lieutenant colonel, Mississippi State Guard, where he serves as commander of a military police battalion; graduate of the Lafayette County Law Enforcement Academy (Mississippi); and graduate of the Law Enforcement Mobile Video Institute. He has also coauthored a variety of peer-reviewed journal articles and conference proceedings. His education consists of a PhD in business administration, Northcentral University; MCJ in homeland security, University of Mississippi; MA in computer resources and information management, Webster University; MBA, Embry-Riddle Aeronautical University; graduate certificate in forensic criminology, University of Massachusetts (Lowell); graduate certificate in nonprofit financial management, University of Maryland (Adelphi); and a BS in computer science with a mathematics minor, Mississippi State University. He is currently pursuing a second doctorate, in police science, with the University of South Africa.

William H. Glover, Jr., JD—He drafts forms, legal digests, and legal summaries for U.S. Legal Forms. He earned his BBA from the University of Mississippi in 1973 and his JD from the University of Mississippi School of Law in 1976. He joined the firm of Wells Marble & Hurst in 1976 as an associate and became a partner in 1979. While at Wells, he supervised major real estate commercial loan transactions and employment law cases. His practice also involved estate administration and general commercial law. Dr. Glover joined the faculty of Belhaven University in Jackson, Mississippi, in 1996 as assistant professor of business administration and university attorney, where he taught business law and business ethics in the BBA and MBA programs until 2004, before a short stay at Wells Marble & Hurst PLLC as general counsel. Dr. Glover is a lieutenant colonel and staff judge advocate for the headquarters of the Mississippi State Guard. He was called to active duty during hurricanes Dennis, Katrina, and Gustav. He received the Magnolia Medal from the Mississippi Army National Guard in 2010.

Rebecca A. Goza, MBA, CIA, CISA, CFE, CRISC, CGEIT—She is the senior director of Internal Audit Services for the American Cancer Society. Ms. Goza is also currently an adjunct professor of accounting at the University of Central Oklahoma. Ms. Goza attended Oklahoma State University in Stillwater, Oklahoma, where she earned her bachelor of science in accounting and a minor in management information systems. Ms. Goza received her MBA in accounting from the University of Central Oklahoma in December 2011 and is currently pursuing a DBA in accounting from Anderson University in Anderson, Indiana. Before joining the American Cancer Society in February 2002, she was employed with Coopers & Lybrand, the Hertz Corporation, and most recently was the director of internal audit at Fleming Companies. Ms. Goza has more than 20 years of experience in internal and external auditing. Ms. Goza has experience in information systems; external, financial, and operational auditing; fraud examination; and compliance auditing. Ms. Goza has been with the American Cancer Society for eleven years and helped create the Internal Audit Services department at the society. While under the direction of Ms. Goza, the American Cancer Society's Internal Audit Services department received the prestigious Institute of Internal Auditors' Recognition of Commitment (ROC) Award, becoming one of only eight internal auditing departments to be honored in 2004. Ms. Goza also received accreditation as an internal assessor/validator from the Institute of Internal Auditors in March 2006, and has served as a volunteer quality reviewer for the Institute of Internal Auditors.

Michael Wigginton, Jr., PhD—His background includes assistant professor of criminal justice and director of the University of Mississippi Master of Criminal Justice Executive Cohort Program, Department of Legal Studies, with the University of Mississippi; former assistant professor, Southeast Louisiana University; adjunct professor, Tulane University; senior special agent, United States Customs Service; special agent, United States Drug Enforcement Administration; detective and state trooper, Louisiana State Police; police officer, New Orleans Police Department; and a U.S. Air Force security police dog handler with service in Vietnam. His education and training include a PhD in criminal justice, University of Southern Mississippi; MS, the University of New Orleans; MS, the University of Alabama; and BA, Loyola University of New Orleans. He is also the author of numerous publications on the criminal justice system.

Introduction

Communication occurs daily within the justice domain. Whether one is dictating a last will and testament or is attempting to sweet talk a patrol officer from issuing a speeding ticket, communication occurs. When reading legal notices in the morning newspaper or listening to traffic reports on the car radio during rush hour, communication occurs. When listening to a candidate for sheriff giving an election speech or reporting a crime via a 911 telephone call, communication occurs. Communication in the justice domain ranges widely from the issuing of Amber alerts to the simple acts of asking a patrol officer for directions to the local park. Regardless of the example, all communication in the justice system is permeated by some straightforward concepts:

- Communication has a catalyst.
- Communication has a human capacity.
- Communication involves mutual understanding.
- Communication has an intended message.
- Communication is continuous.
- Communication occurs everywhere.
- Communication involves form and method.
- Communication often experiences distractions.
- Communication is a process.

Communication occurs in the justice domain because of innumerable reasons. Some may express complaints to commence the lawsuit process or may call a police station to report suspicious activity within a neighborhood. In drastic instances, one may call 911 to report immediate concerns—perhaps a burglar has entered a personal residence while the owner is at home. From a lighter perspective, one may call a police station to learn whether it is sponsoring a little league team this year. Regardless, some reason exists to facilitate such communication within the justice domain.

People communicate. Patrol officers must communicate just as efficiently as any other person in the justice system. Judges must ensure that their jury instructions are clearly stated. When driving during adverse conditions, drivers must see and understand roadway signage that may warn of danger. During divorce proceedings, couples may communicate solely through their respective attorneys. When informing the public of newsworthy trial proceedings, news reporters broadcast their stories to the widest audience possible. Certainly, an infinite array of examples exists that shows the human capacity to communicate directly or indirectly.

When people communicate, some form of messaging occurs. A traffic control officer raises and extends an arm upward to stop traffic. In this case, the message is simple: stop. When a patrol officer is taking a report from someone who witnessed an automobile accident, the message communicated may be a description of the vehicles involved in the accident. When the Supreme Court issues an opinion, it is written and disseminated appropriately. In this case, the message involves expressing an interpretation of law. In any case, human communication, regardless of its modality, involves some type of message.

Communication in the justice domain is unceasing; it occurs continuously. A shift sergeant may commence roll call sharply at 0700 hours. A citizen may report a burglary at any hour of the day or night. A dispatcher may route patrol officers to the scene of an incident at any time. A law enforcement organization may conduct its monthly staff meeting at 3:00 p.m. on the second Monday of each month to discuss the effects of its operations. When one receives a jury summons, a specific date and time for reporting are specified within the court document. Essentially, communication in the justice system occurs all the time.

Such communication occurs everywhere within the justice system. Communication occurs within an open courtroom or within the privacy of a judge's chamber. Communication occurs wherever policing occurs—communication with law enforcement entities exists among neighborhoods and schools; within malls and sporting complexes; among correctional facilities and holding areas; among courtrooms and legal offices; and among roadways, waterways, and airways. Communication exists between attorneys and clients that may be separated by great distances. Basically, communication is not necessarily constrained by geography, and may occur anywhere.

Facilitating justice system communication is accomplished through a variety of modalities. Folks may read crime reports within their local newspaper or view stories about neighborhood watch programs during televised news shows. Someone may use a telephone to summon law enforcement assistance. Police leaders may disseminate organizational directives through the use of electronic mail. Law enforcement vehicles use sirens to gain the attention of motorists. A sheriff may issue a press release to announce the results of an investigation. Certainly, communication within the justice system has many forms and modalities through which messaging is transacted with people.

Communicating is methodical from start to finish. Rarely could it ever be perceived as random. Communicating incorporates a clearly defined process that describes the events that occur between the senders and receivers of messages. Throughout this process, some distractions may inhibit communicating efficiently and effectively. However, all justice system communication occurs methodically and systematically.

The preceding notions are all contained within the following series of questions: why, who, what, when, where, and how? All communication is affected by these queries. Throughout the communications process, someone attempts to convey some intended idea to someone else through a variety of methods. This communications process may occur at any point in time, is geographically unconstrained, and incorporates numerous messaging media.

This text represents an effort to explore these six queries from a variety of perspectives. Certainly, much more is discussed herein that is beyond the scope of these six questions. Regardless, this text represents a robust approach to examining communication within the context of the justice system. Although this book is primarily an introductory discussion of communication, readers are encouraged to explore further the topics introduced herein.

It is the hope of these authors that readers find some meaningful benefit from this book. It is also hoped that the topics herein are sufficiently varied and robust to provide an insightful amalgamation of communication perspectives. Ranging from the mathematics of communication to the influences of ethos, pathos, and logos, it is hoped that readers will discover something new herein. Reader feedback is always encouraged regarding experiences with this book and any suggestions for future revisions. Feel free to contact any of us, and communicate your thoughts!

Dr. Daniel Adrian Doss
Dr. William H. Glover, Jr.
Ms. Rebecca A. Goza
Dr. Michael Wigginton, Jr.

Foundations of Communications

1

> Good communication is just as stimulating as black coffee, and just as hard to sleep after.
> **—Anne Lindbergh (Lindbergh, n.d.)**

Objectives

The objectives of this chapter are to

- Discuss the basic concept of communication
- Discuss the primary attributes of communication
- Introduce the communications process
- Discuss the use of communication in the justice domain
- Discuss the impact of communication in the justice domain

Introduction

Communication inescapably pervades society daily. Each day, humans experience telephones, televisions, radios, computers, personal interactions, and written communications. Silent, nonverbal communications accentuate personal conversations. Such experiences facilitate the transmission of messages between senders and receivers that convey innumerable ideas and concepts among and between communicating entities. Conveying ideas and achieving mutual understanding between the communicating factions is not always easy. For example, communication may occur between members of the justice system and individuals that do not speak, read, or write English. People within the justice system either must have some ability to communicate in a language that is familiar to such an individual or use the services of an interpreter.

Communicating is both an art and a science. Various theories attempt to describe the notions of communications. Theories that encompass social system and languages are referred to as structural theories (Pedersen et al., 2007). Theories reflecting the methods of organizational functioning of systems are referred to as functional theories (Pedersen et al., 2007). Conventional and interactional theories encompass the "process and effects of interaction" (Pedersen et al., 2007). Discovering the meaning "in actions and texts" is deemed to be an interpretive theory (Pedersen et al., 2007). Critical theories are affiliated with "inequality, oppression, and domination" (Pedersen et al., 2007). All of these theories influence the ability of humans to communicate effectively and efficiently.

Communication permeates the justice system and law enforcement organizations. Since its introduction within the policing domain in 1914 by August Vollmer, the use of radio has facilitated law enforcement communications effectively and efficiently (Dinkelspiel, 2010). The use of television communicates depictions of crime scenes, locations of roadway bottlenecks, and information about missing persons and wanted individuals. The use of

911 telephone systems summons law enforcement personnel during emergencies. Court reporters transcribe courtroom events, and may read these statements when asked to do so by judges and attorneys.

Technological advancements have revolutionized communications within the justice system and among law enforcement organizations. Improvements in efficiency and effectiveness have strengthened the abilities of law enforcement organizations to serve their citizenries. However, underlying the basic concept of communication is the human factor. Somewhere, somehow, someone sends a message to someone else that may be received and understood or misunderstood. This human attribute of communicating permeates all law enforcement organizations and justice systems—even during modern times.

Basic Concepts of Communication

Communicating involves the establishment of the mutual understanding and comprehension of a specific message between the sending entity and the receiving entity. Communicating occurs through time, necessitates resources, and involves some specific method. The content of communicated messages is generally purposeful within the justice and law enforcement domains. When considering the act of communicating within the justice system, pertinent questions describe the communications domain: who, what, when, where, why, and how?

Anyone that is arrested must be advised of the Miranda rights before being questioned. This advising of the Miranda warning ensures and protects the constitutional rights of the arrested individual. The Miranda rights consist of the following items:

- The right of the arrestee to remain silent.
- If the arrestee decides to make any statement(s), they can and will be used in a court of law against the arrestee.
- The arrestee may consult an attorney and may have an attorney present during questioning.
- An attorney may be appointed for arrestees that cannot afford an attorney.

Figures 1.1 and 1.2 show the typical Miranda card that is carried by law enforcement personnel.

The informing of the Miranda rights occurred as a result of the 1966 court case involving *Miranda v. Arizona*. The primary functions of communicating the Miranda warning involve protecting both the law enforcement personnel and the accused within the justice system. Furthermore, communicating the Miranda warning contributes toward preserving constitutional rights. The Miranda warning may be considered from the context of the basic questions associated with communications.

Who/Whom?

Two primary factions are associated with communication: senders and receivers. Senders represent the origin points of a message. Receivers represent the recipients of a message. Both individuals and organizations may be the senders and receivers of messages. When

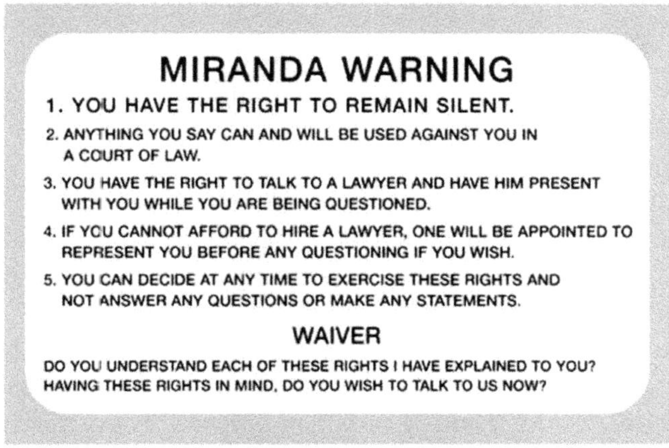
MIRANDA WARNING

1. YOU HAVE THE RIGHT TO REMAIN SILENT.
2. ANYTHING YOU SAY CAN AND WILL BE USED AGAINST YOU IN A COURT OF LAW.
3. YOU HAVE THE RIGHT TO TALK TO A LAWYER AND HAVE HIM PRESENT WITH YOU WHILE YOU ARE BEING QUESTIONED.
4. IF YOU CANNOT AFFORD TO HIRE A LAWYER, ONE WILL BE APPOINTED TO REPRESENT YOU BEFORE ANY QUESTIONING IF YOU WISH.
5. YOU CAN DECIDE AT ANY TIME TO EXERCISE THESE RIGHTS AND NOT ANSWER ANY QUESTIONS OR MAKE ANY STATEMENTS.

WAIVER

DO YOU UNDERSTAND EACH OF THESE RIGHTS I HAVE EXPLAINED TO YOU?
HAVING THESE RIGHTS IN MIND, DO YOU WISH TO TALK TO US NOW?

ENGLISH
(FRONT)

Figure 1.1 Miranda warning card (front). (From http://www.chiefsupply.com/586-Geiger-Miranda-Warning-Card.aspx.)

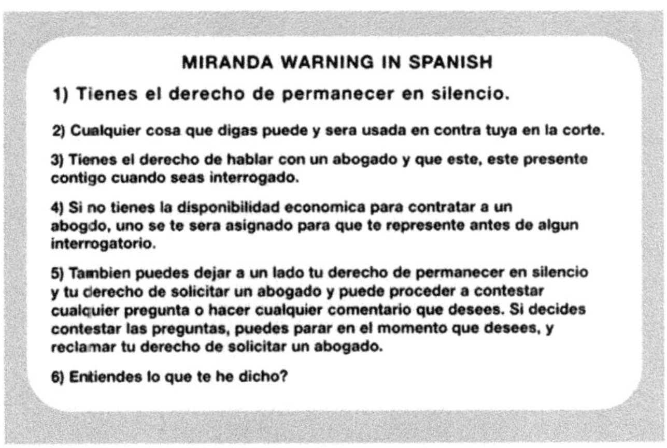
MIRANDA WARNING IN SPANISH

1) Tienes el derecho de permanecer en silencio.

2) Cualquier cosa que digas puede y sera usada en contra tuya en la corte.

3) Tienes el derecho de hablar con un abogado y que este, este presente contigo cuando seas interrogado.

4) Si no tienes la disponibilidad economica para contratar a un abogdo, uno se te sera asignado para que te represente antes de algun interrogatorio.

5) Tambien puedes dejar a un lado tu derecho de permanecer en silencio y tu derecho de solicitar un abogado y puede proceder a contestar cualquier pregunta o hacer cualquier comentario que desees. Si decides contestar las preguntas, puedes parar en el momento que desees, y reclamar tu derecho de solicitar un abogado.

6) Entiendes lo que te he dicho?

SPANISH
(BACK)

Figure 1.2 Miranda warning card (back). Miranda card warnings are often printed in foreign languages. (Courtesy of Chief Supply, http://www.chiefsupply.com/Geiger-Miranda-Warning-Card.html.)

informing arrestees of their Miranda rights, the act of communicating occurs. When informing an arrestee of the Miranda rights, the arresting officer is the sender of the message conveying the informational content. The arrestee is the receiver of the message conveying the informational content.

After the arresting officer informs the arrestee of the informational content of the Miranda warning, the officer may ask whether the arrestee understands the content of the Miranda statements. The arrestee may respond either positively or negatively to indicate whether an understanding of the Miranda rights has occurred, thereby facilitating communication. When responding to the arresting officer's query, the arrestee becomes the sender of a message that conveys whether an understanding of the Miranda rights exists, and the arresting officer becomes the receiver of this message. The arrestee may affirm an understanding of the Miranda rights, affirm a partial understanding that may necessitate additional communication, or may indicate no understanding thereby necessitating further communication.

Certainly, communicating extends beyond the informing of the Miranda rights. For example, when someone calls 911 for assistance, he or she is the sender of the message requesting assistance. When answering the 911 call, the responding telephone operator represents the receiver of the message requesting assistance.

During manhunts for escaped convicts or other wanted individuals, law enforcement organizations may disseminate public warnings through television, radio, Internet, and print media. The sender of the warning is the law enforcement organization, whereas the receivers of the message consist of the members of the general populace that is affected by the warning. During 2011, a manhunt occurred to search for Adam Mayes in Mississippi and Tennessee (Gray, 2012). Mayes was wanted by law enforcement for the crimes of murder and kidnapping (Gray, 2012). National news media broadcast the events of the situation periodically, issued public warnings, and solicited public assistance. The senders of these messages were news media organizations and law enforcement organizations, whereas the receivers of the message consisted of both individuals and organizations nationally. Figure 1.3 shows a roadway billboard communicating pertinent information about Mayes.

There are times when natural disasters or man-made cataclysms may necessitate interactions between senders and receivers. For example, when anticipating the arrival of a hurricane on shorelines, state public safety agencies may send messages to mass audiences within society to facilitate the evacuation of populaces in an attempt to preserve human life. During the events of September 11, 2001, through the use of real-time systems, news media nationally broadcast the tragic events to inform the American populace of the aviation disasters. News media organizations were the senders of the intended messages, whereas the viewers and listeners of the American populace were the receivers of the intended messages.

Figure 1.3 Billboard regarding Adam Mayes. (From http://www1.whdh.com/news/articles/national/12007420153459/wife-mother-of-kidnap-slaying-suspect-arrested/.)

Table 1.1 Communications Cardinalities

Sender	Receiver	Cardinality	Example
1	1	1:1	Dispatcher sends a single police officer to a specific location.
1	N	1:N	Dispatcher sends multiple police officers to a specific location.
N	M	N:M	Many individuals contact multiple law enforcement organizations for assistance during emergencies. For example, many citizens may call both police and sheriff organizations when witnessing a bank robbery.
N	1	N:1	Many citizens may call 911 for assistance when they witness an automobile accident.

The quantitative relationships among communicating entities may be expressed mathematically via the use of cardinality ratios. A cardinality ratio shows the relationship numerically between the members of sets within a given population (Rosen, 1991). Four types of primary cardinality ratios exist: 1:1, 1:N, N:M, and N:1 (Rosen, 1991). These ratios express the following types of relationships:

- One-to-one (1:1)—This relationship involves a single sender and a single receiver. For example, a dispatcher may send a single police officer to a specific location.
- One-to-many (1:N)—This relationship involves a single sender and multiple receivers. For example, a dispatcher sends more than one police officer to a specific location.
- Many-to-many (N:M)—This relationship involves multiple senders and multiple receivers. For example, many citizens may call both police department and sheriff department organizations when witnessing a bank robbery.
- Many-to-one (N:1)—This relationship involves multiple senders and a solitary receiver. Many citizens may call 911 for assistance when they witness an automobile accident.

With respect to the relationships that exist between the senders and the receivers of messages when communicating, the applicable cardinality ratios are expressed in Table 1.1.

What?

A simple question may be posed: what is to be communicated? Messages are communicated between the sender and the receiver. The message purposefully encompasses the concepts and ideas that are portrayed within the intended communication. These notions may be considered from the perspective of the Miranda warning. When communicating the tenets of the Miranda warning, messaging occurs between the sender (i.e., law enforcement personnel) and the receiver (i.e., the arrestee) of the intended message. The content of the message pertaining to the advising of the Miranda warning consists of the basic rights of the arrested individual. Specifically, the content of the message informs the arrestee of the following items:

- The right of the arrestee to remain silent.
- If the arrestee decides to make any statement(s), they can and will be used in a court of law against the arrestee.

- The arrestee may consult an attorney and may have an attorney present during questioning.
- An attorney may be appointed for arrestees that cannot afford an attorney.

When affirming the understanding of the Miranda warning, the messaging between the arrestee and the arresting officer consists of informing the officer whether the arrestee fully understands, partially understands, or does not understand the Miranda warning. Further communications and messaging may occur depending on the understanding of the arrested individual.

Other examples of messages include pleas for assistance when someone experiences an automobile accident or may involve informing the public of a police band concert to benefit a local charity. Messages involve the broadcasting of Amber alerts when a child is missing and the issuing of wanted posters when conducting a fugitive search. In each of these cases, the message serves an intended purpose of informing the receiving party about a specific topic. For communications to be effective, a common understanding and comprehension of the message must occur between the sender and the receiver. Figure 1.4 shows the television communications of an Amber alert notifying the general public of a cancellation.

Feedback and response are considerations of the effectiveness and the efficiency of communicating. The concept of feedback highlights the response of the recipient to a message. Feedback may be verbal, nonverbal, physical, or nonphysical. From the perspective of the Miranda warning, when asked whether the arrestee understands the Miranda rights, the arrestee may say "yes," "no," "maybe," or indicate some other verbal response. Nonverbal, physical responses may consist of the arrestee nodding the head up and down to indicate a positive understanding, vertically back and forth to show some or no understanding, or may not physically move. Depending on the verbal or physical response of the arrestee, additional communication and messaging may be necessary regarding the Miranda rights.

Figure 1.4 Television Amber alert announcement. (From http://www.myfoxdfw.com/story/21422382/amber-alert-canceled-father-arrested.)

When?

The act of communicating occurs through time. Some communication may be almost instantaneous or it may involve significant periods. Three perspectives highlight the chronological aspects of communicating: operational, near-term, or strategic. Varying types of communications highlight these chronological perspectives ranging from organizational strategy documents conveying strategic planning that encompasses an average of five years of intended actions; tactical items that encompass quarterly reports or annual reports of an organization; or operational items that accommodate immediate or daily communications transactions.

From the perspective of the Miranda warning, the timing of communications is practically immediate, and occurs within a real-time scope of activity between the senders and receivers of messages. When asked whether the Miranda rights are understood, an arrestee may respond immediately. In this case, the chronological attribute of communicating is operational because it involves a short-term, immediate perspective.

Strategic plans are a form of expressing the long-term intentions of law enforcement organizations. An example is the strategic plan of the Sarasota County Sheriff's Office (Florida). This plan communicates the "implementation of agency operations from October 1, 2009, through September 30, 2013" (Knight, 2012, p. 4). Furthermore, this plan communicates the vision and mission of the organization throughout the duration of this period. Vision represents the long-term expectation of what the organization hopes to become through time, whereas mission expresses the intent of the organization toward the fulfillment of its vision. Such intent embodies both the goals and the objectives of the organization through time.

Within its strategic documents, the vision of the Sarasota organization is communicated as "a professional agency guided by our values and united with the community to make Sarasota County a safe place to live, work and visit" (Knight, 2012, p. 2). Its organization mission is communicated as "effective and efficient service in partnership with our community" (Knight, 2012, p. 2). The primary goals of the organization are communicated as follows (Knight, 2012, p. 5):

Goal 1: To combat criminal activity and address conditions that foster crime and fear in Sarasota County

Goal 2: To make the roadways and waterways of Sarasota County safe places on which to travel

Goal 3: To recruit, develop, retain, and recognize a diverse, educated, and skilled workforce

Goal 4: To ensure agency and individual accountability by effective and efficient use of personnel, equipment, and technology

Goal 5: To ensure the safety and security of those utilizing court services and in the county's correctional facilities

Additionally, approximately 125 objectives are communicated toward the fulfillment of these five goals (Knight, 2012, p. 5). Within the context of communications, examples of these 125 objectives include the following:

- To clearly articulate the response of the sheriff's office to animal control calls (Knight, 2012, p. 9)

- To enhance the sheriff's office's website and expand its use as a communications vehicle with the community (Knight, 2012, p. 9)
- To enhance the use of commercial television, radio, and local print media (Knight, 2012, p. 10)
- To regularly provide up-to-date information on sexual predators/offenders to school crossing guards (Knight, 2012, p. 10)
- To develop and enhance ongoing information exchange with other criminal justice agencies, including the Department of Juvenile Justice and Department of Corrections, Office of Community Corrections (Knight, 2012, p. 11)

These Sarasota items demonstrate the communications ability of the organization to convey its characteristics that permeate a period of four years. This is a strategic action because strategic plans encompass an average of five years. Some organizations may exhibit strategic periods that are somewhat less than or greater than five years.

However, shorter periods represent the tactical characteristics of the organization. These near-term periods encompass communications activities that influence organizations from anywhere between one to an average of five years. An example of this communication range involves the negotiating of law enforcement contracts. During 2012, in Berkeley, California, police contract negotiations were completed after a period of 15 months (Knobel, 2012). The communications between the factions involved the crafting of three-year contracts that involve "cost of living increases, creates a second tier CalPERS pension formula for new employees, mandates cost sharing by employees in the employer's contribution to CalPERS, and significantly changes retiree health benefits" (Knobel, 2012).

Operational considerations affect the daily and near-term considerations of policing. This type of communication encompasses a variety of police activities. Examples are given as follows:

Dispatching: This type of activity involves "communications center personnel assigned the responsibility for communicating calls-for-service from the communications center to appropriate field units for handling" (Grassie et al., 1978).

Officer safety: The use of "ten-codes" facilitates the use of discreet communications in situations involving "unfavorable information" or wanted suspects as a method of communicating clandestinely to avoid suspects overhearing and understanding the conversation (International Association of Chiefs of Police, 2007).

Contact cards: Some agencies use contact cards as a method of documenting the stopping and questioning of individuals. These cards serve the purpose of documenting events that "typically result in no arrest or charges" (Rankin, 2012).

Office hours and scheduling: Some cities may issue statements indicating the holiday scheduling of city offices, and police departments may announce duty schedules to accommodate holidays. For example, within a weekly report memorandum, the City of Hercules, California, announced that its city offices were to be closed for a brief period during Christmas holidays in 2010 (Nelson, 2010).

Press releases: Press releases are used to facilitate a variety of messages between police organizations and the general public. For example, the Township of Haverford,

> Pennsylvania, issued a 2009 press release that detailed the characteristics of a program designed to deter "underage drinking and dangerous behavior" that contributed to "random acts of vandalism and disorderly behavior" (Glenn, 2009).

Certainly, many more examples may be identified that highlight the strategic, tactical, and operational facets of communications within the policing domain. Some periods have lengthy ramifications (e.g., strategic planning documents), whereas others have immediate implications (e.g., calls for assistance). Strategic communications are characterized by a continuous, ongoing set of activities that contribute toward the fulfilling of the organizational mission through time (Patterson & Radtke, 2009). Short-term communications emphasize activities that support organizational functions that involve durations that are neither strategic nor immediate. Operational communications involve characteristics that affect even shorter periods ranging from immediate circumstances (e.g., 911 assistance) to periodic activities (e.g., annual report releases). Regardless, all communications, whether within the domains of justice and policing, occur through time. Time transcends all forms of communications and their associated activities.

Why?

Communication occurs because some catalyst sparks messaging interaction between the sender of a message and its receiver. There is no solitary reason to necessitate the enacting of communications. Numerous reasons exist, ranging from someone calling 911 for assistance to a police chief mandating the completion of incident reports at the ending of a work shift. Figure 1.5 shows a typical shift briefing that is common among law enforcement agencies.

The instigating of communications may be examined from the perspective of the Miranda warning. Communicating the Miranda warning to an arrestee is necessary before questioning may occur. Such communication is instigated to facilitate the protections granted within the Fourth, Fifth, and Sixth Amendments of the U.S. Constitution.

Figure 1.5 Communicating during a police shift briefing. (From http://www.nwaonline.com/photos/2011/oct/24/120733/.)

Asking an arrestee whether an understanding of the Miranda rights exists is necessary to determine whether further explanation and conversation are required and whether the state must appoint an attorney for the arrestee.

Certainly, other reasons exist to justify the existence of communications. When one applies for a job with a law enforcement organization, an application for employment is usually completed. Employment applications contain a variety of data fields that must be completed and may require the submission of documentation to support the statements that are provided by the applicant. For example, one may have to include letters of recommendation or some proof of law enforcement certification awarded by a state agency. The application and its supporting materials represent a form of written communication through which the law enforcement organization may assess potential candidates for employment.

When an officer responds to an automobile accident, a report must be completed and filed that details the incident. A law enforcement office may interview the individuals involved directly with the accident, record their personal information, verify their identities, and also interview any witnesses who may have observed the accident. These field reports are necessary to show the details of the incident, may be necessary for insurance companies, may be used within further investigations, and may be used during court proceedings. This form of written communication results from its potential use in multiple applications, and may result from departmental mandates regarding the completion and submission of incident reports.

The act of communicating may occur because of a need to inform the general public concerning an array of topics. Such topics may include missing persons, drug reduction programs, safe driving programs, after-school programs for children, enacting of sobriety checkpoints, alternate roadway routes to avoid accident scenes, safety measures for holidays and sporting events, and many others. Within the policing domain, both external and internal communications exist. External communications are associated with messaging between the law enforcement organization and any entity external to the law enforcement organization. Internal communications are associated with messaging that occurs internally within the law enforcement organization.

During 2012, in Mississippi, a police impersonator murdered two individuals during highway stops (Artiles, 2012). After realizing that an imposter was endangering public safety, Mississippi law enforcement organizations "warned motorists that someone may be posing as an officer because the shooting victims had no obvious reason to be stopped on the interstate where they were found" (Artiles, 2012). In this instance, communication with the public was necessitated to warn citizens of the potential danger and to potentially capture the imposter. Warnings were communicated through print, online, television, and radio outlets.

Similarly, during 2003, in Georgia, the City of East Point issued a public service announcement regarding the activities of a different police impersonator within the area of Atlanta. Specifically, the communicated warning stated:

> This is a public safety advisement to all citizens in the City of East Point from Chief Frank L. Brown and all members of the East Point Police Department, due to the recurring crimes in the metro Atlanta area involving police impersonators. The East Point Police Department wants everyone to know we do not have any unmarked vehicles that have the ability or the authority to execute traffic stops in the City of East Point.

> All vehicles that execute traffic stops in the City of East Point are clearly identified with the black and white colors and emergency blue lights on the top of the vehicles. (East Point Police Department, 2003)

These warnings were issued to bolster public safety and security as well as to contribute to the capturing of the imposters. However, they are not the only reasons for communicating within the context of policing. Another reason to spawn communications involves missing persons. One definition of missing person is "someone whose whereabouts is unknown to the reporting party," and may involve "any child who may have run away, been taken involuntary, or may be in need of assistance" (State of California, 2012). In the state of California, "all California police and sheriffs' departments must accept any report, including a report by telephone, of a missing person, including runaways, without delay and will give priority to the handling of the report" (State of California, 2012). In California, this reporting of missing persons involves no minimum waiting period, thereby facilitating quicker communications between the reporting entity and the law enforcement organization.

Each of the preceding examples involves man-made events as catalysts for communications. However, considerations of natural incidents also may necessitate communications. As a precautionary measure, law enforcement organizations may communicate emergency procedures regarding a variety of natural events ranging from earthquakes to flooding (Cornell University, 2012). During Hurricane Gustav, in 2008, the Louisiana State Police provided contact information to the general public, via Internet news media, as a method of disseminating information concerning road closures (Maassen, 2008).

The commencing of communications does not always occur between law enforcement organizations and the public. Instead, factions of law enforcement may communicate internally. When an officer requests assistance at the scene of an incident, one or more officers from the same organization may be dispatched. Such requests are made because of safety concerns. If an officer believes that a dangerous situation may exist, then additional personnel may be summoned. In some cases, departmental policy may dictate that additional law enforcement personnel should be summoned during traffic stops, thereby necessitating communication. These cases are examples of catalysts that invoke internal communications.

Law enforcement agencies may communicate externally with other organizations. When conducting manhunts or missing persons searches that cross jurisdictional boundaries, multiple law enforcement agencies may communicate with each other or with various news media. The incident of Natalee Holloway, who disappeared in Aruba during 2005, is an example of such communication involving multiple entities. The investigation involved "international attention and numerous searches with the help of volunteers, special agents from the FBI, Dutch Soldiers and aircraft, and even divers who examined the ocean floor" (Stein, 2010). Figure 1.6 shows a missing persons poster describing Holloway.

These examples highlight the saliency of communications within the law enforcement domain both externally and internally. In each case, the catalysts instantiating the act of communicating differed, and ranged from public service announcements to missing persons investigations. No solitary catalyst exists to spark communications between senders and receivers of messages. Regardless of the considered circumstance, all acts of communication occur because of some catalyst that instigates messaging activities between senders and receivers within a communications domain.

Figure 1.6 Natalee Holloway missing persons poster. (From http://blog.al.com/wire/2010/11/dutch_to_test_bone_found_on_ar.html.)

How?

The method of transmitting and receiving messages between senders and receivers involves a variety of media. From the perspective of the Miranda warning, the arresting officer may read the Miranda statements from a printed card or may recite them from memory. Informing the arrestee of the Miranda warning may involve a verbal recitation or printed material. Eliciting a response from the arrestee, to determine whether the Miranda warning is understood, may be verbal or nonverbal. Regardless, some method exists through which the act of communicating is facilitated between the arresting officer and the arrestee. Other mediums exist through which communications are facilitated. Such methods involve written media, visual media, auditory media, digital media, human interaction, or combinations of these methods.

The domains of justice and policing use a variety of written media to facilitate a variety of communications. Written media encapsulates the expressed recording of court proceedings, depositions, wills, contracts, complaints, decrees, and warrants; newspaper articles and press releases; copies of missing persons or wanted posters that may be disseminated via postal service; tickets, warnings, and contact cards that are issued during incidents; annual personnel reviews, commendations, recommendations, examinations, or reprimands; operations logs and attendance rosters; and an array of other uses within the context of communications. Figure 1.7 shows a typical commendation certificate.

Visual media encompasses a variety of forms. The use of video pervades policing and law enforcement domains. Examples of this proliferation are given as follows:

- Crime scenes may be photographed or recorded using video equipment.
- Security cameras may be leveraged continuously to monitor and record events among courthouses, prisons, police stations, or other structures.

State of Mississippi
Mississippi Military Department
Certificate of Commendation Ribbon Award

TO ALL WHOM SHALL SEE THESE PRESENTS, GREETINGS:

THIS CERTIFICATE IS HEREBY AWARDED TO

DANIEL ADRIAN DOSS
LIEUTENANT COLONEL (O-5)
SECOND BRIGADE, 210th BATTALION, MILITARY POLICE

FOR THE SUCCESSFUL COMPLETION OF TWO YEARS OF RECRUITING ACTIVITIES AND HONOR GUARD ACTIVITIES, CUMULATIVELY, IN CONJUNCTION WITH THE ARMY NATIONAL GUARD, AIR NATIONAL GUARD, AND CIVILIAN PROFESSIONAL SPORTS AND HIGHER EDUCATION ENTITIES, THAT EXPOSED THE MISSISSIPPI STATE GUARD TO SEVERAL THOUSAND INDIVIDUALS DURING THE PRECEDING TWO YEARS, THAT CULMINATED IN THE SUCCESSFUL RECRUITING AND RETENTION OF PERSONNEL FOR THE STATE GUARD, WHICH PROVIDED BENEFITS FOR THE CITIZENS AND RESIDENTS OF THE GREAT STATE OF MISSISSIPPI AND THE UNITED STATES, WHOSE SERVICE IS A TESTAMENT TO HIS COMMITMENT AND SERVITUDE, AND IS A CREDIT TO THE MILITARY FORCES OF THE NATION AND THE STATE OF MISSISSIPPI, BE IT KNOWN THAT THIS SOLDIER IS HEREBY AWARDED THE

COMMENDATION RIBBON
STATE GUARD OF MISSISSIPPI

PER THE MISSISSIPPI CODE OF 1972, DONE AT THE CITY OF GRENADA, CAMP MCCAIN ARMY NATIONAL GUARD BASE, GIVEN UNDER MY HAND, THIS FIFTEENTH DAY OF MAY, IN THE YEAR OF OUR LORD, TWO THOUSAND AND TEN.

ASHLEY G CULLUM, COLONEL, MSSG
BRIGADE COMMANDER
2BDE HQ CO MP MSSG

Figure 1.7 Commendation certificate.

- Booking photographs are created when processing prisoners and within criminal databases.
- Photographs are used on law enforcement identification cards.
- Among many locales, intersection traffic and public areas may be monitored using video systems.
- Victims of crime may be photographed to document physical injuries.
- Missing persons and wanted posters may be disseminated among the general populace.
- Courtroom artists may hand-sketch images that depict the events of trials and hearings.
- Video systems may be used within patrol cars to document events.
- Charts and graphs may be used to show demographic data or to support statistical analysis.
- Television broadcasts may be used to facilitate public safety.

This listing is not exhaustive. Certainly, many more examples may be identified and listed. The use of visual and video methods may be used in courts as evidence or as historical artifacts within the justice system. Visual imagery is often used to embellish drug reduction, drunk driving reduction, and seat belt safety programs. Television news programs often show scenes from crime scenes or roadway accidents. Regardless of the scenario, visual imagery permeates communications within the justice system.

Auditory resources also facilitate communications within the justice system. Certainly, human speech is the basis of various communications that may be heard within the justice domain, ranging from courtroom questioning to an officer asking a motorist for a driver's licensure as a form of identification. Other forms of auditory communication involve the recording of depositions and witness testimonies, the recording of incidents to record the events of law enforcement responses to dispatch calls, the recording of incoming and outgoing calls to law enforcement agencies and 911 lines, the use of wiretaps to record conversations among target entities, the use of fixed and mobile radios to support communications among law enforcement agencies and personnel, and the use of clandestine recordings to document the conversations of undercover officers during sting operations. Again, such a listing is not exhaustive because many more examples may be cited.

Digital systems also facilitate communications within the justice system. Myriads of messages may be transmitted via electronic mail. Biometric devices may be used to identify law enforcement personnel, prisoners, detainees, and those who have criminal records. The digital displays of radar systems communicate the speed of traveling vehicles. Digital resources provide a basis for editing and analyzing video and audio files through the use of electronic resources. Digital systems also provide the basis for conducting audio and video conferencing via electronic devices. Digital devices form the basis of computer networks through which various communications occur.

Regardless of the situation, the human aspect of communicating must not be discounted. Human interaction is the primary basis of communicating. When performing traffic stops, law enforcement officers often touch the trunk of the stopped vehicle to impart their handprint or fingerprint on the surface of the vehicle. In the event that the officer becomes the victim of an adverse situation, the fingerprint or handprint communicates that fact that the officer was present in the vicinity of the vehicle.

Courtrooms involve much human interaction within the context of communications. Humans may recite their recollections of events as witnesses in a courtroom setting through a session of questions and answers. Attorneys and judges may also interact with witnesses during court proceedings. Shift commanders may provide briefings before deploying patrol units. Officers may periodically provide situational field reports to dispatchers indicating their location, presence, and activities.

These methods may be used independently or they may be combined to facilitate communications. Integrating the methods contributes toward a robust perspective of the communications domain. During periods of societal calamity, multiple methods may be employed to bolster public awareness of threatening situations. During Hurricane Katrina, television, radio, Internet, digital, and human communications were all leveraged as public safety resources to warn society of the danger of the impending storm. Integrating communications resources and methods facilitates the "best possible communications impact for an organization" with respect to its "external audiences" (Cornelissen, 2004).

Noise

Noise may be considered as anything that disrupts or impedes communications. Noise is also defined as "anything that distorts communication or interferes with people's understandings of one another" (Wood, 2010). Noise is also unavoidable within communications systems (Wood, 2010). Within the context of human communications, four categories of noise exist: physiological, physical, psychological, and semantic (Wood, 2010).

Physiological noise encompasses the biological and internal, physical attributes of humans that hamper communications. Specifically, this category of noise represents the "biological influences on a sender or a receiver that interfere with the transmission or reception of a message" (West & Turner, 2011). Examples within this category vary, and include drowsiness, hunger, illness, blindness, deafness, speech impediments, and medical conditions.

Physical noise represents communications barriers that are external to the communicating agents (Samovar et al., 2012). The attributes of this category are physical distracters that impede communication between senders and receivers of intended messages (Collins, 2009). Examples within this category involve an array of distractions, including the lighting or the temperature of the physical environment, sounds of construction masking communications, sirens and gunshots, electronics malfunctions, and crowd chatter.

Psychological noise involves "biases, attitudes, and beliefs" of the individual that impede or affect communications (McKenna, 2000). Specifically, psychological noise represents the "thoughts and feelings" of humans that affect human communication and the interpreting of "others' communication" (Muelhlhoff & Lewis, 2010). Examples within this category include whether one likes the speaker, disdain for the organization that sponsors an event in which communication occurs, and a mistrustfulness of law enforcement personnel or organizations.

The semantic noise category represents language issues that influence communications. Specifically, semantic noise involves any impediment to "word or symbol meanings because of differences in environment, culture, language, pronunciation, values, or experiences" (Metcalfe, 2010). Examples of this type of noise include regional or national accents, jargon, unknown acronyms or abbreviations, unfamiliar terminology, and a lack of understanding of language.

Various examples highlight the noise and communications barriers that affect policing and the justice system. Because of the demographic diversity of the population within San Francisco, California, groups of people often retain the attributes of their native cultures and languages (Gitmed, 2007). This retention of culture and language represents a communications barrier for law enforcement personnel that serve these populations (Gitmed, 2007). During 2012, in the city of Tacoma, Washington, a deaf woman was jailed for "60 hours" without an interpreter after calling the police department to report an assault within her home (Cavaliere, 2012). A witness to the event indicated that "she did not see the officers use hand signals to communicate with White" despite the responding officers stating that they had used appropriate hand signals (Cavaliere, 2012).

Other barriers to communication may affect judgments regarding the guilt or innocence of individuals within the justice system. During 1984, a shooting occurred in New Orleans, Louisiana, in which Curtis Kyles was arrested for the crime (National Registry of Exonerations, 2012). However, during trial proceedings, pertinent information "was never turned over to the defense" regarding the account of someone who had witnessed the event (National Registry of Exonerations, 2012). The appeals reached the Supreme Court. An excerpt from the National Registry of Exonerations describes this situation as follows (National Registry of Exonerations, 2012):

> The U.S. Supreme Court agreed to hear the case and on April 19, 1995, the court overturned Kyles's conviction and ordered a new trial because the prosecution suppressed exculpatory and impeachment evidence. The decision clarified the constitutional duty of the state to disclose exculpatory evidence to the defendant, even if the evidence is in the files of police and unknown to the prosecution. The court held that a review of the suppressed statements of eyewitnesses "reveals that their disclosure not only would have resulted in a markedly weaker case for the prosecution and a markedly stronger one for the defense, but also would have substantially reduced or destroyed the value of the State's two best witnesses." The court also declared that "a recapitulation of the suppressed statements made to the police by (Wallace)—who, by the State's own admission, was essential to its investigation and, indeed, 'made the case' against Kyles—reveals that they were replete with significant inconsistencies and

> affirmatively self-incriminating assertions, that (Wallace) was anxious to see Kyles arrested for the murder, and that the police had a remarkably uncritical attitude toward (Wallace). And the court said that the suppression of the prosecution's list of the cars at the crime scene after the murder tended both to exculpate Kyles, whose license plate was not on the list, and to impeach the prosecution's argument to the jury that the killer left his car at the scene during the investigation and that a grainy photograph of the scene showed Kyles's car in the background. Kyles went on trial again in 1996. One of the original eyewitnesses came forward to recant her identification of Kyles, saying she had implicated him after being pressured by police."

After numerous appeals, mistrials, and convoluted testimonies, Kyles was eventually "released from prison" when the charges against him were dismissed in 1998 (National Registry of Exonerations, 2012). This example demonstrates the potential of communications noise to influence the lives of individuals drastically within the justice system. If evidence had been communicated across both the defense and prosecution, different outcomes may have resulted much earlier in the justice system.

Noise and communication may be considered from the perspective of the Miranda warning. There are no specific wordings or phrasings that are applicable to the stating of the Miranda warning among law enforcement organizations. Although some versions may be longer whereas other versions may be shorter, all versions must contain the basic principles, intent, and content of the Miranda warning. The cognitive and emotional characteristics of arrestees and suspects may affect the communications process that attempts to convey the Miranda warning (Wrightsman & Pitman, 2010, p. 112). Regardless of either a short or long version of the Miranda warning, individuals must "understand and decide upon each of the rights given them" (Wrightsman & Pitman, 2010, p. 112). Although achieving such an understanding may be challenging for many individuals, it is especially challenging for individuals that suffer from mental illness or who have mental handicaps (Wrightsman & Pitman, 2010, p. 112). Such individuals "are highly suggestible," are easily manipulated, and are easily confused (Wrightsman & Pitman, 2010, p. 113). Furthermore, these individuals exhibit "poor communications abilities" and are unable to "reasonably judge and adequately respond to a given situation," thereby contributing to an inability to "grasp the concept of possible future consequences from waiving rights" (Wrightsman & Pitman, 2010, p. 113). Antagonistic behaviors and attitudes of law enforcement personnel may complicate interactions with such individuals when attempting to communicate the Miranda warning (Wrightsman & Pitman, 2010, p. 113).

Another impediment that affects the communicating and understanding of the Miranda warning involves the age of the arrestee or suspect. Youths and juveniles, who are under the age of 16 years, often "do not understand either the language of the Miranda rights or some of the concepts underlying those rights, such as the role of defense counsel in criminal prosecutions" (Ferdico et al., 2009). Additionally, youths who are "preteens or younger lack the intellectual development" that is necessary to render a knowledgeable decision regarding their Miranda rights despite being informed of the contents of the Miranda warning (Ferdico et al., 2009).

Because of the cognitive differences between juveniles and adults, diminishing the effects of such communications barriers may be difficult. Some arguments recommend that interrogation safeguards must exist to accommodate these differences. One recommendation involves the notion that the language of interrogation be simplified and made "more comprehensible to juveniles" (Krzewinski, n.d.).

Communications barriers are unavoidable within the justice system and during policing activities. However, despite the inescapability of noise, its effects may be diminished. Language interpreters may be used when questioning individuals. Braille documents may be used to communicate with blind individuals. Sign language may be used to accommodate the communication needs of deaf individuals. Officers may need to alter their demeanors when communicating with elderly people. Regardless of the efforts made to diminish the negative impacts of communications noise, various impediments shall unceasingly exist within the justice system.

Protocols

Protocols are rules that govern communications, thereby establishing some amounts of standardization and consistency when communicating. The use of protocols lessens confusion and improves the effectiveness and efficiency of communication. Because of such congruency of communications, within the context of public safety and policing, protocols facilitate the "use of standardized language for internal radio communications, which enables public safety agencies to communicate more easily with other agencies and jurisdictions during major emergencies" (U.S. Department of Homeland Security, 2012). When communicating during emergencies, law enforcement agencies are "encouraged to simplify verbal phrases and to use the International Phonetic Alphabet to further improve interoperability" (U.S. Department of Homeland Security, 2012). Furthermore, using such a protocol contributes to conformance to the standards of the National Incident Management System (U.S. Department of Homeland Security, 2012).

After the events of September 11, 2001, some segments of the population were leery of law enforcement organizations (Patterson, 2002). Specifically, female immigrants and refugees, who were victims of domestic violence, were reluctant to seek assistance from law enforcement agencies (Patterson, 2002). This segment of the population exhibited poor or no English proficiency (Patterson, 2002). To serve the needs of these victims of domestic violence, "outreach campaigns" were necessary to link "non-English-speaking victims" to the "services available" from "domestic violence agencies" (Patterson, 2002, p. 1).

Within the programs and services available, the protocol was a consideration of such agencies. Facets of language assistance to facilitate communication included the following items (Patterson, 2002, p. 3):

- Developing policies and procedures for identifying and assessing the language needs of its limited English proficient (LEP) applicants/clients (Patterson, 2002, p. 3)
- Providing for a range of oral language assistance options (Patterson, 2002, p. 3)
- Communicating to LEP persons (either verbally or in written form) their right to language assistance (Patterson, 2002, p. 3)
- Providing written translation of materials that are often used when working with a LEP client (Patterson, 2002, p. 3)

The difficulties of serving a variety of population segments whose English skills are either poor or nonexistent present challenges, obstacles, and dangers for law enforcement organizations and personnel. The ability to communicate using a common paradigm is a component of building trustfulness. Any disconnect between factions that are attempting to communicate poses tremendous implications for law enforcement personnel serving as first responders to incident scenes (Shah et al., 2005, p. 4). If a law enforcement officer is unable to communicate using a common, natural language, it becomes increasingly more difficult to "gather evidence or provide protection" (Shah et al., 2005, p. 4). Because many segments of the population do not speak English, many immigrants may avoid contact with law enforcement officers (Shah et al., 2005, p. 4). Such a discordant circumstance also inhibits the reporting of crime or the calling for assistance by members of the community whose language is not English (Shah et al., 2005, p. 4). Officer safety is also a concern of this language barrier because "being unable to communicate with an armed suspect can dangerously exacerbate a life-or-death situation" (Shah et al., 2005, p. 4).

The traditional mission of policing involves the maintaining of societal order and the deterring of crime. Accomplishing these goals involves trustfulness and cooperativeness between law enforcement organizations and their served communities. Embellishing and forging the relationship between law enforcement organizations and their served communities necessitates "effective and open communications between officers and residents, including those who are not fluent in English" (Shah et al., 2005, p. 5). Furthermore, any law enforcement organization that receives assistance from the federal government must comply with Title VI of the 1964 Civil Rights Act, mandating that they must reasonably "ensure that their services are meaningfully accessible to those who do not speak English well" (Shah et al., 2005, p. 5).

These communication issues are of paramount importance to law enforcement organizations. The use of protocols to overcome language barriers is a necessity to enhance the organizational ability of maintaining societal order and deterring crime among communities. Within the justice domain, it is advisable to develop protocols regarding personnel training emphasizing "language access policy and effective use of the agency's language assistance services" (Shah et al., 2005, p. 10).

Considerations of protocol have implications for the Miranda warning. If a suspect or arrestee does not speak English fluently or does not speak English, then it may be impossible to guarantee that the Miranda concepts are understood. When issuing the Miranda warning, protocols may incorporate "translations of the Miranda warning (for officers who are fluent in those languages), and specific instructions on how to access a telephonic interpreting service" (Shah et al., 2005, p. 11). An additional recommendation states that

> A notation of the fact that a party or witness does not speak English should be included in the witness/victim/suspect information section of the report. Indicate what language was spoken, the name(s) of interpreters, and all vital information about the interpreters, such as social security number, addresses, etc. (LaWall, 2010)

Protocols govern the communications between law enforcement organizations and their serviced communities. Using protocols embellishes the ability of law enforcement organizations and personnel to communicate with diverse population segments. Through the use of protocols, law enforcement entities attempt to strengthen their relationships with their communities. Protocols are applicable to segments of the population that have English fluency or that have constrained English fluency. It is necessary for law enforcement organizations to accommodate both societal population segments when attempting to fulfill the traditional mission of deterring crime and maintaining societal order. Protocols provide a foundation for establishing and maintaining communications with such diverse population segments.

In addition to their traditional roles of enforcing laws, law enforcement organizations are an integral component of emergency response. Protocols also facilitate the communications among first-responder entities during calamities, including law enforcement organizations. Through the use of protocols, communicating becomes more efficient and effective because of standardization among the communicating entities. As a result, the magnitude of responsiveness may be increased regarding operational successfulness.

Protocols permeate this dichotomy of functionality among law enforcement organizations. Protocols establish a foundational basis for standardizing communications during emergencies and provide a basis for accommodating the needs of segments of the population that have poor or no English skills. Given these notions, protocols are an integral aspect of law enforcement communications.

Where?

Acts of communicating occur within the communications domain. The communications domain consists of various attributes that are necessary for communications to occur both efficiently and effectively. It also includes facets of noise as communications barriers. All of the preceding concepts are represented within the communications domain. When taken cumulatively, the notions of who, what, when, how, why, protocols, and noise integrate to establish the attributes of the communications domain. These integrated components represent the environment in which communication occurs.

Communications environments vary; no two are identical. The communications environment of a law enforcement organization serving a small town differs from that of a large, metropolitan police organization. Instead of coordinating the communications of just a few law enforcement personnel within a rural environment, dispatchers may coordinate the communications of thousands of officers within an urban setting. Instead of dealing with a primarily homogenous rural citizenry whose language is overwhelmingly English, urban policing necessitates accommodating numerous languages and a diverse population. Figures 1.8 and 1.9 show maps depicting both English and non-English saturations within the United States.

Within the United States and Puerto Rico, a variety of Native North American languages are spoken. According to the U.S. Census Bureau, the American Community Survey (ACS), conducted between the period of 2006 and 2010, indicated that

> The ACS codes 381 distinct non-English languages, and 169 of these are Native North American languages. Although Native North American languages make up most of the languages coded, the speakers of these languages number less than half a million. The size of the Native North American language speaking population is dwarfed by the 60 million people speaking a different non-English language and the 227 million people who speak English only. (Siebens & Jones, 2011)

Numerous foreign languages are spoken within the United States. Another ACS finding states that

> With 34.5 million speakers, Spanish was by far the most commonly spoken non-English language. Chinese was the only other detailed language with at least 2 million speakers. Even at

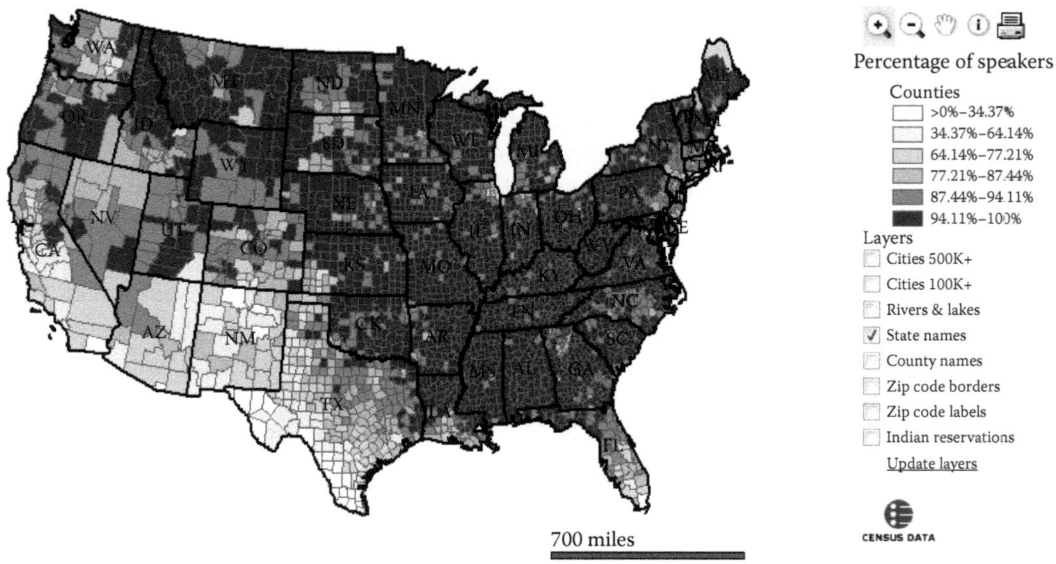

Figure 1.8 English saturation in the United States. (From http://arcgis.mla.org/mla/default.aspx.)

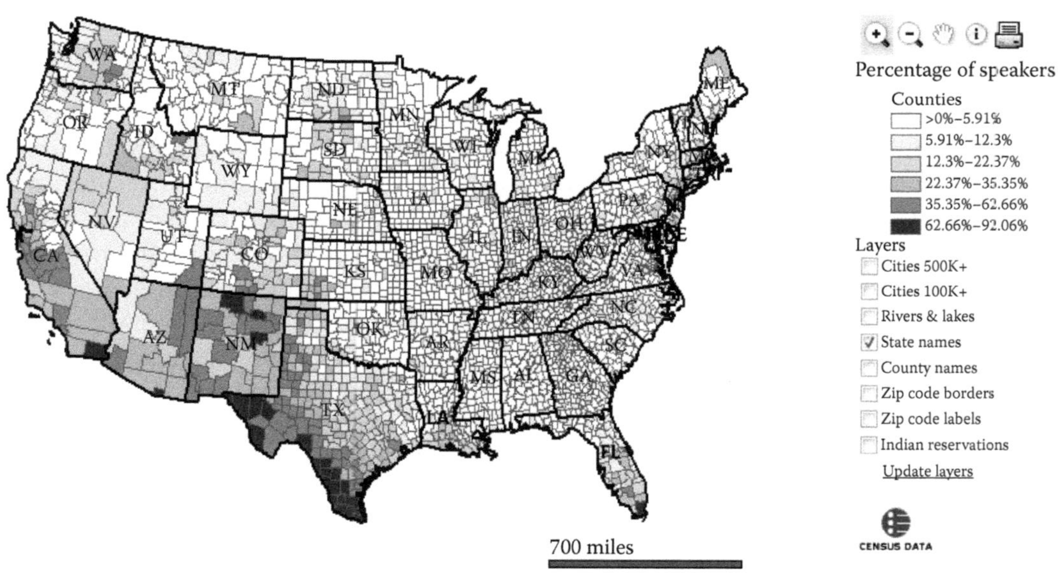

Figure 1.9 Non-English saturation in the United States. (From http://arcgis.mla.org/mla/default.aspx.)

this detailed level, however, there were still five other specific languages with over a million speakers: French, Tagalog, Vietnamese, German, and Korean. The English-speaking ability of the speakers of these specific language groups varied greatly; in some cases, certain groups reported speakers with higher levels of English-speaking ability, while other groups had speakers who were less adept with English. Some groups, such as Spanish, Russian, Chinese, and Vietnamese, showed higher proportions of those speaking English less than "very well" while other languages, such as French, German, Scandinavian, and Hebrew, reported higher than average levels of speaking English "very well." (Shin & Kominski, n.d.)

The ACS findings show that a variety of languages are spoken within the United States and are not necessarily inclusive of dialects. These findings have implications for law enforcement organizations because of the necessity of communicating with diverse population segments. The findings also represent the complexity of the communications environment that affects law enforcement organizations. Although English is deemed to be the dominant language within the United States, law enforcement organizations must grapple with communications barriers within urban areas that host various segments of peoples whose English skills are poor or are nonexistent. For example, within San Diego, for a demographic over the age of five years representing a total population of 2,765,828, the following ACS findings expressed the characteristics of language:

English only: 64.64%
Spanish only: 10.93%
Asian/Pacific Island: 3.41%
Other language: 1.27%
Bilingual: 20.41%

Given these findings, the local law enforcement organizations encounter diverse languages during the courses of their duties. Multiple languages increase the complexity of the communications domain, which affects policing. Further complexities are also interjected by noise barriers that inhibit communications, ranging from the demographics of medical conditions to the attitudes and behaviors of law enforcement personnel. In any case, whether considering national, regional, or local perspectives, communications domains are complex entities that pose numerous challenges, difficulties, and risks for law enforcement organizations and their personnel. Diminishing the effects of such complexities is not an easy endeavor, but it is possible through the uses of mitigation strategies and protocols. Regardless, law enforcement organizations and personnel must acknowledge the attributes of their communications environment and must accommodate the needs of diverse communications requirements.

Success and Failure of Communicating

The notion of successful communication is easily understood. A sender transmits a message via some medium to a receiver. The transmitted message is received by the recipient and is both comprehended and understood faultlessly. Noise may permeate the communications domain. Feedback may occur between the communicating parties thereby instigating another round of communications.

Communications may fail for a variety of reasons. Noise barriers may be so overpowering that communicating becomes impossible. Anything that inhibits the successful sending, transmitting, receiving, processing, and understanding of a message may be deemed as a factor toward communications failure. Failure may occur at any point among the various activities associated with communicating.

Communications Process

When integrated and considered cumulatively, the preceding concepts are components of a communications process. A communications process is synonymous with a communications model. A typical communications process is stated as follows (Smoke, 2010):

Sender: The process of communicating is instigated by the sender. The sender is responsible for formulating the desired contents to be transmitted. The sender also selects the communication method, "forming thoughts," and "expressing these thoughts" via some type of words or symbols (Smoke, 2010).

Message: The message represents the contents that are to be transmitted by the sender. The encoding of the message occurs by using words or symbols. Furthermore, properly selecting the appropriate "message is vital to the communications process" (Smoke, 2010).

Medium: The medium is selected by the sender and represents the "method of transmission" (Smoke, 2010). The medium represents the "means by which the message is transmitted," and consist of oral or written methods (Smoke, 2010). Mediums may also be verbal, nonverbal, or physical.

Receiver: The receiver receives the transmitted message. Decoding of the message occurs upon the receipt of the transmitted message. Receivers are not necessarily inactive within the communications process. Instead, they may instigate some form of feedback regarding the received message.

Feedback: Feedback notifies the sender that the message was received by the receiver. The receiver may indicate an understanding of the message. A lack of feedback may contribute to senders "wondering if the message was received, if it was understood, and if anyone is going to respond" (Smoke, 2010).

Figure 1.10 depicts the typical communication process.

Within the justice domain, this process is implemented continuously among a variety of settings. The communications process occurs each time someone calls 911 for emergency

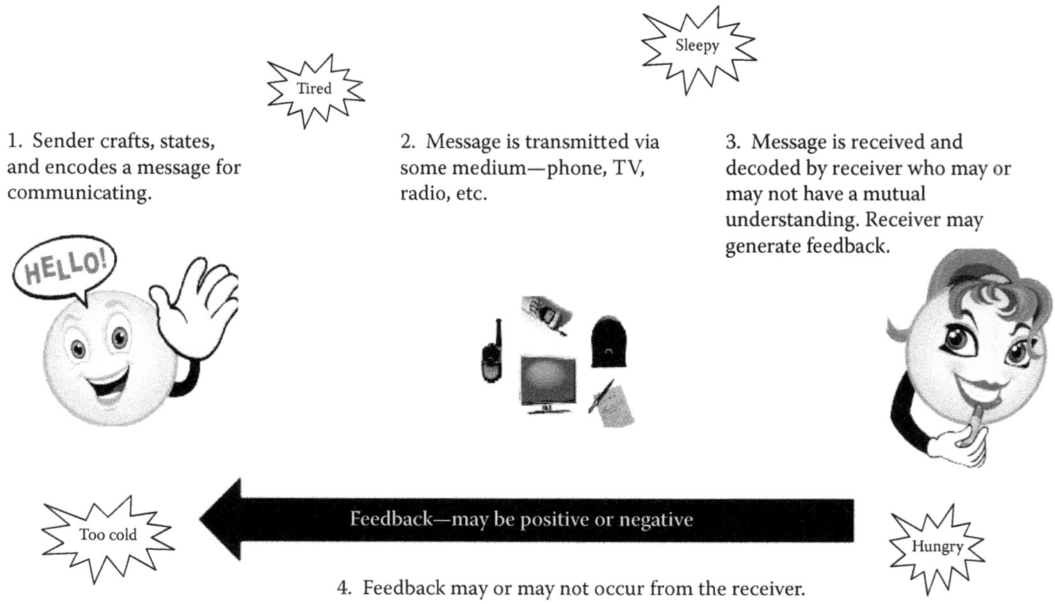

Figure 1.10 Communications process.

assistance, each time that an officer is dispatched to the scene of an incident, each time that an officer issues the Miranda warning, each time that a suspect or arrestee undergoes questioning, and each time that public service announcements are issued by law enforcement organizations. Certainly, many other instances of the communications process may be identified within the justice domain.

Commentary Regarding Communicating in the Justice Domain

A wide variety of examples of communication exist within the justice domain. It is impossible to provide an exhaustive consideration of how communications are leveraged toward deterring crime and maintaining societal order. However, within the justice domain, some acts of communicating have affected the entirety of the nation. One specific example involves the 1963 U.S. Supreme Court case of *Gideon v. Wainwright.*

After being arrested for allegedly breaking into a pool hall, Gideon experienced a trial in which he served as his own defense counsel. Although Gideon made a motion to be represented by legal counsel, it was denied. Gideon was told to represent himself during the court proceedings. Gideon was not an attorney and had no legal training. His ignorance and ineptness resulted in his being imprisoned. In essence, Gideon was "almost illiterate, was charged with a crime he did not commit, represented himself poorly at trial, and then was convicted" (Stocks, 2008). While incarcerated, Gideon educated himself concerning the law, and he "argued his own appeals" (Stocks, 2008). Gideon eventually petitioned the Supreme Court regarding his predicament. Gideon's communication regarding his petitioning of the Supreme Court is summarized as follows:

> After representing himself to the best of his ability, Gideon was pronounced guilty and given the maximum sentence (which is harsh, for a first offense without a lawyer): fifteen years to be served in the Florida department of corrections. When Gideon started to serve his sentence, he decided to do research on his constitutional rights. After appealing to the state and district court of appeals, and being turned down, Gideon proceeded to appeal to the Supreme Court. After a handwritten appeal was written from an indigent man, sitting in a prison cell in Florida, the nine Justices heard the appeal in deliberations and granted the writ of certiorari to Gideon, appointing him an attorney to carry his case. (Rojas, 2009)

Gideon used communication effectively when petitioning the Supreme Court. Although his communication was accomplished manually via hand writing, the end result was that he was appointed legal counsel regarding his case. Essentially, the Supreme Court ruling mandated that "states must provide representation to criminal defendants and ordered a new trial for Gideon" (Stocks, 2008). Moreover, his communication affected American history by altering the perspective of the justice system regarding the appointing of legal counsel for defendants. During modern times, as a result of Gideon's communication with the Supreme Court, public defenders may be appointed for criminal defendants. At the time, his writings may have seemed to be a modest plea for assistance to the highest court in the land. However, this simple act of communicating affected all American courtrooms. Figure 1.11 shows one of Gideon's several petitions in this matter.

During modern times, the use of television beneficially connects the justice system with the general public. For approximately 23 years, before being relegated to a quarterly

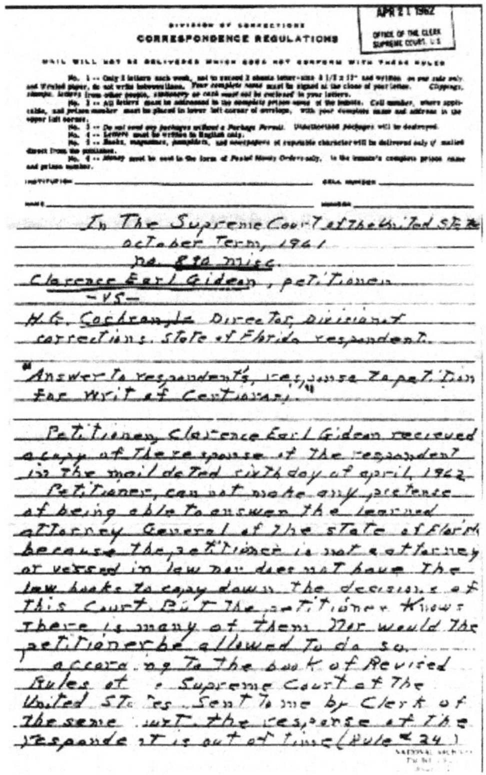

CORRESPONDENCE REGULATIONS

APR 21 1962

OFFICE OF THE CLERK SUPREME COURT, U.S.

In The Supreme Court of the United States
October Term, 1961
No. 890 Misc.
Clarence Earl Gideon, petitioner
-VS-
H.G. Cochran, Jr. Director, Divisions of corrections, State of Florida respondent.

"Answer to respondent's response to petition for writ of certiorari."

Petitioner, Clarence Earl Gideon recieved a copy of the response of the respondent in the mail dated sixth day of april, 1962.
Petitioner, can not make any pretence of being able to answer the learned attorney General of the state of Florida because the petitioner is not a attorney or versed in law nor does not have the law books to copy down the decisions of this Court. But the petitioner knows there is many of them. Nor would the petitioner be allowed to do so.
According to the book of Revised Rules of the Supreme Court of the United States sent to me by Clerk of the same court the response of the respondent is out of time (Rule 24)

Figure 1.11 Gideon's complaint. (From http://www.ct.gov/ocpd/lib/ocpd/images/Gideon%20 Petition.gif.)

special, the America's Most Wanted television show aired weekly episodes featuring stories about "some of the biggest fugitives wanted by the FBI and DEA" (Perricone, 2011). During its tenure, the show offered rewards and contributed to the capturing of approximately 1200 individuals who were wanted by law enforcement agencies (America's Most Wanted, 2012).

Other facets of communication link the justice system with society. Collaborative efforts may occur among "law-enforcement agencies, broadcasters, transportation agencies, and the wireless industry to activate an urgent bulletin in the most serious child-abduction cases" (U.S. Department of Justice, 2012a). This cooperative effort occurs when instigating searches for abducted children in which the circumstances necessitate the issuance of the Amber alert. Details of the missing child are communicated via radio, television, highway signs, lottery tickets, wireless devices, and the Internet (U.S. Department of Justice, 2012b). Communicating through Amber alerts has spared the lives of 595 children nationally (U.S. Department of Justice, 2012b).

Communicating is a vital factor in the success of policing and the functioning of the justice system. Communication must be effective and efficient. All individuals within the justice system must be mindful that the scope and magnitude of their communications have the capacity to affect the lives of others both positively and negatively. Communicating efficiently and effectively can spare lives, can determine whether one lives or dies, can relegate someone to a period of incarceration, or can liberate someone from the punitive attributes of the justice system.

Chapter Comments and Summary

Communicating is an art and science that involves varying periods of time among organizations. Strategic, tactical, and operational periods all are affected by organizational communications. These concepts involve an average of five years for strategic purposes, one to an average of five years for tactical purposes, and immediate to yearly periods for operational purposes. Strategic communications may involve the expression of strategic plans, tactical communications may involve the negotiation of contracts, and operational communication may be the expression of quarterly reports or the issuance of monthly work schedules among local police agencies.

There is no specific reason to begin any form of communications. Communications are justified for a variety of reasons ranging from personal interviews for law enforcement jobs to the issuance of public service announcement and public safety warnings. Individuals may communicate with law enforcement agencies to report suspicious activity, thefts, vandalism, accidents, robberies, missing persons, and a variety of other incidents. Law enforcement agencies may instigate communications to announce the outcome of an investigation, the presence of a sobriety checkpoint, or alternate roadway routes to avoid accident scenes. Policing also involves communicating with diverse groups. Protocols and standards exist to embellish the ability of law enforcement organizations to communicate with different segments of the population.

Various methods exist through which communication is facilitated. These methods include visual, auditory, written, digital, and human resources. These methods may be leveraged independently or they may be integrated to maximize the scope of communications. Regardless, they all serve the function of facilitating communications within the justice domain. However, noise represents impediments that may affect the successfulness of communication either internally or externally.

Implementing these methods, within some communications domain, involves the communications process. This process commences with the formulating and encoding of a message by the sender. Transmitting the desired message occurs through a medium. Receipt and decoding of a message is performed by the receiver. For communication to occur, mutual understanding and comprehension must occur between the sender and the receiver of the message. Feedback occurs when the receiver responds to the sender. Therefore, multiple iterations of the communications process may occur between the sender and the receiver.

The justice system and society are linked through communications. When a child is abducted, Amber alerts may be issued to warn society of a missing child and solicit societal assistance in locating the child. National television shows may also be used to inform the public about criminals and suspects that law enforcement organizations are seeking. Radio broadcasts may be used to facilitate public warning messages. Regardless of the message or medium, communication is a vital characteristic of the justice system and law enforcement organizations.

Terminology

Amber alert
Auditory media
Cardinality

Chronological
Communication
Communications domain
Communications model
Communications process
Concept
Convey
Critical theories
Demographic
Effectiveness
Efficiency
External communications
Failure
Feedback
Functional theories
Gideon v. Wainwright
How
Human interaction
Idea
Interactional theories
Internal communications
Interpretive theories
Message
Miranda v. Arizona
Miranda warning
Near-term
Noise
Operational
Physical barrier/noise
Physiological barrier/noise
Protocol
Psychological barrier/noise
Public service announcement
Receiver
Response
Semantic barrier/noise
Sender
Short-term
Strategic
Strategic plan
Structural theories
Success
Tactical
Time
Transmit
Video media
Visual media

Warning
What
When
Where
Who
Why
Written media

THOUGHT AND DISCUSSION QUESTIONS

1. The 1963 Supreme Court case *Gideon v. Wainwright* involved the simple act of handwritten communication. However, this act affected every American courtroom through the resulting mandate of legal counsel for criminal defendants. Do some research, and determine what other seemingly innocuous acts of communicating have also affected the justice system. Substantively explain and discuss these impacts.
2. Review your local news media. Over the last month, how many news items can you find that were related to the justice system or law enforcement organizations? Substantively discuss whether you believe these items were used effectively.
3. The communications process permeates every courtroom within the United States. Attend a session of your local court, and observe some hearings or trials. On the basis of your observations, write a brief essay that describes the instantiations of the communications processes that you observe. Within your essay, also consider the effects of noise that may have affected the communications process.
4. The communications process may be interrupted or completely abolished for a variety of reasons ranging from equipment failure to inclement weather that impacts electronic devices. Given this notion, write a brief essay that describes how communications systems may be made more robust to facilitate multiple channels to ensure that communication does occur when the primary modality is impeded.

References

America's Most Wanted. (2012). Top stories. Retrieved from http://www.amw.com/ (accessed November 2, 2012).

Artiles, B. (2012). Arrest made in mississippi highway shootings. *WLBT Television.* Retrieved from http://www.wlbt.com/story/18547536/police-impersonator-arrest (accessed November 1, 2012).

Cavaliere, V. (2012). Deaf woman says she was tased by police, jailed for 3 days without interpreter. *New York Daily News.* Retrieved from http://www.nydailynews.com/news/national/deaf-woman-tased-police-jailed-3-days-interpreter-article-1.1130732#ixzz238QK4Qak (accessed November 4, 2012).

Collins, S. (2009). *Interpersonal communication: Listening and responding.* Mason, OH: Southwestern-Cengage Publishing.

Cornelissen, J. (2004). *Corporate communications: Theory and practice* (p. 41). Thousand Oaks, CA: Sage Publications.

Cornell University. (2012). Cornell University police department emergency procedures. Retrieved from http://www.cupolice.cornell.edu/emergency/procedures.cfm (accessed November 2, 2012).

Dinkelspiel, F. (2010). Remembering August Vollmer, the Berkeley police chief who created modern policing. *Berkeleyside*. Retrieved from http://www.berkeleyside.com/2010/01/27/remembering-august-vollmer-the-berkeley-police-chief-who-created-modern-policing/ (accessed November 3, 2012).

East Point Police Department. (2003). Public service announcement. Retrieved from http://www.eastpointpolice.org/PoliceImpersonators.htm (accessed November 3, 2012).

Ferdico, J., Fradella, H., & Trotten, C. (2009). *Criminal procedure for the criminal justice professional* (10th ed., p. 722). Belmont, CA: Wadsworth-Cengage Publishing.

Gitmed, W. (2007). Citizens reporting crimes online: The San Francisco experience. *Police Chief Magazine*. Retrieved from http://www.policechiefmagazine.org/magazine/index.cfm?fuseaction=display_arch&article_id=1248&issue_id=82007 (accessed November 3, 2012).

Glenn, M. (2009). Haverford township police department operation keep safe: A program to reduce underage drinking and dangerous behavior. Retrieved from http://www.haverfordtownship.com/egov/docs/1255370233196.htm (accessed November 3, 2012).

Grassie, R., Sweeney, T., Buzzi, E., Crowe, T., Evans, J., & Wallace, W. (1978). *Integrated criminal apprehension program: The role of communications in managing patrol operations* (pp. 1–18). Washington, DC: U.S. Department of Justice.

Gray, M. (2012). Manhunt on for alleged Tennessee kidnapper. *Time*. Retrieved from http://newsfeed.time.com/2012/05/08/manhunt-on-for-alleged-tennessee-kidnapper/ (accessed October 23, 2012).

International Association of Chiefs of Police. (2007). Use of 10-codes vs. use of plain language in radio communications. *Research Center Perspectives*. Retrieved from http://www.google.com/url?sa=t&rct=j&q=police+communication+operations+ten-code&source=web&cd=2&cad=rja&ved=0CCcQFjAB&url=http%3A%2F%2Fwww.theiacp.org%2FLinkClick.aspx%3Ffileticket%3D5%252B7PC%252ByuYss%253D%26tabid%3D307&ei=P5GVUJzxHYO-8AS-yoDYAg&usg=AFQjCNGV-9G4PmgFiz-9pRilkTY3MyP70g (accessed November 2, 2012).

Knight, T. (2012). *Sarasota county sheriff's office four year strategic plan*. Retrieved from http://www.sarasotasheriff.org/Attachments/Sheriff_Knight/Booklet_sample2.pdf (accessed November 2, 2012).

Knobel, L. (2012). Police contract agreed after 15 months of negotiations. *Berkeleyside*. Retrieved from http://www.berkeleyside.com/2012/08/31/police-city-reach-contract-agreement-after-15-month-negotiation/ (accessed November 2, 2012).

Krzewinski, L. (n.d.). But I didn't do it: Protecting the rights of juveniles during interrogation. Retrieved from http://www.bc.edu/dam/files/schools/law/lawreviews/journals/bctwj/22_2/03_TXT.htm (accessed November 4, 2012).

LaWall, B. (2010). *Domestic violence protocol* (p. 12). Pima County, AZ: Pima County Domestic Violence Task Force.

Lindbergh, A. (n.d.). Anne Morrow Lindbergh quotes. BrainyQuote.com. Retrieved from http://www.brainyquote.com/quotes/quotes/a/annemorrow136164.html (accessed October 23, 2012).

Maassen, P. (2008). Hurricane Gustav announcement/information. WWNO. Retrieved from http://www.wwno.org/post/hurricane-gustav-announcementinformation (accessed November 1, 2012).

McKenna, E. (2000). *Business psychology and organizational behavior* (p. 173). New York: Psychology Press.

Metcalfe, S. (2010). *Building a speech* (7th ed., p. 9). Boston: Wadsworth-Cengage Publishing.

Muelhlhoff, T., & Lewis, T. (2010). *Authentic communication* (p. 40). Downers Grove, IL: InterVarsity Press.

National Registry of Exonerations. (2012). Curtis Kyles. Retrieved from http://www.law.umich.edu/special/exoneration/Pages/casedetail.aspx?caseid=3366 (accessed November 4, 2012).

Nelson, O. (2010). Memorandum. City of Hercules, California. Retrieved from http://www.ci.hercules.ca.us/index.aspx?page=609 (accessed November 2, 2012).

Patterson, L. (2002). *Model protocol on services for limited English proficient immigrant and refugee victims of domestic violence*. Seattle, WA: Washington State Coalition against Domestic Violence.

Patterson, S., & Radtke, J. (2009). *Strategic communications for non-profit organizations: Seven steps to creating a successful plan* (2nd ed.). Hoboken, NJ: John Wiley and Sons Publishing, Inc.

Pedersen, P., Miloch, K., & Laucella, P. (2007). *Strategic sport communication* (p. 77). Champaign, IL: Human Kinetics.

Perricone, K. (2011). 'America's most wanted' canceled after 23 years on the air: Show will become a quarterly special. *New York Daily News*. Retrieved from http://articles.nydailynews.com/2011-05-16/entertainment/29570055_1_amw-fox-entertainment-president-law-enforcement (accessed November 8, 2012).

Rankin, J. (2012). Known to police: No need for review of Toronto police contacts with 'radicalized' youth, act now, says Watchdog Group. *The Star*. Retrieved from http://www.thestar.com/news/gta/article/1150126—known-to-police-no-need-for-review-of-toronto-police-contacts-with-racialized-youth-act-now-says-watchdog-group (accessed November 2, 2012).

Rojas, C. (2009). Gideon v. Wainwright: The decision that changed American history forever. Coconino Community College. Retrieved from http://oldsite.coconino.edu/oncourse/2010/rojas_christian_gideonvwainright.html (accessed November 7, 2012).

Rosen, K. (1991). *Discrete mathematics and its applications* (2nd ed.). New York: McGraw-Hill Publishing.

Samovar, L., Porter, R., & McDaniel, E. (2012). *Intercultural communication: A reader* (p. 10). Boston: Wadsworth-Cengage Publishing.

Shah, S., Rahman, I., & Khashu, A. (2005). *Overcoming language barriers: Solutions for law enforcement*. New York: Vera Institute of Justice.

Shin, H., & Kominski, R. (n.d.). Language use in the United States: 2007. *American Community Survey Reports* (pp. 5–7). Washington, DC: U.S. Census Bureau.

Siebens, J., & Jones, T. (2011). *Native North American languages spoken at home in the United States and Puerto Rico: 2006–2010* (p. 1). Washington, DC: U.S. Census Bureau.

Smoke, C. (2010). *Company officer* (3rd ed., p. 23). Clifton Park, NY: Delmar-Cengage Publishing.

State of California. (2012). California missing persons. Retrieved from http://oag.ca.gov/missing (accessed November 3, 2012).

Stein, D. (2010). Natalee Holloway—Presumption of death: A case study. Harville-Stein Law Offices, LLC. Retrieved from http://www.harvillesteinlawoffices.com/natalee_holloway_case_study.htm (accessed November 1, 2012).

Stocks, J. (2008). *Supreme court decisions: Scenarios, simulations, and activities for understanding and evaluating 14 landmark court cases* (p. 75). Waco, TX: Prufrock Press.

U.S. Department of Homeland Security. (2012). Virginia's common language protocol. Retrieved from http://www.google.com/url?sa=t&rct=j&q=language+protocol+English&source=web&cd=4&cad=rja&ved=0CDMQFjAD&url=http%3A%2F%2Fwww.siec.wa.gov%2Fprojects%2Ffiles%2FLLIS_Common_Language_Protocol_Virginia.pdf&ei=65eWUMbaEJDm8QSZvoCoBA&usg=AFQjCNGPYFOIMSAuT8VbF-7CFF9dQVKBYQ (accessed November 4, 2012).

U.S. Department of Justice. (2012a). AMBER alert—America's missing: Broadcast emergency response. Retrieved from http://www.amberalert.gov/ (accessed November 9, 2012).

U.S. Department of Justice. (2012b). Frequently asked questions. Retrieved from http://www.amberalert.gov/faqs.htm (accessed November 9, 2012).

West, R., & Turner, L. (2011). *Understanding interpersonal communication: Making choices in changing times* (p. 13). Boston: Wadsworth-Cengage Publishing.

Wood, J. (2010). *Interpersonal communications: Everyday encounters* (p. 22). Boston: Wadsworth-Cengage Publishing.

Wrightsman, L., & Pitman, M. (2010). *The Miranda ruling: Its past, present, and future*. New York: Oxford University Press.

Crafting Communication 2

> I learned never to empty the well of my writing, but always to stop when there was still something there in the deep part of the well, and let it refill at night from the springs that fed it.
>
> **—Ernest Hemingway (Hemingway, n.d.)**

Objectives

The objectives of this chapter are to

- Explore the basic questions of gathering information
- Introduce the concept of the writing process
- Introduce the concept of the auditory process
- Introduce the concept of the visual process
- Introduce the concept of the integrated paradigm
- Introduce the notion of perspective

Introduction

A process is defined as "a series of actions or operations conducing to an end" (*Merriam-Webster*, 2012d). This notion is not incommensurate with the attributes of the basic communications process delineated within the preceding chapter. Each stage of the communications process occurs through time. Each stage of the communications process, whether it involves sending, transmitting, or receiving, represents some type of action or operation that is necessary for achieving mutual comprehension and understanding of a message between the sender and the receiver of the message.

Achieving this mutual understanding and comprehension is accomplished through the basic concept of the communications process. However, the communications process may be instantiated among a variety of methods: radio, print, visual, physical, verbal, and nonverbal paradigms. Each method provides a unique fashion through which communication occurs. Integrating the methods of communicating provides law enforcement organizations with a robust capacity of influencing either large or small segments of the populace. However, achieving the desired effect within society, such as leveraging communications to influence others to use seat belts or to report vandalism, occurs through some form of a methodical process. Through such processes, mental imagery is invoked within the mind of the receiver(s) of the intended message.

Invoking the desired mental imagery involves separate or integrated processes through which communications are facilitated. These paradigms involve the writing process, the visual process, the auditory process, the verbal process, or some physical process. In any case, these methods have a commonality: the basic queries of communication. They must all incorporate facets of who/whom, what, when, where, why, and how. Incorporating these basic questions embellishes the communications to bolster the effectiveness of the communication between the sender and the receiver of an intended message.

Communications processes are essential when interfacing between law enforcement organizations and their served populaces. Writing processes methodically contribute to the crafting of press releases, court documents, or contracts. Auditory processes are essential to interpersonal communications ranging from the interviewing of law enforcement officers for news outlets to the interrogating of offenders, suspects, or detainees. Visual processes contribute toward showing the happenings either using real-time or recorded methods. Furthermore, these methods may be used alone or may be integrated when crafting communications.

Regardless of the method used, a baseline of data and information exists when communication occurs between senders and receivers. This information is not random; instead, it is pertinent to the intent of communications. Describing this information is accomplished through the use of the six basic communications queries: who/whom, what, when, where, why, and how? Conveying the obtained information occurs via some means of auditory, written, or visual paradigms. Although the gleaned information may be conveyed, there also is a consideration of purpose underlying the act of communicating. Thus, crafting communications embodies the conveying of information to persuade, inform, instruct, or narrate through the use of auditory, written, and visual fashions.

Such concepts are present from the street patrols of law enforcement officers to the highest echelons of the U.S. Supreme Court. Patrol officers may use video camera and voice recorders to record incidents, whereas arguments before the Supreme Court may involve visual materials, verbal arguments, and auditory communications. Figure 2.1 depicts a courtroom sketch of arguments in the U.S. Supreme Court.

Figure 2.1 Sketch depicting arguments in the U.S. Supreme Court. (From http://www.pbs.org/newshour/rundown/2010/10/inside-the-supreme-court-marcia-coyle-on-military-funeral-protests.html.)

Basic Questions

Regardless of the communications paradigm, all instantiations of the communications process must incorporate the basic questions of who/whom, what, when, where, why, and how. These primary queries may be applied to any event as a method of establishing the basic data that is used within messaging between senders and receivers. Posing these questions provides a baseline of information to spawn the communications process and the content of messages. An example of such application may be considered from the perspective of contemporary events.

During 2012, the citizenries of the states of Colorado and Washington voted to legalize the possession of small amounts of marijuana for recreational purposes (Newsmax, 2012). Punitive measures were dissolved for the personal possession of one ounce or less of marijuana (Newsmax, 2012). Both the states of Washington and Colorado will permit the legal sale and taxing of cannabis trading among "state-licensed stores in a system modeled on what many states have in place for alcohol sales" (Newsmax, 2012). Although the citizens of these states voted to legalize the drug, its possession remains illegal per the federal law. Federal entities have attempted to squelch such trading among dispensaries that act as laundering conduits for the illegal drug trade in states that support the trading of cannabis for medical purposes through dispensaries (Newsmax, 2012). A total of 15 other states and the District of Columbia already have laws that legalize the medical use of marijuana (Newsmax, 2012). In the state of Washington, as a result of Initiative 502, which was "passed with more than 55 percent" of the voters supporting it, prosecutors, in both Pierce and King counties, announced that they were dropping charges involving 225 marijuana possession cases (Newsmax, 2012). Figure 2.2 shows a screen capture from a television news item regarding legalization in Colorado.

Figure 2.2 Colorado news media image concerning marijuana legalization in Colorado. (From http://denver.cbslocal.com/2012/11/06/no-on-64-concedes-colorado-votes-in-favor-of-pot-legal ization/.)

This scenario represents the changing opinion of the American populace in the states of Colorado and Washington. It shows the process of government being exercised by the citizenry through which the justice system is affected by the legalization of marijuana. Although these states legalized the possession and use of small amounts of marijuana, both activities remain illegal by the standards of federal law. Therefore, circumstances exist in which potential conflicts and disputes shall occur between federal and state factions. Such legalizing may affect officer discretion with respect to the enforcement of law, and the opportunity for numerous lawsuits to arise within the justice domain now exists. Furthermore, questions and issues may arise regarding the licensing of dispensaries and taxation. Given such a scenario, ample opportunity exists to employ the six basic queries of communication.

Who/Whom?

This query investigates the personal and organizational attributes of events regarding identity. It provides a basis for understanding the characteristics of the participants involved in the examined situation. Regarding the legalization of marijuana in both Washington and Colorado, the following questions establish basic information and knowledge of the human and organizational aspects of the event domain:

- Who were the voters involved? Demographics of quantities, ages, experiences, affiliations, etc.?
- Who were the leaders of the legalization initiatives?
- Who planned the legalization initiatives?
- Who organized the legalization initiatives?
- Who controlled the legalization initiatives?
- Who supported the legalization initiatives? Any external and internal factions in both states?
- Who helped in the efforts to inform the public regarding the legalization initiatives?
- Who were the prosecutors that dropped the possession cases?
- Who oversaw the voting process?
- Who expressed satisfaction with the legalization of marijuana?
- Who will benefit from the legalization of marijuana in these states?
- Who will not benefit from the legalization of marijuana in these states?
- Who opposed the legalization initiatives?
- Who led the opposition efforts?
- Who planned the opposition efforts?
- Who controlled the opposition efforts?
- Who were the opposition? Demographics of quantities, ages, experiences, affiliations, etc.?
- Who expressed discontent with the legalization of marijuana?

What?

This query investigates the scope and magnitude of events. It provides a basis for understanding the characteristics of the examined situation. Regarding the legalization of marijuana in both Washington and Colorado, the following questions establish some basic information and knowledge of the event domain:

- What instigated the legalization efforts?
- What were the purposes of the legalization efforts?
- What is the history of legalization efforts in Colorado and Washington?
- What challenges occurred during the legalization efforts?
- What method was used to inform the public of the legalization effort?
- What societal benefit will occur from legalization?
- What societal disadvantages will occur from legalization?
- What previous legalization efforts, if any, failed?
- What percentage of the registered voters voted cumulatively?
- What is the policy of the United States versus the policies of those states that have legalized marijuana possession and use?
- What potential medical benefit is associated with legalization?
- What were the terms of the legalization initiatives?
- What are the potential societal ramifications of legalization?
- What business impacts may result from legalization?
- What social impacts may result from legalization?
- What arguments were used to support legalization?
- What arguments were used to oppose legalization?
- What political parties were represented in the legalization efforts?
- What statements were issued after legalization was announced?
- What future effects are anticipated with legalization within the justice system and society?
- What was unique about the legalization efforts?
- What are the potential economic impacts of legalization?
- What are the potential financial impacts of legalization?
- What are the potential political consequences of legalization?
- What licensing issues will affect dispensaries?
- What taxation issues will affect dispensaries and the public?
- What will be the source of legal cannabis products (e.g., suppliers, farms, etc.)?
- What arguments are expected to occur between state and federal factions?

When?

This query investigates the chronological attributes of events. It provides a basis for understanding the characteristics of time and order. Regarding the legalization of marijuana in both Washington and Colorado, the following questions establish some basic information and knowledge of the event domain from the perspectives of past, present, and future queries:

- When was legalization announced?
- When did the legalization initiatives occur?
- When did previous legalization efforts, if any, occur?
- When did the legalization initiatives begin?

- When did the legalization initiatives end?
- When did the constituency first learn about the initiative?
- When did the constituency vote (i.e., open hours of polls)?
- When did the majority of constituents cast their vote?
- When did a perceived need for legalization arise in society?
- When did the organizers of the legalization efforts commence their operations?
- When did other legalization efforts, if any, in other states occur?
- When was legalization announced?
- When are societal benefits expected to be exhibited?
- When are societal disadvantages expected to be exhibited?
- When are existing laws to change officially thereby permitting the possession and use of marijuana?
- When are law enforcement organizations to undergo additional training, if any, associated with the legalization?
- When will defendants be informed that their cases were dropped by prosecutors?
- When did prosecutors decide to drop these cases?
- When will taxation of marijuana sales commence?
- When will taxation benefits derived from legalized sales occur?
- When will economic advantages and disadvantages be exhibited?
- When are political consequences expected to occur?
- When are future challenges and oppositions to legalization anticipated?
- When will licensing issues affect dispensaries?
- When are both dispensaries and marijuana products anticipated to be available?
- When are disputes between state and federal factions expected to occur?

Where?

This query investigates the characteristics of location, place, movement, displacement, or position. It provides a basis for understanding the characteristics of proximity. Regarding the legalization of marijuana in both Washington and Colorado, the following questions establish some basic information and knowledge of the event domain:

- Where did legalization occur?
- Where else have legalization efforts been successful?
- Where have previous or other current legalization efforts failed?
- Where did the legalization efforts originate?
- Where were the greatest quantities supporting legalization represented?
- Where were the least quantities supporting legalization represented?
- Where were the opposition factions?
- Where were polling places located in which demonstrations, if any, occurred?
- Where did any grass-roots campaigns, if any, occur?
- Where else is legalization likely to occur?
- Where did constituents learn of the legalization initiatives?
- Where did organizers of the initiatives travel within the two states?
- Where are any expected advantages of legalization to occur?
- Where are any expected disadvantages of legalization to occur?
- Where are revenues expected to be expended?

- Where are the anticipated locations of dispensaries?
- Where are the sources of legal cannabis products expected to be located (i.e., farms, processing facilities, etc.)?
- Where are the defendants in the dropped cases now? In jail or free?
- Where else may other possession cases be dropped?
- Where will licensing occur (e.g., city, county, state, etc.)?
- Where are anticipated disputes between state and federal factions expected to occur?

Why?

This query investigates the characteristics of causation, relationship, and reasoning. It provides a basis for understanding the characteristics of argumentation. Regarding the legalization of marijuana in both Washington and Colorado, the following questions establish some basic information and knowledge of the event domain:

- Why did legalization occur?
- Why were the legalization efforts successful?
- Why have other legalization efforts, if any, failed?
- Why did the citizens perceive the need to legalize the possession and use of marijuana?
- Why were financial issues expected with legalization?
- Why were taxation issues anticipated with legalization?
- Why were the organizers of the legalization effort motivated to pursue a public forum and initiative?
- Why would someone open a dispensary?
- Why did prosecutors decide to drop their pending cases?
- Why does marijuana use and possession remain illegal per federal law?
- Why are expected disputes between state and federal factions anticipated?
- Why is a licensed dispensary considered to be a necessary location for regulating the trade of cannabis products?

How?

This query investigates the characteristics of methods, procedures, and processes. It provides a basis for understanding the way of doing something. Regarding the legalization of marijuana in both Washington and Colorado, the following questions establish some basic information and knowledge of the event domain:

- How did the organizers of the legalization effort spread their message among constituents?
- How did voting occur (e.g., electronic ballots, hand ballots, etc.)?
- How is a dispensary license obtained?
- How will the legal trading of cannabis products be regulated?
- How will any taxation revenues obtained from the legal trading of products be expended?
- How will production of cannabis products occur?

- How will the distribution of cannabis products occur?
- How will cannabis products be secured among dispensaries?
- How will regulation be implemented?
- How will the justice system be affected?
- How will law enforcement officers determine whether less than an ounce of marijuana is present during searches?
- How will the pricing of cannabis products be determined?
- How will the tax rate be determined?

Crafting Methods

The responses to the aforementioned questions contribute toward understanding the legalization situation from a variety of perspectives. Each question represents a unique view of the problem domain. Certainly, communications may involve any one of these solitary questions. However, integrating these responses formulates a robust view of the problem domain. Expressing this robust perspective or expressing any of the solitary perspectives results from a variety of methods.

If one desires a written expression of the situation, then some method of free writing, brainstorming, outlining, or a formal writing method (that may integrate these activities) may be sufficient. If one desires to communicate through an auditory method, the aforementioned questions must be addressed before broadcasting a news report or giving a public speech. In the case of a visual paradigm, these questions are pertinent with respect to formulating a television newscast or a documentary film. In the cases of auditory and visual methods, one may craft a written response that may be transmitted via radio or that represents the notations that are necessary to prompt television news anchors. Certainly, other combinations are devisable. In any case, some method is employed to provide a basic understanding of the situational domain before the crafting of communication occurs.

Writing Process

The writing process is associated with the generation of printed, expressed communication using some form of language or symbols. The output of the writing process is found among contracts, books, reports, newspapers or newsletters, memorandums, letters, and any other form of written communication. Generating such items is not sporadic; instead, it occurs methodically via the writing process. The writing process consists of the following steps: (1) prewriting, (2) organizing, (3) drafting, (4) revising, (5) editing, and (6) producing a final draft (Wingersky, Boerner, & Holguin-Balogh, 2009). Figure 2.3 shows these basic steps within the writing process.

Prewriting

Prewriting is an activity involving the collecting, organizing, and processing of data and information to facilitate writing (Hibbard & Wagner, 2003). The focus of prewriting identifies the purpose of writing, the characteristics of the receiving audience, the topical

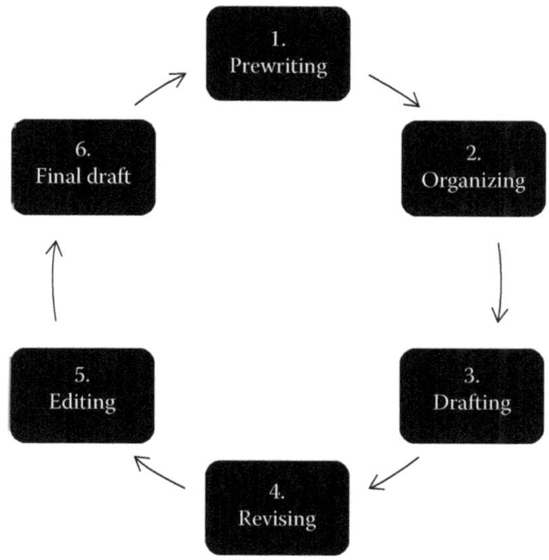

Figure 2.3 Writing process.

constraints, and the writing form (Cohen & Cohen, 2008). Prewriting is an exploratory aspect of the writing process because it facilitates considerations of emotional influences (i.e., feelings and thoughts), the organization of concepts, and the development of a writing strategy (Cohen & Cohen, 2008). These concepts are highlighted as follows:

Purpose: The purpose of writing involves various considerations relating to why the writing occurs. Is the writing intended to entertain, inform, instruct or warn, or persuade? Considering the purpose of the writing answers the question of why the writing occurs.

Audience: The audience consists of those who are intended to read the writing (i.e., the receivers of the intended message). Audiences may comprise the general public, a fellow law enforcement officer, a supervisor, an attorney or client, a judge, someone being served with a court order, news organizations (for press releases), and an array of others.

Topic: The topic limits the scope of the central concept and theme of the writing. Writers must decide exactly what they are writing about, and must limit the writing within these constraints. Therefore, any content must conform to the central theme and primary concept that is expressed within the writing. Ideas that are not within the established scope, concept, and theme are not included within the writing.

Strategy: The strategy consists of organizing and planning the writing (Cohen & Cohen, 2008). It accommodates how content is to be addressed, ordered, and presented within the writing. For example, a writer may use a funneling approach in which a general consideration of the topic is presented, and then the writing quickly targets the most important ideas.

These four concepts may be supplemented by a variety of activities through which writers establish their conceptual frameworks. Examples include the uses of outlining, brainstorming, and concept mapping. These supplements are highlighted as follows:

Outlining: The act of outlining commences with the "first uncertain selection of a topic and organizing assumptions" and is associated with all portions of the established topic (Morahan, 1981). The outline shows the flow of concepts within the writing and the transitions between ideas. It shows the topical relationships that exist within the writing and the groupings of supporting concepts for each of the major points that are to be expressed.

Brainstorming: The act of brainstorming involves the identification and listing of ideas that become mindful regarding the established topic. Basically, the purpose of brainstorming is to "get the ideas flowing" regarding the established topic (Hutchinson, 2005). Brainstorming may occur within groups or may be practiced individually (Hutchinson, 2005).

Concept mapping: The act of mapping concepts involves visually and graphically presenting ideas that are mindful regarding the established topic. The concept map shows pictorially a central idea and the ideas that are directly related to the central idea. The central idea is placed within the center of the map, and the supporting ideas are listed surrounding the central idea. Relationships between the central idea and its supporting ideas are shown via the use of "a series of spokes" (Kopp, 2012).

Organizing

The next step of the writing process is organizing. This consideration of organizing expands the organization that was accomplished within the prewriting stage. Organizing contributes toward the development of a "skeleton" of the writing (Hatcher & Goddard, 2005). Organizing also ensures that complex topics are "clearly communicated" because it incorporates a structuring of ideas and concepts that support the established topic (Putman, 2013). It also presents the primary concept of the writing either directly or indirectly (Guffey & Loewy, 2008). The direct approach involves presenting the primary concept followed by supporting arguments, whereas the indirect method presents the supporting arguments followed by the primary concept (Guffey & Loewy, 2008).

Drafting

Drafting is the third step of the writing process. This stage involves creating an initial copy of the writing and involves various changes to produce succeeding drafts. Drafting incorporates the outputs of the preceding stages to yield "good sentences and paragraphs, storyboarding, and building a tentative argument" via the written word (Blakesley & Hoogeveen, 2011). The outcome of the drafting activities yields the first copy of the written document.

Revising

Revising is the fourth step of the writing process. After an initial draft of the writing is produced, it must be revised. Content may be added, deleted, or altered. Phrasing and wording may be changed. Ideas may be strengthened through the inclusion of additional supporting materials. Structuring may be altered. Revising occurs throughout the writing process and must continuously improve the draft toward the ultimate goal of a refined, finished product. Revisions generally result in the formation of a new draft version of the writing that, in turn, must be revised.

Editing

Editing is the fifth step of the writing process. After a strong draft is fashioned, the draft must be edited. Editing represents the interjecting of quality within the writing through the "imposing of correctness" (Olson, 1987). The activities of editing ensure that the writing conforms to any established format or standards (e.g., Chicago style, organizational paradigms, etc.), contains appropriate content, and ensures conformance with the mechanics of language. When completed, editing represents "quality control for the reader" because its output conforms to any requirements that govern the writing (Kolin, 2012).

Final Draft

The production of a final draft represents the final stage of the writing process. The final draft is the completed document that contains substantive content to support the established topic, a methodical approach to the topic, conforms to standards of quality, and is ready for dissemination within its intended audience. No guarantee exists that the final draft will be perfect; it may contain some errors. However, the final draft represents a written document that has been logically organized and structured, revised and edited, and checked for quality. The final draft is the result of an evolutionary maturing of the written document through the exercising of the writing process over time.

Auditory Process

Although the written word is a powerful form of communication, there are instances when it is inappropriate for communicating. Law enforcement organizations must overcome issues involving communicating with illiterate people or people who do not speak, read, or write the same language. Furthermore, braille translations may be unavailable to support the communications needs of a blind audience. People may communicate orally during interviews or may be guests during radio shows. Press conferences and briefings are conducted orally and experienced through the sense of hearing. Certainly, many more examples of auditory communications may be examined. Given such notions, one may consider the use of auditory communications. The auditory process involves the following steps: (1) topical expression, (2) construction, (3) composing, (4) rehearsal, and (5) presentation. Figure 2.4 shows these steps.

Topical Expression

The first step of the auditory process involves establishing the topic and its associated constraints. Furthermore, one must establish the purpose of the discourse. Topics may be assigned or they may be per the discretion of individuals. When a topic is assigned, it may be the result of a supervisor indicating the need for a briefing to inform the law enforcement organization of new policies and procedures or may be to conduct a press interview. Among courtrooms, attorneys may orally present opening and closing arguments. In other

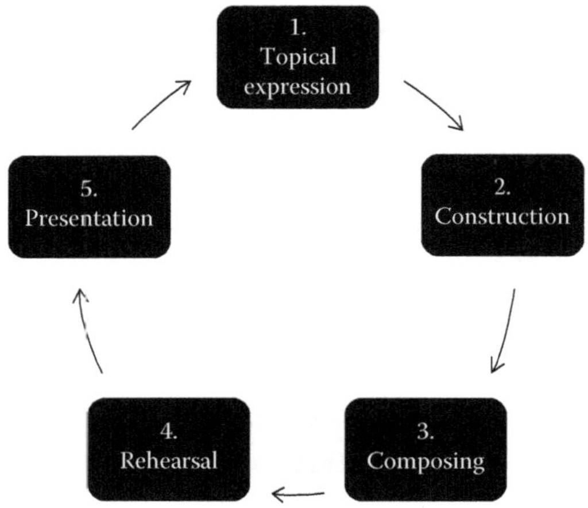

Figure 2.4 Auditory process.

instances, a law enforcement officer may be summoned to speak to a school audience in which one may decide to incorporate personal experiences within a speech. In any case, the topic represents a limited domain of interest.

Construction

After the selection of a topic, construction represents the second stage of the auditory process. Constructing consists of a variety of activities, including outlining, concept mapping, and brainstorming. Constructing also involves performing research to investigate various facets of knowledge regarding the established topic. Organizing occurs to provide some logical, coherent structuring. The descriptions of these activities are identical to those presented within the writing process. This step in the auditory process shares much with the writing process because many discourses are generated via the written word before they are presented orally. The outcome of this step represents the crafting of a framework model from which the bulk of the auditory message may be developed.

Construction also involves considerations of tools that may be used within the discourse. For example, many discourses are supplemented through the uses of presentation software, charts, graphs, and handouts. During the construction stage, these ancillary items may be crafted through analogous methods of revising and editing. Generally, the concepts of these items may be developed concurrently with the construction of the discourse.

Composing

Composing is the third step of the auditory process. The act of composing adheres to the constraints and pattern delineated within the framework model generated from the construction stage. Composing involves adhering to the structuring that was generated within the construction stage. It involves integrating the research sources to strengthen the argumentation of the established topic. It involves the crafting of argumentation, sentences, and paragraphs coherently to convey the primary attributes of the topic.

Drafting, revising, and editing are essential facets of composing. These concepts are identical to those presented within the writing process. These activities develop and mature the content and format of the discourse. They provide a measure of quality assurance to ensure that the discourse adheres to any given requirements. Examples of such requirements include whether the discourse can be presented within a time constraint, whether the content is appropriate, and whether argumentation is logical. The outcome of this step produces a strong draft of the intended discourse.

Composing must also accommodate the potential use of ancillary items. Such supplements may include the use of presentation software, handouts, charts, graphs, figures, and various other items. During the composing stage, these items are finalized and incorporated to facilitate the discourse appropriately.

Rehearsal

Although some discourses may be given extemporaneously, many result from the preceding stages of the auditory process. The fourth step of the auditory process involves rehearsing the intended discourse. Rehearsal is essential as a method of improving the presentation and oratory skills of the presenter. Rehearsing improves the ability to satisfy any time constraints and to improve transitions during the presentation (O'Rourke, 2008). Rehearsing improves the pacing ability of the speaker to modulate the timing of words (i.e., not speaking too slowly or quickly) and ensures that proper phrasing and pronunciation are mastered (O'Rourke, 2008). Rehearsing improves the ability to use any ancillary items (e.g., presentation software, etc.) and improves familiarity with these items.

Rehearsing also improves the verbal and nonverbal characteristics of the presenter. Repetitious vocalizing of the discourse shows the differences between spoken words and written documentation (Barlow, 2002). It provides a method of determining where pauses should occur, embellishes eye movements, and shows when gesturing may be necessary (Barlow, 2002). When rehearsing, it is often beneficial to record versions of the rehearsed discourse and to review them afterward. By doing so, one gains an understanding of where and when verbal, nonverbal, and physical improvements may be made within the discourse (Barlow, 2002). Furthermore, rehearsing also shows where improvements may be made regarding the use, quality, and content of any ancillary tools.

Presentation

Presentation is the final step in the auditory process. This act represents presenting the discourse before its intended audience. Before the presentation, one should arrive early to become familiar with the environment and its potential for various types of noise that may impede communications. If possible, such potential impediments should be remedied before the discourse is given. For example, if a temperature setting is either too hot or too cold, then the environmental temperature may require adjusting. Similarly, lighting may be adjusted or seating may need to be arranged. Regardless, the discourse should demonstrate the seamless integration of tangible and intangible attributes necessary for the success of communications. The discourse itself should exhibit the characteristics of a polished, accomplished performance.

However, not all discourses are perfect. Noise exists within all domains. Various factors affect the presentation of the discourse, ranging from the human fear of speaking in front of others to forgetfulness. Supplemental equipment failures may occur, thereby influencing the dynamics of the discourse. There is always the risk of failing to achieve the ultimate goal of communicating with regard to achieving mutual understanding and comprehending the intended message between the sender and the receiver. Regardless, unless delivered extemporaneously, all discourses involve some facet of methodically crafting auditory communications.

Visual Process—Video

There are situations that necessitate visual communications. In some instances, visual methods may be used to document case studies of events, histories, or to record witness accounts of an incident. Other considerations of visual methods may be to embellish some aspect of argumentation—perhaps an organization wishes to evoke an emotional response from the general public? For example, Mothers Against Drunk Driving (MADD) may appeal to the emotions of the general public during television campaigns that discourage drunk driving. Other cases may serve a different purpose. For example, training videos may be used for instructional reasons.

Regardless of the purpose, visual methods may range from the simple crafting of charts and graphs to support written or oral arguments to the development of films to document case histories or to show crime scenes. Producing the former items is certainly less intensive than producing the latter items. Items necessitating intense efforts are generally crafted through the use of a methodical visual process. The primary steps in this process are as follows: (1) preproduction, (2) production, and (3) postproduction (Shyles, 2007). Figure 2.5 shows these steps.

Preproduction

The first stage of the visual process involves preproduction activities that precede the crafting of visual materials. This stage represents the establishment of the reason for instigating a visual production. It involves the determination of the topic(s) of the visual resource and necessitates much planning (Rosenthal, 2007). The scope of such productions may be rather small, necessitating merely a camcorder and few personnel. Others may necessitate the development of scripts, accommodating of financial budgets to procure requisite equipment and personnel, and significant research concerning the topic of the visual resource. For such complex projects, numerous iterations of revising and editing scripts

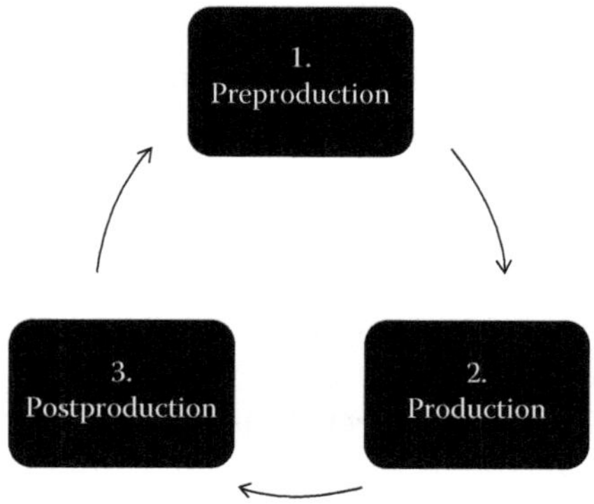

Figure 2.5 Visual process.

may be necessary during the preproduction process (Rosenthal, 2007). This stage is a preparatory phase for the production of the visual resource.

Preproduction exhibits both natural and man-made attributes. Other aspects of preproduction involve determining location, securing filming permissions and permits, considerations of weather for seasonal productions, the availability of personnel, day versus night projects, methods of safety and hazard mitigation, and mapping the concepts associated with the topic of the visual resource. Other factors include various forms of risk assessment that may affect the project. This listing is not exhaustive, and varies with the scope of the intended project. Therefore, many more items may be considered during this stage of the visual process.

Production

The middle stage of the visual process is production. This stage involves the generation of the visual resource (Rosenthal, 2007). It conforms to the specifications of any plans and scripts that were crafted during the preceding stage of preproduction. Directing is an essential component of this stage. Through directing, resources are marshaled, integrated, and used to generate the visual resource. Filming and interviewing (if necessary) occur during this stage. If a satisfactory visual outcome is not generated initially, then filming and interviewing become recursive activities that are exercised until the director is satisfied with the quality of the visual resource. Various activities of editing occur during this stage (Hart, 1999). The required amount of editing time depends on the amount of time that was necessary to record the intended video components and the complexity of the overall project (Hart, 1999).

When producing the intended visual resource, one must be mindful of the purpose of the intended communication. Therefore, three primary questions must be accommodated when producing visual resources (Hart, 1999):

- Explaining the background of potentially complex issues (Hart, 1999)
- Revealing the facts of situations that were previously unknown (Hart, 1999)
- Presenting arguments that show multiple perspectives of an issue (Hart, 1999)

Postproduction

The phase of postproduction is the third stage of the visual paradigm. Postproduction represents a period when "participants can consider what they would like to have done differently" or may contemplate the use of the video resource (Mitchell, 2011). This phase also represents a period in which the "fine-tuning of audio/video footage" occurs to refine its attributes of "sound, visuals, computer graphics, special effects, etc." (Pannu & Tomar, 2010).

Editing techniques continue to occur during this stage (Rose, 2009). Through additional editing and refining, the visual resource is polished to remove defects and to ensure that it conforms to any requirements that were stated initially. These activities also ensure that the video resource adheres to any time constraints.

These aspects of editing are either linear or nonlinear (Worthington, 2009). The linear technique involves editing of a master tape through the sequential ordering of recorded video (Worthington, 2009). The nonlinear technique involves the use of software to perform editing tasks, thereby reducing the amount of time required for editing (Worthington,

2009). During modern times, the nonlinear technique represents a cost-effective paradigm through which the efficiency and effectiveness of generating visual resources are accomplished (Swartz, 2005). The dissemination of the video resource may occur upon the completion of these activities.

Integrated Paradigm

During modern times, the integration of written, auditory, and visual paradigms may be employed to craft communications. This integration is often accomplished through the use of a multimedia paradigm. Essentially, this concept is defined as a system that "exploits a computer to combine text, data, graphics, animation, voice, and video into a single synchronized production or presentation" (Feng, Siu, & Zhang, 2003). In many cases, these systems are interactive. This definition represents the integration of concepts, paradigms, and processes that are associated with the written, auditory, and visual processes described within the preceding sections. Generally, there is no solitary, prescribed method for developing multimedia resources (Khosrow-Pour, 2006). Because of the integrated aspects of writing, audio, and video, the necessary processes may be conducted sequentially or concurrently toward the crafting of a final product.

Perspective

Regardless of the selected process whether one exercises an integrated paradigm, perspective must be considered regarding the final product of communication. Three perspectives exist: (1) personal perspective of the sender of the message, (2) the perspective of the sender toward the receiver of a message, and (3) the perspective about a third party that occurs when senders and receivers communicate. Respectively, these perspectives accommodate pronouns representing the first-person, second-person, and third-person attributes of the communications domain.

First Person

The first-person perspective accommodates a personal view of the communications domain and the characteristics of messaging. When crafting communications, the tenses and words listed in Table 2.1 are associated with the first-person perspective.

Second Person

The second-person perspective accommodates a view of the communications domain and the characteristics of messaging that represents a perspective of the sender toward

Table 2.1 First-Person Perspective

Subjective		Objective		Possessive	
Singular	Plural	Singular	Plural	Singular	Plural
I	We	Me	Us	My, mine	Our, ours

Table 2.2 Second-Person Perspective

Subjective		Objective		Possessive	
Singular	Plural	Singular	Plural	Singular	Plural
You	You	You	You	Your	Your

Table 2.3 Third-Person Perspective

Subjective		Objective		Possessive	
Singular	Plural	Singular	Plural	Singular	Plural
He, she, it	They	Him, her, it	Them	His, her, hers, its	Their, theirs

the receiver of a message. When crafting communications, the tenses and words listed in Table 2.2 are associated with the second-person perspective.

Third Person

The third-person perspective accommodates a view about a third party that occurs when senders and receivers communicate. When crafting communications, the tenses and words listed in Table 2.3 are associated with the third-person perspective.

Considerations of Perspectives

When communicating formally, it is best to avoid the use of first-person and second-person perspectives. Instead, the third-person approach is preferable because it explicitly denotes the attributes of the sender, receiver, and any third parties. The third person is frequently used among a variety of communications ranging from the annual reports of law enforcement organizations to reports that may be required by supervisors. However, there are instances when the first-person and second-person perspectives are appropriate.

When one is giving an acceptance speech because some other notable accomplishment was achieved, then it may be acceptable to communicate using the first-person perspective to show a sense of personal gratitude. An example is seen within the speech given by John Diaz upon entering the office of the chief of police with the Seattle Police Department (McNerthney, 2009):

> I would like to thank Mayor McGinn for the opportunity to continue to lead one of the finest police departments in the country. It is no secret that I feel that policing is one of noblest professions that a person can undertake. It has incredible rewards and responsibilities. I have to thank the great chiefs that I've worked for through my 30 years, from Pat Fitzsimons to Gil Kerlikowske. My nomination sends a powerful message to the newest rookie on up to our most experienced professionals that you can aspire to lead this organization. I started as a patrol officer, I always think of myself as a patrol officer, and now every Seattle Police Officer can see a path in their professional lives that could lead to the Chief's office. This last year has been one of great challenges. We had an eight-day span that started with a neighborhood was paralyzed by fear of a serial arsonist and ending with the calculated execution of Officer Tim Brenton. These horrible crimes were solved quickly with the great work of the officers and the close cooperation of our community. During all of this time we did not have time to grieve. Officers continued to handle 911 calls which continued into December with Officer Ben Kelly stopping a fugitive who had executed the four officers in Lakewood. In the

> midst of all of this we successfully went through our third national accreditation audit by the Commission on Accreditation for Law Enforcement Agencies (CALEA). It is of no surprise to anyone who reads the paper and sees the news that our department has been tested and criticized in recent months. I want you all to know that in a progressive department we take this scrutiny seriously and take the responsibility to address our challenges and shortcomings. The plain truth of it is that no one is harder on the Seattle Police Department than itself. And the other truth is that we can only succeed in keeping our community safe by working with, for and through the community. To this end, we are in the midst of an ambitious initiative to survey every neighborhood in the city to determine the crime and disorder priorities from a community perspective. We call this the "Neighborhood Viewpoint," and it is central to the SPD neighborhood policing plan. This expresses our philosophy that every neighborhood has different needs and priorities and that police services need to be delivered in a way that is responsive to our community. The controversial incidents and the recent upsurge in violence during the late night and early morning weekend hours has my full attention and commitment to address these issues and reaffirm the high standards for which this department is nationally known. And finally this is our opportunity to rededicate our focus on our highest mission—unfailing public safety service to the citizens of Seattle. Thank you again Mayor McGinn, I will go back to my desk this morning as we have deployment issues, budget and other matters to continue to deal with. I cannot end this without thanking my wife Linda, a 23 year veteran of the department for her support. When I put on this uniform every day I can't help but think of the work the men and women of this department do and I can't thank them enough. (McNerthney, 2009)

This speech is permeated with the first-person perspective. Chief Diaz incorporated a personal view within his acceptance speech to express his opinion regarding policing, duties and responsibilities, and gratitude toward others. The use of first person makes his commentary seem warm and enticing instead of cold and objective. First person enhances the conveying of the intended messages to generate feelings of personal expression.

When arrestees are informed of the Miranda warning, the law enforcement officer may generally address the arrestee via the word "you." This reference interjects a second-person perspective within the communications domain. Although the wording of the Miranda warning differs among localities, the intent and content are identical throughout the nation. A typical stating of the Miranda warning is given as follows (Anderson et al., 2002):

> You have the right to remain silent. If you give up that right, anything you say can and will be used against you in a court of law. You have the right to speak with an attorney and to have the attorney present during questioning. If you so desire and cannot afford one, an attorney will be appointed for you without charge before questioning. (Anderson et al., 2002)

These brief statements must be read before questioning occurs, and are essential to inform the accused of pertinent constitutional rights and to protect both the accused and the law enforcement officer. The Miranda warning is permeated with the second-person perspective. It directly addresses the accused through the use of the word "you." Although there is no specificity of person indicated within the statement, the use of "you" is understood because the Miranda warning is read directly to the accused individual.

Descriptions of court proceedings are often expressed through the use of the third-person perspective. An example is found among the writings of the American Center for

Law and Justice involving the 2009 Supreme Court case of *FCC v. Fox Television Stations, Inc.* (American Center for Law and Justice, 2012):

> The Supreme Court ruled that the Federal Communications Commission acted within its statutory power when the regulatory agency declared as indecent the broadcast of expletives from a nationally-televised awards show. The U.S. Court of Appeals for the Second Circuit ruled against the FCC, saying its decision was wrong and it overstepped its authority. The FCC asked the high Court to overturn the lower court decision. The ACLJ represented itself and 18 Members of Congress with its amicus brief filed at the high Court. The brief supported the FCC's position and contended that the indecency policy affords children greater protection from the harm associated by exposure to indecent material without infringing on the constitutional rights of adults. (American Center for Law and Justice, 2012)

Within this excerpt, the use of the third-person perspective eliminates the reflexive and secondary characteristics of communication that are associated with the first-person and second-person perspectives. No personal connotation is ascribed to the third-person perspective. Instead, it details an account of happenings from the external viewpoint of an observer.

Perspective is a powerful tool when communicating. It may be used to show a personal characteristic of the sender or may be used to objectively describe the characteristics of the problem domain from the viewpoint of an observer. Perspective may involve an inherent understanding demonstrated by the receiver of the message. Regardless, perspective must be accommodated when crafting communications.

Other Crafting Paradigms

Other paradigms exist that involve written, auditory, or visual concepts and processes. In some instances, persuasion may be used to sway opinions of individuals and groups. This notion is not uncommon especially among courtrooms in which prosecuting and defending attorneys present arguments on behalf of their clients. Informational paradigms are used to inform an audience regarding the characteristics of some entity. For example, when posting open positions for law enforcement jobs, a personnel department may announce the job requirements and requisite qualifications of applicants through print, visual, and audio media. An instructional use may involve stating the steps of booking and release processes that must be followed during the intake and outtake of prisoners. Furthermore, narration involves the detailing and stating of events from the perspective of an observer or participant. Many courtrooms involve some type of narration to describe witness accounts of events. In any case, these categories may involve the posing of the six basic questions coupled with some form of written, visual, auditory, or integrated paradigm. By doing so, communication between senders and receivers is enhanced greatly.

Persuasion

The concept of persuasion is defined as the "ability to get other people to do what you need, willingly if possible, but certainly without resorting to coercion" (Gurvis, 2008). Communication is often used to influence others regarding their opinion or behavior.

Organizational policies may emphasize the use of persuasion as a method of influencing individuals to comply with the directions of a law enforcement officer. Persuasion may be useful in overcoming any resistance exhibited by others. For example, the Peoria (Arizona) Police Department policy manual incorporates persuasion as follows: "verbal persuasion, negotiation or command instruction or direction from an officer or police services officer (PSO) in the form of verbal statements or commands" (Peoria Police Department, 2009).

Persuasion may be a useful tactic during interrogations depending on the situation and legal constraints (Hart, 1981). Through its use, suspects may yield "incriminating statements" (Leo, 2008). Persuasion may be used to build consensus among the personnel of a law enforcement organization regarding its strategic vision (Isenberg, 2010). It may also be useful when conducting homicide investigations as a method of eliciting of information regarding the crime (Brookman, 2005). Persuasion is useful within the setting of a courtroom. Specifically, it may be leveraged to "enhance motivation, or capacity, for extensive information processing (e.g., reducing distractions, asking questions to elicit thinking) to make it more likely that strong arguments will be understood and accepted" (Schneider & Honeyman, 2006).

Informational

Informing involves the communicating of knowledge, the giving of information "(as of another's wrongdoing) to an authority," or the imparting of "information or knowledge" (*Merriam-Webster*, 2012a). The informational paradigm is expository because it expands upon "ideas and facts" for the purpose of giving and explaining information (Sethi & Adjikari, 2010). This paradigm is not opinionated (Sethi & Adjikari, 2010). Instead, it "states facts" objectively through the logical arranging of arguments and the conveying of ideas "with no bias" (Sethi & Adjikari, 2010).

Examples of this paradigm include the expressing and disseminating of work shift schedules, annual reports of a police organization, quantitative reports showing crime statistics, and so on. The informational paradigm may be used internally or externally. Internal uses may include reports and memos, whereas external uses may include Amber alerts and notifications of sobriety checkpoints. Therefore, informational communication may be directed at a single individual or may accommodate mass audiences.

Instructional

Instructing involves the giving of knowledge, the providing of "authoritative information or advice," or the expressing of "an order or command" (*Merriam-Webster*, 2012b). Instructing expresses "how to do something," and may involve the use of instruction manuals (Means, 2010). This paradigm involves a consideration of communicating the characteristics of processes. It is the expression of the method to show how activities are accomplished. Examples of instructional communication include user manuals showing how to use crime mapping software, self-defense manuals showing how to perform joint locks to subdue attackers, or instructional inserts showing how to clean weapons.

Among courtrooms, judges frequently issue instructions to juries and participants within the proceedings (Lippman, 2011). Such instructions are issued before juries commence deliberations regarding the innocence or guilt of defendants (Lippman, 2011). Typically, the instructions of a judge include the following attributes (Lippman, 2011):

- The jury acts as the "finder of fact," whereas the "judge decides the law" (Lippman, 2011).
- Defendants are "presumed innocent until proven guilty beyond a reasonable doubt" (Lippman, 2011).
- Burden of proof rests with the "prosecution to establish guilt beyond a reasonable doubt" (Lippman, 2011).
- The characteristics of the "crime with which the defendant is charged" (Lippman, 2011).
- Delineation of the "procedures to be followed by the jury" (Lippman, 2011).

Narration

Narration is defined as expressing an account "in detail" or providing a "spoken commentary" (*Merriam-Webster*, 2012c). Narration may be used to convey the elements of personal experiences within the justice domain (Vadackumchery, 2000). Narration may be used among news outlets to convey the attributes of events that occur within the justice domain. For example, accounts of the 1991 beating of Rodney King were narrated among a variety of news outlets, including print and video media (Liebes & Curran, 1998). Newspaper descriptions indicated that the police officers were "irrational and excitable in their work, and as having used their powers illegitimately" (Liebes & Curran, 1998, p. 35).

Narration is also useful among courtroom environments. During court proceedings, narrative statements are often used among opening statements (Bugliosi, 2000). In this sense, the narrative expresses a description of the criminal act "from beginning to end" (Bugliosi, 2000, p. 127). Essentially, narrations of opening statements are used to exclusively present "the facts of the case, which will result in a clearer, more persuasive presentation to the jury" (Bugliosi, 2000, p. 127). Such narratives must "be as interesting as possible," and may involve some aspects of creativity regarding the fashion in which "evidence is presented during the narrative" (Bugliosi, 2000, p. 127). Generally, to achieve a compelling effect within the minds of juries, prosecutors may deliver the narrative as a story so that jurors may "visualize what happened" (Bugliosi, 2000, p. 127). By using narratives, humans gain an understanding of the events that transpired necessitating the court session.

Commentary Regarding Crafting Communications in the Justice Domain

Communicating efficiently and effectively is an art. Much time is expended when crafting communications because of the importance of achieving some mutual understanding between the sender and the receiver of the transmitted message. Successfully communicating implies that both the sender and the receiver share identical mental concepts that are gleaned from the transmitted message.

Achieving this understanding may be difficult. Noise and the complexity of the communications domain may affect the communications process. However, despite these considerations, the sender of a message must make every effort to ensure that the act of communicating is a successful endeavor. Therefore, the crafting of communications is imperative to achieving success regarding the communications process.

Within the justice domain, these considerations are especially important. Before issuing the final draft of an opinion, judges may revise several draft documents before crafting a final version that satisfactorily expresses the desired message using the written word. Video resources may be planned to ensure that a maximum, clear view exists of areas that may need continuous monitoring. Scripts may be prepared to issue general statements or to provide public warnings through radio media. Communicating through the use of multimedia may necessitate additional planning because of the integrated media forms that are used to facilitate communication.

Regardless of the modality of communicating, planning is an essential aspect of the communications process. Although senders may have a concept that they desire to express and transmit, the characteristics of the intended message must be meticulously planned to reduce the potential of failure or the negative effects of impediments. Planning also strengthens the potency of the intended message, and interjects quality within the overall communications process. All communications within the justice system and among law enforcement organizations must incorporate some amounts of planning to maximize the effectiveness and the efficiency of the communications process.

Chapter Comments and Summary

All communications occur because of some catalyst. Numerous paradigms affect communications. Regardless of the modality or the situation involving communications, basic queries are posed to identify salient characteristics of the communications domain. These queries consist of the following: (i) who/whom, (ii) what, (iii) when, (iv) where, (v) why, and (vi) how? These basic questions are applicable to all modalities of communication, including written, auditory, visual, and multimedia paradigms.

Written communications have existed since antiquity. Senders encode, express, and transmit an intended message using the written word. Recipients receive the intended message, perform a decoding process, and gain some understanding from reading the received message. Crafting these written messages is not a spontaneous activity. Instead, it may involve various facets of outlining, free writing, or prewriting.

Similarly, the auditory and visual paradigms invoke the communications process between senders and receivers of intended messages. Planning is an essential component of ensuring the content and quality of scripts that may be broadcast using radio and television resources. Although these modalities may differ in the planning methods, both incorporate planning processes through which quality is interjected within the communications process.

Other factors also affect the crafting of communications. One must be mindful of the formality of writing that is anticipated during the communications process. Therefore, choices must be made regarding first-, second-, or third-person perspectives when crafting messages. One must also consider whether the past, present, or future tense is appropriate. Repetitious acts of proofing and revising may occur to improve the quality of the intended message.

In any case, there is no universal method of crafting communications that is perfect for any given law enforcement organization. All law enforcement organizations and components of the justice system are unique entities. They all have different resources and capacities for crafting communications. They all experience different situations that uniquely influence their respective communications processes. Regardless, they all must accommodate some consideration of crafting communications to achieve the highest levels of efficiency and effectiveness within the communications process.

Terminology

Argument
Audience
Auditory process
Basic queries
Communication failure
Communications process
Communication success
Crafting communications
Crafting paradigm
First person
How
Inform
Instruct
Integrated paradigm
Linear
Message
Multimedia
Narrative
Noise
Nonlinear
Organizing
Perspective
Persuade
Postproduction
Preproduction
Prewriting
Process
Production
Second person
Third person
Visual process
What
When
Where
Who/whom
Why
Writing process

THOUGHT AND DISCUSSION QUESTIONS

1. When accepting or departing a position of leadership within the justice system, personnel may sometimes address constituents via a public forum. It is not uncommon for a newly elected sheriff or judge to give an acceptance speech or to give a speech upon retirement. Do some research within your locale and review the speeches of personnel within the justice system. Apply the basic queries of who/whom, what, when, where, why, and how to your selected speech. Given your examination, discuss how the speech incorporates each of these questions.
2. Review a local newspaper for any articles regarding events within the justice domain. Select an article and analyze its content with respect to the attributes of persuading, informing, instructing, and narrating. Given the descriptions of these concepts contained herein, discuss which category best suits the selected article. Substantively justify the discussions within your response.
3. Review a local television news program for any videos regarding events within the justice domain. Select a video and analyze its content with respect to the attributes of persuading, informing, instructing, and narrating. Given the descriptions of these concepts contained herein, discuss which category best suits the selected video. Substantively justify the discussions within your response.
4. A multimedia approach may be used to communicate with a variety of audiences. Pay close attention to the multimedia modalities that are used in your locality to communicate public safety messages. Write a brief essay that describes the types of media that are used, the message that is communicated, and your opinions of whether you believe the multimedia methods are successfully effective.

References

American Center for Law and Justice. (2012). *Supreme court cases*. Retrieved from http://aclj.org/our-mission/jaysekulow-supremecourt (accessed November 14, 2012).

Anderson, J., Mangels, N., Langsam, A., & Dyson, L. (2002). *Criminal justice and criminology: Concepts and terms* (p. 155). Lanham, MD: University Press of America.

Barlow, B. (2002). *Oral presentations made easy* (p. 22). New York: Scholastic, Inc.

Blakesley, D., & Hoogeveen, J. (2011). *Writing: A manual for the digital age* (p. 12). Boston: Wadsworth-Cengage Publishing.

Brookman, F. (2005). *Understanding homicide*. Thousand Oaks, CA: Sage Publishing.

Bugliosi, J. (2000). *The art of prosecution: Trial advocacy fundamentals from case preparation through summation*. Flushing, NY: Looseleaf Law Publications.

Cohen, V., & Cohen, J. (2008). *Literacy for children in an information age: Teaching, reading, writing, and thinking* (p. 288). Belmont, CA: Thomson-Wadsworth Publishing.

Feng, D., Siu, W. C., & Zhang, H. (2003). *Multimedia information retrieval and management: Technological fundamentals and applications* (p. 327). New York: Springer Publishing.

Guffey, M., & Loewy, D. (2008). *Business communication: Process and product* (7th ed., p. 157). Mason, OH: Thomson-Southwestern Publishing.

Gurvis, S. (2008). *Management basics: A practical guide for managers* (p. 84). Avon, MA: Adams Business.

Hart, C. (1999). *Television program making: Everything you need to know to get started*. Woburn, MA: Focal Press.

Hart, W. (1981). Subtle art of persuasion. *Police Magazine*, *4*(1981), 6–16.

Hatcher, D., & Goddard, L. (2005). *The writing process: A step-by-step approach for everyday writers* (p. 13). Springfield, VA: Landa Books.

Hemingway, E. (n.d.). Writing quotes. BrainyQuote. Retrieved from http://www.brainyquote.com/quotes/keywords/writing.html (accessed November 8, 2012).

Hibbard, K. M., & Wagner, E. (2003). *Assessing and teaching reading comprehension and pre-writing* (Vol. 3, p. 52). Larchmont, NY: Eye on Education Publishing.

Hutchinson, E. (2005). *Beginning writing* (p. 12). Costa Mesa, CA: Saddleback Educational Publishing.

Isenberg, J. (2010). *Police leadership in a democracy: Conversations with America's police chiefs*. Boca Raton, FL: CRC Press.

Khosrow-Pour, M. (2006). *Emerging trends and challenges in information technology management* (p. 2). Hershey, PA: Idea Group Publishing.

Kolin, P. (2012). *Successful writing at work* (3rd ed., p. 41). Boston: Wadswoth-Cengage Publishing.

Kopp, K. (2012). *Strategies for writing in the social studies classroom* (p. 38). Gainesville, FL: Maupin House Publishing.

Leo, R. (2008). *Police interrogation and American justice* (p. 319). Cambridge, MA: Harvard University Press.

Liebes, T., & Curran, J. (1998). *Media, ritual, and identity*. New York: Routledge Publishing.

Lippman, M. (2011). *Criminal procedure* (p. 573). Thousand Oaks, CA: Sage Publications.

McNerthney, C. (2009). Full text of police chief's acceptance speech. *Hearst Seattle Media*. Retrieved from http://blog.seattlepi.com/seattle911/2010/06/24/full-text-of-police-chiefs-acceptance-speech/ (accessed November 14, 2011).

Means, T. (2010). *Business communication* (2nd ed., p. 394). Mason, OH: Cengage Publishing.

Merriam-Webster Dictionary. (2012a). s.v. "inform." Retrieved from http://www.merriam-webster.com/dictionary/inform (accessed November 13, 2012).

Merriam-Webster Dictionary. (2012b). s.v. "instruct." Retrieved from http://www.merriam-webster.com/dictionary/instruct (accessed November 12, 2012).

Merriam-Webster Dictionary. (2012c). s.v. "narrate." Retrieved from http://www.merriam-webster.com/dictionary/narrate?show=0&t=1352870538 (accessed November 15, 2012).

Merriam-Webster Dictionary. (2012d). s.v. "process." Retrieved from http://www.merriam-webster.com/dictionary/process (accessed November 9, 2012).

Mitchell, C. (2011). *Doing visual research* (p. 78). Thousand Oaks, CA: Sage Publications.

Morahan, S. (1981). *A woman's place: Rhetoric and readings for composing yourself and your prose* (p. 174). Albany, NY: State University of New York Press.

Newsmax. (2012). Marijuana Possession Cases in Washington State Going Up in Smoke. Retrieved from http://www.newsmax.com/US/marijuana-cases-washington-state/2012/11/10/id/463603 (accessed November 10, 2012).

Olson, C. (1987). *Practical ideas for teaching writing as a process* (p. 8). Sacramento, CA: California State Department of Education.

O'Rourke, J. (2008). *The truth about confident presenting* (p. 11). Upper Saddle River, NJ: Pearson Education, Inc.

Pannu, P., & Tomar, Y. (2010). *ICT4D: Information communication technology for development* (p. 216). New Delhi, India: I.K. International Publishing House, Ltd.

Peoria Police Department. (2009). *Policy and procedure manual* (p. 1). Peoria, AZ: City of Peoria.

Putman, W. (2013). *Legal analysis and writing* (4th ed., p. 220). Clifton Park, NY: Delmar-Cengage Publishing.

Rose, J. (2009). *Audio postproduction for film and video* (2nd ed.). Burlington, MA: Elsevier Publishing.

Rosenthal, A. (2007). *Writing, directing, and producing documentary film* (4th ed., p. 9). Carbondale, IL: Southern Illinois University Press.

Schneider, A., & Honeyman, C. (2006). *The negotiator's fieldbook: The desk reference for the experienced negotiator* (p. 368). Chicago: American Bar Association.

Sethi, A., & Adjikari, B. (2010). *Business communication* (p. 86). Delhi, India: Tata-McGraw-Hill Publishing.

Shyles, L. (2007). *The art of video production* (p. 23). Thousand Oaks, CA: Sage Publications.

Swartz, C. (2005). *Understanding digital cinema: A professional handbook*. Burlington, MA: Elsevier Publishing.

Vadackumchery, J. (2000). *Human rights friendly police: A myth or reality?* New Delhi, India: A.P.H. Publishing Corporation.

Wingersky, J., Boerner, J., & Holguin-Balogh, D. (2009). *Writing paragraphs and essays: Integrating reading, writing, and grammar skills* (6th ed.). Boston: Wadsworth-Cengage Publishing.

Worthington, C. (2009). *Basic film-making 101: Producing* (p. 28). Casa Postale, Switzerland: AVA Publishing, SA.

Psychological Aspects of Communications

3

Music is the subliminal connecting adhesive in film, or at least in narrative feature films.
—Carter Burwell (Burwell, 2012)

Objectives

The objectives of this chapter are to

- Introduce the psychological attributes of communication
- Introduce communications strategies that use psychology
- Introduce logical reasoning
- Introduce fallacies
- Introduce persuasion
- Introduce behavioral modification
- Introduce subliminal concepts

Introduction

A mental model is defined as "a structural analogue of a real-world or imaginary situation, event, or process that the mind constructs during reasoning" (Nersessian, 2008). Mental models are "private and personal cognitive" representations formed by individuals or groups psychologically (Gilbert, 2001). People psychologically form a variety of mental models involving their surrounding environments. Mental models also may result from the process of communicating. For example, when disseminating a public service announcement informing the public of an Amber alert, the receiver of the message may hear or see a description of the missing child. On the basis of the communicated descriptive attributes, one may interpret the received description to imagine what the missing child looks like. This imagining of the missing child is representative of the formation of a mental model in the mind of the receiver of the message.

Regardless of the method, message, channel, or participants, all communications involve some consideration of achieving a mutual understanding and comprehension of the intended message between the sender and the receiver. Certainly, achieving such mutual comprehension and understanding may be confounded by the presence and the effect of noise that impede communicating. Although noise may be present within the communications environment, receivers formulate some mental representation of the received message. The intangible assessment of the received message contributes toward the crafting of some imagery or concept within the mind of the receiver. Therefore, the importance of mental models must not be discounted when attempting to achieve successful communications.

Regardless of the process used to fashion communications, the end result involves the psychological crafting of a mental model within the mind of the receiver of the message.

Therefore, when performing any instantiation of the communication process, whether it is a single paradigm or an integration of paradigms, the sender must remain mindful of not only the purpose and the method of communicating an intended message but also of the desired concept that is to be imparted within the mind of the receiver to generate the desired effect.

Achieving this end effect involves the use of various strategies to facilitate communications. Humans perform cognitive elements of reasoning involving induction and deduction. Human opinions may be swayed by the use of logic or by emotional appeals. Humans may be bedazzled by the credentials and testimonies of supposed experts that testify during court proceedings. Furthermore, some argumentation may be falsely embellished or twisted convincingly to alter an opinion. These considerations may be integrated within the communications process as a method of attempting to influence the mental model and opinions of individuals and mass audiences. Therefore, regardless of the communications medium, the uses of logos, ethos, and pathos are strategies that embellish the act of communicating and the forming of mental models.

Psychological Strategies

A psychological strategy may be considered as a method of influencing the human "judgment process" (Litwin, 2009). The psychological attributes of communicating may exist either "verbally" or intangibly through the use of "body language" (Rathus, 2005). Incorporating narratives as opening statements during court proceedings embellishes the ability of attorneys to "assign meaning to trial evidence by incorporating it into a plausible account of what happened" (Fulero & Wrightsman, 2009). The use of narratives influences the human ability to "organize information" and may be directly related to the verdicts that are rendered by juries (Fulero & Wrightsman, 2009).

Leveraging psychological strategies affects the perceptions of humans when receiving communicated messages. Depending on the wording selected by the sender of a message, the message may be "received in different ways by the same listener" (Guasco & Robinson, 2007). Both positive and negative perceptions may be achieved through the wording of the intended message (Guasco & Robinson, 2007). Additionally, when communicating within court settings, persuasion may be a tactic through which "reactance effects" may be generated (Lieberman, Arndt, & Vess, 2009).

The use of psychology may be embedded within any form of communication. Written communication may be used to persuade through the telling of a story. Visual imagery may be used to show the effects of a heinous crime. Auditory messaging may incorporate the recorded screams of victims pleading for help. Certainly, these methods may be combined as a method of attempting to strengthen the argumentation of the intended message and the achieving of the desired mental outcome in the mind of the receiver of the message. Regardless, psychological strategies involve some aspects of logical reasoning, emotional appeal, or method of persuasion.

Reasoning Methods

Logical reasoning is the "process of following a set of rigorous steps for reaching valid, or correct, conclusions" (Bernstein, 2010). The act of human reasoning logically occurs

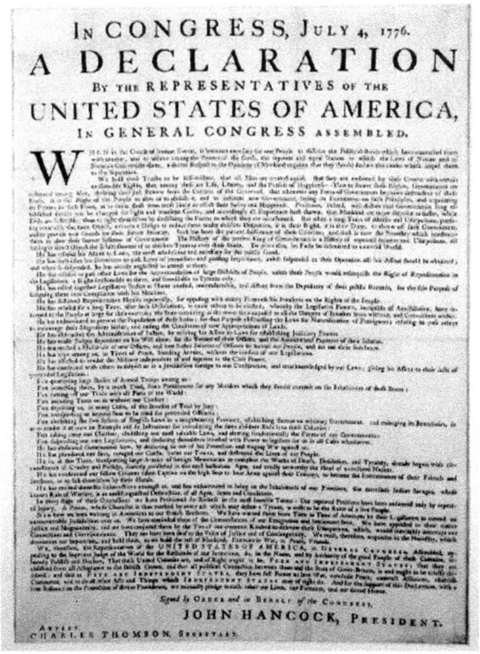

IN CONGRESS, JULY 4, 1776.

A DECLARATION

BY THE REPRESENTATIVES OF THE

UNITED STATES OF AMERICA,

IN GENERAL CONGRESS ASSEMBLED.

JOHN HANCOCK, PRESIDENT.

Figure 3.1 Declaration of Independence. (From http://www.nps.gov/museum/exhibits/revwar/image_gal/indeimg/web_exhibit/declaration.jpg.)

cognitively through the processes of deduction and induction. Deductive reasoning is defined as "the process of reasoning from one or more general statements regarding what is known to reach a logically certain conclusion" (Sternberg, 2009, p. 499). Deductive reasoning facilitates the transitioning from a general perspective of the problem domain to a specific perspective of the problem domain. Inductive reasoning involves moving "from a set of particular observations to the discovery of a pattern that represents some degree of order among the varied events under examination," thereby transitioning from a specific perspective to a general perspective of the problem domain (Sternberg, 2009, p. 22). Both methods may be integrated within communications paradigms.

Within the communications process, both senders and receivers of messages may critically analyze various facets of the communications domain to form some opinion or conclusion thereby influencing any mental model that may exist. Critical analysis and reasoning logically involve a consideration of the concept of logos. Within the context of reasoning, the notion of logos is defined as an "appeal to reason" that "relies on logic or reason" (Purdue University, 2012). Achieving some form of logical reasoning within the human mind occurs through two methods: deduction and induction. Within the sections that follow, these methods are considered with respect to the Declaration of Independence. Figure 3.1 shows the Declaration of Independence.

Deduction

It is assumed that if a deductive argument is valid and the basic premises are truthful, then the "derived conclusion must be true" (Becker, 2009). This derived conclusion does not "imply more" or surpass the basic constraints and attributes of the premises "upon which it is based" (Ericson, 2005). However, the truthfulness of the premises or of the derived conclusion does not imply that the argument itself is valid (Seel, 2012). Therefore, both the conclusion and premises "of a valid argument may all be false" (Seel, 2012).

Deduction involves the use of generalization from which a conclusion is derived. This generalization is the combination of a major and minor argument from which a conclusion is generated. This process of generalization commences with a set of observations to provide a basis for these arguments. An example is given as follows:

- *Major premise*: "The contract of a minor is voidable at the instance of the minor" (Blum, 2007, p. 41).
- *Minor premise*: June Nior is a minor who entered a contract and now seeks to avoid it.
- *Conclusion*: June has the right to avoid the contract.

The form of the premises associated with deductive reasoning is essential with regard to the validity of the conclusion (Blum, 2007, p. 548). The correctness and truthfulness of the considered premises affects the conclusion. An example involving imperfection is given as follows:

- *Major premise*: Prisoners in the local jail were arrested for thievery.
- *Minor premise*: Tom is a prisoner in the local jail.
- *Conclusion*: Tom is a thief.

Although arrested thieves are prisoners in the local jail, other offenders may be jailed for a variety of crimes. Perhaps Tom was arrested for assault or vandalism? Perhaps he was arrested for public drunkenness? Therefore, the form of the premises is important with respect to the validity of the derived conclusion. No guarantee exists that Tom is a thief. Instead, he may be incarcerated for different criminal offenses.

Much of the communication that occurs within the justice system involves written communication. The use of deductive reasoning may be integrated among written documents. When using paragraphs, sentences are used to develop the "main idea," which is "usually expressed by the very first sentence in the paragraph" (Sambey, 1999). This first sentence is referred to as the "topic sentence" (Sambey, 1999). The succeeding sentences must support and embellish the concept expressed within the topic sentence. In essence, they must "expand it in some way" (Sambey, 1999).

These deductive notions of communication are also applicable within the content of messages when communicating with the general public. Entities within the justice system often generate news items for dissemination throughout a variety of channels, including written, auditory, and visual media. The principles of deduction may be used to craft the contents of such items. Incorporating deductive principles adheres to a methodical consideration of the crafting of the intended message.

The crafting of deductive reasoning often involves the use of outlining as a method of stating the desired premises (LeClercq, 1995). An example format is given as follows:

1. Topic sentence of the first major point—states the main idea
   a. Transitioning to the first statement supplementing the main idea

        i. Sentence supporting the topic sentence.
        ii. Other ideas are included in the succeeding sentences.
    b. Transitioning to the next paragraph supplementing the main idea
        i. Sentence supporting the main idea.
        ii. Other ideas are included in the succeeding sentences.
2. Topic sentence of the second major point supporting the main idea
    a. Transitioning to the first statement supplementing the second concept
        i. Sentence supporting the topic sentence.
        ii. Other ideas are included in the succeeding sentences.
    b. Transitioning to the next paragraph supplementing the second concept
        i. Sentence supporting the main idea.
        ii. Other ideas are included in the succeeding sentences.
3. Concluding point supporting the main idea integrating concepts
    a. Transitioning to the first statement supplementing the conclusion
        i. Sentence supporting the conclusion.
        ii. Other ideas are included in the concluding sentences.

These headings and supporting statements are continued until the main ideas and supporting elements of the topic are expressed. Statements that reflect deduction should exhibit "dependent relationships" showing a relationship to the "topic sentence" (LeClercq, 1995, p. 96). Deduction may also be shown through the use of statements such as "for example," "for instance," and so on (LeClercq, 1995, p. 96). Language must be direct and reflective of the premises contained within the concepts being expressed to the receiver of the message.

Deductive reasoning and argumentation were used in the Declaration of Independence. Thomas Jefferson understood the necessity of critical analysis and reasoning to express the justification of separating from England as a method of persuading and convincing the world that the actions of the "American colonies" were justifiable (Kirszner & Mandell, 2011). The arguments of Jefferson are expressed as follows (Kirszner & Mandell, 2011):

- *Major premise*: "When a government oppresses people, the people have a right to abolish that government" (Kirszner & Mandell, 2011).
- *Minor premise*: "The government of England is oppressing the American people" (Kirszner & Mandell, 2011).
- *Conclusion*: "Therefore, the American people have the right to abolish that government" (Kirszner & Mandell, 2011).

Within the Declaration of Independence, the sentence establishing the major premise is, "We hold these truths to be self-evident, that all men are created equal, that they are endowed by their Creator with certain unalienable Rights, that among these are Life, Liberty and the pursuit of Happiness.—That to secure these rights, Governments are instituted among Men, deriving their just powers from the consent of the governed,—That whenever any Form of Government becomes destructive of these ends, it is the Right of the People to alter or to abolish it, and to institute new Government, laying its foundation on such principles and organizing its powers in such form, as to them shall seem most likely to effect their Safety and Happiness" (Independence Hall Association, n.d.).

Within the Declaration of Independence, numerous points supported the minor premise that England was oppressing the colonies. The contents of the points ranged from the imposition of taxes without the consent of the colonies to the deprivation of trial by jury (Independence Hall Association, n.d.). All of these secondary points supported the main premise of the argument to support the notion that separation from England was justifiable. The appendix materials of this text contain the complete text of the Declaration of Independence exhibiting the characteristics of deductive reasoning.

The concluding portion of the Declaration of Independence reinforces the major premise regarding the abolishment of the governmental relationship between the American colonies and England. Specifically, it states, "We, therefore, the Representatives of the united States of America, in General Congress, Assembled, appealing to the Supreme Judge of the world for the rectitude of our intentions, do, in the Name, and by Authority of the good People of these Colonies, solemnly publish and declare, That these united Colonies are, and of Right ought to be Free and Independent States, that they are Absolved from all Allegiance to the British Crown, and that all political connection between them and the State of Great Britain, is and ought to be totally dissolved; and that as Free and Independent States, they have full Power to levy War, conclude Peace, contract Alliances, establish Commerce, and to do all other Acts and Things which Independent States may of right do.—And for the support of this Declaration, with a firm reliance on the protection of Divine Providence, we mutually pledge to each other our Lives, our Fortunes, and our sacred Honor" (Independence Hall Association, n.d.).

Reviewing the Declaration of Independence, contained in Appendix A, shows its conformance to the outlining concept that facilitates deductive reasoning in communication. The introductory statements, representing the major premise, present the case for justifying a separation from England. The minor premises, contained within the facts supporting the argument for separation, are presented and ordered to support the concept represented by the major premise concerning the necessity of separation from England. After the presentation of facts, the concluding statements emphasize and contribute toward the justification of separation.

During modern times, deductive reasoning is as pertinent as it was when the Declaration of Independence was authored. The use of deduction is applicable within the context of written or oral communications within the justice system. Contracts are written, binding legal agreements between at least two parties. Contracts may have the form of an oral agreement or a written agreement. Within the justice system, through the use of deductive reasoning, the "rule of law" may be "applied in a particular case" regarding contracts (Independence Hall Association, n.d.).

Deduction is found within the decisions of the U.S. Supreme Court as well as the lower courts of cities and counties. When judges issue opinions, they often incorporate deductive reasoning to substantiate the foundational basis of their conclusions and decisions. Through the use of deductive reasoning within communications, judges are better able to explain a decision that "adjudicates a live case or controversy that has been presented before a court" (Aldisert, 2009, p. 12).

Deductive reasoning is also used to present arguments for public safety that are espoused by law enforcement organizations. Communicating arguments for the mandatory use of seat belts may incorporate deductive reasoning. Various crime reduction strategies may be examined through the use of deductive reasoning (Klofas, Hipple, & McGarrell, 2010). Certainly, many more examples may be considered from the perspective of deduction. Deductive reasoning is a powerful tool through which numerous issues in the justice domain may be examined, argued, and expressed through multiple media channels.

Induction

Inductive reasoning is a complement to the process of deductive reasoning. Inductive reasoning involves the transitioning "from specific facts or observations to reach a likely conclusion that may explain the facts" (Sternberg, 2009, p. 499). The derived conclusion may be used to speculate "future specific instances" of an event or situation (Sternberg, 2009, p. 499). Essentially, inductive reasoning is a method of crafting generalizations from "specific observations" (Brink, 2006). Within inductive reasoning, the derived conclusions may only be tentative because they are "formed as they are from what has been observed," and may change accordingly when any alterations of observations are manifested (Brain, 2002). Therefore, inductive conclusions are "true" only according to "current experiences" (Brain, 2002). Hence, they may change with the interjecting of a "new experience" or change according to any alterations of an existing observation (Brain, 2002).

Inductive reasoning is useful when communicating within the justice domain. A primary example involves considerations of English contract law. Because the English language has "spread through its colonial history," it has influenced the justice systems of the "United States, Canada, Australia, New Zealand, Hong Kong, and Singapore" (Chen-Wishart, 2012, p. 32). Numerous benefits are associated with English contract law, including the notions that it is "respectful of the agreement and so more certain, and untrammeled by principles of disclosure, good faith, and fair dealing" (Chen-Wishart, 2012, p. 32). Within English contract law, the use of inductive reasoning involves a common law "case-by-case analysis from which general principles may emerge" from a review of previous court documents and rulings (Chen-Wishart, 2012, p. 33).

Among courtrooms, inductive reasoning may be demonstrated within the arguments of attorneys. One may present "all the facts, the logic, and the reasoning first, and then ask the audience, the judge, or a jury to take a particular course of action based on that information" (Dempsey, 2009). Through inductive reasoning, if similarities among cases "strongly predominate," then "the former decision will be deemed to control the decision of the case at bar" (Britton & Bauer, 1922). Such use of inductive reasoning facilitates the influencing of human opinions and behaviors by using facts to support the stated argument, and then deriving a general conclusion based on the presented facts.

Inductive reasoning also influenced the crafting of communications that affected the formation of the United States. Within its written contents, the Declaration of Independence expressed the disgruntlement of the American colonies with Great Britain, and argued for the separation of governments. Although the Declaration of Independence was examined from the perspective of deductive reasoning within the preceding section, it may also be considered from the perspective of inductive reasoning.

The inductive reasoning process incorporates the use of various facts to support argumentation. Within the Declaration of Independence, numerous facts are listed that support the notion that England infringed on the rights and freedoms of the colonies. Excerpted from the Declaration of Independence are the following statements that were presented as factual events to support the argument for separation (National Archives, 1776):

- He has made Judges dependent on his Will alone for the tenure of their offices, and the amount and payment of their salaries.
- He has erected a multitude of New Offices, and sent hither swarms of Officers to harass our people and eat out their substance.
- He has kept among us, in times of peace, Standing Armies without the Consent of our legislatures.
- He has affected to render the Military independent of and superior to the Civil Power.
- He has combined with others to subject us to a jurisdiction foreign to our constitution, and unacknowledged by our laws; giving his Assent to their Acts of pretended Legislation.
- For quartering large bodies of armed troops among us.
- For protecting them, by a mock Trial from punishment for any Murders which they should commit on the Inhabitants of these States.
- For cutting off our Trade with all parts of the world.
- For imposing Taxes on us without our Consent.
- For depriving us in many cases, of the benefit of Trial by Jury.

Certainly, many other items were cited as reasons to justify the notion of separating from Great Britain. Readers may review the entirety of the Declaration of Independence in Appendix A of this book. Cumulatively, such facts provided the argumentative basis for reasoning inductively regarding the notion that the British government and rule were infringing on the rights and freedoms of the American colonies. These facts were also pertinent toward the crafting of a general conclusion regarding the American colonies separating from England. In this case, the use of inductive reasoning also was necessary to support the minor premise of the deductive reasoning process. Specifically, these facts were used to show that "the government of England is oppressing the American people" (Kirszner & Mandell, 2011).

The use of inductive reasoning also permeates the communications of the modern justice system. Similar to the method employed to support the deductive reasoning expressed within the Declaration of Independence, inductive reasoning is "very often used to form either the major of the minor premise" through either analogy or generalization (Aldisert, 2009, p. 163). When writing judicial opinions, this method involves conceptually "connecting the dots" representing "holdings of individual cases, each announcing a specific consequence for a detailed set of facts" (Aldisert, 2009, p. 48). If the writing of a judicial opinion involves analogy, then "resemblances are meticulously compared and special instances of like situations are enumerated" (Aldisert, 2009, p. 48).

Inductive reasoning processes are also appropriate for some law enforcement investigations. When crafting a written report detailing the investigation, one may describe the inductive processes that were used to generate a conclusion. Such reporting may also incorporate a discussion of pertinent facts that were considered during the investigative process that yielded the derived conclusion. For example, such reports may be associated with the concept of inductive profiling within investigations. This method of profiling represents "a process of profiling criminal behavior, crime scenes, and victims from known behaviors and emotions suggested by other criminals, crime scenes, and/or victims" (Aldisert, 2009, p. 72).

When crafting communications, the inductive reasoning process may be used as a solitary method or as a complementary method to deductive reasoning. If it is used alone, then it yields a generalized conclusion that is derived from a considered set of observations. If it is used to complement the method of deductive reasoning, then it may be used to establish the basis of a minor premise. Regardless, inductive reasoning represents a sound tool of logic through which the arguments of messages may be established when communicating within the justice system.

Logical Fallacies

Both deductive reasoning and inductive reasoning use various arguments through which a conclusion may be derived. Within both methods, the validity and truthfulness of facts, premises, and conclusions must be considered with respect to the interjecting of error within the reasoning domain. Such instances necessitate the contemplation of logical fallacies. A logical fallacy is defined as an "argument containing faulty reasoning" (Van Vleet, 2011). Logical fallacies represent "an argument that is usually psychologically persuasive, but logically weak" (Pine, n.d.). Essentially, a logical fallacy influences people to accept arguments and conclusions despite "that people ought not to accept the conclusions of these arguments as strongly supported" (Pine, n.d.). The reasoning associated with a logical fallacy is depicted in Figure 3.2.

Fallacies exist practically everywhere. They may be present within television and radio advertisements in which organizations may attempt to sway public opinion regarding an issue. Political candidates may incorporate logical fallacies to entice voters to believe their position, and to elicit votes from constituents. Numerous fallacies exist representing "perhaps hundreds of logical fallacies and thousands of combinations" (Cournoyer, 2011). It is beyond the scope of this book to consider an exhaustive listing of fallacies that may be used within arguments when communicating. However, numerous examples are readily identifiable. Derived from the University of Texas, some of the fallacies that may influence

Figure 3.2 Logical fallacy reasoning. (From http://www.glasbergen.com.)

communications and the formation of human opinions are described below (University of Texas, 2012):

Ad hominem *argument* (also, "personal attack," "poisoning the well"): The fallacy of attempting to refute an argument by attacking the opposition's personal character or reputation, using a corrupted negative argument from ethos. For example, "He's so evil that you can't believe anything he says." Also applies to cases where potential opposing arguments are brushed aside without comment or consideration, as simply not worth arguing about.

Appeal to closure: The contemporary fallacy that an argument, standpoint, action, or conclusion must be accepted, no matter how questionable, or else the point will remain unsettled and those affected will be denied "closure." This refuses to recognize the truth that some points will indeed remain unsettled, perhaps forever. For example, "Society would be protected, crime would be deterred and justice served if we sentence you to life without parole, but we need to execute you in order to provide some sense of closure."

Appeal to heaven (also, *Deus vult*, *Gott mit uns*, Manifest Destiny, the Special Covenant): An extremely dangerous fallacy (a deluded argument from ethos) of asserting that God (or a higher power) has ordered, supports, or approves one's own standpoint or actions, so no further justification is required and no serious challenge is possible. For example, "God ordered me to kill my children," or "We need to take away your land, since God (or destiny, or fate, or heaven) has given it to us."

Appeal to tradition (also, "If it ain't broke, don't fix it"): The fallacy that a standpoint, situation, or action is right, proper, and correct simply because it has "always" been that way; because people have "always" thought that way; or because it continues to serve one particular group very well. A corrupted argument from ethos (that of past generations). For example, "In America, women have always been paid less, so let's not mess with long-standing tradition."

Argument from ignorance: The fallacy that since we do not know (or can never know, or cannot prove) whether a claim is true or false, it must be false (or that it must be true). Sometimes this also includes "either–or reasoning." For example, "The vet can't find any reasonable explanation for why my dog died. That proves that my neighbor poisoned him! There's no other logical explanation!" A corrupted argument from logos. A fallacy commonly found in American judicial and forensic reasoning.

Argumentum ad baculam (also, "argument from the club"): The fallacy of "persuasion" by force, violence, or threats. For example, "Gimmee your money, or I'll knock your head off!" or "We have the perfect right to take your land, since we have the guns and you don't." This also applies to indirect forms of threat.

Bandwagon (also, argument from common sense, *argumentum ad populum*): The fallacy of arguing that because "everyone" supposedly thinks or does something, it must be right. For example, "Everyone thinks illegal aliens should be deported!" It sometimes also includes lying with statistics. For example, "Surveys show that over 75% of Americans believe Senator Snith is not telling the truth. For anyone with half a brain, that conclusively proves he's a dirty liar!"

Begging the question (also, circular reasoning): Falsely arguing that something is true by repeating the same statement in different words. For example, "The prostitution problem is the most urgent challenge in policing today. Why? Because prostitutes threaten all of our neighborhoods." A corrupt argument from logos. See also "Big lie technique."

Big lie technique (also, "staying on message"): The contemporary fallacy of repeating a lie, slogan, or deceptive half-truth over and over (particularly in the media) until people believe it without further proof or evidence. For example, "What about the Jewish question?" Note that when this particular phony debate was going on, there was no "Jewish question," only a "Nazi question," but hardly anybody in power recognized or wanted to talk about that.

Blind loyalty (also, blind obedience, the "team player" appeal, or the Nuremberg defense): The dangerous fallacy that an argument or action is right simply and solely because a respected leader or source (an expert, parents, one's own "side," team or country, one's boss or commanding officers) say it is right. This is over-reliance on authority and a corrupted argument from ethos that puts loyalty above truth or above one's own reason and conscience. In this case, a person attempts to justify incorrect, stupid, or criminal behavior by whining "That's what I was told to do."

The complex question: The fallacy of demanding a direct answer to a question that cannot be answered without first analyzing or challenging the basis of the question itself. For example, "Why did you rob that bank?" This also applies to situations where one is forced to either accept or reject complex standpoints or propositions containing both acceptable and unacceptable parts.

Essentializing: A fallacy that proposes a person or thing "is what it is and that's all that it is," and at its core will always be what it is right now. For example, "All ex-cons are criminals, and will still be criminals even if they live to be 100." Also refers to the fallacy of arguing that something is a certain way "by nature"; an empty claim that no amount of proof can refute.

False analogy: The fallacy of incorrectly comparing one thing to another in order to draw a false conclusion. For example, "Just like an alley cat needs to prowl, a normal human being can't be tied down to one single lover."

Guilt by association: The fallacy of trying to refute or condemn someone's standpoint, arguments, or actions by evoking the negative ethos of those with whom one associates or a collective to which he or she belongs. A form of *ad hominem* argument. For example, "Don't listen to her. She's an ex-convict, so you can't trust anything she says."

The half truth (also, card stacking, incomplete information): A corrupt argument from logos; the fallacy of telling the truth but deliberately omitting important key details to falsify the larger picture and support a false conclusion. For example, "The truth is that Ciudad Juárez, Mexico, is one of the world's fastest growing cities and can boast of a young, ambitious and hard-working population, mild winters, a dry and sunny climate, low-cost medical and dental care, a multitude of churches and places of worship, delicious local cuisine and a swinging nightclub scene. Taken together, all these facts clearly prove that Juarez is one of the world's most desirable places for young families to live, work and raise a family."

Lying with statistics: Using true figures and numbers to "prove" unrelated claims. For example, "Gas prices have never been lower. When taken as a percentage of the national debt, filling up at your corner gas station is actually far cheaper today than it was in 1965!"

Name calling: A variety of the *ad hominem* argument. The dangerous fallacy that simply because of who you are, any and all arguments, disagreements, or objections against your standpoint or actions are automatically racist, sexist, anti-Semitic, bigoted, discriminatory, or hateful. For example, "My stand on abortion is the only correct one. To disagree with me, argue with me, or to question my judgment in any way would only show what a pig you really are." This also applies to refuting an argument by simply calling it a fallacy or declaring it invalid, without proving why it is invalid.

Overgeneralization (also, hasty generalization): The stupid but common fallacy of incorrectly applying one or two examples to all cases. For example, "Some college student was tailgating me all the way up North Main Street last night. This proves that all college students are lousy drivers, and we should pull their driver's licenses until they either grow up, learn to drive or graduate!"

Political correctness (*PC*): A contemporary fallacy that the nature of a thing or situation can be changed simply by changing its name. For example, "What's going on in Juárez is not a 'war', it is a fight between drug cartels. That means it's not that bad."

Red herring: An irrelevant distraction, attempting to mislead an audience by bringing up an unrelated, but usually emotionally loaded issue. For example, "In regard to my recent indictment for corruption, let's talk about what's really important instead—terrorists are out there, and if we don't stop them we're all gonna die!"

Reductionism (also, oversimplifying, sloganeering): The fallacy of deceiving an audience by giving simple answers or slogans in response to complex questions, especially when appealing to less educated or unsophisticated audiences. For example, "If the glove doesn't fit, you must vote to acquit."

Shifting the burden of proof (see also "Argument from ignorance"): A fallacy that challenges opponents to disprove a claim, rather than asking the person making the claim to defend his/her own argument. For example, "Gang members are everywhere among us, even here on campus, masquerading as students! I dare you prove it isn't so! See? You can't! That means you have to accept that what I say is true."

Slippery slope (also, the domino theory): The common fallacy that "one thing inevitably leads to another." For example, "If you two go and drink coffee together, one thing will lead to another, and soon enough you'll be pregnant and end up spending your life on welfare living in the projects," or "If we cut and run in Iraq or Afghanistan, pretty soon all of southwest Asia will be run by Al-Qaeda."

Snow job: The fallacy of "proving" a claim by overwhelming an audience with mountains of irrelevant facts, numbers, documents, graphs, and statistics that they cannot be expected to understand.

Tu quoque (also, two wrongs make a right): The fallacy of defending a shaky or false standpoint or excusing one's own bad action by pointing out that one's opponent's acts or personal character are also open to question, or even worse. For example, "Sure, we may have tortured prisoners of war, but we didn't cut off heads off like they do!"

Where there's smoke, there's fire (also, hasty conclusion, jumping to a conclusion): The dangerous fallacy of quickly drawing a conclusion and/or taking action without sufficient evidence. For example, "My neighbor has tattoos and piercings, and has different men visiting her all day. Where there's smoke there's fire. That's not right; she's a call girl!"

This listing is not exhaustive. Many other fallacies exist that may be used to negatively embellish message argumentation within the communications process. Readers are encouraged to examine texts in philosophy, persuasion, or psychology for listings and discussions of fallacies that have greater scope and depth.

Fallacies are often referenced among the writings of court proceedings. An example is the California court case of *Bull and Others v. City and County of San Francisco.* This U.S. Ninth Circuit Court of Appeals case involved a dispute regarding the policy and use of prisoner strip searches within San Francisco jails. Invasive searches were performed because contraband was discovered within the jails. The majority opinion expressed that the use of these searches was deemed to be reasonable for "all arrested persons confined in the general jail population" (Samaha, 2012, p. 238). However, the minority opinion disagreed, and referenced logical fallacy as a component of its opinion (Samaha, 2012, p. 240). Excerpts of the dissenting opinion are given as follows (Samaha, 2012, p. 240):

> The majority sweeps away twenty-five years of jurisprudence, giving jailors the unfettered right to conduct mandatory, routine, suspicionless body cavity searches on any citizen who may be arrested for minor offenses, such as violating a leash law or a traffic code, and who pose no credible risk for smuggling contraband into the jail. Under its reconfigured regime, the majority discards Bell's requirement to balance the need for a search against individual privacy and instead blesses a uniform policy of performing body cavity searches on everyone arrested and designated for the general jail population, regardless of the triviality of the charge or the likelihood that the arrestee is hiding contraband.
>
> The rationale for this abrupt precedential departure is founded on quicksand. Indeed, the government's entire argument is based on the logical fallacy that happenstance implies causation. The government argues that contraband has been found in the San Francisco jails. Thus, the government reasons, individuals who are arrested must be smuggling contraband into the jail. Therefore, the government concludes it must body cavity search everyone who is arrested, even those who pose no risk of concealing contraband, much less of trying to smuggle contraband into the jail.
>
> Not all searches are created equal. The Fourth Amendment differentiates between more and less intrusive searches, and requires varying levels of need to justify different kinds of searches. The scope of the particular intrusion, in light of all the exigencies of the case, is a central element in the analysis of reasonableness. Because the Fourth Amendment requires a balancing of the need for the particular search against the invasion of personal rights that the search entails, the most invasive search is justified only by the most compelling need. (Samaha, 2012, p. 240)

The concepts expressed within the dissenting opinion incorporate the examination of logical fallacy versus the basis of the opinion of the majority. The dissenting opinion clearly communicates the basis of the logical fallacy that it believes exists within the majority opinion. Despite the perceived presence of a fallacious bias within the arguments that comprised the majority opinion, the invasive searches were deemed as reasonable, thereby allowing them to continue. Therefore, all persons entering the jail, regardless of cause or their risk of smuggling contraband, are subject to invasive searches.

Another consideration of fallacies involves the 1990s case of O.J. Simpson. During "preliminary hearing," evidence was considered in an isolated fashion instead of being examined from its totality (Rossmo, 2009). This consideration is summarized as follows (Rossmo, 2009):

> The prosecution presented evidence that blood found at the murder scene, when analyzed using conventional grouping techniques, matched that of the accused, with characteristics shared by one in 400 people. The defense argued that an entire football stadium could be filled with those people in Los Angeles who would also match the blood group, and therefore the evidence was useless. (Rossmo, 2009)

Despite the truthfulness of the first portion of the argument, the second portion involving the uselessness of evidence contains a fallacy (Rossmo, 2009). Although the numbers reflecting the quantity of matches is accurate, only a few of those people would have had a relationship with the murdered victims (Rossmo, 2009). Furthermore, even fewer would have a motive for murdering them (Rossmo, 2009). The probability of any individual being represented within "all three categories" is very low (Rossmo, 2009). Therefore, the second portion of the argument, emphasizing the uselessness of the evidence, is incorrect (Rossmo, 2009).

When communicating, fallacies may occur either intentionally or unintentionally (University of Toledo, 2012). When used intentionally, fallacies are integrated within communications for the purpose of persuading "an audience to the writer's point of view" (University of Toledo, 2012). Unintentional uses of fallacies may occur because "the writer is convinced of their truth value" (University of Toledo, 2012). The dangers of fallacies and of human ignorance must not be discounted. Any presence of fallacies tends to interject obscurity within argumentation, to perpetuate falsehoods, thereby derailing "free consent," to encourage humans to render "decisions without understanding" the attributes, presences, and possible availability of "real choices," or to "act hastily when there is actually time to gather more information" and to contemplate the "potential consequences" of choices (University of Toledo, 2012).

Fallacies exist. Given the advent and proliferation of modern communications technologies, senders of messages may attempt to influence the opinions of groups or individuals through broadcasting fallacies among global, national, regional, or local audiences. Excerpts of the 1990s court proceedings involving O.J. Simpson were broadcast and received by audiences both domestically and internationally. Whether fallacies were intentional or unintentional, the opinions of humans were influenced regarding his innocence or guilt.

Within the justice system, both individuals and groups must question the contents of messages that occur between senders and receivers during the communications process. One must be mindful of the power of fallacies, and must question the premises, facts, arguments, and conclusions that are broadcast regarding events within the justice system. Only through vigilant awareness, fostered by a strong knowledge and understanding of fallacies, can groups and individuals critically analyze communications and attempt to formulate objective opinions within the justice system.

Ethos

The word ethos is defined as "the distinguishing character, sentiment, moral nature, or guiding beliefs of a person, group, or institution" (*Merriam-Webster*, 2012a). The characteristics of ethos are applicable to individuals, groups, and organizations. They are also reflective of the senders and receivers of messages within the communications process. During the communications process, senders may exhibit some aspects of their ethos within transmitted messages. Receivers of messages may form some perception and mental model of the sender given the attributes associated with perceptions of ethos.

Ethos permeates communications within the justice domain. One may form an opinion of an individual on the basis of the perceived attributes of experience, knowledge, adherence to a code of ethics, compassionate and benevolent acts, formal credentials, and so on. This notion of ethos is applicable to law enforcement officers, attorneys, judges, various officers of the court, expert witnesses, personal witnesses, jurors, probation officers, and anyone else involved within the justice system. Imparting some aspects of ethos within the communications process may occur through auditory, visual, or written methods.

One consideration of imparting ethos involves the use of expert witnesses during court proceedings. An expert witness appears before tribunals or courts to "provide information not discernible by ordinary means; about matters not within the ken of persons other than those familiar with the science surrounding the issue about which they will speak; and concerning which they have special knowledge by reason of their learning, experience, and particular skill" (Brown & Campbell, 2010). The knowledge of an expert witness is not "expected of a layperson" (James & Nordby, 2005). However, the knowledge of the expert is somehow relevant to the case before the court, and assists the judge or jury in "understanding certain types of evidence" (James & Nordby, 2005). Expert witnesses provide impartial testimony based solely on opinion (James & Nordby, 2005). Although one may have significant knowledge of a topic, the legal designation as an expert witness must be conferred by a court (James & Nordby, 2005).

The ethos of expert witnesses may involve an array of characteristics. Ethos involves an "appeal to the authority of the speaker" (Freedman & Medway, 2005). The ethos of the expert witness involves a consideration of demeanor involving the characteristics of professional credentials, confidence, age, appearance, and competence (Selinger & Crease, 2006). Perceptions of credibility and trustworthiness influence juror perceptions and acceptance of the expert and the communicated testimony (Selinger & Crease, 2006). Influencing jurors to accept the expressed or oral testimony of an expert witness involves a consideration of the presentation style and the ability to relate to others (Walton, 1997). The imparting of ethos is achieved when the "perceived good character" of the expert "creates a positive ambiance" that makes the given opinion "more credible" (Walton, 1997).

Bolstering the perceptions associated with ethos involves a cumulative consideration of the expert. For example, if one employs a physician as an expert, then the showing of a doctor of medicine degree, the type of medical residency, attributes of professional practice that pertain to the court case, continuing education, publications, research activities, membership and participation in professional organizations, and proof of state medical licensing may bolster the credibility of the expert. The characteristics of age, congeniality, vocabulary, familiarity with and ease of explaining concepts, and nonverbal signals also embellish juror perceptions of the physician. The ability to relate to others also may influence juror perceptions.

These considerations of ethos may be appropriate for courtroom settings or visual channels through which communication occurs within the justice system. However, ethos may also be established through writing. Within the Declaration of Independence, attributes of ethos are present. Its contents represent a form of logical appeal expressing the argumentation regarding the validity and credibility of separating from English rule. Its wording and phrasing present the American colonies not as treasonous rebels but as a collective array of victimized people whose cause of liberty was just and righteous. In this respect, the Declaration of Independence is a persuasive document that incorporates ethos to influence its readers via the power of written language.

Ethos is a strong tool that embellishes written, auditory, and visual modalities of communicating. The senders of messages may use it to establish credibility, to achieve trustworthiness, to establish believability, and to persuade the receivers of messages. When used effectively, it may seduce the receiver of the message into feeling that the sender of the message and the contents of the message are appealing.

Pathos

The word pathos is defined as "an element in experience or in artistic representation evoking pity or compassion" and as "an emotion of sympathetic pity" (*Merriam-Webster*, 2012b). Within the communications process, the use of pathos represents an emotional appeal to the mind and senses of the receiver of a message. Leveraging pathos is a method of persuasion involving human feelings, hopes, joys, fears, ambitions, and passions. It may be used to evoke an active response that arouses "a sense of desire, curiosity, excitement, or any other emotion" (Horberry, 2010). Humans may be susceptible to the pathos of arguments through being "moved first by emotion before considering the credibility of the speaker or the facts" of a given situation (Stuart, Sarow, & Stuart, 2007). Pathos is used to influence mental models in the minds of receivers by inciting "evocative and arousing" imageries (Whalen, 1996).

Similar to ethos, the concept of pathos influenced the foundational writings of the American society. Using the Declaration of Independence as an example, the attributes of pathos are easily discovered. Within its opening statements, the sufferings of the American colonies are expressed as follows (National Archives, 1776):

> Prudence, indeed, will dictate that Governments long established should not be changed for light and transient causes; and accordingly all experience hath shewn, that mankind are more disposed to suffer, while evils are sufferable, than to right themselves by abolishing the forms to which they are accustomed. But when a long train of abuses and usurpations, pursuing invariably the same Object evinces a design to reduce them under absolute Despotism, it is their right, it is their duty, to throw off such Government, and to provide new Guards for their future security.—Such has been the patient sufferance of these Colonies; and such is now the necessity which constrains them to alter their former Systems of Government. The history of the present King of Great Britain is a history of repeated injuries and usurpations, all having in direct object the establishment of an absolute Tyranny over these States.

This passage signifies an expression of repeated abuses and exploitations of the American colonies by Great Britain. It shows the long suffering and patience of the American colonies throughout their dismal experience. Although it reflects a period of endurance, it denotes the necessity of separation from England to escape a totalitarian state of tyranny that ensnared the colonies. Cumulatively, these characteristics appeal to the emotion of those who read the document—it incites sympathy and may evoke anger. Through its emotional appeal, it elicits support for the cause of separating from Great Britain. Through the use of pathos, the justification for separating from English rule is bolstered.

During modern times, pathos remains a method of influencing receivers of messages. Within the justice system, pathos is used to influence advocacy for a variety of issues. Pathos may be used to incite an emotional response toward diminishing the instances of drunk driving (Osborn & Osborn, 2000). When considering prostitution, pathos may involve emotional senses of revulsion or may involve eliciting strong advocacy.

Pathos is an aspect concerning opinions regarding crimes of moral turpitude. Caylee Anthony disappeared and died in 2008. Casey Anthony, her mother, did not report Caylee as missing for 31 days, and "repeatedly lied to investigators, parents, and friends, charges for which she would ultimately be convicted" (Garaas-Johnson, 2011). Some of the attributes of the news broadcasts are summarized as follows (Garaas-Johnson, 2011):

> Grace has led the charge to impugn Anthony in the press. Most notably, she received criticism over her decision to refer to Anthony as "Tot Mom," saying it was shorthand for the compressed information area at the bottom of the television screen. Critics see it as a way to remind viewers of the victim, thereby reinforcing an emotional appeal while heaping conjecture and revelation on Anthony. (Garaas-Johnson, 2011)

The broadcasting of the Caylee Anthony situation shocked the American society and evoked an array of emotions nationally. In 2008, Anthony refused an offer of "limited immunity" (Garaas-Johnson, 2011). Prosecutors announced their intention to seek the death penalty for her in 2009 (Garaas-Johnson, 2011). A "death penalty phase hearing" occurred in 2010 (Adams, 2010). She was found not guilty of murder in 2011 (Ablow, 2011). News reports sparked the emotions of the general public nationally regarding the verdict of not guilty, thereby proclaiming her legally innocent of having committed the crime. Communicating the trial outcome via the news media incited acts of violence and threats against Casey, the jurors, the "defense team," and "her parents" (Garaas-Johnson, 2011).

Pathos may be used to incite either positive or negative responses from individuals or mass audiences. The death of Caylee Anthony and the court proceedings of Casey Anthony demonstrate the power of pathos with respect to influencing the emotions of a mass audience within the communications process. Although the range of emotions and resulting actions were most likely unintentional effects of the news stories, public opinion was influenced through periodic communications facilitated by news media. Individuals within society all formed some specific opinion and mental model of the situation. The potential of pathos must not be underestimated when interjecting it within the communications process through which the receivers of messages are influenced.

Behavioral Modification

The psychology of communication is a vital factor when influencing the general public for safety reasons. Cumulatively, the preceding sections represent an array of tools that may be used within the communications process to influence groups and individuals. Within the contexts of the justice domain and law enforcement organizations, these concepts may be used to persuade and alter the behaviors of humans.

Achieving some state of persuasion is "equated with instances of behavioral conversion" (Dillard & Pfau, 2002). Persuasion occurs when individuals "have been induced to abandon one set of behaviors and to adopt another" (Dillard & Pfau, 2002). Persuading the public to alter unsafe behaviors may occur through communications paradigms representing written, auditory, and visual paradigms (or a combination of these methods).

One example involves the methods employed by the North Dakota Department of Transportation (NDDOT). In North Dakota, "the vast majority of motor vehicle fatalities" are the result of "driver behavior including impaired driving, speed, distracted driving, and lack of seat belt use" (North Dakota Department of Transportation, 2012). According to the NDDOT, such behaviors "can be changed through awareness, education, and strict enforcement of traffic safety laws" (North Dakota Department of Transportation, 2012). Educating the public and making it aware of dangerous behaviors occurs through communication.

One method that the NDDOT employs to communicate the dangers and consequences associated with human behavior is the use of multimedia Internet videos. The subjects addressed in these videos include driving under the influence, seat belt use, and motorcycle safety (North Dakota Department of Transportation, 2012). Audiences are encouraged to use the services of designated drivers or taxis, to fasten seat belts before driving, and to wear protective gear and helmets when motorcycling.

The uses of logos, pathos, and ethos are paramount factors of attempting to influence human decisions and behaviors within these videos. Within the motorcycle safety advertisement, an emotional appeal (i.e., pathos) is demonstrated through the presentation of a grieving widow who tearfully reads the obituary of her deceased husband who perished in a motorcycle accident. Another video questions whether one would trust nothing more than an umbrella when skydiving (i.e., logos), and then encourages viewers to use a seat belt when driving automobiles.

An experimental method of altering unsafe behaviors among juveniles involves using electronic monitoring devices to report motorist habits to their parents (Farmer et al., 2010). This experiment involved the electronic monitoring and reporting of the seat belt use of teen drivers to an Internet site that was accessible by their parents (Farmer et al., 2010). The results of the study showed the following:

> Seat belt use improved when violations were reported to the parent websites, and improved even more when in-vehicle alerts were activated. Consistent reductions in speeding were achieved only when teenagers received alerts about their speeding behavior, believed their speeding behavior would not be reported to parents if corrected, and when parents were being notified of such behavior by report cards. (Farmer et al., 2010)

The conclusion of the study suggested that the "electronic monitoring of teenage drivers can reduce the incidence of risky behavior, especially seat belt nonuse" (Farmer et al., 2010). Implementing this study necessitated the use of communications technologies to facilitate the electronic monitoring and reporting of subject data. It also incorporated communications technology to access an Internet site through which parents could review this data. The danger of unsafe behavior was communicated through the use of alert warnings to obtain the attention of the driver to alter any behavior that did not incorporate the use of a seat belt while driving.

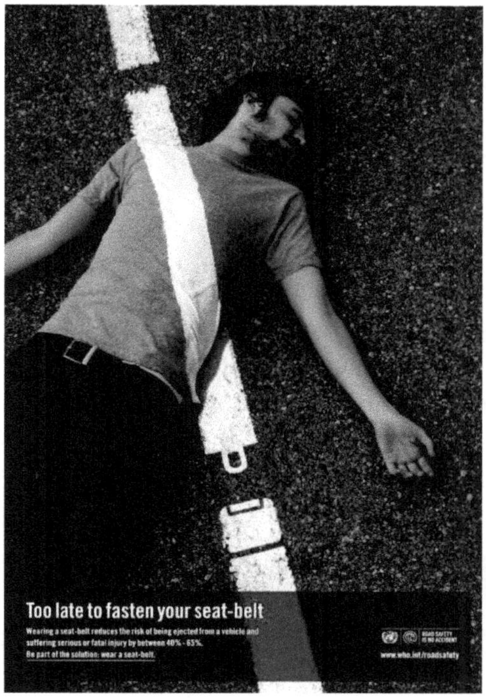

Figure 3.3 Seat belt advertisement. (From http://content.usatoday.com/communities/ondeadline/post/2012/02/vermont-inmates-slip-a-pig-into-state-police-car-decals/1#.UUgCRlehxLE.)

Both groups and individuals are subject to behavioral modification. The use of communication is an essential component of raising awareness concerning a variety of issues that influence the justice domain. When communicating with the general public to achieve behavioral modification, the uses of ethos, pathos, and logos are necessary for inciting some form of analysis or reflective thought in the minds of intended audiences. Through such actions, humans are able to craft mental models concerning the dangers associated with unsafe behaviors. Therefore, after contemplation, humans may alter their behaviors. Figure 3.3 shows a typical seat belt advertisement that attempts to influence human behavior.

Subliminal Concepts

The word subliminal is defined as "existing or functioning below the threshold of consciousness" (*Merriam-Webster*, 2012c). This notion is salient within the context of subliminal communication that may influence the decisions and actions of humans. This type of communication involves "subliminal cues, that is, stimuli presented so rapidly" that humans are unaware of what they have experienced during the communications process (Fiske, 2010). These subliminal cues, "presented at the unconscious level," may affect the "perceptions, feelings, thoughts, and behavior" of humans (Fiske, 2010).

During 2008, prisoners in Vermont who were responsible for making decals for state police vehicles clandestinely placed a subliminal image within several decals that were affixed to approximately 30 police vehicles (Winter, 2012). One of the inmates altered a computer image file and modified a "cow's spots to resemble a pig, the common derogatory term for police" (Winter, 2012). Certainly, this incident was a malicious use of subliminal imagery to insult law enforcement professionals. However, it shows the relative ease with which subliminal imagery may be embedded unnoticed within items that are viewed each day. Figures 3.4 and 3.5 show this alteration.

During the 1970s, when the bind, tie, and kill (BTK) murderer was terrorizing Kansas, the Wichita Police Department attempted to use subliminal messaging as a method of influencing the serial killer to contact law enforcement and turn himself in for having committed the crimes (Bond, 2012). The subliminal messaging was contained within the local news programming of the KAKE television station (Bond, 2012). The message contained one phrase: "contact the chief" (Hewstone, Stroebe, & Jonas, 2012). Despite this attempt to leverage subliminal communication to persuade and influence the behavior of the killer, the messaging was unsuccessful.

Disputes and controversies regarding the use of subliminal communications have been argued within the justice system. During 1990, in the state of Nevada, the surviving

Figure 3.4 Altered spots in subliminal image. (From http://content.usatoday.com/communities/ondeadline/post/2012/02/vermont-inmates-slip-a-pig-into-state-police-car-decals/1#.UUgCRlehxLE.)

Figure 3.5 Closer view of subliminal spot. (From http://content.usatoday.com/communities/ondeadline/post/2012/02/vermont-inmates-slip-a-pig-into-state-police-car-decals/1#.UUgCRlehxLE.)

"family members of two teenage suicide victims" filed a lawsuit against CBS Records and Judas Priest (Harris, 2009). The premise of the lawsuit was that the Judas Priest album *Stained Glass* contained subliminal messaging that influenced the juveniles to commit suicide (Harris, 2009). However, the "judge ruled against the family" (Harris, 2009).

The use of subliminal messaging has also been used as a method of attempting to influence consumer behavior within shopping malls and stores. This use of subliminal messaging embedded various messages such as "I am honest. I will not steal. If I do steal, I will be caught and sent to jail" (Shteir, 2011). However, there is practically no scientific evidence to show that the use of such subliminal messaging effectively deters criminal shoplifting behavior (Carroll, 2003). In fact, "little evidence" exists to show that subliminal messages "transmitted on the auditory channel can bring about desired changes in behavior" (Solomon, 2009).

The failures of attempting to leverage subliminal messaging to capture the BTK killer and to deter theft among retail outlets are unsurprising. The ruling of the judge who presided during the Judas Priest trial is also unsurprising. After over half a century of research and exploration, there is practically no evidence to show the efficacy of subliminal messaging as a tool through which human behavior may be significantly modified. Specifically, there exists practically "no proof that visual or verbal messages presented below the level of conscious awareness have any effect on consumer behavior" (Solomon, 2003).

Commentary Regarding Communications Psychology in the Justice Domain

Incorporating psychological strategies to facilitate the formation of mental models in the minds of individuals or groups and to influence the decisions and behaviors of others is a salient consideration of the communications process. The use of such strategies is not uncommon within society, and has been used to communicate the salient characteristics of a variety of topics, events, and happenings among a variety of different domains. The use of psychological strategies is an essential attribute of the justice domain.

Psychological strategies embellish the ability of attorneys to elicit information or to present their arguments before juries and judges. When one is questioning a juvenile, different uses of ethos, pathos, and logos may be appropriate because of the differences between adult versus juvenile cognitive processes. Similarly, when interacting with elderly people, law enforcement officers may leverage psychological methods during the communications process.

Understanding how the mind forms mental models enhances the ability of law enforcement organizations and entities within the justice system to communicate with others. It also assists in understanding how people form perceptions and opinions of law enforcement personnel and organizations, and of the justice system itself. Leveraging psychological communication strategies assists in the formation of these opinions and perceptions.

Generally, law enforcement organizations wish to communicate overall positive messages regarding public safety and awareness within their served communities. They wish to shape positive opinions and perceptions in the minds of their served populace. Failure to market police services or to make known a police presence within a community contributes to a poor mental model of the law enforcement organization (Doss et al., 2011). If residents have little or no knowledge of the law enforcement agency, then they may have no strong mental model of it or have no opinion. Therefore, communicating with the public is essential in establishing a strong relationship between the law enforcement organization and its served society.

Understanding the psychology of communications also assists in the rendering of human decisions within the justice domain. Courtrooms are permeated constantly with every facet of logical reasoning, ethos, pathos, and persuasion. Judges, juries, and attorneys are all involved somehow with the communications process whether orally via the presentation of cases or silently through the use of nonverbal body language. Through communicating, the rendering of a human decision is embellished. These notions are summarized as follows:

> Judgments and judicial presentations to juries, therefore, are not merely statements of law; they are equally, if not more fundamentally, exercises in rhetoric. To read a judgment in this way is to see it in a new revelatory light that shows the justificatory, if not manipulative, use of language and linguistic devices that are an essential element of the judgment … the judge speaks, the audience listens, and is persuaded: the role of the audience as a participant has been removed and it now merely exists as the passive receiver of the court's decision. (Slapper & Kelly, 2011)

Communicating is an essential component of any justice system, whether federal, state, or local. The ability to influence the minds of jurors and judges is enhanced within the communications process through using psychological strategies to generate mental imagery (i.e., mental model) and perspective of the problem domain. Not only must one master the basic attributes of the communications process, but one must also aptly employ psychological communications strategies to embellish the act of communicating.

Chapter Comments and Summary

This chapter introduced the concepts through which communications processes are essential aspects of fashioning mental imagery among the recipients of messages. Embedded within such communications processes are psychological strategies that are used to influence human decisions, perceptions, and beliefs. The primary methods consist of logos, ethos, and pathos. When communicating, one may desire to elicit emotional responses or some type of analytical response. Some forms of communication are designed to influence and persuade others, thereby representing a form of behavioral modification. In any instance, communicating involves the use of mental models regarding the comprehension and understanding of the intended message.

The notion of logos involves some facets of analytical reasoning that represent both deductive and inductive reasoning. Ethos considers establishing some credibility and the use of expert testimony to appeal to others and to influence and persuade their abilities to render human judgments. Pathos strikes at the very heart of human feelings through emotional appeals that are used to influence human judgments.

Every aspect of the justice domain is permeated by these concepts. Whether a law enforcement officer writes a ticket for a speeding motorist or a judge listens to prosecutorial and defense arguments before rendering a judgment, the communications process must occur. In each instance, the communications process may be embellished through the use of logos, ethos, and pathos.

Terminology

Argument
Behavior
Communication psychology
Conclusion
Credibility
Declaration of Independence
Deductive reasoning
Emotional appeal
Ethos
Expert witness
Fallacy
Fault
Inductive reasoning
Influence
Logical fallacies
Logical reasoning
Logos
Major premise
Mental model
Minor premise
Moral turpitude
Opinion
Pathos
Persuasion
Psychological strategy
Rhetoric
Strategy
Subliminal
Validity

THOUGHT AND DISCUSSION QUESTIONS

1. Do some research, and locate an article in your local newspaper that involves the justice system or some law enforcement organization. On the basis of the discussions within this chapter, what characteristics of logos are present? Substantively discuss how logos is used to influence within your selected article.
2. Do some research, and locate an article in your local newspaper that involves the justice system or some law enforcement organization. On the basis of the discussions within this chapter, what characteristics of ethos are present? Substantively discuss how ethos is used to influence within your selected article.

3. Do some research, and locate an article in your local newspaper that involves the justice system or some law enforcement organization. On the basis of the discussions within this chapter, what characteristics of pathos are present? Substantively discuss how pathos is used to influence within your selected article.
4. On the basis of your selected article, consider how psychological communications strategies may be combined to maximize the effectiveness of the communications process. Substantively discuss how logos, ethos, and pathos are integrated within your selected article.

References

Ablow, K. (2011). Why Casey Anthony's verdict makes sense. *FoxNews*. Retrieved from http://www.foxnews.com/health/2011/07/05/why-casey-anthonys-verdict-makes-sense/ (accessed November 19, 2012).

Adams, C. (2010). Casey Anthony update: See Dec 20, 2010 hearing regarding death penalty phase. *Examiner*. Retrieved from http://www.examiner.com/article/casey-anthony-update-see-dec-20-2010-hearing-regarding-death-penalty-phase (accessed November 19, 2012).

Aldisert, R. (2009). *Opinion writing* (2nd ed.). Bloomington, IN: Authorhouse Publishing.

Becker, R. (2009). *Criminal investigation* (3rd ed., p. 4). Sudbury, MA: Jones and Bartlett Publishers.

Bernstein, D. (2010). *Essentials of psychology* (5th ed., p. 255). Belmont, CA: Wadsworth-Cengage Publishing.

Blum, B. (2007). *Contracts* (4th ed.). New York: Aspen Publishers.

Bond, G. (2012). *North Jersey legacies: Hidden history from the gateway to the skylands* (p. 36). Charleston, SC: The History Press.

Brain, C. (2002). *Advanced psychology: Applications, issues, and perspectives* (p. 63). Cheltenham, UK: Nelson Thomes, Ltd.

Brink, H. (2006). *Fundamentals of research methodology for health care professionals* (2nd ed., p. 6). Cape Town, South Africa: Juta Publishing.

Britton, W., & Bauer, R. (1922). *Cases on business law* (p. 16). St. Paul, MN: West Publishing Company.

Brown, J., & Campbell, E. (2010). *The Cambridge handbook of forensic psychology* (p. 773). Cambridge, UK: Cambridge University Press.

Burwell, C. (2012). Subliminal quotes. BrainyQuote. Retrieved from http://www.brainyquote.com/quotes/keywords/subliminal.html (accessed November 14, 2012).

Carroll, R. (2003). *The skeptic's dictionary: A collection of strange beliefs, amusing deceptions, and dangerous delusions* (p. 225). Hoboken, NJ: John Wiley and Sons Publishing.

Chen-Wishart, M. (2012). *Contract law* (4th ed.). Oxford, UK: Oxford University Press.

Cournoyer, B. (2011). *The social work skills workbook* (p. 61). Belmont, CA: Brooks-Cengage Publishing.

Dempsey, D. (2009). *Legally speaking: 40 powerful presentation principles lawyers need to know* (p. 189). New York: Kaplan Publishing.

Dillard, J., & Pfau, M. (2002). *The persuasion handbook: Developments in theory and practice* (p. 6). Thousand Oaks, CA: Sage Publications.

Doss, D., Guo, C., & Lee, J. (2011). *The business of criminal justice: A guide for theory and practice.* Boca Raton, FL: CRC Press.

Ericson, C. (2005). *Hazard analysis techniques for systems safety* (p. 48). Hoboken, NJ: John Wiley and Sons Publishing.

Farmer, C., Kirley, B., & McCartt, A. (2010). Effects of in-vehicle monitoring on the driving behavior of teenagers. *Journal of Safety Research*, *41*(1), 39–45.

Fiske, S. (2010). *Social beings: Core motives in social psychology* (2nd ed., p. 441). Hoboken, NJ: John Wiley and Sons Publishing.

Freedman, A., & Medway, P. (2005). *Genre in the new rhetoric: Critical perspectives on literacy and education* (p. 106). Bristol, PA: Taylor & Francis Publishing.

Fulero, S., & Wrightsman, L. (2009). *Forensic psychology* (3rd ed., p. 287). Belmont, CA: Wadsworth-Cengage Publishing.

Garaas-Johnson, C. (2011). UND law professor responds to Casey Anthony verdict. The University of North Dakota. Retrieved from http://und.edu/features/2011/07/casey-anthony-verdict.cfm (accessed November 19, 2012).

Gilbert, J. (2001). Towards a unified model of education and entertainment in technology centres. In S. Stocklmayer, M. Gore, & C. Bryant (Eds.), *Science communication in theory and practice* (p. 128). Dordrecht, The Netherlands: Kluwer Academic Publishers.

Guasco, M., & Robinson, P. (2007). *Principles of negotiation* (p. 58). Irvine, CA: Entrepreneur Media.

Harris, R. (2009). *A cognitive psychology of mass communication* (5th ed., p. 129). New York: Taylor and Francis Publishing.

Hewstone, M., Stroebe, W., & Jonas, K. (2012). *An introduction to social psychology* (5th ed., p. 220). West Sussex, UK: John Wiley and Sons Publishing.

Horberry, R. (2010). *Sounds good on paper: How to bring business language to life* (p. 155). London: A&C Black Publishers, Ltd.

Independence Hall Association. (n.d.). The declaration of independence: The want, will, and hopes of the people. Retrieved from http://www.ushistory.org/declaration/document/ (accessed November 19, 2012).

James, S., & Nordby, J. (2005). *Forensic science: An introduction to scientific and investigative techniques* (2nd ed., p. 158). Boca Raton, FL: CRC Press.

Kirszner, L., & Mandell, S. (2011). *Practical argument: A text and anthology* (p. 91). Boston: Bedford/St. Martin's Press.

Klofas, J., Hipple, N., & McGarrell, E. (2010). *The new criminal justice: American communities and the changing world of crime control*. New York: Taylor and Francis Publishing.

LeClercq, T. (1995). *Expert legal writing*. Austin, TX: University of Texas Press.

Lieberman, J., Arndt, J., & Vess, M. (2009). Inadmissible evidence and pretrial publicity: The effects (an ineffectiveness) of admonitions to disregard. In J. Lieberman, & D. Krauss (Eds.), *Jury psychology: Social aspects of trial processes* (p. 82). Burlington, VT: Ashgate Publishing.

Litwin, M. L. (2009). *The public relations practitioner's playbook: A synergized approach to effective two-way communication* (p. 361). Bloomington, IN: Authorhouse Publishing.

Merriam-Webster Dictionary. (2012a). s.v. "ethos." Retrieved from http://www.merriam-webster.com/dictionary/ethos (accessed November 23, 2012).

Merriam-Webster Dictionary. (2012b). s.v. "pathos." Retrieved from http://www.merriam-webster.com/dictionary/pathos (accessed November 22, 2012).

Merriam-Webster Dictionary. (2012c). s.v. "subliminal." Retrieved from http://www.merriam-webster.com/dictionary/subliminal (accessed November 14, 2012).

National Archives. (1776). Declaration of independence. Retrieved from http://www.archives.gov/exhibits/charters/declaration_transcript.html (accessed November 19, 2012).

Nersessian, N. (2008). *Creating scientific concepts* (p. 103). Cambridge, MA: The MIT Press.

North Dakota Department of Transportation. (2012). Traffic safety. Retrieved from http://www.dot.nd.gov/divisions/safety/trafficsafety.htm (accessed November 22, 2012).

Osborn, M., & Osborn, S. (2000). *Public speaking*. Boston: Houghton-Mifflin Publishing.

Pine, R. (n.d.). Essential logic. University of Hawaii. Retrieved from http://home.honolulu.hawaii.edu/~pine/Book2/chap4EL-2.html (accessed November 22, 2012).

Purdue University. (2012). Logos. Retrieved from https://owl.english.purdue.edu/owl/resource/588/04/ (accessed November 22, 2012).

Rathus, S. (2005). *Psychology: Concepts and connections* (9th ed., p. 177). Belmont, CA: Wadsworth-Thomson.

Rossmo, D. K. (2009). *Criminal investigative failures* (p. 45). Boca Raton, FL: CRC Press.

Samaha, J. (2012). *Criminal procedure* (8th ed.). Belmont, CA: Wadsworth-Cengage Publishing.

Sambey, M. (1999). *Business English and communication* (p. 40). Hong Kong: The Chinese University Press.

Seel, N. (2012). *Encyclopedia of the sciences of learning* (p. 911). New York: Springer Publishing.

Selinger, E., & Crease, R. (2006). *The philosophy of expertise*. Columbia, NY: Columbia University Press.

Shteir, R. (2011). *The steal: A cultural history of shoplifting* (p. 221). New York: Penguin Publishing.

Slapper, G., & Kelly, D. (2011). *The English legal system* (12th ed., p. 463). New York: Routledge Publishing.

Solomon, M. (2003). *Conquering consumerspace: Marketing strategies for a branded world* (p. 221). New York: Amacon Publishing.

Solomon, M. (2009). *The truth about what consumers want* (p. 15). Upper Saddle River, NJ: Pearson Publishing.

Sternberg, R. (2009). *Cognitive psychology* (5th ed.). Belmont, CA: Wadsworth Cengage Publishing.

Stuart, B., Sarow, M., & Stuart, L. (2007). *Integrated business communication in a global marketplace* (p. 141). Hoboken, NJ: John Wiley and Sons Publishing.

University of Texas. (2012). Master list of logical fallacies. Retrieved from http://utminers.utep.edu/omwilliamson/ENGL1311/fallacies.htm (accessed November 18, 2012).

University of Toledo. (2012). Logical fallacy. Retrieved from http://www.utoledo.edu/coil/studio/pdf/Logical_Fallacy.pdf (accessed November 19, 2012).

Van Vleet, J. (2011). *Informal logical fallacies: A brief guide* (p. ix). Lanham, MD: University Press of America.

Walton, D. (1997). *Appeal to expert opinion: Arguments from authority* (p. 150). University Park, PA: The Pennsylvania State University Press.

Whalen, D. J. (1996). *I see what you mean: Persuasive business communication* (p. 140). Thousand Oaks, CA: Sage Publishing.

Winter, M. (2012). Vermont inmates slip a pig into state police car decals. *USA Today*. Retrieved from http://content.usatoday.com/communities/ondeadline/post/2012/02/vermont-inmates-slip-a-pig-into-state-police-car-decals/1#.UUgCRlehxLE (accessed March 19, 2013).

Basic Written Communications 4

When you start thinking about taking pictures, sending an e-mail, receiving an e-mail, speaking into your phone and have it transcript voice into text and then sent as an e-mail, it's mind-boggling.

—Steve Largent (Largent, n.d.)

Objectives

The objectives of this chapter are to

- Introduce basic written communications
- Introduce templates for writing
- Discuss electronic mail
- Demonstrate letter and memo formats
- Demonstrate commendation and reprimand formats
- Demonstrate recommendation formats
- Demonstrate operations order formats

Introduction

Written communication is nothing new. Various civilizations and cultures employed the use of written communications throughout antiquity. The Sumerians employed pictographs as the basis of their written communications (Unger, 1988). The first observances of the Sumerian language are traced to approximately "3100 B.C. in southern Mesopotamia" (Kuper, 2011). This age and period of antiquity represent the Sumerian language as the "oldest written language in existence" (Kuper, 2011).

Various forms of written communication pervaded history. Another language of antiquity is Egyptian hieroglyphics. This ancient system of writing was used for approximately 3500 years, and was developed approximately 5000 years ago (Haviland, Prins, Walrath, & McBride, 2011). During 2006, in Mexico, a stone tablet was discovered that contained inscriptions of what is believed to be the Olmec language "dating from around 900 B.C." (Woods & Woods, 2011). In Europe, Greek is the oldest language that is still in use (DuBois, Skoura, & Gatsaniti, 2006). The Aztec Indians used written hieroglyphics to "record history, geography, religion, poetry, public events, and the passage of time" (Waldman, 2006). Asian language has also withstood the test of time and persevered throughout history. The Chinese language is the oldest system of writing that is still used during modern times (Brown, 1998).

Throughout history, communicating through writing has been an essential aspect of human life. It remains so during modern times. Written communication comprises a basis for entertaining and informing, for personal expressions and historical artifacts, for instructing and persuading, and for many other uses. Regardless of the use, written communication incorporates the basic concept of the communications process. Through written communication, the mental concepts of the sender are transmitted via a written medium to a receiver. Although noise may be present within the communications domain, communication is achieved and deemed successful when the receiver understands and comprehends the contents of the written message.

These notions are salient within the context of the justice system. Written communication influences both courts and law enforcement organizations. Through the use of written communication, attorneys may converse with their clients and peers, complaints may be submitted for review and processing, and judicial opinions are expressed through the written word. Law enforcement officers may issue tickets, warnings, or contact cards; field reports may consist of written statements from witnesses who observed an incident; and reports are used to describe incidents that necessitate assistance from law enforcement. Many other forms of written communication pervade law enforcement organizations and the justice system.

This chapter provides an introduction to the types of written communications that influence these domains. Personnel may receive letters for promotions or demotions or they may be commended or reprimanded. Electronic mail (e-mail) may be used to facilitate communications that are both internal and external. Organizations may issue a variety of memorandums or announcements throughout the entirety of the enterprise via written messages. Some law enforcement organizations may maintain operations orders during periods of emergency or for the daily running of the agency. Many other forms of written communication exist that influence individuals and organizations. This chapter explores the primary methods through which communicating occurs using the written fashion.

Electronic Mail

Electronic mail is a form of written communication that is used in conjunction with electronic devices that may be stationary or portable. E-mail is virtually edited, drafted, sent, transmitted, received, and stored using electronic devices. Generally, e-mail is a less formal type of communication through which messages of varying lengths and contents are transmitted. Attachments may be included to the e-mail message that may be more formal than the contents of the body of the e-mail message. For example, one may send a formal report to a supervisor as an attachment to a relatively simple e-mail note.

Some of the benefits of e-mail are as follows:

Mass audience: E-mail allows senders to transmit messages to a mass audience or to the specific members of a group. The use of e-mail transcends both geography and time zones. The senders and receivers of e-mail messages need not be near each other to communicate.

Verification: When sending an electronic message, the sender may specify that a read receipt be specified. The use of a read receipt informs the sender that the message was read by the receiver.

Efficient: The transmission of e-mail between senders and receivers is practically instantaneous. A sender may communicate with only one individual or with a mass audience immediately upon the transmission of the intended message.

Portability: Because of the prevalence of portable electronic devices (e.g., smart phones) that have e-mail capabilities, one may send or receive e-mail messages practically anytime.

Time: Although e-mail messages are transmitted instantaneously, they may not be read immediately. However, the use of e-mail involves an instant sending of messages that incorporates the use of a date and time stamp within the message header. By using a date and time stamp, the senders and receivers of messages know exactly when a message was sent. Date and time stamps are especially helpful when determining whether a message was sent before a specific deadline.

Cost reduction: The use of e-mail lowers organizational administrative costs. Communicating through the use of e-mail eliminates the costs of stamps, envelopes, paper, and human processing.

Encryption: Some e-mail programs facilitate the encrypting of communications. This encrypting of messages bolsters the security of the communications environment between the sender and the receiver of messages. Electronic messages may be encrypted upon their transmission and decrypted upon their receipt. Such encryption requires the use of an encryption key. Sensitive items should be transmitted using encryption to embellish their security.

The use of e-mail represents "progress in communication, both in scope and velocity" that has become "the most popular form of synchronous communication" (Mullen & Daniels, 2009). It is not uncommon for managers to expend approximately two hours daily collecting data for an e-mail message, sending e-mail, or reading e-mail messages (Griffin, 2008). It is common to use e-mail to communicate among departments and between individuals within the justice system and law enforcement agencies. Members of the public and law enforcement organizations may also communicate with each other through the use of e-mail.

The use of e-mail necessitates several considerations to embellish the communications process. These considerations are presented as follows:

Audience: One should consider the receiving audience of the intended message. Depending on the type of audience, sensitive materials may or may not be referenced within the body of the message or attached to the message. The choice of language is also a consideration of the intended audience. Messages may be formal or informal depending on the type of audience.

Header: The e-mail header contains the pertinent addressing information of the intended message. Its contents include fields for the recipient(s) (i.e., the TO: line), the sender (i.e., the FROM: line), chronological data (i.e., the date and time stamp), carbon copy (i.e., the CC: line), blind copy (i.e., the BCC: line), and a message topic (i.e., the SUBJECT line) (Harnal, 2009).

Readability: The body of the e-mail message should be readable. It should not be lethargic, and must have some type of conversational tone to facilitate the ease of response (Logan, 2010). When composing the message content, the recipient should be addressed by name (unless sending to a mass audience), and it should have a personable tone (Jones, 2002). One should get straight to the point quickly without indulging in preamble within the message (Jones, 2002).

Signature: The message signature contains the pertinent information regarding the sender of the message. Signatures should not be long, and must relay quickly details that may facilitate a follow-up conversation through e-mail or other means of communicating. Typically, signatures contain the name and title of the sender, telephone number, fax number, and any other pertinent information that is required by the organization.

Attachments: Any attachments should be referenced within the contents of the message. For example, if one is sending a duty roster to a supervisor, then the body of the e-mail message should contain some statement that a duty roster is attached.

Syntax and semantics: Although short e-mail messages may be composed within an e-mail program, it may be wise to use a word processing program to first compose longer messages. Word processors contain spelling and grammar tools, and multiple drafts of the intended message may be saved to a file and worked on as time permits. Editing, proofreading, and correcting any spelling and grammatical errors are essential to present a professional persona within e-mail messages. When the message is satisfactorily composed, it may be copied and pasted into an e-mail program for transmission to the intended recipients.

Many types of letters and memorandums may be transmitted to individuals or groups through the use of e-mail. These messages may be intended to inform or to persuade. They may be requests for information or may represent simple messages that occur during the daily course of operations within the organization. They may also grant or deny authorization to individuals or organizations. They may be read and discarded immediately or they may be stored in folders within an e-mail program.

Because e-mail is a virtual form of writing, it may be used to transmit letters and memorandums within office environments. However, it has not completely replaced the physical means of written communications using paper distributions of messages among the intended audiences. The succeeding sections introduce the typical forms of written communications that may be used within the justice system or among law enforcement organizations. These items may be transmitted via e-mail messages or may be transmitted through the traditional forms of physical writing.

Memorandums

A memorandum (i.e., memo) is defined as a "written reminder"; "an informal written note of a transaction or proposed instrument"; "a usually brief communication written for interoffice circulation"; or "a communication that contains directive, advisory, or informative matter" (*Merriam-Webster*, 2012g). Memos are relatively short documents that encompass a solitary theme or idea. When constructing memos, they should be concise, complete, clear, correct, and courteous. Generally, memos contain separate components that are similar to the header and body of an e-mail message. These items include the recipient (i.e., TO: line), sender (i.e., FROM: line), date, subject, and contents. Memos are defined by the word "memo" or "memorandum" at the top of the page. Additionally, memos are well suited for electronic communications because of their relatively short length, potential applicability to a mass audience, and have headers that are analogous to an e-mail header.

They are generally used for instructional and informational purposes, to inform personnel of organizational policies, to solicit suggestions from personnel, to make requests, and for reporting purposes (Debasish & Das, 2009). Memos also serve as organizational reminders, requests for assistance, grants or withdrawals of permission, and so on (Debasish & Das, 2009). These concepts are categorized into various types of memos: (1) announcements, (2) authorizations, (3) directives, and (4) persuasive memos.

Announcement Memorandums

An announcement is a form of "notification or declaration" (*Merriam-Webster*, 2012a). Most anything may be announced within organizational settings, ranging from holiday schedules to reminders of visiting dignitaries. These proclamations are accomplished through the use of the announcement memorandum. This type of memorandum may be physically printed and disseminated to the intended audience or it may be disseminated through the use of electronic mail. A sample announcement memorandum is presented in Figure 4.1.

The memorandum in Figure 4.1 is short and direct. It announces the availability of holiday pay for the Thanksgiving weekend, and indicates the proper paperwork that must be submitted. It also directs personnel to contact their supervisor with any questions. This type of communication is efficient and effective because it provides salient information that may be read quickly and understood by departmental personnel.

Authorization Memorandums

Authorization is the sanctioning of "legal authority" or empowerment. Authorization memorandums may convey this sanctioning or may express the denial of authority. This type of memorandum may be physically printed and disseminated to the intended audience or it may be disseminated through the use of electronic mail. A sample authorization memorandum is presented in Figure 4.2.

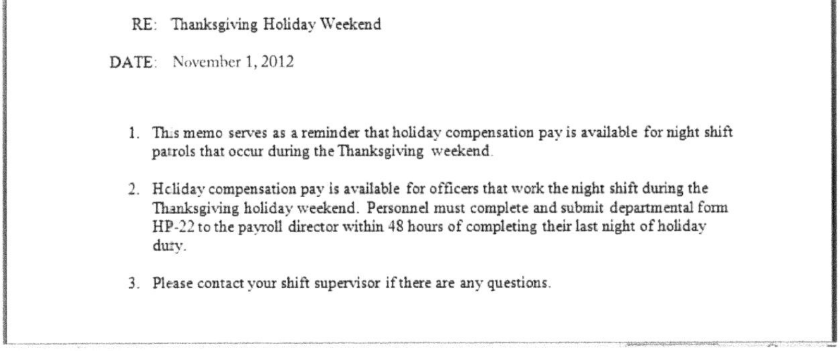
MEMORANDUM

TO: All Hands

CC: Mayor John Smith

FROM: Chief Ima Fake, Somewhere Police Department

RE: Thanksgiving Holiday Weekend

DATE: November 1, 2012

1. This memo serves as a reminder that holiday compensation pay is available for night shift patrols that occur during the Thanksgiving weekend.
2. Holiday compensation pay is available for officers that work the night shift during the Thanksgiving holiday weekend. Personnel must complete and submit departmental form HP-22 to the payroll director within 48 hours of completing their last night of holiday duty.
3. Please contact your shift supervisor if there are any questions.

Figure 4.1 Announcement memorandum.

MEMORANDUM

TO: CPT James Johnson

CC: Mayor John Smith

FROM: Chief Ima Fake, Somewhere Police Department

RE: Firearms Instructor Authorization

DATE: July 11, 2012

1. The personnel department received a copy of your firearms instructor certification.
2. The receipt of this certification qualifies you as a firearms instructor for our local police academy.
3. You are now authorized to conduct firearms training for the police academy. You will be a member of the training staff beginning on 1 AUG 2012. You will instruct the next class of recruits in September. You will receive a training schedule one week before the class begins on 23 SEP 2012.
4. Please contact me if there are any questions.

Figure 4.2 Authorization memorandum.

The memo in Figure 4.2 authorizes an officer to become a certified firearms instructor for the local police academy. Its contents are direct and concise, and provide the basic information necessary to inform the officer of the new empowerment as a firearms instructor. It also communicates the change of status for the officer regarding the inclusion as a training staff member. Although these pertinent details are conveyed through this memo, its primary purpose is to express the granting of authority.

Conversely, the authorization memo may be used to express the denial of authority while retaining the same characteristics of communicating effectively and efficiently. A denial of authority is expressed in the sample memo in Figure 4.3.

MEMORANDUM

TO: CPT James Johnson

CC: Mayor John Smith

FROM: Chief Ima Fake, Somewhere Police Department

RE: Firearms Instructor Authorization

DATE: July 11, 2012

1. The personnel department has not received a copy of your firearms instructor certification. The receipt of this certification is required before you can be classified as a qualified firearms instructor. Because the personnel department has not received a copy of your certification, you are not qualified as a firearms instructor with this department.
2. You are not authorized to conduct firearms training for the police academy.
3. Please request that the State Department of Public Safety send a copy of your firearms instructor certification to the personnel department. After this certification is received, then you may apply again for an instructor status with the police academy.
4. Please contact me if there are any questions.

Figure 4.3 Authorization denied memorandum.

MEMORANDUM

TO: All Personnel

CC: Mayor John Smith

FROM: Chief Ima Fake, Somewhere Police Department

RE: Winter Uniforms

DATE: July 11, 2012

1. The wearing of winter uniforms shall commence on 1 OCT 2012. All personnel will immediately begin wearing their winter issue uniforms on this date.

2. Winter uniforms will consist of the following items:

    - Long-sleeve uniform shirt with dark blue necktie.
    - Field jackets (to be worn when patrolling outdoors).

3. All personnel are required to possess a winter uniform before the mandated change of wear date of 1 OCT 2012.

4. Shift supervisors will verify that all personnel have the appropriate uniform before the change of wear date occurs. Individual personnel are responsible for obtaining the appropriate uniform before the change of wear date implementation.

5. Please contact your shift supervisor if there are any questions.

Figure 4.4 Directive memorandum.

Directive Memorandums

A directive is an edict that serves or intends to "guide, govern, or influence" (*Merriam-Webster*, 2012d). It is used to provide direction that influences the coordinating and controlling of the actions of an individual or of an organization. Analogous to the characteristics of the preceding memorandums, this type of memo communicates concisely and clearly. An example of a directive memo is presented in Figure 4.4.

This memorandum conveys pertinent information for all officers regarding a change of wear date involving winter uniforms. It provides quantifiable deadlines related to the change of uniforms, and provides a listing of the necessary uniform items. Its use of bullet points facilitates a quick scanning of the required items to generate an understanding in the mind of the reader. It also places the responsibility of verifying that personnel have the appropriate uniform upon shift supervisors and places the responsibility for obtaining uniforms upon individual officers. Essentially, it is a statement of what is to happen, when it is to happen, and what resources are necessary. It also specifies the conforming personnel and their specific responsibilities.

Persuasive Memorandums

Persuasion is the art of influencing another "by argument, entreaty, or expostulation to a belief, position, or course of action" (*Merriam-Webster*, 2012h). It seeks to alter the behavior or opinion of someone else or to influence an organization. The use of persuasive memorandums provides a method of persuading both individuals and organizations. Generally, a persuasive memo identifies some problem or issue that influences the organization, its personnel, or stakeholders. It also identifies some recommendation concerning how these challenges may be rectified. The persuasive memo invokes some mental response by expressing the benefit of the recommended solutions. Cumulatively, these attributes contribute toward the influencing of human behaviors and mindsets.

An example of a persuasive memo is given in Figure 4.5.

MEMORANDUM

TO: All Personnel

CC: Mayor John Smith

FROM: Chief Ima Fake, Somewhere Police Department

RE: Physical Fitness

DATE: April 11, 2012

1. Members of the general public are commenting about some of our overweight personnel and question whether they are physically fit to perform policing duties.
2. In order to improve our public image and to provide an opportunity for improved fitness, the department will implement morning runs effective on 18 APR 2012. Morning runs will occur at 0600 hours. Participating employees will have an opportunity to manage their weight and to improve their fitness level.
3. The state requires that all officers pass an annual physical fitness examination. A physical fitness examination will occur on 23 AUG 2012. The officer demonstrating the highest score on the examination will be awarded the departmental physical fitness commendation and its corresponding ribbon.
4. Looking good while in uniform improves our department's public image. I am sure that all officers desire to maintain their best appearance and fitness while in the public eye. Participating in the morning runs will help to improve one's chance of earning the commendation and improve public perceptions thereby reducing negative public commentaries. I look forward to seeing you for the first run next week.
5. Please contact your shift supervisor if there are any questions.

Figure 4.5 Persuasive memo.

Letters

A letter is a "direct or personal written or printed message addressed to a person or organization" (*Merriam-Webster*, 2012f). Letters represent the "most widely or commonly used form of external written communication" (Baraceros, 2000). Generally, letters are no more than two pages in length, and consist of "three or four paragraphs" (Roberts, 1998). They should be concise and clear, and not contain unnecessary information or details (Roberts, 1998). Letters may include the following components:

Heading: The heading consists of pertinent information concerning the sender. This information generally contains an address, "contact details," or organizational "logo" (Roberts, 1998).

Date: This section specifies the date the letter was authored.

Addressee block: This component contains the addressee's contact information. A specific individual is usually identified along with the appropriate title.

Subject: This component identifies the subject of the letter.

Greeting: This component represents the salutation. The addressee is referenced by title and name.

Introductory paragraph: This paragraph states the purpose of the letter succinctly.

Body paragraphs: These paragraphs state the informational content of the letter.

Concluding paragraph: This paragraph may state an appeal to the recipient, summarize the salient content, state a conclusion, or any other relevant closure.

Signature block: This section contains the author's name, title, and position. It requires a hand signature above the author's typed name.

Notifications: This component includes notification of any enclosures, copied recipients, mailing information, or file copies.

Typist: This component may not always be necessary. It contains the initials of the typist and the author.

Overall, a letter must accommodate considerations of the subject, audience, purpose, style, and organization (Carey, 2002). The subject represents the purpose of the letter. The contents of the letter must be related to the subject. Letter subjects may be specified by others (e.g., bosses, colleagues, etc.) or may be associated with some situational event (e.g., holidays, personnel hiring, etc.) (Carey, 2002). Subjects must be expressed concisely and specifically.

Letters must be appropriate for the intended audience or recipient. They may be tailored depending on a variety of factors ranging from the formalness of the communication to the attributes of the receiver. For example, if one is congratulating someone and issuing a commendation letter, then the tone of the letter may be formal. If one is writing to a subject-matter expert, then some technical language may be appropriate. Basically, letters may be suited to the attributes of the receiving audience.

The purpose of the letter must be clear and direct. If not, confusion may occur in the mind of the receiver. As a method of avoiding ambiguity and enhancing clarity, letters should pass the "so what" test (Carey, 2002). This test ensures that the content of the letter is both informational and clear. After reading the letter, the author should ask "so what" to determine whether the contents of the letter sufficiently answer this query (Carey, 2002). If the question cannot be answered clearly, then the letter must be further revised until the question is answerable.

The letter style represents the format of the letter. Letters may use a block style, an indented paragraph style, or a simplified style. The block style accommodates all lines of the letter beginning at the left margin (Guffey & Seefer, 2011). When using the paragraph style, the first line of each paragraph is indented (usually five spaces), and all remaining paragraph lines begin at the left margin (Chaturvedi & Chaturvedi, 2011). All other lines of the paragraph style are indented toward the right of the page (generally beginning in the middle of the page). The simplified letter style has no greeting or closing (a subject line is substituted for the greeting) (Chaturvedi & Chaturvedi, 2011).

Letters must be organized. They must convey the intended message efficiently and effectively. Therefore, the structuring of the letter must be planned in advance to include everything that must be stated within its contents (Geffner, 2010). Essentially, the organization of letters must be "logical, complete, and concise" (Geffner, 2010). Strengthening the organization of a letter improves the chance of eliciting a desired response from its reader (Bowman & Branchaw, 1977).

Letters must be edited and proofread not only for content but also for semantic and syntax errors. Incorrect spelling and grammar detract from the professionalism of the letter regardless of content. Such defects impair the effectiveness of the letter (Bonner, 1974). They also influence the receiver's perceptions of the sender, and are poor reflections of the sender (Wallace & Webber, 2010). Letters may undergo multiple revisions and use multiple reviewers to ensure their correctness for both language and content.

Letters may be used to communicate both internally and externally. This notion differs from the purpose of memorandums because memos are internal documents. The purposes of letters may be varied, and represent both formality and informality. They may be printed and sent via surface mail or transmitted via electronic mail. The succeeding sections present a variety of letters that may be used within the justice system and among law enforcement organizations.

Commendation Letters

Commendation letters may accompany awards for outstanding service or for some recognizable accomplishment. They may originate from either within the organization or externally. A commendation is the recommending of someone as being "worthy of confidence or notice" or the mentioning of something notable "with approbation" (*Merriam-Webster*, 2012c). In short, a commendation letter recognizes the exceptional actions of personnel. A sample commendation letter, using the indented paragraph style, is presented in Figure 4.6.

Transmittal Letters

A transmittal letter expresses the conveying of property from one entity to another entity. Within the justice system, transmittal letters may be used for a variety of purposes internally and externally. Transmittal letters may be used to show the transfer of property between operational shifts or they may be used to show the transfer of prisoners between

DIVISION OF FLORIDA HIGHWAY PATROL

OFFICE OF THE DIRECTOR

October 5, 2012

TO: Lieutenant John Bagnardi

FROM: Colonel David H. Brierton

SUBJECT: 2012 Florida Missing Children's Day

You are commended for your contribution to the *2012 Florida Missing Children's Day*, which was held at the Capitol on September 10, 2012.

It takes a very special person to escort the family members whose loved ones are missing or deceased during this emotional event. Your professionalism during the rehearsal and ceremony created a very positive image for the Florida Highway Patrol.

This work ethic reinforces our belief that the Florida Highway Patrol employs the finest. Once again, thank you for a job well done!

DHB/ndr

cc: Lt. Colonel Ernesto Duarte
Major Ryan Burchnell
Captain Mike Burroughs
Personnel

Figure 4.6 Commendation letter. (From Florida Highway Patrol. 2012. Lieutenant John Bagnardi. http://www.flhsmv.gov/fhp/Recognition/Letters/2012/Bagnardi101912.pdf. Accessed December 9, 2012.)

organizations. They also may be useful when establishing a chain of custody. A transmittal letter may also accompany the presenting of reports or proposals. They also may accompany budget presentations. Essentially, transmittal letters show the movements of items among entities within the justice system.

Transmittal letters may exhibit numerous styles and formats ranging from variations of the block style to the use of indented paragraphs. There are no styles or formats that are common within the justice system for writing transmittal letters. The style and format of a transmittal letter may adhere to municipal or departmental policies, or may represent the preference of the author. Transmittal letters may range in length from only one page to several pages depending on the scope of the material being transferred between entities. Depending on the scope, transmittal letters may incorporate various headings and subheadings to describe the materials being transferred.

Obtained from the Louisville Metro Police Department, an example of a transmittal letter is given in Figure 4.7a through c (Louisville Metro Police Department, 2012). This

(a)

OFFICE OF INTERNAL AUDIT
LOUISVILLE, KENTUCKY

JERRY E. ABRAMSON
MAYOR

THOMAS L. OWEN
PRESIDENT METRO COUNCIL

MICHAEL S. NORMAN, CIA, CFE, CGAP
CHIEF AUDIT EXECUTIVE

Transmittal Letter

February 17, 2010

The Honorable Jerry E. Abramson
Mayor of Louisville Metro
Louisville Metro Hall
Louisville, KY 40202

Subject: Audit of Louisville Metro Police Department's Incentive Pay

Introduction

An audit of the Louisville Metro Police Department's (LMPD) incentive pay was performed. The primary focus of the review was the operational and fiscal administration of incentive pay activity. This included how the activity is processed, recorded, and monitored. The objective was to obtain assurance that the risks are adequately mitigated through the internal control structure.

The audit was conducted in accordance with Government Auditing Standards issued by the Comptroller General of the United States and with the International Standards for the Professional Practice of Internal Auditing issued by the Institute of Internal Auditors.

As a part of the review, the internal control structure was evaluated. The objective of internal control is to provide reasonable, but not absolute, assurance regarding the achievement of objectives in the following categories:

- Achievement of business objectives and goals
- Effectiveness and efficiency of operations
- Reliability of financial reporting
- Compliance with applicable laws and regulations
- Safeguarding of assets

Louisville Metro Police Department – Incentive Pay
February 2010
Page 2 of 12

WWW.LOUISVILLEKY.GOV
609 WEST JEFFERSON STREET LOUISVILLE, KENTUCKY 40202 502.574.3291

Figure 4.7 Transmittal letter. (a) Part 1.

(b)

There are inherent limitations in any system of internal control. Errors may result from misunderstanding of instructions, mistakes of judgment, carelessness, or other personnel factors. Some controls may be circumvented by collusion. Similarly, management may circumvent control procedures by administrative oversight.

Scope

The procedures for administering LMPD incentive pay activity were reviewed through interviews with key personnel. The focus of the review was the operational and fiscal administration of the activity, to include ensuring that eligible LMPD employees were appropriately paid and that Louisville Metro was properly reimbursed from the Kentucky Law Enforcement Council (KLEC). Tests of sample data were performed on activity from May and August 2009. Activity reviewed included payroll system reports of employee earnings, KLEC rosters and corresponding monthly reimbursement documentation, LMPD training records, and Louisville Metro financial system postings.

The review included assessing whether activity was processed, recorded, and monitored accurately and appropriately. The details of the scope and methodology of the review are addressed in the Observations and Recommendations section of this report. The audit would not identify all issues because it was based on a selective review of data.

Opinion

It is our opinion that the administration of LMPD's incentive pay activity needs improvement. The internal control rating is on page 5 of this report. The rating quantifies our opinion regarding the internal controls, and identifies areas requiring corrective action. Opportunities to strengthen the internal control structure were noted. Examples include the following.

- **Monitoring and Reconciliation.** A reconciliation of the monthly reimbursements from KLEC and the corresponding support documentation is not performed to ensure the amount paid is appropriate (i.e., that the detailed listing of officers and reimbursement amounts are appropriate).
    - ➢ Several exceptions were noted during the review of monthly KLEC reimbursements and corresponding payroll activity. Exceptions included reimbursements for officers on unpaid leave or no longer employed by LMPD, no reimbursement for officers receiving incentive pay, reimbursement of the retirement expense for an officer that does not participate in LMPD's retirement program, and inaccurate social security numbers.

      Since there have not been any prior reconciliations of activity, it could not be determined if the exceptions were appropriate.

- **General Administration.** There were some issues noted with the general administration of LMPD's incentive pay activity.
    - ➢ There is not adequate technical support of the database used by LMPD to track officers' training activity. The training database was created prior to the merger of the City and County Police Departments, and the individual that created the

Louisville Metro Police Department – Incentive Pay Page 3 of 12
February 2010

Figure 4.7 (Continued) Transmittal letter. (b) Part 2.

example demonstrates a letter that accompanied a pay audit report. This letter shows a somewhat complex example that incorporates headers to describe an opinion, action plan, control rating, background, and results summary. It uses the indented paragraph style within its body.

Acceptance Letters

An acceptance letter expresses and conveys some fashion of inclusion. Acceptance letters are used for a variety of reasons. For example, a law enforcement organization may opt to participate in a new insurance program or may receive notice that its honor guard was included in a local Christmas parade. Acceptance letters conform to the basic style and

(c)

database is no longer with Metro Government. This creates a risk that training records could be lost in the event of a system failure or glitch.

It should be noted that LMPD Training is currently working with Metro Technology Services to begin using Louisville Metro's PeopleSoft Human Resource System for the tracking of training records. The PeopleSoft system should provide LMPD with more advanced tracking and reporting capabilities, as well as adequate support from Metro Technology Services personnel.

- LMPD does not have documented desktop policies and procedures to guide in the administration of training activity.

The implementation of the recommendations in this report will help improve the internal control structure and effectiveness of the administration of LMPD's incentive pay activity.

Corrective Action Plan

Representatives from the Louisville Metro Police Department have reviewed the results and are committed to addressing the issues noted. LMPD's corrective action plans are included in this report. We will continue to work with LMPD to ensure the actions taken are effective to address the issues noted.

Sincerely,

Michael S Norman

Michael S. Norman, CIA, CFE, CGAP
Chief Audit Executive

cc: Louisville Metro Council Government Accountability and Oversight Committee
Louisville Metro Police Chief
Director of Office of Management and Budget
Louisville Metro External Auditors

Louisville Metro Police Department – Incentive Pay Page 4 of 12
February 2010

Figure 4.7 (Continued) Transmittal letter. (c) Part 3. (From Louisville Metro Police Department. 2012. Incentive Pay. Office of Internal Audit, City of Louisville, Louisville, KY, pp. 2–4.)

format guidelines delineated within the preceding sections. The style and format of an acceptance letter may conform to departmental or municipal policies or may be influenced by the preferences of the author.

Figure 4.8 shows an example of an acceptance letter (National Benefits Programs, 1991). This sample was obtained from the National Benefits Program regarding the acceptance of a benefits program by the Miami (Florida) chapter of the Fraternal Order of Police. Unlike the example of the transmittal letter that showed the paragraph format and style, this acceptance letter invokes the block style. It represents a straightforward acceptance of the program offer using only one page. Although it is a short example, it achieves its purpose directly and succinctly.

FRATERNAL ORDER OF POLICE
WILLIAM NICHOLS LODGE No. 8
999 - 11th STREET (FLAMINGO PARK)
MIAMI BEACH, FLORIDA 33139
531-5636 - 534-2775

August 10, 1991

National Vehicle Programs
Division of Supplemental Benefits
16393 NW 11 Street, Room 120
Pembroke Pines, FL 33028

Attn:Mr.Jerry Cristodero, Ops. Dir.

Dear Mr. Cristodero:

We have received your letter of June 1, 1991 inviting employees of our Department to participate in a discount program already in effect with numerous Federal, State and City agencies.

Please consider this letter a formal acceptance of your offer. We have posted the information requested, and copies have been provided to interested employees.

Thank you for your invitation to join your program, and we look forward to taking advantage of the substantial discounts offered.

Sincerely,

Bernard Winer
Secretary

BW:smd

Figure 4.8 Acceptance letter. (From http://www.nationalbenefitsprograms.com/2010/09/fraternal-order-of-police/.)

Reprimand Letters

There are times when personnel must be reprimanded for their poor behavior and conduct. This action is usually accomplished through the use of a reprimand letter. Reprimand letters generally become part of one's personnel file and exhibit punitive attributes of the organization. The reprimand letter usually describes the incident in which poor behavior or misconduct occurred. They also may serve as warnings to the offending personnel before further punitive measures are taken by the organization.

The format and style characteristics of reprimand letters vary according to departmental or municipal standards. There is no universal format or style that encompasses all reprimands. They may use either the block or indented paragraph methods within the body of the letter. Reprimand letters may be short or long depending on the severity and complexity of the situation. In most cases, the receiver must sign an additional, separate statement indicating the receipt of the reprimand letter.

Figure 4.9a through c shows a sample reprimand letter from the City of Houston (KTRK News, 2012). Its body and components adhere to the block style of writing. It is well organized and presents its arguments methodically to show the characteristics of the reprimand. It contains numerous details of the questionable situation to establish a basis for the reprimand. It also shows why the behavior is unacceptable by including excerpts from the departmental general orders, thereby further strengthening the potency of the reprimand.

(a)

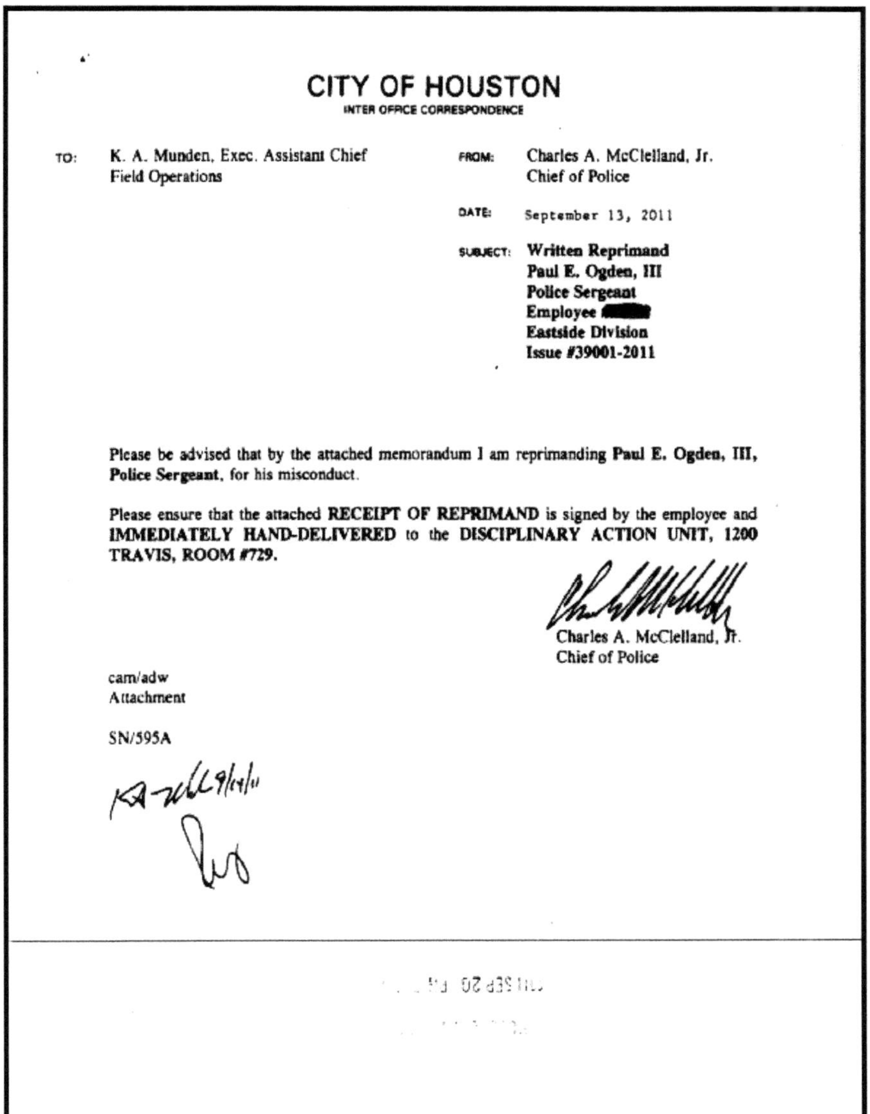

CITY OF HOUSTON
INTER OFFICE CORRESPONDENCE

TO: K. A. Munden, Exec. Assistant Chief
Field Operations

FROM: Charles A. McClelland, Jr.
Chief of Police

DATE: September 13, 2011

SUBJECT: **Written Reprimand**
Paul E. Ogden, III
Police Sergeant
Employee
Eastside Division
Issue #39001-2011

Please be advised that by the attached memorandum I am reprimanding **Paul E. Ogden, III, Police Sergeant**, for his misconduct.

Please ensure that the attached **RECEIPT OF REPRIMAND** is signed by the employee and **IMMEDIATELY HAND-DELIVERED** to the **DISCIPLINARY ACTION UNIT, 1200 TRAVIS, ROOM #729.**

Charles A. McClelland, Jr.
Chief of Police

cam/adw
Attachment

SN/595A

Figure 4.9 Reprimand letter. (a) Part 1.

(b)

CITY OF HOUSTON

INTER OFFICE CORRESPONDENCE

TO:	Paul E. Ogden, III Police Sergeant Employee [redacted] Eastside Division	FROM:	Charles A. McClelland, Jr. Chief of Police
		DATE:	September 13, 2011
VIA:	K. A. Munden, Exec. Assistant Chief Field Operations	SUBJECT:	**Written Reprimand** **Issue #39001-2011**

It has come to my attention that, on or about April 21, 2011, you failed to comply with Houston Police Department rules and regulations regarding **CONDUCT AND AUTHORITY.**

Investigation revealed that, on the above date, you responded to the scene of a vehicle accident involving off-duty Sergeant R. Trejo. While at the scene, you were aware of several wine bottles on the floorboard of Sergeant Trejo's vehicle. Also, you were aware that allegations had been made that alcohol may have been a factor in the accident and you failed to exercise appropriate supervisory conduct when you neglected to ensure that the wine, potential evidence, was properly tagged and secured in a manner consistent with department evidence handling policy and practice.

Additionally, you failed to use sound judgment when you covered the bottles with a cloth to prevent them from being seen by any members of the public.

It has been determined that, by your actions, you have violated the following:

GENERAL ORDERS

Conduct and Authority, Order No. 200-08, dated September 28, 2005, states in part, but is not limited to:

1 **CONDUCT AND BEHAVIOR**

Sound Judgment

Employees' behavior will be limited to conduct which is reasonable and prudent. No employee will commit any act on-duty or off-duty in an official or private capacity that tends to bring reproach, discredit, or embarrassment to the department. ~~Employees are expected to exercise sound judgment at all times.~~

Figure 4.9 (Continued) Reprimand letter. (b) Part 2.

Gratitude Letters

Gratitude letters express some sense of appreciation and thankfulness. They may originate internally or externally in relation to the justice system or law enforcement organizations. Letters of gratitude may show an appreciation for personnel who have contributed meaningfully to the law enforcement organization or to its societal stakeholders. They may also be sent to a law enforcement organization from members of the general public or from some organization that has received some benefit from the services of a law enforcement organization.

(c)

Paul E. Ogden, III, Police Sergeant - 2 -
RE: Written Reprimand

8 **SUPERVISORY CONDUCT**

Supervisors will actively enforce the law and the policies and procedures of the Houston Police Department. Supervisors will not permit or otherwise fail to prevent violations of the law or the rules, regulations, policies, and procedures of the Houston Police Department by any employee.

Supervisors who fail to take appropriate action when they are aware or should have been aware an employee was in violation of the law or department policy will be held accountable.

Supervisors will report violations of law and department policy to the employee's immediate supervisor without delay. If the employee is a subordinate of the supervisor, the remainder of the employee's chain of command will be notified, as required by General order 200-03, **Investigation of Employee Misconduct.**

Consequently, you should consider this memorandum, a **reprimand** regarding your misconduct, and notice that repetition of such violations will not be tolerated.

Charles A. McClelland, Jr.
Chief of Police

cam/adw

SN/595A

Figure 4.9 (Continued) Reprimand letter. (c) Part 3. (From http://dig.abclocal.go.com/ktrk/PICS/SEPTEMBER11/Ogden_appeal.pdf.)

No specific format exists regarding the crafting of a gratitude letter. Such letters may follow the block or indented paragraph style. Its contents are generally a heartfelt expression of thanks and appreciation. The lengths of gratitude letters vary according to the complexity of the situation and the depth of details contained within the body of the letter.

Figure 4.10 shows a letter of gratitude received by the Florida Highway Patrol. Although it is a short letter, its contents express the thankfulness of a school group that was visited by a patrolman from the Florida Highway Patrol. This letter conforms to the aforementioned block style of writing. It contents exhibit the gratefulness of the author, and cite details of the situation involving the Florida Highway Patrol.

Temple Terrace Presbyterian Church
420 Bullard Parkway
Temple Terrace, Florida 33617
(813) 988-3514

Rev. Elizabeth B. Kuehl, Pastor

July 25, 2012

Date
AUG 2 2012
Office of the Director

Colonel David H. Brierton
Florida Highway Patrol
Neil Kirkman Building
2900 Apalachee Parkway
Tallahassee, Florida 32399

Dear Colonel Brierton:
We are indebted to Mr. Buck Justice, retired Florida Highway Patrol, for contacting Captain Jackie Freeman to arrange for Trooper Jesse Lopez to visit our campus and provide the children with an exciting, colorful and educational program.

Imagine their surprise as Trooper Lopez arrived on his motorcycle replete with red and blue flashing lights and of course the siren! The children range in age from 2 to 9 and Trooper Lopez captured their imagination as he taught them about the highway patrol. They were intrigued by his uniform and equipment and he was patient with all their questions.

I am grateful to you and ask that you extend our gratitude to Captain Freeman and Trooper Lopez for taking the time to help us create an experience that the children will long remember. We appreciate all you do for us on the roads and in the schools.

Sincerely,

Elizabeth Kuehl

Elizabeth Kuehl

Figure 4.10 Gratitude letter. (From Temple Terrance Presbyterian Church, Temple Terrace, FL.)

Response Letters

Response letters represent a written response to some query of the justice system or of law enforcement organizations. They may also represent a written response by some organization or individual that is queried by some entity within the justice system or law enforcement organization. Response letters are generally cordial and informative written materials that directly address a specific question. They may be associated with practically any type of query ranging from a request for incident reports to complaint resolution.

Figure 4.11 shows a sample response letter obtained from Brockton, Massachusetts, regarding a query of auditing its water and sewer department (Brockton Post, 2010). This response letter conforms to the indented paragraph style and format. It provides detailed information as a basis for its response to the query regarding the auditing of the water and sewer department. It provides references to complaints filed by Brockton residents. Furthermore, it expresses multiple resolutions that may rectify the situation.

City of Brockton

Law Department

LINDA M. BALZOTTI
MAYOR

PHILIP C. NESSRALLA, JR.
CITY SOLICITOR

KATHERINE M. FEODOROFF
GILBERT J. SCHIPANI
CAITLIN E. LEACH
ASSISTANT CITY SOLICITORS

PATRICIA A. FLORIO
PARALEGAL

MARY T. MILLIGAN
WORKER'S COMPENSATION AGENT
(508) 580-7821

October 14, 2010

Martha Coakley, Attorney General
Commonwealth of Massachusetts
One Ashburton Place
Boston, MA 02108

Re: Open Meeting Law Complaint – Brockton Water Commission

Dear Attorney General Coakley:

In accordance with the statutory guidelines of the Open Meeting Law, enclosed please find copies of several complaints filed by City of Brockton residents regarding a Water Commission Executive Session meeting on August 30, 2010. As City Solicitor for the City of Brockton I am authorized by law to represent the Water Commission in this matter.

In response to these complaints, I offer the following in resolution of the issues. After review of the complaint allegations, the Brockton Water Commission agrees to undergo training relative to the Open Meeting Law and any other rules or regulations related thereto. Said training will be in the form of course books on Open Meeting Law, review, analysis and discussion of statutory language with either a representative of the Brockton City Solicitor's office or the Attorney General's office. The Commission will further examine, after the completion of its training, whether any future decisions on calling Executive Session should be preceded by consultation with the office of the Brockton City Solicitor. The Commission after completion of its training and in-depth analysis of the Open Meeting Law will determine whether or not any past sessions failed to adhere to said law.

I look forward to working with your office to ensure that the City of Brockton and its boards, commissions and departments are in full compliance with the Open Meeting Law and all other laws of the Commonwealth. Thank you for your courtesy and attention in this matter.

Yours truly,

PHILIP C. NESSRALLA, JR.
City Solicitor

PCN:paf
cc: Mayor Linda M. Balzotti
Bruce Malcolm, Chairman, Brockton Water Commission

BROCKTON CITY HALL ▪ 45 SCHOOL STREET ▪ BROCKTON, MASSACHUSETTS 02301
TEL: (508) 580-7110 FAX: (508) 580-7112
law@cobma.us

Figure 4.11 Response letter. (From http://www.brocktonpost.com/2010_10_01_archive.html.)

Delinquency Letters

A delinquency letter is used to inform an individual or an organization of its failure to satisfy some requirement of the justice system. Delinquency letters are mailed after some event that transpires that may be classified as either a civil or criminal infraction. The appearance and organization of delinquency letters generally adhere to a standard fashion that is specified by the state or municipality. The contents of delinquency letters express the details of the alleged infraction and the associated punitive consequences. They may also include some reference of laws that express the illegality of the alleged infraction. Delinquency letters also incorporate some request for the individual or the organization to contact the justice system, and provide the appropriate contact information.

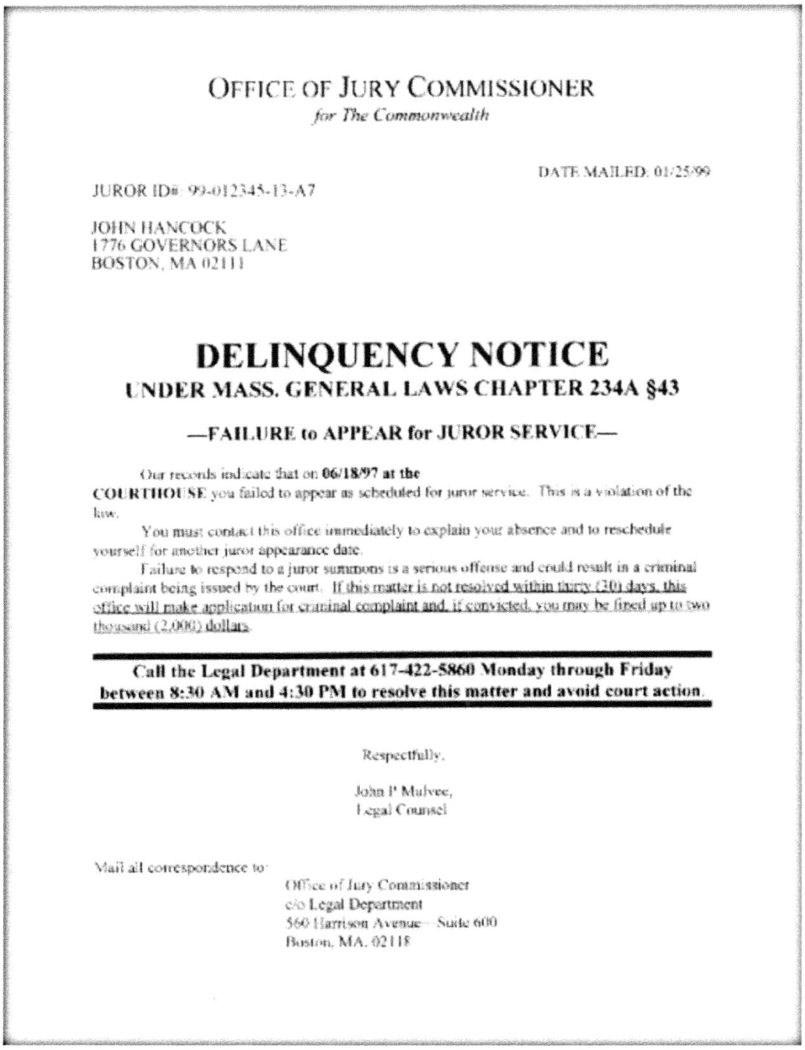

OFFICE OF JURY COMMISSIONER
for The Commonwealth

DATE MAILED: 01/25/99

JUROR ID#: 99-012345-13-A7

JOHN HANCOCK
1776 GOVERNORS LANE
BOSTON, MA 02111

DELINQUENCY NOTICE
UNDER MASS. GENERAL LAWS CHAPTER 234A §43

—FAILURE to APPEAR for JUROR SERVICE—

Our records indicate that on **06/18/97 at the COURTHOUSE** you failed to appear as scheduled for juror service. This is a violation of the law.

You must contact this office immediately to explain your absence and to reschedule yourself for another juror appearance date.

Failure to respond to a juror summons is a serious offense and could result in a criminal complaint being issued by the court. If this matter is not resolved within thirty (30) days, this office will make application for criminal complaint and, if convicted, you may be fined up to two thousand (2,000) dollars.

Call the Legal Department at 617-422-5860 Monday through Friday between 8:30 AM and 4:30 PM to resolve this matter and avoid court action.

Respectfully,

John P Mulvee,
Legal Counsel

Mail all correspondence to:

Office of Jury Commissioner
c/o Legal Department
560 Harrison Avenue—Suite 600
Boston, MA. 02118

Figure 4.12 Delinquency letter. (From http://www.mass.gov/courts/docs/jury/legal-delinquency-notice-redacted.pdf.)

Delinquency letters are both informational and are designed to elicit a response from the intended recipient. Therefore, the style and format of the delinquency letter may emphasize the use of boldface, large font to highlight the urgency and importance of the intended message. Depending on the template used by the municipality or the state, variations of the block style or indented paragraph style may be used. An example of a delinquency letter is presented in Figure 4.12.

Handbills

A handbill is a "small, printed sheet to be distributed (as for advertising) by hand" (*Merriam-Webster*, 2012e). The term handbill is synonymous with the term "flyer." Handbills may be used for many purposes ranging from the advertising of a police band concert to the dissemination of public notices. They may be used as fact sheets detailing some facets of the

NEW JERSEY TURNPIKE AUTHORITY
NOTICE OF PUBLIC HEARING
GARDEN STATE PARKWAY
INTERCHANGES 41 and 44 IMPROVEMENTS PROJECT
TOWNSHIP OF GALLOWAY, ATLANTIC COUNTY

NOTICE IS HEREBY GIVEN that the New Jersey Turnpike Authority will hold a public hearing in compliance with Executive Order 172 on the proposed Garden State Parkway Interchanges 41 and 44 improvements project ("Project") in Galloway Township, Atlantic County. At Interchange 41, the Authority proposes to construct new northbound and southbound entrance and exit ramps, realign the existing access road, and construct improvements along Jimmie Leeds Road (CR 561)(including widening and traffic signalization). At Interchange 44, the Authority proposes to construct a new southbound parkway entrance ramp and a new northbound parkway exit ramp to create a full interchange, replace the Pomona Road (CR 575) overpass, and construct improvements along Pomona Road (including widening and traffic signalization).

Figure 4.13 Handbill. (From http://www.gallowaytwp-nj.gov/.)

police organization or its operations. They represent a form of informational writing in which the pertinent details of some situations or events are expressed.

The organization, styles, and formats of handbills may vary according to organizational or municipal policies. They may also be influenced by the preferences of the authors. Regardless, handbills serve the purpose of conveying information to a specific group or to the general public. Figure 4.13 shows an example of a handbill obtained from Galloway, New Jersey (New Jersey Turnpike Authority, 2012).

Cards

A card is defined as "a flat, stiff usually small and rectangular piece of material (as paper, cardboard, or plastic) usually bearing information" (*Merriam-Webster*, 2012b). Two types of cards generally exist within the justice domain: business cards and post cards. Business cards may be disseminated with letters and other mailings, and may be passed from person to person. Post cards may be disseminated through the postal service.

Business cards are small, distributable paper instruments through which one expresses personal or professional details. They are often carried in wallets or purses, and may be stored in rolodexes. Typically, the dimensions of business cards are 2″ by 3.5″, and have a "landscape (horizontal) orientation" (Oliver, 2010). Business card colors "should be white, off-white, or ivory" to ensure that legibility is enhanced, and should use only one font type (Oliver, 2010). The content of a business card is informational. It generally presents a name, title, organizational affiliation, telephone and fax numbers, postal address, and electronic mail address. The name is generally centered in the middle of the card, the organizational information is contained within the lower left-hand side, and contact information is contained within the lower right-hand side of the card (Oliver, 2010).

Business cards may be disseminated for a variety of purposes. Officers may give them to business owners that own shops along a patrol route, disseminate them among charitable organizations, provide them after visiting the scene of an accident or crime to potential witnesses and the affected parties, or disseminate them to anyone whom the officer deems is necessary. Attorneys may disseminate business cards to clients and potential clients, judges, and other attorneys. Basically, the purpose of a business card is to serve as a physical instrument that communicates the pertinent contact information of someone within the justice system or among law enforcement agencies. An example of a business card is presented in Figure 4.14 (PoliceBusinessCards.com, 2012).

Post cards are larger than business cards. The largest size of post cards for regular postage is 4.5″ by 6″, whereas the largest size of post cards for first-class postage is 6.125″ by 11.5″ (Lander, 2005). Among law enforcement organizations, post cards may be used to inform the public of ongoing policing programs within the community, to serve as reminders, or to serve as public warnings. In Maryland, post cards are used to diminish the chance of theft of personal property among vehicles (Montgomery County Maryland Government, 2008). Police patrols send post cards to residents when they can observe plain-view items that may be easily stolen from unattended vehicles (Montgomery County Maryland Government, 2008). An example of the Maryland post card is shown in Figure 4.15 (Connected Communities Newswire, 2008).

Within the justice system, post cards are used to convey information quickly and effectively. Because they differ from letters, there is no consideration of block style or paragraph indentation. Instead, sentences are short, and the body of the message may incorporate the use of a bulleted list that highlights the salient points of the intended message. No specific

Figure 4.14 Business card. (From http://www.policebusinesscards.com/display_bcards.asp?CardType=Law%20Enforcement&Country=United%20States&Region=Federal&Agency=US%20Army%20Military%20Police.)

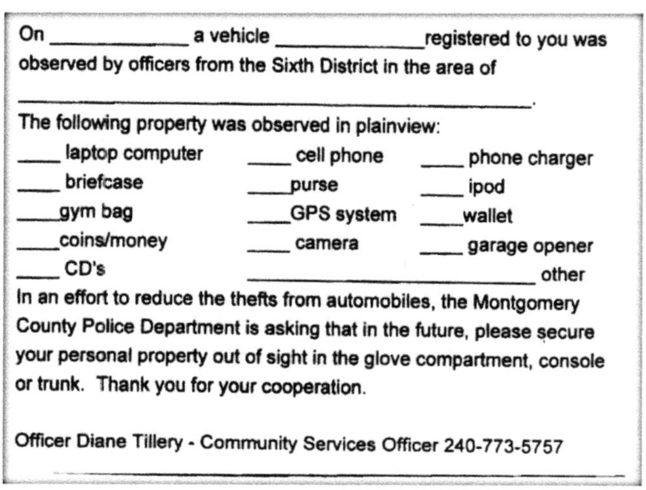
On ____________ a vehicle ______________registered to you was observed by officers from the Sixth District in the area of

____.

The following property was observed in plainview:

____ laptop computer ____ cell phone ____ phone charger
____ briefcase ____purse ____ ipod
____gym bag ____GPS system ____wallet
____coins/money ____ camera ____garage opener
____ CD's ____________________ other

In an effort to reduce the thefts from automobiles, the Montgomery County Police Department is asking that in the future, please secure your personal property out of sight in the glove compartment, console or trunk. Thank you for your cooperation.

Officer Diane Tillery - Community Services Officer 240-773-5757

Figure 4.15 Post card. (From http://connectedcommunities.us/showthread.php?t=22716.)

appearance or presentation of information exists for post cards within the justice system. Instead, a postcard template may conform to any standards that may be implemented by the state or the municipality.

Post cards may be used to facilitate communications with potential jurors. In Lassen County, California, post cards are used to elicit postponement responses to jury summons (The Superior Court of California, County of Lassen, 2012). In Massachusetts, residents may be notified of jury service through the use of post cards (State of Massachusetts, 2012b). Massachusetts citizens may also be notified of their failure to appear for jury service through the use of post cards (State of Massachusetts, 2012a). Examples of jury post cards are presented in Figures 4.16 and 4.17.

OFFICE OF JURY COMMISSIONER FOR THE COMMONWEALTH
500 Harrison Avenue, Suite 600, Boston, Massachusetts 02118-2447

SUMMONS for JUROR SERVICE

You are hereby summonsed to serve as a **GRAND JUROR** commencing on:

FRIDAY, JANUARY 8, 1999 AT 9:00 AM
PLYMOUTH COUNTY GRAND JURY, LOWER LEVEL
36 MAIN STREET, BROCKTON MA 02401

- You may postpone your juror service, if necessary, to a time within 12 months.
- You will receive an informational notice approximately 5 days before your scheduled date. It will contain a map and directions to the courthouse.
- A knowing failure to obey this summons without a justifiable excuse is a crime which, upon conviction, is punishable by a fine of not more than $2000.
- Please display this card where it will remind you when you must appear.

JUROR ID# = 99-004583-12-45

If a courthouse is wheelchair-accessible, you will find the wheelchair symbol to the right of the courthouse name wherever it appears. Where no symbol is shown, that courthouse is not wheelchair-accessible.

PAGE 1

VERY IMPORTANT: You must COMPLETE, DETACH, and MAIL the Juror Confirmation Form (page 3 below) Within 10 Days.

Figure 4.16 Jury summons post card. (From http://www.mass.gov/courts/jury-info/mass-jury-system/about-the-ojc/.)

NOTICE OF FAILURE TO APPEAR FOR JUROR SERVICE

Our records indicate that on the date, time, and location shown below, you failed to appear as scheduled. This is a violation of the law.

You must contact this office immediately to explain your absence and to reschedule yourself for another date of appearance.

You may respond by using the attached postcard, or you may call us at 1-800-THE-JURY, Monday through Friday, 9:00 AM to 4:30 PM. Please be very patient. We receive as many as 1500 phone calls per day.

Failure to respond to this notice may result in a fine of not more than $2000.

Respectfully,
Jury Commissioner
for the Commonwealth

APPEAR: Friday, September 10, 1999 AT 8:00 Am
John W. Mccormack P.O. & Courthouse
Room 328
90 Devonshire Stree
Boston Ma 02109

Figure 4.17 Failure to appear post card. (From http://www.mass.gov/courts/docs/jury/legal-failure-to-appear-postcard.pdf.)

Operations Orders

An operations order is defined as "a standard format for organizing and planning police action and use of force" (May & Headley, 2008). They may be useful in many situations, and are "crucial whenever any law enforcement officer or agency responds to crown control or siege incident" (May & Headley, 2008). Various operations orders are passed through the respective chains-of-commands among law enforcement organizations. They may instigate the commencement of a complex operation, or they may direct an individual to appear before a superior officer for some reason. Operations orders standardize the responses and actions of larger units or organizations, and improve the efficiency and effectiveness of police responses and operations (May & Headley, 2008).

Operations orders generally follow a template that incorporates the various factors that influence the conduction of the intended operation. The primary components of an operations order are given as follows:

Situation: This component describes a synopsis of the situation in which the operations order is executed and conducted.

Mission: This component expresses succinctly exactly what is to be accomplished through the conduction of the operation.

Administration and logistics (i.e., execution): This component details exactly how the activities of the operation are to occur. It encompasses the primary queries of who, what, when, where, and how.

Budget: This component details the financing of the operation.

Command and control: This component details the appropriate chain of command, authority, and responsibility of the leadership factions of the participating units and personnel.

Inclement weather: This component details the considerations of weather and incorporates considerations of how weather will affect the conduction of the operation.

Contingencies: This component considers what might possibly go wrong during the operation, and how such events will be accommodated. Basically, it expresses an alternative course of action that might occur if contingencies are encountered.

Communications: This component expresses the characteristics of communications that will occur during the operation.

All operations are unique. Therefore, not all of the preceding sections may be contained within an operations order. Departments also vary in their uses of operations order templates. Therefore, the template used by one law enforcement organization may differ slightly or drastically from the operations order template of another law enforcement organization. Furthermore, the operations order may use formal headings or subheadings, and it may incorporate facets of the block style or indented paragraph style of writing. Operations orders may also be used by law enforcement organizations of any size.

In Figures 4.18 and 4.19a through c, two different formats are presented for operations orders. Figure 4.18 shows the paragraph style used by the New York Police

OPERATIONS ORDER

SUBJECT: CHARGING STANDARDS FOR POSSESSION OF MARIHUANA IN A PUBLIC PLACE OPEN TO PUBLIC VIEW	
DATE ISSUED:	NUMBER:
09-19-11	49

1. Questions have been raised about the processing of certain marihuana arrests. At issue is whether the circumstances under which uniformed members of the service recover small amounts of marihuana (less than 25 grams) from subjects in a public place support the charge of Criminal Possession of Marihuana in the Fifth Degree Penal Law section 221.10 (1) (CPM 5th).

2. The specific circumstances in question include occasions when the officers recover marihuana pursuant to a search of the subject's person or upon direction of the subject to surrender the contents of his/her pockets or other closed container. A crime will not be charged to an individual who is requested or compelled to engage in the behavior that results in the public display of marihuana. Such circumstances may constitute a violation of Penal Law section 221.05 - Unlawful Possession of Marihuana, a violation *not* Penal Law section 221.10 (1) – Criminal Possession of Marihuana in the 5th degree, a class B misdemeanor.

3. To support a charge of PL 221.10 (1) the public display of marihuana must be an activity undertaken of the subject's own volition. Thus, uniformed members of the service lawfully exercising their police powers during a stop *may not* charge the individual with PL 221.10(1) CPM 5th if the marihuana recovered was disclosed to public view at an officer's direction.

4. In such situations, uniformed members of the service must charge the violation, Unlawful Possession of Marihuana (UPM), Penal Law section 221.05. Unlawful Possession of Marihuana is a non-fingerprintable offense and is punishable by a fine. As a general matter, the defendant is entitled to a criminal court summons for the violation Unlawful Possession of Marihuana. Alternately, *Patrol Guide 208-27, "Desk Appearance-General Procedure"* (see *NOTE* at the top of page "6"), provides for the defendant to be released when $100 pre-arraignment bail is posted under certain circumstances. Finally, a field test on the recovered substance must be conducted pursuant to *Patrol Guide 218-08, "Field Testing of Marijuana by Selected Uniformed Members of the Service Within the Patrol Services and Housing Bureaus."*

5. Where there is uncertainty regarding what provision of Penal Law Article 221 Offenses Involving Marihuana to charge, members of the service are directed to contact the Legal Bureau.

6. Commanding officers will ensure a sufficient supply of marihuana field test kits are available at their commands. Additionally, commanding officers will ensure and sufficient personnel are trained and available on all tours to conduct marihuana field tests and prepare the relevant reports.

7. Commanding officers will ensure that the contents of this Order are brought to the attention of members of their commands.

BY DIRECTION OF THE POLICE COMMISSIONER

DISTRIBUTION
All Commands

1 of 1

Figure 4.18 New York Police Department operations order. (From http://marijuana-arrests.com/docs/NYPD-ORDER-RE-MARIJUANA-ARRESTS-SEPT-19-2011.pdf.)

Department (NYPD). Figure 4.19a through c shows the style used by the U.S. Department of Homeland Security (DHS) Bureau of Customs and Border Protection (CBP). The formats, styles, and organizations of these examples differ. The NYPD example is fairly short, and expresses the salient characteristics of what is to be done regarding marijuana arrests. The CBP example shows a lengthy template that accommodates a variety of data fields representing an order that may express the attributes of complex operations. In both cases, the operations order is used to direct and control the actions of the respective organizations.

(a)

FY 2010 OPERATION STONEGARDEN (OPSG) OPERATIONS ORDER AND BUDGET TEMPLATE

U.S. DEPARTMENT OF HOMELAND SECURITY BUREAU OF CUSTOMS AND BORDER PROTECTION

Op Order Name:	Operation	
Op Order Number:	<Completed by CBP>	
Op Dates:	From:	To:
Report Date:		

Executive Summary
I. SITUATION
A. General Situation:

B. Terrain/Weather:

C. Criminal Element:

D. Friendly Forces:

II. MISSION

III. EXECUTION
A. Management/Supervisor Intent:

B. General Concept:

C. Specific Responsibilities:
1.

2.

3.

D. Coordinating Instructions:

Figure 4.19 Federal operations order template. (a) Part 1.

Planning Written Communications

Crafting a letter, memorandum, or post card is not always extemporaneous. Generally, much thought is required to produce effective messages and written documents to facilitate communications within the justice system and among law enforcement organizations. One writes for a reader. Therefore, when crafting written communications, attention must be given to the perspective of the reader of the intended message. Such attentiveness occurs

(b)

IV. BUDGET
Within the Operations Order, include budgets and operative spending plans in one-year increments (Year 1, Year 2, and Year 3). The annual operations should be practical and able to be completed within the 36-month period of performance. Grantees may not begin operations, obligate, or expend any funds until the final Operations Order and embedded budget has been approved by FEMA GPD and CBP/BP Headquarters and any existing special conditions and/or restrictions are removed.

The sample table provided below may be used as a guide to the applicant in the preparation of the budget and Operations Order to be submitted. Using the table below, compute the total estimated cost under the Narrative Justification column and indicates the amount of Federal funds requested under the Federal Request column that will support the project.

A.1 Example - Cost Estimates/Funding Requests (Year 1):

Administration/Logistics/Budget Request		Narrative Justification (Computation of Items)	Federal Request
Law Enforcement Operational Overtime		$50 per hour OT rate x 11 personnel x 10 hours x 3 day detail x 4 quarters per year x 2 years	$132,000.00
Fringe Benefits for Law Enforcement		$27.55/hr x 1.5 OT = ($41.33/hr) x (.062) = ($2.56/hr FICA) x 5840 hrs/yr x 2 yrs	$29,925.92
Travel, Lodging, and Per Diem for deployed LE and/or Federally sponsored (DHS/FEMA) border security task forces, conferences and/or mandatory training		Federal or below: approx miles of 3,500, 15 days single Occupancy @ $150 for 5 people	$1,750.00
General Equipment		Lines, personal flotation devices, GPS software updates, marine batteries, thermal imaging system	
Special Equipment (Requiring separate waiver i.e., Planes, boats, vehicles, SUVs, etc.)		Sea Hawk Boat, Explorer 4x4 Police with Package	$75,000.00
Part-Time to Full-Time Law Enforcement Personnel			
Activated Reserve Law Enforcement Personnel			
Vehicles:	Vehicle Maintenance	46,800 miles per year x .18 cents per mile = $8,424.00 x 2 yrs Tires, engine repair, other	$16,848.00
	Fuel Cost	3,342 x $4.50 per gallon = $15,043/yr x 2 yrs	$30,086.00
Total			$285,609.92

Figure 4.19 (Continued) Federal operations order template. (b) Part 2.

during a planning period in which the salient characteristics of the written communication are identified and established.

Specifying the essential attributes of written communication may be embellished through the use of planning tools. Figure 4.20a through d shows a sample worksheet that may be incorporated during the planning of written communications. This worksheet accommodates the basic elements of crafting written communications. It contains data fields that are helpful when identifying the primary characteristics of the written document, the intended recipient(s), the content of the message, the organization of the

(c)

A.2 Cost Estimates/Funding Requests (Year 2):
< INSERT COST ESTIMATES AND FUNDING REQUESTS TABLE >

A.3 Cost Estimates/Funding Requests (Year 3):
< INSERT COST ESTIMATES AND FUNDING REQUESTS TABLE >

V. COMMAND/CONTROL/COMMUNICATION
A. Chain of Command:

B. Unit Command:

C. Communications Detail:

D. Map Coordinates:
Notes:

Longitude:	Latitude:	
Degrees:	Minutes:	Seconds:
Decimal:		
Location Zone:		

ANNEX
A. Administration Annex:

B. Execution Annex:

C. Command Annex:
Media Action Plan:

Legal Review:

Risks:

Photos:

Figure 4.19 (Continued) Federal operations order template. (c) Part 3. (From http://www.fema.gov/pdf/government/grant/2012/fy12_hsgp_operations.pdf.)

message, the style and format of the written communication, the purpose and approach of the communication, the deadlines, and the attributes of mailing the completed written document.

Using this type of worksheet interjects quality within the overall writing process through which a final document is produced. It serves as a mechanism through which the author is challenged to provide the relevant details that will affect the crafting of the written document. Because it necessitates the stating of specific items and specific responses to writing queries, it ensures that the author does not forget to include anything that affects the written document, its contents, or its associated administrative functions (e.g., mailing).

(a)

Written Communications Worksheet

What is the tracking number of this communication?

What is the intended date of the communication?

For whom is the communication intended?

What is the title of the intended recipient?

What is the contact information for the intended recipient?

E-Mail:
Fax:
Telephone:
Cell Phone:
P.O. Box:
Mail Station:
Street Address:
Zip Code:

What is the subject of the communication?

Which Style? __ Block Style __ Modified Block Style __ Indented Paragraph Style

What is the primary purpose of this communication?

What is the secondary purpose (if any) of this communication?

If a response to another communication, what does the entity want to know?

Writing Planning Sheet Page 1

Figure 4.20 Writing worksheet. (a) Part 1.

Commentary Regarding Writing in the Criminal Justice Domain

The basic notion of written communication is unchanged since antiquity. Simply, among themselves, humans express concepts through the written word. During the Whiskey Rebellion of 1794, President George Washington used writing to record his daily accounts of the incident (The Papers of George Washington, 2012). This event was the first intervention of militia forces to internally suppress insurrection within the United States regarding the Excise Act of 1791 (The Papers of George Washington, 2012).

The 1800s amassed a variety of written documents within the justice system and among law enforcement organizations. The recorded opinions within the court systems

(b)

Written Communications Worksheet

What are the main points that must be contained within this written communication?

1
2
3
4
5
6
7

How does the reader benefit from this communication?

1
2
3
4
5
6
7

What approach(es) should be taken with this communication? Circle all that are applicable.

Admitting Guilt	Humor
Announcement	Obtain Response
Apology	Order
Appreciation	Personal/Confidential
Arouse Curiosity	Regret
Ask Question(s)	Reprimand
Awareness of an Issue	Request Assistance
Bad News	Update Status
Commendation	Urgent/Emergency
Compliment or Congratulate	Transmittal
Confirmation	Warning
Good News	*OTHER*

Writing Planning Sheet Page 2

Figure 4.20 (Continued) Writing worksheet. (b) Part 2.

provide historical artifacts of the writing styles and formats that were popular during this period. Wanted posters delineated and communicated the characteristics of criminals. Various advertisements expressed the need and opportunities for law enforcement officers.

The 1900s witnessed the writings of August Vollmer. This period also exhibited the societal prevalence of the written word through which acts of crime, the activities of law enforcement organizations, and the events of the justice system were presented within newspapers and magazines. These modalities of writing quickly disseminated information regarding historical events, such as the kidnappings of the Lindbergh baby and Patricia Hurst, the shooting of President Reagan, the news of the Watergate scandal, and the heinous deeds of the Rosenbergs.

(c)

Written Communications Worksheet

If another approach(es) is/are necessary, then specify:

How can the approach(es) be phrased to maximize the reader's attention?

1
2
3
4
5
6
7

Who will sign this communication?

What is the title of the person signing this letter?

What organization does the signatory represent?

What is the contact information for the signatory?

E-Mail:
Fax:
Telephone:
Cell Phone:
P.O. Box:
Mail Station:
Street Address:
Zip Code:

Writing Planning Sheet Page 3

Figure 4.20 (Continued) Writing worksheet. (c) Part 3.

The 2000s also are rife with writings denoting events within the justice system and among law enforcement organizations. Americans were repulsed by reading about the treason of Robert Hanssen and of the horrific terrorist events of September 11, 2001. Americans were elated to read about the death of Osama bin Laden. Additionally, the U.S. Supreme Court expressed its written opinion regarding nationalized health care.

Throughout American history, writing has been an essential form of communicating and documenting events within the justice system and among law enforcement agencies. The need for written expression that existed during the period of President George Washington remains unchanged during modern times. The act of humans writing for other humans is unchanged. The necessity of ensuring the quality of message contents is unchanged. The basic premise of the communications process is unchanged.

(d)

Written Communications Worksheet

What typist information must be included?

What distributions of this communication are appropriate?

What is the deadline for this communication?

Will this communication be sent before the specified deadline? YES NO

What type of mailing is appropriate? Circle the appropriate choice.

First Class Mail	Standard Mail
Internal Mail	Parcel
Electronic Mail	Priority Mail
Postage Due	Express Mail
Overnight Delivery	Certified Mail
Two-Day Delivery	Return Receipt
3-5 Day Delivery	Private Courier
Air Mail	General Delivery

What holidays or other interruptions may affect the mailing?

What is the cost of mailing and delivery?

Writing Planning Sheet Page 4

Figure 4.20 (Continued) Writing worksheet. (d) Part 4.

The attributes of written communication are essentially unchanged. Although cultural norms and technology have changed since the time of President Washington, the human characteristics of communicating through writing are relatively unchanged. The necessity of President George Washington to write persuasively is representative of the same notions of persuasive writing strategies that affect modern communications within the justice system and among law enforcement organizations.

During modern times, written communication pervades the justice system and law enforcement organizations. Law enforcement officers write frequently when performing their duties. After being called to the scene of an incident, some type of report is generally filed afterward, stating the officer's account of the event. Attorneys use written documents to communicate with clients, colleagues, and judges. Members of the general public often state their complaints or praises through the use of written documents. These considerations are not exhaustive; many other types of written expression may be identified among law enforcement organizations and within the justice system.

Communicating within the justice system involves the language skills and acumen of both the senders and receivers of messages. Messages should be reviewed to ensure that their content is appropriate and adequately encompasses the desired concepts that are to be communicated. Proofreading and editing are essential to ensure that written documents have little, if any, defects that may diminish the understanding of the message. These actions also must occur to improve the efficiency and effectiveness of communications. When crafting messages, authors must be vigilantly mindful of the mindset and perspective of the reader.

Regardless of the type of communication and whether it is conducted through electronic mail, letter, memorandum, or card formats, authors must strive to maximize the influence that it has on readers. Psychological strategies discussed within Chapter 3 may be incorporated within the written document to influence readers. Furthermore, within the justice system and among law enforcement organizations, all written communication must conform to the communications process introduced within Chapters 1, 2, and 3.

Chapter Comments and Summary

This chapter introduced the primary forms of written communications within the justice system and among law enforcement organizations: memorandums, letters, cards, and handbills. Each of these items demonstrates some facet of using the written word as an instantiated modality within the communications process. Writing is an effective method of conveying the thoughts of one individual or organization into the mind of another entity.

Writing effectively and efficiently to generate a desired understanding in the mind of the reader and to influence human behavior is an artful endeavor. No perfect method exists, and most all writing is influenced by situational characteristics and the attributes of the author. Within the justice system and among law enforcement organizations, writing may be influenced by policy.

Memorandums, letters, cards, and handbills are crafted to satisfy a myriad of purposes and requirements. Memorandums serve as information resources, announcements, notifications, and confirmations. Letters may be used to reprimand or commend personnel for the conduct and behavior, to seek assistance or pose queries, and for a variety of different purposes. Cards may act as quick informational references through which individuals may communicate their contact information and relevant affiliations. Handbills may be used to disseminate information to the general public.

There is no universal format, style, or organizational method of communicating via the written word within the justice system or among law enforcement organizations. Because these entities are unique and must conform to different policies and governances, their methods of written communications are unique. Despite such uniqueness, most communications within the justice domain and among law enforcement organizations incorporate some facets of the block, modified block, or indented paragraph styles of writing.

Communication is an essential aspect of organizational operations. Communicating efficiently and effectively improves the coordination and command of an organization and its endeavors. The use of an operations order facilitates communications that influence the operational functions of an organization. Generally, most operations orders adhere to a basic information template in which headings and subheadings may be varied with respect to the uniqueness of the endeavor and the organization.

Written communication is an inescapable reality of the justice system and law enforcement organizations. Although writing has occurred traditionally via printed media, the use of electronic mail accommodates much of the written communication within the justice domain. Electronic mail is a virtual entity. However, the principles that affect written communication are most certainly applicable to the electronic domain. When using electronic mail, people may also incorporate style, organization, format, and writing strategies.

Writing is not always spontaneous. Instead, it results from a methodical planning process through which messages are crafted and finalized before being transmitted to a receiver. Using a planning worksheet assists authors to identify and specify the essential characteristics of written communication that influence the communications process. Additionally, one must be mindful of correctness regarding the semantics, syntax, grammar, and spelling of the written language. Interjecting quality within the written document improves the perceptions of the reader and embellishes the understandability of the final document.

Terminology

Acceptance letter
Announcement memo
Attachment
Audience
Authorization memo
Body
Business card
Commendation letter
Conversational
Directive memo
Electronic mail
Encryption
Encryption key
Header
Language
Letter
Mass audience
Memo
Memorandum
Message body
Operations order
Organization
Persuasive memo
Planning worksheet
Post card
Reprimand letter
Response letter

Security
Signature
Style
Subject
Transmittal letter
Virtual
Writing worksheet
Written communication

THOUGHT AND DISCUSSION QUESTIONS

1. Written communication accommodates the use of strategy when composing messages. Given the contents of all preceding chapters and the discussion of writing letters within this chapter, draft a letter that attempts to persuade a local entity to donate some of its old resources to a police charity.
2. Do some research and determine what types of written communication are used by local law enforcement organizations. Compare and contrast these responses to identify the commonness of the written communications. Discuss these similarities and differences.
3. Assume that a local law enforcement organization has changed its fuel supplier because of pricing changes. The old fuel supplier was BigFuel Inc., whereas the new supplier is NowFuel Inc. The effective date of change is November 22. All personnel must return their fuel cards to the motor pool and obtain new fuel cards. Write a memorandum that informs the personnel of the law enforcement organization of this change.
4. You are a candidate for the office of sheriff for your county. Compose a handbill that you can use to support your campaign. Incorporate the basic reasons why you should be elected, personal and professional characteristics that qualify you for the job, and the date of the election. Include any other information that you deem is necessary.

References

Baraceros, E. (2000). *Business correspondence* (p. 4). Manila, Philippines: Rex Book Store, Inc.

Bonner, W. (1974). *Better business writing*. Homewood, IL: R.D. Irwin Publishing.

Bowman, J., & Branchaw, B. (1977). *Understanding and using communication in business*. San Francisco: Canfield Press.

Brockton Post. (2010). Open meeting law complaint—Brockton water commission. City of Brockton. Retrieved from http://www.brocktonpost.com/2010_10_01_archive.html (accessed December 9, 2012).

Brown, M. (1998). *The British guide to writing and scripts: History and techniques* (p. 20). London: The British Library.

Carey, J. (2002). *Business letters for busy people* (p. 2). Franklin Lakes, NJ: The Career Press, Inc.

Chaturvedi, P. D., & Chaturvedi, M. (2011). *Business communication: Concepts, cases, and applications* (2nd ed., p. 145). New Delhi, India: Pearson.

Connected Communities Newswire. (2008). Community and public safety newswire. Montgomery County, Maryland. Retrieved from http://connectedcommunities.us/showthread.php?t=22716 (accessed December 10, 2012).

Debasish, S., & Das, B. (2009). *Business communication* (p. 252). New Delhi, India: PHI Learning Private Limited.
DuBois, J., Skoura, X., & Gatsaniti, O. (2006). *Cultures of the world: Greece* (p. 87). Tarrytown, NY: Marshall Cavendish Benchmark.
Florida Highway Patrol. (2012). Lieutenant John Bagnardi. Retrieved from http://www.flhsmv.gov/fhp/Recognition/Letters/2012/Bagnardi101912.pdf (accessed December 9, 2012).
Geffner, A. (2010). *Business English: The writing skills you need for today's workplace* (p. 167). Hauppauge, NY: Barron's Educational Service.
Griffin, R. (2008). *Fundamentals of management* (5th ed.). Boston: Houghton-Mifflin Publishing.
Guffey, M., & Seefer, C. (2011). *Business English* (10th ed., p. 60). Mason, OH: Cengage Learning.
Harnal, A. (2009). *Linux: Applications and administration* (p. 227). New Delhi, India: Tata-McGraw-Hill Publishing.
Haviland, W., Prins, H., Walrath, D., & McBride, B. (2011). *Anthropology: The human challenge* (p. 391). Mason, OH: Cengage Publishing.
Jones, G. (2002). *Effective email* (p. 23). Reading, England: Graham Jones.
KTRK News. (2012). Ogden appeal. City of Houston. Retrieved from http://dig.abclocal.go.com/ktrk/PICS/SEPTEMBER11/Ogden_appeal.pdf (accessed December 9, 2012).
Kuper, K. (2011). *Mesopotamia: The world's earliest civilization* (p. 42). New York: Britannica Publishing.
Lander, J. (2005). *All I need is money: How to finance your invention* (p. 7/13). Berkeley, CA: Nolo Press.
Largent, S. (n.d.). Steve Largent quotes. Brainyquote. Retrieved from http://www.brainyquote.com/quotes/quotes/s/stevelarge353506.html (accessed November 23, 2012).
Logan, R. (2010). *Understanding new media: Extending Marshall McLuhan* (p. 252). New York: Peter Lang Publishing.
Louisville Metro Police Department. (2012). *Incentive pay* (pp. 2–4). Louisville, KY: Office of Internal Audit. City of Louisville.
May, D., & Headley, J. (2008). *Reasonable use of force by police: Seizures, firearms, and high-speed chases* (p. 60). New York: Peter Lang Publishing.
Merriam-Webster Dictionary. (2012a). s.v. "announcement." Retrieved from http://www.merriam-webster.com/dictionary/announcement (accessed December 7, 2012).
Merriam-Webster Dictionary. (2012b). s.v. "card." Retrieved from http://www.merriam-webster.com/dictionary/card (accessed December 9, 2012).
Merriam-Webster Dictionary. (2012c). s.v. "commend." Retrieved from http://www.merriam-webster.com/dictionary/commends?show=0&t=1355103723 (accessed December 8, 2012).
Merriam-Webster Dictionary. (2012d). s.v. "directive." Retrieved from http://www.merriam-webster.com/dictionary/directive (accessed December 8, 2012).
Merriam-Webster Dictionary. (2012e). s.v. "handbill." Retrieved from http://www.merriam-webster.com/dictionary/handbill (accessed December 9, 2012).
Merriam-Webster Dictionary. (2012f). s.v. "letter." Retrieved from http://www.merriam-webster.com/dictionary/letter (accessed December 8, 2012).
Merriam-Webster Dictionary. (2012g). s.v. "memorandum." Retrieved from http://www.merriam-webster.com/dictionary/memorandum (accessed November 27, 2012).
Merriam-Webster Dictionary. (2012h). s.v. "persuade." Retrieved from http://www.merriam-webster.com/dictionary/persuade (accessed December 8, 2012).
Montgomery County Maryland Government. (2008). Montgomery county police employ post card initiative for theft from vehicle prevention. Department of Police. Retrieved from http://www6.montgomerycountymd.gov/Apps/Police/News/NA_details.asp?NaID=4474 (accessed December 10, 2012).
Mullen, J., & Daniels, D. (2009). *Email marketing: An hour a day* (p. 2). Indianapolis, IN: Wiley Publishing.
National Benefits Programs. (1991). Fraternal order of police. Retrieved from http://www.nationalbenefitsprograms.com/2010/09/fraternal-order-of-police/ (accessed December 9, 2012).

New Jersey Turnpike Authority. (2012). Notice of public hearing. Retrieved from http://www.gallowaytwp-nj.gov/ (accessed December 9, 2012).

Oliver, V. (2010). *301 smart answers to tough business etiquette questions* (p. 54). New York: Skyhorse Publishing.

PoliceBusinessCards.com. (2012). Business card designs for United States/Federal. Retrieved from http://www.policebusinesscards.com/display_bcards.asp?CardType=Law%20Enforcement&Country=United%20States&Region=Federal&Agency=US%20Army%20Military%20Police (accessed December 10, 2012).

Roberts, J. (1998). *Business letter writing: Your questions and answers* (p. 6). Surrey, Great Britain: Trotman and Company, Ltd.

State of Massachusetts. (2012a). If you have received a 'failure to appear' postcard. Retrieved from http://www.mass.gov/courts/jury/FailureForms.htm (accessed December 10, 2012).

State of Massachusetts. (2012b). The process: Summonsing to service. Retrieved from http://www.mass.gov/courts/jury/summons.htm (accessed December 10, 2012).

The Papers of George Washington. (2012). University of Virginia. Retrieved from http://gwpapers.virginia.edu/documents/whiskey/index.html (accessed December 10, 2012).

The Superior Court of California, County of Lassen. (2012). Juror service. Retrieved from http://www.lassencourt.ca.gov/index.php?option=com_content&view=category&layout=blog&id=42&Itemid=92 (accessed December 10, 2012).

Unger, M. (1988). *The new Unger's bible dictionary*. Chicago: The Moody Bible Institute.

Waldman, C. (2006). *Encyclopedia of Native American tribes* (3rd ed., p. 12). New York: Checkmark Books.

Wallace, M., & Webber, L. (2010). *IT governance: Policies & procedure* (p. 843). New York: Aspen Publishers.

Woods, M., & Woods, M. (2011). *Ancient communication technology: From hieroglyphs to scrolls* (p. 52). Minneapolis, MB: Twenty-First Century Books.

Visuals and Graphical Communication

5

A film is never really good unless the camera is an eye in the head of a poet.
—**Orson Welles (Welles, n.d.)**

Objectives

The objectives of this chapter are to

- Discuss the use of charts and graphs
- Discuss the use of diagrams and figures
- Discuss the use of tables
- Discuss the use of visual imagery
- Discuss the use of animation and video resources

Introduction

A picture is supposedly worth a thousand words. The potency of imagery must not be discounted when communicating. Visual depictions may instantly convey a message between senders and receivers. Visual imagery may enhance written communications or it may be a complement to auditory communication. Visual imagery may convey concepts that may be inadequately expressed through the written word with respect to the intent of the sender of the message. It shows relationships among data sets and can be useful when attempting to understand complex concepts. Visual imagery may be used to show the relationships that exist among organizational components or it may be used to show process steps. Graphics and visual resources both complement written language through "clarifying complex figures and helping readers visualize major points" (Lehman & DuFrene, 2008). In any case, the use of graphic and visual imagery represents a powerful resource through which communications occurs.

Within the justice system and among law enforcement organizations, the use of visual imagery facilitates a variety of communications. Both adults and children are encouraged to "take a bite out of crime" through the use of television commercials that incorporate the animated crime dog "McGruff" (Miller, Hess, & Orthmann, 2011). Crime mapping tools incorporate visualizations of geographic data to show the relationships between incidents of crime (Boba, 2005). Tables are used to delineate the increases in various crime rates over decades (Davey, 1998). Wanted posters have been used since the period of the Old West until modern times to depict the image and pertinent details of criminals that are wanted by law enforcement organizations (Hall, 2009).

Visual imagery has generally always involved two dimensions. However, given the proliferation and advent of modern computing devices, visualization of three dimensions has greatly improved the capacity of law enforcement organizations to employ crime mapping tools to analyze and evaluate crime within geographic regions. Three-dimensional tools also have greatly improved the capabilities of terrain mapping functions through which search and rescue missions may be embellished.

Visual imagery improves the ability to recognize missing individuals. Instead of a written description that may invoke somewhat different mental models within the minds of readers, presenting a photograph of the missing person provides a basis for immediate recognition. The photographs of numerous missing persons are presented on milk cartons and grocery bags in the hope that someone will recognize the missing individual and will alert the appropriate authorities regarding the location of the missing person (Cutler, 2002).

Erecting buildings to house administrative offices, courts, jails, and police departments is not accomplished haphazardly and randomly. Instead, the use of architectural blueprints provides a foundational basis for showing the building plans of these structures. Through the use of such blueprints, construction firms are able to erect buildings according to the requirements of the blueprint. Architectural blueprints are a form of imagery that represents technical design.

Using graphics and visual imagery enhances the written word. Such items are used to simplify and quickly convey concepts that might necessitate many paragraphs or pages of written language. Incorporating graphics and visual imagery may strengthen the ability of readers to conceptualize and understand the contents expressed by the written word. In such instances, tables, figures, graphs, charts, and photographs are supplements through which such communications occurs.

Graphics and visual imagery are not new concepts. Some of the earliest human communications incorporated the use of visual imagery. Cave paintings represent one of the oldest forms of human communication (Ryan & Conover, 2004). These images originated approximately 25,000 years ago during the Paleolithic age and continued into the Neolithic age (Ryan & Conover, 2004). Remnants of these drawings permeate caverns globally (Ryan & Conover, 2004).

During approximately 1500 B.C., the Egyptians began using hieroglyphics whose basis was pictographs that represents both sounds and words (Ryan & Conover, 2004). The Egyptian culture also invented a type of paper known as papyrus (Ryan & Conover, 2004). These observations suggest that ancient Egypt was the first culture to "produce manuscripts in which words and images were combined to document and communicate information with such sophistication and detail" (Ryan & Conover, 2004). The use of visual imagery and graphics has continued to permeate human history.

Combining such imagery with written text or with auditory communication also permeates modern society. Within the justice system and among law enforcement organizations, charts and graphs may be nestled among the paragraphs of an annual financial report detailing the operating expenses of the organization. Video and photographic resources may be used to record the details of crime scenes. The use of multidimensional data generates maps through which evacuation route planning is accomplished or to embellish patrol routes for responding officers. Certainly, many more examples of visual imagery and graphics are mindful within the contexts of the justice system and among law enforcement organizations. In short, these forms of communication pervade human activities and endeavors within the justice domain.

Visibility and Conspicuity

Visuals and graphics should be incorporated to achieve the highest and best effect of communicating within the mind of the receiver. This notion necessitates considerations of visibility and conspicuity. Visibility alludes to "how well" visual and graphic imagery "can be seen," whereas conspicuity represents the effectiveness of visual and graphic imagery to "attract attention" (Proctor & van Zandt, 2008). Determinations of visibility and conspicuity are associated with the location of graphic and visual imagery, how well they attract attention, and the "environmental conditions" of the communications domain (Proctor & van Zandt, 2008).

Law enforcement vehicles exemplify the concepts of visibility and conspicuity. Because they are emergency vehicles, they must be seen clearly and must be instantly recognizable. Therefore, they are generally black and white (or other contrasting colors), have loud sirens, and possess blue flashing lights. They also have some type of easily recognizable writing or symbols that identify them as police vehicles. Usually, their markings incorporate the words "POLICE" or "SHERIFF" along both sides of the vehicle using large, bold font type. In many cases, law enforcement vehicles show the traditional police badge or sheriff's star somewhere along the doors or sides of the vehicle where the symbol can easily be seen. They also may exhibit some types of "retroreflective materials" (Federal Emergency Management Agency, 2009, p. 19). Because blue flashing lights are reserved only for law enforcement vehicles, the use of blue lights further uniquely identifies law enforcement vehicles.

These factors cumulatively contribute toward the recognition of a law enforcement vehicle. Therefore, this combination of attributes communicates the notion that the vehicle is a law enforcement vehicle. Although noise within the communications domain may interfere with the recognition of a law enforcement vehicle from a distance, there must be no mistaking the correct type of vehicle, especially during emergencies. Therefore, law enforcement vehicles must be recognizable during poor and severe weather; conditions of fogginess, rain, and snow; at night; and when sunlight may impair clear views. Figure 5.1 shows a typical law enforcement vehicle.

Figure 5.1 Law enforcement vehicle. (From http://www.bridgeportwv.com/images/PoliceCar.jpg.)

These characteristics of visibility and conspicuity are applicable for all uses of visuals and graphics within the justice domain. Law enforcement is concerned with the rules of the road with respect to ensuring public safety. Another example of visibility and conspicuity is the typical traffic signal. Generally, traffic signals are placed high above intersecting roads or near street corners where they are easily seen. Because of their bright colors, overall physical design, and location, they attract the attention of motorists. Their typical colors of red, yellow, and green communicate when drivers must stop, clear the intersection, or proceed. They must be visible and understandable in all forms of weather, at night, and during day hours. Figure 5.2 shows a typical traffic signal.

During 2008, commensurate with findings of the preceding decade, "more law enforcement" personnel perished because of "traffic-related incidents than from any other cause" (Federal Emergency Management Agency, 2009, p. 5). In Houston, Texas, between 2008 and 2012, approximately 155 traffic accidents involved law enforcement vehicles (Rogalski, 2012). Such accidents cause traffic bottlenecks, contribute to the public disfavoring law enforcement organizations, and generate lawsuits within the justice system. Visibility and conspicuity affect human life. If law enforcement vehicles or traffic signals are not visible and conspicuous, then accidents may occur that result in death or serious injury.

Visibility and conspicuity also affect policing in a variety of ways. These characteristics of policing deter crime and show a police presence within society (Siegel & Worrall, 2013). Furthermore, law enforcement vehicles that are "highly visible" tend to "promote better officer presence than low-visibility police cars" (Thomas & Williams, 2012). These notions are essential aspects of community-oriented policing programs in which communicating with the members of society is essential in diminishing crime rates and maintaining societal order (Thomas & Williams, 2012).

Visibility and conspicuity are relevant characteristics of communication. They embellish the ability to generate an understanding within the minds of message recipients. They direct the attention of message receivers purposefully with respect to the importance of the intended message. They embellish the recognition of the intended message despite the presence of noise within the communications domain. Essentially, they strengthen the potency of the intended message and improve the chance of achieving a mutual understanding

Figure 5.2 Traffic signal. (From http://www.ci.missoula.mt.us/index.aspx?nid=461.)

Figure 5.3 Police car visibility and conspicuity (day and night hours). (From Federal Emergency Management Agency. 2009. Emergency Vehicle Visibility and Conspicuity Study. U.S. Government, Washington, DC. p. 17.)

between the senders and receivers of messages within the communications domain. When leveraging visibility and conspicuity, law enforcement entities must deliberately plan their use to maximize the impact of the communicated message. Figure 5.3 shows the potency of visibility and conspicuity during both day and night periods.

Design Characteristics of Visuals and Graphics

Designing visuals and graphics necessitates meticulous considerations of their uses to gain the highest and best impacts of their affiliated messages within the communications domain. Several factors affect the designing of visual and graphic imagery to achieve a maximal effectiveness when messages are received. The following characteristics affect the designing of visuals and graphics:

Conspicuity: Visuals and graphics must be conspicuous to attract attention. The attributes of "prominence, novelty, and relevance" are essential design considerations (Proctor & van Zandt, 2008).

Visibility: Visuals and graphics must be seen. They must be visible in all forms of weather, lighting conditions, and so on.

Legibility: Optimal legibility may be achieved through embellishing the "contrast ratio of the characters against the background" and through the use of "type fonts" that are easily readable (Proctor & van Zandt, 2008). Figure 5.3 shows an example of legibility during both day and night hours.

Maintainability: Depending on the type of resource in which they are used, visuals and graphics must be made from materials that are resistant to the detrimental effects of "aging and wear" that may result from "sunlight, rain, cleaning detergents, soil, vandalism, and so forth" (Proctor & van Zandt, 2008). Such considerations are appropriate for vehicles, traffic sign, and like items. However, when using visuals and graphics among paper documents, maintainability is much more difficult to achieve because of the frailty of paper.

Standardization and consistency: Graphics and visuals should be unchanging when attempting to portray a branded image in society. Therefore, with the exception of vehicle and tag numbers, patrol cars are generally always identical. Similarly, police uniforms are identical among individual organizations or departments. Such uniformity communicates the easily recognizable message of a police presence within society.

Emphasis: The dominant theme within the graphic or visual resource should be emphasized (Bovee & Thill, 2012, p. 342). For example, in Figure 5.3, the use of the words "Highway Patrol" and the symbolic badge emphasize the importance of the message that the vehicle is a law enforcement patrol car.

Convention: Designing visual and graphic imagery is "guided by a variety of generally accepted rules or conventions" that influence practically all facets of design (Bovee & Thill, 2012, p. 342). For example, using the English language necessitates reading from left to right (Bovee & Thill, 2012, p. 342). When designing organizational charts for law enforcement organizations, the highest position is presented at the top of the chart and the subordinate positions are drawn appropriately below the highest position within the hierarchical chain of command.

Simplicity: Visuals and graphic imagery must convey information succinctly without extra embellishment. For example, in Figure 5.3, the use of the symbolic badge instantly communicates that the vehicle has some law enforcement affiliation.

Communicating with graphics and visual resources must convey information effectively and efficiently. Designing these resources necessitates contemplations of the preceding factors in conjunction with the "principles of line, mass, space, size, color, pattern, and texture" (Bovee & Thill, 2012, p. 341). Graphic and visual resources must "clarify, reinforce, or emphasize a particular idea" and must facilitate a cumulative understanding of the intended message between senders and receivers within the communications domain (Lehman & DuFrene, 2008). In any case, the use of graphic and visual resources must contribute meaningfully and substantially to the communications process.

Visualizing Data

Four types of data exist: nominal, ordinal, interval, and ratio. These categories of data are defined as follows:

Nominal: This type represents "names, labels, or categories" in which there are "no implied criteria by which the data can be ordered from smallest to largest" (Brase & Brase, 2013). Names, such as the Meridian Police Department and the Livingston Police Department, are examples of nominal data.

Ordinal: This type represents arrangements of data that can be ordered, and any "differences between data values either cannot be determined or are meaningless" (Brase & Brase, 2013). The class rankings for a graduating police academy class are examples of ordinal data. For example, out of a class of 30 folks, Smith was second, Jones was tenth, and Mason was twentieth.

Interval: This type represents arrangements of data that can be ordered, and any "differences between data values are meaningful" (Brase & Brase, 2013). Within the justice system, differences in pay scales for different categories of personnel are representative of interval data.

Ratio: This type represents data that can be ordered, and "both differences between data values and ratios of data values are meaningful" (Brase & Brase, 2013). The physical sizes and measurements of personnel are examples of ratio data. For example, Smith is 5′11″, whereas Jones is 5′3″ with respect to their heights. A negative height would be impossible. This measurement involves quantity, equality of measurement units, and a measurement that cannot be below the value of zero.

Certainly, the use of written language may be used to describe and express the salient characteristics of these types of data. However, such writings may become lengthy and confusing. As a method of simplifying, embellishing, or replacing the written word, graphic and visual resources may be used to communicate the salient characteristics of data. Accomplishing these tasks is performed through the incorporation of charts, graphs, diagrams, tables, and figures within messages when communicating between senders and receivers.

Charts

Charts are used to show the relationships between sets of data visually, chronological periods versus tasking, or they may be used to show the steps of a process. All charts should be appropriately labeled to show the relevant variable names, measurement units, titles, and differences between data sets. Any use of colors, shading, and textures within charts should effectively differentiate the considered data sets and measurements. Typically, communicating may be embellished through the use of bar charts, pie charts, Gantt charts, flow charts, and organizational charts. Each chart is used to satisfy a particular purpose.

Bar Chart

A bar chart is a visual resource that depicts summaries for two or more data variables. Bar charts can be easily generated through the use of contemporary spreadsheets or statistical packages. The city of Tucson, Arizona, uses a variety of bar charts to show changes in crime over time. An example is presented in Figure 5.4.

This chart uses vertical bars to show crime rate quantities annually for the period between 1997 and 2011. The bar chart consists of two dimensions in which time, measured in years, represents the *x*-axis and the variable of crimes per 100,000 persons represents the *y*-axis. The chart uses appropriate labels for the *x*-axis and *y*-axis to denote these variables. The labeled title for the chart is atop the image and denotes the material presented within the chart. The source of the data contained within the chart is appropriately referenced and cited with respect to its origin within the Tucson Police Data sections of the Uniform Crime Reports.

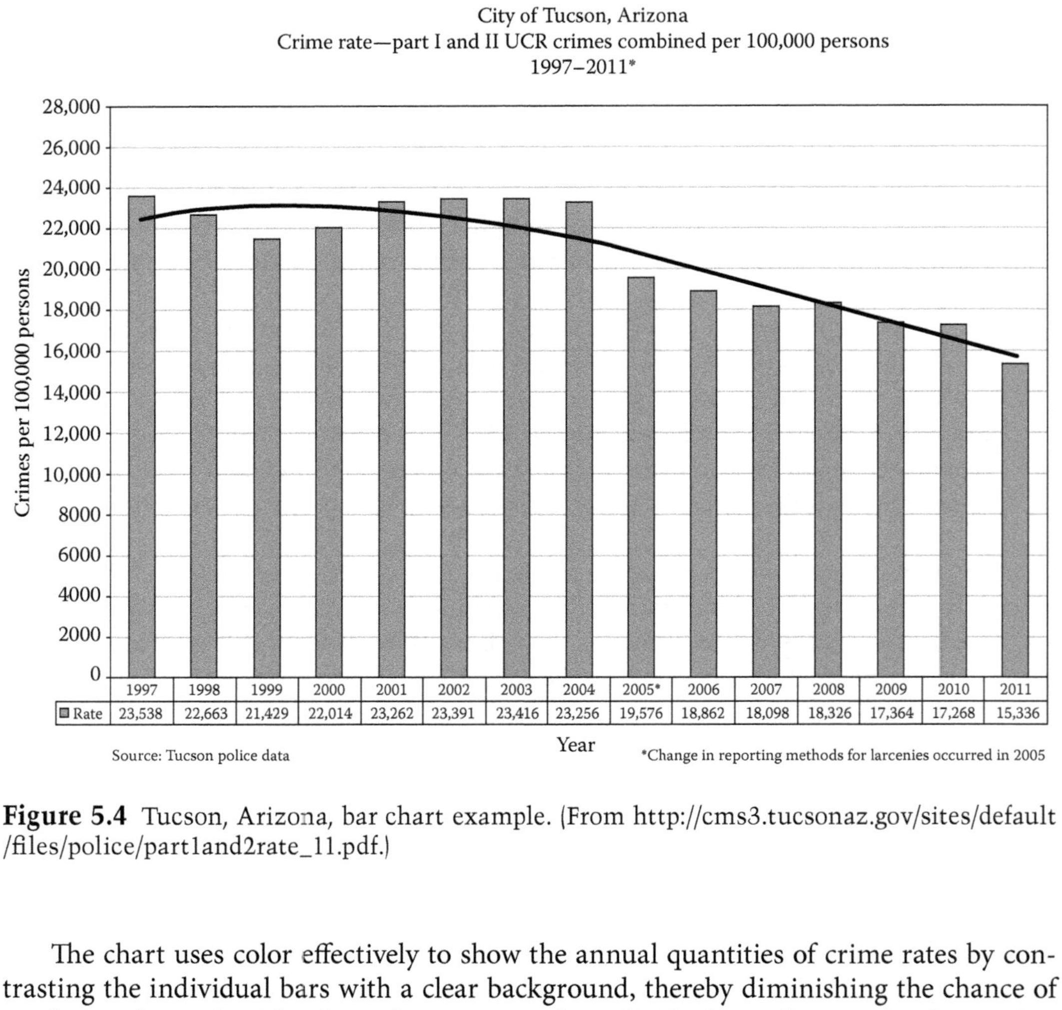

Figure 5.4 Tucson, Arizona, bar chart example. (From http://cms3.tucsonaz.gov/sites/default/files/police/part1and2rate_11.pdf.)

The chart uses color effectively to show the annual quantities of crime rates by contrasting the individual bars with a clear background, thereby diminishing the chance of confusing the reader. The chart also separates the individual bars from each other so that they are clearly seen and understood. Furthermore, the chart incorporates grid lines to show individual crime rate quantities horizontally across the image, thereby giving the reader some perspective of the quantities and their relationship with time. Additionally, the chart depicts the appropriate curve indicating the overall trend of crime through time.

Using written English to describe, compare, and contrast the data sets to convey the same message that is readily obtainable from the chart would be lethargic and cumbersome. Conveying the intended message is accomplished rather easily through the chart, and it facilitates an understanding of the data comparisons within the mind of the reader. This example exhibits the characteristics of design and represents a graphical resource that visually helps to facilitate an understanding in the mind of the reader.

Pie Chart

Pie charts are another resource through which communication is enhanced to visualize data. Pie charts are round images that are used to compare proportions of two or more variables. They may be divided into many sections to show the proportions. A typical pie chart is presented in Figure 5.5.

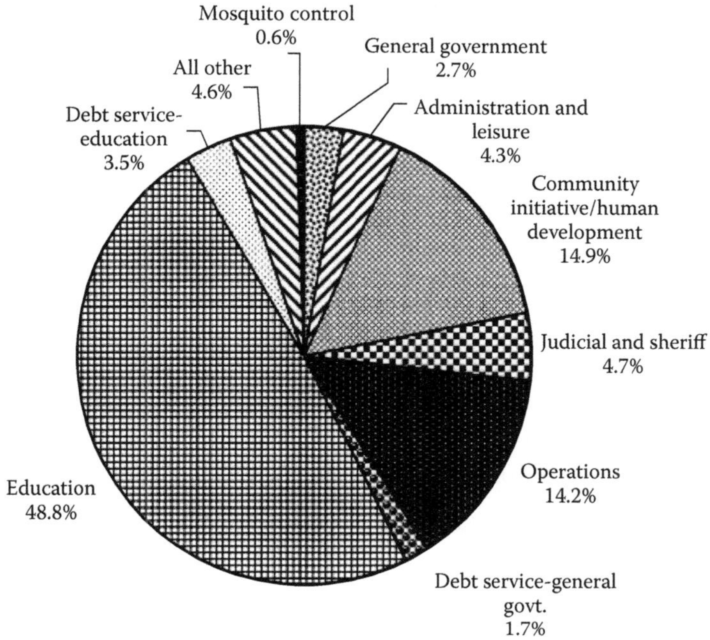

Figure 5.5 Chesapeake, Virginia, pie chart example. (From http://www.cityofchesapeake.net/Government/City-Departments/Departments/Budget-Department/Approved-Budget-FY-2009-10/Budget-Summary-for-Fiscal-Year-Beginning-2009.htm#.)

Pie charts may use different, contrasting colors or different pattern textures to denote their various proportions of variables. Within Figure 5.5, patterned textures are used to show these differences. The pie chart contains label names that represent the separate variables (e.g., operations, education, etc.). Within Figure 5.5, percentages are used to show the mathematical proportion that is represented by the specific variables comprising the pie chart. If a variable name is too long or too large to fit adjacent to its respective proportional section, then lines are drawn between the variable name and the associated section within the pie chart. Within Figure 5.5, lines are present to affiliate variables with small proportions. Figure 5.5 shows a pie chart using two dimensions. The use of three dimensions may also artistically embellish pie charts. Regardless of textures versus colors or two versus three dimensions, pie charts are useful resources through which proportionality among variables may be exhibited within the communications domain.

Gantt Chart

Another graphic and visual resource is the Gantt chart. This type of chart is commonly used within the contexts of organizational and project management. It is used when scheduling projects and incorporates a chronological aspect of the cumulative endeavor. Specifically, Gantt charts are used to visually show the "scheduling of tasks that go into completing a project" (Schermerhorn, 2010). The use of contemporary project management software may easily generate Gantt charts.

Using Gantt charts facilitates the scheduling of quality periodically within the scheduling of an endeavor (Schermerhorn, 2010). Through the use of Gantt charts, project managers may identify the salient tasks and their necessary periods for completion, deadlines,

Task Name	Start	Finish
1.1 Contract with Technical Assistant	6/1/05	12/30/05
1.2 Oversee Tech Assist Contract	1/2/06	3/14/08
1.3 Prepare and Maintain SEMP	1/2/06	4/7/06
1.4 Develop Concept of Operations	1/2/06	4/7/06
1.5 Identify System Requirements	4/10/06	6/23/06
1.6 Develop the Verification Plan	5/22/06	6/30/06
1.7 Develop Other Specific Plans	2/10/06	9/7/06
2.1 Develop a High Level Design	6/26/06	9/8/06
2.2 Contract with System Integrator	9/11/06	3/30/07
2.3 Oversee the System Integrator	4/2/07	3/14/08
2.4 Identity Detailed Requirements	4/2/07	5/11/07
2.5 Prepare Detailed Design	5/14/07	7/20/07
3.1 Build the Initial System	7/23/07	1/4/08
3.2 Verify (Test) Initial System	11/1/07	3/12/08
3.3 Train Agency Personnel	11/1/07	2/20/08
3.4 Add STARNET to Op Procedures	11/1/07	1/23/08
3.5 Document Compliance w OFR 940	9/3/07	10/5/07
3.6 Validate Initial Implementation	10/1/08	12/23/08
Operation of STARNET	1/7/08	12/26/08

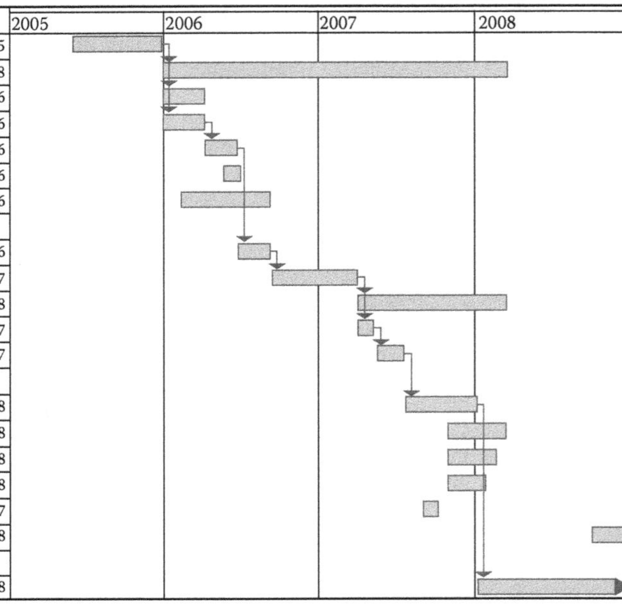

Figure 5.6 FDOT Gantt chart. (From http://www.fhwa.dot.gov/cadiv/segb/files/starnet/STARNET%20Systems%20Engineering%20Management%20Plan%20v1-0_files/image004.gif.)

milestones, dependencies, concurrency of activities, and sequencing of events that are necessary for the successful and timely completion of an endeavor. The characteristics of both long-term and short-term projects may be expressed through Gantt charts. Figure 5.6 depicts an excerpt from a project Gantt chart representing a project with the Florida Department of Transportation (FDOT).

The excerpt presented in Figure 5.6 shows a typical project schedule via the use of a Gantt chart. It encompasses a period of four years ranging between 2005 and 2008, and the colored lines horizontally show the timings of activities during these years. The first column identifies the specific tasks that must be accomplished during the course of the project and assigns a unique number to each task. The second column contains the starting dates of each task, and the third column shows the ending dates of each task. Such detail allows for easily identifying tasks that are overlapping. Columns four through seven represent the period of years that encompass the cumulative endeavor.

Flow Chart

Flow charts are diagrams that graphically and visually depict "the steps of a particular job in sequence" (Amsden, Butler, & Amsden, 1998). They are also used to pictorially show the various steps within a process from beginning to end. Flow charts improve the ability of humans to control processes and understand process flows, information processing, and decisions. Flow charts consist of various symbols and lines to denote various facets and relationships within a given domain. These symbols and lines are defined as follows:

Terminator: Indicates the beginning or the ending of an activity. The terminator is expressed graphically by using an elongated oval.

Input/output: Indicates the point of incoming data or the point of outgoing data. The input/output symbol is denoted by a parallelogram.

Process: Indicates the presence of some type of process. The process symbol is denoted by a rectangle.

Decision: Indicates some type of decision involving one or more alternative choices. The decision symbol is denoted with a diamond.

Reference or control point: Indicates the presence of some type of control mechanism. This item is generally denoted with a circle.

Lines: Lines are used to show the relationships between these basic symbols.

Figure 5.7 shows the basic symbols that are commonly used within flow charts.

Organizational processes may be modeled and communicated through the use of flow charts. Figure 5.8 shows the planning and development process of the U.S. DOT Federal Transit Administration (FTA). Using the process depicted by this flow chart results in "the identification and prioritization of transportation corridors in greatest need of more detailed planning and analysis" (U.S. Department of Transportation, 2012a). An analysis of the possible alternatives yields "a specific transportation need (or set of needs), identifies alternative actions to address these needs, and generates information needed to select an option for further engineering and implementation" (U.S. Department of Transportation, 2012a). After selecting an alternative, preliminary engineering may be requested to signify "the beginning of FTA's project management oversight function" (U.S. Department of Transportation, 2012a). Upon entering the final design stage, "candidate projects are considered by FTA for a Full Funding Grant Agreement" (U.S. Department of Transportation, 2012a).

The process depicted by the flow chart in Figure 5.8 exhibits significant aspects of detailed design. The flow chart expresses the life cycle stages that result in the construction

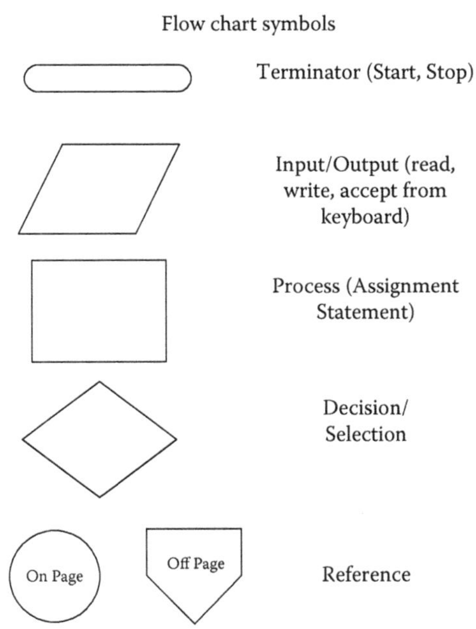

Figure 5.7 Flow-chart symbols. (From http://virtual.parkland.edu/kcouch/CIS122/Week1/FlowchartSymbols.htm.)

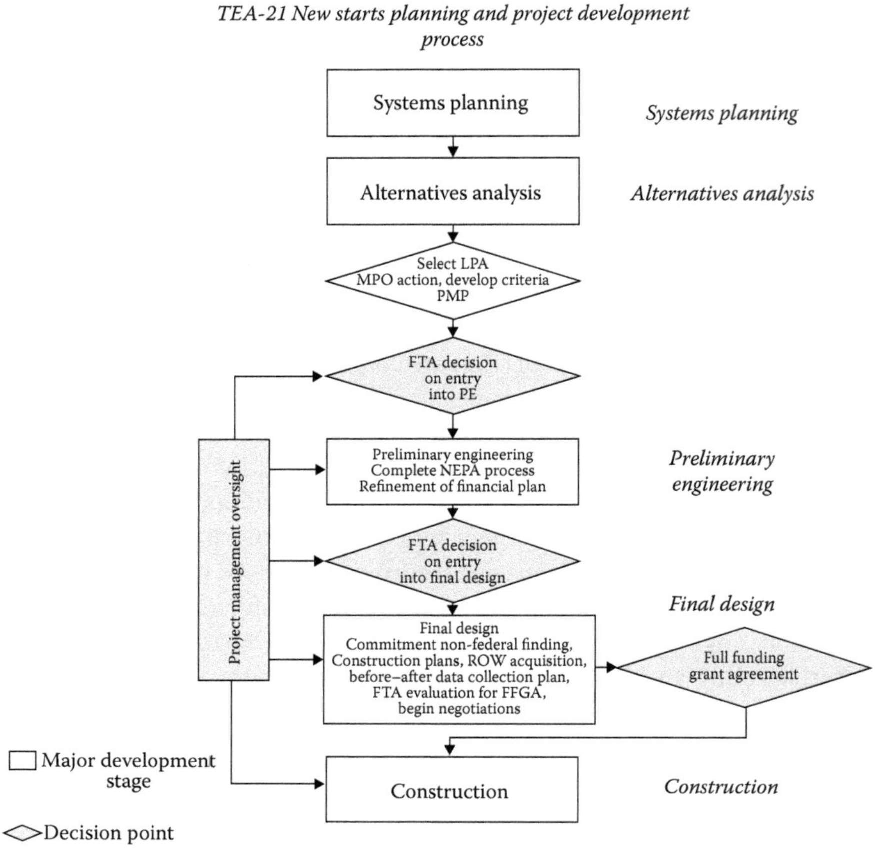

Figure 5.8 Planning and development process flow chart. (From http://www.fta.dot.gov/12304_2610.html.)

phase involving transportation corridors. It accommodates facets of planning and the evaluation of alternative courses of action, engineering, design, and construction phases. Processes, such as systems planning, are denoted by rectangles. Decisions are expressed with diamonds (e.g., entries into succeeding phases), and lines are used to show the flows of decisions and their resulting processes. Cumulatively, the flow chart also expresses the actions and related decisions that occur through time.

Organizational Chart

Representing the relationships that exist among organizational structures is accomplished through the use of an organizational chart. This type of chart depicts hierarchical chains of command and the relationships among organizational positions or components. It also represents the design of the organization and the associated responsibilities within the chain of command. Specifically, an organizational chart shows a "visual representation of the structure of an agency" by providing a "blueprint of the agency showing the different components and the subdivisions relating to it" (Stering, 2008). Figure 5.9 shows the organizational chart for the Dayton (Ohio) Police Department.

This organizational chart shows graphically the structuring of the organization. It shows the respective components of the organization and their associated subcomponents,

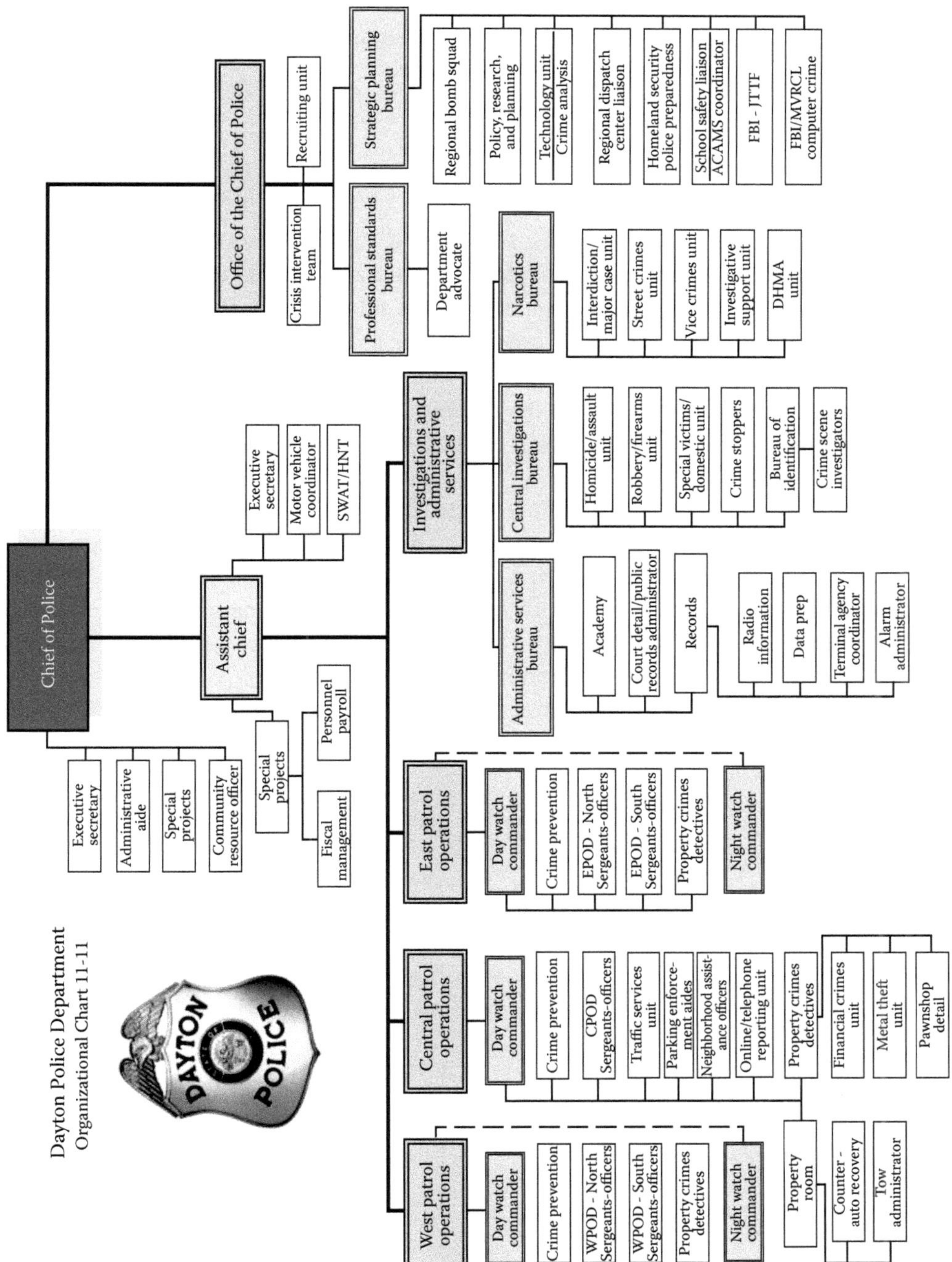

Figure 5.9 Dayton (Ohio) Police Department organizational chart. (From http://www.cityofdayton.org/departments/police/pages/default.aspx.)

and shows personnel titles along with subordinate personnel within the respective chains of command. Positions and components are depicted by using rectangles. Relationships between positions or components are shown through the use of lines to connect the appropriate rectangles. Communications must flow through the appropriate chain of command within the organization. Through using the organizational chart, law enforcement personnel, the municipality, the public, and any other entity can clearly determine how information flows within the organization.

Line Graphs

A line graph is used to show data relationships in two or three dimensions. Two-dimensional graphs involve considerations of data representing an *x*-axis versus the *y*-axis. Basically, line graphs are used to show the data relationships of multiple variables (Cole, Smith, & DeJong, 2013). The individual points that comprise line graphs are determined by the data representing corresponding points between the considered axis variables. Connecting these individual data points will result in the fashioning of a line. Line graphs may be easily produced through the use of spreadsheet or statistical programs. An example of a line graph is presented in Figure 5.10.

The line graph depicted in Figure 5.10 represents a two-dimensional consideration of data. It shows the interval of "cumulative time of collapse-to-arrival" regarding patient emergency calls. It accommodates considerations of both police and emergency medical services (EMS) personnel. The *x*-axis represents the period of time after the collapsing of a patient, whereas the *y*-axis represents a percentage of emergency personnel arrivals. This graph contains three separate lines showing EMS arrivals, police arrivals, and both EMS and police arrivals. It uses open diamonds, closed diamonds, and dots to differentiate

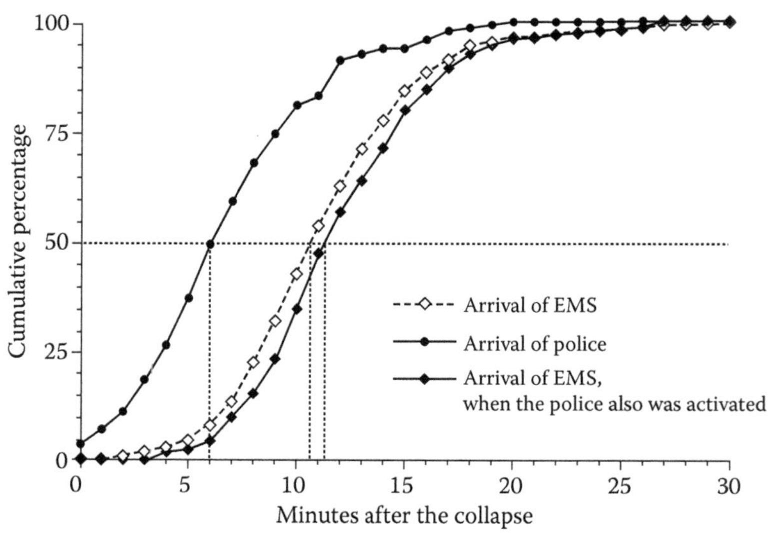

Figure 5.10 Example of a line graph. (From http://www.sciencedirect.com/science/article/pii/S0300957298001026.)

among these types of arrivals. The graph also incorporates a legend that denotes the different symbols used to portray the data points that comprise each of the lines.

Integrating Charts and Graphs

In some cases, it may be appropriate to integrate charts and graphs to produce a visual representation to embellish communications. This type of visual incorporates the attributes of both charts and line graph data. Figure 5.11 presents this form of integrated visual imagery.

The visual imagery presented in Figure 5.11 incorporates both line graphs and bar charts to show the relationships among data sets. By doing so, viewers are able to grasp both measurable quantities through time as well as various trends that were exhibited through time simultaneously.

Diagrams

A diagram is "a graphic that explains rather than represents" and may generally be "a drawing that shows arrangement and relations" (*Merriam-Webster*, 2012a). A variety of diagrams may be used to graphically and visually embellish communications. Some of the typical types of diagrams are summarized as follows:

Scatter-plot diagram: This type of diagram is associated with the analytical methods of mathematical regression and correlation (Walker & Maddan, 2013). It is helpful when visually determining whether there is an association between two variables and may also exhibit the "nature of the relationship" (Walker & Maddan,

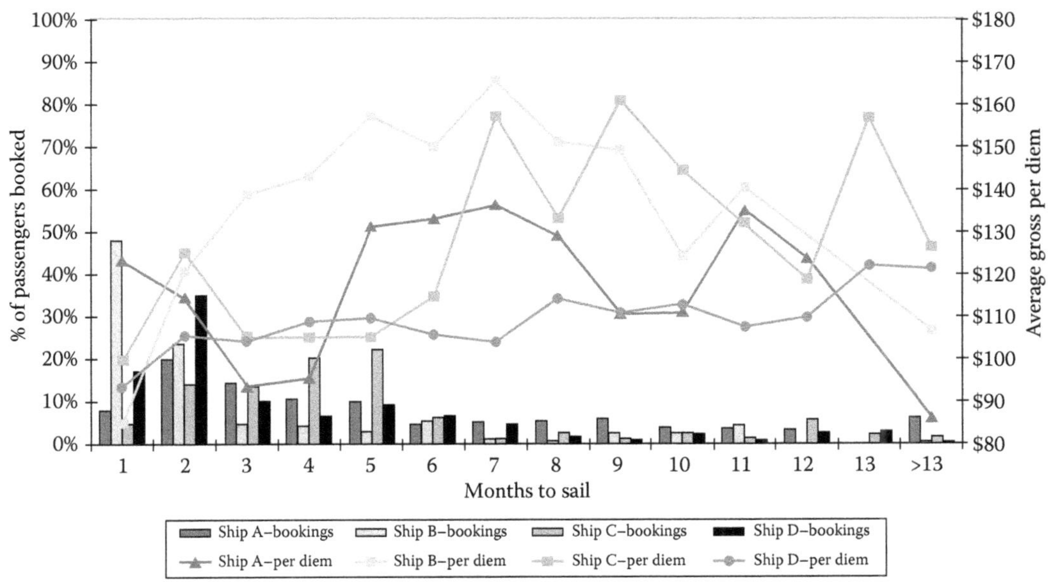

Figure 5.11 Example of integrating charts and line graphs. (From http://www.justice.gov/atr/public/workshops/docs/202661.htm.)

2013). Visually, scatter plots may also show whether any outlying data points exist that may affect the considered distribution and may be helpful when examining whether "there is a curvilinear relationship that may be adversely influencing the correlation" (Walker & Maddan, 2013). Merely viewing a scatter-plot diagram is insufficient to determine whether a relationship exists within the considered data. Instead, mathematical analysis must be performed.

Process diagram: A process diagram "provides a visual representation of a process by defining a process and demonstrating the relationships between input and output elements" (Basu, 2004). Process diagrams show the methodical flow of activities that occur through time in order to accomplish a specific endeavor or activity.

Technical diagrams: A technical diagram is "a representation of a physical object" (Pfeiffer, 2003). Technical diagrams may be illustrated from numerous perspectives and may involve "'exploded' views" (Pfeiffer, 2003).

Scatter-Plot Diagram

A typical scatter-plot diagram is shown in Figure 5.12. This scatter-plot diagram shows the mapping of data with regard to an *x*-axis and a *y*-axis. The *x*-axis represents metropolitan percentages, whereas the *y*-axis represents the rates of violent crime. The data points contained within the diagram represent the corresponding *x*-axis and *y*-axis coordinates. This scatter plot only shows the data points between the variables. Further mathematical analysis is necessary to determine the effects of regression and correlation.

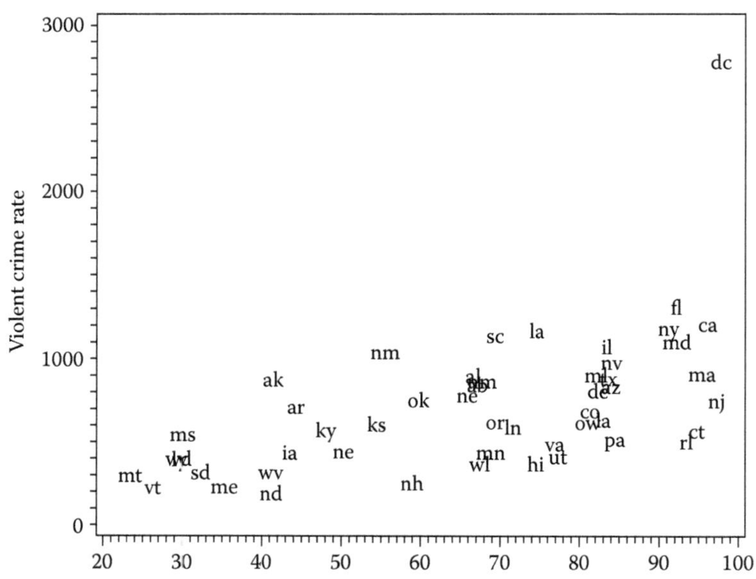

Figure 5.12 Scatter-plot diagram example. (From http://www.ats.ucla.edu/stat/sas/webbooks/reg/chapter2/sasreg2.htm.)

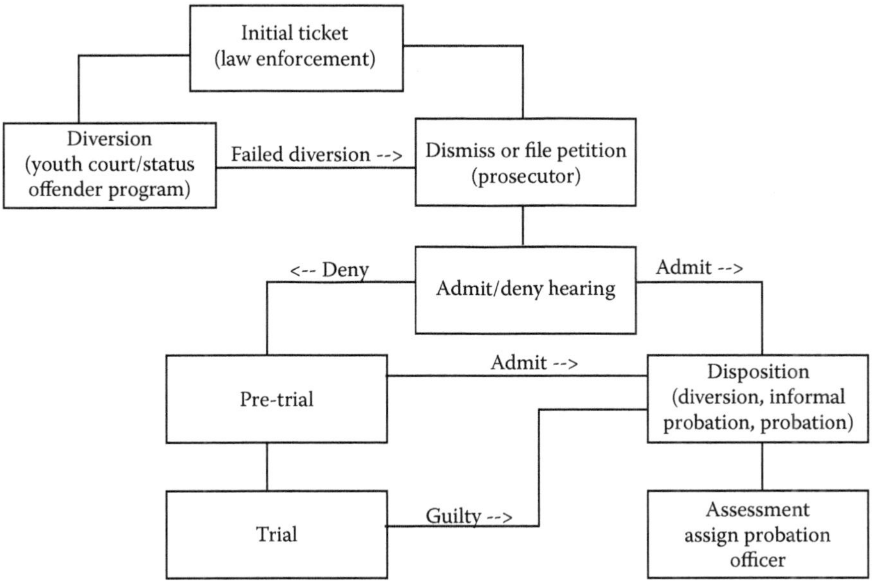

Figure 5.13 Bannock County, Idaho, process diagram. (From http://www.bannockcounty.us/juvenile/court_process.html.)

Process Diagram

A typical process diagram is shown in Figure 5.13. This process diagram represents the processing mechanism of the Bannock County (Idaho) Juvenile Court system. This diagram shows the entry point into the juvenile system, the succeeding processes, and the eventual assigning of a probation officer. It is representative of a logical process flow throughout the juvenile justice system and shows the routes that may be taken before a probation officer is eventually assigned. Within Figure 5.13, the individual process components and stages of the justice system are denoted by rectangles. Lines are used to connect the specific process components. Arrows are used to show the directionality of the process flow within the system.

Technical Diagram

Technical diagrams are used to depict an innumerable variety of physical entities. Everything from building blueprints to electronic circuitry may involve some aspects of technical diagrams. Within the justice domain, technical diagrams are used when designing vehicles, radio systems, buildings, weapons, computer systems, jails and prisons, aviation resources, maritime resources, camera and video systems, and many others. A technical diagram may express the characteristics of physical objects to embellish construction. Through using technical diagrams, a measure of quality may be interjected when generating physical products. Technical diagrams also may enhance standardization during the crafting and developing of physical entities. Furthermore, technical diagrams may accompany patent documentation. An example of a technical diagram is given in Figure 5.14.

Main instrument panel

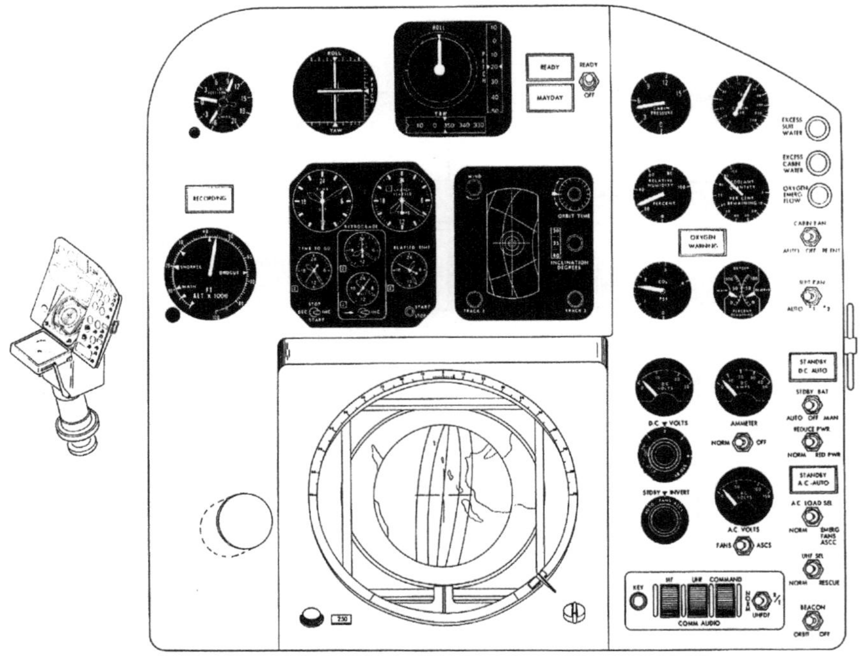

Figure 5.14 Example of technical diagram. (From http://history.nasa.gov/diagrams/mercury.html.)

Tables and Figures

Tables are visual resources through which information is compared and contrasted in a columnar fashion. Tables must present their contents both simply and briefly (National Aeronautics and Space Administration, 2012). An excerpt from a National Aeronautics and Space Administration technical writing manual describes the use of tables as follows (National Aeronautics and Space Administration, 2012):

> Present tabulated material in an organized manner. Like elements should read down, not across. Variables are usually given in columns topped by boxheads, with the constants given in the first, or stub, column. Boxheads should be brief; if necessary, they may be amplified by footnotes. Boxheads usually contain a word description of a concept or quantity, its symbol, and its unit, separated by commas; symbols must be defined when they are used. Arrange tabulated data in a logical order that your readers can easily recognize. Usually this arrangement is an ascending or descending order of value for the prime parameter. The order is necessary to clarify trends. You can also help your readers see relations and comparisons of data by carefully wording the boxheads and the stub column. Put items to be compared in adjacent columns. Generally numbers in columns are more easily compared than numbers in rows. Another type of table is the leaderwork table, in which dissimilar data are listed in rows with leader dots connecting each parameter with the corresponding value. Give conditions that apply to an entire table in a headnote. Indicate footnote citations by lower-case letters (superscripts) ordered across the table from left to right and top to bottom. (National Aeronautics and Space Administration, 2012)

Table 5.1 Sample Table

Officer Name	Marksmanship Score	Aptitude Test Score
Jones	95	88.0%
Smith	95	93.0%
Mason	88	84.0%
Monroe	90	72.5%

Tables are usually presented near their textual references within written communications or they may be contained within an appendix. Within written communications, tables are not to be placed before its initial referencing within a composition. Each column within a table should have a heading denoting the materials contain therein. Generally, tables are one page or less in size. If the information contained within a table exceeds one page, then it is advisable to use separate tables to present the information. A sample table is presented in Table 5.1.

Figures differ from tables. Figures encompass a variety of visual forms. They may include photographs, drawings, art, technical diagrams, charts, graphs, or any other visual entity that is not a table. Figures generally contain headings that consist of a figure number and a figure title that are below the figure. Figures should be limited to the size of one page or less. Legends may be used to clarify various points of visual imagery that are contained within the figure. Within a written composition, figures should not be placed before their point of referencing within the written language. Instead, they should be placed immediately succeeding the point of reference. The figures contained within this book are examples of various types of figures that enhance the message expressed by written language.

Video and Animation

Video and animation are powerful tools through which senders may convey their messages visually and graphically. The receivers of messages see exactly what the sender of the message conveys within the communications domain. Videos and animations may incorporate the characteristics of "images, text, and scenes" to project visually a message to an intended audience (Friedmann, 2010). Videos and animations may be used to compel audiences toward a certain perspective or viewpoint or they may be used to objectively document events within the justice system or society.

Videos of events are memorable and may influence mass audiences. The video broadcasting of the events of September 11, 2011, the assassination of President John F. Kennedy, the aftermath of the Oklahoma City bombing, and the court proceedings of O.J. Simpson and Casey Anthony affected both national and global audiences. Each of these events affected society and influenced human opinions and perceptions. Depending on the method of presenting such events, videos may be used to hold the attention of audiences when communicating (Friedmann, 2010). This technique is referred to as visual seduction (Friedmann, 2010).

The use of video also facilitates the historical documenting of events for archival purposes. Other purposes of communication may be satisfied through the use of video. For example, instructional videos may show proper methods of handcuffing. In some cases, videos are used to influence human behaviors, such as seat belt law conformance and reduction of drunk driving. The animated McGruff the Crime Dog media campaign emphasized community participation to reduce crime.

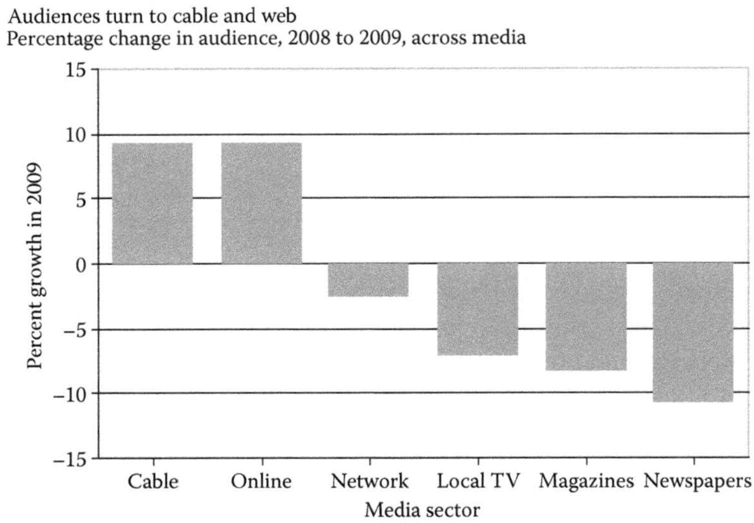

Figure 5.15 Comparing media sectors. (From http://stateofthemedia.org/2010/overview-3/key-findings/.)

In some instances, the use of video and animation represents a method of communicating that may be superior to the solitary use of written language. American audiences now seek news sources that offer instant gratification (Pew Research Center's Project for Excellence in journalism, 2012). Figure 5.15 shows comparisons among contemporary news sources.

During the period between 2008 and 2009, print media magazine and newspaper outlets saw a reduction in attention, whereas online Internet and cable sources exhibited an increase in interest. Similar trends have been witnessed during recent years. According to the findings of a 2012 poll conducted by the Pew Research Center, which involved a survey of 3003 adults, the 2012 quantity of Americans obtaining news from printed newspapers was approximately 23%, whereas approximately 55% "watched the news or a news program on television" (Pew Research Center, 2012). Therefore, opportunity exists to leverage video and animation as a strong method of communicating events within the justice system or among law enforcement organizations using Internet media and cable television outlets.

Maps and Geographic Attributes

Maps are another form of visual resources that are used to embellish communications. A map is defined as "a representation, usually on a flat surface, of the whole or a part of an area" (*Merriam-Webster*, 2012b). A primary purpose of maps is to "communicate in ways that support meanderings and mobilities, including routine and extraordinary movements" (Adams, 2009). Maps are used to portray a variety of geographic data that embellishes navigation or may serve instructional purposes of exhibiting traveling directions between points. Map data may be crucial when performing activities associated with disaster planning and management. For example, an impending storm may necessitate the evacuation of thousands of people within a very short period. Map data may be used to plan primary and alternative evacuation routes.

Mapping data is used in conjunction with geographic information systems and interactive software programs that allow users to query databases to determine the locations of sexual offenders. One example is the ClearMap system implemented by the Chicago (Illinois) Police Department. This mapping system allows users to search geographic region mapping data using the search fields of "address, community area, ward, police beat and district, and around a school or park" (Chicago Police Department, 2012). The locations of offenders are communicated immediately, thereby informing users of any registered sexual offenders that may be near their specific location.

Maps may be used to show the potential effects of natural events. Maps may be used to communicate the risks associated with such hazards. Through the use of hazard maps, the "location and probability" of potentially hazardous events may be depicted thereby informing viewers of potential dangers (National Academy of Sciences, 2009). Communicating through such maps facilitates the crafting of mitigation strategies (National Academy of Sciences, 2009). For example, maps are useful when examining the risks of potential flooding events and crafting appropriate mitigation strategies (National Academy of Sciences, 2009).

Another example of using maps to communicate the dangers of natural hazards involves seismic activity. The U.S. Geological Survey (USGS) generates maps that are used to "display earthquake ground motions for various probability levels across the United States and are applied in seismic provisions of building codes, insurance rate structures, risk assessments, and other public policy" (U.S. Geological Survey, 2012). Such maps may communicate probabilistic and scenario information (U.S. Geological Survey, 2012). A sample map is presented in Figure 5.16.

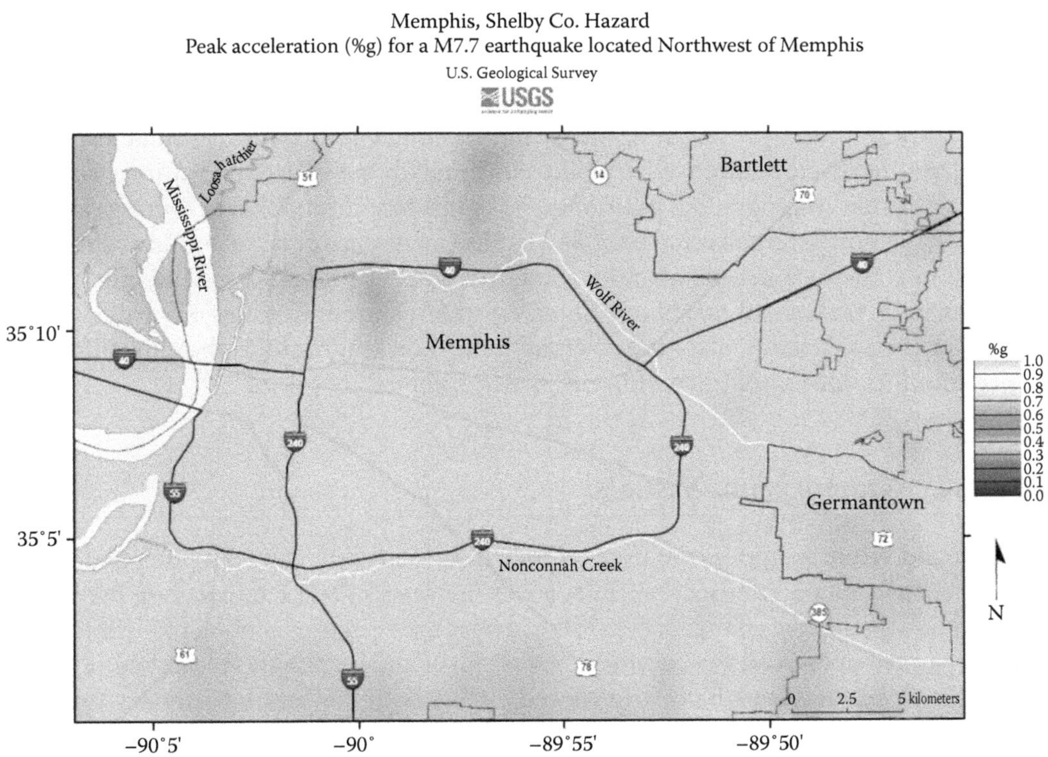

Figure 5.16 USGS hazard map example. (From http://earthquake.usgs.gov/regional/ceus/products/download/graphic/pdf/ncs7p7_pga.pdf.)

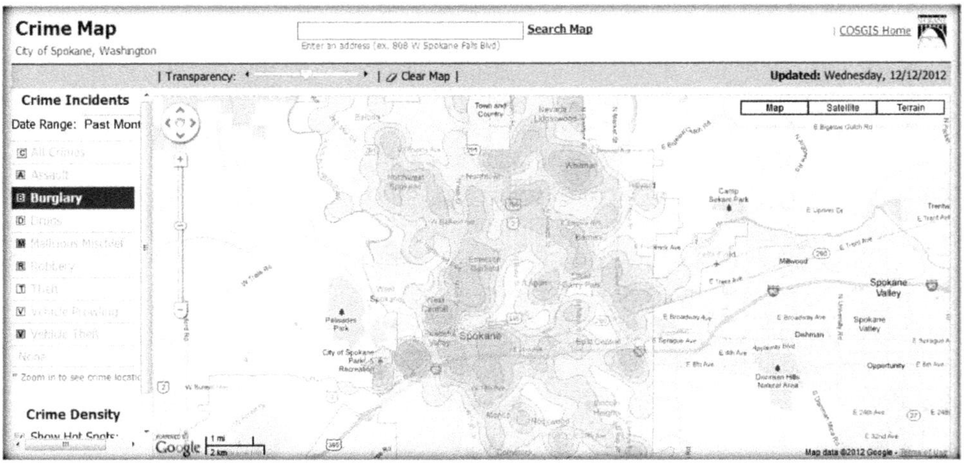

Figure 5.17 Crime map for Spokane, Washington. (From http://www.spokanegis.org/crimemap2/default.htm.)

Maps are also used within the contexts of crime mapping functions. Crime mapping is an analytical method of examining the geographic characteristics of crime within a given region. Maps are used to show the locations of criminal events. Within crime mapping applications, criminal events may be depicted geographically by the types of specific crimes or by the cumulative incidents of criminal offenses that occurred within a specific time period. Figure 5.17 shows an example of a crime map depicting burglaries in the region of Spokane, Washington.

Communicating through maps is essential within the contexts of the justice system and among law enforcement organizations. The locations of offenders or incidents of crime may be conveyed through the use of maps. The use of mapping data may embellish patrol route planning or may improve the ability to mitigate the effects of natural and other disasters. The use of geographic positioning systems may communicate routing data that supports emergency responses among law enforcement personnel to minimize the time required to arrive at the scene of an incident. Maps may be incorporated among Internet sites or within traditional forms of printed, written communications. Regardless of the context or the application, maps are essential visual and graphic tools that embellish various communications activities within the justice domain.

Roadway Graphics and Visuals

Graphic and visual imageries are used to embellish roadways. They provide public safety messages, navigational information, and convey messages of law. Examples are the posting of speed limits and lane change signs. These images are presented among roadway signage and are painted upon roadway pavement. Figure 5.18a and b present typical roadway signs.

Highway signage must be clearly viewed during both day and night hours, and during all types of weather. Therefore, they must be sturdy and robust, and may be painted with retroreflective materials. Roadway signs must be both conspicuous and visible. The bright colors attract attention and convey messages using contrasting colors. Throughout the nation, signage is generally standardized to ensure that motorists have a common

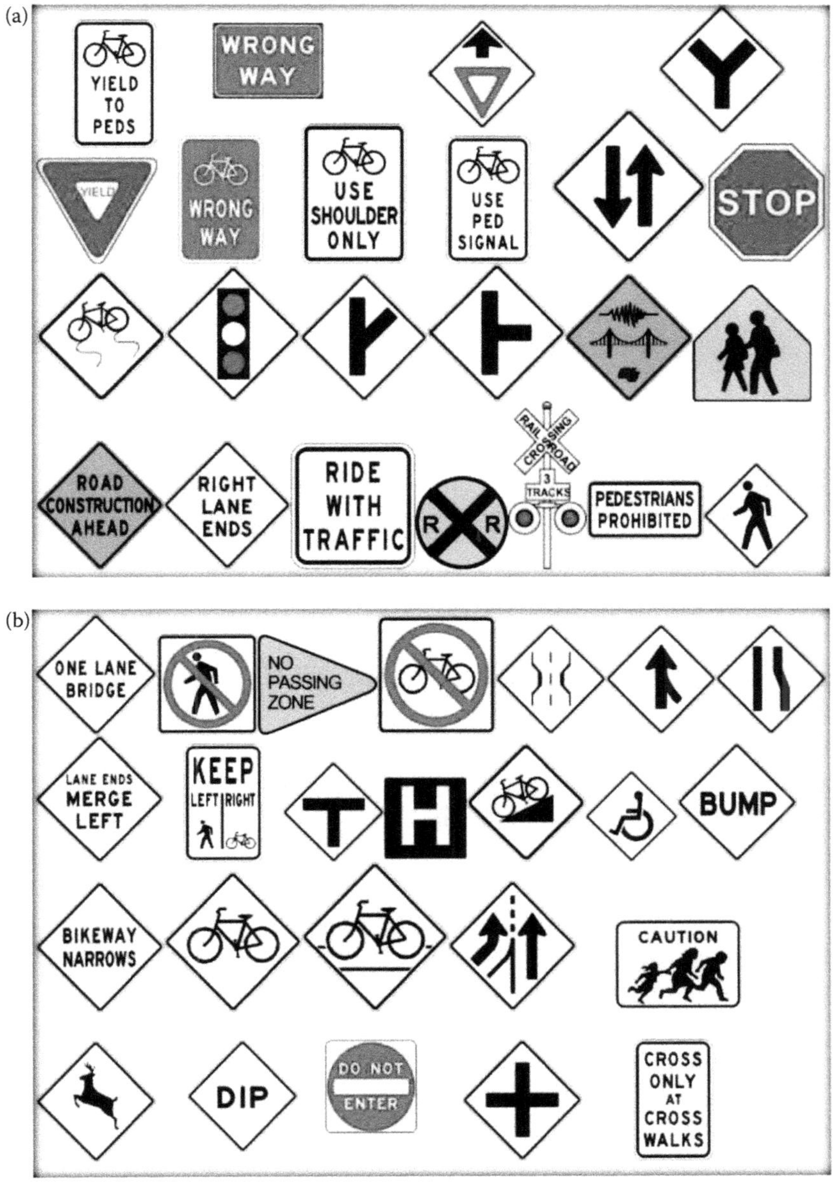

Figure 5.18 (a, b) Roadway signs. (From http://safety.fhwa.dot.gov/ped_bike/hispanic/fhwanhtsa/appendix6.cfm.)

understanding of the intended message communicated through graphic visual imagery. Therefore, a stop sign in Montana is identical to a stop sign in Maine.

Within the United States, five categories of signage exist: (1) regulatory signs, (2) warning signs and object markers, (3) guide signs, (4) temporary traffic control signs, and (5) school signs (U.S. Department of Transportation, 2012b). Regulatory signs communicate the attributes of regulations or laws (e.g., speed limit 70) (U.S. Department of Transportation, 2012b). Warning signs and object markers communicate the attributes of possible dangers and conditions that may affect travel (e.g., slippery when wet) (U.S. Department of Transportation, 2012b). Guide signs communicate navigational information

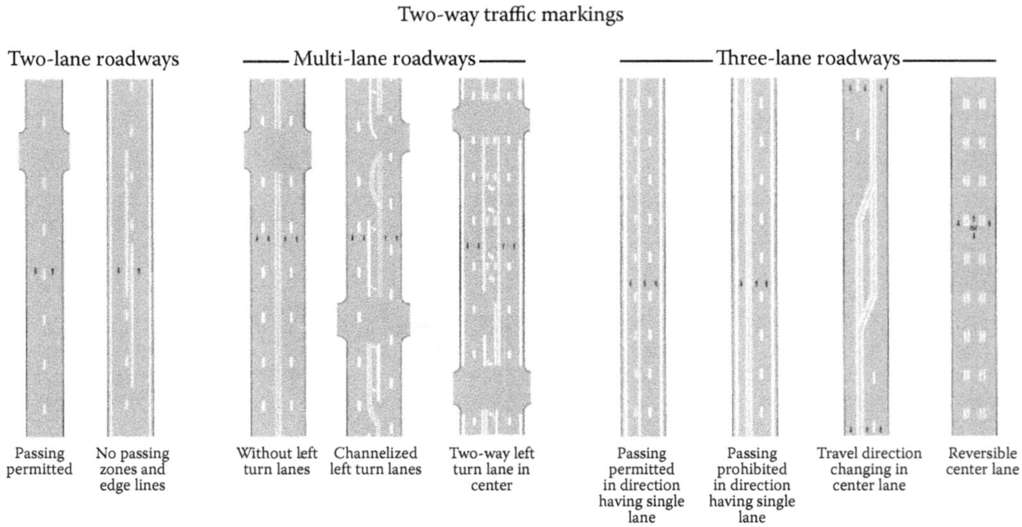

Figure 5.19 Pavement markings. (From http://mutcd.fhwa.dot.gov/services/publications/fhwaop02090/index.htm.)

(e.g., routing information such as street names or distance data) (U.S. Department of Transportation, 2012b). Temporary traffic control signs communicate conditions that may temporarily affect travel (e.g., detour) (U.S. Department of Transportation, 2012b). School signs communicate information concerning school areas (e.g., end school speed limit) (U.S. Department of Transportation, 2012b).

Pavement markings also communicate pertinent information that affects travel. Analogous with the messages of roadway signs, pavement markings communicate public safety information. They must be visible and conspicuous, and may be painted using retroreflective materials. They must be visible in all types of weather, and during both night and day hours. Pavement markings denote crosswalks, passing lanes, no passing lanes, bike lanes, no parking zones, parking spaces, and a variety of other conditions that affect motorists, bikers, and pedestrians. Pavement markings "indicate which part of the road to use, provide information about conditions ahead, and indicate where passing is allowed" (U.S. Department of Transportation, 2002). Figure 5.19 shows typical American pavement markings.

Aviation Graphics and Visuals

Some law enforcement organizations have aviation units or share aviation resources with other organizations. Therefore, they must consider communications with respect to the types of runway and aviation markings that permeate airport and airfield environments. Analogous with roadway markings, aviation markings must be visible and conspicuous to attract attention. They must effectively communicate information succinctly and immediately. These markings must be visible and conspicuous in all types of weather, and during day and night hours. Their composition must resist both physical and natural forces to bolster their maintainability.

Airway markings differ from their roadway counterparts. Because of the potential of foreign object damage, they must be constructed from materials that do not deteriorate easily or that may become loose and endanger humans or aircraft. Airports may implement a "numbering system or alphanumeric system that is located in a corner of the surface marking" as a method of facilitating the "daily inspection, scheduled maintenance, necessary repairs, etc., for surface markings" (Federal Aviation Administration, 2010, p. 2). Various markings appear in or around aviation environments. For example, runway landing designator markings identify and communicate the ending of a runway (Federal Aviation Administration, 2010, p. 9). These markings are white and consist of "a single number or two numbers," and in the event of parallel runways, "the number(s) are further supplemented with a letter" (Federal Aviation Administration, 2010, p. 9).

Another example involves taxiways. Specifically, taxiway shoulder markings use "a perpendicular reference line drawn from the taxiway centerline" (Federal Aviation Administration, 2010, p. 47). These markings are "uniformly spaced," and do not "exceed 50 feet (15 m) between two adjacent markings measured at the largest gap of the radially spaced markings" (Federal Aviation Administration, 2010, p. 47). The color of taxiway shoulder markings is yellow (Federal Aviation Administration, 2010, p. 47). Figure 5.20 displays taxi marking characteristics.

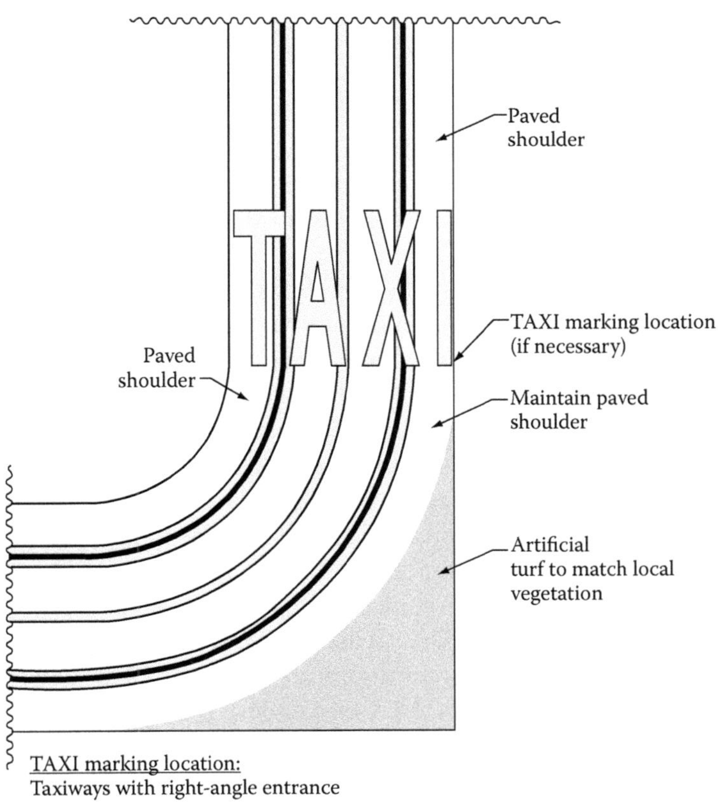

Figure 5.20 Aviation taxi marking. (From http://www.faa.gov/airports/resources/advisory_circulars/index.cfm/go/document.current/documentNumber/150_5340-1.)

Maritime Graphics and Visuals

Law enforcement missions are not limited to ground and air operations. Many law enforcement organizations employ some maritime resources. Examples of such entities include facets of the U.S. Coast Guard and various port authorities that operate along rivers, inland waterways, beaches, and lakes. In such instances, law enforcement resources, such as patrol boats, may be marked with graphics and visuals that uniquely identify the vessel as a law enforcement resource.

Marking maritime vessels with graphic and visual items is essential for conveying the message that the vessel is a law enforcement entity. Floating buoys and moorings also must be clearly identifiable. Among waterways, graphic and visual displays may indicate hazards that affect travel and sailing, such as sunken vessels or other obstructions that may be concealed by water, and communicate waterway navigational route information. Similar to the conspicuity and visibility concepts that are applicable to land and aviation resources, maritime vessels and waterway safety and navigational aids must be clearly seen. Therefore, markings must attract attention and must endure various types of weather and other natural elements (especially water). They must also be visible during day and night hours.

Among maritime environments, several items are used to communicate a variety of messages. Certainly, law enforcement resources may be clearly identified by displaying a symbolic badge, using blue lights, and by expressing boldly and prominently the organizational identifier in writing on the vessel (e.g., writing the word police). Additional items include the following:

Lateral aids to navigation: These items "show the sides of a navigable channel, mark junctions and forks or splits in the channel, indicate the safe side to pass a hazard to navigation, and mark the safe centerline on wide bodies of water" (U.S. Coast Guard, 2012, p. 6).

Preferred channel aids: The buoy and beacon items communicate navigational information "via shape, color, light, and/or audible signal" (U.S. Coast Guard, 2012, p. 4). These items may employ a red and green color scheme (U.S. Coast Guard, 2012, p. 4).

Nonlateral aids to navigation: These items represent maritime versions of the "informational, regulatory, and warning signs encountered on the road" (U.S. Coast Guard, 2012, p. 4). Diamond-shaped versions of dayboards often represent "informational signboards" that communicate location information (U.S. Coast Guard, 2012, p. 4).

Safe water marks: These items communicate the presence of "fairways, mid-channels, and offshore approach points" (U.S. Coast Guard, 2012, p. 4).

Isolated danger marks: These items communicate the presence of "an isolated danger that may be passed on all sides" (U.S. Coast Guard, 2012, p. 4).

Range dayboard: These items communicate navigational information to "help the vessel operator maintain a straight and safe course within a navigable channel" (U.S. Coast Guard, 2012, p. 4). These items are generally mounted along shorelines (U.S. Coast Guard, 2012, p. 4).

Nautical charts: A nautical chart is the maritime "equivalent of road maps," and communicates "an aerial view of a waterway with its aids to navigation, landmarks, and bridges, as well as information on water depth, latitude, and longitude, and a variety of other important navigational information" (U.S. Coast Guard, 2012, p. 4).

Information and regulatory marks: These items are colored using an orange and white scheme. They communicate information "to alert vessel operators to various warnings and regulations" (U.S. Coast Guard, 2012, p. 9).

According to the Bureau of Transportation Statistics, during 2010, there were 41 fatalities related to waterway incidents (Bureau of Transportation Statistics, 2012). A total of 159 waterway injuries and a total of 5427 accidents occurred in 2010 (Bureau of Transportation Statistics, 2012). Cumulatively, 6788 vessels were involved in these incidents (Bureau of Transportation Statistics, 2012). The financial amount of the 2010 associated damages was approximately $106.7 million (Bureau of Transportation Statistics, 2012). Maritime environments have some dangers that must be acknowledged by law enforcement organizations whose missions involve some aspects of maritime functions.

The safety and security of waterways must not be discounted in comparison to the dangers of roadways and airways. All three modalities are dangerous, and public safety organizations must communicate these dangers to all travelers. Law enforcement entities must be visible and conspicuous within such environments. Figure 5.21 depicts an example of markings through which the communicating of maritime information occurs.

Commentary Regarding Visual Paradigms and the Justice Domain

Law enforcement organizations fulfill missions among land, maritime, and aviation environments. They must communicate within all three settings efficiently and effectively. The use of graphic and visual resources embellishes the ability to communicate among these environments. Communicating in these environments involves messaging with society, messaging among other law enforcement entities, and messaging with any supporting entities.

Within the justice system, graphic and visual resources are present. Courtrooms may incorporate the use of numerous diagrams and figures to support expert witness testimonies. Photographs and video resources may be examined as evidence through which attorneys embellish their arguments. Signage may permeate courthouses to communicate emergency exits and building evacuation routes. Wanted posters may communicate photographs of wanted individuals to law enforcement organizations and within society.

Maintaining a strong relationship with society is an essential aspect of successful policing. The use of visual and graphic resources may enhance community policing programs to foster communications. Such imagery is also necessary when attempting to modify societal behaviors and when attempting to build trust between society and law enforcement organizations. The use of graphics and visual imagery may be incorporated within written

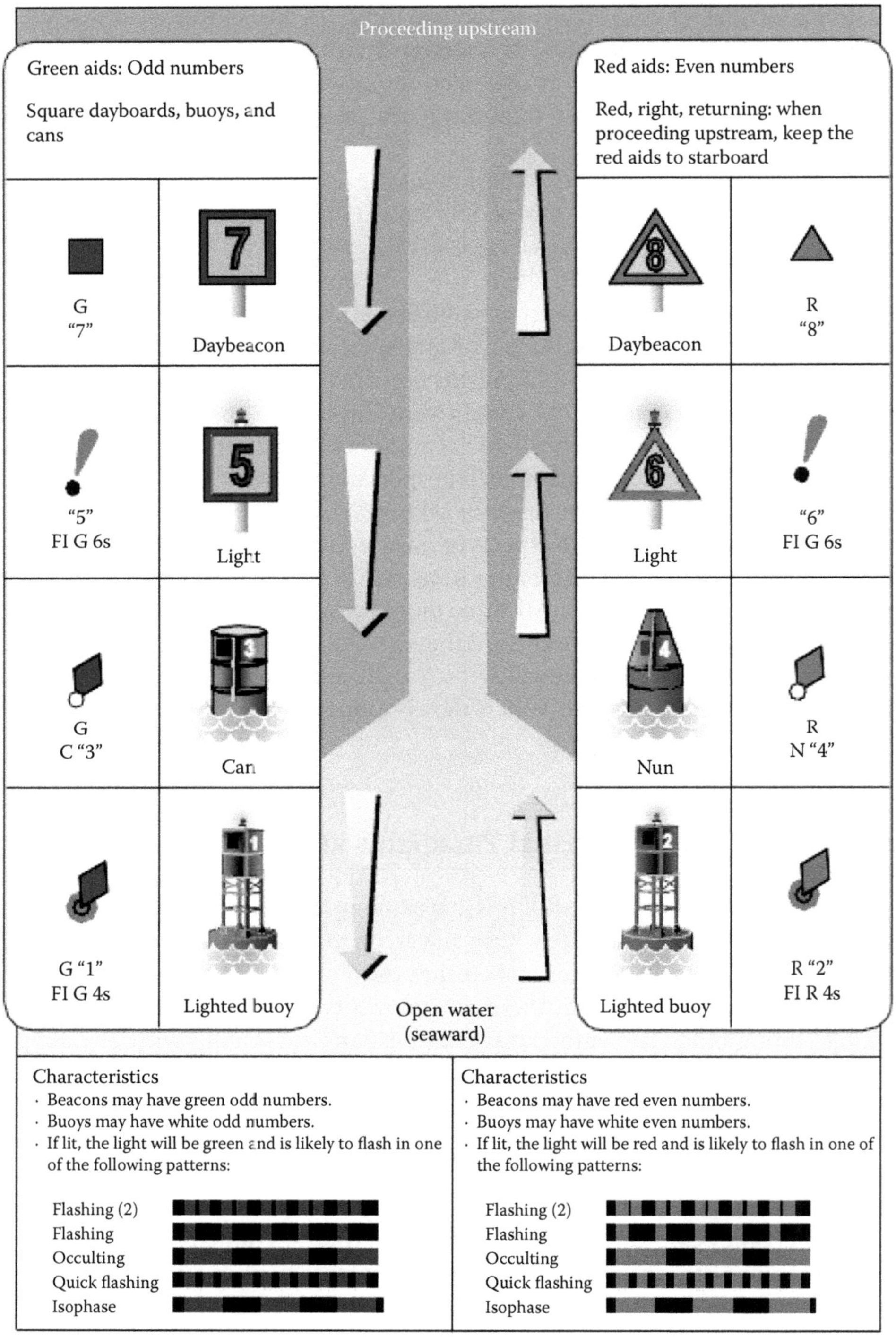

Figure 5.21 Example of maritime markings. (From http://www.uscg.mil/d13/dpw/docs/usaidstonavigationsystembooklet23dec03.pdf.)

Figure 5.22 Imagery supporting community policing. (From http://www.msubillings.edu/police/.)

documents or broadcast media. Figure 5.22 depicts the use of such imagery to facilitate public interaction and community policing.

The justice domain has many tensions and conflicts. After all, the court system is a construct through which dispute resolution occurs. From the perspective of criminal offenses and cases, entering the court system involves some type of contact with law enforcement entities. Within civil proceedings, entering the court system involves some contact with an officer of the court, a court administrator, or some other civil authority. Communicating is necessary in both civil and criminal court proceedings. The use of graphic and visual resources may contribute toward the resolution of disputes in both criminal and civil matters.

Chapter Comments and Summary

This chapter introduced the concepts of graphic and visual communication resources. The use of such imagery bolsters the scope and magnitude of communications methods through providing items that are viewable. Such items may be used objectively or influentially when communicating. Objective uses include documenting and archiving incidents within the justice domain for historical purposes. Influential uses include incorporating visual and graphic imagery for the purposes of societal behavior modification. In any case, the use of graphic and visual resources is a powerful method of embellishing communications.

Written language may be supplemented through the use of graphic and visual imagery. Within documents, tables and figures may be used to enhance the contents of the written word. Humans may find it easier to view an image to gain an understanding of a concept instead of reading a lengthy section of text. The use of tables, figures, diagrams, charts, graphs, photographs, etc., contributes toward embellishing the written word.

Both visibility and conspicuity are of paramount importance to law enforcement organizations. Resources must clearly, efficiently, and effectively communicate the presence of a law enforcement entity. Therefore, any graphics and visuals must quickly gain and hold the attention of viewers. Furthermore, they must robustly endure a variety of conditions involving all kinds of weather and both day and night hours.

The functions of ensuring public safety are embellished through the ability to communicate. Law enforcement vehicles are often equipped with flashing blue lights as a unique identifier. Route maps may be disseminated to refugees during periods of natural or man-made disasters that necessitate evacuation. Certainly, more uses of graphic and visual tools may be identified that improve the ability of law enforcement organizations to communicate with society, thereby bolstering public safety.

In essence, graphic and visual resources are communicative tools that supplement other communications paradigms. Although they may be used as a solitary method of communicating, they are not to be deemed always as total replacements for other attributes or forms of communication. Therefore, they may be used in conjunction with their peer methods. Graphic and visual resources are tools through which other forms of communicating may be complemented and embellished.

Terminology

Airway communication
Animation
Architectural blueprint
Attention
Bar chart
Bubble diagram
Chart
Conspicuity
Graph
Data flow diagram
Design
Dimensions
Entity–relationship diagram
Evacuation
Flow chart
Gantt chart
Geographic information system
Geographic positioning system
Line chart
Map
Markings
Maritime communication
Organizational chart
Pie chart
Process diagram
Roadway communication
Routing
Scatter-plot diagram
Technical diagram

Terrain
Video
Visibility
Visual seduction

THOUGHT AND DISCUSSION QUESTIONS

1. This chapter introduced a variety of campaigns in which animation or visual resources were used to influence public behavior. Another well-known figure is Smokey Bear. The Smokey Bear campaign is the "longest running" public service announcement "campaign in U.S. history" (Smokey Bear, 2012). Do some research, and substantively discuss how the Smokey Bear campaign leverages video and graphic resources to deterring wildfire. The Smokey Bear material is available from http://www.smokeybear.com/.
2. Graphic and visual resources are not total replacement for other attributes or methods of communication even though they may be used by themselves to communicate an intended message. Do some research in your locale, and determine how graphic and video resources are used to supplement other modes of communicating within the justice domain. Write a brief essay that discusses your opinions of the efficiency and effectiveness of using these graphic and video resources.
3. Communicating is an essential characteristic of community-oriented policing. Do some research in your locale, and determine how graphic and visual resources are integrated and leveraged to support community policing endeavors. Write a brief essay that discusses how graphic and visual resources are used to facilitate your selected example of community policing.
4. Some may argue that there is no "best" method of communicating when comparing and contrasting auditory, written, and visual methods. Consider the advantages and disadvantages of each method. Briefly discuss which method you believe is best when compared with the uses of visual and graphic imagery.

References

Adams, P. (2009). *Geographies of media and communication* (p. 193). West Sussex, UK: Wiley-Blackwell Publishing.

Amsden, R., Butler, H., & Amsden, D. (1998). *SPC simplified: Practical steps to quality* (p. 169). Portland, OR: Productivity, Inc.

Basu, R. (2004). *Implementing quality* (p. 53). London: Thomson Learning.

Boba, R. (2005). *Crime analysis and crime mapping* (p. 54). Thousand Oaks, CA: Sage Publications.

Bovee, C., & Thill, J. (2012). *Business communication today* (11th ed.). Upper Saddle River, NJ: Pearson Publishing.

Brase, C., & Brase, C. (2013). *Understanding basic statistics* (p. 7). Boston: Brooks/Cole Publishing.

Bureau of Transportation Statistics. (2012). Table 2-45: Waterborne transportation safety and property damage data related to vessel casualties. Retrieved from http://www.bts.gov/publications/national_transportation_statistics/html/table_02_45.html (accessed December 13, 2012).

Chicago Police Department. (2012). ClearMap. Retrieved from http://gis.chicagopolice.org/ (accessed December 12, 2012).

Cole, G., Smith, C., & DeJong, C. (2013). *The American system of criminal justice* (13th ed., p. 731). Belmont, CA: Wadsworth-Cengage.

Cutler, B. (2002). *With rose-colored glasses removed.* Lincoln, NE: iUniverse.

Davey, J. (1998). *The politics of prison expansion: Winning elections by waging war on crime* (p. 32). Westport, CT: Greenwood Publishing.

Federal Aviation Administration. (2010). *150/5340-1K—Standards for airport markings.* Washington, DC: U.S. Government.

Federal Emergency Management Agency. (2009). *Emergency vehicle visibility and conspicuity study.* Washington, DC: U.S. Government.

Friedmann, A. (2010). *Writing for visual media* (3rd ed., p. 129). Burlington, MA: Focal Press.

Hall, R. (2009). *Wanted: The outlaw in American visual culture.* Charlottesville, VA: University of Virginia Press.

Lehman, C., & DuFrene, D. (2008). *Business communication* (16th ed., p. 369). Mason, OH: Southwestern-Cengage Publishing.

Merriam-Webster Dictionary. (2012a). s.v. "diagram." Retrieved from http://www.merriam-webster.com/dictionary/diagram (accessed December 12, 2012).

Merriam-Webster Dictionary. (2012b). s.v. "map." Retrieved from http://www.merriam-webster.com/dictionary/map (accessed December 12, 2012).

Miller, L., Hess, K., & Orthmann, C. (2011). *Community policing: Partnerships for problem solving* (p. 256). Clifton Park, NY: Delmar-Cengage.

National Academy of Sciences. (2009). *Mapping the zone: Improving flood map accuracy* (p. 91). Washington, DC: The National Academies Press.

National Aeronautics and Space Administration. (2012). *NASA TM-105419.* Retrieved from http://grcpublishing.grc.nasa.gov/editing/chp2.CFM (accessed December 12, 2012).

Pew Research Center. (2012). In changing news landscape, even television is vulnerable. Retrieved from http://www.people-press.org/2012/09/27/in-changing-news-landscape-even-televisionis-vulnerable/ (accessed December 12, 2012).

Pew Research Center's Project for Excellence in Journalism. (2012). The State of the News Media. Retrieved from http://stateofthemedia.org/2010/overview-3/key-findings/ (accessed December 12, 2012).

Pfeiffer, W. (2003). *Technical writing* (5th ed., p. 113). Upper Saddle River, NJ: Pearson Education.

Proctor, R., & van Zandt, T. (2008). *Human factors in simple and complex systems* (2nd ed., p. 197). Boca Raton, FL: CRC Press.

Rogalski, J. (2012). Crashes caused by cops leave victims wanting justice. *KHOU News.* Retrieved from http://www.khou.com/news/ITeamHPDAccidents-149102875.html (accessed December 12, 2012).

Ryan, W., & Conover, T. (2004). *Graphic communications today* (4th ed., p. 40). Clifton Park, NY: Delmar-Cengage Publishing.

Schermerhorn, J. (2010). *Exploring management* (2nd ed., p. 127). Hoboken, NJ: John Wiley and Sons Publishing.

Siegel, L., & Worrall, J. (2013). *Essentials of criminal justice* (8th ed., p. 98). Belmont, CA: Wadsworth-Cengage Publishing.

Smokey Bear. (2012). *Welcome. Smokey Bear campaign.* Retrieved from http://www.smokeybear.com/vault/?js=1 (accessed December 12, 2012).

Stering, R. (2008). *Police officer's handbook: An analytical and administrative guide* (p. 33). Sudbury, MA: Jones and Bartlett Publishers.

Thomas, M., & Williams, C. (2012). Police car visibility: Detection, categorization, and defining components. *The Journal of Law Enforcement, 2*(3), 1–29.

U.S. Coast Guard. (2012). *U.S. aids to navigation system: What you need to know about the markers on the water.* Washington, DC: U.S. Government.

U.S. Department of Transportation. (2002). *United States pavement markings* (p. 2). Washington, DC: U.S. Government.

U.S. Department of Transportation. (2012a). New starts planning and project development process. Retrieved from http://www.fta.dot.gov/12304_2610.html (accessed December 12, 2012).

U.S. Department of Transportation. (2012b). *Standard highway signs including pavement markings and standard alphabets—2012 supplement*. Washington, DC: U.S. Government.

U.S. Geological Survey. (2012). Hazard mapping images and data. Retrieved from http://earthquake.usgs.gov/hazards/products/ (accessed December 12, 2012).

Walker, J., & Maddan, S. (2013). *Statistics in criminology and criminal justice: Analysis and interpretation* (4th ed., p. 78). Burlington, MA: Jones and Bartlett Publishing.

Welles, O. (n.d.). Film quotes. BrainyQuote.com. Retrieved from http://www.brainyquote.com/quotes/keywords/film.html (accessed December 10, 2012).

Reporting and Technical Communication

6

This report, by its very length, defends itself against the risk of being read.
—Winston Churchill (Churchill, n.d.)

Objectives

The objectives of this chapter are to

- Introduce the writing of reports
- Introduce informal reporting
- Introduce formal reporting
- Introduce reporting formats
- Introduce technical documentation
- Introduce proposals

Introduction

Reporting occurs throughout the justice domain. Law enforcement officers may submit incident reports after servicing a call for assistance. Members of the general public may submit a written report to an attorney or a law enforcement officer detailing their accounts of an incident. Supervisors may require their subordinates to submit periodic progress reports. Law enforcement organizations may issue an annual report that details the characteristics of their primary operations and financing during the preceding year.

Technical documents also permeate the justice domain. User manuals may accompany software packages used for crime mapping and criminal databases. They may discuss the procedures necessary for installing, operating, and maintaining a new radio communications system. The manufacturers of automobiles distribute printed manuals that discuss and explain the characteristics of vehicles that may be used to operate and maintain police cars.

Within the corrections system, there are basic needs for medical care and foodstuffs. Numerous vendors may be candidates for providing such services and products. Prisons, jails, and detention centers may issue a request for proposal (RFP) that solicits business proposals and bids competitively to amass a pool of potential vendors that may satisfy these needs. Applicant organizations may submit a proposal delineating their ability to uniquely satisfy the requirements of the entity that issued the RFP.

Other forms of reports exist within the justice system. Investigators may provide periodic reports that detail their activities and findings both during and after their investigations are completed. Such reports may originate within the justice system or they may originate from private investigators. Expert witnesses may prepare and submit a report of their findings as evidence during court proceedings. These submissions may vary in detail and are objective documents that show their investigative queries, methodologies used, findings, interpretations of outcomes, conclusions, and recommendations.

Law enforcement organizations are unique throughout the nation. No two organizations are exactly alike, and their administrative processes differ according to the needs of the organization. Therefore, they exhibit unique processes that may have some commonness or may drastically differ. The written policies of the organization may detail the steps of processes that affect the administrative functioning of the organization. Documenting these processes represents a form of communicating through technical writing.

Within the justice domain, communicating with reports may be formal or informal. The scope and magnitude of reporting also varies with respect to the complexity of the situation. Technical documentation may also be formal or informal, and also varies with the complexity of the considered service or product. In any case, expressing either formal or informal concepts through the written word is a salient consideration of the justice system and of law enforcement organizations.

Formal Documents and Reports

A formal report is a written document that provides information that may facilitate the rendering of human decisions. In some cases, they may contain "only information" or they may provide some type of quantitative analysis and "make recommendations" (Guffey & Almonte, 2010, p. 253). Formal reports vary in length, and may necessitate only a few pages or more than 200 pages (Guffey & Almonte, 2010, p. 253). Formal reports are also associated with projects and endeavors that exhibit a great amount of complexity (Guffey & Almonte, 2010, p. 253). Formal report documents are written using the third-person perspective.

They are also extensively detailed, and incorporate a variety of contents, referencing methods, and sections. Typically, the initial items consist of a cover page, an executive summary, contents and lists of supporting materials, and author credentials and contact information. The primary body of a formal report document consists of introductory materials, posed queries, methodology, findings, conclusion(s), recommendation(s), and considerations of factors that constrain or influence the endeavor.

Not all of these sections are contained within all formal documents. Only those sections that are necessary are contained within the formal document. Some departments and organizations may have formal report templates that contain minimum sections that must be included because of policy reasons. Depending on the situation, they may remain the confidential and proprietary property of an organization or they may be released for public review. Furthermore, when submitted to the requesting authority, formal reports and documents are generally accompanied by a transmittal letter. The succeeding sections describe these sections and transmittal letter.

Letter of Transmittal

Transmittal letters were introduced and discussed within Chapter 4. Simply, a transmittal letter shows the movement of an item between the sending party and the receiving party. When used within the context of formal communications, the transmittal letter shows the transfer of the formal report document from the author(s) to the requesting entity. Through the certified receipt of a transmittal letter, proof is obtained to show that the transfer of the formal report actually transpired. Figure 4.7 in Chapter 4 shows an example of a transmittal letter.

Cover Page

The cover page of a formal report document conveys the pertinent details of the item being submitted to the requesting authority. It generally contains the title of the report document and the date of the submission. The cover page also incorporates any other required or necessary information (e.g., author information, document tracking number, organizational information). Figure 6.1 depicts a typical formal report cover page.

Unless governed by some organizational policy, the preferences and requirements of the requesting entity, or the preference of the author, there is no universal standard for report cover pages. Numerous ways of designing and crafting a cover page exist. Figure 6.2 shows another example of a report cover page.

Both Figures 6.1 and 6.2 incorporate the use of graphic and visual imagery to enhance the presentation of the cover page. However, there is no mandate that such imagery be a part of the cover design. Instead, a simple, typed sheet will also suffice.

Figure 6.1 Example of a formal report cover page. (From http://www.oig.dhs.gov/assets/Mgmt/2012/OIG_12-69_Mar12.pdf.)

Figure 6.2 Stanford University report cover page. (From http://www.stanford.edu/group/SUDPS/safety-report/Almanac.pdf.)

Executive Summary

The executive summary represents a succinct synopsis of the contents of the formal report document. An executive summary is synonymous with an abstract. Executive summaries are generally contained within longer report documents. Their use is highly functional in that readers gain the highlights of the material by reading the executive summary without having to read the entire document. By doing so, administrators and managers require less time to gain an initial understanding of the purpose of the report.

The contents of the executive summary are concise. They often contain some mention of the problem or issue, might have a methodological overview, and generally contain the highlights of the work, including some discussion points from the findings, and reviews of the conclusions and recommendations. The executive summary considers events that have already occurred. Therefore, they are generally written using the past or present tenses. Because executive summaries are summations, they should be constrained to one or two pages in length.

Executive summaries should be considered as documents that may exist individually although they are contained within formal report documents. It should be assumed that readers will not read the entirety of the formal report document, and will access its contents only if necessary, out of curiosity, or if they have some reasons for reading the formal report in its entirety. Therefore, when crafting an executive summary, one should incorporate only the most relevant and salient issues that demand the attention of readers.

An example of an executive summary is presented in Figure 6.3.

OIG

Department of Homeland Security
Office of Inspector General

Executive Summary

The *American Recovery and Reinvestment Act of 2009* (Recovery Act) provided $787 billion to the federal government to stimulate the U.S. economy. Of that amount, the Department of Homeland Security received $2.75 billion for various projects run by the Office of the Under Secretary for Management, U.S. Customs and Border Protection, U.S. Immigration and Customs Enforcement, Transportation Security Administration, the U.S. Coast Guard, and the Federal Emergency Management Agency.

At the request of the Recovery Accountability and Transparency Board, we conducted a review to determine whether the department has established a process to perform limited data quality reviews of reports submitted by recipients of Recovery Act funds administered by the department to identify material omissions and/or significant reporting errors, and to notify the recipients of the need to make appropriate and timely changes.

The department process for verifying the completeness and accuracy of data reported by recipients is evolving. The department issued general guidance on reviewing contractor reports on September 15, 2009. Also, four of five components developed approaches for substantiating the accuracy of recipient reporting. Later, the department headquarters developed a method to identify non-registrants and began providing that information to its components. However, the department has not yet issued detailed procedures for performing limited data quality reviews of recipient reporting to identify material omissions and significant reporting errors.

To improve the process, we are recommending that the department issue formal policy and procedures to guide the agency. In an October 28, 2009 response to the draft report (Appendix B), the department generally concurred with the finding and recommendation. Based on the response, we consider the recommendation resolved but not implemented. The recommendation will remain open until we receive a copy of the department-wide policy and procedures.

Process Used by the Department of Homeland Security to Monitor Reporting by Recipients of American Recovery and Reinvestment Act of 2009 Funds

1

Figure 6.3 Example of an executive summary. (From http://permanent.access.gpo.gov/gpo31464/OIG_10-08_Oct09.pdf.)

Author Qualifications and Contact Information

An optional section within formal report documents is the author qualifications and contact information section. Generally, it is wise to include the authorship and contact information; however, it is unnecessary to always include some discussion of qualifications and certifications. In the case of expert testimony, it may be required and beneficial to include the credentials and experiences of the expert in addition to the appropriate contact information. This section may denote higher education, completion of training programs, professional certifications, and any other information that contributes toward establishing the professional acumen of the author(s).

Some formal report documents are produced by think tanks, government entities, or other professional organizations. In such cases, the specific individuals that contributed to the authoring of the formal report may be unlisted within the document. However, some organizations may list and describe the contributing authors or may only indicate by name only the contributing authors. These situations may involve the sponsoring organization listing a brief description of its mission and history. Generally, most organizations will include some method of contacting them, including mailing address, electronic mail address, and telephone numbers.

Table of Contents

The formal report document should always contain a table of contents. This section shows the page numbers of the specific chapters, sections, and headings that comprise the overall document. Within the table of contents, the titles of chapters, sections, and headings are identical to those contained within the body of the document. It provides a method of quickly examining the contents of the report to determine the materials therein, and provides information through which they are easily accessed. Generally, the table of contents is located in the front of the formal report document. The table of contents within this book is representative of a table of contents that is appropriate for a formal report document. Generating a table of contents is accomplished easily through the use of the word processing software in which the formal report document is created.

Listing Pertinent Information

Formal report documents generally contain lists of pertinent information contained within the overall document. Lists are generally contained to denote the graphic and visual imagery or other supporting materials that are contained within the formal report document. Using such lists provides readers with a quick method of determining which pages contain certain supporting materials. Generally, most formal report documents contain lists of figures, diagrams, exhibits, photographs, and tables.

Many formal report documents incorporate abbreviations or acronyms as a method of shortening long terms, phrases, or words that are repeated within the text of the document. For example, the phrase Department of Homeland Security would be shortened to simply DHS. By including a listing of abbreviations and acronyms, readers gain an understanding of any shortened words, terms, or phrases that may be encountered when reading the text of the document.

Another listing involves a consideration of relevant terms. In some cases, formal report documents may contain a terminological section that lists and briefly defines terms that are used within the text of the document. Within the front materials of this book, the list of abbreviations and acronyms is typical of this type of listing. Such a listing assists when contributing to an understanding of the technical language that is pertinent to the problem domain. For example, someone who has no medical education or background may find a coroner's report to be confusing. However, through the inclusion of a brief listing and defining of pertinent medical terminology, readers may gain some understanding of the words and phrases that are contained within the text of the coroner's report.

The use of lists is guided by the contents of the formal report document. If a visual or graphic image is included within the body of the document, then it should be included within the appropriate listing within this section near the front of the formal report document. This notion is true for all supplementary materials that are contained within the text of the formal report document.

Introduction

The introduction section establishes a basis for the work described within the formal report document. It provides background information that describes the problem domain and presents any research questions that were investigated. By reading the introduction, readers gain a familiarity with the salient reasoning that justified the work discussed within the formal report document. The length of the introduction section varies according to the scope and magnitude of the endeavor that was accomplished. It should be sufficient in depth and detail to provide a good understanding of why the endeavor was worthy of pursuit. Headings and subheadings are usually numbered. Graphic and visual aids are used as necessary to support the written text.

The introduction section also is informative for other purposes. It may identify the sponsoring organization, and expresses any necessary authorizations. It may discuss any previous studies that occurred, and how the current study or project complements or relates to previous findings. It may also allude to the highlights of the methodology, bias, and constraints that were observed during the progression of the study or project. The introduction may also include an overview of a chronological timeline that shows milestones and when activities were completed with respect to the completion of the study or project.

The introduction section also may express the highlights of the design and methodology of the study or project. Designs may be either qualitative or quantitative. Qualitative designs would necessitate descriptions of case studies, historical summaries, and so forth. Quantitative designs would necessitate descriptions of mathematical analysis. Referencing the methodology would describe the method through which the study or project was conducted.

Other topics that may be included within the introduction may involve aspects of summarizing financial resources and required equipment. The characteristics of costs and budgetary concerns may be highlighted as well as the types and forms of equipment that were necessary during the conduction of the research. However, unless deemed necessary by the sponsoring organization, by organizational policy, or by the situation itself, discussions of these topics are not always required within the introduction section.

Scope and Limitations

The scope and limitations section represents a consideration of anything that constrained the conduction of the project or research study. Every research study or project is unique. The constraining factors that limited one study or project may be completely irrelevant for another study or project. A practically innumerable array of factors may influence studies and projects. Examples include funding, human expertise, equipment, time, access to populations and samples, stratifications, and many others.

Identifying and expressing the scope and limitations is important to clarify the reach and vastness of the study or project. For example, if it is merely a pilot study, then it should be repeated using a much larger population and sample. This status should be clearly identified so that readers will understand that the study or project is only a small endeavor, and that a larger effort may generate different outcomes thereby necessitating changes to the conclusions and recommendations. Headings and subheadings within this section are usually numbered. Graphic and visual aids are used as necessary to support the written text.

Bias

Although "bias" is a short word, it may have a tremendous impact on the research study or project. Bias may be conceptualized and perceived as anything that negatively influences the study or project. Sources of bias exist everywhere; there is no perfect study or project. Acknowledging the potential influences of bias represents an awareness of the influences that may have affected the study or project. This section of a formal report document alludes to the imperfections that may influence the study or project. Headings and subheadings within this section are usually numbered. Graphic and visual aids are used as necessary to support the written text.

Bias originates from a variety of factors. When using sampling methods, the size of the population or sample may be inappropriate, the research design and method may be flawed, the author may interject some personal bias, the calibration of equipment may interject bias, poor response rates to surveys may show bias, and so on. It is beyond the scope of this textbook to provide a lengthy elucidation of bias factors that may influence a study or project. Readers are encouraged to consult a research methods textbook for more information regarding the influence of bias.

Methodology

The methodology section describes the processes and procedures that governed the conduction of the study or project. Essentially, a methodology represents the "rationale for the application" of the methods employed during the study or project (Hammond & Wellington, 2012). It describes how data were collected, handled, processed, and interpreted. The methodology of one study or project may be completely inappropriate for a different study or project. Therefore, methodologies are unique for the considered study or project. Headings and subheadings within the methodology section are usually numbered. Graphic and visual aids are used as necessary to support the written text.

This uniqueness contributes toward page length. Methodological descriptions may be short or long depending on the complexity of the study or project. Regardless of the length, the methodology section must adequately provide sufficient details of how the study or project was conducted. The methodology section must be detailed enough to allow others to repeat the study or project, if necessary.

Body and Supporting Discussions

The body of the formal report document contains the primary discussions affiliated with the study or project. It discusses and answers the pertinent inquiries that were investigated or resolved. With respect to the queries of who, what, when, where, why, and how, the discussions of this section provide a meaningful consideration of each question. Reading this section of the formal report document facilitates a strong understanding of the study or project and its importance. It further establishes the saliency of the cumulative study or project as well as incorporates a consideration of consequences.

All of the primary, secondary, and tertiary discussions are contained within this section. These discussions are generally ordered by numbered sections and subsections. Graphic and visual aids are used as necessary to support the written text. The length of this section varies according to the complexity of the study or project. The body and supporting discussions may range from only a few pages to hundreds of pages in length. Regardless, its informational content must provide a solid understanding of the problem domain.

Findings

The findings section of the formal report document accommodates a discussion of the outcomes of the study or the project. Some formal report documents may title this section as "Results" or "Outcomes." Depending on the approach taken to this section, merely a presentation of descriptive statistics and discussions may be used to portray the findings of the study or project. Otherwise, a deeper discussion of the findings may be appropriate to consider their meaning.

Furthermore, any interpretation of the outcomes of the study or project is contained within the findings section. For instance, if a study or project incorporated an analysis of variance (ANOVA) method, then the appropriate ANOVA tables and interpretations would be contained within the findings section. If a study or project incorporated some aspect of case studies within its method, then the cases must be appropriately analyzed and interpreted within the findings section.

Headings and subheadings within the findings section are usually numbered. Graphic and visual aids are used as necessary to support the written text. The length of the findings section varies according to the complexity of the problem domain and the tools through which outcomes are displayed. Depending on the methodology, findings may be presented using tables, charts, graphs, or any other method that is deemed appropriate for the study or project in accordance with the methodology.

Conclusions and Recommendations

This section of the formal report document presents and discusses the conclusions that were derived from the interpretation of the findings. For each conclusion, one or more recommendation(s) should be crafted. In some cases, the recommendations may be actionable through which change is instigated within the problem domain. In others, perhaps no action is warranted. Regardless, the contents of this section provide the information that is necessary to support the rendering of human decisions through time.

The headings and subheadings of this section are numbered. Graphic and visual aids are used as necessary to support the written text. The length of this section varies depending on the complexity and number of conclusions and offered recommendations. Furthermore, the contents of this section are unique, and are generated from a consideration of the preceding section that discusses the findings and their interpretation.

Appendix

The appendix materials of a formal report contain any supplementary items that embellish the discussions contained within the document. Practically any type of written material or graphic or visual aid can be contained within the appendix materials. For example, if a study or report involves a financial emphasis, then amortization schedules or time value of money tabulations may be contained within the appendix materials.

The length of an appendix varies according to the complexity of the study or project. Letter headings within the appendix materials are generally alphabetized. Terms and words contained within the appendix materials are appropriately referenced within the main body of discussions that comprise the study or project document.

Index

The index materials of a formal report document provide references to the pages in which key terms are located. The appendix contains an alphabetical listing of the key terms and phrases that were used within the document. The size of the appendix varies according to the quantity of terms and words contained therein.

Reference Materials

The reference materials of the document contain a collection of the articles, magazines, books, pamphlets, sources of graphic and visual resources, Internet materials, and any other materials that were used in creating the formal report document. Referencing these items may conform to some established style (e.g., *The Chicago Manual of Style*) or they may conform to some organizational referencing style. Regardless, all sources of information and materials must be contained within this section.

Informal Documents and Reports

Informal report documents are less complex and lengthy when compared with their formal report counterparts. Informal reports may be grouped into six categories as follows (Guffey & Almonte, 2010, p. 224):

Informational reports: This category represents reports that address a specific issue and serve a specific purpose. Although they may contain information, such reports do not necessarily provide an analysis of their informational content (Guffey & Almonte, 2010, p. 224). They may serve an operational function within the organization and may record "daily, weekly, and monthly" activities (Guffey & Almonte, 2010, p. 224).

Progress report: This type of report provides a status update regarding what has or has not been accomplished regarding some endeavor. These reports also "monitor unusual or nonroutine activities" (Guffey & Almonte, 2010, p. 224). They generally provide information regarding whether a task is proceeding according to schedule, whether additional measures are necessary, and whether alternative courses of action are warranted (Guffey & Almonte, 2010, p. 224).

Justification or recommendation reports: This type of report presents various types of information, and also provides some type of analysis regarding the information. They are helpful with respect to the rendering of organizational decisions. They consider options evaluation and offer recommendations as problem solutions (Guffey & Almonte, 2010, p. 224).

Feasibility report: This type of report may succeed some type of formal report that was previously completed. A feasibility report considers whether a potential endeavor may be pursued with some measure of success.

Summary report: This type of report "condenses the primary ideas, conclusions, and recommendations of a longer report or publication." It presents the highlights of an issue or concept, and tends to serve informational purposes.

Meeting minutes: This type of a report expresses the happenings and records the events that transpired during a meeting. Copies of this report may be disseminated to the individuals that participated in the meeting after they are transcribed (Guffey & Almonte, 2010, p. 224).

Oral report: This type of report does not necessitate written documentation and generally does not require transcribing. This type of report may be given physically in person or through other media forms of telephone or video conferencing. However, in some cases, oral reports may be transcribed for historical and archival purposes.

The lengths of informal reports may require only a few pages, and they may not always incorporate the use of graphic or visual tools to embellish written language. They are generally specific, and serve the near-term needs and requirements of the organization. In some cases, they may not adhere to any specific document format and may have few, if any, sections within their primary contents.

Some types of informal reports may be generated quickly and disseminated easily, whereas others may require more time and depth. For example, if a supervisor requests an update regarding a specific community policing activity, then an officer may send a response using an electronic mail message or may opt to update the supervisor via telephone. In contrast, a feasibility study may necessitate many pages of discussion before providing a conclusion and recommendation to facilitate the rendering of a human decision. Therefore, although both examples demonstrate the use of informal reports, they differ in modality and complexity. However, in most cases, informal reports can be expressed through a "short letter or memorandum" (Rodriques, 1992).

Formal versus Informal Paradigms

Reporting is a useful function among organizations. All organizations have a need for some type of reporting mechanism through which information flows among the components of the organization and along chains of command. Both formal and informal reporting modalities satisfy the requirements of reporting within organizations. However, there are differences between these reporting paradigms. Examples of the primary differences are given as follows:

- Formal reports are written in the third-person perspective to enhance objectivity, whereas informal reports may incorporate the uses of first-person and second-person perspectives when communicating.
- Formal reports are generally complex and lengthy, whereas informal reports can be short enough to necessitate their conveyance through a letter or memorandum.
- Formal reports contain numerous sections and front materials, whereas informal reports may contain none of these items (depending on the type of informal report).
- Formal reports may be so lengthy and cumbersome that one may assume that they be unread, whereas informal reports are so short (e.g., e-mail messages) that one can assume that they are read in their entirety.
- Formal reports may describe complex endeavors that necessitate research design and mathematical analysis, whereas informal reports may have simplicity and little design.
- Formal reports usually are accompanied by transmittal letters, whereas informal reports generally do not have this requirement.

Delineating Processes and Procedures

Regardless of the type of report, whether formal or informal, or the type of document being produced, there are times when one must express the steps that comprise a specific process or processes. A process is defined as "a series of actions or operations conducing to an end" (*Merriam-Webster*, 2012). Explaining, discussing, and describing processes is helpful when crafting report methodologies, and is useful when drafting user manuals and other forms of instructional documentation.

Process writing incorporates a chronological approach to the sequencing of activities that comprise a process. It identifies each of the steps that are necessary for a process to occur, and expresses them in their correct sequence. These instructions should be so exact and precise that someone unfamiliar with the concept can understand the process, and implement it from start to finish successfully. Therefore, written instructions must be absolutely clear to facilitate an understanding in the mind of the reader.

When constructing process delineation, one of the initial considerations involves an evaluation of the potential audience for whom the instructions are intended. Generally, it should be assumed that readers have little, if any, knowledge of how the process is to be performed. Therefore, language should be simple and direct, and should be unambiguous. Humans are imperfect creatures, and make mistakes. Therefore, ensure that all of the steps of the written process are present and are encountered in their correct sequence. When writing processes and procedures, the following attributes should be kept in mind (Rog & Kropp, 2004):

- Use a "factual language and tone" (Rog & Kropp, 2004).
- Disallow unnecessary details or descriptions (Rog & Kropp, 2004).
- Adjust vocabulary for the audience (Rog & Kropp, 2004).
- Use a second-person perspective (Rog & Kropp, 2004).
- Use "imperative sentences," with the subject implicitly understood (Rog & Kropp, 2004).
- Use chronological transitions, such as "first, next, after that," (Rog & Kropp, 2004).
- Outline and organize the process steps before beginning writing.
- Create a flow chart or a process diagram to show the overall process in its entirety. When writing begins, refer to this image to ensure that steps are accounted for and presented in the correct order within the written document.
- Explain any technical terminology in order to embellish the reader's understanding of the instructions.
- Assume that the reader will make a mistake when attempting to perform the process. Therefore, incorporate contingency directions as corrective measures so that readers can rectify their situation and eliminate confusion.
- Some processes are complex. Dealing with complexity is best done by breaking down concepts of great complexity into smaller components.
- Test the written process before it is released to others. Testing the written instructions ensures that all of the process steps are listed in their correct order and are present within the process. Missing steps will result in a failed process and a confused reader.
- Within the written document, process steps should be listed numerically.

- It may be helpful to incorporate the use of checkboxes to show which steps have been completed and which are uncompleted.
- Use graphics and visual resources for clarification.

Figure 6.4a and b depict a National Aeronautics and Space Administration (NASA) electronics process. This process shows good design and forethought. It incorporates a checklist to ensure that the individual steps are satisfied. It also uses a document status to record the history of the document and any revisions. Furthermore, it also shows individual steps of the electronics process in their correct sequencing. Each of these steps is numbered with respect to its location within the sequence. Additionally, the separate phases of the process are expressed and categorized to include their relevant process steps.

(a)

Process Checklist for Implementation Phase	
Overview	In the Implementation phase, the design is mapped to the internal structure of the chip and the device is programmed with the design. The Implementation process includes: • Place and Route • Floorplanning • Device programming • Post layout and programming tests
Entrance Criteria	The following criteria should be met prior to beginning the Implementation phase for complex electronics: • The design is reviewed and approved. • Design synthesis was successful. • Design verification and simulation was successfully performed.
Responsible Personnel	Design Engineer – Final implementation activities; device programming. Quality Assurance – Perform the process and product assurance activities listed below.
Not all steps listed below have to be completed sequentially. When a step is finished, the completion date is added to the table below, along with initials of the assurance representative.	

ID	Process Step	Completion Date	QA
1	**Entrance Criteria are met.**		
2	Assess the implementation of the detailed design.		
3	Witness the programming of the device (if programmed in-house). Ensure that process plans are used for repeatable programming. Ensure that the proper, configuration-controlled design is used.		
4	Verify that post-programming tests are performed. Witness the test if any requirements are verified.		
5	Review problem reports and anomalies related to complex electronics (or with devices that include CE). Ensure adequate root cause analysis was performed and corrective actions are implemented.		
QA Analyses			
6a	Problem Trend Analysis		
6b	Process Verifications (list the audits, etc. performed)		
6c	Update Risk Analysis		
Review the following documents (or information included within higher-level documents) that are created at this phase. Approve where authorized.			
7	Process Plans or Procedures for programming the device		
Review any updates to these plans. Ensure that new information is incorporated in the plans.			
8	Complex Electronics Design Document		
9	Complex Electronics Model		
10	Test Files/Data and Simulation Specifications		

Figure 6.4 NASA electronics process template. (a) Part 1.

(b)

ID	Process Step	Completion Date	QA
11	Maintenance Manual		
12	Operations or User Manual		
13	Training Plan		
14	Implementation Plan		
15	Testing Plan		
16	Verification and Validation Plan		
17	Safety Plan		
18	**Exit Criteria are met.**		

Exit Criteria	At the end of the Implementation phase, the following criteria should be met: • The device is programmed with the design.

Documentation Status			
Document ID	Document Name	Revision	Date
	Process Plan for programming the device		
	Maintenance Manual (or Plan)		
	Operations or User Manual		
	Training Plan		
	Complex Electronics Design Document		
	Complex Electronics Model		
	Test Files/Data and Simulation Specifications		
	Implementation Plan		
	Complex Electronics Testing Plan		
	Verification and Validation Plan		
	Safety Plan		

Figure 6.4 (Continued) NASA electronics process template. (b) Part 2. (From http://www.hq.nasa.gov/office/codeq/software/ComplexElectronics/checklists.htm.)

The material preceding the process steps helps clarify concepts that aid in understanding the process cumulatively. It also provides specifications of the roles and responsibilities of pertinent individuals. Furthermore, the necessary entrance criteria are expressed before the beginning of the process, and the appropriate exit criteria are expressed after the process steps. Specifying the exit criteria expresses a definition of success if the process was properly implemented and executed.

Processes also permeate the justice domain. Figures 6.5 through 6.6a and b show a graphical view of the steps for a court transcript redaction process and its associated expression in written language. Within these figures, the flow-chart image and its associated process delineation are affiliated with the U.S. Bankruptcy Court (Ohio). These items also exhibit the characteristics of thoughtful design, and represent a different approach to specifying the considered process that what was seen in the preceding NASA example.

Figure 6.5 shows a court transcript redaction process. It represents the graphic and visual imagery from which Figure 6.6a and b are derived. The steps contained within the written process are commensurate with the flow-chart image that is depicted in Figure 6.5. Each step contains some amount of embellishment to clarify its meaning and to indicate any applicable constraints. The precursor material specifies the limitation of responsibility regarding court personnel and establishes a redaction purpose. The materials succeeding the process provide additional information that further detail chronological aspects of the redaction process and solidify deadlines. The use of such embellishment clarifies

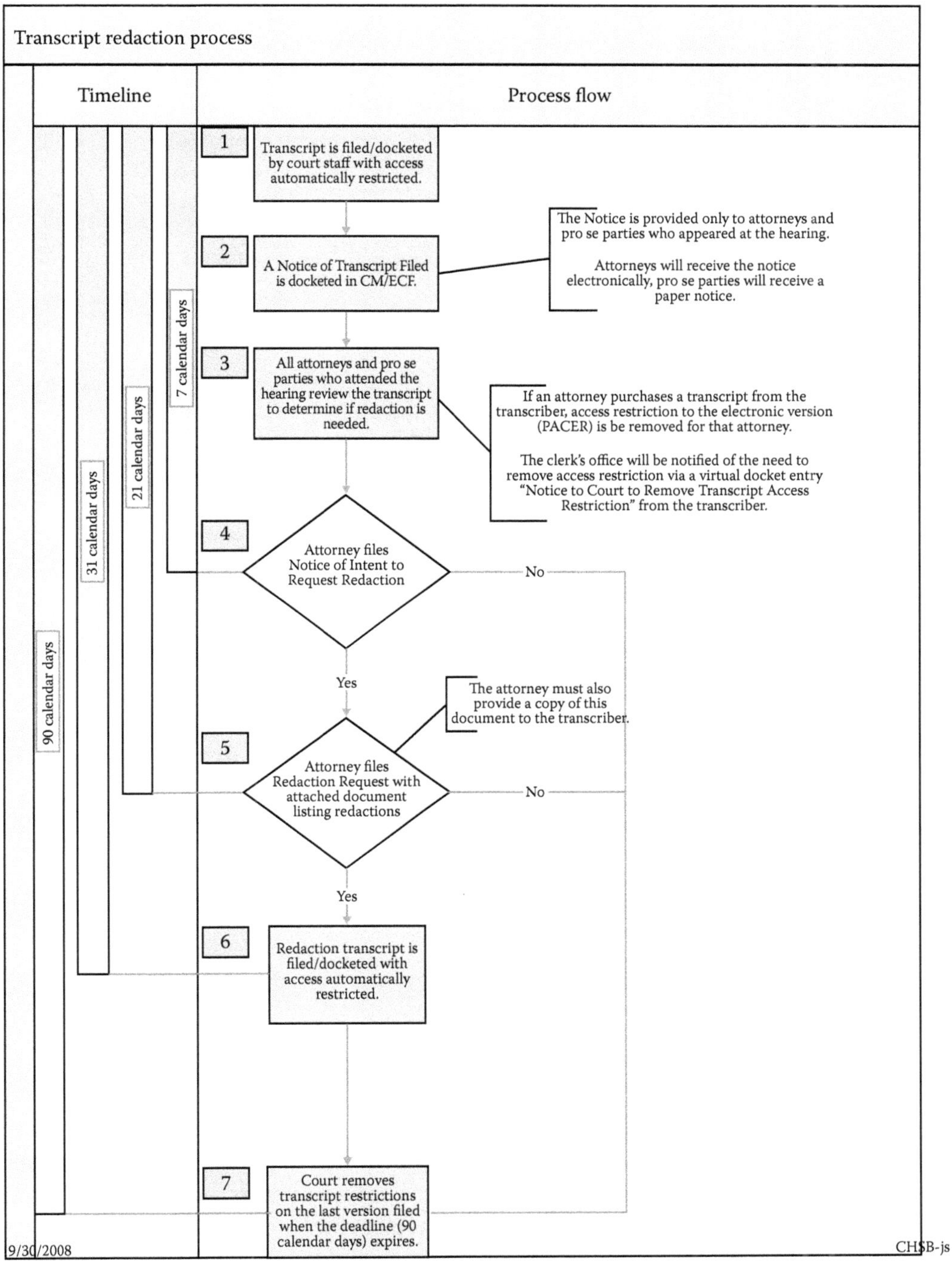

Figure 6.5 Transcript redaction flow chart. (From www.ohsb.uscourts.gov/pdffiles/TranscriptRedactionInfoRA.pdf.)

the redaction process and helps reduce any confusion or questions that readers may have regarding the process.

Both the NASA example and the court transcript redaction example highlight their respective processes. Although they are completely different processes, the expression of the respective processes exhibits some commonness. Both provide adequate details to

(a)

TRANSCRIPT REDACTION PROCESS

With the installation of ECF v.3.2 comes the functionality that will permit the court to implement the Judiciary's privacy policy as it applies to the electronic availability of transcripts. At the outset, a few observations about responsibilities need to be made. When a transcript is filed with the court, the attorneys and *pro se* parties who attended the hearing are solely responsible for redaction of the information described in Rule 9037. Redaction is accomplished only with their input. Transcribers are not responsible for identifying a need for redaction. The clerk is not required to review documents for compliance with Bankruptcy Rule 9037. The court's responsibility is to provide public access to the transcript and restrict access in accordance with the Judiciary's privacy policy.

<u>Snapshot of Transcript Redaction Process</u>

The following information embellishes that contained in the flowchart outlining the transcript redaction process:

Step 1) Submission of Transcript to Court.

Transcribers will be required to electronically submit their transcripts to the court via CM/ECF. Once the transcript is docketed by court personnel, access to the transcript is automatically restricted to court staff and public terminal users. However, neither a public terminal user nor court staff may copy or print a copy of the transcript during a 90-day restriction period.

Step 2) "Notice of Transcript Filed" is Docketed in CM/ECF

In addition to setting forth the date a transcript of a proceeding was filed, the notice will contain deadlines related to restrictions and redaction. Only attorneys and *pro se* parties who actually appeared at the hearing will be provided with this notice. Attorneys will receive an electronic notice, and *pro se* parties will receive notice by U.S. mail.

Step 3) 7-Day Review Period.

During the 7-day period following the docketing of the transcript, attorneys and *pro se* parties are responsible for reviewing a transcript for information that should be redacted under the Judicial Conference's privacy policy, i.e., Social Security numbers (last 4 digits only), birth dates (only the year), minors (refer to with initials), and financial account numbers (last 4 digits only).

Step 4) "Notice of Intent to Request Redaction"

By the end of 7 calendar days after the transcript is docketed, if an attorney intends to redact material from the transcript, she must file a "Notice of Intent to Request Redaction" of information from the transcript. An attorney is responsible for reviewing the opening and closing statement made on behalf of the party he represents, any statements made by the party, and testimony of any witness called by the party.

If no notice is filed by the end of this 7-day period, the court may assume that redaction of personal data is not necessary and may make the transcript electronically available to the public at the end of 90 days.

Figure 6.6 Transcript redaction process. (a) Part 1.

exercise both processes. Both use some type of embellishment to clarify any points that may confuse readers. Both are representative of thoughtful design and a logical ordering of sequenced steps chronologically. In both cases, a sufficient amount of explanation and information is provided so that the processes are repeatable.

Expressing processes through written language requires an exceptional and meticulous attention to the details of the considered process. Authors must also consider the characteristics of the user for whom they are expressing the process, and must accommodate a range of various knowledge levels regarding the subject domain. Although authors may have some assumptions regarding their target audience, no guarantee exists that readers will completely understand the message they are attempting to convey via written language. Regardless, authors must make every effort to ensure that processes and their component steps are explicitly delineated with plenty of details to diminish the chance of reader confusion.

(b)

Step 5) Redaction Request.

If a "Notice of Intent to Request Redaction" has been filed, the attorney has whatever remains of a 21 calendar day period (following the docketing of the transcript) to file a "Redaction Request." Attached to the "Redaction Request" will be a document which lists the places in the transcript where the personal data to be redacted appears. The transcriber must then redact the identifiers as directed by the party.

Step 6) Docketing of Redacted Transcript.

Within 31 calendar days of the transcript being docketed, a redacted version of a transcript must be filed with the court by the transcriber.

Step 7) Removal of Transcript Restrictions.

Finally, at the end of the 90 day period after the docketing of the original transcript, the court removes transcript restrictions on the last version of the transcript filed.

Other Information:

1. A transcript provided to the court by a transcriber will be available at the clerk's office for inspection only for a period of 90 days after it's docketed.

2. During the 90-day period, a copy of the transcript may be obtained from the court transcriber at the rate established by the Judicial Conference. The transcript will be available within the court for internal use, and an attorney who obtains the transcript from the transcriber may obtain remote electronic access to the transcript through the court's CM/ECF system.

3. After the 90-day period has ended, the filed transcript will be available for inspection and copying in the clerk's office and for downloading from the court's CM/ECF system through the judiciary's PACER system.

Figure 6.6 (Continued) Transcript redaction process. (b) Part 2. (From www.ohsb.uscourts.gov/pdffiles/TranscriptRedactionInfoRA.pdf.)

User Manuals and Instructional Documentation

A user manual is defined as "a document created by the manufacturer of a device that provides detailed installation and operation instructions" (ToolingU, 2012). User manuals are a form of instructional documentation through which users gain an understanding of how to operate some entity. User manuals must express the functionality of the considered system or device succinctly and clearly. Graphic and visual resources may embellish the contents of user manuals. Furthermore, user manuals may contain one or more process delineations regarding the working and operation of the considered system or device. User manuals are targeted toward both unskilled and skilled personnel, and "provide instructions for the setup, operation, and maintenance" of a system or device (Alred, Brusaw, & Oliu, 2012). They also contain "safety precautions and troubleshooting charts and guides" (Alred, Brusaw, & Oliu, 2012).

User manuals are generally created through multiple iterations of the writing process. The length of the user manual is influenced by the complexity of the considered system or device. Several drafts of the user manual may be generated before a final version is released. The timing of finalization and release of the user manual is especially important because it must coincide with the release date of the product or system. Authors and organizations must interject quality within the user manual by testing it against operational versions of the product or system. Performing such tests shows where discussions and materials are absent that must be included within the user manual.

Annual Reports

Annual reports are another type of informational document that provide business, management, administrative, management, financial, and accounting information for the public and organizational stakeholders. As their name implies, annual reports are generated at the end of each fiscal year of operation. Their contents show the activities of the organization that occurred during the preceding year. Annual reports usually contain the balance sheet, statement of retained earnings, income statement, and statement of cash flows for an organization (Brigham & Daves, 2010). Cumulatively, these items provide a perspective of the "operations and financial position" of the organization (Brigham & Daves, 2010). A letter from an executive officer of the organization is included within the annual report to describe the "operating results during the past year" and to discuss "new developments that will affect future operations" (Brigham & Daves, 2010).

These concepts are common among most organizational annual reports. However, because all organizations are unique, the presentation of the materials and their associated discussions are also presented uniquely. Annual reports can be quite lengthy, spanning hundreds of pages, and contain numerous sections. Although these reports contain a large amount of accounting and financial information, it is presented and embellished with written language to convey the pertinent concepts. Within the justice domain, one example of an annual report is that of Securitas Corporation (2012).

The 2011 Securitas Annual Report (Securitas Corporation, 2012) contains 146 pages through which the operational and administrative functions of the organization are communicated to stakeholders. It has several major sections representing a corporate overview, statement from the Chief Executive Officer (CEO), a competitive market synopsis, equity share distributions, governance and management, details of the annual report, quarterly data, and future opportunities. Many other subsections are contained within the annual report.

Throughout this document, the concepts of communicating with graphics and visual imagery and with written language are integrated. An excerpt from the CEO statement is presented in Figure 6.7.

Figure 6.7 contains several elements of communicating effectively and efficiently. It contains the use of a numbered list to show the expected factors for future success. It incorporates a photograph of the CEO to convey a sense of congeniality and personable ambiance. Its opening statement, using larger, bold font, clearly acknowledges a downfall in corporate performance, whereas the succeeding statements lay the groundwork for future improvement. Figure 6.7 exhibits dark letters that contrast with a clear background, thereby improving the readability of the document. A margin note is used to denote and emphasize the key factors related to the future success of the organization in due time.

The bottom Figure 6.7 shows a graphic image of a line graph to visually and immediately convey performance information through time. Through the line graph, readers can view and understand the changes in performance that affected the corporation over time. Furthermore, the line graph conveys not only annual performance information but also the quarterly performance information of the organization. The use of the line graph reinforces the content expressed by the written language.

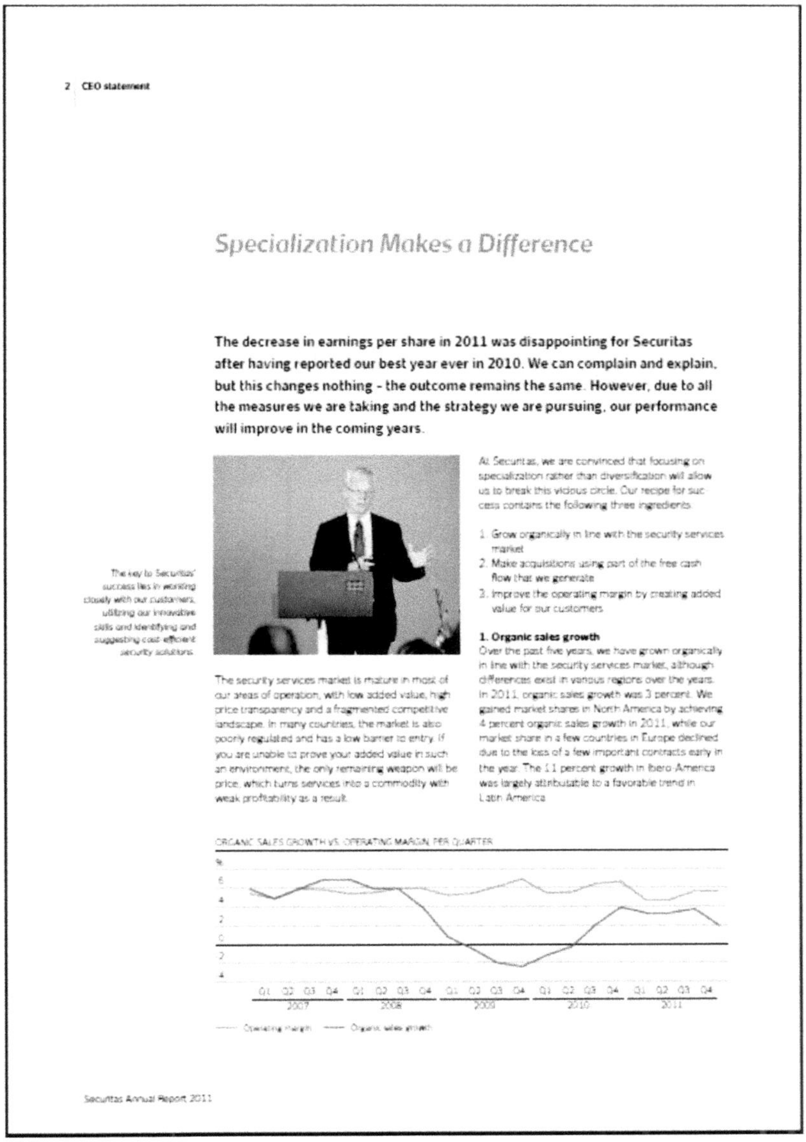

2 CEO statement

Specialization Makes a Difference

The decrease in earnings per share in 2011 was disappointing for Securitas after having reported our best year ever in 2010. We can complain and explain, but this changes nothing - the outcome remains the same. However, due to all the measures we are taking and the strategy we are pursuing, our performance will improve in the coming years.

The key to Securitas' success lies in working closely with our customers, utilizing our innovative skills and identifying and suggesting cost-efficient security solutions.

The security services market is mature in most of our areas of operation, with low added value, high price transparency and a fragmented competitive landscape. In many countries, the market is also poorly regulated and has a low barrier to entry. If you are unable to prove your added value in such an environment, the only remaining weapon will be price, which turns services into a commodity with weak profitability as a result.

At Securitas, we are convinced that focusing on specialization rather than diversification will allow us to break this vicious circle. Our recipe for success contains the following three ingredients:

1. Grow organically in line with the security services market
2. Make acquisitions using part of the free cash flow that we generate
3. Improve the operating margin by creating added value for our customers

1. Organic sales growth
Over the past five years, we have grown organically in line with the security services market, although differences exist in various regions over the years. In 2011, organic sales growth was 3 percent. We gained market shares in North America by achieving 4 percent organic sales growth in 2011, while our market share in a few countries in Europe declined due to the loss of a few important contracts early in the year. The 11 percent growth in Ibero-America was largely attributable to a favorable trend in Latin America.

Securitas Annual Report 2011

Figure 6.7 Excerpt from the 2011 Securitas Annual Report—CEO statement. (From 2011 Securitas Annual Report.)

The remainder of the report contains similar uses of graphic and visual resources to efficiently and effectively communicate the pertinent financial and accounting details of the organization. In Figure 6.8, another excerpt from the 2011 Securitas Annual Report shows the use of a tabular format to present financial information. In this case, contrasting colors are used within the tabular resource to show different categories of financial and accounting data. Additionally, the table shown in Figure 6.8 contains an appropriate header to denote its function and type of information conveyed. The text of the table shown in Figure 6.8 also contrasts with the clear background of the page, thereby enhancing the readability of the document.

These uses of graphics and visual resources instantly provide the details of financial and accounting data that are relevant to the consolidated statement of income. The various categories and their associated data contents are easily recognizable and viewable. The use

Annual Report 71
Consolidated financial statements

Securitas' financial model - consolidated statement of income

Supplementary information

MSEK	2011	2010	2009
Sales	58 995.6	59 097.5	61 216.7
Sales, acquired business	5 061.5	2 242.3	1 450.0
Total sales	**64 057.1**	**61 339.8**	**62 666.7**
Organic sales growth, %	*3*	*1*	*-1*
Production expenses	-52 977.4	-50 076.0	-50 983.9
Gross income	**11 079.7**	**11 263.8**	**11 682.8**
Gross margin, %	*17.3*	*18.4*	*18.6*
Expenses for branch offices	-3 621.2	-3 656.3	-3 822.2
Other selling and administrative expenses	-4 145.7	-3 895.0	-4 111.3
Total expenses	**-7 766.9**	**-7 551.3**	**-7 933.5**
Other operating income	74.3	12.7	11.3
Share in income of associated companies	-2.4	-1.0	-4.1
Operating income before amortization	**3 384.7**	**3 724.2**	**3 756.5**
Operating margin, %	*5.3*	*6.1*	*6.0*
Amortization of acquisition related intangible assets	-218.2	-164.3	-138.3
Acquisition related costs	-193.5	-89.6	-5.9
Operating income after amortization	**2 973.0**	**3 470.3**	**3 612.3**
Financial income and expenses	-493.0	-502.3	-589.8
Income before taxes	**2 480.0**	**2 968.0**	**3 022.5**
Net margin, %	*3.9*	*4.8*	*4.8*
Taxes	-741.4	-887.2	-904.5
Net income for the year	**1 738.6**	**2 080.8**	**2 118.0**

Operating items. Net debt-related items. Goodwill, taxes and non-operating items. Items related to shareholders' equity.

Securitas' financial model is described on pages 54–55.

Figure 6.8 Securitas 2011 Annual Report excerpt—consolidated data. (From 2011 Securitas Annual Report.)

of contrasting colors within the separate lines easily groups categories of data together. Therefore, readers experience less confusion when viewing the tabular graphic.

The Securitas Annual Report successfully leverages the characteristics of integrating graphic and visual resources with the written word to effectively and efficiently communicate with stakeholders and potential investors. The overall design of the document lends itself to a high level of readability and accessibility of information.

Quarterly Reports

Some corporate reports are issued with greater frequency than that of an annual report. Quarterly reports are issued four times per fiscal year. Their content is similar to that of an annual report but only considers the organizational performance that was exhibited during the preceding quarter of operations. An example of a quarterly report is that of the Corrections Corporation of America (CCA). Figure 6.9 shows an excerpt from the third-quarter 2012 CCA report.

This excerpt presents financial and accounting data using the traditional tabular format that is common among business settings. It is appropriately labeled at the top of the excerpt to denote is functional purpose involving data representing the condensed consolidated balance sheet. The columnar format facilitates the categorization of data chronologically across the considered quarterly period. Rows show the specific data fields and the corresponding data values.

CORRECTIONS CORPORATION OF AMERICA AND SUBSIDIARIES
CONDENSED CONSOLIDATED BALANCE SHEETS
(UNAUDITED AND AMOUNTS IN THOUSANDS, EXCEPT PER SHARE AMOUNTS)

ASSETS	September 30, 2012	December 31, 2011
Cash and cash equivalents	$ 59,242	$ 55,802
Accounts receivable, net of allowance of $1,155 and $1,218, respectively	239,233	269,685
Deferred tax assets	7,947	11,768
Prepaid expenses and other current assets	23,807	18,676
Current assets of discontinued operations	12	3,498
Total current assets	330,241	359,429
Property and equipment, net	2,582,019	2,608,740
Restricted cash	5,020	5,013
Investment in direct financing lease	7,928	9,233
Goodwill	11,988	11,988
Other assets	30,479	25,047
Non-current assets of discontinued operations	-	181
Total assets	$ 2,967,675	$ 3,019,631
LIABILITIES AND STOCKHOLDERS' EQUITY		
Accounts payable and accrued expenses	$ 171,048	$ 195,726
Income taxes payable	98	605
Current liabilities of discontinued operations	963	2,031
Total current liabilities	172,109	198,362
Long-term debt	1,131,152	1,245,014
Deferred tax liabilities	137,276	136,503
Other liabilities	35,060	31,730

Figure 6.9 CCA quarterly report excerpt. (From http://ir.correctionscorp.com/phoenix.zhtml?c=117983&p=irol-newsArticle&id=1755801.)

The graphic image leverages contrasting colors to improve readability. The use of dark text against a clear background sharply contrasts the written language with the background of the image. The use of bold text, denoting the latest quarter of performance results, gains and holds the attention of the reader. Overall, the presentation of quarterly information is very simple and straightforward. No excessive imagery or other embellishments exist to obscure the communicated message. Although the CCA excerpt differs from the Securitas example with respect to graphic and visual imagery, it still conveys effectively and efficiently its intended information.

Crime, Field, and Incident Reports

Among law enforcement agencies and within the justice system, a common type of report is the incident report (also referred to as a field report or crime report). This type of report is generally issued anytime an officer services a call for assistance in which public interaction is involved. The law enforcement organization retains a copy and the civilian that requested assistance also receives a copy. Figure 6.10 shows an incident report that may be used to report instances of hate crime.

Figure 1. Hate Crime Incident Report Form, Federal Bureau of Investigation

1-699 (Rev. 7-23-96)

Form Approval
OMB No. 1110-0015

HATE CRIME INCIDENT REPORT

Initial ☐ Adjustment ☐ ORI ☐☐☐☐☐☐☐☐☐ Date of Incident ___/___/___

Incident No. ☐☐☐☐☐☐☐☐☐☐☐☐ **Page** ☐ **of** ☐ **of Same Incident**

UCR Offense

	UCR Code	# of victims		UCR Code	# of victims
#1	☐☐	☐☐☐	#4	☐☐	☐☐☐
#2	☐☐	☐☐☐	#5	☐☐	☐☐☐
#3	☐☐	☐☐☐	#6	☐☐	☐☐☐

Offense Code

01 Murder
02 Forcible Rape
03 Robbery
04 Aggravated Assault
05 Burglary
06 Larceny-Theft
07 Motor Vehicle Theft
08 Arson
09 Simple Assault
10 Intimidation
11 Destruction/Damage/ Vandalism

Location *(Check one for Offense #1)*

01 ☐ Air/ Bus / Train Terminal
02 ☐ Bank / Savings and Loan
03 ☐ Bar / Night Club
04 ☐ Church / Synagogue / Temple
05 ☐ Commercial / Office Building
06 ☐ Construction Site
07 ☐ Convenience Store
08 ☐ Department / Discount Store
09 ☐ Drug Store / Dr.'s Office / Hospital
10 ☐ Field / Woods
11 ☐ Government / Public Building
12 ☐ Grocery / Supermarket
13 ☐ Highway / Road / Alley / Street
14 ☐ Hotel /Motel / etc.
15 ☐ Jail / Prison
16 ☐ Lake / Waterway
17 ☐ Liquor Store
18 ☐ Parking Lot / Garage
19 ☐ Rental Storage Facility
20 ☐ Residence / Home
21 ☐ Restaurant
22 ☐ School / College
23 ☐ Service / Gas Station
24 ☐ Specialty Store (TV, Fur, etc.)
25 ☐ Other / Unknown

Enter Location **Code** if Different from Offense #1

#2 ☐☐
#3 ☐☐
#4 ☐☐
#5 ☐☐
#6 ☐☐

Bias Motivation *(Check one for Offense #1)*

Racial
11 Anti-White
12 Anti-Black
13 Anti-American Indian/ Alaskan Native
14 Anti-Asian/Pacific Islander
15 Anti-Multi-Racial Group

Ethnicity/National Origin
32 Anti-Hispanic
33 Anti - Other Ethnicity/ National Origin
Specify __________

Religious
21 Anti-Jewish
22 Anti-Catholic
23 Anti-Protestant
24 Anti-Islamic (Moslem)
25 Anti-Other Religion
26 Anti-Multi-Religious Group
27 Anti-Atheism/Agnosticism

Sexual
41 Anti-Male Homosexual
42 Anti-Female Homosexual (Lesbian)
43 Anti-Homosexual (Gay & Lesbian)
44 Anti-Heterosexual
45 Anti-Bisexual

Disability
51 Anti-Physical Disability
52 Anti-Mental Disability

Enter Bias Motivation **Code** if Different from Offense #1

#2 ☐☐
#3 ☐☐
#4 ☐☐
#5 ☐☐
#6 ☐☐

Victim Type: For each offense code listed above, check all applicable victim types

Victim Type:	Offense Code #1	Offense Code #2	Offense Code #3	Offense Code #4	Offense Code #5	Offense Code #6		Offense Code #1	Offense Code #2	Offense Code #3	Offense Code #4	Offense Code #5	Offense Code #6
1. Individual*	☐	☐	☐	☐	☐	☐	1. Religious Organization	☐	☐	☐	☐	☐	☐
2. Business	☐	☐	☐	☐	☐	☐	2. Society	☐	☐	☐	☐	☐	☐
3. Financial Institution	☐	☐	☐	☐	☐	☐	3. Other	☐	☐	☐	☐	☐	☐
4. Government	☐	☐	☐	☐	☐	☐	4. Unknown	☐	☐	☐	☐	☐	☐

*Indicate the total number of individual victims involved in the incident. ☐☐☐

Number of Offenders ☐☐ **(Use "00" for "Unknown")**

Suspected Offender's Race as a Group (Check one)

1 ☐ White
2 ☐ Black
3 ☐ American Indian / Alaskan Native
4 ☐ Asian / Pacific Islander
5 ☐ Multi-Racial Group
6 ☐ Unknown

Figure 6.10 Incident report example. (From http://justice.uaa.alaska.edu/forum/18/1spring2001/a_hate.html.)

This report incorporates the use of graphic and visuals to improve communication. For example, square checkboxes are associated with various data fields to indicate exactly where individual characters are to be placed within the form. Square checkboxes are also used as tools through which the reporting officer may indicate a variety of data characteristics regarding the incident. For example, within the Victim Type section, the reporting officer can select the appropriate square to indicate the type of victim and the corresponding offense code.

The form also shows multiple categories in which related fields of data are grouped. Such grouping facilitates ease of entry of data within the form. It also minimizes the time necessary to locate a specific data field and its corresponding entry point. Within each category, the specific data fields are presented by using numbered lists to denote specific characteristics of the incident. Using such checkboxes interjects standardization within the form and limits the areas in which writing is supposed to occur.

The overall design of the form is concise. It facilitates a quick, efficient recording of data effectively. No embellishments are present that obscure the viewing of data categories. An understanding of the contents of the form may be gained by quickly scanning the responses indicated within the sectioned categories. The form consists of only one page, thereby eliminating the necessity of tracking multiple pages of an incident report that could be easily lost or misplaced before they are further processed within the justice system.

These notions are applicable to the designs of most incident reports used by law enforcement organizations. When servicing a call for assistance, law enforcement officers may have limited time or may work in adverse weather conditions. Forms must be designed to record data efficiently and effectively. The design of the form must also convey the recorded data efficiently and effectively. When an officer submits the incident report through the appropriate chain of command, transcriptionists must be able to quickly read the form and transcribe its contents into a database system for further processing within the justice system.

Some incident reports are not constrained to solely one page. Instead, some law enforcement organizations may use forms that involve multiple pages. When considering incident reports, the use of multiple pages increases the chance of items becoming lost or misplaced, thereby inciting a failure to communicate all of the pertinent data regarding the incident in a timely fashion.

Some incident reports contain sections in which officers may freely write the characteristics of the event or in which civilians may hand write a statement of their account of the incident. Although open sections may demonstrate the ability to collect additional details of the incident, they also interject noise within the communications domain because of difficulties associated with reading poor handwriting or when carbon copies fail to produce readable copies of the form.

Although the form presented in Figure 6.10 is in black and white, many incident reports consist of carbon-copied pages of different colors. For example, the responding officer may retain an original top, white copy; the civilian requesting assistance may be given a yellow carbon copy; and components of the justice system may be forwarded a pink carbon copy.

Regardless, in any case, incident reports serve a valuable purpose within the justice system. They represent an initial method of collecting data regarding the incident and communicating it through the succeeding components of the justice system. After data is recorded within the incident report, the report itself becomes an artifact that may be referenced at some future point during court proceedings.

Other Types of Reports

Many other report types exist. Because each department and organization has its own reporting policies and requirements, it is impossible to present an exhaustive consideration of additional reports. However, other forms of reporting include a variety of formal and informal reports. Such reports may be highly analytical and complex, or they may be operational and are used during the day-to-day operations of the organization.

Some municipalities may issue an annual departmental or organizational status report that may necessitate formal reporting practices. Other examples of formal reports may include some types of economic analysis to investigate the impacts of crime with respect to increases or decreases of law enforcement resources, forecasting to investigate and speculate the future needs of a municipality concerning its law enforcement resources, or composing reports that summarize the activities that occurred during the deployment of law enforcement resources during an actual emergency situation.

Two types of reports show high complexity and formality: analysis of strengths, weaknesses, opportunities, and threats (SWOT) and an after-action-review (AAR) that may be necessitated after serious incidents (e.g., flooding, chemical train explosions, terrorist events) that necessitate the deployment of law enforcement resources. Both SWOT analysis and the AAR may be used to examine the performance characteristics of an organization after an incident. Through the use of these items, organizations may improve the efficiency and effectiveness of their responses to both natural and man-made events.

Both SWOT and AAR reports may be lengthy and complex. They must be objective because their primary purpose is to yield information that will contribute to the bettering and improving of the organization. In some cases, they may be scathing when poor performance is observed and documented. Other reviews may be positive and recommend only minimal changes within the law enforcement organization. Regardless, both forms of reports are formal tools through which the efficiency and effectiveness of organizations may be improved.

Other forms of informal reports are diverse. Each law enforcement entity may have its own reporting requirements and policies that affect the types, styles, and quantities of reports that are submitted. For example, an organization may mandate that officers provide a hand signature within a personnel roster to signify their presence during shift meetings. Although it is a simple concept, the collection of signatures represents a report that informally communicates attendance. Some organizations may implement a sign-in/sign-out sheet for civilians who visit jails, when they arrive or depart a visiting area.

Regardless of the formalness of a report, its intended purpose is to communicate information. Some may be archived for long periods or they may be used immediately. Some may have long-term, strategic purposes (e.g., crafting of strategy) or others may serve operational purposes of the daily functioning of the organization (e.g., sign-in sheets). In any case, reports are tools through which organizations may express purposeful information to satisfy a variety of purposes.

Commentary Regarding Reporting in the Justice Domain

Reporting is nothing new. During the American Revolution, reports were passed along chains of command to facilitate a hierarchical flow of information for command and control purposes. Generals and their subordinate commanders shared information among themselves. For example, on Monday, April 28, 1777, at Morristown, General George Washington provided the following report to General McDougall (Baker, 1892):

> At three o'clock this morning, I received your favor of the 27th. The intelligence it contains is interesting and truly distressing. By this time, I fear the enemy have effected their purpose and destroyed all the stores at Danbury.

Even General Washington both received and gave reports. Since the colonial period, the need for effectively communicating organizationally and the necessity of sharing information both remain unabated. During modern times, law enforcement organizations communicate daily using a variety of modalities, and facilitate numerous reporting endeavors. Reporting occurs at all levels of organizations and affects all types of law enforcement entities.

Two famous reports are the report of the Warren Commission discussing the assassination of President John F. Kennedy and the 9/11 Commission Report. Both influenced American society and remain the subjects of much debate. Although the reports of most law enforcement organizations will neither achieve such notoriety nor spur national curiosity, their reports fulfill their unique requirements. Reporting is a common fact of life for law enforcement organizations and their personnel. The ability to communicate effectively and efficiently, through reports, is a skill that must be mastered by the individuals that comprise law enforcement organizations and the justice system.

Chapter Comments and Summary

This chapter introduced formal and informal methods of writing that permeate the justice system and law enforcement organizations. Formal report documents may be complex and lengthy. They may contain numbers sections, headings, and subheadings, and are generally accompanied by a transmittal letter. Conversely, informal reports can be quite simple and often may be expressed through a short letter or electronic mail note. Both formal and informal methods of reporting are methods through which communication occurs internally or externally among law enforcement organizations and the justice system.

Formal and informal writing may also encompass the expression of processes and procedures. This type of writing is instructional and informative, and expresses the steps that enable readers to accomplish some task or activity. Before expressing processes via written language, it is advisable to delineate the considered process within a flow chart as a method of showing the specific actions, decisions, and steps that comprise the process. After crafting the flow chart, it may be referred to when composing the steps of the process using written language. Care must be taken to ensure that the written language contains all of the correct steps sequenced chronologically. Process writing is useful when composing user manuals. A user manual communicates how to install, configure, operate, and maintain equipment.

A variety of other reports exist. From the organizational perspective, entities within the justice domain may issue annual reports that discuss the characteristics of their operations during the preceding year. Quarterly reports provide similar information, but only for the preceding quarter. Incident or field reports are issued when a law enforcement officer must service a call for assistance. Organizations may also have reports that are uniquely crafted to satisfy their respective needs.

Among reports, written language may be embellished by the use of graphic and visual resources. These items strengthen the conveyed message within the report, and allow readers to quickly gain an understanding of the discussed concepts. Basically, they reinforce the contents of the written language.

Reporting permeates the justice domain, and affects all law enforcement organizations and justice systems. Within American society, the use of reporting is historically seen in the writings of George Washington during his service in the American Revolution as a general officer. A need for reporting existed during his time period. Similarly, modern organizations also have a similar need for reporting. Although technologies have changed through time, the need for reporting communications through hierarchical chains of command is unchanged.

Terminology

AAR
Analysis
Annual report
Artifact
Bias
Clarity
Complexity
Concise
Constraints
Cover page
Field report
Form
Formal report
Graphic imagery
Historical
Incident report
Informal report
Instructions
Instructional documentation
Introduction section
List of figures
List of illustrations
List of tables
Methodology
Process
Qualitative
Quantitative
Quarterly report
Report
Research design
Scope and limitations
Transcription
User manual
Visual resource
SWOT

THOUGHT AND DISCUSSION QUESTIONS

1. View a copy of an incident report that is used by your local law enforcement organization. Compare and contrast it with the example presented herein. Discuss substantively the similarities and differences that are observable.
2. Interview your local law enforcement personnel to determine what types of formal reports they use regarding the functioning of the law enforcement organization. Discuss how these reports contribute to the functioning of the organization. Within your discussion, consider the chain of command that uses these reports.

3. Interview your local law enforcement personnel to determine what types of informal reports they use regarding the functioning of the law enforcement organization. Discuss how these reports contribute to the functioning of the organization. Within your discussion, consider the chain of command that uses these reports.
4. Interview your local law enforcement personnel to determine what kinds of equipment they use during a typical shift of work. If possible, view the user manuals that accompany these pieces of equipment. Discuss how these manuals effectively and efficiently present the methods through which pieces of equipment are installed, configured, operated, and maintained.

References

Alred, G., Brusaw, C., & Oliu, W. (2012). *Handbook of technical writing* (10th ed., p. 332). Boston: Bedford/St. Martin's Press.

Baker, W. (1892). *Itinerary of General Washington from June 15, 1775 to December 23, 1783* (p. 72). Philadelphia, PA: J. B. Lippincott Co.

Brigham, E., & Daves, P. (2010). *Intermediate financial management* (10th ed., p. 217). Mason, OH: South-Western Cengage Publishing.

Churchill, W. (n.d.). Report quotes. Retrieved from http://www.brainyquote.com/quotes/keywords/report.html (accessed December 13, 2012).

Guffey, M., & Almonte, R. (2010). *Essentials of business communication* (6th ed.). Toronto, Canada: Nelson Education.

Hammond, M., & Wellington, J. (2012). *Research methods: The key concepts* (p. 109). New York: Routledge Publishing.

Merriam-Webster Dictionary. (2012). s.v. "process." Retrieved from http://www.merriam-webster.com/dictionary/process (accessed December 12, 2012).

Rodriques, M. (1992). *Effective business communication* (p. 422). New Delhi, India: New Concept Publishing Company.

Rog, L., & Kropp, P. (2004). *The write genre: Classroom activities and mini-lessons that promote writing with clarity, style, and flashes of brilliance* (p. 127). Ontario, Canada: Markham Publishers.

Securitas Corporation. (2012). *Annual Report 2011*. Retrieved from http://www.securitas.com/Global/_DotCom/Annual%20reports/Annual_Report_2011.pdf (accessed June 5, 2014).

ToolingU. (2012). PLCs Training. Retrieved from http://www.toolingu.com/definition-450280-39961-user-manual.html (accessed December 13, 2012).

Oral Communications and Interpersonal Behaviors

7

There are two things that are more difficult than making an after-dinner speech: climbing a wall which is leaning toward you and kissing a girl who is leaning away from you.

—Winston Churchill (Churchill, n.d.)

Objectives

The objectives of this chapter are to

- Introduce the oral communications process
- Introduce persuading or informing verbally
- Introduce extemporaneous speeches
- Discuss truthfulness versus deception verbally
- Discuss oral communications in the justice domain

Introduction

Historically, before the advent of modern electronic technologies, television, telephones, and radio systems, written and auditory communications prevailed as the dominant forms of communication within the justice domain. During the colonial period, communicating orally was a necessary method of disseminating information among regions, locales, and people. Specifically, town criers were tasked with the responsibility of disseminating information orally. For example, town criers were "allowed to disturb the peace" after 9:00 p.m., and "only with official news" that had been previously authorized (Pencak, 2011).

During modern times, communicating orally is an innate characteristic of the justice domain. Attorneys argue in courtrooms to either prosecute or defend an individual, witnesses are verbally questioned and must provide verbal responses, judges provide oral instructions, and jurors debate what they heard through verbal discussions. When one makes a 911 telephone call, the request for assistance occurs orally. Dispatchers interact with members of the public and law enforcement personnel orally.

When touring a national park, park rangers conduct tours and verbally inform the audience regarding a variety of historical and current topics. The touring audience may interact with the park ranger by asking initial and follow-up questions. The park ranger guide answers these questions. The flow of such communication is both conversational and informative. In some cases, it may be entertaining especially when the speech is tailored for children. Interaction between the park ranger and the touring audience is usually informal and may involve nonverbal cues.

Communicating verbally occurs either between individuals or with audiences of varying size. Person-to-person contact occurs daily within the justice system. Attorneys ask questions of witnesses among courtrooms. Patrol officers verbally interact with motorists during traffic stops. Charitable events may necessitate a police chief or sheriff giving a speech to small or large audiences. During periods of calamity, municipal leaders may orally warn residents of impending dangers and provide informative statements regarding actions that are to be taken when necessary. Such oral messages may be disseminated through the use of radio systems or television stations.

Debating occurs frequently during political campaigns. Among locales where constables, police chiefs, or sheriffs are elected by the populace, spirited debates may occur among the candidates. In such cases, the verbal communication may be both informative and persuasive. Candidates attempt to inform an audience regarding their viewpoints and beliefs regarding certain issues that affect the public, and attempt to persuade people to vote for them.

Communicating verbally also necessitates a consideration of human behavior. The body language of listeners provides cues regarding their perceptions when hearing speeches. Although this type of audience feedback is silent, it provides valuable information for speakers. Through the provision of such feedback, speakers may adjust their delivery of the speech to affect the audience.

Verbal communications are powerful. Judges may read aloud jury verdicts that sentence someone to death row or they may pronounce someone as being found not guilty of a criminal offense. Such announcements may invoke depression and shock, or they may incite shouts of joy within a court setting. These scenarios may elicit verbal comments either affirming or condemning the outcome.

Certainly, many more examples of oral communication may be identified and considered within the contexts of the justice system and law enforcement organizations. Verbal communications affects every facet of policing and every case that is processed within the justice system. Verbal communications are innate communication methods within the justice system and law enforcement organizations, and are probably the most dominant form of communication among these domains. Figure 7.1 shows U.S. Supreme Court Chief Justice John Roberts giving a speech.

Figure 7.1 U.S. Supreme Court Chief Justice John Roberts delivering a commencement address at Georgetown University. (From http://www.c-spanvideo.org/program/192685-1.)

Oral Communications Process

Chapter 4 introduced the writing process through which written communications are crafted. Similarly, formal settings and occasions may necessitate crafting oral communications through a methodical process. Informal settings and occasions may be appropriate for an extemporaneous speech. Regardless of the situation, some varying amounts of thoughtfulness affect the crafting of oral communications whether they are targeted for a formal event (e.g., retirement ceremonies) or arise as an impromptu conversation near the departmental water cooler.

Every person is unique. Individuals may have different writing styles and methods of expressing themselves when communicating. This notion also applies to the crafting of oral communications. Some people may benefit from using a complex process to author speeches, whereas others may prefer less structure. Some people may prefer to use lengthy outlines that contain a significant quantity of topics, whereas others may prefer to use only note cards containing only bulleted lists. Some people may prefer brainstorming for ideas when crafting oral communications, whereas others exercise meticulous research. Given these notions, different people may craft oral communications using different methods.

Despite these differences, a methodical process can be identified and expressed through which oral communications may be crafted. Within the context of a formal situation, the crafting of oral communication often involves a methodical process. The steps of such a process are expressed as follows:

1. Analysis of the audience
2. Requirements
3. Design
4. Development
5. Testing
6. Delivery
7. Feedback

Analysis of the Audience

After one is invited, is ordered or directed, or has volunteered to speak before a group, some knowledge of the expected audience is necessary to influence the crafting of the intended speech. Before crafting oral communications, several queries may be contemplated to gain an understanding of the expected audience. Some points to remember when crafting oral communications include the following items:

Demographics: What are the demographics of the intended audience? Are they senior citizens or high school students? Are they white-collar professionals or blue-collar workers? Are they employed or unemployed?

Interest level: Will the audience be interested? Are they required to attend the speech or did they freely choose to attend? Is the interest level anticipated to be merely cursory or will it be a strong interest?

Knowledge level: What level of knowledge is the audience expected to have? Are they to be experts or novices? Are they experienced or inexperienced? Does the knowledge level vary among these categories?

Affiliations: What audience affiliations exist? Are they peer colleagues or do they represent an unrelated vocation or profession? Is there any commonness with the expected audience?
Attitudes: Does the audience favor or disfavor a certain topic? Does the audience have any reason to unjustly scrutinize the speaker or will it be amiable?
Setting and venue: Will the audience be seated or standing? Will it be formal or informal? Will the audience be indoors or outdoors?

Certainly, many more points and associated questions may be imagined. Some thought will generate additional questions within each of these categories. Before designing any type of oral communication, speakers must have a basic understanding of the characteristics of the intended audience. Speakers must carefully avoid stereotyping the audience. Stereotyping is the assumption that "all members of a group have similar behaviors or beliefs simply because they belong to the group" (Verderber, Sellnow, & Verdeber, 2012, p. 64).

Various sources may be used to investigate these questions. Surveys, talking with the person that invited the speaker, and talking with others who have already spoke before the group are sources of information. The questions contained within these items are sufficient for speakers to begin conceptualizing the initial requirements and designs for oral communications.

Requirements

An understanding of the primary questions contained within the audience analysis enables speakers to specify the requirements for the intended oral communications. However, besides the audience analysis, some additional information is required to establish a strong set of requirements for the speech. Some points to remember when establishing requirements include the following items:

Emphasis: Does the intended oral communication inform, entertain, or persuade?
Purpose: Why is the oral communication occurring? Is this a special occasion? If so, what type of occasion?
Topic: What is the whole point of the oral communication? After understanding the purpose and emphasis, one must identify the main theme of the oral communication. The main theme can usually be expressed with a single sentence for clarity. This item should involve determining the major point of the intended communication.
Subtopics: Once the major point of the intended communication is established, any supporting subtopics should be identified. These items address the secondary and tertiary points of the intended oral communication.
Research: Performing research to gain an understanding of the subject of the intended communication. It involves a variety of questions regarding the major point of the intended oral communication. What is the background of the issue? Why is the major point an issue? What statistics can be included? What are the consequences? What has already been accomplished? What benefits may be derived? What alternatives are available?

Sponsors: Some events have sponsors. Determine whether any sponsors must be mentioned and credited. Any mentioning of sponsors may occur, and the beginning or the ending of an oral communication.

Environment: Environmental characteristics may affect both the speaker and the audience. Examples include speaking in light versus dark settings; day versus night hours; controlled or uncontrolled temperatures; speaking before, during, or after a meal; weather conditions; and so forth.

Time: Will the oral communication occur during morning, noon, or night hours? What is the scheduled time to begin? If using video conferencing, one must also consider time differences when different time zones are involved.

Constraints: What are the constraining factors that affect speaking? What is the maximum length of time for the talk? Is there a minimum length of time for the talk? Are there budgetary constraints? Are there any physical limitations of the environment? Are there any subjects to include or avoid? Are there any equipment constraints?

Technology and equipment: What technological resources are available? Are computers, projectors, and screens available? Are laser pointers available? Are conferencing resources available? Are recording resources available? Are microphones available? Is a podium or lectern available?

Supplemental materials: Are any supplemental materials required? Are graphic and visual resources necessary? Are handouts of presentation slides necessary? Are door prizes necessary? If presenting awards or certificates, are they available?

Interaction: Is audience participation permissible? When are questions and answers hosted? Is audience interaction necessary? Is the event a closed or open forum?

Certainly, many more questions may be imagined and expressed within all of these categories. Answering these questions provides information from which a baseline set of requirements can be crafted. Establishing a strong set of requirements helps speakers to adjust and tune the design of their oral communications to maximize the effectiveness and the efficiency of the oral communication.

Design

Design is defined as the "clarity of the organizational pattern used by the speaker" (Steinberg, 2000). The design of the speech is fashioned according to the stated requirements of the anticipated oral communication. Designing oral communication includes a variety of functions and related activities through which an initial framework of the intended speech is produced. Activities that contribute to designing the oral communication include the following:

Organization: This activity consists of identifying the primary concepts that are part of the cumulative oral communication. The sequential ordering of these concepts should be specified. Consideration should be given to the preamble, introduction, supporting points, closure, and follow-up components of the oral communication.

Outlining: This activity expands on the sequencing of concepts. The outlining methods presented within Chapter 2 are acceptable methods of crafting this outline.

This activity involves stating the major point and supporting points using a written outline format. It incorporates any research items that are necessary to support the major point and subpoints. It shows the logical ordering of topics, represents continuance and transitional flows, and serves the purpose of expressing the organization of the oral communication.

Planning visual and auditory resources: This activity uses the generated outline to determine where and when visual and auditory resources are necessary within the oral communication. It also must include a consideration of the types and ordering of presentation slides that are used when speaking. This activity complements the planning of equipment and technological resources.

Planning equipment and technological resources: This activity accommodates the availability of technology and equipment during the oral communication. It ensures the compatibility of software items and hardware items. It considers the types and sizes of sound systems that are necessary for speaking. It considers the video resources that are necessary for showing any supplemental films or videos. This activity complements the designing of visual and graphic resources.

Planning supplements: This activity accommodates the designing of supplemental materials. For example, if audience handouts of presentation materials are necessary, will they be color or black-and-white copies? How many copies are necessary? How many slides are printed on a page of paper? Colors and fonts should also be contemplated when designing supplemental materials.

Quality and feedback: After an initial design is specified, some measures of quality and feedback must be effected to improve the overall design. Quality and feedback ensure that the design conforms to the specifications that are contained within the requirements. Checklists may be used to determine whether all of the necessary items were incorporated within the outlined contents of the speech. Peer review may provide critical feedback and commentaries that may be used to improve the outline.

This phase must produce a design that adheres to any constraints that were specified within the requirements. Basically, it leverages the outcome of the requirements phase to produce a viable construct that serves as a blueprint for developing the presentation of the oral communication. Therefore, meticulous planning must occur to ensure the development of a presentation and oral communication that exhibit high levels of quality.

Development

The development phase involves the full construction of the oral communication and its supplements. It uses the blueprint outline that was fashioned in the design phase, and expounds on it to generate a full-length speech and presentation materials. Development uses the fashioned outline to produce a complete, written document that represents the full text of the oral communication. It uses the fashioned design of graphic and visual resources to produce graphic and visual resources that will be used during the actual speaking. Development also encompasses the crafting of any ancillary items that may be disseminated during a presentation, briefing, or speech, such as handouts.

Quality and feedback are also pertinent considerations of development. After the initial draft of the actual oral communication and its supplementary materials are developed, they may undergo various revisions. Speakers must ensure that spelling errors are absent within the written speech, and that it includes all of the necessary topics and information. Speakers must ensure that their speech conveys the intended information, and that they have an understanding of the correct pronouncements of words and phrases.

A peer review of the output of this phase embellishes quality. Feedback may be solicited to generate comments and observations that may be used to improve the quality of the products. Numerous editors may be used to examine the syntax and semantics of language and to ensure that appropriate content exists within the written speech. Peer review may also ensure that the developed speech and supplements conform to the specifications that are delineated within the requirements document.

Testing and Rehearsing

Integration testing and systems testing embellish considerations of quality before the final product is approved and released for implementation (Stair & Reynolds, 2010). These notions are useful when crafting oral communications. After a written speech and its supplemental materials are developed, they must exhibit characteristics of quality. Testing and rehearsing are methods through which quality goals may be achieved.

Speakers may desire to test their speech before a sample audience before the actual speaking event occurs. This audience may be composed of just about anyone ranging from off-duty police personnel to the members of the speaker's family. If possible, the speaker should attempt to test the implementation of the oral communication in the actual venue or a similar venue before the speaking event occurs. Doing so will incite a sense of familiarity with the setting and will facilitate an awareness of the setting in the mind of the speaker. This form of testing also allows the speaker to practice using any technology and equipment items that are necessary during the delivery of the intended speech.

Rehearsing a speech repetitively is essential with respect to improving the potential effectiveness of the oral communication (Verderber, Verderber, & Sellnow, 2012). Speakers should record and review their delivery of the intended speech multiple times (Verderber, Verderber et al., 2012). When a speaker hears the recording, any impediments, errors of phrasing, or mispronunciations may be discovered and corrected. Frequent rehearsals also increase the speaker's familiarity with the contents and improve the ability to recall memorable information. Such practice also helps speakers adjust their presentation so that it conforms to any time constraints.

Speakers may also rehearse their speeches in a variety of ways. Some people may rehearse using a mirror, whereas others may simply practice while imagining an audience in their living rooms. Regardless of the available resources, rehearsing any intended oral communication is necessary for refining delivery skills and for improving one's familiarity with the intended materials. Figure 7.2 shows someone rehearsing while using a washroom mirror.

Testing and rehearsing also improve the quality of visual and graphic resources. A sample audience should be able to indicate whether imagery is clear and large enough to be viewed satisfactorily when projected against a screen. The feedback from a sample audience should also indicate whether colors sufficiently contrast so that written text is clearly and easily readable.

Testing and rehearsing provide an integrative, systemic approach to improving the presentation before the actual oral communication occurs. Through these activities, speakers

Figure 7.2 Using a mirror to practice oral communication. (From http://www.masterfile.com/stock-photography/image/649-01610217/Man-practicing- speech-in-office-washroom-mirror.)

must not only practice communicating orally but must also improve their ability to multitask by using equipment and any other pertinent resources simultaneously. These activities also improve the ability of the speaker to effectively and efficiently blend the tangible and intangible attributes of presentation to convey the intended message. Through practice and rehearsal, speakers may master the characteristics of delivery that affect the actual event.

Delivery

The completion of the quality phase generates a product that may be presented orally. Delivering oral communications is defined as how "a message is communicated orally and visually through" the uses of both "voice and body" (Verderber, Sellnow et al., 2012, p. 206). Although one may have a quality speech and excellent supporting materials, humans may experience difficulty when presenting orally. Glossophobia is a human fallibility that impedes the ability to publically speak in front of others (i.e., fear of public speaking) (Tofanelli, 2012). Essentially, it is speech anxiety (Tofanelli, 2012).

Various methods exist to counter the negative effects of speech anxiety. Nervousness should be viewed as a positive feeling that incites an attitude of excitement regarding the speech (Bovee, 2003). Speakers should focus their mind toward conveying the content of the intended message (Bovee, 2003). Frequently rehearsing and practicing the speech, visualizing successfulness, and projecting a countenance of confidence may also alleviate feelings of anxiety (Bovee, 2003). An old adage says that practice makes perfect. The one more speaks in public, the more one becomes comfortable when speaking in front of others. Therefore, the level of comfortableness increases with experience. Speakers desiring to diminish the effects of glossophobia should seek and pursue numerous opportunities to publically speak in front of others (Bovee, 2003).

Other methods exist through which the effects of speech anxiety may be diminished. Maintaining eye contact with the members of the audience also may embellish the ability to speak in public (Bovee, 2003). Eye contact with others should be maintained for a period ranging between five to seven seconds per individual (Acello, 2005). Being enthusiastic about the topic and event is important because "enthusiasm can replace fear" when speaking publically (Kline, 2001). Having a good attitude toward the listening audience also may alleviate speech anxiety. Speakers should remember that listeners are the same folks with whom they would probably converse normally within informal settings, and that they have some amount of empathy for the speaker (Kline, 2001). Breathing deeply and speaking slowly may also be beneficial practices (Kline, 2001).

The characteristics of body language also may influence oral communications. Approximately 90% of what people perceive during oral communications is expressed through body language, whereas the remaining 10% is attributed to the "actual words" used during communication (Mathew, 2011). Body language represents a form of unknowingly influencing communications subconsciously. As a form of body language, the use of calculated pauses give speakers "a chance to breathe deeply," may incite relaxation, and help to "pace the speech well" (Dowis, 2000).

Other nonverbal factors affect the communications domain when presenting orally. Facial expressions also affect the conveyance of the intended message. Facial expressions include movements of eyes, eyebrows, and mouth to convey emotions and reactions (Griffin, 2009). Speakers can use facial expressions to communicate their interest in the subject matter, disagreement or agreement with various discussion points, attitude toward ideas, and "feelings about an issue" (Griffin, 2009).

The choice of clothing also influences the delivery of oral communications subconsciously. Shirts and trousers must be clean, neat, pressed, and creased. Ties should be straight with a full knot, and collar material should not be seen above the knot of the tie. A tie clasp or tie tack should be used to hold the necktie in place. Tie lengths should not appear as being too long or too short. Gig lines, aligning the trouser fly, shirt, and edge of the belt buckle, must always be straight. Among formal settings, the choice of clothing must express professionalism. Individuals should inspect themselves before conducting any type of oral communication involving an audience to ensure they are neat and groomed.

Audience interaction may be part of oral communications depending on the formality of the situation. Depending on the scenario, audience members may be requested to ask questions at the end of the delivery or may be allowed to ask questions during the delivery. The former method allows a speaker to complete a speech within any time constraints, whereas the latter method may increase the time required to deliver a speech.

Many other factors may positively or negatively affect the delivery of oral communications (e.g., posture and presence). It is beyond the scope of this introductory text to consider an exhaustive array of such factors. Readers are encouraged to consult other literature sources that address the psychological and material aspects of public speaking for lengthier discussions of these concepts.

Delivering oral communications embodies numerous complexities of tangible and intangible characteristics that affect the communications domain. Everything from a personal fear of speaking in front of others to the personal appearance of a speaker affects oral communications. Taking advantage of speaking opportunities improves the skills of a speaker through time, and allows speakers to alter their personal appearances to enhance the subconscious aspects of communication. Additional improvements may be facilitated through the use of audience feedback.

Feedback

Feedback is defined as the transmission of any "evaluative or corrective information about an action, event, or process to the original or controlling source" (*Merriam-Webster*, 2012a). Simply, feedback occurs when a speaker requests that the audience provide information regarding the oral communication, and receives the requested information shortly thereafter. Feedback is a mechanism through which future presentations may be improved by examining the information that is collected from an audience.

Feedback may be collected by disseminating a survey to the audience. Various questions may address perceptions regarding the topic, the attributes of the speech, the attributes of the setting and environment, the attributes of the graphic and visual materials, and the attributes of the speaker. Surveys may poll an audience regarding its perceptions of any number of other factors. Surveys may be conducted online via the Internet or may be physically disseminated to an audience immediately after the presentation.

Another method of obtaining feedback may be to talk directly with members of the audience after the presentation is completed. This type of communication becomes more personal, and facilitates a conversational style of questioning. Queries may be open-ended, thereby allowing respondents an opportunity to express themselves fully. Speakers, in turn, may ask follow-up questions to investigate further any given responses.

Feedback should not be considered a punitive or negative activity. Instead, it should be perceived as an act through which valuable information is obtained that may be used to alter the characteristics of the speaker, the presentation, any supplementary materials, or any aspect of the speech for improvement purposes. Essentially, the use of feedback is a measure through which the overall quality of oral communications may be improved through time.

Speaking Paradigms

Oral communication encompasses three paradigms: informing, persuading, and entertaining. Informing consists of conveying messages that are informational. For example, during a press conference, a police chief may periodically inform the public regarding the status of an ongoing manhunt, issue a safety warning, and describe the physical appearance and last known location of a wanted individual. Oral persuasion represents an attempt to alter the opinions and behaviors of individuals or groups. Certainly, radio commercials and individuals speaking at public events to advocate deterring drug use or seat belt use both involve persuasive speaking. The basic concepts of informative and persuasive methods were presented in Chapter 3.

The third paradigm, entertaining, may seem odd within the context of the justice domain. However, speaking to entertain may be considered within the contexts of the justice system and law enforcement organizations. Entities within the justice system often provide speakers for events involving young children. In such cases, personnel may need to convey messages through entertaining speeches that hold the attention of youths. For example, personnel may wear Smokey Bear or Ranger Smith costumes and use humor when orally delivering public safety messages within school settings.

Logical Arguments

Chapter 3 also introduced the basic concepts of logical arguments (i.e., logos, pathos, and ethos). These concepts are also applicable within the context of oral communications. Speakers may need to establish some commonness with their audience or establish themselves as experts within a domain. Before giving a speech, speakers may briefly review their credentials as a method of indicating their expertise and knowledge. Doing so may embellish perceptions of credibility regarding the speaker. When speaking, one may invoke an emotional appeal to incite some type of public reaction (e.g., calming and dispersing crowds). Law enforcement personnel may opt to use integrative, logical arguments to persuade the crowd to calm and disperse.

Effective Language

The ability to use language effectively is a paramount consideration of oral communications. Regardless of the topic or venue, the speaker must be mindful of the phrases and words that are contained within speeches or other forms of oral communication. Some typical considerations of the effective use of language are given as follows:

- Grammar and vocabulary should match the audience and the occasion, and should be adapted to suit the demographic characteristics of the audience (Jaffe, 2007). Speaking in front of a group of well-educated physicians necessitates a different level of vocabulary than does speaking in front of automobile mechanics whose formal education may be limited.
- Demeaning language and profanity should be omitted when speaking publically (Jaffe, 2007).
- Words and phrases must be understandable, and terms that are familiar to audiences should be used (Jaffe, 2007).
- Slang should either be omitted or minimized (Jaffe, 2007). Public venues reflect a higher level of formality than do "everyday" interactions and conversations between individuals (Jaffe, 2007).
- Increasing the clarity of communicating orally may be accomplished by avoiding extreme generalizations (Wood, 2009).
- Words should be correctly pronounced, the tone of voice should be altered as necessary, and stalling tactics should be avoided (Hayes & Ninemeier, 2009). Stalling tactics consists of expressions that generate thinking time, show nervousness or unpreparedness, or make the speaker seem unprofessional. Examples include phrases such as "like, you know" and use of "ummmm" or "ahhhh" when speaking (Hayes & Ninemeier, 2009).

Extemporaneous Communication

The oral communications process is certainly appropriate for constructing oral presentations and supplemental materials that represent a structured approach to crafting communication. However, there are times when communication may be less structured or even unstructured. In such cases, an extemporaneous delivery of the intended speech occurs. An extemporaneous speech is defined as "one where the ideas are prepared, but the language is definitely composed only at the moment of delivery" (Gupit, 1986).

Extemporaneous speeches are neither memorized nor read from a written version (Gupit, 1986). The delivery of an extemporaneous speech occurs either with or without the use of notations (Gupit, 1986). If notations are unused, then the speaker must have a good memory to recall the sequencing of the points that are to be discussed within the speech (Gupit, 1986). In some cases, this type of speaking exhibits an advantage of "spontaneity and naturalness" without seeming disorderly (Gupit, 1986).

Speaking Organizations and Training

The improvement of speaking skills requires time, effort, and practice. All speakers have some area(s) in which they can improve their oral communications skills. Various organizations and training programs exist through which individuals can improve their skills and gain experience speaking in front of others. Some of these organizations are local groups of enthusiasts, whereas others involve nationally recognized entities. Examples include Toastmasters International and the National Speakers Association.

Both organizations provide ample opportunities for speaking practice. Toastmasters International has approximately 280,000 members distributed among "13,500 clubs in 116 countries" (Toastmasters International, 2012). Participating in Toastmasters International provides opportunities to "give impromptu talks on assigned topics, conduct meetings, and develop skills related to timekeeping, grammar and parliamentary procedure" (Toastmasters International, 2012). The National Speakers Association provides similar opportunities but is targeted toward subject matter experts. Within the United States, the organization has chapters "in most major markets" (National Speakers Association, 2012). It attempts to improve speaking skills in the areas of eloquence, expertise, enterprise, and ethics (National Speakers Association, 2012).

Novice speakers that wish to improve their skills may find Toastmasters International to be a beneficial starting point through which they may gain experience and sharpen their skills. After gaining some experience, specific domain knowledge, and notoriety, one may consider an affiliation with the National Speakers Association. Practice is essential when attempting to improve speaking skills. Law enforcement personnel desiring to enhance their speaking abilities may wish to explore the opportunities offered by these (and other) organizations.

Oral Communication, the U.S. Constitution, and the Justice System

Oral communication is common within all professions whether it occurs between individuals or involves some form of group presentation. Oral communication pervades every facet of modern society. These notions affect the justice domain. The components of the justice system communicate both internally and externally. Any oral communications occurring within the justice system must be commensurate with expressed laws. Various amendments of the U.S. Constitution influence both policing and the justice system. Specifically, the First, Fourth, Fifth, Sixth, and Fourteenth Amendments have implications for speech and oral communications.

The First Amendment guarantees the right of having the freedom of speech within American society. The First Amendment is stated as follows:

> Congress shall make no law respecting an establishment of religion, or prohibiting the free exercise thereof; or abridging the freedom of speech, or of the press; or the right of the people peaceably to assemble, and to petition the Government for a redress of grievances. (National Archives, 2012)

This right facilitates the freedom of expression without vast government restraints or limitations (Legal Information Institute, 2012). In some cases, in which speech may "cause a breach of the peace or cause violence," government interference may be necessary (Legal Information Institute, 2012). When these scenarios occur, the government must render "substantial justification" for its actions limiting free speech (Legal Information Institute, 2012). The classic example of yelling "fire" in a crowded theatre is the primary example of this concept.

The Fourth Amendment guarantees various rights. These rights include being secure from "unreasonable searches and seizures" by the government unless "probable cause" exists to justify the issuing of a warrant (National Archives, 2012). The invoking of such a warrant is preceded by an "Oath or affirmation, and particularly describing the place to be searched, and the persons or things to be seized" (National Archives, 2012). Such oaths or affirmations may be expressed orally and later expressed through writing. The Fourth Amendment is stated as follows:

> The right of the people to be secure in their persons, houses, papers, and effects, against unreasonable searches and seizures, shall not be violated, and no Warrants shall issue, but upon probable cause, supported by Oath or affirmation, and particularly describing the place to be searched, and the persons or things to be seized. (National Archives, 2012)

Contacting a judge to obtain a search warrant may necessitate a visit with the judge by law enforcement personnel to request a search warrant. This meeting may involve short or long discussions that occur personally and verbally, thereby representing oral communication. After the reasoning supporting the request for a warrant is explained orally, the salient points of reasoning may be expressed via written statements. This scenario represents an instance in which oral communication is necessary to initially begin the process of obtaining a search warrant.

When considering allegations of a very serious nature, the Fifth Amendment guarantees the use of a Grand Jury before one is summoned before a court, and guarantees protectiveness against self-incrimination. The protections of the Fifth Amendment are commonly known as the right to silence. The Fifth Amendment is stated as follows:

> No person shall be held to answer for a capital, or otherwise infamous crime, unless on a presentment or indictment of a Grand Jury, except in cases arising in the land or naval forces, or in the Militia, when in actual service in time of War or public danger; nor shall any person be subject for the same offence to be twice put in jeopardy of life or limb; nor shall be compelled in any criminal case to be a witness against himself, nor be deprived of life, liberty, or property, without due process of law; nor shall private property be taken for public use, without just compensation. (National Archives, 2012)

The Fifth Amendment is profound within the context of the justice domain. Although individuals may be questioned during criminal case proceedings, they may invoke the

Fifth Amendment to avoid incriminating themselves. However, any invoking of the Fifth Amendment is specific to the allegations of a certain offense. This issue was addressed in 1990 during 501 U.S. 171, *McNeil v. Wisconsin*. Specifically, this court case showed that invoking the "Fifth Amendment right to remain silent with regard to a particular offense does not constitute an invocation for other offenses for which the suspect has not yet been charged" and that the "right against self-incrimination is specific to an offense" (Becker & Dutelle, 2013).

The Sixth Amendment guarantees the right of being informed of any allegations that may be leveled against someone and to be confronted by any witnesses regarding the issues associated with the allegations. The Sixth Amendment is stated as follows:

> In all criminal prosecutions, the accused shall enjoy the right to a speedy and public trial, by an impartial jury of the State and district wherein the crime shall have been committed, which district shall have been previously ascertained by law, and to be informed of the nature and cause of the accusation; to be confronted with the witnesses against him; to have compulsory process for obtaining witnesses in his favor, and to have the Assistance of Counsel for his defence. (National Archives, 2012)

Certainly, one may be served with a written court summons via a process server and various types of warrants may be expressed through written language. The use of oral communication may complement these written expressions. For example, when serving a warrant or summons, law enforcement personnel may orally inform the suspect of the existence of the warrant or summons and the contents of the documents. Witnesses may present oral testimony publically within court settings, and may be orally examined by attorneys representing both the prosecution and the defense.

The Fourteenth Amendment contains five sections, one of which accommodates some aspect of oral communication. Section 3 of the Fourteenth Amendment is stated as follows:

> No person shall be a Senator or Representative in Congress, or elector of President and Vice-President, or hold any office, civil or military, under the United States, or under any State, who, having previously taken an oath, as a member of Congress, or as an officer of the United States, or as a member of any State legislature, or as an executive or judicial officer of any State, to support the Constitution of the United States, shall have engaged in insurrection or rebellion against the same, or given aid or comfort to the enemies thereof. But Congress may by a vote of two-thirds of each House, remove such disability. (Archives.gov, 2012)

The Fourteenth Amendment specifies various oaths and qualifications that are necessary for entering public office. An oath is "a solemn usually formal calling upon God or a god to witness to the truth of what one says or to witness that one sincerely intends to do what one says" and is a "solemn attestation of the truth or inviolability of one's words" (*Merriam-Webster*, 2012c). Fox example, when one accepts an appointment as a commissioned officer within the U.S. Army, the following oath is administered:

> I, <Name>, having been appointed an officer in the Army of the United States, as indicated above in the grade of <Grade> do solemnly swear (or affirm) that I will defend the Constitution of the United States against all enemies, foreign or domestic, that I will bear true faith and allegiance to the same; that I take this obligation freely, without any mental reservations or purpose of evasion; and that I will well and faithfully discharge the duties of the office upon which I am about to enter; so help me God. (Morris, 2010)

Figure 7.3 Administration of the U.S. Army commissioning oath. (From http://www.army.mil/media/304778.)

This oath is administered orally. After completing this oath, army officers have a fiduciary obligation of accountability to the "American people" and the "military profession" (Felice, 2009). It orally expresses the transitioning "from civilian to solider," and signifies the acceptance of "both the duty to obey orders and the duty to obey the Constitution" (Felice, 2009). Administering this oath orally represents the "legal and moral" obligations of the commissioned officer to adhere to military rules and constitutional defense (Felice, 2009). Figure 7.3 shows the administration of the commissioning oath.

Both civilian and military organizations must adhere to the restraints of the U.S. Constitution. The deeds of any law enforcement organization or personnel, whether civilian or military, must be constitutional. With respect to the notion of oral communication, many actions that occur with the justice domain are verbal. All these verbal actions, whether they involve witness questioning during court proceedings or entering the military, must conform to the principles established within the U.S. Constitution.

Policing and Oral Communication

Oral communication affects the daily activities of policing. It ranges from talking with citizens during traffic stops or community events to ordering suspects to submit to police authority during emergency situations. Traffic stops and traffic control points (TCPs) can be very dangerous. Any call for assistance has the potential to develop into a scenario in which human life may be threatened. Although a scene may seem innocuous upon the initial arrival of law enforcement personnel, there is no guarantee that the circumstances will not become very dangerous.

The initial arrival of an officer at the scene of an incident or a TCP communicates the presence of law enforcement personnel. People generally recognize the message conveyed by flashing blue lights or a uniformed officer. Once a law enforcement officer engages in oral communication, the law enforcement officer may use spoken language to generate compliance. For example, terms such as "hands in the air," "freeze," and "don't move" are verbal commands that represent "the least forceful method of gaining subject compliance" (O'Brien, 2008). Others may be phrased within simple conversations that occur during public interaction. A classic example involves the law enforcement officer asking a motorist for a driver's license, proof of insurance, and registration.

Such verbal commands represent a method of attempting concise and clear communications. The use of verbal commands is a method of attempting to manage the behavior of the subject (Machovec, 2006). These commands may be issued softly or loudly; may be "friendly, firm, or authoritative"; and may be complemented by nonverbal gestures (e.g., waving a hand) (Machovec, 2006). Both the feasibility and the clarity of oral commands are salient attributes of "eliciting compliance" (Schwarzkopf et al., 2008). Failing to orally communicate concisely and clearly tends to "exacerbate negative interactions" (Schwarzkopf et al., 2008). Such failure then necessitates a greater level of forcefulness to obtain the compliance of the subject (Alpert & Dunham, 2004).

Another aspect of policing and oral communication involves deception and untruthfulness. Polygraph examinations may be administered to individuals who are attempting to secure employment with law enforcement organizations and to suspects who are being investigated by law enforcement organizations. A polygraph machine is a "scientifically calibrated instrument that records physiological changes in respiration (pneumograph), electrical resistance of the skin (galvanograph), and changes in blood pressure and pulse rate (cardiosphygmograph)" (Conser, Paynich, & Gingerich, 2013). These three forms of measurement data are independently recorded via the use of "three pen-like devices on graph paper" within the polygraph machine (Conser et al., 2013).

Two types of polygraph testing exist: the Control Question Test (CQT) and the Guilty Knowledge Test (GKT). The CQT uses a series of control questions that are "designed to tap a probable lie" (Rogers, 2008). The scoring of the CQT involves a consideration that innocent people may be concerned with the likelihood of lying during the asking of a preliminary question that may be embarrassing (Rogers, 2008). Contrastingly, guilty individuals may emphasize "more weight to their lies to the relevant questions and thus respond more strongly to them" because they know they actually committed criminal offenses (Rogers, 2008).

The GKT is not designed to identify probable lies. Instead, it is designed to identify knowledge that would be possessed only by someone that committed a crime or "knows only facts a criminal would know" (Costanzo & Krauss, 2012). The GKT assumes that "a guilty person will recognize scenes and events from the crime that an innocent person will not recognize" (Costanzo & Krauss, 2012). Recognizing these attributes is assumed to yield "elevated physiological arousal" (Costanzo & Krauss, 2012).

Polygraph examinations are not infallible and are imperfect. Examiner or operator error may affect the testing outcomes (Furnham & Taylor, 2011). False polygraph outcomes may occur because the polygraph examination itself frightens innocent people (Albrecht, Albrecht, Albrecht, & Zimbelman, 2012). Also, polygraph examinations may fail to detect

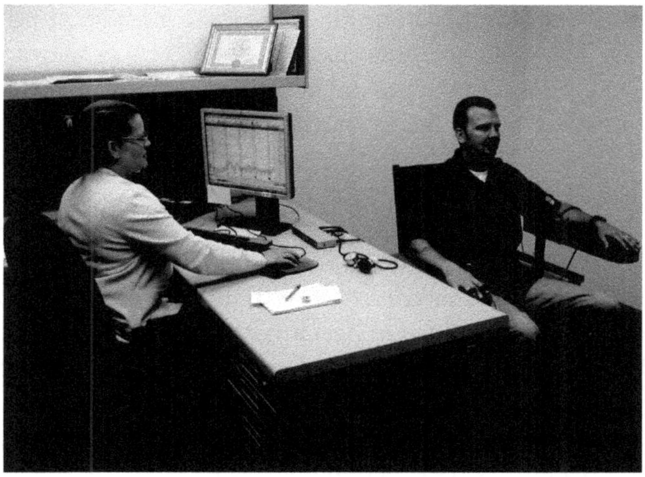

Figure 7.4 Administration of a polygraph examination. (From http://www.co.washington.or.us/Sheriff/FightingCrime/CriminalInvestigations/polygraph-services.cfm.)

"psychopathic liars" because such individuals are unstressed "when they lie as they have suppressed their conscience to the point that they no longer feel stress" (Albrecht et al., 2012). A failure to pass a polygraph examination does not always "imply certain guilt" (Albrecht et al., 2012). The passing of a polygraph examination also does not always imply innocence. Regardless, despite imperfections that are associated with polygraph testing, it represents a tool through which oral communication occurs within the justice system (Figure 7.4).

Oral communication certainly occurs between law enforcement officers and other humans. It also occurs between law enforcement officers and animals. For instance, some law enforcement officers are members of canine units in which verbal commands are essential in directing canine actions and influencing the behaviors of police dogs. Canines may be trained to respond to commands using English, a foreign language, or a combination of languages.

Numerous other modalities of oral communication occur within the justice domain. Supervisors may converse with subordinates amiably when conducting periodic performance reviews. Law enforcement personnel may use a gentle tone when speaking with little children. When interacting with people whose native tongue is not English, law enforcement personnel may communicate through some other language (e.g., Spanish). If the officer is unfamiliar or unknowledgeable regarding the language of the suspect, then an interpreter may be used. Regardless, oral communication permeates law enforcement organizations and the justice system in a variety of fashions.

Informing the Public: Announcements and Conferences

Events of national, regional, and local interests are announced through news and press conferences. News and press conferences are occasions in which organizational leadership orally makes a statement regarding some issue, and hosts a period of questions and answers afterward (if deemed appropriate). Many of these events are affiliated with some aspect of the justice system. When making oral announcement through news and press conferences, the basic reasoning and arguments of logic must be mindful. Ethos, pathos, and logos are strong tools in oral communication. Public venues may be influential, informative, or both. Speaking before the general public also may necessitate the incorporation of logos, ethos, and pathos within the intended message that is conveyed through the oral communication.

These concepts are integrated throughout the conferences and announcements that occurred during the 1970s in conjunction with the Watergate scandal. President Richard M. Nixon was the only U.S. president to resign from office. He did so because of the Watergate events. His resignation succeeded a vote of the Judiciary Committee of the House of Representatives "to recommend his impeachment" (The History Place, 1974). President Nixon resigned on August 8, 1974 (The History Place, 1974). One month later, President Gerald R. Ford did the unthinkable (according to some opinions) and startled the nation by pardoning former President Richard M. Nixon during the aftermath of the Watergate scandal. President Ford addressed the nation unexpectedly on September 8, 1974 to inform the American people of his decision to pardon former President Nixon (Ford, 1974). The text of this announcement is presented as follows:

> Ladies and gentlemen: I have come to a decision which I felt I should tell you and all of my fellow American citizens, as soon as I was certain in my own mind and in my own conscience that it is the right thing to do. I have learned already in this office that the difficult decisions always come to this desk. I must admit that many of them do not look at all the same as the hypothetical questions that I have answered freely and perhaps too fast on previous occasions.
>
> My customary policy is to try and get all the facts and to consider the opinions of my countrymen and to take counsel with my most valued friends. But these seldom agree, and in the end, the decision is mine. To procrastinate, to agonize, and to wait for a more favorable turn of events that may never come or more compelling external pressures that may as well be wrong as right, is itself a decision of sorts and a weak and potentially dangerous course for a President to follow.
>
> I have promised to uphold the Constitution, to do what is right as God gives me to see the right, and to do the very best that I can for America. I have asked your help and your prayers, not only when I became President but many times since. The Constitution is the supreme law of our land, and it governs our actions as citizens. Only the laws of God, which govern our consciences, are superior to it.
>
> As we are a nation under God, so I am sworn to uphold our laws with the help of God. And I have sought such guidance and searched my own conscience with special diligence to determine the right thing for me to do with respect to my predecessor in this place, Richard Nixon, and his loyal wife and family. Theirs is an American tragedy in which we all—all have played a part. It could go on and on and on, or someone must write the end to it. I have concluded that only I can do that, and if I can, I must.
>
> There are no historic or legal precedents to which I can turn in this matter, none that precisely fit the circumstances of a private citizen who has resigned the Presidency of the United States. But it is common knowledge that serious allegations and accusations hang like a sword over our former President's head, threatening his health as he tries to reshape his life, a great part of which was spent in the service of this country and by the mandate of its people.
>
> After years of bitter controversy and divisive national debate, I have been advised, and I am compelled to conclude that many months and perhaps more years will have to pass before Richard Nixon could obtain a fair trial by jury in any jurisdiction of the United States under governing decisions of the Supreme Court. I deeply believe in equal justice for all Americans,

> whatever their station or former station. The law, whether human or divine, is no respecter of persons; but the law is a respecter of reality.
>
> The facts, as I see them, are that a former President of the United States, instead of enjoying equal treatment with any other citizen accused of violating the law, would be cruelly and excessively penalized either in preserving the presumption of his innocence or in obtaining a speedy determination of his guilt in order to repay a legal debt to society. During this long period of delay and potential litigation, ugly passions would again be aroused. And our people would again be polarized in their opinions. And the credibility of our free institutions of government would again be challenged at home and abroad. In the end, the courts might well hold that Richard Nixon had been denied due process, and the verdict of history would even more be inconclusive with respect to those charges arising out of the period of his Presidency, of which I am presently aware.
>
> But it is not the ultimate fate of Richard Nixon that most concerns me, though surely it deeply troubles every decent and every compassionate person. My concern is the immediate future of this great country. In this, I dare not depend upon my personal sympathy as a long-time friend of the former President, nor my professional judgment as a lawyer, and I do not.
>
> As President, my primary concern must always be the greatest good of all the people of the United States whose servant I am. As a man, my first consideration is to be true to my own convictions and my own conscience. My conscience tells me clearly and certainly that I cannot prolong the bad dreams that continue to reopen a chapter that is closed. My conscience tells me that only I, as President, have the constitutional power to firmly shut and seal this book. My conscience tells me it is my duty, not merely to proclaim domestic tranquility but to use every means that I have to insure it.
>
> I do believe that the buck stops here, that I cannot rely upon public opinion polls to tell me what is right. I do believe that right makes might and that if I am wrong, ten angels swearing I was right would make no difference. I do believe, with all my heart and mind and spirit, that I, not as President but as a humble servant of God, will receive justice without mercy if I fail to show mercy. Finally, I feel that Richard Nixon and his loved ones have suffered enough and will continue to suffer, no matter what I do, no matter what we, as a great and good nation, can do together to make his goal of peace come true.
>
> Now, therefore, I, Gerald R. Ford, President of the United States, pursuant to the pardon power conferred upon me by Article II, Section 2, of the Constitution, have granted and by these presents do grant a full, free, and absolute pardon unto Richard Nixon for all offenses against the United States which he, Richard Nixon, has committed or may have committed or taken part in during the period from July 20, 1969 through August 9, 1974. In witness whereof, I have hereunto set my hand this eighth day of September, in the year of our Lord nineteen hundred and seventy-four, and of the Independence of the United States of America the one hundred and ninety-ninth.

This announcement shows a thoughtful approach to informing the general public regarding the pardoning of former President Nixon. Its contents are informative and incorporate forms of logical reasoning as methods through which justification of the pardoning was attempted. Obviously, the primary message conveyed through the use of informational characteristics regarded the pardoning of Nixon. The speech also makes it known that no precedents existed through which the current situation could be benchmarked. After all, Nixon was the first president to resign from the presidency. Figure 7.5 depicts President Ford addressing the nation.

Logos exists within this speech because it informs the public regarding the reasons for issuing a pardon. For example, President Ford indicated that "that a former President

Figure 7.5 President Ford verbally informing the nation of Nixon's pardon. (From http://www.fordlibrarymuseum.gov/avproj/nixon.htm.)

of the United States, instead of enjoying equal treatment with any other citizen accused of violating the law, would be cruelly and excessively penalized either in preserving the presumption of his innocence or in obtaining a speedy determination of his guilt in order to repay a legal debt to society" (Ford, 1974). Not all Americans would necessarily agree with this sentiment, but President Ford stated it as a basis to justify his pardoning of Nixon.

President Ford also stated that "In the end, the courts might well hold that Richard Nixon had been denied due process, and the verdict of history would even more be inconclusive with respect to those charges arising out of the period of his Presidency, of which I am presently aware" (Ford, 1974). The reasoning associated with this statement was because of his perceptions regarding the amount of time that would need to pass before Nixon could have a fair and speedy trial. Healing occurs through time; revisiting the issue after an amount of time would again necessitate painful considerations of the Watergate scandal in the minds of Americans and the peoples of other nations. Therefore, granting the pardon would possibly avoid future issues and deter the possibility of negative judgments of the American government and justice system by other nations.

Ethos exists within this speech. The use of ethos involves the characteristics of ideology and beliefs to justify the behavior of President Ford regarding the decision to pardon Nixon. Within the speech, President Ford alluded to his religious convictions and beliefs that guided his decision to pardon former President Nixon. He reminded the viewing audience of his fiduciary obligation to uphold American laws "with the help of God," and that he had "sought such guidance" and personally contemplated his "own conscience with special diligence" regarding his actions and decision to pardon Nixon (Ford, 1974). These references show the integration of ethos within the speech.

Pathos exists within this speech. The use of pathos represents an appeal to the emotions of the audience. President Ford stated that "Theirs is an American tragedy in which we all—all have played a part. It could go on and on and on, or someone must write the end to it. I have concluded that only I can do that, and if I can, I must" (Ford, 1974). This passage attempts to establish a common sentiment within the minds of the audience members by indicating that all Americans and their government had a stake in the tragedy. It shows the endlessness of the situation if it was unstopped. President Ford also stated that "But it is common knowledge that serious allegations and accusations hang like a sword over our former President's head, threatening his health as he tries to reshape his life, a great part of which was spent in the service of this country and by the mandate of its people."

Reminding the audience of Nixon's public service and the potentially detrimental consequences to his health played at the hearts and minds of all Americans. Using the phrase "all have played" a part not only insinuates that government entities have a shared responsibility, but also alludes to a shared commonness with all Americans. The uses of these references represent attempts to elicit empathy and sympathy from the audience.

Announcements made through public forums may often have repercussions. The announcement of the pardon destroyed the credibility of the Ford administration (President Profiles, 2012). Almost overnight, the approval rating of President Ford decreased from 71% to 50% (President Profiles, 2012). The efforts to persuade public opinion were unsuccessful because many believed that corrupt dealings had occurred between the current and former presidents (President Profiles, 2012). These notions are summarized as follows (President Profiles, 2012):

> It was virtually impossible to convince the public that the pardon had not resulted from a secret, if not corrupt, deal. Not only did public opinion surveys reflect powerful anger about pardoning Nixon before he could even be indicted but, by Ford's own admission, there were only seven hundred favorable letters among the four thousand received by the White House within the next few days. The Ford honeymoon was over. (President Profiles, 2012)

The pardon was an attempt to "spare the nation any legal accounting of the former President's own participation in Watergate" (Renka, 2010). During the Watergate scandal, Nixon had "led a systematic cover-up of presidential and White House involvement in a break-in and bugging of telephones at the Democratic National Committee (DNC) headquarters housed in the Watergate Hotel on the Potomac River waterfront" (Renka, 2010). The Ford administration did not survive the next election. Instead, the American people elected Jimmy Carter as the next president.

Within the justice system, it is not uncommon for municipal leaders, chiefs of police, and sheriffs to speak during press and news conferences. During 2012, Police Chief Dan Oates addressed a grieving society during the aftermath of the Aurora, Colorado, shootings in which 71 people were wounded and 12 were killed by gunman James Holmes (Stein & Foley, 2012). The event occurred at a movie theater where *The Dark Knight Rises* movie was showing (Stein & Foley, 2012). Figure 7.6 shows a television excerpt of Chief Oates discussing the tragic event.

Familiar examples are notable. Another 2012 incident involved the retirement of Detroit (Michigan) Police Chief Ralph Godbee because of "allegations that he engaged in a relationship with a subordinate female police officer" (NBC News, 2012). In this case, the press conference speaker was facilitated by a municipal leader, Detroit Mayor Dave Bing (NBC News, 2012). After Hurricane Sandy ravaged the East Coast, during a press conference, Toms River Township, New Jersey Police Chief Michael Mastronardy spoke to residents who were "frustrated that they couldn't get on the island to see their homes" (Bello, 2012).

Press and news conferences occur to facilitate the oral announcement of a variety of events and incidents. They may be related to heinous deeds, natural disasters, ceremonial events, fugitive searches, or for a variety of other reasons. Although the examples considered herein were of national notoriety, not all such events have such prominence and

Figure 7.6 Chief Oates discussing the Aurora, Colorado, shooting incident. (From http://foxnewsinsider.com/tag/dan-oates/.)

interest. Others may be localized regarding the events in small communities—perhaps the retirement of a sheriff and the election of a new one. In any case, sheriffs, during news and press conferences, police chiefs, and municipal leaders orally communicate with an audience to provide information. Such information may simply be to provide a status update regarding some situation or may be to advise residents regarding potential endangerments. Regardless, press and news conferences are oral communications events that permeate the legal system and law enforcement organizations.

Commentary Regarding Oral and Interpersonal Communications

Within the justice system and among law enforcement organizations, oral communication is essential and inescapable. Strong oral communication skills are necessary for interviewing potential law enforcement candidates, questioning witnesses, speaking during special occasions, interacting with the members of the general public, interrogating suspects, dispatching 911 emergency assistance, speaking during shift briefings, facilitating press and news conferences, and so forth. All personnel within the justice system and among law enforcement organizations must continuously attempt to refine their oral communications skills.

However, despite one's best efforts to facilitate meaningful and effective oral communications, barriers exist that impede the communications process. Various barriers include the following items:

Speaker attributes: Poor grammar and pronunciation skills may negatively affect the listening audience. A speaker's unfamiliarity with terminology and poor phrasing also are perceived negatively. A lack of exuding confidence and enthusiasm are also impediments.

Appearance: If the appearance of a speaker is either "unattractive or unacceptable" to the audience, then the "credibility of an oral message can be reduced" (Krizan,

Merrier, Logan, & Williams, 2011). Furthermore, "unintended nonverbal signals" may be distractions that negatively influence the receiving of oral messages (Krizan et al., 2011).

Environment: The tangible and intangible characteristics of the environment may impede oral communications. The locations and distances of physical objects and considerations of "room temperature, odor, light, and color" also affect oral communications (Krizan et al., 2011).

Receiver attributes: The characteristics of the receiving individual also affect oral communications. Emotional mindsets, disabilities, interest, subject knowledge, cultural biases, language issues, and so forth also can be impediments to oral communication (Krizan et al., 2011).

Supplements: Ancillary items must be of high quality. Language errors, incorrect mathematics, or other errata contained within presentation slides are perceived negatively.

No speakers or situations are absolutely perfect. Impediments and noise exist within the communications process, thereby affecting oral communications. Regardless, speakers must be well prepared and must attempt to craft oral communications that exhibit high quality. Preparation is essential when considering the successfulness and effectiveness of oral communications. Exercising the communications process discussed herein provides a foundational baseline through which oral communications may be crafted to achieve some measures of preparedness and successfulness.

Speakers can prepare by rehearsing and refining their materials and presentations. However, no speaker can fully control the attributes that generate successfulness. Speakers cannot control the weather or the thoughts of the individuals comprising the listening audience. Equipment can malfunction during the discourse. Absenteeism may affect the listening audience. Speaking events may be cancelled or postponed. Medical emergencies may arise during a presentation. Any number of other uncontrollable events may be imaged that affect the successfulness of oral communication.

Within the justice system and among law enforcement organizations, people must also be mindful of the impact of words and the potency of oral communication. Negotiations are examples of such power. Negotiating is a "conferring with others so as to arrive at the settlement of some matter" (*Merriam-Webster*, 2012b). Crisis negotiation represents a type of "bargaining where it is important to solve the crisis quickly (often within hours)" (Spoelstra & Pienaar, 1996). Legal negotiating involves using oral communication to "persuade the opposition to adopt a new position closer to your own" (Frascogna & Hetherington, 2001). Hostage negotiators must "talk with the hostage taker, keep him or her talking, establish rapport if possible, and let the hostage taker vent his or her anger and frustration (which in itself can often defuse the situation)" (Snow, 2002).

Many other contexts and examples may be identified and considered regarding the power of oral communication within the justice domain. Oral communication is everywhere—from the lowest officer patrolling a local street to the highest echelons of the Federal Bureau of Investigation and the Central Intelligence Agency (CIA). It permeates all situations from simple office conversations to hostage negotiations. It involves all types of personnel from patrol officers performing traffic stops to police chiefs providing briefings during press conferences (Figure 7.7). Regardless of the scenario, oral communication is an essential and omnipresent characteristic of the justice domain.

Figure 7.7 Resignation of CIA Director Petraeus. (From http://nbclatino.com/2012/11/09/cia-director-david-petraeus-resigns-cites-extramarital-affair/.)

Chapter Comments and Summary

This chapter introduces oral communications. Communicating orally is a method of communication that complements the auditory and written modalities. Oral communication permeates every facet of the justice system and law enforcement organizations. Attorneys present their arguments in court and patrol officers interact daily with the members of their served populaces. Judges verbally instruct jurors, and jurors debate among themselves the merits of a case that decide the fate of an accused individual.

Crafting oral communications may be accomplished through a methodical process. The process delineated within this chapter represents a process through which oral communications can be crafted to achieve some level of successfulness and effectiveness. This process begins with an analysis of the audience and culminates in the collection of feedback data through which improvement may be obtained. The intermediary steps encompass design, development, and testing of the oral communication.

Humans are unique creatures. All humans have different capacities for speaking in front of others. Some folks may naturally adapt to public speaking immediately, whereas others may exhibit symptoms of glossophobia (i.e., speech anxiety). Overcoming the fear of speaking in front of others may be accomplished through using various tactics ranging from envisioning successfulness to managing breathing. No one method is universal. Individual humans must determine the method that is personally the most beneficial.

Oral communication within the justice domain must conform to the principles established within the U.S. Constitution. Several constitutional amendments accommodate some aspects of oral communication. These considerations range from the right of freedom of speech to avoiding self-incrimination. Oaths of office for public service are also addressed within the U.S. Constitution.

Oral communication has the capacity to influence national interests. The Watergate scandal involved the resignation of President Richard Nixon and the pardoning of Nixon by President Gerald Ford. Both events necessitated various announcements that were delivered orally. Within the pardon of Nixon, various characteristics of ethos, pathos, and logos were used to express the foundational concepts of the pardon.

Noise exists within the communications domain. Barriers and impediments are characterized by the attributes of the listener as well as the speaking environment. Barriers may be tangible and intangible. The locations of physical objects are examples of tangible barriers, whereas room temperatures are representative of intangible barriers. Regardless, every effort must be made to minimize the effects of noise and barriers within the communications domain.

Oral communications are complex, and involve numerous dynamics of human nature and uncontrollable events. Equipment may fail, and medical emergencies may interrupt speakers. Regardless, speakers must acknowledge the constraints and limitations that affect their personal performance and of the speaking environment. Any consideration of complexity must also acknowledge the permeation of oral communication within the justice domain. It exists everywhere from the highest levels of law enforcement administration to the lowest levels of street patrols. In any case, oral communication is a primary form of communicating within the justice system and among law enforcement organizations.

Terminology

Announcement
Audience analysis
Barrier
Body language
Breathing
Control Question Test
Deception
Delivery
Design
Development
Equipment
Extemporaneous
Eye contact
Fear
Fifth Amendment
First Amendment
Formal speech
Fourteenth Amendment
Fourth Amendment
Glossophobia
Guilty Knowledge Test
Impediment
Inform
Informal speech
Integration
Negotiation
News conference
Nonverbal
Oath
Oral command

Oral communication
Outline
Pacing
Pardon
Pause
Peer review
Perjury
Persuade
Polygraph
Press conference
Rehearsal
Requirements
Sixth Amendment
Speech
Speech anxiety
Technology
Testing
Town crier
Truthfulness
Verbal command
Verbal communication

THOUGHT AND DISCUSSION QUESTIONS

1. Compare and contrast oral communication with the other modalities of written expression and visual communication. Discuss the similarities and differences that exist between these methods.
2. Do some research, and consider the advantages and disadvantages of oral communications. Discuss whether you believe oral communication is more personable than the methods of written expression and visual communication.
3. A copy of President Ford's news conference is contained within the appendix materials of this book. Read and review this material, and write an essay that discusses your opinion of the elements of persuading and informing that exist within this transcript. Furthermore, within your essay, discuss your perceptions of whether it includes logos, ethos, or pathos (or all three).
4. Contact your local law enforcement agency and interview some of the personnel. Determine what types of oral communication are used in the daily operations of the organization. Within your essay, consider the effectiveness and the efficiency of such communications with respect to communicating with other officers and the general public.

References

Acello, B. (2005). *Nursing assisting: Essentials for long-term care* (2nd ed., p. 122). Clifton Park, NY: Thomson-Delmar Publishing.

Albrecht, S., Albrecht, C., Albrecht, C., & Zimbelman, M. (2012). *Fraud examination* (4th ed., p. 309). Mason, OH: South-Western Publishing.

Alpert, G., & Dunham, R. (2004). *Understanding police use of force: Officers, suspects, and reciprocity* (p. 60). New York: Cambridge University Press.
Archives.gov. (2012). Constitution of the United States: Amendments 11–27. *The Charters of Freedom. National Archives.* Retrieved from http://www.archives.gov/exhibits/charters/constitution_amendments_11-27.html (accessed December 19, 2012).
Becker, R., & Dutelle, A. (2013). *Criminal investigation* (4th ed., p. 189). Burlington, MA: Jones and Bartlett Publishers.
Bello, M. (2012). Jersey police chief is force of calm in Sandy's wake. *USA Today.* Retrieved from http://www.usatoday.com/story/news/nation/2012/11/02/toms-river-police-chief-michael-mastronardy/1675345/ (accessed December 18, 2012).
Bovee, C. (2003). *Contemporary public speaking* (2nd ed., p. 25). San Diego, CA: The Collegiate Publishing Group.
Churchill, W. (n.d.). Speech quotes. BrainyQuote.com. Retrieved from http://www.brainyquote.com/quotes/keywords/speech.html (accessed December 14, 2012).
Conser, J., Paynich, R., & Gingerich, T. (2013). *Law enforcement in the United States* (3rd ed., p. 165). Burlington, MA: Jones and Bartlett Publishing.
Costanzo, M., & Krauss, D. (2012). *Forensic and legal psychology: Psychological science applied to law* (p. 63). New York: Worth Publishers.
Dowis, R. (2000). *The lost art of the great speech: How to write one—How to deliver it* (p. 215). New York: American Management Association.
Felice, W. (2009). *How do I save my honor? War, moral integrity, and principled resignation* (p. 125). Lanham, MD: Rowman and Littlefield Publishers.
Ford, G. (1974). Address to the nation pardoning Richard M. Nixon. *American Rhetoric.* Retrieved from http://www.americanrhetoric.com/speeches/geraldfordpardonofnixon.htm (accessed December 19, 2012).
Frascogna, X., & Hetherington, H. L. (2001). *The lawyer's guide to negotiation: A strategic approach to better contracts and settlements* (p. 116). Chicago: American Bar Association.
Furnham, A., & Taylor, J. (2011). *Bad apples: Identify, prevent, and management negative behavior at work* (p. 221). New York: Palgrave-MacMillan Publishing.
Griffin, C. (2009). *Invitation to public speaking* (3rd ed., p. 277). Boston: Wadsworth-Cengage.
Gupit, F. (1986). *Elements of public speaking* (4th ed., p. 29). Manila, Philippines: REX.
Hayes, D., & Ninemeier, J. (2009). *Human resources management in the hospitality industry* (p. 238). Hoboken, NJ: John Wiley and Sons.
The History Place. (1974). Richard M. Nixon: Resigning the Presidency. Retrieved from http://www.historyplace.com/speeches/nixon.htm (accessed December 19, 2012).
Jaffe, C. (2007). *Public speaking: Concepts and skills for a diverse society* (5th ed., p. 24). Belmont, CA: Thomson Wadsworth.
Kline, J. (2001). *The essentials of effective public speaking: Quick access to the important rules and techniques for successful speaking* (p. 65). Piscataway, NJ: Research & Education Association.
Krizan, B., Merrier, P., Logan, J., & Williams, K. (2011). *Business communication* (8th ed., p. 19). Mason, OH: South-Western Cengage Publishing.
Legal Information Institute. (2012). First amendment: An overview. Cornell University. Retrieved from http://www.law.cornell.edu/wex/first_amendment (accessed December 18, 2012).
Machovec, F. (2006). *Private investigation and security science: A scientific approach* (3rd ed., p. 68). Springfield, IL: Charles C. Thomas Publishing.
Mathew, S. (2011). *The act of change management: A principled approach for leaders* (p. 40). Bloomington, IN: Iuniverse Publising.
Merriam-Webster Dictionary. (2012a). s.v. "feedback." Retrieved from http://www.merriam-webster.com/dictionary/feedback (accessed December 15, 2012).
Merriam-Webster Dictionary. (2012b). s.v. "negotiate." Retrieved from http://www.merriam-webster.com/dictionary/negotiate?show=0&t=1355823830 (accessed December 18, 2012).

Merriam-Webster Dictionary. (2012c). s.v. "oath." Retrieved from http://www.merriam-webster.com/dictionary/oath (accessed December 19, 2012).

Morris, L. (2010). *Military justice: A reference handbook* (p. 13). Santa Barbara, CA: ABC-CLIO Publishing.

National Archives. (2012). Bill of Rights. *The Charters of Freedom*. Retrieved from http://www.archives.gov/exhibits/charters/bill_of_rights_transcript.html (accessed December 18, 2012).

National Speakers Association. (2012). Advancing the speaking profession since 1973. Retrieved from http://www.nsaspeaker.org/about (accessed December 15, 2012).

NBC News. (2012). Detroit police chief Ralph Godbee resigns amid sex scandal. Retrieved from http://usnews.nbcnews.com/_news/2012/10/08/14298235-detroit-police-chief-ralph-godbeeresigns-amid-sex-scandal?lite (accessed November 19, 2012).

O'Brien, R. (2008). Verbal commands: How does your team gain control of subjects? *Police Magazine*. Retrieved from http://www.policemag.com/blog/swat/story/2008/11/verbal-commands.aspx (accessed December 19, 2012).

Pencak, W. (2011). *Contested commonwealth: Essays in American history* (p. 63). Lanham, MD: Lehigh University Press.

President Profiles. (2012). Gerald R. Ford—The Nixon pardon. Retrieved from http://www.presidentprofiles.com/Kennedy-Bush/Gerald-R-Ford-The-nixon-pardon.html (accessed December 19, 2012).

Renka, R. (2010). Nixon's fall and the ford and carter interregnum. Southeast Missouri State University. Retrieved from http://cstl-cla.semo.edu/renka/ui320-75/presidents/nixon/nixon%27sfall.asp (accessed December 19, 2012).

Rogers, R. (2008). *Clinical assessment of malingering and deception* (3rd ed., p. 257). New York: The Guilford Press.

Schwarzkopf, E., Houlihan, D., Kolb, K., Lewinski, W., Buchanan, J., & Christenson, A. (2008). Command types used in police encounters. *Law Enforcement Executive Forum*, *8*(2), 100.

Snow, R. (2002). *The complete guide to personal and home safety: What you need to know* (p. 104). Cambridge, MA: Perseus Books.

Spoelstra, M., & Pienaar, W. (1996). *Negotiation: Theories, strategies, and skills* (2nd ed., p. 225). Cape Town, South Africa: Juta and Company.

Stair, R., & Reynolds, G. (2010). *Principles of information systems* (9th ed., p. 559). Boston: Course Technology.

Stein, S., & Foley, E. (2012). Colorado shooting news conference: Aurora police chief speaks on tragedy. *The Huffington Post*. Retrieved from http://www.huffingtonpost.com/2012/07/20/colorado-shooting-news-conference_n_1690270.html (accessed December 19, 2012).

Steinberg, S. (2000). *Persuasive communication skills: Public speaking* (p. 259). Claremont, South Africa: Juta and Co. Publishing.

Toastmasters International. (2012). Welcome to Toastmasters International. Retrieved from http://www.toastmasters.org/ (accessed December 14, 2012).

Tofanelli, D. (2012). *Communication in organizations* (p. 88). Bloomington, IN: Authorhouse Publishing.

Verderber, R., Sellnow, D., & Verdeber, K. (2012). *The challenge of effective speaking*. Boston: Wadsworth-Cengage.

Verderber, R., Verderber, K., & Sellnow, D. (2012). *Speak* (p. 153). Boston: Wadsworth-Cengage.

Wood, J. (2009). *Communication in our lives* (5th ed., p. 124). Boston: Wadsworth-Cengage Publishing.

Communications Technology 8

There was a time when nails were high-tech. There was a time when people had to be told how to use a telephone. Technology is just a tool. People use tools to improve their lives.
—Tom Clancy (Clancy, n.d.)

Objectives

The objectives of this chapter are to

- Define communications technology
- Discuss technological advancement and police communication
- Discuss historical aspects of communications technology and policing
- Discuss current uses of communications technology and policing
- Discuss the concept of technology as a tool to embellish human activities

Introduction

Technology is defined as "the practical application of knowledge especially in a particular area"; "a capability given by the practical application of knowledge"; "a manner of accomplishing a task especially using technical processes, methods, or knowledge"; or the "specialized aspects of a particular field of endeavor" (*Merriam-Webster*, 2012b). Another perspective of technology is stated as follows:

> ... application of knowledge to the practical aims of human life or to changing and manipulating the human environment. Technology includes the use of materials, tools, techniques, and sources of power to make life easier or more pleasant and work more productive. Whereas science is concerned with how and why things happen, technology focuses on making things happen. Technology began to influence human endeavour as soon as people began using tools. (*Merriam-Webster*, 2012b)

These definitions and insights allude to the notion that technology embellishes human existence beneficially. Technologies permeate modern lifestyles in a variety of ways—washing machines, traffic signals, cellular phones, computers, cranes and roadway equipment, trains, airplanes, ships, x-ray machines, blood analysis machines, television, radio, and practically an innumerable array of other examples. Each day, within the societies of most developed countries, modern technology influences practically everyone in some capacity whether from merely listening to a radio or viewing air traffic control monitor screens.

Technology is a tool that enhances the rendering of human decisions and the performance of human activities. Numerous examples exist to explain this concept. Among manufacturers that produce automobiles, processes and procedures may be made more efficient and effective through the use of robotic automation instead of manual human labor (Pride, Hughes, & Kapoor, 2013). Among hospital environments, some organizations use "pharmacy robots that stock and retrieve drugs" without inciting "additional labor expenses" while simultaneously increasing production (Madura, 2007). Some businesses leverage sales automation and Internet resources to generate large increases of sales volume (Thompson, 2005). Human decisions are embellished through the use of decision support systems to support a variety of choices ranging from human resources and personnel applications to choices involving the managing of an organization (Stair & Reynolds, 2010).

These notions also affect the communications domain. Within this context, communication technology exists to embellish a variety of human processes, procedures, and activities. In this context, the appropriate term to represent this use of technology within the communications domain is communications technology. Technology is leveraged in a variety of ways to support communications. Again, numerous examples exist to explain this concept.

Many radio stations use automation to support their overnight programming for radio broadcasts (Keith, 2012). Mass media leverages technology to facilitate communication with a vast audience (e.g., Internet sites) (Klopfenstein, 1997). Landline telephones and cellular telephones enable communication between people regardless of physical distance (Grant & Meadows, 2008). Television facilitates communications broadcasts to "all corners of the world" (Pannu & Tomar, 2010). Social networking has decentralized communications such that practically any entity can communicate with any other entity and transmit practically any message (Blanchard, 2011). Essentially, modern technologies have revolutionized the ability of humans to communicate efficiently and effectively, and to transmit a variety of messages to any number of receivers.

These notions have implications for law enforcement organizations and the justice system. Law enforcement officers receive assistance call information from dispatchers through the use of radio systems. News media may broadcast the details of heroic incidents involving law enforcement officers (e.g., saving a life) to a mass audience. Law enforcement personnel may use loudspeakers to broadcast their voices when dealing with crowds or environments in which there is interfering noise within the communications domain. Cyber crime may also be perpetrated through the use of communications technology (Pattavina, 2005). Law enforcement organizations may use communications technology to conduct surveillance operations (Knepper, Doak, & Shapland, 2009). Numerous laws, regulations, and policies exist that govern the actions that are facilitated through the use of technology within the justice domain. Certainly, many other considerations of communications technology are pertinent to the communications domain within the contexts of the justice system and law enforcement organizations.

Brief History of Communications Technologies

Traditional forms of communications technologies have varied throughout history. Each period exhibited its own form of communications technology. Some of the earliest forms of communications technologies were land vehicles and maritime vessels that were used to transport messages across great distances geographically (Witzel, 2009). These technological advancements increased the speed of human communication (Witzel, 2009). Maritime vessels facilitated the communications that occurred among various peoples continentally between land masses across oceans. During the middle of the fifteenth century, Johann Gutenberg introduced the printing press, thereby improving printed communication.

During the late 1700s, the use of communications signaling was used within military organizations. These forms of technology included human couriers, "signal flags for tactical messages," and the use of "postal coaches" for messages of diplomacy and for messages having a strategic intent (Sterling, 2008). Semaphore messaging was also used during this period. The armies of Napoleon leveraged semaphores to send messages quickly among components of the military (Sterling, 2008). The French system implemented the Chappe semaphore system to facilitate communication between Paris and field units of the military (Sterling, 2008). The Chappe semaphore system was capable of transmitting message speeds "as high as 120 miles per hour in ideal conditions" (Sterling, 2008). Figure 8.1 shows the basic Chappe semaphore network.

In England, during 1841, semaphore systems were implemented among railway lines (Bianculli, 2003, p. 169). This event represented the initial use of semaphores to facilitate communications among railway lines (Bianculli, 2003, p. 169). Eventually, these systems were slowly implemented among American railway lines during the 1870s and 1880s (Bianculli, 2003, p. 171). However, within the United States, each railroad company designed its own semaphore coding system, thereby causing much confusion when communicating with trains (Bianculli, 2003, p. 173).

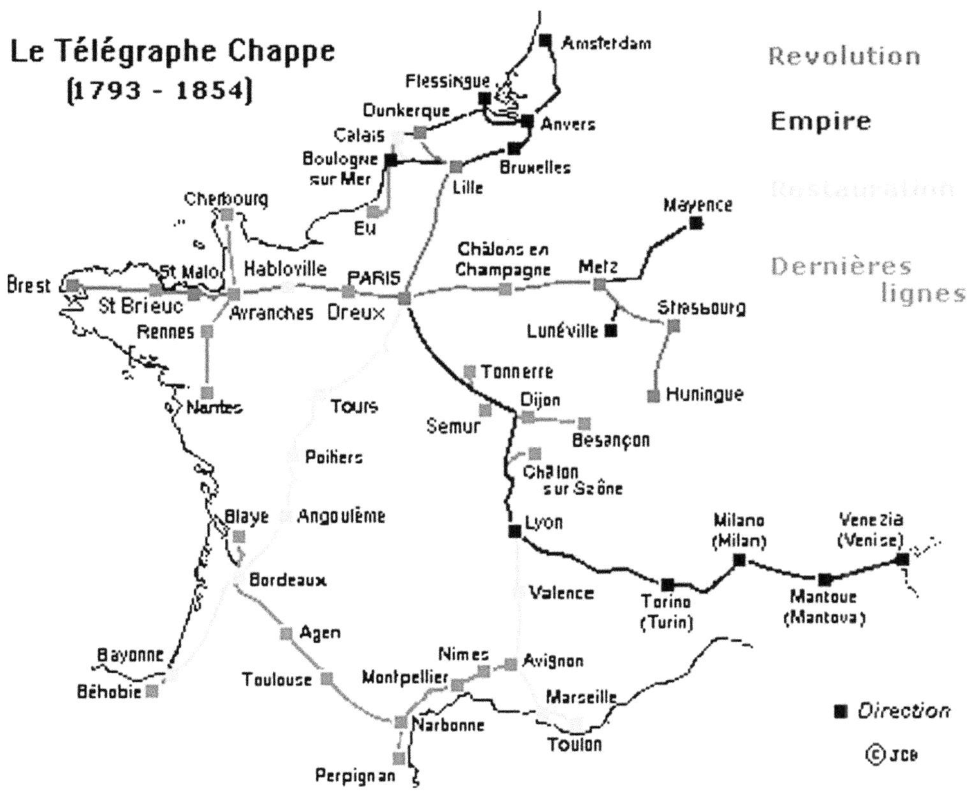

Figure 8.1 Chappe semaphore network of the eighteenth century. (From http://www.rienadire.fr/wordpress/?p=1039.)

The invention of the telegraph also improved human communications technologically. The telegraph system was developed by Samuel Morse in 1844 (U.S. Department of Transportation, 1997). The telegraph enabled communications between senders and receivers of messages without the use of transportation (U.S. Department of Transportation, 1997). Essentially, the messenger and message were separated by this invention (U.S. Department of Transportation, 1997). Telegraph communication systems were developed to control operational aspects of railways (Tiffin & Kissling, 2007). However, its use spread to facilitate communications among various other unrelated domains. Before the end of the 1860s, all of the continents were connected telegraphically through the use of telegraph machines and "submarine cable" (Tiffin & Kissling, 2007). This expanding of telegraph systems facilitated communications quickly across the globe.

Other early inventions ushered significant advances in communications technologies. Thomas Edison introduced the phonograph in 1877, thereby ushering recording technology to facilitate communication (Morton, 2004). The invention of the camera, during the 1890s, by Oskar Messter, ushered new advances in communicating through imagery and led to the initial crafting of newsreels (Welch, 2000). During 1896, Guglielmo Marconi "sent and received" messages across a "distance of two miles" via a system of "wireless telegraphy" (Willis, 2010). This device led to the development of radio communications (Willis, 2010). During 1929, the introduction of the kinescope contributed toward the eventual development of television (Abramson, 2003).

These initial devices and inventions provided a framework for communication in auditory, visual, oral, and printed modalities. Since their respective introductions, numerous advances have occurred through which human communication is embellished among these domains. During modern times, organizations are permeated by a variety of communications technologies representing these primary modalities. Faxes, telephones, computers, social media, radios, televisions, personal communications devices, and an array of other resources are common among modern lifestyles. These modern devices all owe their existence to historical accomplishments that introduced or improved on the communications paradigms of their respective periods.

Forms of Communications Technologies

There exists no solitary instantiation of communications technology. Instead, it ubiquitously pervades modern society in a variety of forms. Such items consist of telephones and facsimile machines, electronic billboards, radio systems, television systems, sound systems at public venues, Internet and intranet resources, both stationary and mobile computing devices and their supporting networks, tracking systems, and surveillance systems. Many other instantiations could be imagined and identified. Regardless, they all exist to embellish the communications process between humans.

Network Technology

A network is "an interconnected or interrelated chain, group, or system"; "a system of computers, peripherals, terminals, and databases connected by communications lines"; or a "group of radio or television stations linked by wire or radio delay" (*Merriam-Webster*, 2012a). Electronic networks represent the conversion of "useful sound or data into electrical impulses" and are "capable of transmitting both voice and nonvoice messages (e.g., telex, telegrams, data)" (Dagostino & Wujek, 2005). Electronic networks are the logical and physical constructs through which computers, telephones, and so forth are networked and connected together to facilitate communication. Internet and intranet resources are examples of networks.

Two methods of establishing connectivity via networking exist: wired and wireless. A wired network is defined as "one that uses cables to connect network devices" (Parsons & Oja, 2012, p. 256). Many desktop computers and their associated machineries (e.g., scanners and printers) are connected through the use of wired networks. Although this type of networking is common among office settings and generally has great speed when exchanging data, the linked devices are relatively stationary with little mobility because the networked devices are linked through cables (Parsons & Oja, 2012, p. 256). One generally does not tend to move such items frequently, and such items usually do not necessitate a large amount of mobility.

A wireless network is defined as one that "transports data from one device to another without the use of cables or wires," and range in size from local areas to wide areas (Parsons & Oja, 2012, p. 165). Wireless networks are not connected through the use of cables. Instead, connectivity is established through the use of "radio signals, microwaves, and infrared light" (Parsons & Oja, 2012, p. 165). A wireless network facilitates the mobility of its connected devices. For example, cellular telephones may be carried anywhere. However, wireless networks may be more expensive financially than their wired counterparts, have a limited range of communications, may pose greater security risks than wired networks, and may exhibit slower speeds of exchanging data among the devices that are interconnected within the network (Parsons & Oja, 2012, p. 165).

Mass Media Technology

Mass media represents the "types of media that reach mass audiences" (Misiroglu, 2002). Examples of mass media include "television, radio, film, books, magazines, newspapers, and the Internet" (Misiroglu, 2002). Other examples of mass media include billboards and recordings (Wimmer & Dominick, 2011). Many forms of print communication that were popular and well-known newspapers, magazines, journals, and so forth are now available through the Internet. Mass media advantageously facilitates the communication of a message to a vast audience within a limited amount of time (Duncan & Goddard, 2011). Through the use of mass media, human behavior may also be altered (Duncan & Goddard, 2011). Additionally, the use of mass media may also be leveraged to influence public opinion regarding a variety of topics (Pedersen, Miloch, & Laucella, 2007).

Although the use of mass media is advantageous when communicating a message to a mass audience, it also has disadvantages. Mass media is disadvantageous because "large corporations own media outlets, and control" the information that is disseminated through their respective channels; the financial cost of mass media is often a constraint; and mass media is generally inappropriate when attempting to effectively communicate with "specific, target populations" (Murphy, 2013).

Social Network Technology

A social network is defined as "a set of social actors, or nodes, members that are connected by one or more types of relations" (Furht, 2010). More specifically, a social network represents "a social structure made by individuals and organizations," and the foundational connect comprises "individuals and more specific types of interdependency, such as friendship, common interest, and relationships of beliefs" (Pho, Han, & Kang, 2011). Both Facebook and MySpace are popular Internet instantiations of social networking resources. Social media is a multimedia communications experience that facilitates human interaction and communication using imagery, text, video, and audio resources among individuals that share similar interests.

Social networks have some advantages. Some of the most common advantages are given as follows:

- Social networks are "free to join and easy to use" instead of being constrained by the costs that are associated with creating and maintaining websites (Hart, Greenfield, MacLaughlin, & Geier, 2010).
- Social networks facilitate existing and new relationships among entities, and keep "external entities and partners informed" (Hart et al., 2010).
- Social networks have the capacity to reach "target audiences around the clock" (Hart et al., 2010).
- Social networks may generate a "loyal following" by informing regularly about the activities of an organization (Hart et al., 2010).

Social networking represents a form of communication in which individuals may communicate with merely one person or millions of people. For example, within five years of its founding in 2003, the Facebook Internet social network has amassed approximately "100 million users," and had approximately "half-a-billion members networking in 40 languages" by the middle of 2010 (Baran & Davis, 2012). Although social networking is an electronic, virtual form of communication, its use also facilitates human bonding (Pease, Rowe, & Cooper, 2007). It may be used to communicate personally or professionally; numerous individuals, groups, and organizations communicate through social networking.

Print Media Technology

Print media represents a variety of forms ranging from daily newspapers and magazines to handbills and traffic tickets. Essentially, print media represents the use of the written word to communicate between senders and receivers of an intended message. The technology associated with print media "involves the production of printed material using an offset sheet-fed press and other equipment to create finished, printed products" (World Skills International, 2012). Generally, printing technology incorporates the use of relief printing, letterpress printing, intaglio printing, offset printing, screen printing, lithographic printing, and electrostatic printing. These types are summarized as follows:

- *Relief printing*: Relief printing represents the "oldest printing method," and uses an "image carrier on which the image areas are raised above the non-image areas" (Ohta & Rosen, 2006).
- *Letterpress printing*: Letterpress printing is synonymous with relief printing (Ryan & Conover, 2004). However, it represents an antiquated method of printing with limited uses during modern times (Ryan & Conover, 2004).

- *Intaglio printing*: This type of printing "involves an image that is depressed" within a "printing plate" (Lokensgard, 2004). The surface area of the plate is coated with ink, any excess ink is removed by a scraping mechanism, and printing occurs when the "ink left in the sunken areas is transferred" to the printed product (Lokensgard, 2004).
- *Offset printing*: This form of printing is a very common method. It is used to produce an array of items, including "business cards, brochures, magazines, and newspapers" (Johansson, Lundberg, & Ryberg, 2012).
- *Screen printing*: Screen printing represents a "generic" method in which "stencil-like processes are used to print textiles and wallpapers, either by hand or by machine" (Jackson, 2002).
- *Lithographic printing*: This method involves the "chemical principle that grease and water are mutually repellant." Both non-image and image areas of a printing plate reside in the "same plane," and the areas denoting the image are "treated to render them receptive to ink, and the non-image or nonprinting areas are treated to make them receptive to water" (Sward & Gardner, 1972).
- *Electrostatic printing*: This method involves paper touching a "photoreceptor and the back of the paper is flooded with ions carrying a charge opposite that of the toner" (Romano, 2000). The toner is attracted to the "image areas" by the "opposite charge," thereby ensuring that the toner adheres to the "surface with the strongest attraction." This adhesion forms a printed image.

Video Media Technology

During modern times, the technology of video media encompasses a wide range of items that are used to produce videos. Such technologies may represent rather complex systems found in large, sophisticated studio environments or it may be as simple as the camera and recording system within a cellular telephone or computer system. It also encompasses items through which videos are edited and viewed. Essentially, video technology enables the inputting, editing, managing, publishing, and sharing of "video production projects" (Shelly, Cashman, Gunter, & Gunter, 2007).

The video development process was delineated within Chapter 5. However, there are numerous types of video technology that may be used to produce video products. Although the discussions herein are not exhaustive regarding these items, some of the recent technological advancements involve digital video systems. The use of digital systems now easily accommodates a variety of video editing and producing functions. Simple films can be augmented to include "scrolling titles and transitions, cutting out or adding scenes, and adding background music and voice-over narration" (Shelly & Vermaat, 2012). Figure 8.2 depicts the digital editing and revising of video materials.

Audio Media Technology

Audio technologies involve a variety of items ranging from tangible voice recorders and editing equipment to intangible software programs. Examples include compact discs (CDs), mini-discs, super audio CDs, digital audio recording systems, digital audio tape, and the audio characteristics of digital versatile discs (Sony Service Centre, 2001). Other items include resources to influence audio (e.g., absorbers, reflectors, and diffusers) and

Figure 8.2 Video editing. (From http://www.adobe.com/sea/products/premiere.html.)

to project sound (e.g., loudspeakers, headphones, and earphones) (Kleiner, 2012). Among many electronic devices, sound cards "are responsible for digitizing, recording, and compressing" various "sound files" (Parekh, 2006). Such items represent tangible audio technology resources.

Software represents the intangible attributes of audio technologies. A variety of software programs exist to create audio productions and to control audio equipment. Audio software enables one to "cut and crop the audio track, loop the music track, bring up or down the volume levels, and clean up the overall recording" (Allen, 2012). Software also facilitates the ability to change "voice tones and pitch" (Allen, 2012). It also may be used to create and store files of various audio formats. Figure 8.3 shows a typical user interface of audio software.

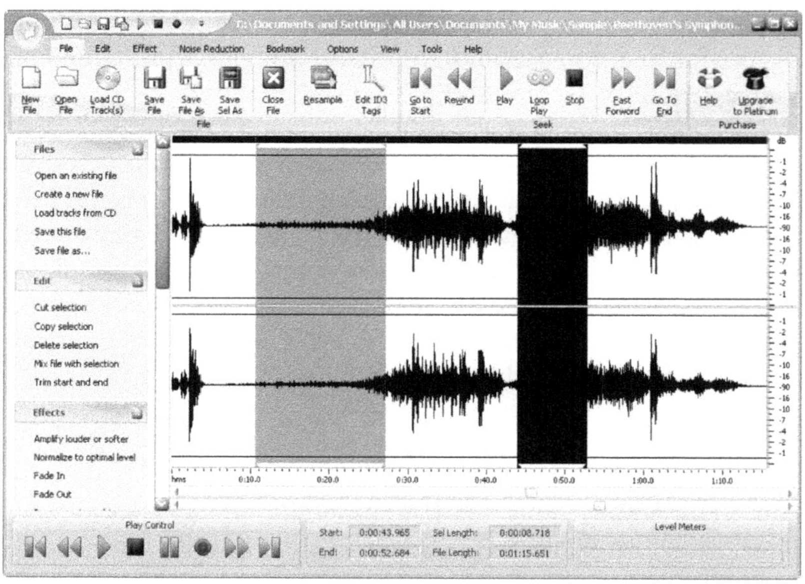

Figure 8.3 Audio software interface. (From http://www.bluechillies.com/screenshot/45137.html.)

Multimedia Technology

Multimedia systems embellish the human experience with a variety of technological systems. Multimedia systems are now prevalent among the domains of "video conferencing, online shopping in virtual environments, video-on-demand services, and e-learning to remote health care" (Feng, 2008). Multimedia technologies incorporate an integration of visual, graphic, audio, and written resources to facilitate communications. Multimedia products may also be interactive depending on the type of application and its functional requirements. The primary goal of multimedia technology is to "use sight, sounds, and animation to make computer output look as much like real life as possible" (Andrews, 2009).

Satellite Technology

Satellite technology facilitates communication locally, regionally, internationally, and globally. These tools are the communications foundation for assisting "ships and aircraft to navigate safely in all weather conditions" (Maini & Agrawal, 2007). Satellites also assist the navigation of various missile weaponries as well as represent the basis for geographic positioning systems (Maini & Agrawal, 2007). Satellite technology is also used to monitor ankle tag bracelets among criminal offenders (Watt, 2012). Satellites are the backbone of many telephone communications systems, and they contributed to the antiquating of oceanic cables as forms of communications systems (Morton & Gabriel, 2004).

Other Forms of Communications Technology

Modern communications is facilitated by a range of different resources. These items represent auditory, visual, print, and multimedia modalities of communication. Examples include telephones, faxes, electronic mail, videos, public address systems, cellular telephones and land-based telephones, satellite networks, undersea constructs, and so forth. Given the advent and proliferation of electronic technologies within the communications domain, it is impossible to provide an exhaustive listing of all types of applications and devices that exist to support the communications needs of both individuals and organizations. However, numerous forms of communications technology exist.

Policy and Communications Technology

Various definitions of policy exist. Policy is "a relatively stable, purposive course of action or inaction followed by an actor or set of actors in dealing with a problem or matter of concern" (Anderson, 2011). Policy is also defined as "a broad statement of principle that presents management's position for a defined control area" (Tipton & Krause, 2007). From an organizational perspective, policy also represents the "intent of a senior management" (Limaye, 2009). Essentially, policy represents the expression of acceptable and unacceptable actions, behaviors, and deeds within an organizational setting.

Various perspectives of policy exist that influence both the justice system and law enforcement organizations. In some cases, financial and economic policies exist to influence the methods through which such organizations are funded. Budgetary policies may constrain how any allocated funds are expended. Personnel policies may influence codes of conduct during working hours. Security policies may influence the accessing of controlled information and physical resources. Policy also influences communications technologies within the justice domain.

Within the justice domain and among law enforcement organizations, policies may influence the use of communications technology. During modern times, many law enforcement organizations and personnel advocate the use of camera systems for individual officers, vehicles, and buildings. Officer safety, public safety, and overall security are primary reasons for the crafting of such policies. Using camera technologies provides a means of recording events as they occur, and recording them for later use involving a variety of reasons. For example, such videos may be used during court proceedings to communicate the salient facts of a situation or for training purposes among police academies.

The use of video technology records the details of both benevolence and disaster among law enforcement scenarios. When reviewed, the details of the recorded event are communicated to the viewing audience with greater power and clarity than mere words can express. The following notion highlights the importance of this concept: "Videos depicting the last moments of an officer's life are always shocking, explicit, and immensely disturbing, yet they are often the only voices that officers have when they can no longer speak for themselves" (Fredericks, 2008). During 2008, such a tragic incident occurred in Arkansas when two West Memphis police officers were murdered. The follow excerpt summarizes this account:

> … in-car video showed a 16 year old exiting the passenger side of a vehicle while shooting at the officers with an AK-47. "Since the officers are no longer available, I have to let the dash-cam video speak for itself," stated Prosecutor Mike Walden. (Fredericks, 2008)

This incident shows the importance of vehicular video technologies to record policing events. However, such video technologies must be employed and deployed in accordance with a stated organizational policy. The leaders of law enforcement organizations must craft clear, understandable policies and procedures regarding the use of such technologies (Westphal, 2004). Policies must address issues involving "when the video system must be in record mode, when the tapes should be replaced, how the tapes are reused, how the chain of evidence is maintained with the tapes, and how the tapes are stored" (Westphal, 2004). No solitary policy is universal to accommodate the needs of all law enforcement organizations. Instead, each separate organization must craft its own policy regarding such issues. Figure 8.4 shows a dash-mounted video system that is typical of such devices that are deployed among police vehicles.

Complaints are a fact of life among law enforcement organizations and their personnel. Many invalid complaints arise because members of the public misunderstand the actions of law enforcement personnel or because they file totally false complaints. The use of vehicular video technologies tends to reduce the progression of such complaints after filing. Many such complaints may be "dismissed on the spot" or may be resolved "at the first line supervisory level because the in-car recording enabled involved parties to review the evidence of the contact" (International Association of Police Chiefs, 2003).

Organizational policies must address issues of complaints. In some cases, policy may dictate that an investigating supervisor initially review the associated video in which the event was recorded "before calling any witnesses or interviewing the officer" (Westphal, 2004). This review contributes toward "determining whether the allegation requires further

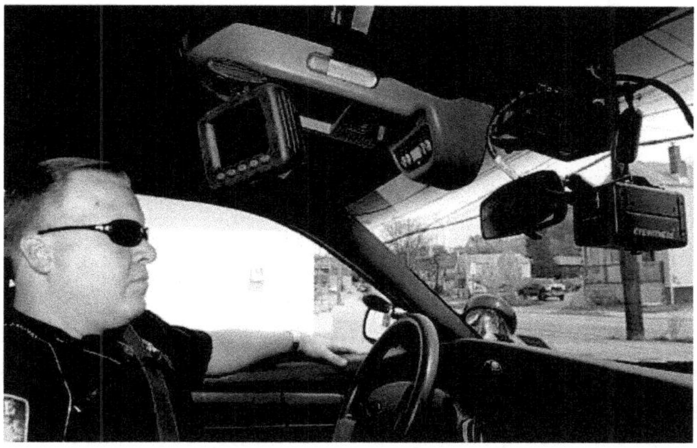

Figure 8.4 Dash-mounted police video system. (From http://www.post-gazette.com/local/north/2010/04/15/Caught-on-camera-Suburban-police-departments-realize-benefits-of-cruiser-cams/stories/201004150267.)

investigation" and communicating the notification of the findings (Westphal, 2004). A policy must be crafted and expressed that delineates the methodical process through which the reviewing of recordings produced by video resources occurs, and through which the findings are communicated to the vested parties. Through crafting, stating, establishing, and employing such a policy, events "can be reviewed and dealt with in a factual manner and addressed appropriately when there is a camera present" (Westphal, 2004).

Communicating the mandatory and optional situations in which the use of video technology is appropriate is accomplished through the written expression of organizational policy. An example of such policy tenets involves the *Municipal Police Institute In-Car Video Recording Policy and Procedure No. 4.14* (Municipal Police Institute, n.d.). Instances of mandatory situations are described as follows (Municipal Police Institute, n.d.):

1. "MANDATORY RECORDING: Officers assigned to vehicles with video recording equipment will activate the same to record the following:
   a. Traffic stops (to include, but not be limited to, traffic violations, stranded motorist assistance and all crime interdiction stops);
   b. Priority responses;
   c. Vehicle pursuits;
   d. Prisoner transports; and
   e. Crimes in progress" (Municipal Police Institute, n.d.).

Another excerpt from the policy describes situations in which the use of video technology may be optional. These considerations are described as follows (Municipal Police Institute, n.d.):

2. "OPTIONAL RECORDING: Officers, at their discretion, may record any situation or incident that the officer, through training and experience, believes should be [audibly and] visually recorded.
   NOTE: Officers may audibly and visually record any incident in which all involved parties consent. At the beginning of any public contact or traffic stop, the officer

> shall notify the citizen that the events are being audibly and visually recorded. This notification does not apply to crimes in progress or similar situations where notification is impractical." (Municipal Police Institute, n.d.)

These policy excerpts provide a clear distinction regarding the use of video technology between mandatory and optional situations. There exists no ambiguity regarding the details of mandatory versus optional scenarios during which video technology may be employed. It also specifies what information is to be communicated to the members of the public regarding any recordings. It also addresses the impractical attributes of scenarios that may pose significant risk to law enforcement personnel or the general public (e.g., shootings or bank robbery).* In any case, the policy ensures that all members of the public are treated identically, and provides a baseline of behavior to which law enforcement personnel must adhere during the course of their duties.

Communication policy certainly accommodates the use of radio technologies. Radio devices may be mounted within vehicles, or they may be portable and worn by individual officers as a component of uniform equipment. Organizational policy may govern the procurement, issuance, use, storage, and maintenance of such equipment. Additionally, policy may govern the communicated messages that are transmitted and received by radio technologies, and also the senders, receivers, and intermediaries that are involved with messaging.

An example of communications technology policy considerations is expressed within the policy manual of the Seattle (Washington) Police Department. This policy expresses radio procedures that are required to facilitate effective, efficient communications among law enforcement personnel. It also incorporates considerations of officer safety by delineating the proper method of reporting arrivals at the scene of an incident, assigning unit radio numbers, reporting the service status, and acknowledging the service assignments that are received from dispatchers. Figure 8.5 shows an excerpt from the policy manual.

The policy manual dictates acceptable and unacceptable behaviors that are to be exhibited by law enforcement personnel when using radio communication technology. For example, arguments between law enforcement personnel and dispatchers are disallowed. This restriction ensures that radio traffic conforms to only messaging that is pertinent to the functioning of law enforcement functions and messaging that is required to facilitate law enforcement operations. Any disputes or disagreements can later be discussed and resolved personally among affected personnel.

Implications for the hierarchical chain of command are also incorporated within the policy. Any violations of the policy are to be resolved through the appropriate chain of command within the organization. This specification of policy ensures that a method exists through which any issues that are associated with the abuse of radio technologies can be addressed organizationally through a methodical process.

The radio communications policy also contains clauses that enhance officer safety. Law enforcement officers are required to report their service status and are required to report their location and associated activities. By doing so, dispatchers know where the

* The policy expounds upon these primary tenets, and provides much greater detail regarding such incidents. Readers are encouraged to view the policy or to consult similar policies regarding the recording of incidents using video technology. The policy is available at Municipal Police Institute (n.d.).

III. Radio Procedures

A. Portable radios are assigned to specific units, sections, or positions. If a portable radio is required in an assignment, one will be provided to the employee by that unit or section. Employees must return their portable radios when they are reassigned or promoted.

Exception: All Commanders shall be assigned their own radio.

B. Unit radio numbers are assigned to each unit according to its function in the Department, for purposes of mobile communications. The Communications Captain maintains the list of radio assignment numbers.

C. When communicating by radio, field units shall first give their assigned unit radio number as identification. Communications between field units and Radio shall be conducted in a business-like manner, using proper language and correct procedures.

D. Field units shall keep the Communications Dispatcher advised of their "in" and "out of service" status during the entire time the mobile unit is assigned to field duty.

E. Officers comprising field units who receive a call from the Communications Dispatcher shall respond by giving their radio assignment number and their current location. If the call is received via Video Mobile Data Terminal (VMDT), officers may indicate that they are enroute viaVMDT.

F. Assignments from the dispatcher shall be acknowledged without further comment unless additional information is needed.

G. Field units responding to a dispatched call will advise the Communications Dispatcher of their arrival at the assigned location.

H. Whenever a field unit goes "out of service" for any reason except in response to a radio dispatched assignment, that unit shall notify the dispatcher by radio or VMDT that they intend to go "out of service," give the location, and briefly state the nature of the activity. The VMDT may be used to log oneself to on-view incidents and traffic stops. All coffee breaks and lunch breaks must be approved by the dispatcher.

I. Officers shall not argue with the Communications Dispatchers.

J. Violations of radio procedures or other causes for complaint, from either the dispatchers or field units, will be reported to the complainant's unit commander and processed through the proper channels.

K. Unit commanders are charged with the responsibility of ensuring that all complaints and violations noted are fully processed.

L. All employees of the Department are reminded of the limits of authority and responsibility within which they are assigned and that any unjustified attempts to breach them may result in discipline.

M. The Communications Section, in cooperation with the King County 800Mhz Regional Communications Board, has authority over the utilization of all Seattle Police Department 800 MHz talk groups.

Figure 8.5 Seattle, Washington, policy excerpt. (From Seattle Police Department. 2012. Policy and Procedure Manual, http://www.seattle.gov/police/publications/manual/, accessed December 27, 2012.)

officer is located and what activity they are pursuing. Having this knowledge betters the potential of dispatchers to allocate additional resources and to know the location of an officer if assistance is required.

Every law enforcement organization is different; no two are identical. The leadership of such organizations must craft policies that govern and influence communications technology resources. Although policies may be expressed, they must be understood throughout the entirety of the organization. Therefore, the leadership of law enforcement organizations must strive to ensure that all personnel are knowledgeable regarding the contents of organizational policy. Even though a policy must exist, the leadership of law enforcement organizations must also ensure an adherence to the policies of the organization. Therefore, some method of informing, enforcing, and addressing issues of policy must be accommodated throughout the entirety of the law enforcement organization.

Communications Technology in the Justice Domain

Communications technology has existed within the justice domain since its inception whether communication was facilitated by manual couriers and methods or through the use of modern electronic devices. During the nineteenth century, one of the earliest instances of using communications technology occurred in London, England, during 1845

(Packer, 2008). This incident involved the transmission of the location of a "train-bound murderer" through "wireless telegraph to police" across a distance of 18 miles (Packer, 2008). The murderer was "apprehended" when he departed the train (Packer, 2008).

The twentieth century witnessed numerous improvements in communications technology and policing. Within the United States, August Vollmer served as the Berkeley (California) Chief of Police between the years 1909 and 1932 (Cole & Smith, 2008). During his tenure, he advocated and heralded significant advancements in policing, including the use of motorcycle patrols, analysis of handwriting, and the use of fingerprints (Cole & Smith, 2008). Although these advancements improved policing methods, one of his most notable accomplishments was the integration of radio communications technology within the law enforcement domain.

The initial use of radio facilitated continuous communication between the Berkeley police headquarters and its police field units (Cole & Smith, 1928). All police routes were patrolled with vehicles that contained radio systems that consisted of "a radio receiver, with a loud speaker mounted just behind the steering wheel, and also headphones" if an officer preferred to "use them" (Cole & Smith, 1928). A "red light" was mounted within the vehicle through which an officer could be summoned if a Morse code wireless telegraph message was sent from headquarters (Cole & Smith, 1928). The radio system functioned perfectly at speeds of fifty miles an hour, and within three to five minutes the "entire force" could be "assembled at the scene of an alarm" (Cole & Smith, 1928).

Since the introduction of such radio equipment, the communications technology resources used within policing have continuously improved. Through time, each generation of police organizations has adapted the communications technology of the period to satisfy its requirements. Through the use of modern communications technology, law enforcement organizations can efficiently, effectively, and quickly "disseminate information" (Newburn & Neyroud, 2008).

The current instantiation of modern policing differs from those of its predecessors. Unlike policing paradigms of the 1970s in which "police officers thought they were doing a fine job if they responded quickly to calls for service and investigated crimes thoroughly," modern policing exhibits a greater focus toward deterring crime and maintaining societal order (Police Executive Research Forum, 2012). This change of perspective necessitates a greater and closer relationship between law enforcement organizations and their served communities (Police Executive Research Forum, 2012).

One of the methods through which this occurs involves the use of social networks as a communications tool. Many police departments are joining social networking sites as a method of maintaining a virtual presence through which they may interact and communicate with their respective populaces. Daily news may be posted to inform citizens of community events and the actions of the law enforcement organization. Social networking sites may be used to recruit candidate law enforcement officers by advertising open positions or class formations for upcoming police academies, may be used to request citizen assistance in solving crimes, and may be used as a community-oriented policing resource. Citizens may post commentaries and experience virtual discussions within the social network site, communicate with police personnel, or communicate with other citizens. Through the use of social networking, law enforcement organizations gain the ability to communicate with both a mass audience and individuals. This perspective of law enforcement organizations leveraging social media as a communications resource is primarily benevolent and demonstrates community outreach.

However, instead of primarily disseminating information, law enforcement organizations may retrieve information from social networks that may be critical when solving crimes. A strong example of the potency of using social networks to deter and counter criminal activity and organizations is the 2008 dismantling of a street gang in Cincinnati, Ohio. In this incident, a total of 71 people were arrested in conjunction with a nine-month investigation that involved the use of social media (Kelly, 2012). The Cincinnati police "created databases of information scraped from social networks, existing police records and phone records, then used software to analyze the data and establish links between suspects" (Kelly, 2012). Members of the criminal organization used social network media to communicate various details of their criminal deeds: "set up drug deals, brag about wrongdoings, and even upload incriminating videos" (Kelly, 2012).

This Cincinnati example highlights the saliency of using social media to conduct data mining, crime analysis, and crime mapping functions to establish necessary relationships within a collected set of data to show potential criminal attributes. This use of social media by law enforcement is not uncommon. During 2012, approximately 80% of law enforcement organizations indicated that they "use social media to assist in criminal investigations" (Thompson, 2012).

Another communications technology resource is the license plate reader (LPR). The LPR is an automated device that retrieves and displays vehicle ownership information electronically. An LPR "uses cameras to scan license plates within its field of vision, matches the scanned images against national crime databases, and alerts the officer" to pertinent crime attributes that may necessitate attention (Smith, 2012). These attributes may consist of outstanding warrants, stolen vehicles, criminal background of the owner of the vehicle, and known associates of the owner of the vehicle (Priest & Arkin, 2011). An LPR system is capable of processing approximately "1800 license plates per minute" (American Civil Liberties Union, 2012). More than one-third of "large U.S. police agencies," representing approximately 37%, implement some type of LPR system (Angwin & Valentino-Devries, 2012). Figure 8.6 depicts an LPR network system.

Although communication technologies provide law enforcement organizations with a vast plethora of information, they are not without debate and dispute. Constitutional issues are associated with the use of these communications technologies. During 2012, the American Civil Liberties Union (ACLU) filed a lawsuit against the Department of Homeland Security and the Department of Justice regarding the use of federal LPR systems (American Civil Liberties Union, 2012). This dispute involves privacy considerations of individuals potentially being tracked that are not being investigated for criminal offenses or who have no criminal record. Specifically, the lawsuit requests information regarding the following issues (American Civil Liberties Union, 2012):

- Do federal agencies operate their own LPRs?
- How long do they keep data?
- With whom do they share LPR data?
- How secure is the data?
- Are privacy policies in place to protect drivers?

License plate data is generally not considered to be a form of public information, and is accessible by law enforcement organizations. Collecting and processing of license plate data occurs daily throughout the nation without incident. However, the use of LPR systems

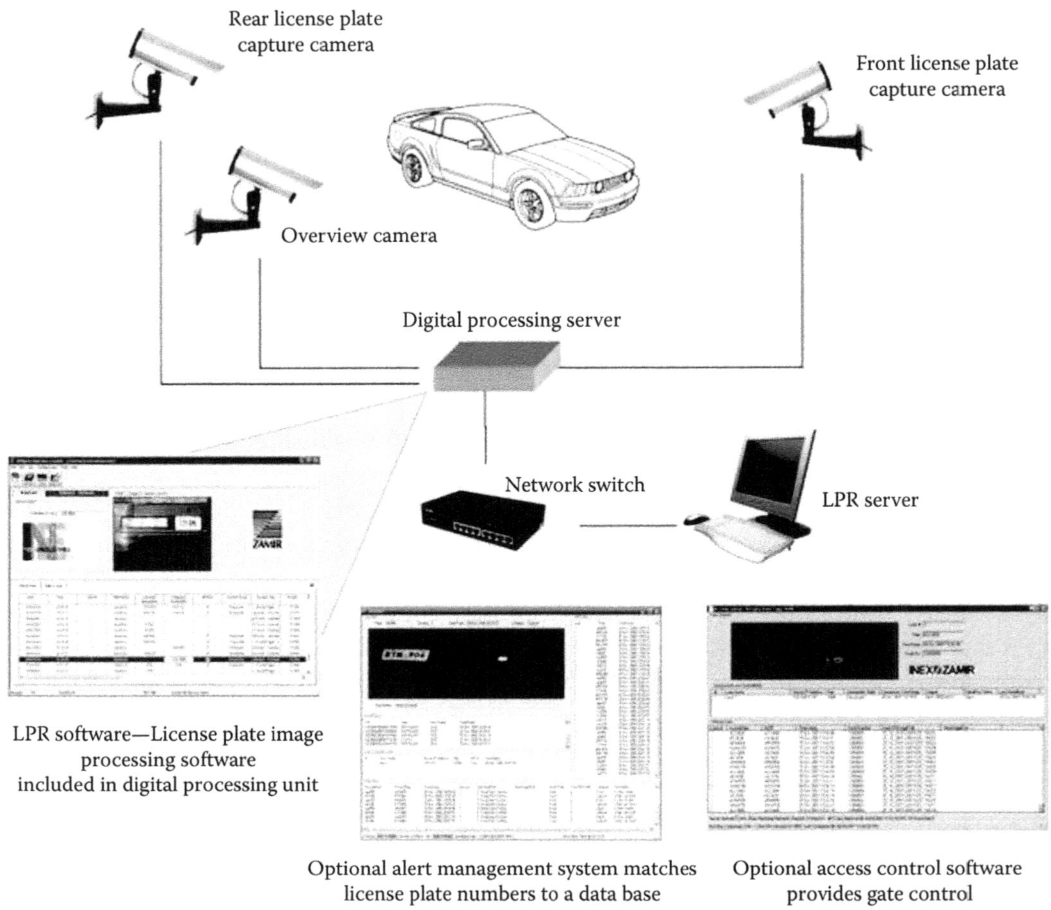

Figure 8.6 Networked LPR system. (From http://www.kintronics.com/lpr/lpr.html.)

also records and stores "the time, date, and location of each vehicle" (Insinna, 2012). The ACLU is concerned because the ability to collect and store such information facilitates an ability to create unnecessary profiles of individuals by "tracking the movements of citizens, which it believes would be a major invasion of privacy" (Insinna, 2012).

These observations are salient with respect to issues of security versus privacy within the domain of communications technology. The use of LPR equipment communicates the pertinent details of vehicle ownership. However, through the use of LPR technology, additional data is collected that is immaterial to ascertaining the ownership of a vehicle—namely, characteristics of date, time, and location regarding the collecting and the processing of the vehicular tag number. Concerns are associated with the potential for abusing LPR technology because "Privacy advocates counter that widespread license-plate tracking could have a chilling effect on private business conducted in public—such as parking outside counseling meetings, doctors' offices, or political protests" (Sussex County Angel, 2012).

Communications technology is a powerful resource within the domain of policing. Gone are the days of August Vollmer in which a relatively simple radio system was necessary for communicating among law enforcement entities. Modern times are rife with electronic technologies and sophisticated information processing systems through which communications are facilitated between entities. Although the introduction of radio technology to facilitate law enforcement communications greatly improved the ability of law enforcement organizations to serve communities, it did not necessarily incite large national debates and disputes regarding privacy versus security interests that are associated with modern technologies (e.g., LPRs). Regardless, communications technology is now tightly and seamlessly integrated among modern law enforcement organizations.

Through the use of such technologies, communicating is an instantaneous event that affects mass audiences as well as individuals. Because of the scope and magnitude of modern communications technologies, law enforcement organizations are better able to serve their respective communities, more efficiently and effectively than ever before. As new communications technologies emerge, they will also be integrated among law enforcement environment in due time to further improve these abilities. Each succeeding generation will adapt its communication technology to satisfy the needs of law enforcement to deter crime and to maintain societal order.

Commentary Regarding Communications Technology

Each generation has adapted the technology of its respective period within the justice domain. Through time, technology has changed and advanced with respect to the influences of new innovations. Incorporating new technologies within the policing domain has generated many improvements in the efficiency and effectiveness of law enforcement organizations regarding their ability to communicate both internally and externally. This integration of new technology also improves the ability of law enforcement organizations to serve society by deterring crime and maintaining societal order.

Regardless of the time periods or of the emerging of new technologies, the use of communications technology must adhere to the tenets and principles established within the U.S. Constitution. Law enforcement organizations and entities within the justice system must not transgress the laws they uphold daily when using communications technologies. Essentially, all uses of communications technologies must be legally conducted within the limits of expressed law.

The constitutionality of modern communications technologies often involves a consideration of both First Amendment and Fourth Amendment freedoms and rights. Citizens of the United States have the freedom of speech and the right not to experience and endure unreasonable searches and seizures. During modern times, the use of communications technologies often incites numerous issues, debates, and disputes regarding these basic freedoms.

One such incident involved a 2012 lawsuit in which "a gun-advocacy group" filed a lawsuit regarding allegations of "violations of the First Amendment, claiming Honolulu police arbitrarily delete posts and ban those who comment unfavorably about the department on the social media site" (Associated Press, 2012). A primary consideration of the argument involved the notion of whether the Facebook page was "government speech" or a "public forum" (Associated Press, 2012). As a result, the Honolulu police altered its "posting rules" to accommodate "unrestricted posting on the page" (Associated Press, 2012). At the time of this writing, the lawsuit is still pending and has not reached a conclusion.

The basic premise of the lawsuit is interesting. Public forums allow the responsible use of free speech. Therefore, theoretically, users of the forum should be able to responsibly entertain various discussions and postings. However, if the site is deemed to be a form of "government speech," then the governmental entity "has the right to control what speech it wants to support" (Associated Press, 2012). These notions are unchanged since the founding of the nation. The only change that has occurred through time represents technological advancements in communications technology through which humans send and receive messages.

This lawsuit is significant because it represents the newness of debates and disputes that accompany emerging technologies within the virtual domain. More specifically, in this case, the considered technology is communications technology. The outcome of this lawsuit will undoubtedly set a precedent that may affect many other future lawsuits and perspectives of social media within the justice domain.

Other issues of constitutionality, involving modern communications technology, have already been resolved within the court system. Such disputes involve a consideration of the Fourth Amendment versus personal privacy within the virtual domain of social networks. A recent 2012 lawsuit involved Melvin Colon regarding his postings of "public photos on Facebook that showed him flashing gang signs, but made private more incriminating posts, including references to past violent crimes and threats against others" (Kelly, 2012). Regarding this matter, any "legitimate expectation of privacy ended" when Colon "disseminated posts to his 'friends' because those 'friends' were free to use the information however they wanted—including sharing it with the government" (Kelly, 2012). The criminal charges against Colon involved narcotics offenses, weapons offenses, and murder (Kelly, 2012).

This lawsuit also represents the disputes and questions that surround the maturing of the uses of modern communications technologies. Its content clarifies the expectations of privacy that exist within the virtual domain regarding social networking resources and the consequences and ramifications of expressing written material that may be incriminating. Such material may be used as evidence during court proceedings.

Technology continues to advance. Modern technology will be antiquated by the capabilities and standards of future technologies. Regardless, the use of future technologies must also be constitutional, and will also raise legal questions involving an array of disputes and debates.

Additionally, the use of communications technology must also adhere to the constraints and mandates imposed by government factions. One such government entity is the Federal Communications Commission (FCC). The FCC oversees and "regulates interstate and international communications by radio, television, wire, satellite, and cable in all 50 states, the District of Columbia and U.S. territories" (Federal Communications Commission, 2012). It exists as an independent agency, and is "overseen by Congress" (Federal Communications Commission, 2012). The FCC originated as a result of the Communications Act of 1934 (Federal Communications Commission, 2012). This legislation integrated "combined and organized federal regulation of telephone, telegraph, and radio communications" (U.S. Department of Justice, 2012a).

Other uses of communications technology are influenced by different aspects of legislation. For instance, using communications technology to perform wiretapping activities must adhere to the constraints of federal law and the obtaining of warrants properly. Such activities are governed by the Electronic Communications Privacy Act (ECPA) of 1986.

The ECPA collectively "protects wire, oral, and electronic communications while those communications are being made, are in transit, and when they are stored on computers," and also "applies to e-mail, telephone conversations, and data stored electronically" (U.S. Department of Justice, 2012b).

To use communications technology to perform a variety of surveillance functions electronically, additional pieces of legislation must be considered. Some of the pertinent legislations that address the uses of communications technology involve considerations of the Communications Assistance for Law Enforcement Act (CALEA) of 2006 and the Foreign Intelligence Surveillance Act (FISA). Both pieces of legislation embellish the ability of law enforcement organizations to investigate domestic and international cases.

The CALEA "mandates the telecommunication companies' cooperation when law enforcement engages in a wiretap" by providing "access to the systems and facilities necessary to track the communication of one subscriber without infringing on the privacy of another subscriber" (Cornell University Law School, 2012). The FISA "authorizes the President to use warrantless wiretapping if it relates to protecting the United States against a potential grave attack, sabotage, or espionage, on the that the government does not tap any U.S. citizen" (Cornell University Law School, 2012). The FISA also allows law enforcement organizations to "obtain a warrant for foreign intelligence taps that do not meet the criteria of the first situation" (Cornell University Law School, 2012).

Law enforcement organizations admirably pursue the traditional goals of deterring crime and maintaining societal order. Leveraging communications technology is a method of fulfilling this fiduciary obligation to society. The uses range from merely informational and interactive through social networking or surveillance to collect and gather data from electronic communications. Regardless of the communication technology employed, whether telephonic, social network, or any other fashion, its use must be legally employed within the constraints of expressed law.

Chapter Comments and Summary

This chapter is devoted to discussing the technological frameworks through which human communication is facilitated. Although humans may communicate manually, manual communication is impeded by geographic distance and the time required for communicating effectively and efficiently. Through the passage of time and technological advancements, the efficiency and effectiveness of human communication has improved significantly. From the perspective of the communications process, these technological advancements are referred to as communications technology.

The historical advancements of technology were each incorporated within the justice domain generationally. Each generation has integrated its communications technology to satisfy the needs and requirements of law enforcement organizations. The use of a semaphore system was considered to be cutting edge during its period; today, its use is antiqued and barely remembered. Similarly, other instances of what was once considered to be advanced communications technology are now relegated to museums and history books. Although Vollmer's radio system was functional and effective, its scope and magnitude are humbled when compared with the characteristics of modern communications technologies.

Communications technology is nearly inescapable during modern times. It is present among social media, radio systems, tracking systems, telephone systems, video systems, audio systems, LPRs, and so forth. Therefore, modern communications technology represents an array of different functions and instantiations that permeate practically every facet of modern lifestyles and policing activities. Its power is immense, and it can facilitate communication with individuals and mass audiences instantaneously.

The use of modern communications technology also is the foundation of many debates regarding security versus privacy. Modern technology may be used to determine any number of personal attributes based on the specification of very little initial information (e.g., vehicular tag numbers). Many privacy concerns are addressed through the court system regarding the constitutionality of such uses and regarding the potential conditions that may facilitate the abuse of communications technology for illicit purposes.

Terminology

Audio technology
August Vollmer
Automation
Camera
Communication technology
Communications Act of 1934
Communications Assistance for Law Enforcement Act of 2006
Electronic Communications Privacy Act of 1986
Electronic network
Federal Communications Commission
Foreign Intelligence Surveillance Act
Generation
Legislation
License plate reader
Mass audience
Mass media
Mobility
Multimedia technology
Network
Phonograph
Policy
Printing technology
Privacy
Radio
Regulation
Satellite technology
Security
Semaphore
Social media
Social network
Surveillance

Technology
Telegraph
Television
Video technology
Wired network
Wireless network
Wireless telegraphy

THOUGHT AND DISCUSSION QUESTIONS

1. Human nature and the primary tenets of the U.S. Constitution are unchanged since the founding of the nation. However, communications technology has changed greatly over the years. Do some research, and investigate the characteristics of two technologies that were presented within the historical discussions of this chapter. Write an essay that discusses how these pieces of historical technology contributed toward the crafting of modern communications technologies.
2. Technology is continuously changing through time. Do some research, and investigate the potential technologies that are expected to improve future instantiations of communications technology. Write an essay that discusses two emerging technologies that you believe will influence future communications within the justice domain.
3. This chapter introduced the notion that the use of undersea communications cables was replaced with the use of satellite systems. Do some research, and determine what other technological advancements contributed to the antiquating of technologies that were used by law enforcement organizations during the latter half of the twentieth century. Write an essay that discusses your findings.
4. This chapter introduces various debates and issues that are associated with emerging technologies within the contexts of the communications domain and law enforcement. The discussions herein primarily examine First Amendment and Fourth Amendment freedoms. From the perspective of the characteristics of modern communications technologies, write an essay that discusses how some of the other amendments may be debated within the context of law enforcement.

References

Abramson, A. (2003). *The history of television, 1942–2000*. Jefferson, NC: McFarland and Company, Inc.

Allen, M. (2012). *Michael Allen's 2012 e-Learning annual* (p. 35). San Francisco: Pfeiffer Publishing.

American Civil Liberties Union. (2012). ACLU sues federal agencies over license plate reader information. Retrieved from http://www.aclu.org/national-security/aclu-sues-federal-agencies-over-license-plate-reader-information (accessed December 29, 2012).

Anderson, J. (2011). *Public policymaking: An introduction* (p. 6). Boston: Wadsworth Publishing.

Andrews, J. (2009). *A+ guide to managing and maintaining your PC* (6th ed., p. 434). Boston: Cengage.

Angwin, J., & Valentino-Devries, J. (2012). New tracking frontier: Your license plates. *The Wall Street Journal*. Retrieved from http://online.wsj.com/article/SB10000872396390443995604578004723603576296.html (accessed December 29, 2012).

Associated Press. (2012). Hawaii gun group sues police over deleted facebook posts. First Amendment Center. Retrieved from http://www.firstamendmentcenter.org/hawaii-gun-group-sues-police-over-deleted-facebook-posts (accessed December 29, 2012).

Baran, S., & Davis, D. (2012). *Mass communication theory: Foundations, ferment, and future* (6th ed., p. 19). Boston: Wadsworth-Cengage.

Bianculli, A. (2003). *Trains and technology: The American railroad in the nineteenth century*. Cranbury, NJ: Associated University Presses.

Blanchard, O. (2011). *Social media ROI: Managing and measuring social media efforts in your organization*. Boston: Pearson Education Publishing.

Clancy, T. (n.d.). Technology quotes. Brainyquote. Retrieved from http://www.brainyquote.com/quotes/keywords/technology_4.html (accessed December 24, 2012).

Cole, G., & Smith, C. (1928). Radio police patrol city of eighty thousand. *Popular Mechanics Magazine, 49*(2), 185.

Cole, G., & Smith, C. (2008). *Criminal justice in America* (5th ed., p. 94). Belmont, CA: Thomson Higher Education.

Cornell University Law School. (2012). Electronic surveillance. Retrieved from http://www.law.cornell.edu/wex/electronic_surveillance (accessed December 29, 2012).

Dagostino, F., & Wujek, J. (2005). *Mechanical and electrical systems in construction and architecture* (p. 695). Upper Saddle River, NJ: Prentice-Hall Publishing.

Duncan, S., & Goddard, H. W. (2011). *Family life education: Principles and practices for effective outreach* (2nd ed.). Thousand Oaks, CA: Sage Publishing.

Federal Communications Commission. (2012). What we do. Retrieved from http://www.fcc.gov/what-we-do (accessed December 28, 2012).

Feng, D. (2008). *Biomedical information technology* (p. 497). Burlington, MA: Academic Press.

Fredericks, G. (2008). Caught on camera: The clear capture of officer murders is a grim reality of this powerful technology. *Evidence Technology Magazine*. Retrieved from http://www.evidencemagazine.com/index.php?option=com_content&task=view&id=431 (accessed December 17, 2012).

Furht, B. (2010). *Handbook of social network technologies and applications* (p. 4). New York: Springer Publishing.

Grant, A., & Meadows, J. (2008). *Communications technology: Update and fundamentals* (11th ed.). Burlington, MA: Focal Press.

Hart, T., Greenfield, J., MacLaughlin, S., & Geier, P. (2010). *Internet management for nonprofits: Strategies, tools, and trade secrets* (p. 167). Hoboken, NJ: John Wiley & Sons Publishing.

Insinna, V. (2012). License plate reader technology sparks lawsuit. National Defense Industrial Association. Retrieved from http://www.nationaldefensemagazine.org/archive/2012/November/Pages/LicensePlateReaderTechnologySparksLawsuit.aspx (accessed December 29, 2012).

International Association of Police Chiefs. (2003). The impact of video evidence on modern policing. Retrieved from http://www.cops.usdoj.gov/Publications/video_evidence.txt (accessed December 27, 2012).

Jackson, L. (2002). *Twentieth century pattern design* (p. 219). New York: Princeton Architectural Press.

Johansson, K., Lundberg, P., & Ryberg, R. (2012). *A guide to graphic print production* (3rd ed., p. 303). Hoboken, NJ: John Wiley & Sons Publishing.

Keith, M. (2012). *The radio station: Broadcast, satellite, and internet* (8th ed., p. 294). Burlington, MA: Focal Press.

Kelly, H. (2012). Police embrace social media as crime-fighting tool. CNN News. Retrieved from http://www.cnn.com/2012/08/30/tech/social-media/fighting-crime-social-media/index.html (accessed December 29, 2012).

Kleiner, M. (2012). *Acoustics and audio technology* (3rd ed.). Ft. Lauderdale, FL: J. Ross Publishing.

Klopfenstein, B. (1997). New technology and the future of the media. In A. Wells, & E. Hakanen (Eds.), *Mass media and society* (pp. 19–49). Greenwich, CT: Ablex Publishing Corporation.

Knepper, P., Doak, J., & Shapland, J. (2009). *Urban crime prevention, surveillance, and restorative justice: Effects of social technologies*. Boca Raton, FL: CRC Press.

Limaye, M. G. (2009). *Software testing: Principles, techniques, and tools* (p. 509). New Delhi, India: Tata McGraw-Hill Publishing.

Lokensgard, E. (2004). *Industrial plastics: Theory and application* (4th ed., p. 329). Clifton Park, NY: Delmar Learning.

Madura, J. (2007). *Introduction to business* (4th ed., p. 340). Mason, OH: Thomson South-Western Publishing.

Maini, A., & Agrawal, V. (2007). *Satellite technology: Principles and applications* (p. 4). Hoboken, NJ: John Wiley & Sons Publishing.

Merriam-Webster Dictionary. (2012a). s.v. "network." Retrieved from http://www.merriam-webster.com/dictionary/network (accessed December 24, 2012).

Merriam-Webster Dictionary. (2012b). s.v. "technology." Retrieved from http://www.merriam-webster.com/dictionary/technology?show=0&t=1356414184 (accessed December 24, 2012).

Misiroglu, G. (2002). *The handy politics answer book* (p. 143). Canton, MI: Visible Ink Press.

Morton, D. (2004). *Sound recording: The life story of a technology*. Westport, CT: Greenwood Publishing.

Morton, D., & Gabriel, J. (2004). *Electronics: The life story of a technology*. Baltimore, MD: The Johns Hopkins University Press.

Municipal Police Institute. (n.d.). In-car video recording. Policy & Procedure No. 4.14. Grafton, MA. p. 5. Retrieved from http://www.google.com/url?sa=t&rct=j&q=police+policy+in-car&source=web&cd=1&cad=rja&ved=0CDoQFjAA&url=http%3A%2F%2Fwww.municipalpoliceinstitute.org%2Fdocuments%2F4.14%2520In-Car%2520Video%2520Recording.doc&ei=4PjbUNeCK4zy9gTB7YCwBA&usg=AFQjCNGKx_ohxPSPZcRwRKtgpxn_3az5Kw&bvm=bv.1355534169,d.eWU (accessed December 28, 2012).

Murphy, F. (2013). *Community engagement, organization, and development for public health practice* (p. 249). New York: Springer Publishing.

Newburn, T., & Neyroud, P. (2008). *Dictionary of policing* (p. 273). Portland, OR: Willan Publishing.

Ohta, B., & Rosen, M. (2006). *Color desktop printer technology* (p. 4). Boca Raton, FL: CRC Press.

Packer, J. (2008). *Mobility without mayhem: Safety, cars, and citizenship* (p. 170). Durham, NC: Duke University Press.

Pannu, P., & Tomar, Y. (2010). *ICT4D: Information communication technology for development* (p. 224). New Delhi, India: I.K. International Publishing House Pvt., Ltd.

Parekh, R. (2006). *Principles of multimedia* (p. 220). New Delhi, India: Tata McGraw-Hill.

Parsons, J., & Oja, D. (2012). *New perspectives on computer concepts 2012: Comprehensive*. Boston: Course Technology.

Pattavina, A. (2005). *Information technology and the criminal justice system*. Thousand Oaks, CA: Sage Publishing.

Pease, W., Rowe, M., & Cooper, M. (2007). *Information and communication technologies in support of the tourism industry*. Hershey, PA: Idea Group Publishing.

Pedersen, P., Miloch, K., & Laucella, P. (2007). *Strategic sport communication*. Champaign, IL: Human Kinetics Publishing.

Pho, H., Han, S., & Kang, B. (2011). Emergency-affected identification notification by using online social networks. In T.-H. Kim, H. Adeli, H.-K. Kim, H.-J. Kang, K. Kim, A. Kim, & B.-H. Kang (Eds.), *Software engineering, business continuity, and education* (p. 543). New York: Springer Publishing.

Police Executive Research Forum. (2012). *How are innovations in technology transforming policing?* (p. iii). Washington, DC: Police Executive Research Forum.

Pride, W., Hughes, R., & Kapoor, R. (2013). *Foundations of business* (3rd ed., p. 231). Mason, OH: South-Western Publishing.

Priest, D., & Arkin, W. (2011). *Top secret America: The rise of the new American security state*. New York: Hatchette.

Romano, F. (2000). *Digital printing: Mastering on-demand and variable data printing for profit* (p. 155). San Diego, CA: Windsor Professional Information.

Ryan, W., & Conover, T. (2004). *Graphic communications today* (4th ed., p. 301). Clifton Park, NY: Delmar Learning.

Seattle Police Department. (2012). Policy and procedure manual. Retrieved from http://www.seattle.gov/police/publications/policy/spd_manual.pdf (accessed December 27, 2012).

Shelly, G., & Vermaat, M. (2012). *Discovering computers complete: Your interactive guide to the digital world* (p. 345). Boston: Course Technology.

Shelly, G., Cashman, T., Gunter, G., & Gunter, R. (2007). *Teachers discovering computers: Integrating technology and digital media in the classroom* (p. 318). Independence, KY: Cengage, Learning.

Smith, D. (2012). Police license-plate scanners raise privacy concerns. *The Sacramento Bee*. Retrieved from http://www.sacbee.com/2012/11/28/5014520/police-license-plate-scanners.html (accessed December 29, 2012).

Sony Service Centre. (2001). *Digital audio technology: A guide to CD, MiniDisc, SACD, DVD(A), MP3, and DAT*. Woburn, MA: Focal Press.

Stair, R., & Reynolds, G. (2010). *Principles of information systems* (9th ed.). Boston: Cengage Publishing.

Sterling, C. (2008). *Military communications: From ancient times to the 21st century* (p. 311). Santa Barbara, CA: ABC-CLIO Publishing.

Sussex County Angel. (2012). Police using license plate readers are creating a national database of our movements. Retrieved from http://sussexcountyangel.wordpress.com/2012/09/08/police-using-license-plate-readers-are-creating-a-national-database-of-our-movements (accessed June 5, 2014).

Sward, G. G., & Gardner, H. A. (1972). *Paint testing manual: Physical and chemical examination of paints, varnishes, lacquers, and colors* (13th ed., p. 490). West Conshohocken, PA: American Society for Testing and Materials.

Thompson, C. (2012). Busted! Police turn to social media to fight crime. *CNBC News*. Retrieved from http://www.cnbc.com/id/48232039/Busted_Police_Turn_to_Social_Media_to_Fight_Crime (accessed December 28, 2012).

Thompson, K. (2005). *Sales automation done right: Selling in the digital age*. Ontario, Canada: SalesWays Press.

Tiffin, J., & Kissling, C. (2007). *Transport communications: Understanding global networks enabling transport* (p. 91). Philadelphia, PA: Kogan Page Publishing.

Tipton, H., & Krause, M. (2007). *Information security management handbook* (p. 378). Boca Raton, FL: Auerbach Publications.

U.S. Department of Justice. (2012a). The Communications Act of 1934. Retrieved from http://www.it.ojp.gov/default.aspx?area=privacy&page=1288 (accessed December 29, 2012).

U.S. Department of Justice. (2012b). Electronic Communications Privacy Act of 1986. Retrieved from http://www.it.ojp.gov/default.aspx?area=privacy&page=1285#contentTop (accessed December 29, 2012).

U.S. Department of Transportation. (1997). *Transportation statistics annual report 1997* (p. 269). Washington, DC: U.S. Government.

Watt, N. (2012). 'Sobriety bracelets' to monitor offenders in alcohol-related cases. *The Guardian*. Retrieved from http://www.guardian.co.uk/law/2012/mar/17/sobriety-bracelets-alcohol-related-crimes (accessed December 26, 2012).

Welch, D. (2000). *Germany, propaganda, and total war, 1914–1918: The sins of omission*. Brunswick, NJ: Rutgers University Press.

Westphal, L. (2004). The in-car camera: Value and impact. *Police Chief Magazine*. Retrieved from http://www.policechiefmagazine.org/magazine/index.cfm?fuseaction=display_arch&article_id=358&issue_id=82004 (accessed December 17, 2012).

Willis, J. (2010). *100 media moments that changed America* (p. 43). Santa Barbara, CA: ABC-CLIO Publishing.

Wimmer, R., & Dominick, J. (2011). *Mass media research: An introduction* (9th ed.). Boston: Wadsworth Cengage Publishing.

Witzel, M. (2009). *Management history: Text and cases* (p. 279). New York: Routledge Publishing.

World Skills International. (2012). Print Media Technology. Retrieved from http://www.worldskills.org/index.php?option=com_content&task=view&id=303&Itemid=429 (accessed December 26, 2012).

Organizational Communication 9

Think like a wise man but communicate in the language of the people.
—William Butler Yeats (Yeats, n.d.)

Objectives

The objectives of this chapter are to

- Discuss Maslow's hierarchy of needs
- Discuss communications directionality
- Discuss conflict resolution
- Discuss networks and channels
- Discuss communication styles
- Discuss communications failure
- Discuss communications policy

Introduction

All organizations are unique; no two are identical. Each organization is composed of individuals whose skills, knowledge, experiences, and personal characteristics individually contribute uniquely to the whole of the organization. The most valuable asset that any organization possesses is its people. Organizations are no better than the people that comprise them, ranging from the lowest janitor to the highest-ranking officer within the organizational hierarchy. Regardless of the station, tenure, or affiliation with an organization, people will communicate. Among organizations, people are the catalysts of communication.

Within organizational settings, people may communicate as individuals or as groups. Communications may be sent and received on behalf of organizations. Messaging may flow either externally or internally with respect to organizational boundaries. Internally, communication flows in multiple directions. Externally, communication occurs between different organizations. In any case, organizations have a need to communicate.

This need to communicate arises from a variety of origins; there is no solitary cause. Managing directors may receive monthly reports from any number of subordinate work groups. Status meetings may involve representation from numerous department heads who must communicate with each other regarding the progress of their respective departments. Organizations may issue official announcements through the conduction of press conferences or press releases. Different work groups and teams may communicate with each other. Certainly, many other examples may be identified. Regardless, communication occurs internally among organizations and externally with other entities.

Organizations are dynamic entities. They change through time according to the influences of a variety of factors. Within the justice system, such factors may include the election of new judges or chiefs of police; retirements and replacements of personnel; formation or dissolution of organizations or their components; changes of laws, policies, and regulations; integration of new technologies; and a myriad of other factors. Regardless, such characteristics influence and necessitate communication among organizational structures.

Organizational communication is complex. Conflicts may arise between individuals or among groups that necessitate quick resolution. Managers may solicit advice from their subordinates before making decisions. Methods of evaluation may exist organizationally that necessitate communication. Gender differences may influence communication within the organizational structure. Misunderstandings of messages often occur among organizations, thereby affecting their efficiency and effectiveness. Personal biases may affect organizational communication. Communications networks may be disabled, thereby either impeding or completely eliminating the ability to communicate organizationally.

Organizational communication represents an array of woven facets that present different, complex perspectives of communicating with humans. Regardless of whether one must facilitate communication to resolve dispute between work groups or invoke an appropriate chain of command for communication among the various layers of the organizational structure, humans are associated with the relevant communications processes. Essentially, organizational communication represents another perspective of human communication.

Maslow and Communication

Abraham Maslow published a hierarchy of human needs during the 1940s. This hierarchy begins with the basic motivational needs of physiological human existence and progress through the highest motivational stage of human self-actualization. Maslow developed and expressed this hierarchical needs theory because other theories of human motivation were limited and constrained to "basic physiological needs," and did not accommodate considerations of human "personal growth" (Eysenck, 2004). Beginning with its lowest level, the hierarchy developed and posed by Maslow is presented in Table 9.1.

Table 9.1 Maslow's Hierarchy of Human Needs

Level	Layer	Description
1	Survival	Lowest level representing physiological needs such as "food, drink, shelter, sleep, etc." (Federal Bureau of Investigation, 2012)
2	Safety	Security concerns—consist of needs such as stability, environmental predictability, freedom of "physical, economic, or psychological anxiety" (Federal Bureau of Investigation, 2012)
3	Inclusion/belonging	Personal concerns—consist of needs for "affection, and intimacy from partners, family, and group" (Federal Bureau of Investigation, 2012)
4	Esteem	Personal concerns—consist of needs such as "self-confidence, recognition, appreciation, and respect from others" (Federal Bureau of Investigation, 2012)
5	Self-actualization	Highest level representing needs of "discovering and fulfilling one's own potential" (Federal Bureau of Investigation, 2012)

This hierarchy is relatively easy to understand. It is a progressive hierarchy in which the needs of the lowest level must be satisfied before the higher needs can be satisfied. The needs of any one level must be satisfied before progression to the next highest level occurs. For example, within the lowest level of the hierarchy, humans must sleep and eat to ensure the proper functioning and survival of their bodies, whereas the highest level of the hierarchy represents the fulfillment of human potential. Attaining the highest level necessitates the progression of each stage of the hierarchy successively. After the basic human needs for survival are satisfied, the human needs of security and safety, belonging, esteem, and self-actualization occur progressively through time.

Progressing through the stages of the hierarchy has implications for communication. Humans must communicate to obtain the resources that are necessary for survival. Humans must communicate their requirements for ensuring safety and security (e.g., completing a job interview to obtain employment). Humans must interact and communicate with others in group settings to facilitate a sense of belonging and inclusion. Communication occurs to show the recognition of human accomplishments and rewards. All of these successive progressions culminate in self-actualization.

Maslow's hierarchy has implications for organizations. Organizations are composed of humans and incorporate the characteristics and influences of human nature within their components and structures. Therefore, all organizations are influenced by the needs of humans throughout their breadth and depth, and among their activities and functions. The hierarchy developed and posed by Maslow can be embellished to portray the organizational perspective incorporating the influences of human needs. Beginning from the lowest level of needs, the embellished hierarchy is presented in Table 9.2.

Commensurate with the original hierarchy established by Maslow, the organizational version commences with the notions of basic survival needs and progresses successively through each of the separate stages to culminate in self-actualization through time. The initial, lowest level signifies the need of humans to earn financial resources that are sufficient to procure the basic essentials of life, including the purchasing of food, shelter, and clothing. The second level represents work environments that pose few physical threats to workers. The third level represents the human interactions that occur among peer employees within an organization. The fourth level represents the acknowledgment and recognition of accomplishments and outcomes within the work setting. The highest level represents self-actualization through which some level of control is exhibited through the liberty of creativity.

Table 9.2 Organizational Perspective of Maslow's Hierarchy

Level	Layer	Description
1	Survival	Lowest level representing needs of "a 'living wage' to allow purchase of food and clothing" (Miller, 2012, p. 41)
2	Safety	Represents needs of work environments that are "physically safe" (Miller, 2012, p. 41)
3	Inclusion/belonging	Represents needs of "social relationships" among peer workers (Miller, 2012, p. 41)
4	Esteem	Represents needs of "rewarding work" and "bonus pay" (Miller, 2012, p. 41)
5	Self-actualization	Highest level representing needs of "work allowing the exercise of creativity" (Miller, 2012, p. 41)

Within the justice domain, this enhancement of Maslow's hierarchy has implications for organizations. Within the lowest level, justice system personnel must earn sufficient money to pay for their basic costs of living. For example, local market rates may influence the rates attorneys may charge clients for their services, thereby justifying their rates. The next level incorporates work environments that are reasonably safe to prevent harm from occurring to personnel within the justice system. Scanning mechanisms may be used to screen people for potential weapons or dangerous objects before entering courtrooms.

The middle level represents human relationships among justice system personnel. Attorneys, judges, clients, and law enforcement personnel interact and communicate with each other cooperatively and collaboratively. This interaction leads to the next stage involving the esteem of personnel. Recognizing the accomplishments of personnel may be done both internally and externally through the announcement of awards or certificates earned through hard work, commitment, and merit. The final stage culminates in self-actualization within the organization in which personnel have some control and creativity.

Within the justice system, communication occurs throughout this enhanced model of Maslow's hierarchy. Working wages are generally communicated orally or in writing during personnel job interviews. Organizational policies are written and disseminated throughout organizations to bolster environmental safety and security by clarifying what behaviors are acceptable and unacceptable. Through time, personnel achieve a variety of accomplishments that contribute toward the improvement of esteem and confidence. Publishing promotions, retirements, or heroics both internally and externally regarding an organization contributes to satisfying the need for human esteem. Some individuals may be promoted into leadership and assume positions of responsibility within the organization that involve large amounts of power and influence over others. These individuals communicate their vision and orders throughout the organization. Achieving this level of status may incite self-actualization in which the potential of personnel is realized.

Although organizations may be established through the crafting of artificial entities (e.g., corporations, government agencies, and special interest groups), their basic, primary unit is the solitary human. During their association with an organization, humans have various needs that require fulfilling through time, ranging from basic survival to the manifestation of their aspirations involving self-actualization. Regardless, to have these needs satisfied, whether individually or organizationally, communication must occur with others.

Such communication may be as simple as asking for a pay raise or asking a coworker for assistance. From the cumulative perspective of organizations, it may be exhibited through the public announcement of a joint venture or a strategic partnership in which different organizations collaborate mutually to attain some long-term, strategic goals and objectives. In any case, communication must occur between and among humans with respect to the fulfillment of some need whether personally or organizationally.

Organizational Directionality of Communication

Directionality is defined as "operating most effectively in a particular direction" or "relating to direction or guidance especially of thought or effort" (*Merriam-Webster*, 2012a). This definition has implications for communicating among law enforcement organizations and within the justice system. Personnel may communicate with subordinates to direct their actions. Others may communicate by sending reports to supervisors within their established chain of command. Personnel may communicate and collaborate with their immediate or distant peers to resolve some issue.

Although the communications process occurs between the sender and the receivers of an intended message, it involves some notion of direction regarding the flow of communication. The preceding scenarios demonstrate three perspectives of directionality within the communications process: downwardly, upwardly, and horizontally. Generally, the directionality of communication within organizations occurs in accordance with the scope of the established chain of command.

Communicating Downwardly

Communicating downwardly involves a top–down perspective regarding the organizational chain of command. This type of downward communication is defined as flowing from "supervisor to subordinate" (Hitt et al., 2009, p. 298). Within the justice domain, numerous examples of downward communication are present. On example involves the use of patrol scripts to control policing activities among communities. This concept is expressed as follows (Rivero & Pepper, 2010):

> Crime data and event data can be obtained, aggregated, and plotted on a unique daily patrol script by the department's crime prevention professionals and shift sergeants prior to the start of the shift. The patrol officers then know ahead of time who, what, when, where, why, and how proactive patrols need to be conducted for that shift. (Rivero & Pepper, 2010)

The use of patrol scripts shows a downward flow of information organizationally. Data is collected, analyzed, and interpreted, and the concluding outcomes are then forwarded to shift supervisors. These shift supervisors then disseminate this information to their subordinate patrol officers. After receiving this information, patrol officers are better informed during the course of their duty shifts. The downward flow of communicating occurs between supervisors and subordinates. Within this flow of communication are contained the primary six questions, discussed within the preceding chapters, that provide a good amount of information that may assist individual patrol officers when performing their duties in the field.

Communicating Upwardly

Communicating upwardly involves a bottom–up perspective regarding the organizational chain of command. This type of upward communication is defined as flowing from "subordinates to supervisors" (Hitt et al., 2009, p. 298). This type of communication is present among law enforcement organizations and within the justice system. One example involves the periodic reporting of the status of training regarding law enforcement personnel. In the state of Indiana, such periodic reports are required annually (State of Indiana, 2012). The state of Indiana expresses this reporting requirement as follows:

> "Annual training status report" means the report that the chief executive officer of every department or agency in Indiana must submit, to the executive director of the board, detailing the training received by all of that department's law enforcement officers and reserve police officers during the previous calendar year. (State of Indiana, 2012)

This type of reporting represents an upward flow of communication from local agencies to a higher authority regarding training issues. Individual law enforcement organizations are subordinate to the Law Enforcement Training Board (LETB) regarding training issues, and must adhere to its tenets and mandates. Submitting the required reports periodically informs the LETB of the readiness and ability of personnel and individual law enforcement organizations.

Such reporting is not uncommon within the justice domain. This type of reporting shows the attributes of the organization regarding its ability to effectively and efficiently render public service. In some cases, if deficiencies are found, then they may be rectified accordingly. In other cases, if any awards for exemplary training performance are necessary, then they may be conferred accordingly. Regardless, this type of reporting demonstrates an upward flow of communication because it commences with subordinate entities, and is forwarded to a higher level of administrative structuring.

Communicating Horizontally

The act of communicating horizontally occurs between equivalent levels or entities within an organization. Specifically, it is defined as communicating "between associates at the same level" within an organization (Hitt et al., 2009, p. 299). Another definition expresses that it is messaging "within or across work units" (Gaines & Worrell, 2012). Regardless of the definition, a solitary concept is present: horizontal communication is neither downward nor upward organizationally; it is linear.

Among law enforcement organizations and within the justice system, such communication is prevalent. Within law enforcement organizations, it may occur between day-shift and night-shift supervisors. Horizontal communication may occur among individual patrol officers when they speak and interact among themselves. Within the justice system, attorneys may communicate directly with each other to achieve some consensus before court appearances. Regardless of the consideration, horizontal communication occurs directly across organizational boundaries without any upward or downward communications flow.

Communications Networks and Channels

The notions of communicating upwardly, downwardly, and horizontally contribute to the notion of a communications network. A communication network represents the entities (both senders and receivers) that are involved in the conduction of communications and the paths through which communication flows among these entities. Although upward, downward, and horizontal communication represents the three primary directions of communications flow organizationally, they also are representative of a communications network.

Communications networks are either internal or external (Sen, 2007). Internal networks comprise only senders, receivers, and transmissions pathways that are within the boundaries of a solitary organization. For example, shift supervisors may communicate with their respective patrol personnel. External networks represent senders, receivers, and pathways that exist between completely different organizations. For example, a local law enforcement agency may need to communicate with a federal law enforcement agency. These perspectives of internal and external communication also represent instantiations of communications

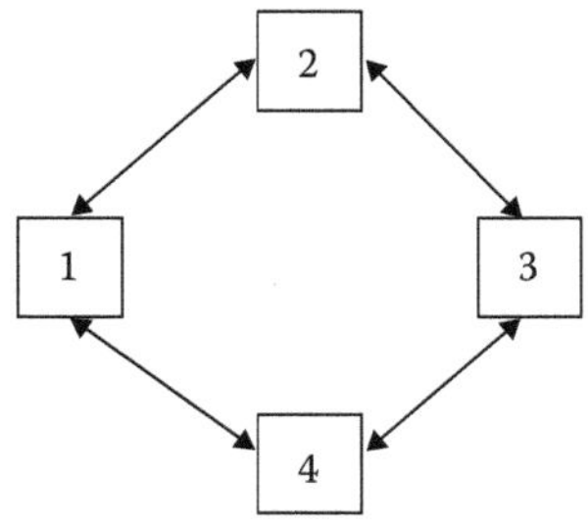

Figure 9.1 Sample communications network.

networks. The former instance is representative of an internal communications network, whereas the latter instance is representative of an external communications network.

Communications networks may be expressed graphically and analyzed mathematically. Within a communications network, points and lines exist to denote the pertinent senders, receivers, and paths that exist within the networked infrastructure. Senders and receivers are denoted by points, whereas pathways showing connectivity are denoted by lines. Within a communications network, points denoting senders and receivers are referred to as nodes. Lines denoting pathways between nodes are referred to as connections. Figure 9.1 shows this concept.

Graphically displaying the network shows the infrastructure of the connected environment. Within Figure 9.1, nodes are denoted by numbered squares. The numbers may be used to denote specific individuals or departments within an organization. Connections are denoted by lines connecting the individual nodes. The directionality of communication flows is denoted by the arrows contained within the connecting lines.

Communications networks may be analyzed mathematically. It is possible to determine quantitatively the number of connections that may exist within a network provided that the population size is known. The mathematical formula for calculating the number of channels that exist within a given population is stated as follows (Richardson, 2010):

$$C = N\frac{(N-1)}{2} \tag{9.1}$$

The following variable descriptions are pertinent when understanding this formula:

C = quantity of channels
N = population size

A straightforward example may be used to show this concept. If a group has 14 members that may all communicate with each other directly, then the number of channels for communicating directly is calculated as follows:

$$C = N\frac{(N-1)}{2}$$

$$C = (14)\frac{(14-1)}{2}$$

$$C = 240$$

Understanding how to mathematically calculate communications paths quantitatively has implications for planning and managing of organizational growth through time. For example, if an organization is anticipating growth through time, then knowing its expected communications path requirements contributes toward the financing and obtaining of additional resources through time to facilitate connectivity among personnel.

These considerations of connectivity also incorporate considerations of whether all members within a population are capable of directly communicating with each other. From a mathematical perspective, this consideration of networks involves two classifications: fully connected and partially connected. Fully connected networks are constructs in which "each node is connected to all the others" (Vervest et al., 2005). Partially connected networks are constructs in which not all of the nodes are directly connected to each other. However, any node within the partial construct has the capability to communicate with any other node within the network either directly or indirectly.

Theoretically, among mission-critical communications environments, communications networks must be robust enough to endure calamities to facilitate the continuity of communications during man-made or natural incidents. This notion is referred to as fault tolerance. Essentially, a fault-tolerant network is one whose design is fashioned to accommodate a variety of potential events that endanger communications. In many cases, redundant communications channels and alternative modalities of transmitting messages may be incorporated within the design of the communications network to improve its robustness.

Communications networks also may be formal or informal. Formal communications networks exhibit an established chain of command and adhere to the formal structuring of the organization. Most all of the preceding examples represent some aspects of formal networks. Informal networks are rather different because they may be loosely coupled, cross-organizational boundaries; have no adherence to the structure of the organization; and may be influenced by personal contacts. Informal networks invoke the "natural desire of people" to "interact and communicate" among themselves regarding "the latest information or event" (Jayarum & Kotwani, 2012). An example of an informal network is the typical office grapevine. The grapevine represents a "universal method of transmitting messages of unofficial means," generally "quickly and accurately" (Sims, 2002).

Communication is an essential attribute of any organization. All organizations possess channels of communication both formally and informally. Organizations are also affected by both internal and external communications. People will disseminate information either through official means within an organization or unofficially via the informal methods of a grapevine. Regardless of the context, communicating is an essential function of all components of an organization and of all humans within an organization. Only through leveraging communications networks appropriately can organizations function effectively and efficiently.

Conflict Resolution and Communication

Within organizations and between different organizations, various conflicts and disputes may arise through time. Communication is an essential and critical aspect of resolving such issues. Certainly, the court system is a domain in which conflicts and disputes are resolved. However, it is not the only method of resolving conflicts in which communicating is necessary between the affected rivals. Four other methods exist: arbitration, mediation, negotiation, and facilitation.

Arbitration

Arbitration is defined as the "action of arbitrating," involving the "hearing and determination of a case in controversy by an arbiter" (*Merriam-Webster*, 2012b). Generally, arbitration involves a "neutral, third party" or a panel of "neutral parties" rendering a decision regarding the "merits" of the considered situation (Fiadjoe, 2004). Essentially, arbitration is an alternative to litigation that may occur within traditional court settings, and its outcomes are either binding or nonbinding agreements. Among many international settings and controversies, arbitration may be preferred to traditional litigation because "it may be possible to pick a seat for the arbitration that allows the parties to be represented by their regular counsel," which may not be possible in foreign court systems (Moses, 2012).

The use of arbitration also may involve "rules of evidence," and is similar to a traditional court hearing (Cross & Miller, 2012). The disputing parties may "frame" the considered issues, and express any constraints that are applicable to the arbitrator (Cross & Miller, 2012). If the arbitration decision is binding upon the affected parties, then any appeal options may be limited (Cross & Miller, 2012). In many contracts, clauses may exist in which the parties agree to not pursue any traditional litigation but invoke some type of arbitration as a method of dispute resolution.

Mediation

Mediation is another form of dispute resolution that necessitates communication between affected rivals. Mediation is defined as the "act or process of mediating" or "intervention between conflicting parties to promote reconciliation, settlement, or compromise" (*Merriam-Webster*, 2012c). Mediation represents an alternative to the traditional form of litigation.

Within the United States, much mediation is facilitated through the National Mediation Board (NMB). The NMB generally facilitates mediation within the transportation industry to ensure the efficient and effective functioning of railways and airways (National Mediation Board, 2012). The NMB has an astounding rate of success. Approximately 97% of its mediated cases were resolved without impeding American public service (National Mediation Board, 2012). It has exhibited approximately a 99% rate of success after 1980 (National Mediation Board, 2012).

Mediation typically involves some form of systematic process to generate dispute resolution. In the case of the NMB, the process begins with the affected parties exchanging notices before entering some type of negotiations. As a result of negotiations, the affected parties may or may not reach an agreement. If an agreement is not reached, then a variety of succeeding processes may occur. Figure 9.2 shows the cumulative mediation process of the NMB.

Negotiation

Negotiation is probably the best known of the alternative methods of resolving disputes in which communication is necessitated. Negotiation is defined as the "action or process of negotiating or being negotiated" (*Merriam-Webster*, 2012d). Another definition

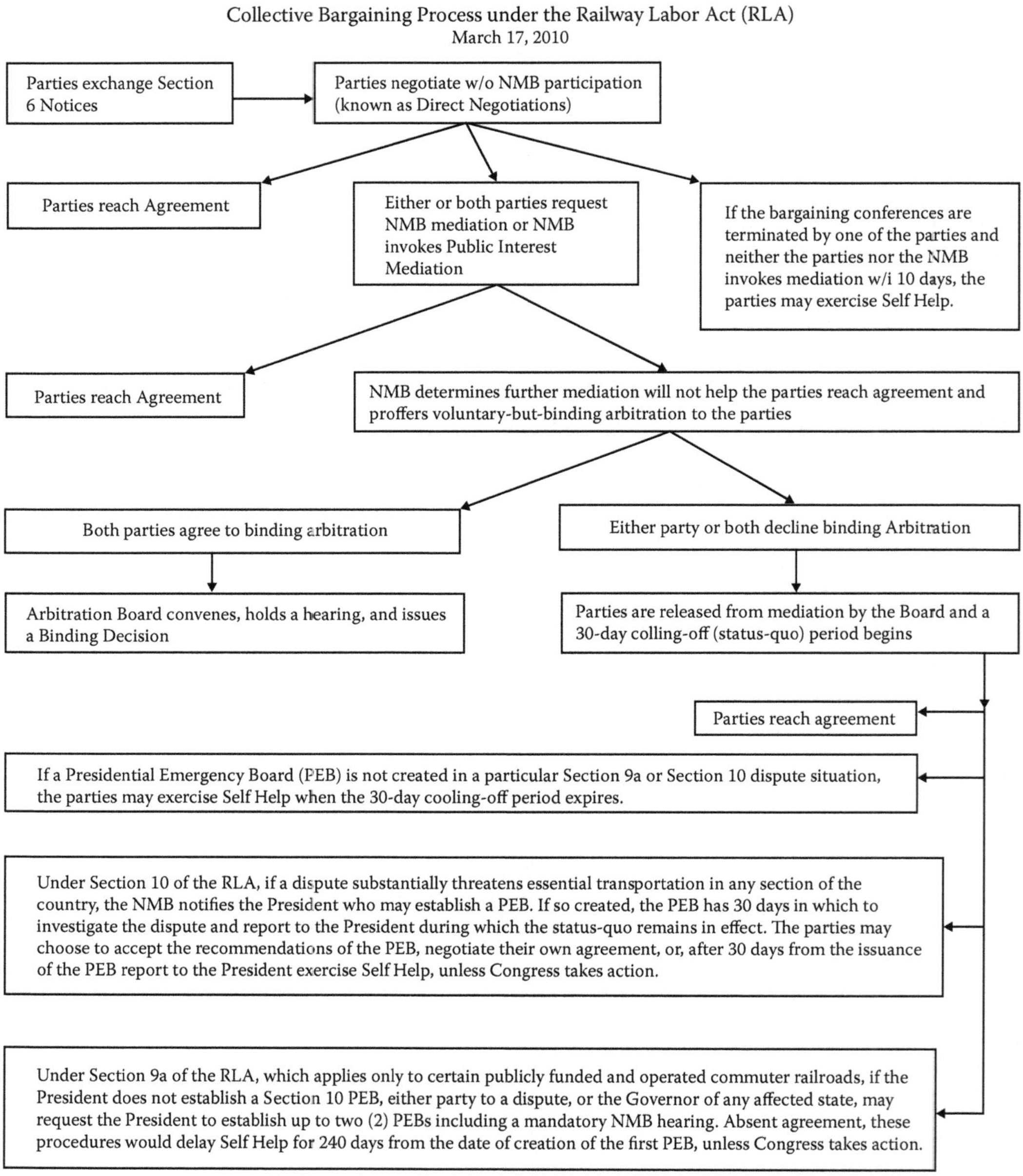

Figure 9.2 Mediation process (collective bargaining). (From http://www.nmb.gov/publicinfo/collbarg2.pdf.)

of negotiation indicates that it is a "process of bargaining in which two parties, each of which has something that the other wants, try to reach an agreement on mutually accepted terms" (Chaturvedi & Chaturvedi, 2011). In a sense, negotiation results in some type of compromise occurring between the disputing parties.

Negotiation is not spontaneous; it follows some form of methodical process. One such process is highlighted in Table 9.3 (Smutko, 2012).

Table 9.3 Negotiation Process

Step	Action	Characteristics
1	Establish procedures	Develop protocols and rules, and express them in a charter
2	Educate each other	Share concerns; identify and share interests—reasons, needs, concerns, and motivations underlying participants' positions—rather than assert positions; identify what items are understood and given
3	Problem definition	Define present situation and desired future
4	Specify information needs	Technical background information; available information and information that is needed; agree on methods for generating answers to relevant technical questions, or a path to follow even if no technical consensus exists
5	Further education	Field visits, data collection, briefings, interviews, etc.
6	Generate options	Brainstorming, public opinion, expert opinions, etc.
7	Develop criteria for evaluating options	Feasibility, fairness, efficiency, etc.
8	Reach agreements	Single text, building blocks, agreement in principle, etc.
9	Develop a written plan	Document areas of agreement; common understandings; develop action plan

Facilitation

Another method of resolving disputes through communication is facilitation. This method is defined as using "techniques to improve the flow of information in a meeting between parties to a dispute" (U.S. Office of Personnel Management, 2012). Facilitation differs from mediation because it is focused more toward the overall process enacted to reach a resolution outcome (U.S. Office of Personnel Management, 2012). Mutual communication occurs among the participants in a facilitation meeting to efficiently complete problem-solving activities to yield a "jointly agreed upon goal" (U.S. Office of Personnel Management, 2012). According to the U.S. Office of Personnel Management, facilitation is most appropriate during the following situations (U.S. Office of Personnel Management, 2012):

1. The intensity of the parties' emotions about the issues in dispute are low to moderate.
2. The parties or issues are not extremely polarized.
3. The parties have enough trust in each other that they can work together to develop a mutually acceptable solution.
4. The parties are in a common predicament, and they need or will benefit from a jointly acceptable outcome.

Communication Styles

Every individual person is unique and has a different capacity for communicating effectively and efficiently with others. Some folks are easier to communicate with than others, and some people are better at instigating and performing communications than others. Such differences may be influenced by the personal characteristics of the individual or may be influenced by culture or situation. These notions introduce the concept of communication style. Communication style is composed of both the verbal and nonverbal attributes of people that emphasize "personhood versus situation or status" (De Mooij, 2005).

Within the justice domain, a variety of communication styles are present. Agents within the justice system and law enforcement organizations must interact with a variety of entities. The United States represents a diverse array of demographic characteristics that may affect the communication styles of law enforcement entities and the justice system. Figure 9.3 shows recent demographics expressed by the U.S. Census Bureau (U.S. Census Bureau, 2012).

Communication style differs from culture to culture. No one communication style is either better or worse. Instead, communication styles are merely different among different peoples. Methods and modes of communication that are considered to be comfortable for Americans may be uncomfortable for people from different cultures. This notion is salient for law enforcement personnel and entities within the justice system given their potentials of interacting with different people and cultures.

The communication style of North America is generally familiar to most all American law enforcement organizations and its justice system. This style of communicating with others is very straightforward (Guffey & Loewy, 2008). Any form of perceived evasion may invoke suspicion within the communications process (Guffey & Loewy, 2008). Any perception of a "hidden agenda" may spark feelings of distrust within the communications process (Guffey & Loewy, 2008, p. 18). When communicating, silence and delays may incite feelings of discomfort and impatience (Guffey & Loewy, 2008, p. 18).

The Native American communication style also exhibits different characteristics. Among some tribes, silence is a method of dealing with "ambiguity" (Neuliep, 2009). This communication style is also very succinct and "concise" (Neuliep, 2009). It may also involve some facets of directness within the communications process (Dana et al., 2008). Furthermore, this communication style is "characterized by speaking softly and slowly," "does not interject," and avoids "eye contact" (James, 2013). It also incorporates "subtle expressions and gestures, as well as silences" (Milian & Erin, 2001).

The African American communication style is also different. It may be fluid and adapted to the communication style of an organization (Keyton, 2005). It also exhibits a "spontaneity and optimism related to overcoming feelings of adversity" (Ray, 2009). When

People QuickFacts	USA
Population, 2011 estimate	311,591,917
Population, 2010 (April 1) estimates base	308,745,538
Population, percent change, April 1, 2010 to July 1, 2011	0.9%
Population, 2010	308,745,538
Persons under 5 years, percent, 2011	6.5%
Persons under 18 years, percent, 2011	23.7%
Persons 65 years and over, percent, 2011	13.3%
Female persons, percent, 2011	50.8%
White persons, percent, 2011 (a)	78.1%
Black persons, percent, 2011 (a)	13.1%
American Indian and Alaska Native persons, percent, 2011 (a)	1.2%
Asian persons, percent, 2011 (a)	5.0%
Native Hawaiian and Other Pacific Islander persons, percent, 2011 (a)	0.2%
Persons reporting two or more races, percent, 2011	2.3%
Persons of Hispanic or Latino Origin, percent, 2011 (b)	16.7%
White persons not Hispanic, percent, 2011	63.4%

Figure 9.3 United States demographics overview. (From http://quickfacts.census.gov/qfd/states/00000.html.)

speaking, the distinctiveness of vocal pitch may attribute precise meaning to words when communicating (Holloway, 2005).

Asian culture involves a communication style that avoids “causing shame or loss of face to themselves and others to maintain harmonious relations” that may not emphasize directness and assertiveness when communicating (Pedersen et al., 2008). The Asian communication style is also characterized as “collectivist,” and contributes toward maintaining “peace and tranquility” (Gudykunst, 2003). Within this culture, certain nonverbal cues, such as eye contact, may be used less to regulate and embellish communication (Wood, 2011).

Hispanic communication style is different from that typically found in mainstream American culture (Neuliep, 2009). Within the Hispanic culture, oral communication may occur through the use of the Spanish or English languages. The use of Spanglish (i.e., English–Spanish hybrid language) also represents a hybrid language that may be used to communicate (Neuliep, 2009). The emergence of such hybrid linguistics may occur naturally because of the integration of cultures between American and Spanish societies (Neuliep, 2009). Additionally, nonverbal cues may emphasize communication through physical touching, hugging, or cheek kissing (Neuliep, 2009).

Many more communication styles exist globally. Regardless, they all have their own innate characteristics through which humans communicate personally and organizationally. Differences in communications styles are pertinent considerations of the justice system and law enforcement organizations. Myriads of people are interacted with and processed by both entities daily. Understanding the characteristics of communications style improves the ability of law enforcement organizations and the justice system to render public service.

Virtual Organizations and Communication

Some incidents and relationships within the justice domain may necessitate virtual communication. This type of communicating occurs when the affected parties must work together but are separated by some geographic distance that impedes their frequent personal interaction. Collaborations between state and federal agencies may exhibit this type of organization. Although distances between the peer entities may be merely a few miles or may be thousands of miles, communication must occur. Below are some suggestions to enhance communication within a virtual context:

Set a foundation for handling unknowns: Supervisors are unable to view “body language and facial expressions” within the virtual experience (Gray & Larson, 2003). Therefore, during the communications process, supervisors must “probe deeper” in order to make personnel “explain their viewpoints, actions, and concerns more clearly” (Gray & Larson, 2003).

Information sharing: Personnel must achieve some consensus regarding “what, when, where, and how information will be shared” as well as “how and when they will respond to it” (Gray & Larson, 2003).

Periodic updates: Communicate frequently with personnel to inform them of any scheduling changes or other pertinent information. This may be accomplished through the use of some virtual “central access point” such as a “website” (Gray & Larson, 2003).

Tracking personnel and activities: Virtual entities may experience communications difficulties. Some issues may be averted or deterred by using "scheduling software" to track calendar dates and events that affect personnel within the virtual environment (Gray & Larson, 2003).

Occasional physical presence: Although the organizational experience is primarily virtual, the incorporation of periodic physical meetings or other gatherings may enhance communication. Such an event helps personnel to "meet each other and socialize" (Gray & Larson, 2003). Such meetings should occur "at key junctures" (Gray & Larson, 2003).

Communications Failure

Despite the highest and best efforts to facilitate communications organizationally, there are times when the communications process may fail completely or it may experience various impediments. Every organization is unique and experiences its own set of factors that may diminish the scope, magnitude, and potency of its communications. There exists no one, specific cause that will influence communicating negatively within the organizational environment; instead, there exist many such reasons. Below are some of the primary considerations that organizations experience when communications either fail or experience impediments:

Misunderstanding and ambiguity: Although senders of messages may state clearly and completely the content of their transmitted messages, receivers may have a different interpretation of the messages than was intended by the sender. In some cases, the wording and phrasing of the message contents may be ambiguous, thereby generating confusion in the mind of the receiver.

Equipment: Equipment has limitations. It must be maintained and properly operated. In some cases, it may be damaged or completely destroyed either accidentally or because of the circumstances of an incident. Radio systems may fail because of an electrical short within their circuitry, or cell phone communications may fail when a signal is lost because of weather or geography. Regardless, any failure of equipment hampers the ability to communicate.

Language: Language is an essential aspect of communicating orally. Law enforcement officers whose primary language is English may experience difficulty when attempting to communicate with people whose English skills are either limited or nonexistent. Certainly, such a scenario also affects the court system.

Organizational attributes: Various organizational attributes may influence communicating. Errors may be made when transcribing and disseminating work schedules. Personnel may be absent during shift briefings when pertinent information is expressed and disseminated. New personnel may have to experience a learning curve to learn the terminology of the organization. Any number of organizational characteristics may affect communicating.

Human attributes: Certainly, the human barriers to communication delineated in Chapter 3 may negatively influence the communications process. Humans may experience a wide variety of factors that influence communicating, ranging from hunger and tiredness to illness and hearing impairments.

Listening skills: Listening skills are essential when communicating via any medium that incorporates some facet of auditory characteristics. Listening should be conducted actively, and not passively. Methods of embellishing listening may involve the taking of notes during a briefing, asking questions to clarify points to ensure certainty and accuracy, and so forth.

Organizational Policy and Communication

Chapter 1 introduced and defined the notion of organizational policy, and delineated various contexts in which policy affects communications. Policy may also be considered from the perspective of organizational communications. Organizational policy influences communication by governing what actions and resources are appropriate or inappropriate within the communications process. Generally, organizational communications policies must accommodate the following concepts: who, what, when, where, why, and how?

An example of an organizational communications process policy is that of the Truro (Massachusetts) Police Department. Figures 9.4 and 9.5 display excerpts from this communications policy (Truro Police Department, 2006).

These excerpts highlight rules and protocols that govern and influence organizational communications within the law enforcement organization. All of the primary queries are addressed within these excerpts. The policy addresses the senders and receivers of the messages, and expresses how they are to be designated (e.g., using the proper call sign). Each call sign is unique; therefore, senders and receivers are clearly identified without ambiguity or confusion. The policy also addresses the content of the message. Examples are the planning of messages before they are transmitted, the disallowing of personal names, and the voicing of messages using plain English.

Chronological aspects of communicating are also addressed within the policy. It mandates that military time is used to express all times (i.e., 24-hour clock). Location is also addressed within the policy. It mandates that the arrival to the scene of an incident is to be reported immediately. The policy also accommodates a methodical process for transmissions procedures detailing how communication occurs. Furthermore, the policy also justifies some of its tenets. Specifically, it mandates the use of plain English when communicating as a method of conforming to the requirements of the National Incident Management System (NIMS) protocols.

This policy is expressed straightforwardly and understandably. It addresses the basics of communications protocols that are necessary for communicating efficiently and effectively while minimizing the time required for the communications process to occur. It provides constraints regarding the spoken language so that the chance of confusion is minimized regarding the transmitted message. It also embellishes officer safety and the safety of the general public by disallowing the use of personal names regarding law enforcement personnel and by minimizing the use of complainant names when communicating.

This policy also alludes to communications that may occur externally regarding the organization. The NIMS compliance necessitates the use of plain English when communicating. By incorporating this mandate, the law enforcement organization is capable of communication with other law enforcement agencies, various first responder organizations, and other entities, should collaboration with other organizations become necessary.

COMMUNICATIONS ADM-2.02

Department business only. Unnecessary communications will not be allowed.

1. All FCC rules and regulations (located in Communications Center) will be adhered to.

2. Military time shall be used in all transmissions.

3. Messages are to be clear, concise, and accurate so that transmission time is kept at a minimum, in plain English. *(Revised March 28, 2006)*

4. Courtesy is most essential for the efficient and effective operation of the radio system. Discourtesy, sarcasm, or arguments will not be tolerated.

5. **Personal names will not be used during transmissions.** Officers and Telecommunicators will use and identify each other and other stations by assigned call signs. *(Revised September 12, 2003)*

6. Profane and obscene language is a violation of FCC rules and regulations. Employees must not use loud, uncivil, indecent, or profane language even under the greatest provocation.

7. Officers and Telecommunicators will be responsible for proper radio communications. *(Revised September 12, 2003)*

8. The names of complainants shall not be broadcast over the air unless it is necessary as a part of the call or assignment. Officers and Telecommunicators shall use discretion in the use of complainant names, keeping in mind that in order to prevent retaliation in some cases, we should maintain the confidentiality of the names of a complainant or witness. In doubtful cases the shift Commander should be consulted on this issue. *(Revised September 12, 2003)*

9. In order to conform with *NIMS*, the Truro Police Department will use plain English for all radio traffic with the exception of signing on the air (ZERO-1). *(Added March 28, 2006)*

F. **TRANSMISSION PROCEDURES:** Before transmitting, officers and Telecommunicators should: *(Revised September 12, 2003)*

1. Plan the message before transmitting, when possible.

2. Listen to make sure another message is not being interrupted.

3. Hold the mike 1 - 3 inches from the mouth. Do not attempt to transmit with the mike still attached to the dashboard or radio console.

4. Depress the transmit button and wait 3 seconds (it takes 2 - 3 seconds for

TRURO POLICE DEPARTMENT MANUAL 5

Figure 9.4 Excerpt no. 1 from Truro Police Department communications policy. (From http://www.truropolice.org/On%20Line%20Manuals/Communications.pdf.)

For example, if an earthquake, hurricane, or other severe incident occurs that necessitates an emergency response, the law enforcement entity may communicate with other organizations using plain English.

Communications policy is essential for any law enforcement organization. Through the use of a communications policy, organizations may express the behaviors that are allowable and disallowable when communicating. Communications policies affect all levels of the organizational hierarchy, as well as the breadth and depth of the organization. They also dictate operationally how communications resources are to be used and operated when communicating.

Such policies also are protective because they provide a foundational baseline of procedures and processes that influence organizational communications. For example, the anonymity of law enforcement personnel is protected when communicating and the disuse of personal names also bolsters operational security. In any case, law enforcement

COMMUNICATIONS ADM-2.02

identification mode in the radio to transmit). Any verbal transmission during this time period will be lost.

5. Speak normally and clearly, using an evenly modulated tone of voice, as in a phone conversation. Avoid vocal displays of emotion such as loss of temper, nervous excitement, sullenness, etc., which tend to distort a radio transmission.

6. Identify the officer or station by using the proper call sign. *(revised September 12, 2003)*

7. Officers should give Telecommunicators reasonable time to acknowledge the transmission, as well as giving officers reasonable time to answer. *Rrevised September 12, 2003)*

8. Avoid, if possible, lengthy messages. If the message is long, transmit a portion of it to ensure that it has been acknowledged, and then continue.

9. Acknowledge all calls promptly.

10. Report arrival at the scene promptly.
Example: 700, Baker 4 is on location. *(Revised March 29, 2006)*

11. Clear the call promptly.
Example: 700, Baker 4 is clear. *(Revised March 29, 2006)*

12. Officers shall advise the Telecommunicator when they are going out of service and returning to service. *The Telecommunicator shall record and track each officer's status.*

G. SPECIAL TRANSMISSION PROCEDURES: On those occasions when a sensitive message must be delivered over the radio and it is desirable to minimize outside monitoring, the following procedures will be followed:

a. The Telecommunicator will contact a specific officer and instruct them to switch to channel 4 on CODE. This will enable encrypted conversations *(Revised Jan 1, 2003)*

c. Both the Telecommunicator and the unit will turn to Channel 4.

d. The Telecommunicator will then contact the officer and deliver the message. *(Revised Jan 1, 2003)*

e. Both officer and desk will then return to normal channels. *(Revised Jan 1, 2003)*

TRURO POLICE DEPARTMENT MANUAL 6

Figure 9.5 Excerpt no. 2 from Truro Police Department communications policy. (From http://www.truropolice.org/On%20Line%20Manuals/Communications.pdf.)

organizations and justice system entities should craft, express, and maintain a communications policy.

Commentary Regarding Organizational Communication

An organization is defined as "an administrative and functional structure" including its "personnel" (*Merriam-Webster*, 2012e). The discussions of this chapter consider communication from the perspectives of the justice system and law enforcement organizations. However, all organizations experience some form of communication whether or not they are members of the justice domain. All commercial and government organizations exhibit the characteristics of the communications process.

Given these notions, one may also consider organizational communication from the perspectives of darker organizations whose existence threaten society. Within the United States, numerous illicit organizations employ various types of communications for criminal purposes. Examples include factions of organized crime, terrorist organizations, street gangs, and motorcycle gangs.

Communicating among such entities often involves the use of clandestine functions. In some cases, gang writing and symbols encode messages and affiliations through the use of various ciphers and alphabets that are innate to the organization. Within the United States, "every state and major city" is "plagued with local, loosely structured, street gangs that are mainly motivated by drug sales" (Florida Department of Corrections, 2012a). Such organizations form because of "common interests and a sense of loyalty to individuals from their city, neighborhood, street, or housing complex" (Florida Department of Corrections, 2012a). As the organization grows and matures, it may affiliate with "a national street gang such as the Bloods, Crips, or Chicago-based Folk Nation and People Nation sets and use their symbols and identifiers" (Florida Department of Corrections, 2012a).

Graffiti comprises a good amount of gang communications. Graffiti may express a variety of messages despite any innocuous appearances. These notions are expressed as follows:

> As gang activity increases so does their graffiti. Graffiti has been called the "newspaper of the streets." Each gang has its unique symbols and cryptic types of writing. Graffiti is *not art work;* it is sophisticated communication that publicizes the gang's power, status, delineates territory, sends messages, and warns intruders. Graffiti upside down or crossed out is generally a "put down" or threat to a rival gang or person. "Death warrants" for police officers are known to have been posted with graffiti. (Florida Department of Corrections, 2012b)

Within the United States, there exists an astounding quantity of approximately "33,000 violent street gangs, motorcycle gangs, and prison gangs" (Federal Bureau of Investigation, 2012). Among these organizations are approximately "1.4 million members" that are "criminally active" (Federal Bureau of Investigation, 2012). Many of these organizations exhibit a high level of sophistication and organization (Federal Bureau of Investigation, 2012). All of these organizations leverage violence as a method of controlling "neighborhoods" and increasing their illegal cash flows though criminal activities (Federal Bureau of Investigation, 2012). Such activities involve "robbery, drug and gun trafficking, fraud, extortion, and prostitution rings" (Federal Bureau of Investigation, 2012).

Regardless of the type, size, scope, and magnitude of the instantiations of criminal organizations, they all have a need to communicate. Communication flows between and among the individuals that comprise the organizations and among the components of the organizations. Communication flows throughout the respective chains of command. Essentially, communication flows between and among the organizations both externally and internally. Each one exhibits the characteristics of organizational communications that are discussed herein through some variant of the communications process.

All organizations, whether legal or illegal, are composed of individual humans who are the catalysts of communication. Therefore, the concepts underlying organizational communication are not relegated solely to the justice system and law enforcement organizations. They apply to any organization whether it is a little league team or a global, corporate conglomerate. They also apply to the shadier domains of criminal activity. Any organizational structure, regardless of its purpose, size, location, or functions, has a need to communicate.

Chapter Comments and Summary

This chapter introduced various perspectives of organizational communications. Examining the communications process from an organizational perspective increases the complexity of communications. Organizations are composed of individuals that communicate with each other. Organizations have various components that also must communicate internally. External communication occurs between one or more different organizations. Within an organization, communication may flow upwardly, downwardly, and across boundaries either formally or informally. Throughout this myriad of communications, both individuals and organizations may be examined from the perspective of Maslow's needs hierarchy.

This flowing of communication occurs within a network. Networks represent the amalgamation of senders, receivers, messages, and resources that are necessary for the conduction of organizational communications. Networks may be graphically displayed and modeled mathematically. The complexity of a network increases with its size, scope, and magnitude of communications.

All organizations experience some type of conflicts both internally and externally through time. Resolving conflicts necessitates communication between the disputing parties. Although the criminal justice system is an entity through which disputes are resolved traditionally and legally, there exist alternative forms of resolving disputes through which communicating is necessary. These include arbitration, mediation, facilitation, and negotiation.

Law enforcement organizations and the justice system must accommodate communications regarding a wide variety of cultures and peoples. Within the United States, such facets of organizational communication encompass groups of North American, African American, Native American, Asian American, and Hispanic audiences. Performing communications efficiently and effectively with such groups involves a consideration of communication style.

Despite the best efforts of an organization to pursue successful communications, there are times when communication is unsuccessful. Failure within the communications process may arise from a myriad of origins. Examples include equipment failure, human misunderstandings and fallibilities, environmental factors, language issues, listening skills, and so forth. In some cases, failure may be completely unavoidable or it may be averted.

Communication within an organization is governed and influenced by organizational communications policy. All organizations should craft, express, and maintain realistic policies regarding communication to delineate what behaviors and resources are appropriate for conducting communication. Such policies are protective, and embellish officer safety and operations security.

Both legal and illegal domains exhibit the characteristics of organizational communication. Gang symbols and language are methods through which criminal organizations perform communications both internally and externally. Within the United States, every state exhibits some aspect of organizational communication that is leveraged to facilitate criminal activities.

All organizations are composed of humans. The most important resource of any organization is its people. Some folks exhibit greater abilities of communication than do others. In any case, humans are the catalysts of organizational communication. Therefore, all organizational communication is dependent on human beings to send, transmit, and receive messages either internally or externally. Essentially, all organizations exhibit the characteristics of communication both internally and externally and both formally or informally.

Terminology

Arbitration
Communication failure
Communication network
Communication policy
Communication style
Connection
Cultural effects
Downward communication
External communication
Facilitation
Fault tolerance
Formal network
Gang communication
Grapevine
Horizontal communication
Informal network
Internal communication
Maslow's hierarchy of needs
Mediation
National Mediation Board
Negotiation
Node
Officer security
Operational security
Organization
Organizational communication
Upward communication
Virtual organization

THOUGHT AND DISCUSSION QUESTIONS

1. This chapter examined the Truro Police Department policy regarding organizational communications. Do some research, and locate other communications policies from different law enforcement organizations throughout the nation. Compare and contrast these communications policies. Write a brief essay that discusses the similarities and differences regarding the discovered policies.

2. Interview some of the personnel from your local law enforcement organizations. Ask what organizational attributes hinder the communications process. Write a brief essay that discusses your findings. Within your discussion, incorporate some recommendations for improving the communications of your local law enforcement organization.
3. Communications policy also contributes toward the bolstering of operational security when managing incidents. Other than the example presented herein, write a brief essay that identifies and discusses three other ways in which a communications policy may be used to strengthen operations security among law enforcement organizations.
4. Communications policy also contributes toward the bolstering of officer safety when managing incidents. Other than the example presented herein, write a brief essay that identifies and discusses three other ways in which a communications policy may be used to strengthen officer safety among law enforcement organizations.

References

Chaturvedi, P. T., & Chaturvedi, M. (2011). *Business communication: Concepts, cases, and applications* (2nd ed., p. 193). New Delhi, India: Dorling Kindersley.

Cross, F., & Miller, R. (2012). *The legal environment of business: Text and cases—Ethical, regulatory, global, and corporate issues* (8th ed., p. 60). Mason, OH: South-Western Cengage Publishing.

Dana, R., Gamst, G., & Der-Karabetian, A. (2008). *CBMCS multicultural training program* (p. 514). Thousand Oaks, CA: Sage Publishing.

De Mooij, M. (2005). *Global marketing and advertising: Understanding cultural paradoxes* (p. 137). Thousand Oaks, CA: Sage Publishing.

Eysenck, M. (2004). *Psychology: An international perspective* (p. 66). East Sussex, UK: Psychology Press.

Federal Bureau of Investigation. (2012). They poison our streets with drugs, violence, and all manner of crime. Retrieved from http://www.fbi.gov/about-us/investigate/vc_majorthefts/gangs/gangs (accessed December 30, 2012).

Fiadjoe, A. (2004). *Alternative dispute resolution: A developing world perspective* (p. 27). London: Cavendish Publishing.

Florida Department of Corrections. (2012a). Gangs in Florida. Retrieved from http://www.dc.state.fl.us/pub/gangs/fl.html (accessed December 20, 2012).

Florida Department of Corrections. (2012b). Parent and community awareness strategies. Retrieved from http://www.dc.state.fl.us/pub/gangs/awareness2.html (accessed December 30, 2012).

Gaines, L., & Worrell, J. (2012). *Police administration* (3rd ed., p. 211). Clifton Park, NY: Delmar Cengage Publishing.

Gray, C., & Larson, E. (2003). *Project management: The managerial process* (2nd ed., p. 373). New York: McGraw-Hill Publishing.

Gudykunst, W. (2003). *Cross-cultural and intercultural communication* (p. 134). Thousand Oaks, CA: Sage Publications.

Guffey, M., & Loewy, D. (2008). *Essentials of business communication* (9th ed.). Mason, OH: South-Western Publishing.

Hitt, M., Miller, C., & Colella, A. (2009). *Organizational behavior: A strategic approach* (2nd ed.). Hoboken, NJ: John Wiley & Sons Publishing.

Holloway, J. (2005). *Africanisms in American culture* (p. 72). Bloomington, IN: Indiana University Press.

James, A. (2013). *Survive and thrive as a physical educator: Strategies for the first year and beyond* (p. 122). Champaign, IL: Human Kinetics.

Jayarum, R., & Kotwani, N. (2012). *Industrial economics and telecommunication regulations* (p. 165). New Delhi, India: PHI Learning Private, Ltd.

Keyton, J. (2005). *Communication and organizational culture: A key to understanding work experiences* (p. 110). Thousand Oaks, CA: Sage Publishing.

Merriam-Webster Dictionary. (2012a). s.v. "arbitration." Retrieved from http://www.merriam-webster.com/dictionary/arbitration (accessed December 29, 2012).

Merriam-Webster Dictionary. (2012b). s.v. "directionality." Retrieved from http://www.merriam-webster.com/dictionary/directionality (accessed December 29, 2012).

Merriam-Webster Dictionary. (2012c). s.v. "mediation." Retrieved from http://www.merriam-webster.com/dictionary/mediation?show=0&t=1356761051 (accessed December 29, 2012).

Merriam-Webster Dictionary. (2012d). s.v. "negotiation." Retrieved from http://www.merriam-webster.com/dictionary/negotiation (accessed December 29, 2012).

Merriam-Webster Dictionary. (2012e). s.v. "organization." Retrieved from http://www.merriam-webster. com/dictionary/organization (accessed December 30, 2012).

Milian, M., & Erin, J. (2001). *Diversity and visual impairment: The influence of race, gender, religion, and ethnicity on the individual* (p. 389). New York: AFB Press.

Miller, K. (2012). *Organizational communication: Approaches and processes* (6th ed., p. 41). Boston: Wadsworth Cengage Publishing.

Moses, M. (2012). *The principles and practice of international commercial arbitration* (2nd ed., p. xix). New York: Cambridge University Press.

National Mediation Board. (2012). Mediation: NMB responsibilities and activities. Retrieved from http://www.nmb.gov/mediation/mrna.html (accessed December 29, 2012).

Neuliep, J. (2009). *Intercultural communication: A contextual approach* (4th ed., pp. 102, 228). Thousand Oaks, CA: Sage Publishing.

Pedersen, P., Draguns, J., Lonner, W., & Trimble, J. (2008). *Counseling across cultures* (6th ed., p. 117). Thousand Oaks, CA: Sage Publishing.

Ray, G. (2009). *Language and interracial communication in the United States: Speaking in black and white* (p. 68). New York: Peter Lang Publishing.

Richardson, G. (2010). *Project management: Theory and practice* (p. 237). Boca Raton, FL: CRC Press.

Rivero, D., & Pepper, J. (2010). Proactive patrolling through the use of patrol scripts. *Police Chief Magazine*. Retrieved from http://www.policechiefmagazine.org/magazine/index.cfm?fuseaction=display_arch&article_id=2202&issue_id=92010 (accessed December 29, 2012).

Sen, L. (2007). *Communication skills* (2nd ed.). New Delhi, India: Prentice Hall Publishing.

Sims, R. (2002). *Managing organizational behavior* (p. 155). Westport, CT: Quorum Books.

Smutko, L. S. (2012). Collaborative watershed planning in North Carolina. North Carolina State University. Retrieved from http://www.ces.ncsu.edu/depts/agecon/WECO/publication/WatershedSearching.PDF (accessed December 30, 2012).

State of Indiana. (2012). Article 2: General provisions. *Indiana Administrative Code*. Retrieved from http://www.in.gov/legislative/iac/T02500/A00020.PDF (accessed December 29, 2012).

Truro Police Department. (2006). *Truro Police Department Communications*. Retrieved from http://www.truropolice.org/On%20Line%20Manuals/Communications.pdf (accessed December 30, 2012).

U.S. Census Bureau. (2012). State and county quick facts. Retrieved from http://quickfacts.census.gov/qfd/states/00000.html (accessed December 29, 2012).

U.S. Office of Personnel Management. (2012). Alternative dispute resolution guide. Retrieved from http://www.opm.gov/er/adrguide/section1-a.asp (accessed December 30, 2012).

Vervest, P., van Heck, E., Preiss, K., & Pau, L.-F. (2005). *Smart business networks* (p. 20). Heidelberg, Germany: Springer-Berlin.

Wood, J. (2011). *Communication mosaics: An introduction to the field of communication* (6th ed., p. 97). Boston: Wadsworth Cengage Publishing.

Yeats, W. (n.d.). Communication quotes. Brainyquote.com. Retrieved from http://www.brainyquote.com/quotes/keywords/communicate.html (accessed December 28, 2012).

Marketing and Advertising Communications 10

Advertising is the art of convincing people to spend money they don't have for something they don't need.

—Will Rogers (Rogers, n.d.)

Objectives

The objectives of this chapter are to

- Introduce the concept of marketing communication
- Define the concepts of marketing and advertising
- Introduce the marketing process
- Discuss public service communication
- Discuss applications of marketing communication in policing
- Discuss applications of advertising communication in policing

Introduction

Someone requesting assistance from a law enforcement entity must have faith and confidence that assistance will be rendered efficiently and effectively within an acceptable period of time. Before someone can summon assistance from a law enforcement organization, some knowledge and understanding regarding the presence of the law enforcement organization must be present in the mind of the individual that requests assistance. Although such knowledge and understanding may be gained from personal experience with a law enforcement organization or its personnel, it may also be gained from a variety of public safety marketing and advertising campaigns.

These notions introduce the concept of marketing communication. Marketing communication is defined as "the coordination of promotion efforts to ensure their maximal informational and persuasive impact" (Pride et al., 2012). These promotions occur through all sorts of media venues. Such promotions may inform citizens of neighborhood watch programs, after-school programs, missing persons, and so forth. They may also be used for behavioral modification. Within this context, advertisements regarding seat belt use and drunk-driving checkpoints may be communicated through many venues to enhance public awareness of these issues and influence public opinions. Not only do they attempt to influence the pubic mindset regarding issues, but they may also influence public perceptions of law enforcement organizations and personnel.

Influencing Public Perceptions

Law enforcement and criminal justice organizations are subject to a myriad of perceptions among their served public markets. These perceptions are influenced through the use of communication. The use of marketing communication influences the formation of such perceptions and opinions within both the public and private sectors of society. Some connotations may be highly positive, facilitating a trustful public relationship, whereas others may be significantly negative, facilitating significant distrust of law enforcement organizations.

During 1992, the Los Angeles riots culminated in various debates regarding the actions of the police department that occurred during the aftermath of the Rodney King incident. According to the State of California (2010), "During the riots, former Police Chief Daryl Gates was widely criticized for failing to send in a sufficient number of police soon enough to prevent bloodshed and looting." This civil unrest and violence was broadcast both nationally and internationally, among a variety of media outlets, and the associated media content contributed to the negative formation of numerous perceptions and opinions regarding the Los Angeles Police Department (LAPD). Through the use of media, the reputations of the LAPD and its personnel were both tarnished and questioned.

Conversely, positive connotations of law enforcement and criminal justice organizations may be derived through the use of media. During 2009, a renegade soldier assaulted, wounded, and killed his fellow U.S. Army soldiers at Fort Hood, Texas. This terrorist was a commissioned officer serving in the U.S. Army. According to the U.S. Department of Defense (2009), "Army Maj. Nidal Malik Hasan, a psychiatrist at Carl R. Darnall Army Medical Center, allegedly shot and killed 13 soldiers and wounded 43 others." Civilian law enforcement officers subdued Hasan after the murderous rampage. The civilian officers, Kimberly Munley and Mark Todd, were deemed as heroes, and they received high accolades from the U.S. Army (U.S. Department of Defense, 2009). News reports of this event were broadcast across a variety of media outlets nationally and internationally. Through the use of media, the reputation of the Fort Hood civilian police force was embellished positively. Figure 10.1 shows Officer Munley being visited by Defense Secretary Robert Gates following the tragic attack.

These scenarios are examples of many such other incidents in which law enforcement entities may be viewed either positively or negatively by their served public markets. The use of media influences perceptions that may either strengthen relationships between law enforcement entities and their served markets, or that may diminish the strength of such relationships. Through the use of media, trust may also be strengthened or weakened between law enforcement entities and their served public markets. The Los Angeles riots and Fort Hood terrorism events are demonstrative of the leveraging of media resources to inform and influence public perceptions.

However, law enforcement and criminal justice entities may also leverage the potential of contemporary media outlets to facilitate relationships and enhance their provision of services among a myriad of public markets. Someone may hear a radio advertisement announcing the opening of a new policy academy class. Someone may view a television commercial reminding the public to wear seat belts. Other examples may be the advertising of neighborhood watch programs. Certainly, most all police vehicles have a large, blatant 911 painted visibly and clearly along their sides. These considerations of leveraging are accomplished through the communicative methods of marketing, advertising, and branding.

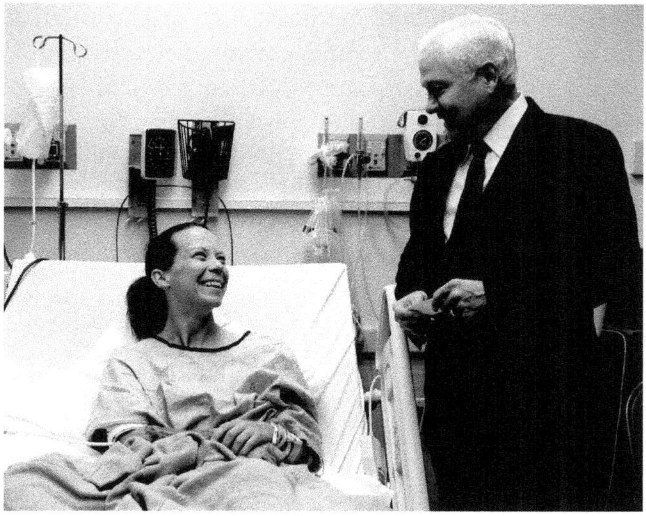

Figure 10.1 Officer Munley being visited by Defense Secretary Robert Gates after the Fort Hood attack. (From http://blog.mysanantonio.com/education/2010/01/fort-hood-heroes-trained-at-texas-state/.)

Marketing and Advertising Concepts

The basic concept and premise of marketing may be perceived as a process that necessitates planning and facilitates the distribution of products or services from producers to consumers. It also incorporates some facets of communicating to make the public aware of the product or service, and lure the public to partake of the products or services. An examination of these concepts yields some interesting observations. The concept of marketing involves multiple entities within the context of some specific relationship. One set of entities may be considered as the originators of products and services, whereas the second set of entities are the consumers of such products and services. Between these two sets of entities exists some form of contextual relationship that provides the basis for facilitating the transference of goods and services in return for any associated compensation. Before such transactions occur, some information regarding the product or service must be publically communicated to create awareness and to influence personal opinions and decisions.

Advertising is defined as "calling the attention of people to a commodity, and inducing them to buy the commodity" (Starch, 1910). Although this definition was specified nearly a century ago, its content and intent remain unchanged. An examination of the definition of the term advertising yields an analogous construct when compared with the concept of marketing. Advertising also involves the interactions, between multiple entities, that associate these entities through some form of a relationship. A first set of entities demonstrates the announcing and persuading behaviors that are necessary to influence the second set of entities to partake of a certain commodity.

Given these definitions, the concepts of marketing and advertising differ significantly. On the basis of the notions of the preceding definitions, advertising is a subset of marketing. The use of advertising demonstrates the function through which effective and efficient marketing activities may occur through time. Such effectiveness and efficiency are achieved through the use of systematic, methodical research initiatives and the crafting and implementation of commensurate strategic plans through time. The culmination of these efforts facilitates the provision of law enforcement services within society, and influences public perceptions of the agency and the provided service.

Examples of these concepts are common. The use of marketing and advertising may appeal to local, regional, national, international, or global audiences. The use of marketing and advertising may be to simply communicatively inform populaces regarding some event (e.g., tornado or hurricane) or to sway public opinion regarding a societal issue (e.g., drunk driving). The use of marketing and advertising may occur singly or it may be part of a collaborative effort among multiple law enforcement organizations.

Within the context of public safety, one example of leveraging communication to enact marketing and advertising functions involves a consideration of vehicular safety. Vehicle awareness information is disseminated, via the Internet, through the U.S. government. A benefit of disseminating driver education materials is the provision of resources that inform the general public regarding vehicle safety issues. These issues include considerations of child passenger safety, defective vehicle manufacturing and affiliated recall programs, the basic safety of passengers, and tools through which vehicle histories may be investigated (National Highway Transportation and Safety Administration, 2010b). This information may improve the awareness of drivers, may provide the resources necessary through which fraudulent vehicle sales may be avoided, or may preserve human life.

The National Highway Transportation Safety Administration also leverages media outlets to communicate public safety and awareness information. Such endeavors include communicating information regarding booster seats and seat belt initiatives (National Highway Transportation and Safety Administration, 2010a). Informing society of the proper transition between booster seats and seat belts propagates a valuable public service message, and is a reminder of the necessity of complying with driving laws. It also encourages the use of seat belts as a method of influencing the behaviors of drivers. This information also provides a means through which human life may be preserved when it is heeded within society. Figure 10.2 shows a typical advertisement informing the public regarding safety seat characteristics.

According to the U.S. Department of Transportation, sobriety checkpoints may be communicated through a variety of media outlets and the Internet to inform the public of potential traffic delays and safety initiatives (National Highway Transportation and Safety Administration, 2001). Announcing checkpoints is a reminder concerning the intolerance of law enforcement agencies regarding instances of inebriated driving within society. Communicating this information warns the general public of the consequences affiliated with driving when influenced by alcohol or drugs. These announcements also may provide routing information that is necessary for logistics and shipping companies to adjust their schedules and routes accordingly to minimize any impediments to their business operations.

The Federal Bureau of Investigation (FBI) communicates a variety of missing persons and "most wanted" announcements across a variety of law enforcement agencies and within its Internet site (Federal Bureau of Investigation, 2010). Physical descriptions and pictures of offenders and missing individuals may be provided as resources through which the proper identification may occur of specific individuals. These FBI announcements may yield the arrest of offenders and may prevent further instances of crime. Such announcements inform society of dangerous individuals that pose threats to human life

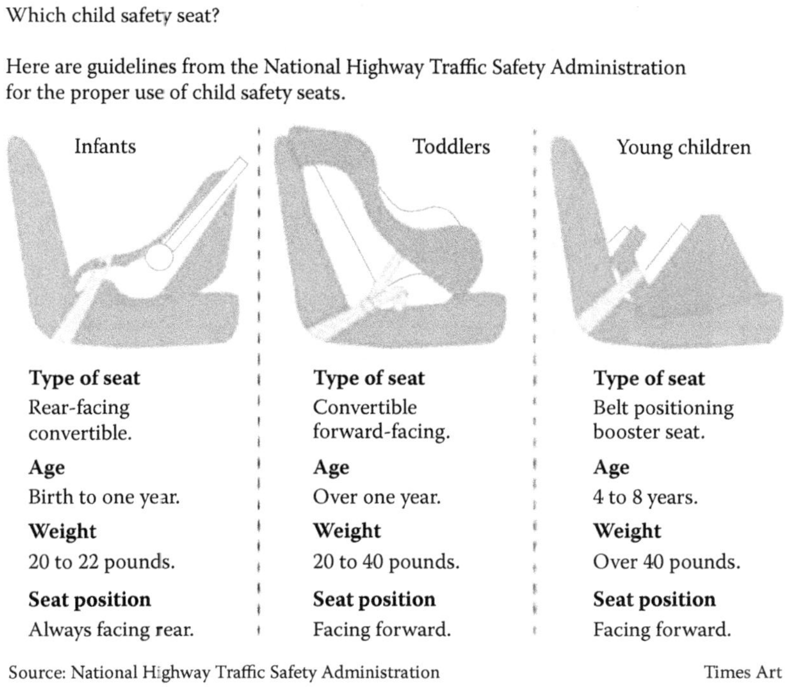

Figure 10.2 Child safety seat characteristics. (From http://www.sptimes.com/2003/06/03/Northpinellas/Crash_injures_girl_de.shtml.)

and property. These announcements may also include the promise of a reward for information that facilitates the capture of wanted individuals (Federal Bureau of Investigation, 2010). Because of the promise of such rewards, human behavior may be influenced to provide clues that divulge the identities or locations of offenders or missing persons. Such announcements are applicable to a variety of criminal offenses.

Many municipalities announce offenders, within news media, who were arrested for crimes involving prostitution. The city of Tampa, Florida, issues press releases that highlight such criminal offenses (City of Tampa, 2010). Specific press release announcements, detailing the affiliated sting operations and resulting arrests of offenders, are distributed among media outlets to inform society of such offenses (City of Tampa, 2010). Because of the motivation and nature of their criminal offenses, this form of marketing and advertising incites personal shame and disrepute, among offenders, through which their behaviors may be modified. Because of such publicity, societal opinions of these individuals may disrupt their personal and professional lives, and influence a change of behavior. Therefore, this form of media announcement serves as a modern version of the antiquated, scarlet letter approach to publicly identifying sexual offenders. Figure 10.3 shows an excerpt from a television news broadcast that informs the public of such an arrest.

Many other uses of marketing and advertising may be identified. Law enforcement agencies may announce their participation in community events and fund-raisers. The promotions of officers may be announced publicly. Agency recruiting initiatives may be embellished through public calls for employment. Crime statistics may be openly and publicly reported. Announcements regarding community-based policing activities may facilitate increased societal participation (e.g., neighborhood meeting announcements).

Figure 10.3 Excerpt of news television broadcast announcing a prostitution arrest. (From http://dakota.kstp.com/news/crime/186329-hill-murray-football-coach-arrested-fridley-prostitution-sting.)

Regardless, any marketing and advertising communication initiative must be well planned and well executed to embellish its efficiency and effectiveness within society. Given these notions, communicating via marketing and advertising is a powerful tool through which law enforcement entities may contribute toward the attainment of the goals of objectives of their missions while simultaneously providing societal benefits through time.

Traditional versus Service Paradigms

Many perceptions and mental images are invoked regarding the terms marketing and advertising. Common marketing and advertising activities permeate contemporary society both inconspicuously and blatantly. Constantly and daily, humans are targeted with a variety of marketing and advertising phenomena, ranging from subtle logos to bright, flashy billboards that attempt to persuade individuals to partake of various products and services. These products and services include a variety of entities—colas, clothing, restaurants, automobiles, sporting events, medicines, religious events, nursing homes, motion pictures, concerts, toys, candies, and an array of countless other entities. A significant purpose of marketing and advertising is to persuade consumers to partake of such entities, through the use of various media and messages influentially, as a method of providing mutual value to both organizations and consumers. Regardless of the market system and strategic approach, consumers must make a decision, of their own volition, regarding whether to purchase an item or to participate in an activity. These concepts are certainly applicable among the traditional sales initiatives of both for-profit and nonprofit entities.

However, these concepts are equally significant regarding the activities of law enforcement and criminal justice entities with respect to their crafting of services, provision of services, and influencing of public image through time. Although the preceding connotations are generally associated with the for-profit motive of organizations, the nonprofit aspects of marketing and advertising must not be ignored. In most cases, law enforcement and criminal justice entities are extensions of governmental bodies and are representative of nonprofit entities. Therefore, law enforcement and criminal justice entities are oriented toward the marketing and advertising of services that provide benefit to society and are indicative of the fulfillment of organizational mission. Examples of such service marketing initiatives

Figure 10.4 Neighborhood watch announcement. (From http://www.sandyspringspolice.org/neighborhoodwatch.)

are not uncommon among law enforcement and criminal justice entities. Figure 10.4 shows a public notice of the Sandy Springs (Georgia) Police Department announcing a neighborhood watch program and soliciting the public to summon police if necessary.

The Milwaukee (Wisconsin) Police Department (MPD) leverages media communications outlets to express the benefits of its community partnerships to deter acts of crime. According to the MPD, "block watch groups and neighborhood associations are the key to crime prevention in Milwaukee" (City of Milwaukee, 2012). The MPD also indicates that "what we do together with the community matters and we can prove it" (City of Milwaukee, 2012). When compared with 2009 Milwaukee crime statistics, the outcomes of this community relationship demonstrated a "12.3 percent reduction in violent crime since last year and a 31 percent reduction over the last three years" (City of Milwaukee, 2012). The use of media communications provides a means through which the benefits of service-based policing are marketed and advertised. Because of such media announcements, citizens gain both understanding and appreciation of the services rendered by law enforcement entities, and have knowledge of whether their tax dollars are expended effectively.

The U.S. Department of Justice (DOJ) also leverages media outlets to demonstrate the benefits of its community-oriented policing programs. The goals and objectives of such programs are designed to maximize monies invested in marketing and advertising to influence youth behaviors. These concepts are useful among youth programs. For example, in San Francisco, California, Foster Youth Services advertises its beneficial outcomes of expended grant funds received from the DOJ via the Internet (Foster Youth Services, 2012). These grant funds were used within the local school systems (Foster Youth Services, 2012). These outcomes show that "32% of participants have had a decrease in unexcused absences" and that "30% of participants have shown an increase" regarding grade point average (Foster Youth Services, 2012).

The marketing and advertising of such programs facilitate opportunities for youths to avoid criminal influences and pursue courses of actions that may provide meaningful futures. Furthermore, the use of media provides a tool through which law enforcement may emphasize a commitment among local communities and to the future successes of societal children. Through the use of such media, law enforcement organizations may influence public perceptions and opinions regarding service programs, and may improve public trust regarding law enforcement entities.

The marketing and advertising characteristics of both the Milwaukee and DOJ examples are representative of the service aspects of community-oriented policing initiatives. Both examples show community benefits within their respective societies. Although service programs may differ given the myriad of locales that are served by community-oriented policing, both examples are indicative of emphasizing and announcing crime prevention and deterrence. Both examples highlight the effectiveness of their respective services through time, and allude to the perpetuations of their services within their respective communities. The use of media communication provides a resource through which the descriptions of success, opportunities of police partnerships, and rendered services may influence societal perceptions of both law enforcement entities.

However, to facilitate a strong public perception of these programs, the marketing and advertising characteristics of both programs must be meticulously planned, executed, and maintained through time. Therefore, a systematic approach to the functions of marketing and advertising is necessitated before any information is communicated to the public. The long-term, strategic characteristics; the short-term, tactical characteristics; and the near-term, operational aspects of service paradigms must also be contained within this approach. Such an approach may be facilitated through an application of a specific, formal marketing process through time.

Marketing Process

Marketing and advertising are not uncommon attributes within the domains of law enforcement and criminal justice entities. Both types of organizations may leverage marketing and advertising to influence public opinion and to build a strong trust relationship within their served public markets. Both marketing and advertising functions may be used to generate negative connotations, among society, whether accidentally or purposefully. Regardless, the use of marketing and advertising provides a powerful means through which the leaders of law enforcement and criminal justice organizations may embellish their obligations of public service. The leaders of law enforcement and criminal justice organizations must render a conscious decision to pursue marketing and advertising efforts toward some stated purpose or fulfillment of service within society. This pursuance is facilitated through the marketing process.

The rendering of a decision to pursue marketing and advertising initiatives must occur through a methodical, systematic mechanism in which a variety of requirements, analysis, development, design, testing, implementation, and feedback activities occur through time. The characteristics of long-term, strategic activities; short-term, tactical activities; and near-term, operational activities must be integrated within this mechanism. Such a mechanism must also incorporate functions of quality assurance and control, requirements analysis and specification, service development and refinement, financial decisions, and considerations of public interaction.

The workings of such a process may be expressed methodically through defining the various stages and states of existence that occur through time to pursue marketing and advertising initiatives. The use of a systematic marketing process is critical to the implementation, evaluation, and adjustment of any marketing and advertising initiatives. Such a process may be derived from the descriptions of strategic marketing processes given by the U.S. Department of Agriculture (U.S. Department of Agriculture, 2008b), the U.S. Small Business Administration (U.S. Small Business Administration, 2010), and the U.S. Department of Transportation (U.S. Department of Transportation, 2010). The following discussions highlight such a marketing process.

Within any systematic marketing process, a delineation of separate stages must specify the activities and goals of each marketing phase. Therefore, specification must occur of the stages and activities that comprise the cumulative marketing process. When crafting a marketing process, these stages may be primarily sequential. Some stages may be repeated until a satisfactory output is produced from each stage before progression to the next stage of the process may occur in due time. Therefore, a satisfactory output is required, per stage, before progression to the succeeding stage may occur through time. Furthermore, a marketing process must incorporate a variety of qualitative and quantitative activities that culminate in the manifestation of media marketing and advertising strategically, tactically, and operationally.

Societal Commencement

The marketing process begins with society. Within society, various human needs and wants exist. With respect to the terms of the basic question of economics, law enforcement entities must attempt to satisfy the unlimited needs and wants of humans with resources that are scarce. Therefore, not all public service initiatives and programs may be pursued simultaneously given the scarcity and availability of resources that are required for their design, development, and implementation. Hence, the marketing process begins with queries regarding what services and programs must be crafted, for whom such services and programs are intended within the public sector, and the magnitude and scope of such programs and services. These queries provide the foundation for detailing the proposed initiative, and recommending it for further analysis both internally and externally. Administrators and leaders must determine which programs will be selected and implemented.

Requirements

The second stage of the marketing process encompasses research analysis and the specification of the requirements that define and describe the potential initiative. During this stage, the characteristics of the intended market are examined and determined with respect to the intended service or program. The organizational capacity to pursue the proposed initiative is also examined. This stage of the marketing process may also involve the use of feasibility studies to determine whether the proposed initiative is possible and viable. Per the discussions in Chapter 1, the requirements specifications must address the following questions: how, who, what, when, where, and why? The output of this stage represents a written document that expresses all of the requirements that must be satisfied within the campaign.

Resource Analysis

The third stage of the marketing process involves resource analysis. This stage is highly quantitative and may involve the use of multiple forecasting methods. Such analysis may encompass examining the future, expected population demographics versus the commensurate quantities of resources that are required to support the policing initiative through time. These resources may include signage, television outlets, print media outlets, Internet presence, community events, cosponsors, etc. If the outcomes of the analysis are indicative of a realistic condition that may be supported through time, then the initiative enters the fourth stage of the marketing process.

Design

The fourth stage of the marketing process involves a consideration of design. This stage encompasses the crafting of a cumulative blueprint that provides a foundation for the entirety of the marketing and advertising campaign. The design of the marketing and advertising campaign is derived from the requirements that were expressed within step two of the process. Within the design, the basic queries of communication must be addressed: who, what, when, where, why, and how?

Development

The fifth stage of the marketing process involves the actual development and crafting of the service. This phase occurs with respect to the requirements that were crafted during the second stage of the marketing process. During the development activities, the crafting of the service must occur in accordance with the specifications delineated within the requirements documentation. Frequently and periodically, the development of the service may be benchmarked against the requirements specification to ensure that little, if any, deviation occurs regarding the characteristics of the initiative being developed. This action also provides measures of quality assurance and quality control within this stage of the marketing process.

Financial Management

The sixth stage of the marketing process considers the monetary aspects of the initiative. During this stage, various facets of capital budgeting analysis may be performed to determine whether the designed service is financially and economically worthwhile. Within this stage, the quantitative tools of net present value analysis, internal rate of return analysis, payback time analysis, and profitability index analysis may be used concurrently to determine whether the initiative should be pursued financially. From the economic perspective, the quantitative tools of break-even analysis and cost–benefit analysis may occur to determine the worthiness of the initiative. If the outcomes of these analyses indicate that the initiative is worthwhile financially and economically, then the initiative may be considered for pursuance.

Initiative Decision

The seventh stage of the marketing process involves the rendering of a human decision to either pursue or discard the initiative. This decision integrates the outcomes of each of the preceding stages of the marketing process, and it incorporates considerations of personnel, intelligence, operations, training, resource availability, logistics, financial and economic factors, feasibility, and societal and organizational characteristics. If any of these categories are significantly deficient, then the initiative may be discarded. Otherwise, the initiative may be pursued.

Commit Organizational Resources

The eighth stage of the marketing process is indicative of a conscious decision to commit organizational resources toward the pursuance of the initiative through time. Personnel are assigned to the initiative. This stage also obliges the expending of financial monies toward the fulfillment of the successful implementation of the developed service. Within this stage, the crafting of public relations activities, tactics, and strategies occurs with respect to the methods through which information regarding the initiative will be introduced and disseminated among its served populace.

Strategies and Tactics

The ninth stage of the marketing process involves advertising and marketing strategies and tactics. It is during this stage that the public market is enticed and influenced to generate positive connotations and mental models of the initiative. The activities of this stage may incorporate the use of radio, television, Internet, and print media resources to disseminate information regarding the initiative. Public events and word-of-mouth activities may also embellish marketing and advertising activities. The anticipated effect of the marketing and advertising activities is that of public support and partaking of the service.

Implementation

The tenth stage of the marketing process represents the implementation of the initiative. Once public knowledge and understanding of the initiative are manifested within the served populace, the law enforcement agency must support its initiative across any participating entities and geographic regions. This stage involves the distribution of any necessary resources that are required to support the implementation of the initiative. During this stage, the actual implementation and provision of communication occurs through time. It is during this period that the marketing and advertising activities occur to generate public awareness of some issue.

Feedback

The eleventh stage of the marketing process involves the collection and processing of feedback to adjust the characteristics of the service. This feedback analysis may occur both internally and externally. Internal analysis may facilitate policy decisions or operational decisions. External analysis may be used to examine the receptiveness and public perceptions that exist regarding the marketing and advertising campaign. Feedback activities may involve examining response times to distress calls, shift work schedules, reductions among rates of crime, and an array of other attributes within the service domain. Feedback data may be collected through a variety of methods ranging from Internet surveys to telephone interviews with citizens. The purpose of feedback analysis is to generate improvements in efficiency and effectiveness of the service initiative to yield benefits for both the law enforcement agency and society.

Evaluation

Evaluation represents the conclusion of the marketing process before it is iteratively influenced by the characteristics of society. Evaluation is defined as a determination of "the significance, worth, or condition of, usually by careful appraisal and study" (*Merriam-Webster*, 2012). All marketing and advertising campaigns may be evaluated to determine whether they may be continued without any alterations, be continued with some alterations, or be discontinued. Any number of factors may affect decisions during a period of evaluation. Funding may be insufficient to continue a campaign; societal demographics may change thereby affecting marketing and advertising; and so forth. Every facet of the marketing and advertising campaign should be evaluated from a variety of perspectives ranging from public opinions to financial management.

Characteristics of the Marketing Process

An examination of these stages indicates that the marketing process is cyclical and demonstrates economic characteristics. It commences with an examination of human needs and wants within society, and demonstrates fruition through the satisfaction of these human needs and wants through time. Although it is primarily a sequential process, various stages within its construct may be repeated as necessary. Such repetition is manifested greatly among the first six stages of the marketing process.

A potential manifestation of repetitiveness occurs regarding the development stage. Once the development of the service occurs, any defects must be corrected through a comparison with the stated requirements that were generated within the second stage of the marketing process. If corrections are extremely difficult or may be impossible given the resources of the law enforcement agency, a condition may arise in which alterations of the stated requirements are necessary provided that the intended function of the service is unchanged. Therefore, the entire marketing process defaults to the second stage of requirements analysis, and must proceed sequentially according to the prescribed, succeeding stages.

Another potential manifestation of repetitiveness occurs regarding the financial and cost analysis stage of the marketing process. If the financial or economic analyses outcomes indicate that the initiative is not worthwhile, then alterations of the requirements may be necessary. Any such alterations must not change the intended function of the service initiative but should be representative of an approach that demonstrates lowered costs monetarily. Any different approach must be delineated within the requirements of the initiative. Therefore, the entire marketing process defaults to the second stage of requirements analysis, and must proceed sequentially according to the prescribed, succeeding stages.

The decision to either pursue or discard the initiative presents the potential of repetitiveness among the stages of the marketing process. If the initiative is rejected, for any reason, it may not be completely eliminated from consideration if its importance dictates that it may potentially provide great benefit within society. If such a condition occurs, then organizational leaders may examine the stated requirements of the service and consider whether alterations are necessary without compromising the intended function. If the intended function of the service may be uncompromised, then the requirements may be altered as necessary. Therefore, the entire marketing process defaults to the second stage of requirements analysis, and must proceed sequentially according to the prescribed, succeeding stages.

Any service initiative must be approached both systematically and methodically. Although many law enforcement agencies may informally craft and provide services among small initiatives, the implementation of larger initiatives may benefit from the use of a formal methodology. The marketing process represents such a formal methodology. Through the use of the marketing process, law enforcement entities may not only craft services, but may also improve their capacity to control, lead, organize, plan, and coordinate their intended services within society.

Service Marketing and the Justice Domain

Within the context of traditional marketing paradigms, a profit motive is associated with the marketing process of services. With respect to nonprofit organizations, the fulfillment of mission and the provision of societal benefits are motives that underlie the marketing process of services. Regardless of whether the motives of an organization are based on profits or societal benefits, the services marketing process necessitates a variety of business decisions among law enforcement and criminal justice entities. These decisions are associated with the organizational capacity to render the offered service and the perspectives of the public market.

On the basis of the collective writings of the National Library of Medicine (National Library of Medicine, 2005), the U.S. Department of Agriculture (U.S. Department of Agriculture, 2008a), and the California Prison Industry Authority (California Prison Industry Authority, 2011), the following attributes must be considered among marketing initiatives: (1) price, (2) promotion, (3) product, (4) position, (5) physicality, (6) processes, and (7) people. The service perspective of business decisions is manifested in prisoner work programs among for-profit prisons and corrections entities. The category of price involves the fees charged to house and maintain inmates during the period of incarceration. The promotion attributes include forging relationships among host work environments that employ inmates. The product category may be the end state of the prisoner because a rehabilitated individual may result from experiencing the service-based work program. Positioning may involve a determination of where the work program is to be performed. Physicality involves determining any tangible resources that are necessary for providing the service (e.g., prison clothes washers or call center). Processes include crafting any methods that are necessary for generating the service, management decision models, determining reporting methods, and influencing distribution methods that exist within the work environment or served market. The category of people is inclusive of decisions regarding the inmates providing the service, personnel who oversee the work program, and the individuals of the market for whom the service is provided.

Customer satisfaction involves determining whether the satisfaction of market consumers is fulfilled regarding the service offering. The use of customer feedback and commensurate adjustments to the service offered may facilitate customer satisfaction. Determinations of cost influence whether market consumers perceive and believe that the service is worthwhile, and is worth the amount of money that is paid for the service. Decisions regarding service convenience are various, and must provide ease and benefit for market consumers. Within a prisoner work program setting, factors such as whether the operational environment is unimpeded and workers are readily available may contribute to consumer perceptions of convenience. Communication decisions must provide mutual benefit for both the provider and the consumers of the service. Service announcements and periodic status meetings may be used to facilitate communications between the service provider and the market consumers.

The marketing of prisoner work programs provides mutual benefit for both the provider of the service and society. The design and marketing of such services must complement the organizational capacity to provide quality services through time. Certainly, the outcome of the marketing process may be communicated via the Internet to show the benefits of inmate labor programs. This notion is corroborated through an examination of work programs offered by Mississippi Prison Industries. According to the Mississippi Department of Corrections, its prisoner worker service program offerings "adopted strategies to make business more efficient by balancing operations in keeping with the needs of the customers, reducing waste, making the most of resources available while refraining from unreasonably competing with Mississippi's private sector manufacturers" (Mississippi Department of Corrections, 2010). Through the use of the marketing process, organizational leaders may incorporate such considerations across all stages of the crafting of the service offering. Furthermore, the use of the marketing process provides a method through which service decisions may be specified and refined through time to provide a robust, quality benefit among market consumers and society.

Branding

Across the nation, police departments exist in market conditions that are quite monopolistic. Within a county or parish, police departments are generally responsible for preventing crime and maintaining order within their established jurisdictions. Because of their uniqueness as public entities, any existence of competing entities is very limited. However, jurisdictions may overlap in some regions and locales via the provisions of services by both city police and county or parish sheriff's departments. Because of this situation, the marketing and advertising of law enforcement services may be limited or nonexistent. However, neglecting these activities does not facilitate a strong mental model of policing among the populace.

Law enforcement organizations may consider branding decisions as methods of engraining themselves within their served communities. Branding provides familiarity and immediate recognition within the serviced market. Branding demonstrates a method through which law enforcement organizations may embellish community-oriented policing initiatives. Branding is a tool through which communication and knowledge may be shared within the serviced market. Therefore, branding represents an increased capacity to manifest public service.

The decision to pursue a branding strategy provides law enforcement organizations with a myriad of considerations regarding its community presence. Branding emphasizes name recognition (U.S. Navy, 2010). Therefore, branding may be used to facilitate an awareness of organizational mission and services provided among communities. Because of branding, the public gains an understanding of the role and function of community policing. On the basis of audits of the U.S. Office of the Inspector General, branding involves realism (Office of the Inspector General, 2010). Law enforcement entities must not promise public services that cannot be provided, and must fulfill their public service obligations effectively and efficiently.

Therefore, law enforcement entities must carefully consider whether they have sufficient resources available before committing themselves to a public service endeavor.

Specialty advertising decisions are tools through which branding occurs (U.S. Federal Trade Commission, 2010). Because of the categorization of advertising functions as subsets of branding strategies, they are used to disseminate branding messages and familiarity among communities. Such goals may be accomplished through the use of T-shirts, ball caps, etc. (U.S. Federal Trade Commission, 2010). Branding also involves a consistent structure. Consistency reinforces the identity and message of the law enforcement organization within its serviced community. This consistency presents a common appearance among personnel and resources.

The concepts of branding are applicable to both the for-profit and nonprofit entities. The common theme, among both for-profit and nonprofit entities, within the context of law enforcement, is to prevent crime and to maintain order within society. Therefore, regardless of whether a law enforcement or criminal justice entity has a profit motive, the use of branding familiarizes society with the functions and presence of the law enforcement entity.

With respect to the for-profit entities, among security services, an example is the Wackenhut Corporation. This entity leverages a variety of relationships and activities through which it embellishes its market recognition and familiarization through branding. According to the Savannah River Site of the U.S. Department of Energy, Wackenhut participates during high school events to assist in influencing the decisions of American youths to attend college and compete for scholarship funds (U.S. Department of Energy, 2013). Such activities interject the Wackenhut name among youths who will evaluate employers upon graduation. Because of such activities, Wackenhut familiarizes its name among younger generations.

Nonprofit law enforcement and criminal justice entities may also benefit from decisions to pursue branding strategies. The Community-Oriented Policing Services (COPS) component of the DOJ represents such an entity. The COPS organization strategically identifies and brands itself through the slogan of "building relationships, solving problems" (U.S. Department of Justice, 2013). The context of the slogan may be viewed from both community and law enforcement perspectives. The COPS organization is recognized as a resource through which local law enforcement entities may obtain funding, assistance, and information to embellish their community-oriented policing initiatives. Because of COPS partnerships, communities benefit from strengthened relationships between the served populace and law enforcement entity, which are necessary for the success of community-oriented policing. The use of community-oriented policing contributes toward the building of trust between law enforcement entities and their served populaces. Figure 10.5 shows the COPS slogan used as a branding mechanism.

Both for-profit and nonprofit law enforcement and criminal justice entities may implement branding strategies. The development of a brand requires time, and it must be implemented strategically. Branding must contribute toward the long-term pursuit of strategic vision, and must incorporate a variety of advertising and marketing goals and objectives. Any branding strategy must be flexible to accommodate fluctuations regarding the preferences of

Figure 10.5 COPS branding slogan. (From http://www.cops.usdoj.gov/.)

the serviced public market. Therefore, branding decisions must incorporate feedback gained from observations of its serviced populace, and must be rendered appropriately to facilitate the highest and best relationships between the organization and the community.

Regardless of such considerations, organizational leaders must contemplate branding decisions from the perspective of providing benefit for both the organization itself and the served community. Each populace demonstrates its own culture and attributes of crime. Therefore, each law enforcement organization must develop a unique branding strategy, with respect to the demographic characteristics of its serviced populace, which contributes toward the prevention of crime and maintenance of order within society. The success of such branding is accomplished through the building of trust and the influencing of positive perceptions among society members.

Marketing Process Evaluation

Evaluation must permeate all phases of marketing, advertising, and branding functions. Initially, evaluation may be used to explore and identify the demographic characteristics of the serviced community. The determination of such demographic attributes contributes toward the crafting of strategies through which policing services are marketed and advertised within society. Furthermore, such determination also contributes toward the crafting of branding strategies through which familiarity and trust are established between law enforcement entities and their serviced communities. Evaluation may occur through a variety of methods.

One method of evaluation examines the strengths, weaknesses, opportunities, and threats (SWOT) of the serviced market. This SWOT analysis may be used to implement and adjust marketing, advertising, and branding strategies according to the dynamic characteristics of the serviced market environment. Both for-profit and nonprofit law enforcement organizations may implement SWOT analysis.

Market strengths may be examined through queries regarding whether sufficient resources exist to pursue the desired initiative. Resources may include squad cars, personnel, weapons, and incarceration facilities. Market weaknesses may be examined through queries regarding whether any impedances hamper the progression of the desired initiative. Weaknesses may include a lack of cooperation between the serviced market and police departments, lack of training resources, lack of funds, or a lack of personnel. Market opportunities may be examined through queries regarding whether additional services may be provided within the serviced market. Opportunities may include the addition of personnel, school programs, and increases of scheduled patrols. Market threats may be examined through queries regarding whether any forces exist that may diminish or nullify the effectiveness and efficiency of the provided services. Threats may include reductions in personnel, an elimination of funding, or political disagreements.

This type of SWOT analysis may be used to embellish the crafting, implementing, and adjusting of marketing, advertising, or branding functions. The use of SWOT allows organizational leaders an opportunity to evaluate the status of their initiatives, and to render decisions regarding any contingencies that may be manifested within the serviced market. Through the use of SWOT analysis, organizations may improve the efficiency and effectiveness of their public service functions and operational capacities.

The use of SWOT analysis is not the only form of evaluation that may improve the functions of marketing, advertising, or branding. Other methods may include quantitative analysis (e.g., chi-square methods) or the use of qualitative analysis (e.g., case studies). Additional functions of evaluation may include organizational benchmarking, financial ratio analysis, or the use of quality control paradigms. Because each law enforcement organization is unique, no solitary method of evaluation exists that is completely appropriate regarding all situations. Therefore, when considering evaluation, each individual department must determine the requirements of evaluation with respect to its intended marketing, advertising, or branding initiative, and craft evaluation functions accordingly. Hence, evaluation of marketing initiatives is highly situational, and may vary among serviced, public markets.

Public Service Campaigns and Advertisements

Public service campaigns (PSCs) and public service advertisements (PSAs) are designed to communicate information that is in the best interests of the public. Specifically, such concepts are expressed as "any announcement for which no charge is made and which promotes programs, activities or services of federal, state or local governments or the programs, activities, or services of nonprofit organizations" (*WJBK News*, 2012). This notion also applies to "other announcements regarded as serving community interests" (*WJBK News*, 2012). Both PSCs and PSAs are not uncommon within the justice domain.

The foremost example involves the Smokey Bear campaign that informs the public regarding the danger of wildfires and wildfire prevention. The program is "managed by the U.S. Forest Service in cooperation with the Advertising Council Inc. and the National Association of State Foresters" (U.S. Forest Service, 2009). The National Park Service (and other organizations) leverages Smokey Bear to create awareness of fire within national parks (National Park Service, 1994). The marketing and advertising of Smokey Bear represents the "longest running PSA campaign in U.S. history" (Smokey Bear, 2012). The effectiveness of this campaign is unquestionable. Since its origination during the 1940s, it has reduced the quantity of "acres lost annually to fire in the United States from 22 million" to approximately 4 million acres (Ehrlich et al., 2007). The campaign is targeted toward both adults and children (Hammari, 2007).

Another campaign that attempts to influence public behavior through marketing and advertising involves the Mothers Against Drunk Drivers (MADD) organization. For nearly one-third of a century, since 1980, MADD has attempted to diminish the effects and reduce the instances of drunken driving on American roadways (Mothers against Drunk Driving, 2012). This campaign involves a strong Internet presence through which information is disseminated regarding the methods through which drunken driving may be curtailed. It also incorporates social networking as a method of further communicating the salient aspects of its messages.

Both the Smokey Bear and the MADD campaigns have national appeal and outreach. Their messages are presented to mass audiences nationally. However, not all PSCs and PSAs have a national interest. Some may have only a regional or local interest and audience. The campaign of Howard County, Maryland, represents such an example. In this case, marketing and advertising communications are targeted toward audiences near the locality. Figure 10.6 shows an example of this type of communications effort (Howard County Police Department, 2007).

Practically any topic regarding public safety and public awareness may be communicated through marketing and advertising methods. When a child is missing or abducted, it

Figure 10.6 Howard County campaign. (From http://www.hcdrugfree.org/images/trafficsafetycampaign.pdf.)

is common for Amber alerts to be issued to inform the general public regarding the appearance of the child, last known location, name of the child, and contact information for law enforcement authorities. When such alerts are issued, they involve collaboration and cooperation between multiple news organizations and law enforcement entities (Murphy, 2007).

Regardless of the message conveyed through public service communications, they all serve the primary purpose of generating public benefit. Informing the public concerning calamities or merely providing a reminder of the presence of police is a fiduciary responsibility of public safety entities and law enforcement organizations. Through leveraging marketing and advertising effectively and efficiently, a mass audience may be communicated with for a variety of purposes ranging from behavioral modification to warnings of public dangers. In any instance, PSCs and PSAs are strong tools through which law enforcement organizations may communicate with mass audiences.

Commentary Regarding Marketing and Advertising Communications

From the perspectives of law enforcement organizations and the justice system, communications marketing and advertising are pursued cooperatively and collaboratively with external media organizations. Among localities, when inclement situations arise that endanger the public, or to promote some other type of topical awareness, local television and radio stations may be used to communicate with the public. In and of themselves, local law enforcement organizations do not have resources through which PSAs and PSCs may be pursued.

Some aspects of communicating with the public necessitate a national campaign and commensurate appeal to convey messages. One entity through which this collaboration occurs is the Ad Council. This organization describes itself as follows (Ad Council, 2012a):

> The Ad Council is a private, non-profit organization that marshals volunteer talent from the advertising and communications industries, the facilities of the media, and the resources of the business and non-profit communities to deliver critical messages to the American public. The Ad Council produces, distributes and promotes public service campaigns on behalf of non-profit organizations and government agencies in issue areas such as improving the quality of life for children, preventive health, education, community well being and strengthening families. The Ad Council has endeavored to improve the lives of all Americans since first creating the category of public service advertising in 1942.

Incidents involving children often may involve communicating with a mass audience. Notifications regarding situations that endanger children may originate with social workers from "juvenile detectives" and "juvenile probation officers" (Roberts & Springer, 2007). Certain situations may necessitate "police social worker" interventions during night hours (Roberts & Springer, 2007). Depending on the outcome of a situation, a child may be placed in foster care or may eventually be adopted.

It is not uncommon for components of the justice system to partner with the Ad Council to pursue various public awareness campaigns regarding issues involving children. One issue that affects the justice system involves the adoption of foster children. Through Ad Council initiatives, the American public is made aware that "there are around 400,000 children in the U.S. foster care system; 104,000 of these children are waiting for families to adopt them" (Ad Council, 2012b). This use of Ad Council marketing and advertising is targeted toward audiences nationally. The campaign conveys the following message:

> "You don't have to be perfect to be a perfect parent." Humor is brought to the seemingly challenging task of adopting a child from foster care, to reassure prospective parents that even if not "perfect," they have the ability to provide the stability and security that a child needs and deserves. (Ad Council, 2012b)

Another consideration of marketing and advertising communication involves regional, state, or local perspectives. In such instances, law enforcement organizations may be concerned with roadway safety. For example, such marketing and advertising campaigns may involve considerations of how to alter the perceptions and behaviors of speeding motorists. The city of Seattle, Washington, implements a public safety campaign through which citizens are informed of the dangers of speeding and its potentially fatal consequences. The campaign also provides information for motorists to inform them of how they can reduce speeding on roadways. Figure 10.7 shows the salient Internet components of this campaign (City of Seattle, 2012).

Local marketing and advertising campaigns are leveraged by law enforcement organizations to inform the public regarding a variety of issues. Through marketing and advertising to fulfill a public service function, law enforcement organizations are better able to pursue the goals of deterring crime and maintaining societal order. Communicating through the resources of marketing and advertising represents a method of influencing behavior and generating public awareness through which messages are methodically crafted and conveyed. In any case, within the justice domain, such messaging represents a benevolent use of marketing and advertising communications.

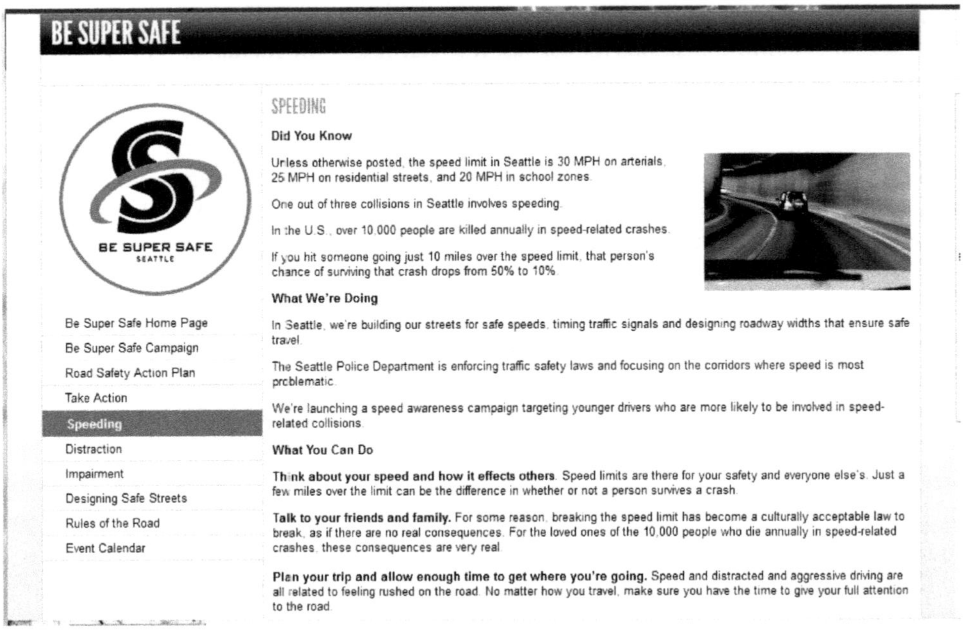

Figure 10.7 Seattle, Washington, speeding campaign. (From http://www.seattle.gov/beSuperSafe/speeding.htm.)

Chapter Comments and Summary

Entities within the justice system and law enforcement organizations must often need to communicate with various public audiences. Marketing, advertising, and branding are salient aspects of informing the public regarding some event or to generate some type of awareness within the public mindset. These methods also contribute toward the influencing of societal perceptions of law enforcement and criminal justice entities through time. These tools may be leveraged to craft, implement, and adjust the strategic, tactical, and operational functions of both for-profit and nonprofit law enforcement and criminal justice organizations. Such tools are not used randomly and indiscriminately. Instead, their mechanisms must be specifically planned and crafted to satisfy a specific purpose toward the fulfillment of identified, anticipated outcomes. Therefore, the use of a marketing process satisfies this requirement.

Invoking the tools of marketing and advertising is systematic and methodical. The marketing process exists as a sequential process through which marketing and advertising activities are performed through time to convey some message to a public audience. Societal attributes contribute toward the instigation of the marketing process. Upon its completion, numerous activities of evaluation must occur before a new cycle of the marketing process commences.

Influencing behaviors and conveying information to the public are also considerations of marketing and advertising. These campaigns exist to bolster public safety through time. For example, to reduce speeding or drunken driving, law enforcement organizations may employ a marketing or advertising campaign to generate public awareness and to alter the behavior of citizens. Such campaigns are generally accomplished in conjunction with external entities such as the Ad Council or local marketing and advertising organizations.

Regardless of the initiative, law enforcement entity, or serviced market, evaluation is an important tool that must not be neglected. Evaluation is used to refine the crafting of marketing, advertising, and branding initiatives before they are implemented. Once implemented, evaluation is the function through which determinations may be made regarding the efficiency and effectiveness of marketing initiatives through time. On the basis of the outcomes of evaluation assessments, organizational leaders may adjust their activities and strategies accordingly to provide the highest and best services possible.

Regardless of a for-profit (e.g., security firm or for-profit prison) or nonprofit status (e.g., youth programs or police departments) within the justice domain, marketing and advertising are useful methods of communicating with the public to provide information regarding a variety of events or to solicit public feedback and assistance. Marketing and advertising may be used as warning mechanisms through which the public becomes informed about entities that may be harmful, whether tangible or intangible. In any case, each law enforcement organization must determine how it may uniquely leverage marketing and advertising to communicate with its served public (Figure 10.8).

Figure 10.8 IC3 cyber crime poster communicating a public warning. (From http://www.ic3.gov/media/IC3-Poster.pdf.)

Terminology

Ad Council
Advertisement
Advertising
Awareness
Behavioral modification
Branding
Consumer
Decision
Evaluation
Feedback
Financial management
Influence
Marketing
Marketing communication
Marketing process
Mass audience
Product marketing
Public awareness
Public benefit
Public opinion
Public safety
Public service announcement
Public service campaign
Service marketing
Smokey Bear
SWOT

THOUGHT AND DISCUSSION QUESTIONS

1. Within your local area, identify three types of advertising that communicate a law enforcement or criminal justice message. Do you believe these types of advertising are effective or ineffective? Please justify and substantiate your response.
2. This chapter presented a marketing process. Although this marketing process is an adequate method of facilitating the development, implementation, and adjustment of a marketing campaign, what other types of marketing processes are suitable for achieving the same purpose? Please justify and substantiate your response.
3. Branding facilitates familiarity and understanding within serviced public markets. Within your local area, identify three types of law enforcement or criminal justice branding initiatives that are prevalent. Do you believe these types of advertising are effective or ineffective? Please justify and substantiate your response.
4. Evaluation is a salient component of strategy. On the basis of your responses to the preceding questions, identify and discuss evaluation methods that are used to refine your identified activities of marketing, advertising, and branding. Please justify and substantiate your response.

References

Ad Council. (2012a). About us. Retrieved from http://www.adcouncil.org/About-Us (accessed December 29, 2012).

Ad Council. (2012b). Adoption from foster care. Retrieved from http://www.adcouncil.org/Our-Work/Current-Work/Family-Community/Adoption-from-Foster-Care (accessed December 29, 2012).

California Prison Industry Authority. (2011). Joint/Free venture program summary. Retrieved from http://www.pia.ca.gov/Inmate_Development/JointVenture.html (accessed January 20, 2011).

City of Milwaukee. (2012). Welcome to the Milwaukee police department. Retrieved from http://www.milwaukee.gov/police (accessed December 30, 2012).

City of Seattle. (2012). Speeding. Retrieved from http://www.seattle.gov/beSuperSafe/speeding.htm (accessed December 29, 2012).

City of Tampa. (2010). 'Patrol like you live there' operation nets 10 prostitution arrests. Retrieved from http://www.tampagov.net/appl_tampa_announcements/ViewRelease.asp?ReleaseID=5679 (accessed December 30, 2012).

Ehrlich, D., Minton, A., & Story, D. (2007). *Smokey, Rosie, and you!: The history and practice of marketing public programs* (p. 67). McLean, VA: The Track Group.

Federal Bureau of Investigation. (2010). Wanted by the FBI. Retrieved from http://www.fbi.gov/wanted.htm (accessed December 30, 2012).

Foster Youth Services. (2012). What's new. Retrieved from http://www.healthiersf.org/fys/News/whatsnew.php (accessed December 29, 2012).

Hammari, J. (2007). Nature's graphics: Graphic design's historic influence on American behavior in the outdoors. Retrieved from http://www.d.umn.edu/~hamma036/NaturesGraphicsS.pdf (accessed December 29, 2012).

Howard County Police Department. (2007). Traffic safety public service campaign. Retrieved from http://www.hcdrugfree.org/images/trafficsafetycampaign.pdf (accessed December 29, 2012).

Merriam-Webster Dictionary. (2012). s.v. "evaluate." Retrieved from http://www.merriam-webster.com/dictionary/evaluation (accessed December 30, 2012).

Mississippi Department of Corrections. (2010). Mississippi prison industries. Retrieved from http://www.mdoc.state.ms.us/mississippi_prison_industries.htm (accessed December 30, 2012).

Mothers against Drunk Driving. (2012). History of MADD. Retrieved from http://www.madd.org/about-us/history/ (accessed December 21, 2012).

Murphy, P. (2007). Double whammy against child abductors: Child abduction team and public service campaign launched. Retrieved from http://attorneygeneral.utah.gov/196.html (accessed December 29, 2012).

National Highway Transportation and Safety Administration. (2001). Alcohol and safety 2001: A review of the state of knowledge. Retrieved from http://www.nhtsa.gov/people/injury/research/AlcoholHighway/5_dealing_w_problem.htm (accessed December 30, 2012).

National Highway Transportation and Safety Administration. (2010a). *Report to congress: Improving the safety of child restraints—Booster seat study*. Retrieved from http://www.nhtsa.gov/DOT/NHTSA/NRD/Multimedia/PDFs/Crashworthiness/Booster%20Seat%20Study%20Report%20to%20Congress.pdf (accessed December 30, 2012).

National Highway Transportation and Safety Administration. (2010b). Safercar.gov. Retrieved from http://www.safercar.gov (accessed December 30, 2012).

National Library of Medicine. (2005). Social marketing: Planning before conceiving preconception care. Retrieved from http://www.ncbi.nlm.nih.gov/pmc/articles/PMC1592143/ (accessed December 30, 2012).

National Park Service. (1994). Spanning the gap—50 years of fire prevention: Smokey Bear celebrates a big birthday. Retrieved from http://www.nps.gov/dewa/naturescience/upload/cmsstg SMOKY.pdf (accessed December 30, 2012).

Office of the Inspector General. (2010). *Audit of USAID/MALI's education program*. Retrieved from http://www.usaid.gov/oig/public/fy10rpts/7-688-10-004-p.pdf (accessed December 29, 2012).

Pride, W., Hughes, R., & Kapoor, J. (2012). *Business* (11th ed., p. 431). Mason, OH: South-Western Cengage Publishing.

Roberts, A., & Springer, D. (2007). *Social work in juvenile and criminal settings* (p. 129). Springfield, IL: Charles C. Thomas Publishers.

Rogers, W. (n.d.). Advertising quotes. Brainyquote.com. Retrieved from http://www.brainyquote.com/quotes/keywords/advertising.html (accessed December 30, 2012).

Smokey Bear. (2012). Welcome. Only you can prevent wildfires. Retrieved from http://www.smokeybear.com/vault/?js=1 (accessed December 28, 2012).

Starch, D. (1910). *Principles of advertising: A systematic syllabus of the fundamental principles of advertising.* Madison, WI: The University Cooperative Co.

State of California. (2010). *Evaluating California's boards and commissions—California performance review.* Retrieved from http://cpr.ca.gov/CPR_Report/Form_Follows_Function/Evaluating_Boards_and_Commissions.html (accessed December 30, 2010 and December 30, 2012).

U.S. Department of Agriculture. (2008a). The dynamics of change in the U.S. food marketing environment. Retrieved from http://www.ams.usda.gov/AMSv1.0/getfile?dDocName=STELPRDC5070995 (accessed December 30, 2012).

U.S. Department of Agriculture. (2008b). *Supply chain basics: The dynamics of change in the U.S. food marketing environment.* Retrieved from http://www.ams.usda.gov/AMSv1.0/getfile?dDocName=STELPRDC5070995 (accessed December 30, 2012).

U.S. Department of Defense. (2009). Fort Hood first responders save lives. Retrieved from http://www.defense.gov/news/newsarticle.aspx?id=56583 (accessed December 30, 2012).

U.S. Department of Energy. (2013). News from the Savannah river site. Retrieved from http://www.srs.gov/general/news/releases/NR2008_CollegeNightScholarships.pdf (accessed January 2, 2013).

U.S. Department of Justice. (2013). Community-oriented policing services. Retrieved from http://www.cops.usdoj.gov/ (accessed January 2, 2013).

U.S. Department of Transportation. (2010). Highways for life. Retrieved from http://www.fhwa.dot.gov/hfl/pres08.cfm (accessed December 30, 2012).

U.S. Federal Trade Commission. (2010). FTC report to congress for 1994 concerning cigarette sales, advertising, and promotion, pursuant to the Federal Cigarette Labeling and Advertising Act. Retrieved from http://www.ftc.gov/os/1996/10/94cigrp.htm (accessed December 27, 2012).

U.S. Forest Service. (2009). Smokey Bear guidelines. Retrieved from http://www.fs.fed.us/fire/prev_ed/smokeybearawards/Smokey_Bear_Guidelines.pdf (accessed December 29, 2012).

U.S. Navy. (2010). Benefits of branding. Retrieved from http://www.mwr.navy.mil/mwrprgms/brandedfood.htm (accessed December 29, 2012).

U.S. Small Business Administration. (2010). Programs and services to help you, start, grow, and succeed. Retrieved from http://www.sba.gov/smallbusinessplanner/plan/writeabusinessplan/serv_bp_marksale.html (accessed December 30, 2012).

WJBK News. (2012). WJBK Fox 2 PSA Policy. Retrieved from http://www.myfoxdetroit.com/story/18770304/wjbk (accessed December 29, 2012).

Emergency and Public Communication

11

Do what you can, with what you have, where you are.

—President Theodore Roosevelt (Roosevelt, n.d.)

Objectives

The objectives of this chapter are to

- Understand the necessity of public warning
- Understand the use of information systems regarding informing the public of danger
- Understand the methods of using information systems to facilitate public warning
- Understand the technologies that form the basis of information systems that facilitate public warning
- Understand the shortcomings of such technologies

Introduction

Various threats arise from man-made and natural origins. Emergency communications networks are critical in facilitating incident responsiveness efficiently and effectively. The use of public warning systems (PWS) is critical to communicating with citizens regarding perilous situations. The communication of information may involve crucial implications for life or death. Warnings may or may not precede man-made and natural disasters.

In some cases, public warnings may be communicated with a sufficient amount of time to evacuate citizens from potential incident locations. When hurricanes develop within the ocean, they may be observed and tracked for days before landfall occurs. This period of time often involves the warning of the citizenry across potential landfall locations. Other situations may demonstrate a period of time that is insufficient to generate public warnings. When tornadoes develop and destroy physical infrastructure and cause death or injuries, an insufficient amount of time may exist to warn the general public of the perilous situation. Numerous situations exist that necessitate the communication of public warnings and advisories.

The spring of 2011 manifested numerous natural disasters. The state of Mississippi experienced flooding, severe storms, and tornadoes that gouged the state and obliterated entire towns. Specifically, the town of Smithville, Mississippi, was completely destroyed. After the storms destroyed the town, Mississippi experienced flooding nearly three weeks later. Progressive flooding occurred in many cities, towns, and rural areas along the length of the Mississippi River. The flooding began in the northern United States, and flowed south along the course of the river. Regions of the Mississippi Delta were completely flooded. As Mississippi was recovering from storms and tornadoes, in advance of the impending flooding, Mississippi Governor Haley Barbour issued a warning regarding the rising waters of the Mississippi River. Specifically, Governor Barbour stated

> Hopefully we're not going to have an issue in this part of the state, but over the next few weeks on the Mississippi, we're going to have what could be record levels of the Mississippi, which is going to result in flooding in a great deal of the western part of the state. We're going to put all the resources we got into these tornado areas, but there are going people who are watching on television who live in areas affected by the Mississippi River. And they need to understand right now is the time for them to start protecting themselves, that they need to start taking care of their property, moving property, moving furniture, moving things that can be moved, things that can be elevated, because three weeks from now, we're going to have a tremendous amount of water in places where there's never been water in my lifetime, and I'm 63 years old. (Blitzer, 2011)

Governor Barbour's warning was witnessed nationally via the CNN. His warning of flooding became reality. A city that experienced this flooding was Vicksburg, Mississippi. Residents were warned regarding the coming flood using a variety of methods ranging from traditional newspapers to Internet announcements. These public warnings were issued through the use of communications systems involving the networks of telephone or satellite systems, thereby communicating with a mass audience.

Other situations may involve an unwarned citizenry before the occurrence of a cataclysm. During 2010, a British Petroleum (BP) oil well, located within the Gulf of Mexico, exploded and caused the largest oil spill in American history. This event was not preceded with any notice or warning among the communities of the Gulf Coast. Certainly, after the incident, emergency measures ensued regarding response and recovery initiatives. Along the Gulf Coast, communities and citizens received appropriate warnings during the aftermath of the event.

News of the BP incident was disseminated globally through the use of a variety of methods. Newspapers, radio, and television documented the events as they occurred through time. The communication of public warnings and advisories that succeeded the incident conveyed pertinent instructions within the affected populaces of the Gulf Coast and among maritime entities traversing along its waters. Figure 11.1 depicts an excerpt from television news communicating this incident.

The preceding examples show the need for communicating with the public regarding emergency incidents and the necessity of communications among emergency responders. These emergency communications resources are items that are necessary for communicating accurate and timely information to the public during crisis or emergency situations (Walsh et al., 2011). The use of such communication systems provides a basis for communicating warnings before incidents (if time allows), public advisories, and instructions regarding hazardous events.

It is imperative to maintain functional, efficient, and effective emergency communications resources throughout American society. During 2006, Executive Order 13407 mandated the "United States to have an effective, reliable, integrated, flexible, and comprehensive system to alert and warn the American people in situations of war, terrorist attack, natural disaster, or other hazards to public safety and well-being (public alert and warning system), taking appropriate account of the functions, capabilities, and needs of the private sector and of all levels of government in our Federal system, and to ensure that under

Figure 11.1 BP oil spill. (From http://www.habitat.noaa.gov/highlights/hldeepwaterhorizon.html.)

all conditions the President can communicate with the American people" (Federation of American Scientists, 2006).

This policy mandate necessitates the conception and construction of robust communication infrastructures throughout the United States. Such communication resources facilitate emergency communications nationally, regionally, and locally among emergency incident locations. The technologies and policies that are affiliated with these resources are varied given the different needs of communities and localities within the American populace. A myriad of communications technologies support the satisfaction of these needs. In every instance, all of these resources serve a common purpose: contributing toward the safety and security of society.

National Incident Management System

The National Incident Management System (NIMS) is a framework that facilitates a methodical, "proactive approach" to assisting government entities, the commercial sector, and other organizations to collaboratively integrate resources and to perform together for the prevention, protection against, response to, and mitigation of the "effects of incidents, regardless of cause, size, location or complexity, in order to reduce the loss of life and property and harm to the environment" (Federal Emergency Management Agency, 2012b). Across the nation, the use of NIMS working environments fosters the seamless integration of resources to increase the efficiency and effectiveness of incident preparedness, response, and recovery initiatives. Basically, NIMS enhances collaboration among emergency responders to maximize the potency, scope, and magnitude of incident preparedness, response, and recovery initiatives. It also establishes a common foundation for conducting communications.

The use of communication is essential to facilitate common understanding and situational awareness among responding entities and between responding entities and the general public. Disseminating information to the public is crucial during disasters.

Communicating timely, accurate, and informative warnings may save lives and improve the efficiency and effectiveness of response and recovery initiatives.

Within the NIMS architecture, the use of public information officers (PIOs) is essential when managing information for public dissemination, and when interacting with the public. The Federal Emergency Management Agency (FEMA) describes the role and responsibilities of the PIO as follows (Federal Emergency Management Agency, 2008):

> The Public Information Officer is responsible for interfacing with the public and media and/or with other agencies with incident-related information requirements. The Public Information Officer gathers, verifies, coordinates, and disseminates accurate, accessible, and timely information on the incident's cause, size, and current situation; resources committed; and other matters of general interest for both internal and external audiences. The Public Information Officer may also perform a key public information-monitoring role. Whether the command structure is single or unified, only one Public Information Officer should be designated per incident. Assistants may be assigned from other involved agencies, departments, or organizations. The IC/UC must approve the release of all incident-related information. In large-scale incidents or where multiple command posts are established, the Public Information Officer should participate in or lead the Joint Information Center (JIC) in order to ensure consistency in the provision of information to the public. (Federal Emergency Management Agency, 2008)

Within the NIMS framework, the PIO position is associated with the command staff and personnel. The PIO performs an advisory role toward the incident commander (IC) about any issues regarding public information associated with the management of the incident or the affiliated information systems involved with the public dissemination of information. According to FEMA, such public information should concern the "cause, size, and current situation" of an incident; the commitment of resources; and "other matters of general interest to the public, responders, and additional stakeholders (both directly affected and indirectly affected)" (Emergency Management Institute, 2010). The scope of the responsibilities of the PIO also encompasses "inquiries from the media, the public, and elected officials; emergency public information and warnings; rumor monitoring and response; media relations; and other functions required to gather, verify, coordinate, and disseminate accurate, accessible, and timely information related to the incident" (Federal Emergency Management Agency, 2008). Figure 11.2 shows a PIO being interviewed by news media.

During April 2010, the regions of Imperial County and Baja California experienced a magnitude 7.2 earthquake. The use of the PIO position embellished the period of response and recovery through the management and dissemination of public information. Public information consisted of announcements regarding the availabilities, locations, and hours of operations of local assistance centers and the collaborating agencies through which earthquake refugees could obtain transportation and obtain financial assistance (Imperial County Office of Education, 2010). The National Aeronautics and Space Administration (NOAA) and the National Weather Service (NWS) also issued a public statement regarding the potential of local tsunamis developing as a result of the earthquake (*Santa Barbara Independent*, 2010).

From the NIMS perspective, these public statements satisfied the fiduciary obligations of the PIO, and satisfied the aforementioned description of public information. The definitive contents of these public statements also served to quell public fears through the provision of informative material that could be understood, comprehended, and actively used within the general public.

Figure 11.2 PIO news media interview. (From http://www.fema.gov/photolibrary/photo_details.do?id=42157.)

The releasing of such public statements is methodical, and often involves the management and synthesization of data from numerous sources. Furthermore, the transmission of such public statements may involve numerous recipients across vast areas besides those of the local incident area. For example, the NOAA/NWS statement affected the entirety of the American and Canadian coastlines along the Pacific Ocean. These observations show the potential of PIOs to affect large geographic regions and mass quantities of people. With respect to NIMS, the release of such statements must be methodical involving standardization among the processes of any associated PIOs and their mechanisms.

Because of the NIMS tenets, multiple sources of data, and potentials of PIO influence, the strict control and sound management of information are both required and necessitated to ensure the integrities of information and public awareness within the incident domain. These functions of controlling and managing are satisfied through the uses of joint information centers and joint information systems. Both entities are accommodated within the overall NIMS framework.

Public Warning Systems

PWS are entities that collect and analyze data regarding a potential or actual incident, analyze this data, interpret the outcomes of analysis to derive a course of action, and communicate an appropriate warning or advisory within the populace to incite appropriate actions with respect to the characteristics of the incident domain. The use of PWS resources should be leveraged to reach a mass audience, and to maximize the communicating of warning information among the members of the general public. Therefore, the use of PWS should be directed to reach as many people as possible with information regarding an incident. The use of such resources is designed to be scalable to disseminate information locally, regionally, or nationally.

During modern times, it is common to hear such warnings among radio broadcasts, to view television broadcasts containing warning information, or to receive warning information through the use of mobile electronic devices. These resources are descended from the efforts of decades of research and applications of communications technologies to warn the public regarding endangerments. Although modern warning systems involve various digital technologies and software products, the origins of PWS and PIS were primitive.

During 1948, Tinker Air Force Base, located in Oklahoma, experienced a tornado that devastated the military installation. This incident occurred on March 20, 1948. After this tornado occurred, the Air Force commenced research to investigate the potential of forecasting tornadoes. Ernest J. Fawbush and Robert C. Miller, two Air Force officers, both serving as meteorologists, contributed to the "first publicly broadcast tornado forecast and warning, issued at Tinker for the air base on March 25, 1948" (Oklahoma Historical Society, 2012). This event instigated the development of "future warning systems" such as "Doppler radar, NEXRAD, satellite imaging, and storm tracking" (Oklahoma Historical Society, 2012). Furthermore, in time, Oklahoma became the host for the National Severe Storms Laboratory and the Storm Prediction Center of the NOAA and the Regional Forecast Center of the NWS (Oklahoma Historical Society, 2012).

Although the technologies and methods of public warning have improved, incidents occur that involve little or no time with which to implement warning processes and procedures before the incident occurs. The completely accurate prediction of such events may be impossible. Examples of such incidents include natural disasters (e.g., tornadoes) and man-made events (e.g., terrorist events). However, during the progression and aftermath of such incidents, it is possible that PWS warnings and advisories may be broadcast accordingly to facilitate public safety and awareness.

The preceding considerations of public warning are indicative of three periods during which the use of PWS resources may occur: (1) preceding incidents, (2) during the occurrences of incidents, and (3) after the occurrences of incidents. Depending on the type of incident and scenario, differing amounts of time may exist within each of these periods. Each of these periods represents a unique dimension of the incident domain that necessitates different types of public warning information or that necessitates various types of technologies when implementing warning processes and procedures.

These periods must be considered when designing, implementing, managing, and evaluating PWS and PIS. Throughout each of these periods, the leveraging of PWS and PIS must be maximized to reach a mass audience. Multiple methods of communicating with the public and communicating among responding entities must exist to facilitate public safety and organizational functioning. The infrastructures of these communication methods must be designed for survivability, and to also generate warnings across multiple technological platforms that may integrate multiple information systems. They must also be designed to serve a populace that demonstrates varying demographics. For example, warnings must be disseminated among disabled people and among those who reside in environments for the invalid. Warning messages must also be communicated among populations of varying ethnicities. Therefore, the designs of such systems and their technological infrastructures must accommodate a variety of audiences. Regardless of the audience served, the contents of warning messages must be unique and distinct to generate a distinguishable message that signals danger and provides instructions.

Commercial Mobile Alert System

According to the Federal Communications Commission (FCC), the Commercial Mobile Alert System (CMAS) is a public safety resource allowing "customers who own an enabled mobile device to receive geographically targeted, text-like messages alerting them of imminent threats to safety" that exist within their geographic location (Federal Communications Commission, 2012a). This concept targets specific target populations within the affected danger locations through the use of cellular towers to disseminate information among "dedicated receivers in CMAS-enabled mobile devices" (Federal Communications Commission, 2012a). Participation is voluntary among the providers of wireless telecommunications services. The administration and coordination of the communication system represents collaboration among the FCC, FEMA, and the commercial wireless industry (e.g., AT&T or Verizon) for the purpose of enhancing public safety.

This communication system is complementary to the existing resources of communicating information within society. The technological framework leverages communication resources to facilitate the issuance of warning messages among affected regions of "critical emergency incidents" (Federal Communications Commission, 2012a). Only individuals within identified danger zones receive messages through the communications system. To receive such alerts, these individuals must be subscribers of a telecommunications organization that participates in the communications system. The receipt of messages is free for the subscribers of participating telecommunications companies. Because the underlying algorithms comprising the communication systems involve geographic targeting of the incident area, subscribers who exit the affected incident region will not receive an alert message because they are not physically present within the danger zone. Although only recipients that are within the incident area will receive alerts, the system is incapable of tracking the locations of alert recipients.

Limited forms of alerts are disseminated by the communications system. Only critical emergencies necessitate the generation of warnings. According to the FCC, these types of alert messages are as follows (Federal Communications Commission, 2012a):

1. Alerts issued by the president
2. Alerts involving imminent threats to safety or life
3. Amber alerts

Integrated Public Alert and Warning System

The Integrated Public Alert and Warning System (IPAWS) satisfies the policy of maintaining an American emergency warning system (EWS) that is mandated within Executive Order 13407. The IPAWS exists as a resource to issue timely alerts and warnings to the American populace for the purpose of preserving "life and property" (Federal Emergency Management Agency, 2012a). Administrating this policy necessitates collaboration between the FEMA and various organizations. The array of federal organizations that collaborate with FEMA to administer IPAWS consists of the FCC, the NOAA's NWS, and the Science and Technology Directorate of the Department of Homeland Security. These organizations are cooperatively transforming the existing "national alert and warning system to enable rapid dissemination of authenticated alert information over as many communications channels as possible" (Federal Emergency Management Agency, 2012a). The scope and magnitude of IPAWS facilitates the integration of capabilities and services among federal, state, and local entities to disseminate information to citizens using multiple methods of communications. Figure 11.3 shows the basic IPAWS concept.

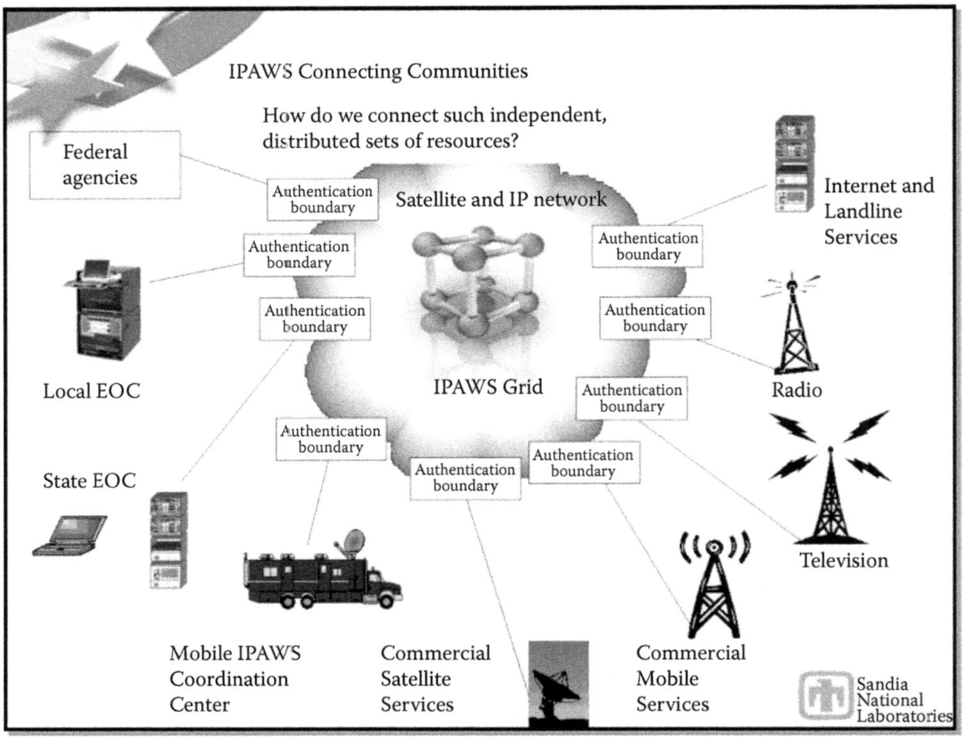

Figure 11.3 Basic IPAWS concept. (From http://www.emforum.org/vforum/IPAWS/slide04.htm.)

The communication of emergency IPAWS messages permeates society using various methods. The EWS may leverage resources such as AM/FM satellite radio, satellite television, digital television, cable television, and analog methods. The use of mobile services involves the dissemination of emergency messaging through the use of cellular devices. Internet resources may consist of emergency warnings posted within public safety websites. NOAA resources may include various newscasts and radio transmissions. Unique information resources may include the use of digital billboards along highways or digital signage on public buildings or siren warning systems. The use of computer networks and software products forms the basis of delivering warning alerts throughout the entirety of this system. The use of communication alert protocols facilitates the interoperability of the IPAWS resource.

The use of IPAWS satisfies three strategic goals associated with government policy (Federal Emergency Management Agency, 2012a):

1. Create and maintain an integrated interoperable environment for alert and warning.
2. Make alert and warning more effective.
3. Strengthen the resilience of IPAWS infrastructure.

One perspective of the requirements involves a consideration of the demographics of the affected population with whom communication occurs. For example, although emergency alerts may be received within a targeted area, they must be understood to be effective. Individuals who do not speak or read English may not understand any received alert warnings despite their access to multiple information devices through which alerts are disseminated (e.g., cell phone, television, or radio). Therefore, a method of improving effectiveness involves disseminating alert messages using multiple languages across multiple information outlets. This characteristic of disseminating warning alerts maximizes the effectiveness of informing as many people as possible during emergencies.

The third goal permeates each of the preceding concepts. The IPAWS framework leverages multiple methods of collecting and disseminating warning alerts within its PIS and PWS structures. The use of multiple methods improves the capacity of generating effectiveness throughout the architecture of the IPAWS construct. Natural disasters often destroy physical resources that are used by emergency responders (e.g., cell towers or telephone networks). Such losses impede the ability to communicate with responding entities and with the general public.

However, through the use of multiple information systems, the IPAWS improves the potential of survivability of the PIS and PWS functions because of the existence of alternative methods of collecting, processing, and disseminating incident information. Effectiveness may be improved because of the leveraging of multiple and alternative methods of facilitating PWS and PIS functions. Such robustness contributes toward an increased probability of emergency information being received within the general public and among responding entities. Therefore, because the chances of emergency communications are actually sent and received, the effectiveness of alerts may be improved.

The IPAWS goals and resources involve considerations of communication's strategic value. According to the FEMA, the benefits of IPAWS are summarized as follows (Federal Emergency Management Agency, 2012a):

- Allows the president of the United States to speak to the American people under all emergency circumstances, including situations of war, terrorist attack, natural disaster, or other hazards
- Builds and maintains an effective, reliable, integrated, flexible, and comprehensive alert and warning system
- Enables federal, state, territorial, tribal, and local alert and warning emergency communication officials to access multiple broadcast and other communications pathways for the purpose of creating and activating alert and warning messages related to any hazard affecting public safety and well-being
- Informs the American public before, during, and after a disaster through as many means as possible
- Diversifies and modernizes the Emergency Alert System (EAS)
- Creates an interoperability framework by establishing or adopting standards such as the common alerting protocol (CAP)
- Enables alert and warning to those with disabilities and to those without an understanding of the English language
- Partners with the NOAA to enable seamless integration of message transmission through national networks

The use of IPAWS provides national benefit through leveraging communications resources to facilitate alert and warning communications during periods of emergencies. Communicating with the general public is a paramount concern when inclement circumstances arise, and necessitates the highest and best of communication technologies. However, the IPAWS is still subject to human limitations. When reporting incidents or receiving incident reports, errors may occur during the transcribing of data among human personnel. Human operators of the IPAWS may have varying levels of understanding of the software and hardware interfaces that comprise the IPAWS construct. Regardless, IPAWS represents a significant communications resource through which public safety may be embellished.

Emergency Alert System

The EAS is defined as a "national public warning system that requires broadcasters, cable television systems, wireless cable systems, satellite digital audio radio service providers, and direct broadcast satellite providers to provide the communications capability to the president to address the American public during a national emergency" (Federal Communications Commission, 2012b). The EAS succeeded and replaced the emergency broadcast service that served as the resource through which emergency information was disseminated during the twentieth century. Considerations of these resources are discussed further within the succeeding sections of this chapter.

The EAS exists as a communications resource through which information may be disseminated quickly throughout the populace during emergencies. Examples of its use include the issuance of Amber alerts, informing about cataclysmic accidents (e.g., chemical spills resulting from train derailment), and the dissemination of information regarding dangerous weather conditions. The EAS may also be implemented among regional, state, and local authorities to disseminate targeted announcements.

Federally, the EAS is administered collaboratively via the joint contributions of the FEMA, the NOAA's NWS, and the FCC (Federal Communications Commission, 2012b). Nationally, the authority to determine when any activation of the EAS occurs is allocated to the president, and this authority may also be delegated to the FEMA director. The responsibility of national testing, activating, and exercising of EAS resources is allocated to the FEMA.

The NWS provides weather information regarding emergency incidents to be disseminated within the populace. The contribution of the FCC involves "prescribing rules that establish technical standards for the EAS, procedures for EAS participants to follow in the event the EAS is activated, and EAS testing protocols" (Federal Communications Commission, 2012b). The FCC also "ensures that the EAS state and local plans developed by industry conform to FCC EAS rules and regulations" (Federal Communications Commission, 2012b).

The EAS serves as America's notification system regarding both man-made and natural disasters. The use of EAS resources may be targets to accommodate the requirements of each specific incident ranging from national to local scopes of disseminating information within the considered populace. The use of EAS resources often acts as both preventive and responsive functions through which human life may be spared with regard to dangerous incidents. The timeliness of disseminating information assists humans with rendering decisions regarding measures to bolster safety and security, thereby potentially sparing human lives. Figure 11.4 shows a typical EAS television broadcast that occurs when emergency circumstances necessitate public warnings.

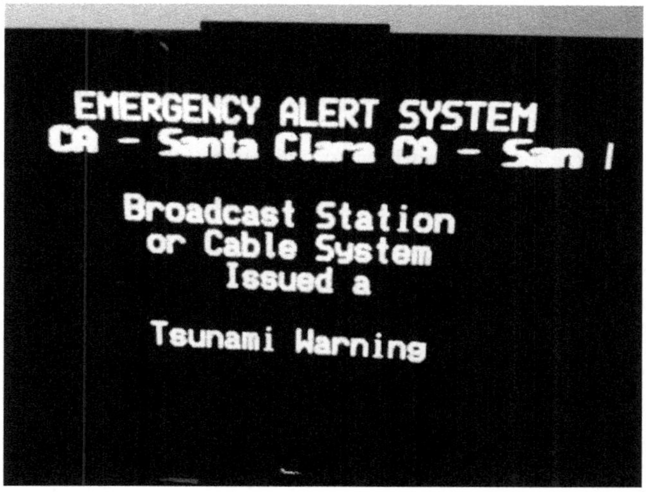

Figure 11.4 EAS television broadcast. (From http://www.scpr.org/news/2011/11/08/29773/only-test/.)

Common Alert Protocol

Modern communications systems involve a variety of different technological hardware platforms and software products. These platforms encompass numerous resources, including cellular devices, transmitters, receivers, processors, television, radio, and other digital systems. Independently and individually, some of the messaging contents of these items may be incompatible with the resources that are used by peer agencies. In some cases, they may even be incompatible within individual organizations. Therefore, a method of providing messaging commonness among these different resources must exist within the architecting of communications resources.

The necessary commonness is achieved through the CAP. The CAP is a "general format for exchanging all-hazard emergency alerts and public warnings over all kinds of networks" (Jones & Botterell, 2005). The CAP resource provides consistency of messaging across many different hardware and software platforms that comprise communications frameworks. Basically, CAP messaging represents a tool through which interoperability is achieved among communications infrastructures.

This commonness of messaging, across different platforms, ensures that a consistent message is broadcast to the affected populace. Such messaging occurs simultaneously across different communications resources. Because messaging commonness is achieved among many different communications resources, the efficiency and effectiveness of issuing warning alerts and emergency notifications are improved. As a result, emergency responders increase the probability of communicating with a maximized quantity of individuals and organizations within the affected populace.

The messaging of the CAP is utilized to generate a "single input to activate all kinds of alerting and public warning systems" (Jones & Botterell, 2005). Because of this use, reductions of work occur among multiple platforms and systems within PIS and PWS environments. Therefore, from an operations perspective of issuing public service information, the use of CAP messaging facilitates improvements in efficiency and effectiveness.

CAP messaging also provides a method of amalgamating and normalizing notification and alert messages. This action occurs to support analytical comparisons involving "situational awareness and pattern detection" (Jones & Botterell, 2005). Through its normalization and commonness among platforms, CAP messaging contributes to a mutual understanding of the incident domain among responding entities and within the affected populace.

CAP messaging is an integral component of the IPAWS infrastructure. Essentially, CAP is a resource that IPAWS implements to broadcast information through "radio, TV, cable systems, etc." (Thurst, 2010). CAP messaging accommodates all types of mediums for disseminating information during emergencies. Examples include "cellphone, texting, e-mail, and landline phone calling" (Thurst, 2010). The relationship between CAP and IPAWS is described as follows:

> CAP messaging acts as a method to move data between IPAWS and EAS. The basic CAP converter polls a CAP server, somewhere, for messages. When a message for a geographic area is received, the CAP converter processes it and converts it to an EAS format, which is then sent via high level audio to the station's EAS encoder decoder unit. The EAS unit receives the information and then has the final say (or station personnel, if the EAS unit is in manual) as to whether the EAS message gets transmitted. (Thurst, 2010)

The use of CAP provides emergency responders with a common basis for sharing information during emergencies. It facilitates the interoperability of messaging resources among communications actions ranging from the initial reporting through the managing of the incident itself. The use of CAP contributes to the commonness of the understanding of the incident domain among responders, and improves the ability of authorities to disseminate information efficiently and effectively to the general public using a variety of resources (e.g., cellular devices, radio, or television).

National Communications System

The National Communications System (NCS) exists as a resource through which assistance is rendered to the "President, the National Security Staff, the Director of the Office of Science and Technology Policy and the Director of the Office of Management and Budget in: (1) the exercise of the telecommunications functions and responsibilities, and (2) the coordination of the planning for and provision of national security and emergency preparedness communications for the Federal government under all circumstances, including crisis or emergency, attack & recovery and reconstitution" (National Communications System, 2012b).

The origin of the NCS occurred in conjunction with the Cuban missile crisis. The tension of the situation was heightened because of communication difficulties among factions of the "United States, the Union of Soviet Socialist Republics, the North Atlantic Treaty Organization, and foreign heads of state" (National Communications System, 2012b). Because of the seriousness of the event and the difficulty of communications, President Kennedy mandated an analysis of "national security communications" (National Communications System, 2012b). As a result of this analysis, it was recommended that an entity be formed to serve "the President, Department of Defense, diplomatic and intelligence activities, and civilian leaders" through a unified, solitary "communications system" (National Communications System, 2012b). President Kennedy authorized the formation of the NCS during 1963, and mandated that it link, improve, and extend the "communications facilities and components of various federal agencies, focusing on interconnectivity and survivability" (National Communications System, 2012b).

The NCS experienced numerous organizational changes and increases of responsibility during the succeeding presidential administrations. During modern times, it now encompasses a variety of primary services. These services include the responsibilities of maintaining and implementing the following services and programs:

- Government Emergency Telecommunications Service (GETS)
- Telecommunications Service Priority (TSP)
- Wireless Priority Service (WPS)
- Shared Resources High Frequency Radio Program (SHARES)
- Route Diversity Program (RDP)

Government Emergency Telecommunications Service

The GETS entity is described through the following statements (National Communications System, 2012a):

> The Government Emergency Telecommunications Service (GETS) is a White House–directed emergency phone service provided by the National Communications System (NCS) in the Office of Cybersecurity and Communications Division, National Protection and Programs Directorate, Department of Homeland Security. GETS supports Federal, State, local, and tribal government, industry, and non-governmental organization (NGO) personnel in performing their National Security and Emergency Preparedness (NS/EP) missions. GETS provides emergency access and priority processing in the local and long distance segments of the Public Switched Telephone Network (PSTN). It is intended to be used in an emergency or crisis situation when the PSTN is congested and the probability of completing a call over normal or other alternate telecommunication means has significantly decreased. (National Communications System, 2012a)

The importance and relevance of GETS cannot be understated because of the pervasiveness of modern technologies across communications infrastructures. The economics of pricing and technological advances in computer software and hardware make the GETS resource both feasible and practical. However, given the growth of networked infrastructures and communications systems, the GETS resource is susceptible to both systemic failure and network congestion despite redundancies within its architecture. Such failures may result from both man-made and natural events. Examples range from disastrous earthquakes that sever communications pathways to human error within or when using software programs.

GETS uses these major types of networks (National Communications System, 2012a):

1. The local networks provided by local exchange carriers and wireless providers, such as cellular carriers and personal communications services (PCS)
2. The major long-distance networks provided by interexchange carriers—AT&T, Verizon Business, and Sprint—including their international services
3. Government-leased networks, such as the Federal Technology Service, the Diplomatic Telecommunication Service, and the Defense Switched Network

GETS is accessed through a universal access number using common telephone equipment such as a standard desk set, facsimile, modem, or wireless phone. A prompt directs the entry of an individual personal identification number (PIN) and the destination telephone number. After authentication occurs, the call is identified as national security or emergency priority call, thereby facilitating special treatment (National Communications System, 2012a).

Wireless Priority Service

The FCC describes the WPS entity through the following statements (Federal Communications Commission, 2012c):

> WPS is a federal program that authorizes cellular communications service providers to prioritize calls over wireless networks. Participation in the WPS program is voluntary. Participating service providers typically deploy WPS in stages until service is available in most coverage areas and functionality has reached full operating capability. Authorized users dial *272 on a WPS enabled device to receive calling queue priority. WPS calls do not preempt calls in progress, but provide priority status over cellular communications networks. To get priority status over the wireline communications network, you need to use the Government Emergency Telecommunications Service (GETS). WPS and GETS can be used in combination program in combination with WPS. The FCC sets the rules and policies for the WPS program; the National Communications System, a part of the U.S. Department of Homeland Security, manages the WPS program. The WPS program is in effect all the time—it is not contingent on a major disaster or attack taking place. WPS is widely available from Alltel, AT&T (formerly Cingular Wireless), Cellular South, Edge Wireless, SouthernLINC, Sprint Nextel, Sprint PCS, T-Mobile, and Verizon Wireless.

The WPS is a resource involving additional communications features, requiring subscription, on a per–cell phone basis, that integrates with existing cell phone networks that enable WPS technologies. The WPS resource prioritizes emergency calls through an array of special cellular network attributes that are analogous with the characteristics of GETS. These features are described as follows:

- *Originating Radio Channel Priority*: WPS addresses congestion in the local radio access channel (or cell), which is often the reason that cellular calls cannot be made during heavy calling periods or when damage to network infrastructure occurs. WPS automatically provides priority access to local radio channels, placing WPS calls in queue for the next available channel if a channel is not immediately available. Originating Radio Channel Priority requires WPS feature activation on the calling cellular phone. WPS calls do not preempt calls in progress nor will WPS users monopolize all available cellular resources (National Communications System, 2012c).
- *High Probability of Completion Features*: When a radio access channel becomes available and the call proceeds, WPS calls are assigned a unique "NS/EP" call marking by the cellular network switching equipment. This marking triggers industry standard High Probability of Completion (HPC) features residing in most U.S.

telecommunications networks as calls are routed from the originating cell to the called cellular or landline phone. These HPC features significantly increase the probability of call completion should the call encounter network congestion or blockage beyond the originating cell. Thus, WPS calls receive similar "across the network" priority as GETS calls without having to dial the GETS access number and PIN (National Communications System, 2012c).

- *Terminating Radio Channel Priority*: Incoming WPS (and GETS) calls to cell phones served by WPS-enabled cellular networks automatically receive priority access to local radio channels, placing incoming GETS and WPS calls in queue for the next available channel if a channel is not immediately available. Terminating Radio Channel Priority does not require the called cellular phone to be subscribed to WPS. Incoming GETS and WPS calls do not preempt cellular calls in progress nor will they monopolize all available cellular resources (National Communications System, 2012c).

Designated personnel among federal, state, local, and tribal governments have eligibility to use WPS resources. Furthermore, some personnel across facets of the critical infrastructure also qualify to use WPS resources. The eligibility of personnel is evaluated according to the following (National Communications System, 2012c):

- Executive leadership and policy makers
- Disaster response/military command and control
- Public health, safety, and law enforcement command
- Public services/utilities and public welfare
- Disaster recovery

These categories are also used for queue prioritization with respect to incoming calls within the originating queue. Regardless, all calls within the WPS and GETS resources receive identical priorities and attentiveness among networked infrastructures and within the call queue (National Communications System, 2012c).

Ten-Codes

Communicating among law enforcement organizations and personnel tends to involve the use of ten-codes for reasons of "brevity, not privacy" (Miletich, 2003). The concept of ten-codes originated in 1937, and was improved upon in "1974 by the Association of Public-Safety Communications Officials-International to allow for brevity and standardization of message traffic" (Mack, 2009). The initial efforts represented the first effort to "address the need for standards in radio-use language" (Association of Public-Safety Communications Officials, 2012).

Ten-codes are a form of oral communication that convey messages using the number 10 as the first set of digits that are succeeded by another number (Miletich, 2003). Using this nomenclature facilitates quick communication among law enforcement personnel and organizations. For example, if an officer requires "immediate assistance," then a ten-code may be voiced as 10–50 (Miletich, 2003). Communicating in this way is both "quicker and faster" than speaking the phrase "officer needs immediate assistance" (Miletich, 2003). Generally, ten-codes are used within Canada and the United States (Miletich, 2003). Figure 11.5 shows an excerpt of ten-codes specified by Davidson County, North Carolina (Davidson County, 2012).

There is no set of universal ten-codes that are used by all law enforcement organizations. Instead, ten-code formats differ per each individual law enforcement organization and jurisdiction. The code 10–50 in one law enforcement organization may have an entirely different meaning within another law enforcement organization. Although communicating through the use of ten-codes may be efficient for individual law enforcement organizations, these differences and uniqueness pose problems when interaction with other law enforcement organizations is necessary. Because multiple ten-code formats exist, law

Official Ten Code List

10-0 Use Caution
10-1 Signal Weak
10-2 Signal Strong
10-3 Stop Transmitting
10-4 Affirmative (OK)
10-5 Relay To
10-6 Busy
10-7 Out of Service
10-8 In Service
10-9 Repeat
10-10 Negative
10-11 —On Duty
10-12 Standby
10-13 Existing Conditions
10-14 Message/Information
10-15 Message Delivered
10-16 Reply to Message
10-17 Enroute
10-18 Urgent
10-19 (In) Contact
10-20 Location
10-21 Call By Phone
10-22 Disregard
10-23 Arrived at Scene
10-24 Assignment Complete
10-25 Report to (Meet)
10-26 Estimated Time Arrival
10-27 License/Permit Info
10-28 Vehicle Info
10-29 Records Check
10-30 Danger/Caution
10-31 Pick Up
10-32 —Units Needed
10-33 EMERGENCY
10-34 Time
10-35 Alarm/Silent
10-36 Domestic
10-37 Civil Dispute
10-38 Man with a Gun
10-39 Urgent Use Lights/Sirens
10-40 Fight in Progress
10-41 Beginning Tour of Duty
10-42 Ending Tour of Duty
10-43 Chase
10-44 Riot
10-45 Bomb Threat
10-46 Assault
10-47 Complete Quickly
10-48 Drug Involvment
10-49 Drag Racing/C&R Driving
10-50 Accident PD,PI,F
10-51 Wrecker Needed
10-52 Ambulance Needed
10-53 Road locked
10-54 Hit & Run PD,PI,F
10-55 Intoxicated Driver
10-56 Intoxicated Pedestrian
10-57 Request Breathalyzer
10-58 Direct Traffic
10-59 Convoy or Escort
10-60 Suspicious Vehicle
10-61 Vehicle Stop
10-62 Breaking & Entering
10-63 Investigate
10-64 Crime in Progress
10-65 Armed Robbery
10-66 Notify Coroner
10-67 Report of Death
10-68 Livestock in Roadway
10-69 Advise Phone Number
10-70 Improperly Parked Car
10-71 Inproper Use of Radio
10-72 Prisoner in Custody
10-73 Mental Subject
10-74 Prison or Jail Break
10-75 Indicated Wanted/Stolen
10-76 Prowler
10-77 Assist Fire Department
10-78 Unlock Vehicle
10-79 Hostage Situation
10-80 Silent Run/No Lights-Sirens
10-84 Area Survey
10-86 Larceny
10-88 Shoplifting
10-91 Rape/Sexual Offense
10-93 Open Garage Door
10-94 Close Garage Door
10-99 Out of Radio Contact

Disposition & Other Codes

C1 Report & Arrest
C2 Citation Issued/Warrant Served
C3 False Alarm
C4 Picked Up
C5 Field Contact
C6 BOLO
C7 Report Filed
C8 Alarm
C9 Property Check
C10 Service Rendered
C11 Advised Rights to Warrant
C12 Unfounded
C13 Verbal Warning
C14 Referred to Other
C15 Domestic Violence
C16 Lexington Magistrate/SD
C17 Thomasville Magistrate/SD
C20 Car Wash
C21 Cleared No OCA
C22 Written Warning
C27 Unable to Locate
C39 Attempt Suicide
C44 DOA
C47 CPR in Progress

Out of Service & Other

S1 At the Station
S2 Meal Break
S3 Secure Radio
S4 Fuel
S7 Meet With
S8 Equipment
S9 Alarm/Keyholder Info
S10 10-7 Personal/Residence
S12 Out of the City
S13 Revoked all Other
S14 Revoked DWI
S15 Flat Tire
S20 Calls Pending
S25 Officer Needs Help
S26 DCI Down
S37 N & S Out of District

Figure 11.5 Davidson County, North Carolina, ten-code listing. (From http://www.co.davidson.nc.us/media/PDFs/5/10-codelist.pdf.)

enforcement personnel may become easily confused when communicating with different agencies. This notion is summarized as follows (Mack, 2009):

> Over time, the meanings of the codes have become different for different agencies. For example, if a Washington County deputy got into an accident with his cruiser today, he would report to the communications center that he was 10–50. But in Virginia, a 10–50 means an officer needs assistance. In Maryland, it means a traffic accident with injuries. In New York, 10–50 means a disorderly person. A 10–79 call, depending on where it is made, can mean anything from a bomb threat to a missing bicycle.

This potential for confusion has fostered a change of communications policy among many law enforcement organizations. Notable examples involve the states of Virginia and Maryland. During 2006, the state of Virginia abandoned its use of ten-codes (Weil, 2012). The state of Maryland abandoned the practice of using ten-codes within the Maryland State Police in 2012 (Weil, 2012). Both Virginia and Maryland cited the potential for confusion when communicating with other organizations as the reasoning for abandoning their respective ten-code formats (Weil, 2012).

The tragic events of September 11, 2001, and Hurricane Katrina demonstrated the potential effects of confusion that arise when multiple ten-code formats are used when communicating among multiple organizations. In the case of the terrorist attack of September 11, 2001, "agencies had difficulty communicating because they used different codes or signals" (Department of Maryland State Police, 2012). During Hurricane Katrina in 2005, responders that cooperated from numerous organizations throughout the nation were ordered to "revert to plain language to avoid misunderstanding emergency calls" that could have arisen from confusion involving the use of ten-codes (Mack, 2009).

Some law enforcement organizations choose to retain their use of ten-codes. The reasons vary ranging from confidentiality of communication to officer safety. Regardless, during modern times, an increasing quantity of law enforcement organizations and first-responder entities are abandoning the use of ten-codes in favor of natural language because of the potential confusion that may arise from using ten-codes when interacting with multiple organizations.

Common Language Protocol

Many law enforcement organizations and first-responder entities have abandoned the use of ten-codes in favor of natural language when communicating. The use of this natural language is referred to as the Common Language Protocol, and represents a "system of radio communications that emphasizes plain language" (Byrnes, 2013). The events of the first decade of the twenty-first century heralded a need for some common frames of understanding when communicating among law enforcement organizations and first-responder entities. This need is associated with the benefit of "public safety," the safety of any responding personnel, and the safety of "those affected by the incident" (Federal Emergency Management Agency, 2006).

Plain language is a form of communicating that "can be understood by the intended audience and meets the purpose of the communicator" (U.S. Department of Homeland Security, 2010, p. 5). Using plain language improves the ability of multiple organizations to interact and collaborate operationally (Federal Emergency Management Agency,

2006). Through the use of plain language, responders improve their chances of coordinating responses effectively regardless of the "size, scope, or complexity of the incident" (Federal Emergency Management Agency, 2006). Through using plain language, responding entities, including law enforcement organizations, comply with NIMS tenets regarding communication among multiple organizations during inclement situations (Federal Emergency Management Agency, 2006).

This compatibility of communications improves the efficiency and effectiveness of response operations because "plain language replaces coded substitutions with common terminology and definitions that can be understood by individuals from all responder disciplines and across jurisdictions" through the use of "normally used words and phrases" (U.S. Department of Homeland Security, 2010, p. 5). Some arguments exist regarding the terminology of "plain language" because it may be interpreted as either language that is analogous with everyday speech or interpreted as speech that is "unique to one jurisdiction or discipline and, therefore, may not be common to others outside of that group" (U.S. Department of Homeland Security, 2010, p. 5).

Regardless of any debate concerning the interpretation of meaning, emergency communication must be recognizable and understandable by all entities that participate in an emergency response. The use of common language replaces any encoded communications paradigms (e.g., ten-codes) with phrases and terms that are germane to natural human language and speech. Through the use of such commonness of language, less failure is experienced within the communications process. The use of common language improves the chance of establishing a mutual understanding of the intended message between both the sender and receiver of the message.

Encoded Language versus Common Language

Although emergency responders and law enforcement organizations are encouraged to use common language when responding to incidents that involve multiple organizations, some debate exists regarding encoded messaging (e.g., ten-codes) versus common language. Two perspectives may be considered regarding this debate: messaging time and personnel safety. Various opinions exist regarding these perspectives.

Within the state of Colorado, a prominent study occurred in 1975 that examined the messaging and communicating time requirements of encoded language versus common language within law enforcement communications. The findings of the study showed that using clear speech transmissions produced fewer errors than using a coded transmission system when communicating (Brooks, 1975). Specifically, through a period of twenty-four hours, communicating through clear speech yielded time savings of "two hours, 52.8 minutes" provided that "transmission continued" throughout the period "uninterrupted" (Brooks, 1975, p. 7). This same study also explored error rates when communicating using plain language versus coded language. The use of clear speech communication exhibited an error rate of 7.0%, whereas coded language transmission exhibited an error rate of 42.5% (Brooks, 1975, p. 4). This study provides some quantitative consideration that the use of plain language is superior to the use of coded transmissions.

Another perspective of the debate between using plain language versus coded language when communicating involves considerations of personnel safety and operations security. Debate exists whether the use of plain language either compromises or improves "responder safety" and "security and privacy" (U.S. Department of Homeland Security, 2010, p. 8). Some fear that the use of plain language reveals pertinent details of operations when communicating, thereby compromising both security and safety (U.S. Department of Homeland Security, 2010, p. 8). However, such arguments are countered through considerations of modern technology. During modern times, the use of "ear buds" and "cellular telephones" provide "a mechanism to transmit information to only the responder which helps protect responders" (U.S. Department of Homeland Security, 2010, p. 9). By using such modern technologies, operations security is also embellished because only pertinent responding personnel hear the communications activity.

The decision whether to incorporate the use of plain language versus coded language within law enforcement communication is unique for every law enforcement organization. The uniqueness of situations and circumstances affecting individual law enforcement organizations affect this decision. A decision that is preferable for one law enforcement organization may be completely inappropriate for a different law enforcement organization. Regardless, an increasing quantity of law enforcement organizations are beginning to favor plain language transmissions instead of coded language transmissions when communicating (U.S. Department of Homeland Security, 2010, p. 9).

Emergency Communications Planning

Many folks associate law enforcement organizations with the deterrence of crime. However, law enforcement organizations also have a fiduciary responsibility of maintaining societal order. Therefore, they may be leveraged as resources during a variety of situations and events that are not associated with criminal activity. Examples include the use of law enforcement organizations during severe weather events, public health endangerments (e.g., epidemics), and various forms of accidents (e.g., airline crashes or train wrecks). Regardless of the leveraging of law enforcement organizations, communication is necessary to conduct operations effectively and efficiently.

The instantiation of such communication is not random. Instead, it involves methodical planning with respect to the potentials of a variety of contingencies that may affect society. This planning must incorporate some consideration of interoperability to promote "future vision for communications interoperability within the state or territory" and should "should align emergency response agencies with the goals, objectives, and initiatives for achieving that vision" (U.S. Department of Homeland Security, 2013). Generally, such planning accommodates organizational preparation for communicating, considerations of communications domain risk, public communication strategies, and methods of communicating with other agencies (Brito, Luna, & Sanberg, 2009).

Communication planning represents a preparatory exercise that affects the strategic aspects of an organization (Ferguson, 1999). Planning provides a baseline of communications processes and procedures that may be implemented during a variety of situations. The communications plan must include the names and contact information for personnel and responding organizations that must be contacted when emergencies arise (Cross, 2008). Such information must be amalgamated and located with a "central source" to ensure its accessibility (Cross, 2008). Contacting the appropriate individuals and organizations may be accomplished through the use of a call tree or a recall list that includes verification that pertinent entities were contacted and notified of the emergency situation.

Risk communication is a salient consideration of law enforcement organizations. The communicating of risk occurs as a method of conveying "information about a specific risk to achieve a desired result, typically behavioral change" (Brito et al., 2009, p. 5). The informational content and the formats of emergency messages are very specific and are influenced by the attributes of the emergency situation and its circumstances (Brito et al., 2009, p. 5). The communicating of risk to the general public is significant because it is a method of "maintaining public order and helping residents protect themselves and support their neighbors as much as possible" (Brito et al., 2009, p. 6).

Any emergency communications plan must incorporate some methods through which communication occurs with the general public. The use of radio, television, social media, and various Internet presences is a method of disseminating information and facilitating public information. Both one-way and two-way communications should also be considered within a communications plan. Certainly, within the communications process, a function of sending messages to the receiving public facilitates public awareness of an event, and provides relevant information through which members of the public can make choices that affect their individual situations and reduce feelings of uncertainty during chaos.

However, some consideration of two-way communication involves the notion that members of the public can query a public organization regarding the ongoing situation or event. For example, telephone lines can be established to support both voice and facsimile communications. Using such telephone communication facilitates the "transmission of documents or information" and allows members of the public to "send comments to an agency" (U.S. Department of Transportation, 2013). These methods accommodate the conveying of "prerecorded answers or responses to common inquiries" (U.S. Department of Transportation, 2013).

Communications planning must also identify and specify methods of communicating with other organizations that may be used during emergency responses. Such entities include departments of transportation, emergency operations centers, news media, ambulance services and hospitals, other law enforcement organizations, fire departments, and so forth. Establishing a foundational set of communication protocols is an essential aspect of communicating efficiently and effectively with other organizations. Therefore, communications plans should consider the use of plain language as a method of oral communication. It should also incorporate a consideration of the various technologies and personnel that are used to facilitate communication among the pertinent organizations.

A primary example of communications planning is the National Emergency Communications Plan (NECP). The NECP fulfills the purpose of promoting the "ability of emergency response providers and relevant government officials to continue to communicate in the event of natural disasters, acts of terrorism, and other man-made disasters and to ensure, accelerate, and attain interoperable emergency communications nationwide" (U.S. Department of Homeland Security, 2008). This plan accommodates several communications objectives, including the structuring of governance and leadership, coordination of federal activities, protocols for planning and operations, communications technologies, life cycle analysis, personnel capabilities and skills, and communications capabilities for disastrous events (U.S. Department of Homeland Security, 2008). The NECP also includes provisions for its implementation and its evaluation through metrics analysis (U.S. Department of Homeland Security, 2008).

Crafting an emergency communications plan is a preparatory endeavor that may diminish the effects of various incidents that endanger society and that improves the ability of an organization to communicate clearly, efficiently, and effectively. Such plans must be maintained and updated frequently to ensure their correctness and appropriateness for the organization. To invoke a sense of familiarity with the plan, organizations may have practice drills to ensure that personnel are trained and aware of the tenets of the plan. Such exercises also show shortcomings that may be rectified, thereby improving the capability and readiness of the communications capacities of an organization.

The planning of communication is also unique. Each individual law enforcement organization has different personnel and resources, and experiences different environmental factors that represent differing threats among communities. Each law enforcement organization also has a unique policy that governs its communications practices. A communications plan that is appropriate for one organization may be completely inappropriate for a different law enforcement organization. Therefore, when crafting a communications plan, the unique characteristics of the communication and organizational domains must be considered.

Commentary Regarding Emergency and Public Communications

No nation, region, state, or locale is insusceptible to the effects of criminal activities or disastrous incidents. During such events, law enforcement organizations and personnel must communicate effectively and efficiently. Performing the daily operational activities of law enforcement necessitates communicating efficiently and effectively. Regardless of the circumstance or the scenario, all law enforcement organizations must communicate understandably using clear and timely transmissions of information.

Within the context of law enforcement organization, communicating occurs both internally and externally. Internal communication may involve dispatchers allocating and directing law enforcement resources to the scene of an incident or the location of a service call. External communication may involve communicating with the general public for a variety of reasons ranging from issuing mass audience warnings before, during, and after severe weather incidents or to inform the public of anticipated drunken driving checkpoints.

The former scenario involves a consideration of emergency communication. Numerous communications infrastructures exist through which the president of the United States may send and receive messages regarding incidents of national scope and magnitude as well as infrastructures through which local mayors may warn residents of local incidents that constitute emergency conditions (e.g., gas leaks). Regardless of the scope of such emergency scenarios, any responding law enforcement organizations must communicate. Such communication may involve only one responding law enforcement organization or it may involve communicating with other law enforcement organizations and responding entities.

Regardless of the quantity of responding entities, the attributes of emergency communications must conform to the foundational principles of communicating succinctly, clearly, and understandably. Essentially, such communications must be effective and efficient with respect to facilitating a mutual understanding of the intended message between the senders and receivers that are involved within the communications process. Such factors contribute toward the crafting and fielding of emergency responses that are successful.

Chapter Comments and Summary

Communicating with and disseminating information among populaces is a critical aspect of preparedness, reaction, and response. Through the use of various resources, emergency personnel may facilitate communications among themselves or with their served populaces. The contents of public service messages, warnings, and alerts must be relevant and timely to support the rendering of human decisions regarding courses of actions during emergency situations. Such characteristics are also critical to rendering decisions that may spare human life before, during, and after calamities.

The NIMS is a framework that facilitates a methodical, "proactive approach" to assisting government entities, the commercial sector, and other organizations to collaboratively integrate resources and to perform together for the prevention, protection against, response to, and mitigation of the "effects of incidents, regardless of cause, size, location or complexity, in order to reduce the loss of life and property and harm to the environment" (Federal Emergency Management Agency, 2013). Basically, NIMS is a management paradigm that embellishes the effectiveness and efficiency of managing disaster responses.

PWS are entities that collect and analyze data regarding a potential or actual incident, analyze this data, interpret the outcomes of analysis to derive a course of action, and disseminate an appropriate warning or advisory within the populace to incite appropriate actions with respect to the characteristics of the incident domain. The use of PWS resources should be leveraged to reach a mass audience, and to maximize the dissemination of warning information among the members of the general public. Therefore, the use of PWS should be directed to reach as many people as possible with information regarding an incident. The use of PWS resources is designed to be scalable to disseminate information locally, regionally, or nationally.

According to the FCC, the CMAS is synonymous with the Personal Localized Alerting Network (Federal Communications Commission, 2013). The CMAS exists as a resource through which the "transmittal of emergency alerts, by commercial mobile service providers to their subscribers," occurs during periods of emergencies (Moore, 2010). Other technologies and resources complement the CMAS framework. These additional developments include the IPAWS. Such improvements are representative of the progression and betterment of warning systems and technologies through time. Figure 11.6 shows the progression of warning systems that resulted in the crafting of IPAWS.

These systems leverage the use of modern digital technologies to disseminate alerts, warning, and public service information among affected populaces during emergency incidents. Radio and television now broadcast digitally, and are integral components of IPAWS. Cellular telephone networks and the Internet are also components of these systems. Through the use of these systems, emergency authorities embellish their ability to maximize the warning of citizens regarding calamities.

Survivability and maintaining communications among federal, state, regional, local, and government entities is a concern regarding emergency situations. The NCS exists as a resource through which such communications may be facilitated during times of emergency continuously. The NCS accomplishes its mission through the organizational components of GETS, WPS, RDP, SHARES, and TSP.

Communicating among law enforcement organizations and with other entities must occur clearly, succinctly, efficiently, and effectively. However, the use of ten-codes and

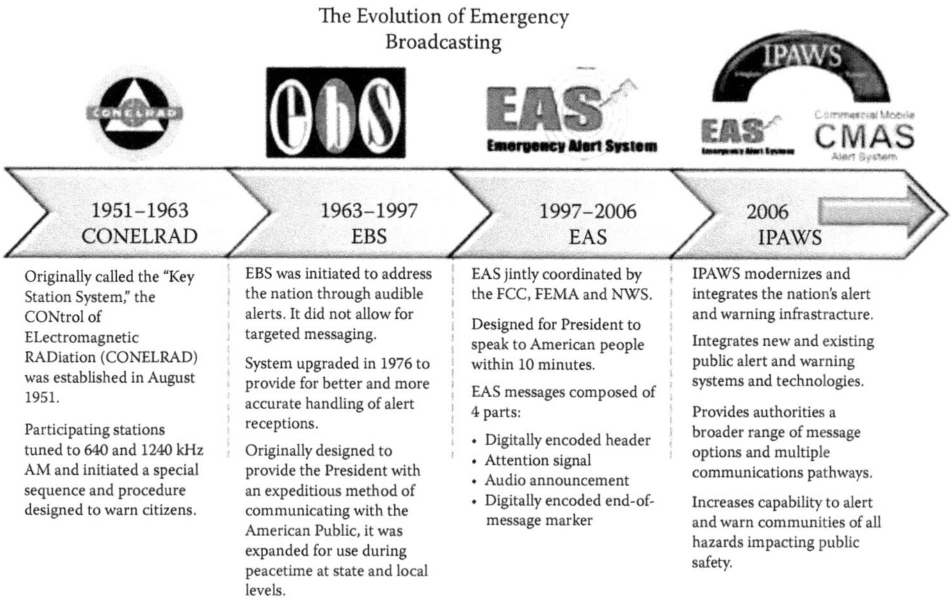

Figure 11.6 Development of public warning systems. (From http://www.fema.gov/pdf/emergency/ipaws/ipaws_the_evolution_of_emergency_broadcasting.pdf)

other coded language formats may impede the accomplishment of these goals. Therefore, it is advocated that plain language be used when communicating among law enforcement entities.

Communications planning is an essential aspect of emergency preparedness. Organizations must uniquely craft emergency communications plans that accommodate communicating with the general public as well as with other organizations that may be used to respond to man-made and natural incidents. Each emergency communications plan is unique because of the differences that exist among the communications domains federally, regionally, and locally.

Terminology

Association of Public-Safety Communications Officials
Cellular resource
Clear speech
Common Alerting Protocol
Common language
Common Language Protocol
Communication planning
Emergency Alert System
Federal Communications Commission
Federal Emergency Management Agency
Government Emergency Telecommunications Service
Integrated Public Alert and Warning System

Interactive communication
Mass audience
National Communications System
National Emergency Communications Plan
National Oceanic and Atmospheric Administration
National Weather Service
Network
National Incident Management System
National Weather Service
NOAA radio
Personal Localized Alerting Network
Plain language
Public safety
Public warning system
Redundancy
Scalable
Survivability
Targeted audience
Ten-codes
Wireless communications

THOUGHT AND DISCUSSION QUESTIONS

1. The uses of communication systems are varied across the nation. Every situation is unique that involves the use of communication resources. Within your locality, select examples of communications resources that are components of emergency management. Critically analyze the use of these resources within the function of emergency management, and discuss how they are leveraged to disseminate information among emergency responders and how they are used to warn a maximum of entities within the populace.
2. Have a discussion with your local emergency management director or law enforcement organization. Within this discussion, identify the strengths, weaknesses, threats, and opportunities that exist regarding the communications resources that are implemented within your locality. On the basis of the outcomes of this analysis, what recommendations can you offer to improve the characteristics of emergency management within you locality?
3. Radio has long been a resource for disseminating public service information quickly among mass audiences. During modern times, this concept remains viable with respect to both man-made and natural disasters. Radio technologies have improved and matured through time to yield specific emergency radios that embellish response efforts during the aftermaths of incidents and that are used to warn the general public. Select three types of emergency radios that are publically available, compare and contrast their salient features, and discuss substantively the advantages and disadvantages of each type of radio.
4. This chapter introduced the debate between common language and encoded language that may be used when responding to emergency incidents and service calls for assistance. Do some research to determine the perceptions of your local law

enforcement organization regarding the debate between common language versus encoded language. Write a brief essay that describes the policy of your local law enforcement agency regarding its use of common language and encoded language during emergency responses and daily operations.

References

Association of Public-Safety Communications Officials. (2012). APCO projects. Retrieved from http://www.apco911.org/about-apco/apco-projects.html (accessed January 1, 2013).

Blitzer, W. (2011). The situation room. *CNN Transcripts*. Retrieved from http://transcripts.cnn.com/TRANSCRIPTS/1104/29/sitroom.02.html (accessed December 31, 2012).

Brito, C., Luna, A., & Sanberg, E. (2009). *Public health emergencies: A guide for law enforcement*. Washington, DC: U.S. Government.

Brooks, P. (1975). *Ten code versus clear speech communication*. Lakewood, CO: Public Safety Department.

Byrnes, K. (2013). County police departments move to common language protocol. *Eldersburg Patch*. Retrieved from http://eldersburg.patch.com/articles/county-police-departments-move-to-common-language-protocol (accessed January 1, 2013).

Cross, M. (2008). *Scene of the cybercrime* (2nd ed., p. 226). Burlington, MA: Syngress Publishing.

Davidson County. (2012). Official Ten Code List. North Carolina. Retrieved from http://www.co.davidson.nc.us/ (accessed January 1, 2013).

Department of Maryland State Police. (2012). Starting today, common language protocol will be used by Maryland State police. Retrieved from http://www.mdsp.org/Home/tabid/40/ctl/Detail/mid/1226/xmid/20538/xmfid/4/Default.aspx (accessed January 1, 2013).

Emergency Management Institute. (2010). IS 702. Retrieved from http://training.fema.gov/emiweb/is/is702a.asp (accessed December 31, 2012).

Federal Communications Commission. (2012a). Commercial mobile alert system. Retrieved from http://www.fcc.gov/guides/commercial-mobile-alert-system-cmas (accessed December 31, 2012).

Federal Communications Commission. (2012b). Emergency alert system. Retrieved from http://transition.fcc.gov/pshs/services/eas/ (accessed December 31, 2012).

Federal Communications Commission. (2012c). Wireless priority service (WPS). Retrieved from http://transition.fcc.gov/pshs/emergency/wps.html (accessed December 31, 2012).

Federal Communications Commission. (2013). Commercial mobile alert system (CMAS). Retrieved from http://www.fcc.gov/guides/commercial-mobile-alert-system-cmas (accessed January 1, 2013).

Federal Emergency Management Agency. (2006). NIMS alert: NIMS and use of plain language. Retrieved from http://www.fema.gov/pdf/emergency/nims/plain_lang.pdf (accessed January 1, 2013).

Federal Emergency Management Agency. (2008). National Incident Management System (NIMS). Retrieved from http://www.fema.gov/pdf/emergency/nims/NIMS_core.pdf (accessed December 31, 2012).

Federal Emergency Management Agency. (2012a). Integrated public alert and warning system. Retrieved from http://www.fema.gov/emergency/ipaws/ (accessed December 31, 2012).

Federal Emergency Management Agency. (2012b). National Incident Management System (NIMS). Retrieved from http://www.fema.gov/emergency/nims/AboutNIMS.shtm (accessed December 31, 2012).

Federal Emergency Management Agency. (2013). Lesson 1: Understanding NIMS. Retrieved from http://emilms.fema.gov/IS700aNEW/NIMS0101summary.htm (accessed January 1, 2013).

Federation of American Scientists. (2006). Executive Order 13407. Retrieved from http://www.fas.org/irp/offdocs/eo/eo-13407.htm (accessed December 31, 2012).

Ferguson, S. (1999). *Communication planning: An integrated approach*. Thousand Oaks, CA: Sage Publishing.

Imperial County Office of Education. (2010). Announcement of local assistance center for imperial county residents and business community. Retrieved from http://www.icoe.org/webfm_send/4540 (accessed December 31, 2012).

Jones, E., & Botterell, A. (2005). CAP: The Common Alerting Protocol, v. 1.1. *OASIS.* Retrieved from http://www.oasis-open.org/committees/download.php/15135/emergency-CAPv1.1-Corrected_DOM.pdf (accessed December 31, 2012).

Mack, S. (2009). Police shift to plain language. *Bangor Daily News.* Retrieved from http://bangordailynews.com/2009/12/30/news/police-shift-to-plain-language/ (accessed January 1, 2013).

Miletich, J. (2003). *Homicide investigation: An introduction* (p. 49). Lanham, MD: Scarecrow Press.

Moore, L. (2010). *The emergency alert system (EAS) and all-hazard warnings.* Washington, DC: Congressional Research Service.

National Communications System. (2012a). Gets program information. Retrieved from http://gets.ncs.gov/program_info.html (accessed December 31, 2012).

National Communications System. (2012b). Welcome to the National Communications System. Retrieved from http://www.ncs.gov/ (accessed December 31, 2012).

National Communications System. (2012c). Wireless priority service. Retrieved from http://wps.ncs.gov/program_info.html (accessed December 31, 2012).

Oklahoma Historical Society. (2012). Encyclopedia of Oklahoma history & culture. Oklahoma State University. Retrieved from http://digital.library.okstate.edu/encyclopedia/entries/T/TO008.html (accessed December 31, 2012).

Roosevelt, T. (n.d.). Theodore Roosevelt quotes. Brainyquote.com. Retrieved from http://www.brainyquote.com/quotes/authors/t/theodore_roosevelt.html (accessed December 31, 2012).

Santa Barbara Independent. (2010). Easter Earthquake Rumble. Retrieved from http://www.independent.com/news/2010/apr/04/easter-earthquake-rumble/ (accessed December 31, 2012).

Thurst, P. (2010). Common alert protocol. Engineering Radio. Retrieved from http://www.engineeringradio.us/blog/2010/10/common-alert-protocol-cap/ (accessed December 31, 2012).

U.S. Department of Homeland Security. (2008). *National emergency communications plan* (p. 1). Washington, DC: U.S. Government.

U.S. Department of Homeland Security. (2010). *Plain language frequently asked questions (FAQs).* Washington, DC: U.S. Government.

U.S. Department of Homeland Security. (2013). Statewide communication interoperability plans. Retrieved from http://www.dhs.gov/statewide-communication-interoperability-plans (accessed January 1, 2013).

U.S. Department of Transportation. (2013). Using special techniques to enhance participation. Retrieved from http://www.planning.dot.gov/PublicInvolvement/pi_documents/toc-foreword.asp (accessed January 1, 2013).

Walsh, D., Christen, H., Callsen, C., Miller, G., Maniscalco, P., Lord, G., & Dolan, N. (2011). *National incident management system: Principles and practice* (2nd ed.). Sudbury, MA: Jones & Bartlett Publishers, Inc.

Weil, M. (2012). Maryland State police abandon 'ten code' radio communications such as '10-4.' *The Washington Post.* Retrieved from http://articles.washingtonpost.com/2012-02-04/local/35445190_1_code-lore-and-legend-police-agencies (accessed January 1, 2013).

12 Employment Communication

My agent said, "You aren't good enough for movies." I said, "You're fired."
—Sally Field (Field, n.d.)

Objectives

The objectives of this chapter are to

- Discuss legislation that influences employment communication
- Discuss employment announcements and postings
- Discuss cover letters
- Discuss employment interviewing techniques
- Discuss resumes
- Discuss employment offer and rejection letters
- Discuss termination of employment letters

Introduction

Communication permeates all work environments. Both organizations and individuals have a need to communicate regarding employment issues. Within the justice domain, employers must communicate with the general public and various staffing agencies to announce job openings. Individuals and staffing agencies must communicate with potential employers regarding any interest in these announced positions. During this act of communicating, numerous instances of electronic mail and other written communications, telephone conversations, and personal interviews may be necessary to screen applicants during the hiring process.

Both federal and state legislation influences the acts of communicating that occur among work environments. Minimum wage requirements must be expressed and placed so that they may be viewed openly. Evacuation plans may be visibly posted so that people may exit structures in the event of an emergency. Safety and health-care posters must be visible and accessible among work environments. These postings may involve the use of multiple languages to accommodate an audience of varied demographics.

Employment communication may be considered from an internal perspective. Internally, the crafting and announcing of open job positions occurs. Written policy manuals exist that express the management practices and guidelines of the organization. Personnel records are either paper or electronic, and communicate the salient aspects of employment history for an individual personnel. Annual performance reviews may involve oral discussions between supervisors and subordinates, and may be documented using proprietary forms and paperwork. Corporate executives, directors, and managers may facilitate staff meetings in which verbal and visual communication occurs. Staff meetings may incorporate open forums to discuss pertinent issues that affect individuals and work groups.

Employment communication may be considered from an external perspective. Externally, organizations may announce their open job positions through the use of newspapers, newsletters, magazines, and Internet postings. They may also leverage Internet methods of providing online job applications or host discussion forums for job candidates. Organizations may also conduct telephone interviews with job applicants before hosting a personal interview with a selected pool of specific candidates. Conducting a telephone interview before hosting a personal interview may reduce the costs of employee recruitment because no costs are incurred for travel and lodging. Organizations may also communicate with various staffing services to coordinate the screening of applicants. Organizations may also leverage news releases to announce certain events of downsizing, hiring, and personnel accomplishments.

Organizational policy also affects communications regarding work environments. In some instances, personnel must read and sign a confidentiality agreement or a noncompete agreement that communicates the expectations of the employer regarding personnel conduct and behavior both when at work and away from the workplace. Through signing such agreements, in most cases, personnel agree to not disclose any proprietary information that could compromise the competitiveness or trade secrets of the organization. Therefore, individuals would be disallowed from communicating such information to any other entity.

Communication pervades work settings continuously. Whether one discusses pay raises or promotion opportunities with supervisors, it involves communicating. Dismissing and counseling employees regarding their job performance involves communicating. Soliciting and evaluating resumes of candidate employees require communication. Certainly, many more examples of workplace communication may be identified and discussed. Regardless, among work environments, communication occurs to facilitate the daily operations and transactions of employers.

Fair Labor and Standards Act of 1938

The Fair Labor and Standards Act (FLSA) of 1938 established standards regarding minimum wage, compensation for employee overtime, the keeping of records, and "child labor" (U.S. Department of Labor, 2013b). Since its initial version of 1938, this legislation has experienced several changes. However, during modern times, a total of approximately "130 million" employees are affected by this legislation (U.S. Department of Labor, 2013b). It is applicable to both public and private employers, and encompasses both full-time and part-time personnel (U.S. Department of Labor, 2013b). Although various exemptions regarding minimum wage are accommodated by this legislation, it is applicable to a large array of occupations (U.S. Department of Labor, 2013b).*

The FLSA may be considered from the perspective of communication. Every employer that is covered by the FLSA requirements must visibly post a notice that explains its

* Some types of jobs are not covered by the minimum wage provisions of FSLA. Readers desiring a greater knowledge of this legislation may review its pertinent details via: http://www.dol.gov/compliance/guide/minwage.htm.

primary tenets conspicuously where it may be "readily read" (U.S. Department of Labor, 2013b). This posting must be maintained continuously. Posters are available in the Spanish, Chinese, Russian, Thai, Hmong, Vietnamese, and Korean languages (U.S. Department of Labor, 2013b). The only required language within the posting is English. Additionally, customized signage may be designed for specific industries regarding the tenets of the FLSA. Examples of these specific domains include agriculture and both state and local governments.

Various court cases have considered merits of the FLSA with respect to some attributes of communication. During 2009, the *Agui v. T-Mobile USA Inc.* case involved the claims of former T-Mobile personnel that the "company provided Blackberrys or other smart devices to them, and required them to respond to work-related emails and text messages at all hours" (Silverglate & Salner, 2011, p. 43). These former employees indicated that they used their communications devices approximately ten to fifteen hours each week (Silverglate & Salner, 2011, p. 43). This case was settled before any "dispositive motions" were filed (Silverglate & Salner, 2011, p. 43).

Another 2009 case is that of *Kuebel v. Black & Decker (U.S.) Inc.* This case involved some allegations of FLSA violations regarding "employee commutes to and from work in conjunction with the time employees spent at home before and after work syncing their company-provided PDAs and responding to e-mail" (Silverglate & Salner, 2011, pp. 43–44). An initial outcome of this case awarded a partial judgment in favor of the employer because the use of the communications devices "at home did not contribute to the employees' principal activity of maintaining product displays in their stores" (Silverglate & Salner, 2011, p. 44).

These court cases show the effects of changing communications technologies within both society and work settings. When the original legislation was crafted during 1938, modern cellular telephones and other mobile personal communications devices did not exist. During modern times, employees do not always have to be physically present within their work settings to conduct communications on the behalf of their employers. Through the use of mobile technologies, work-related communications may be performed from any location. Such portability has prompted numerous debates concerning work functions versus compensation.

Although the FLSA primarily encompasses various facets of labor law, it also involves a consideration of the communications that affect work settings. Regardless, all employers must maintain postings that describe the primary tenets of the FLSA. Through such postings, personnel are aware of their rights and employer responsibilities concerning compensation and hours worked—including those times that incorporate work-related communication. Figure 12.1 shows the typical signage that is associated with the FLSA (U.S. Department of Labor, 2013i).

Occupational Safety and Health Act

The Occupational Safety and Health Act (OSHA) is another piece of legislation whose primary tenets must be communicated throughout organizational structures. The two primary functions of this legislation consist of "setting standards and conducting inspections to ensure that employers are providing safe and healthful workplaces" (U.S. Department of Labor, 2013h). The OSHA may be considered from a communications perspective.

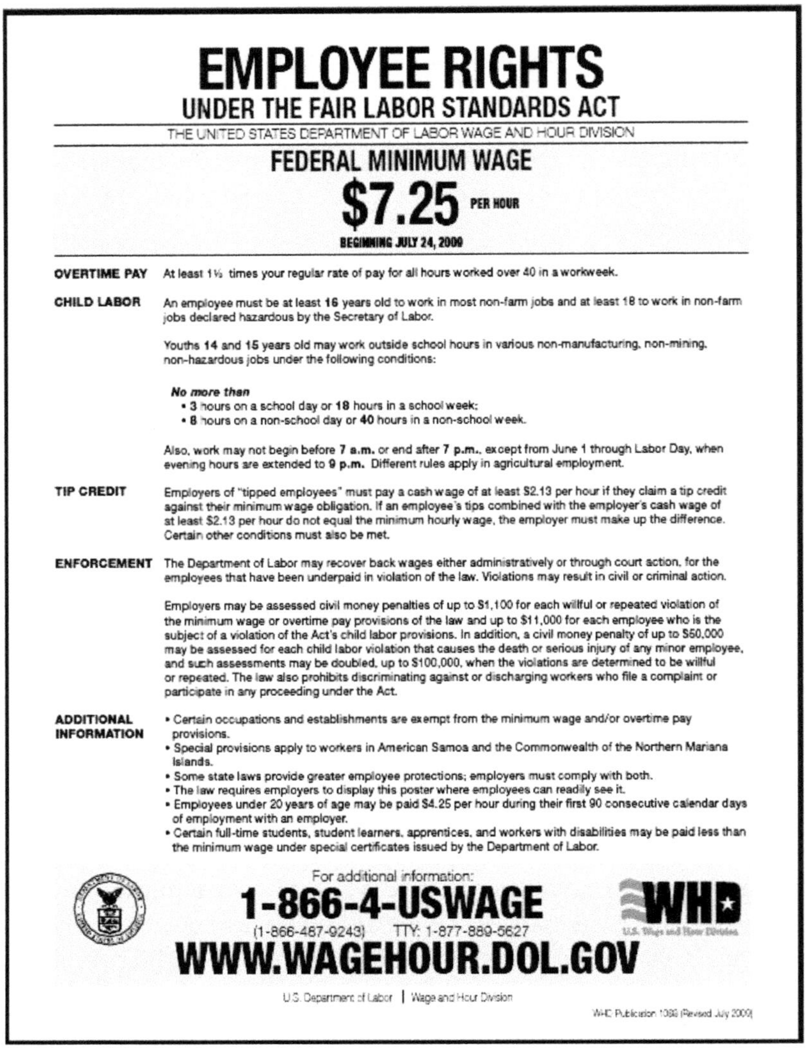

EMPLOYEE RIGHTS

UNDER THE FAIR LABOR STANDARDS ACT

THE UNITED STATES DEPARTMENT OF LABOR WAGE AND HOUR DIVISION

FEDERAL MINIMUM WAGE

$7.25 PER HOUR

BEGINNING JULY 24, 2009

OVERTIME PAY At least 1½ times your regular rate of pay for all hours worked over 40 in a workweek.

CHILD LABOR An employee must be at least **16** years old to work in most non-farm jobs and at least 18 to work in non-farm jobs declared hazardous by the Secretary of Labor.

Youths **14** and **15** years old may work outside school hours in various non-manufacturing, non-mining, non-hazardous jobs under the following conditions:

No more than
- **3** hours on a school day or **18** hours in a school week;
- **8** hours on a non-school day or **40** hours in a non-school week.

Also, work may not begin before **7 a.m.** or end after **7 p.m.**, except from June 1 through Labor Day, when evening hours are extended to **9 p.m.** Different rules apply in agricultural employment.

TIP CREDIT Employers of "tipped employees" must pay a cash wage of at least $2.13 per hour if they claim a tip credit against their minimum wage obligation. If an employee's tips combined with the employer's cash wage of at least $2.13 per hour do not equal the minimum hourly wage, the employer must make up the difference. Certain other conditions must also be met.

ENFORCEMENT The Department of Labor may recover back wages either administratively or through court action, for the employees that have been underpaid in violation of the law. Violations may result in civil or criminal action.

Employers may be assessed civil money penalties of up to $1,100 for each willful or repeated violation of the minimum wage or overtime pay provisions of the law and up to $11,000 for each employee who is the subject of a violation of the Act's child labor provisions. In addition, a civil money penalty of up to $50,000 may be assessed for each child labor violation that causes the death or serious injury of any minor employee, and such assessments may be doubled, up to $100,000, when the violations are determined to be willful or repeated. The law also prohibits discriminating against or discharging workers who file a complaint or participate in any proceeding under the Act.

ADDITIONAL INFORMATION
- Certain occupations and establishments are exempt from the minimum wage and/or overtime pay provisions.
- Special provisions apply to workers in American Samoa and the Commonwealth of the Northern Mariana Islands.
- Some state laws provide greater employee protections; employers must comply with both.
- The law requires employers to display this poster where employees can readily see it.
- Employees under 20 years of age may be paid $4.25 per hour during their first 90 consecutive calendar days of employment with an employer.
- Certain full-time students, student learners, apprentices, and workers with disabilities may be paid less than the minimum wage under special certificates issued by the Department of Labor.

For additional information:

1-866-4-USWAGE

(1-866-487-9243) TTY: 1-877-889-5627

WWW.WAGEHOUR.DOL.GOV

WHD

U.S. Department of Labor | Wage and Hour Division

WHD Publication 1088 (Revised July 2009)

Figure 12.1 Typical FLSA poster. (From http://www.dol.gov/whd/regs/compliance/posters/flsa.htm#.UPjUP2ffQbQ.)

Specifically, the OSHA tenets require the producers and "importers of hazardous materials" to evaluate their manufactured or imported products (U.S. Department of Labor, 2013h). If an item is deemed to be hazardous, then it must be appropriately labeled to communicate the possible danger. Labeling occurs "on containers of the material," and the initial "shipment of the material to a new customer must include a material safety data sheet (MSDS)" (U.S. Department of Labor, 2013h). These MSDS resources are also used within personnel training to communicate hazards recognition and avoidance regarding the considered items (U.S. Department of Labor, 2013h).

The primary tenets of the OSHA must also be communicated organizationally among work settings. Employers that are covered by OSHA requirements must openly display and maintain conspicuously visible posters where personnel may view them (U.S. Department of Labor, 2013h). Any facsimiles or reproductions of the poster must adhere to "at least 8 1/2 by 14 inches with 10 point type" (U.S. Department of Labor, 2013h). Such posters may be obtained in both the English and Spanish languages. The only mandated language to be used within OSHA posters is English (U.S. Department of Labor, 2013h). Figure 12.2 depicts a typical OSHA poster (U.S. Department of Labor, 2013f).

The displaying of OSHA posters also may result from the outcomes of court proceedings through the issuing of court orders that ensure OSHA posters are displayed or disseminated among personnel. During 2009, the Southern Air cargo airline was ordered to "withdraw a lawsuit it filed against nine former employees and pay them more than $7.9 million in wages, damages, and legal fees" (Walter, 2009). An additional mandate of this case involved ensuring that personnel were aware of OSHA provisions. In order to

Figure 12.2 Typical OSHA poster. (From http://www.osha.gov/Publications/poster.html.)

accomplish this task, the airline was ordered to "provide all Southern Air crew members with copies of the FAA Whistleblower Protection Program poster and OSHA's notice to employees, and post these in each Southern Air facility" (Walter, 2009).

Migrant and Seasonal Agricultural Worker Protection Act

The Migrant and Seasonal Agricultural Worker Protection Act (MSPA) safeguards various "migrant and seasonal agricultural workers" regarding their activities and associations with "farm labor contractors, agricultural employers, agricultural associations, and providers of migrant housing" (U.S. Department of Labor, 2013j). This legislation is also pertinent concerning a communications perspective because it mandates that various written disclosures be provided when recruiting potential workers. This disclosure must express the "terms and conditions" of employment, and must be provided "upon request" when "offering employment" (U.S. Department of Labor, 2013j). Additionally, the disclosure must be stated in the language of the employee (U.S. Department of Labor, 2013j).

The MSPA also mandates that employers post and conspicuously maintain signage that expresses its basic tenets. This signage must be posted within the work location. Essentially, this signage expresses the "rights and protections that the MSPA affords workers" (U.S. Department of Labor, 2013j). Under the terms of the MSPA legislation, the details of housing must also be communicated to workers. Specifically, the "terms and conditions of occupancy" must be expressed and communicated to tenants (U.S. Department

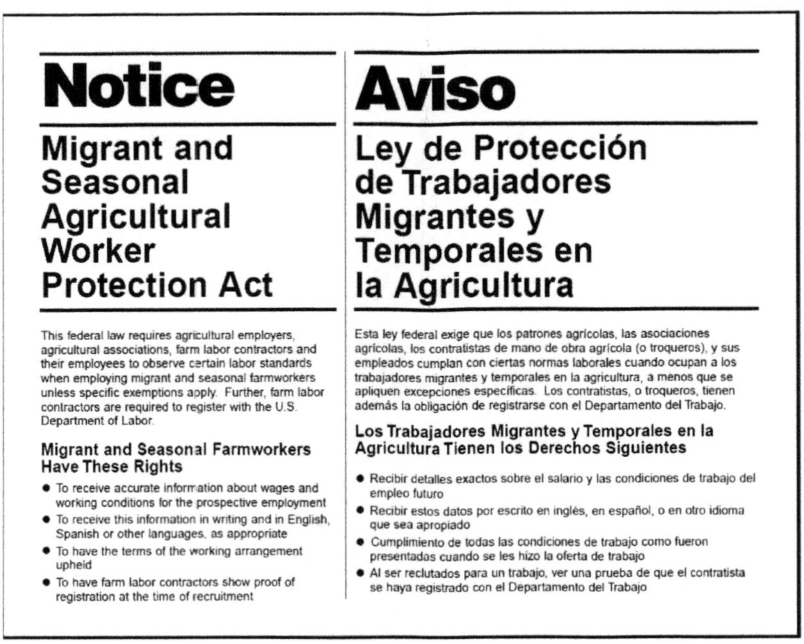

Notice

Migrant and Seasonal Agricultural Worker Protection Act

This federal law requires agricultural employers, agricultural associations, farm labor contractors and their employees to observe certain labor standards when employing migrant and seasonal farmworkers unless specific exemptions apply. Further, farm labor contractors are required to register with the U.S. Department of Labor.

Migrant and Seasonal Farmworkers Have These Rights

- To receive accurate information about wages and working conditions for the prospective employment
- To receive this information in writing and in English, Spanish or other languages, as appropriate
- To have the terms of the working arrangement upheld
- To have farm labor contractors show proof of registration at the time of recruitment

Aviso

Ley de Protección de Trabajadores Migrantes y Temporales en la Agricultura

Esta ley federal exige que los patrones agrícolas, las asociaciones agrícolas, los contratistas de mano de obra agrícola (o troqueros), y sus empleados cumplan con ciertas normas laborales cuando ocupan a los trabajadores migrantes y temporales en la agricultura, a menos que se apliquen excepciones específicas. Los contratistas, o troqueros, tienen además la obligación de registrarse con el Departamento del Trabajo.

Los Trabajadores Migrantes y Temporales en la Agricultura Tienen los Derechos Siguientes

- Recibir detalles exactos sobre el salario y las condiciones de trabajo del empleo futuro
- Recibir estos datos por escrito en inglés, en español, o en otro idioma que sea apropiado
- Cumplimiento de todas las condiciones de trabajo como fueron presentadas cuando se les hizo la oferta de trabajo
- Al ser reclutados para un trabajo, ver una prueba de que el contratista se haya registrado con el Departamento del Trabajo

Figure 12.3 Typical MSPA poster. (From http://www.dol.gov/whd/regs/compliance/posters/mspaenspbw.pdf.)

of Labor, 2013j). Figure 12.3 shows the typical MSPA signage (U.S. Department of Labor, 2013e).

Family Medical and Leave Act

The Family Medical and Leave Act (FMLA) encompasses "all public agencies (state and local governments) and local education agencies (schools, whether public or private)" (U.S. Department of Labor, 2013d). This legislation is also applicable within the private sector. Essentially, this legislation provides a basis for establishing and providing "job-protected leave for qualifying events without interference or restraint from their employers" (U.S. Department of Labor, 2013d). Employers are required to communicate the salient details of this act to their employees.

During 2007, a dispute regarding FMLA requirements (*Barthalow v. David Martin Excavating*, No. 1:05-CV-2593, MD PA, 2007) involved the absenteeism of an employee "whose wife had a heart ailment and sometimes needed his care, was terminated" (Business Management Daily, 2007). Although the poster was posted conspicuously, the employee did not see it and was ignorant of how to request time to tend to his wife (Business Management Daily, 2007). The court ruled that "that the company should have let Barthalow know how to ask for FMLA leave after it learned about his wife's illness" (Business Management Daily, 2007). This case shows that although FMLA posters may be conspicuously posted, they may not be seen by personnel and that personnel may be unaware of FMLA requirements and its associated processes for requesting leave time. Once an employer is aware of personal situations that may necessitate FMLA leave, they should inform employees of appropriate requirements, processes, and procedures.

Communicating FMLA details occurs through the posting and maintaining of conspicuous signage within the work environment. Employers covered by this legislation must display the signage "even if no employees are eligible for the FMLA leave" (U.S. Department of Labor, 2013d). If the majority of an organizational workforce is not English literate, then the appropriate signage may be posted using "a language in which the employees are literate" (U.S. Department of Labor, 2013d). Figure 12.4 shows the typical FMLA signage (U.S. Department of Labor, 2013c).

Employee Polygraph Protection Act

The Employee Polygraph Protection Act (EPAA) is applicable to only employers within the private sector. It does not apply to the work settings of "federal, state, and local government agencies" (U.S. Department of Labor, 2013g). The basic purpose of this legislation prohibits the use of polygraph examinations during hiring practices of "most private employers" or "during the course of employment" (U.S. Department of Labor, 2013g). Generally, employers may not request that personnel take a polygraph examination or discriminate against personnel that refuse to take such examinations (U.S. Department of Labor, 2013g).

Any failure of private employers to abide by the EPAA may result in legal ramifications. During 2012, eight individuals filed a lawsuit against Metropolitan Interpreters and Translators Inc. (MetLang) involving allegations that they were subjected to "illegal

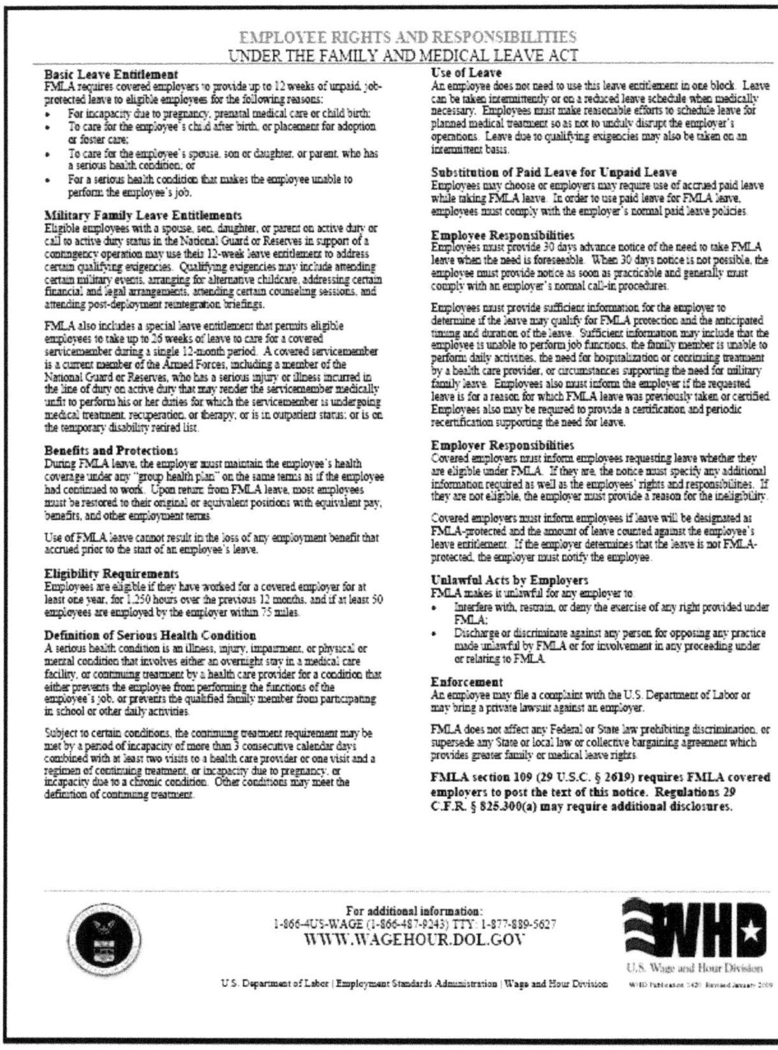

EMPLOYEE RIGHTS AND RESPONSIBILITIES
UNDER THE FAMILY AND MEDICAL LEAVE ACT

Basic Leave Entitlement
FMLA requires covered employers to provide up to 12 weeks of unpaid, job-protected leave to eligible employees for the following reasons:

- For incapacity due to pregnancy, prenatal medical care or child birth;
- To care for the employee's child after birth, or placement for adoption or foster care;
- To care for the employee's spouse, son or daughter, or parent, who has a serious health condition; or
- For a serious health condition that makes the employee unable to perform the employee's job.

Military Family Leave Entitlements
Eligible employees with a spouse, son, daughter, or parent on active duty or call to active duty status in the National Guard or Reserves in support of a contingency operation may use their 12-week leave entitlement to address certain qualifying exigencies. Qualifying exigencies may include attending certain military events, arranging for alternative childcare, addressing certain financial and legal arrangements, attending certain counseling sessions, and attending post-deployment reintegration briefings.

FMLA also includes a special leave entitlement that permits eligible employees to take up to 26 weeks of leave to care for a covered servicemember during a single 12-month period. A covered servicemember is a current member of the Armed Forces, including a member of the National Guard or Reserves, who has a serious injury or illness incurred in the line of duty on active duty that may render the servicemember medically unfit to perform his or her duties for which the servicemember is undergoing medical treatment, recuperation, or therapy; or is in outpatient status; or is on the temporary disability retired list.

Benefits and Protections
During FMLA leave, the employer must maintain the employee's health coverage under any "group health plan" on the same terms as if the employee had continued to work. Upon return from FMLA leave, most employees must be restored to their original or equivalent positions with equivalent pay, benefits, and other employment terms.

Use of FMLA leave cannot result in the loss of any employment benefit that accrued prior to the start of an employee's leave.

Eligibility Requirements
Employees are eligible if they have worked for a covered employer for at least one year, for 1,250 hours over the previous 12 months, and if at least 50 employees are employed by the employer within 75 miles.

Definition of Serious Health Condition
A serious health condition is an illness, injury, impairment, or physical or mental condition that involves either an overnight stay in a medical care facility, or continuing treatment by a health care provider for a condition that either prevents the employee from performing the functions of the employee's job, or prevents the qualified family member from participating in school or other daily activities.

Subject to certain conditions, the continuing treatment requirement may be met by a period of incapacity of more than 3 consecutive calendar days combined with at least two visits to a health care provider or one visit and a regimen of continuing treatment, or incapacity due to pregnancy, or incapacity due to a chronic condition. Other conditions may meet the definition of continuing treatment.

Use of Leave
An employee does not need to use this leave entitlement in one block. Leave can be taken intermittently or on a reduced leave schedule when medically necessary. Employees must make reasonable efforts to schedule leave for planned medical treatment so as not to unduly disrupt the employer's operations. Leave due to qualifying exigencies may also be taken on an intermittent basis.

Substitution of Paid Leave for Unpaid Leave
Employees may choose or employers may require use of accrued paid leave while taking FMLA leave. In order to use paid leave for FMLA leave, employees must comply with the employer's normal paid leave policies.

Employee Responsibilities
Employees must provide 30 days advance notice of the need to take FMLA leave when the need is foreseeable. When 30 days notice is not possible, the employee must provide notice as soon as practicable and generally must comply with an employer's normal call-in procedures.

Employees must provide sufficient information for the employer to determine if the leave may qualify for FMLA protection and the anticipated timing and duration of the leave. Sufficient information may include that the employee is unable to perform job functions, the family member is unable to perform daily activities, the need for hospitalization or continuing treatment by a health care provider, or circumstances supporting the need for military family leave. Employees also must inform the employer if the requested leave is for a reason for which FMLA leave was previously taken or certified. Employees also may be required to provide a certification and periodic recertification supporting the need for leave.

Employer Responsibilities
Covered employers must inform employees requesting leave whether they are eligible under FMLA. If they are, the notice must specify any additional information required as well as the employees' rights and responsibilities. If they are not eligible, the employer must provide a reason for the ineligibility.

Covered employers must inform employees if leave will be designated as FMLA-protected and the amount of leave counted against the employee's leave entitlement. If the employer determines that the leave is not FMLA-protected, the employer must notify the employee.

Unlawful Acts by Employers
FMLA makes it unlawful for any employer to:

- Interfere with, restrain, or deny the exercise of any right provided under FMLA;
- Discharge or discriminate against any person for opposing any practice made unlawful by FMLA or for involvement in any proceeding under or relating to FMLA.

Enforcement
An employee may file a complaint with the U.S. Department of Labor or may bring a private lawsuit against an employer.

FMLA does not affect any Federal or State law prohibiting discrimination, or supersede any State or local law or collective bargaining agreement which provides greater family or medical leave rights.

FMLA section 109 (29 U.S.C. § 2619) requires FMLA covered employers to post the text of this notice. Regulations 29 C.F.R. § 825.300(a) may require additional disclosures.

For additional information:
1-866-4US-WAGE (1-866-487-9243) TTY: 1-877-889-5627
WWW.WAGEHOUR.DOL.GOV

U.S. Department of Labor | Employment Standards Administration | Wage and Hour Division

WHD
U.S. Wage and Hour Division

Figure 12.4 FMLA signage. (From http://www.dol.gov/whd/regs/compliance/posters/fmla.htm#.UPjk22ffQbQ.)

polygraph tests that included questions about infidelity and bestiality" (Maass, 2012). These personnel were employed among criminal cases for the Immigrations and Customs Enforcement and the U.S. Drug Enforcement Agency (Maass, 2012). The group alleges that they were fired from employment "after they supposedly failed flawed lie-detectors, received inconclusive results or outright refused to submit to them" (Maass, 2012). The group is seeking punitive damages and attorneys' fees (Maass, 2012). Time will tell the outcome of this case.

The basic tenets of the EPAA should be communicated among organizational employees. Such communication is achieved through the use of conspicuous signage that is accessible and continuously present within the work setting. Posters detailing the basic tenets of the EPAA are available in both the English and Spanish languages (U.S. Department of Labor, 2013a). Figure 12.5 depicts the typical EPAA signage (U.S. Department of Labor, 2013a).

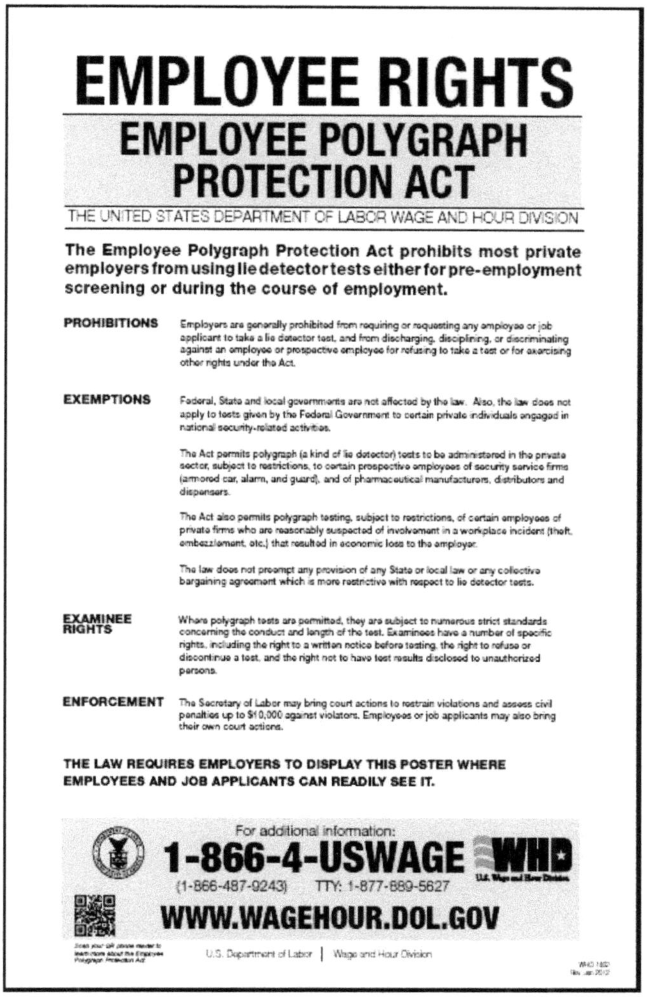

Figure 12.5 Typical EPAA signage. (From http://www.dol.gov/whd/regs/compliance/posters/eppa.htm#.)

Other Legislation and Communication

The preceding laws are not the only pieces of legislation that involve some aspect of communication. Many other legislative acts mandate that their primary tenets be visibly and conspicuously communicated among organizational personnel. Generally, in most cases, the salient points of employment laws are communicated through signage within the workplace. The U.S. Department of Labor maintains a listing of employment laws that contain Internet links to appropriate signage. This resource collection may be accessed at http://www.dol.gov/compliance/guide/.

Employment Postings

The announcement of employment opportunities may occur through a variety of methods that incorporate oral, written, or video forms of communicating. A job posting is an announcement that communicates the "qualifications and skills" for which the employer is searching (Walker, 2011). Job postings may be small advertisements in the back of a trade journal or they may be full-size newspaper advertisements. They may be broadcast during radio and television shows or commercials. Some employers may opt to announce publically their openings through the Internet or internally via an organizational intranet. Figure 12.6 shows an Internet job posting for the Broken Arrow (Oklahoma) Police Department (City of Broken Arrow, 2013).

The job posting in Figure 12.6 shows the desired qualifications of the police department and the conditions of initial employment. It delineates the steps of the hiring process and the geographic area that is patrolled by the department. The posting communicates the necessity of specialized qualifications within the candidate pool, thereby excluding applicants that do not possess the requisite credentials. The job posting also contains multiple methods of contacting the police department through either surface mail or telephone. Additional contact information is provided for the human resources department of the municipality. Overall, the posting is short and succinct through which the pertinent details of the desired applicant, the department, and the necessary contact information are communicated to the general public.

Job postings may be of all shapes, sizes, and lengths. Regardless, their purpose is to attract the attention of potential candidates and to communicate the employment requirements and contact details of the employer. Furthermore, job postings provide a means of establishing communication between potential applicants and employers. The specificity of job details is essential to distinguish applicants who are qualified from those

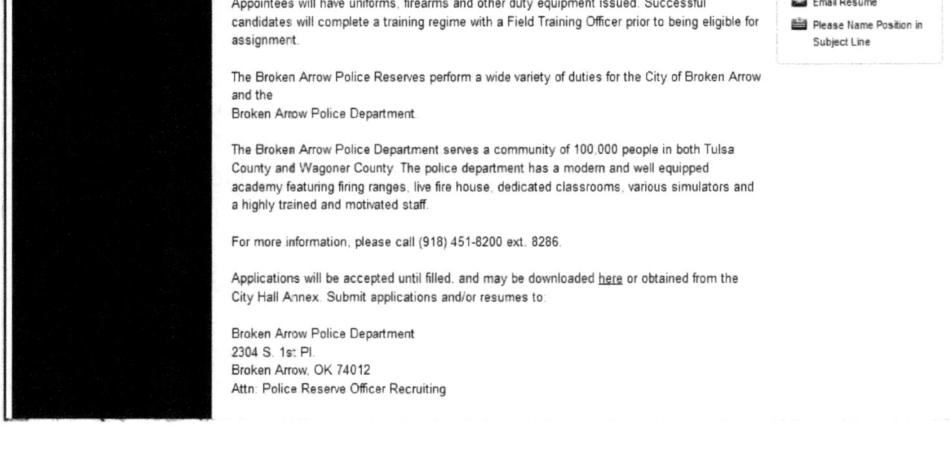
Permit Center
Police
Fire

◄ Back to All Categories

Police Reserve Officers

The Broken Arrow Police Department is currently seeking to increase its number of CLEET certified police reserve officers. At this time, interested applicants must at least hold reserve officer certification from CLEET. Further, applicants would undergo a multi-step hiring process similar to the one in place for full time officers. The hiring process will include: 1) interviews, 2) thorough background investigation, 3) polygraph examination, 4) physical agility/obstacle course (for orientation purposes only) and 5) standardized law enforcement psychological testing (MMPI).

Appointees will have uniforms, firearms and other duty equipment issued. Successful candidates will complete a training regime with a Field Training Officer prior to being eligible for assignment.

The Broken Arrow Police Reserves perform a wide variety of duties for the City of Broken Arrow and the
Broken Arrow Police Department.

The Broken Arrow Police Department serves a community of 100,000 people in both Tulsa County and Wagoner County. The police department has a modern and well equipped academy featuring firing ranges, live fire house, dedicated classrooms, various simulators and a highly trained and motivated staff.

For more information, please call (918) 451-8200 ext. 8286.

Applications will be accepted until filled, and may be downloaded here or obtained from the City Hall Annex. Submit applications and/or resumes to:

Broken Arrow Police Department
2304 S. 1st Pl.
Broken Arrow, OK 74012
Attn: Police Reserve Officer Recruiting

Category
Police Department
Status
Open
Published
September 21, 2012 3:00 PM
Closing
Open Until Filled

Tools
Download Application
Email Resume
Please Name Position in Subject Line

Figure 12.6 Broken Arrow, Oklahoma, law enforcement job posting. (From http://www.brokenarrowok.gov/Jobs.aspx?UniqueId=97&From=All&CommunityJobs=False&JobID=Police-Reserve-Officers-64.)

individuals who are unqualified. This segregating of applicants eliminates unnecessary and burdensome reviews of materials during the hiring process.

Cover Letter

When communicating with potential employers, a cover letter may be necessary to accompany materials that are required within the hiring process. A cover letter is a short, introductory note that communicates the positive intentions of the candidate regarding the employment opportunity. It may incorporate some facets of education, skills, and experience that satisfy the requirements of the job posting. Generally, cover letters are limited to one page in length.

The cover letter has a primary purpose: to gain the attention and the interest of the potential employer. Certain key words may be integrated within the contents of the cover letter to convey a sense of appropriateness regarding the qualifications stated within the commensurate job posting. If possible, cover letters should be addressed to a specific individual within the organization. If a specific individual is not listed within the job posting, then it may be worthwhile to contact the organization and determine the name of the appropriate recipient of the cover letter. Cover letters should also be succinct and should have no grammar or spelling errors.

Cover letters may also be targeted toward the specific requirements of the job posting. Generic cover letters may be very ineffective at gaining the attention and interest of potential employers. The targeted approach should delineate how an applicant satisfies the requirements of the job posting. Cover letters also express how the applicant can contribute positively, meaningfully, and beneficially to the hiring organization, and how the applicant can be distinguished from others that may be applying for the same position. Furthermore, cover letters may express a desire for an interview appointment with potential employers. Courtesy and formality are necessary when composing cover letters. One should ensure that appropriate titles and courtesies are rendered properly within the cover letter, and that the tone of the writing style exhibits the characteristics of professionalism.

Essentially, the preceding concepts may be itemized within four categories: address and salutation, opening, main body, and closure (Sethi & Adhikari, 2010). The address and salutation provide routing information and a greeting for the receiver of the intended message conveyed within the cover letter. Many job postings of larger organizations (e.g., Federal Bureau of Investigation and Customs and Border Protection) may not have listed a specific individual, and contacting such organizations to determine a specific hiring manager may be fruitless. Therefore, in such cases, the typical "Dear Sir" approach is acceptable (Sethi & Adhikari, 2010). However, if possible, cover letters should be specifically addressed to an appropriate hiring manager.

The opening of the cover letter is designed to attract the "attention of the reader" (Sethi & Adhikari, 2010). It must also identify the specific position for which the applicant is applying, and generally refers to the original advertising of the open position (Sethi & Adhikari, 2010). Unsolicited communication with a potential employer may include the reasons why an applicant is seeking employment with the organization (Sethi & Adhikari, 2010).

The body of the cover letter is relatively short and contains merely a couple of paragraphs. This instance is one in which size does not matter—it is quality, not quantity, that counts! Within these paragraphs, the applicant must present briefly why he or she is an exceptional candidate for the job. Highlight any salient skills, experience, and credentials that are pertinent for the job listing. Essentially, this section represents "strengths" and "suitability" for the considered employment opening (Sethi & Adhikari, 2010).

The closure of a cover letter represents the ending of the note and includes final comments. The closure should specifically request that an interview be granted regarding the job opening (Sethi & Adhikari, 2010). Closing points also may express gratitude for a reader to have reviewed the documents, and may also reference any enclosures that are transmitted and conveyed with the cover letter. Certainly, the enclosures would contain the resume and any required copies of training transcripts (or certificates).

Cover letters may be drafted using any of the letter styles and formats presented in Chapter 4. Regardless of the selected style or format, they must always be concise and limited to a page. Figure 12.7 shows a sample cover letter.

When crafting cover letters, one should be mindful of the perspective and constraints of the reader and the screening process. An application package may be processed through electronic information systems that query key words and phrases. Within the sample cover letter, such words include "certification" and "degree." Human resources and personnel departments may eliminate unqualified applicants before qualified packages are forwarded

January 20, 2013

Chief Yuar Aperson
Big City Police Department
P.O. Box 2013
Big City, MS 55555

Chief Aperson,

I am applying for the position of Patrol Supervisor that was listed in the January 7, 2013 edition of the *Daily Babbler* newspaper. The primary qualifications were stated as state law enforcement certification, 10 years of law enforcement management experience, and a successful career history of organizational improvement and leadership. I am qualified for this position, and am available immediately. The following items highlight my qualifications:

- 15 years of law enforcement management experience.
- Graduate of the State Police Academy (certification no. 29292).
- Bachelor of Science degree in Police Science.
- Awarded $75,000 in grant funding for community policing initiatives last year.
- Improved departmental efficiency rating by 15% over the last two years.

The newspaper listing requested copies of certifications, training transcripts, work history, and professional references. These items and a current resume are enclosed within this application package.

I am a qualified, seasoned officer that can contribute meaningfully to the Big City Police Department. I request that an interview appointment be granted to discuss this opportunity. I shall contact you within the next two weeks to follow-up this application package.

Thank you for your time and attention to this matter.

Yours Sincerely,
Ima Person
Ima Person

P.O. Box 1414
Big City, MS 55555
(555)-555-5555

Enclosures
IP: jd

Figure 12.7 Sample cover letter.

to hiring managers or are retained in application pools. Applicants must also assume that they are not the only applicant for the position. Therefore, readers may parse and maintain stacks of cover letters, resume, and supporting documents, thereby generating a large amount of materials that must be evaluated (Pfeiffer, 1993, p. 561).

Readers may be both impatient and tired (Pfeiffer, 1993, p. 561). Hiring managers do not have time to read every word of every page of applications materials, and have only sufficient time to scan and spot read materials. Hiring managers may also receive application packages near the end of a "busy day" or during evening hours, necessitating additional work at home (Pfeiffer, 1993, p. 561). Therefore, information within cover letters must be conveyed quickly and clearly to gain the attention of readers.

If an application package gains the interest of a reviewer, then it must exhibit a fine quality of writing style and language use (Pfeiffer, 1993, p. 561). The cover letter represents an initial method of communicating with hiring managers and generates a first impression in the mind of the reader. Materials that are difficult to read or that contain errors in grammar, syntax, semantics, spelling, or phrases may be discarded immediately. If an application package contains such errors, then a hiring manager or reviewer may assume that a similar quality of work-related performance may be exhibited if the applicant is hired. Therefore, it is imperative that cover letters and applications materials have no defects.

Resumes

A resume is defined as a summary that details a "set of accomplishments" (*Merriam-Webster*, 2013). A resume is usually a short, written document that communicates the professional accomplishments of an individual. The basic function of a resume is to "show the reader" what a prospective employee is capable of doing, and acts as a "selling document" to identify the applicant as the person for whom the employer is specifically searching (Debasish & Das, 2009). Therefore, a resume is a marketing resource that advertises the selling points of a job candidate through communicating via written language.

Generally, depending on the experience, qualifications, and credentials of an individual, resumes are no more than a couple of pages in length. There is no one solitary, perfect format for crafting a resume. Instead, many formats may be used to convey the accomplishments of a lifetime. Resumes may also be customized per the requirements of a job advertisement or posting. Regardless, in any case, a resume must communicate clearly, concisely, efficiently, and effectively the message that a sender wishes to convey to a receiver regarding some aspect of employment.

Although a resume may be drafted in just about any fashion, three primary types of resume organization exist: (1) chronological, (2) functional, and (3) hybrid. The chronological organization delineates accomplishments using a "reverse chronological order" (Cazenovia College, 2013). This method expresses the "most recent work experience first" succeeded by the previous experience and accomplishments (Cazenovia College, 2013). Generally, most employers prefer this resume organization because it is read and interpreted easily. The functional organization emphasizes job functions instead of "chronological order" Cazenovia College, 2013). Within this type of resume, the attributes of "skills, abilities, and areas of expertise" are highlighted categorically instead of itemizing "career history" (Cazenovia College, 2013). This fashion of resume organization may be disfavored by employers because it may be difficult and confusing to determine where and when functional areas of experience occurred through time. The hybrid organization method integrates the characteristics of both the chronological and functional resume organizations. Using this fashion may facilitate great specificity to express the pertinent details one wishes to convey. Through the hybrid approach, "an applicant who has had a position with varied responsibilities can list the tasks by category" instead of using a listing of unrelated "tasks and responsibilities" (Cazenovia College, 2013).

A resume must exhibit professionalism. Regardless of the organizational format of a resume, it must facilitate the act of communicating both effectively and efficiently while exhibiting pleasing aesthetics. Care must be taken to ensure that a resume document reflects "current formatting and production standards while maintaining a distinctive conservative tone" (Lehman & Dufrene, 2011, p. 489). Resumes are usually created using 8.5″ × 11.0″ paper of a "neutral color (white, buff, or gray)," and that is of "high quality (preferably 24-pound, 100-percent cotton fiber)" (Lehman & Dufrene, 2011, p. 490). Font sizes within the body of the resume document should be 12 point or 10 point, and fonts should be conservative (e.g., Times New Roman). Larger font sizes (but not excessively large) may be used to identify the candidate.

Figure 12.8 shows a typical resume format. This resume example is clear, concise, and neatly arranged to provide a quick accessing of information. Its columnar format

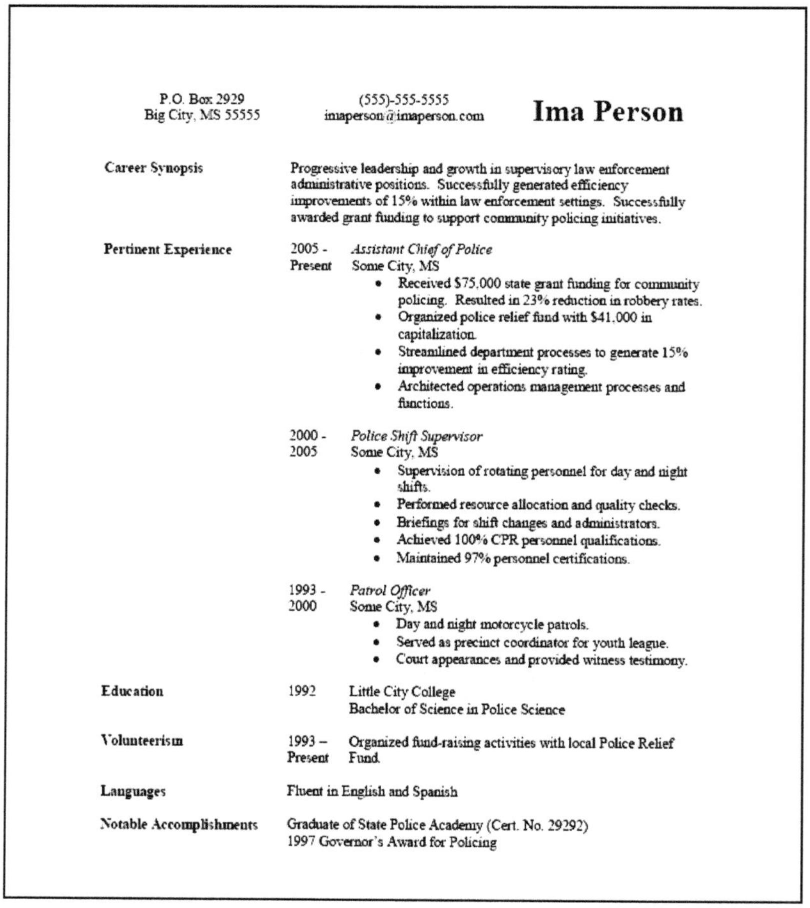

P.O. Box 2929
Big City, MS 55555

(555)-555-5555
imaperson@imaperson.com

Ima Person

Career Synopsis
Progressive leadership and growth in supervisory law enforcement administrative positions. Successfully generated efficiency improvements of 15% within law enforcement settings. Successfully awarded grant funding to support community policing initiatives.

Pertinent Experience

2005 - Present *Assistant Chief of Police*
Some City, MS
- Received $75,000 state grant funding for community policing. Resulted in 23% reduction in robbery rates.
- Organized police relief fund with $41,000 in capitalization.
- Streamlined department processes to generate 15% improvement in efficiency rating.
- Architected operations management processes and functions.

2000 - 2005 *Police Shift Supervisor*
Some City, MS
- Supervision of rotating personnel for day and night shifts.
- Performed resource allocation and quality checks.
- Briefings for shift changes and administrators.
- Achieved 100% CPR personnel qualifications.
- Maintained 97% personnel certifications.

1993 - 2000 *Patrol Officer*
Some City, MS
- Day and night motorcycle patrols.
- Served as precinct coordinator for youth league.
- Court appearances and provided witness testimony.

Education
1992 Little City College
Bachelor of Science in Police Science

Volunteerism
1993 – Present Organized fund-raising activities with local Police Relief Fund.

Languages
Fluent in English and Spanish

Notable Accomplishments
Graduate of State Police Academy (Cert. No. 29292)
1997 Governor's Award for Policing

Figure 12.8 Sample resume.

provides listings for categories (e.g., languages and pertinent experience), chronological periods encompassing specific experiences, and descriptions of achievements and accomplishments. This example resume begins with a high-level overview of the most salient accomplishments of the candidate. The remaining sections provide greater details and clarifications that support the high-level description of experience. The remaining sections also introduce ancillary characteristics of the candidate such as volunteerism and notable achievements. The inclusion of such additional items provides a more robust description of the candidate. Although the example resume is limited to a single page, it facilitates the pertinent details of the candidate that a hiring manager may find attractive.

The example resume also contains a header that provides the identity of the candidate and multiple methods of contact, including surface mail, telephone, and electronic mail. The name of the candidate is visibly obvious and attracts attention in the upper right-hand corner of the page. Such positioning and sizing are purposeful and functional. Approximately 90% of humans are right-handed, whereas roughly 10% are left-handed (Coon, Mitterer, Brown, Malik, & McKenzie, 2010). Therefore, reviewers may hold a stack of resumes in their left hand and thumb through them using their right hand. By having the name of the job candidate expressed visibly and boldly within the upper right-hand corner of the page, the resume may be noticed prominently and identified easily when compared with other resumes.

Another interesting observation regarding the sample resume involves the English language. The example incorporates the use of sentence fragments or short sentences to convey pertinent information concisely. The use of complete sentences is unnecessary when crafting resumes (Statsky, 2009). The use of sentence fragments is acceptable, provided that English language rules of parallelism are invoked (Statsky, 2009).

Resumes should describe successfulness throughout a career. Therefore, the language should also incorporate "action words" that show the candidate is capable of performing successfully to "get things done" (Chiagouris, 2010). Examples of such words include the following: accomplished, developed, operated, reduced, improved, supervised, investigated, transformed, strengthened, and so forth (Bovee & Thill, 2012). Essentially, the wording and phrasing of a resume must "show results" that were successfully accomplished by the candidate (Bovee & Thill, 2012).

Although paper resumes are quite useful, many resumes are now submitted, maintained, and reviewed electronically. Mobile devices, such as iPads, may be used to transmit and receive resumes (and certainly other documents). Resumes may also be transmitted and received through electronic mail. Additionally, if one produces a paper resume, then it must be of such quality that it may be scanned and stored electronically. Another consideration of the electronic domain involves social networking. Many social networking sites may host resumes, thereby exposing one's qualifications and work history to a mass audience.

Resumes represent a written advocacy of a job candidate. They must be detailed sufficiently and truthfully to communicate the pertinent details of a job candidate that are commensurate with the requirements of prospective employment. Crafting a resume is not always easy. Some people may be poor writers and others may find it troublesome to constrain their accomplishments within a one- or two-page document. Customizing a resume to the specific requirements of a certain job posting may result in the crafting and maintaining of many different versions of a resume.

Regardless, crafting a resume may be made less tedious by adhering to the steps of the writing process delineated in Chapter 4. Resumes are written documents that must be edited, revised, proofed, and evaluated for accuracy and quality several times before they are forwarded to prospective employers. By adhering to the steps of the writing process, job candidates may improve the efficiency and effectiveness of communicating through resumes.

Employment Interviews

Employment interviews are events in which prospective employees are screened, questioned, and evaluated to make a determination regarding the suitability as a potential employee with an organization. Simultaneously, an employment interview is an event in which a prospective employee may make a similar determination concerning whether the organization would be a suitable employer. Therefore, an employment interview is conceptually a "two-way conversation" through which employers and job candidates learn about each other (Dlabay, Burrow, & Kleindl, 2009).

Employment interviews normally encompass four steps: (1) planning, (2) beginning, (3) questioning, and (4) closing (Narayan, 1999). The initial step of planning consists of determining the "criteria by which the applicant will be judged" (Narayan, 1999, p. 158). Many activities occur during this because it represents the precursor for the interview in which the tools and resources for evaluating candidates are identified. The methods of how these tools and resources are to be implemented during the interview are also identified within this stage of the interview process. Additionally, this step of the interview process accommodates considerations of the job requirements versus the characteristics of the person to be interviewed (Narayan, 1999, p. 158). During this step, the credentials, resume, and supporting documents of a prospective employee are also reviewed to ensure some familiarity exists regarding the applicant before the interview occurs (Narayan, 1999, p. 158). Essentially, the planning stage provides a basis for establishing structure throughout the interview process.

The second step of the interview process represents the commencement of the interview. It represents a welcoming phase in which the interviewee is met initially and greeted appropriately. Interviewers should introduce themselves, and address the interviewee "by name" (Narayan, 1999, p. 158). This step involves "breaking the ice" congenially as a method of establishing a relaxed environment (Narayan, 1999, p. 158). During this step, some informal conversation may occur as a method of relaxing the interviewee (Narayan, 1999, p. 158).

The third step of the interview process consists of interviewing the applicant through questioning. This questioning may occur through the use of panel interviews or solitary interviewers. Panel interviews consist of questioning the interviewee by multiple people either concurrently as a group or sequentially with specific appointment times. Solitary interviews consist of questioning the interviewee by only one person for a length of time. Federal rules constrain the types and topics of questions that may be posed during job interviews. Within the United States, such restrictions include queries regarding "spiritual life or religion," "ethnic or cultural background, sexual orientation, age, or handicapping condition" (Everett, 2007).

Given these federal constraints, the line of interview questioning should be restricted to only those queries that are associated with the requirements of the intended employment. The attributes of the posted job description should heavily influence the questions that are asked during the employment interview (Colaprete, 2012). Careful attention must be given to the questions that are posed during employment interviews. Presenting unrelated or illegal queries, such as questions concerning religion or disability, may result in legal disputes and lawsuits against the employer. Such questions not only have the potential of liability and legal consequences but also may "force the organization into a position to hire an otherwise unqualified or unfit candidate" (Colaprete, 2012).

Therefore, the line of questioning during interviews must be constructed to explore facets of the interviewee that are related to the posted job announcement and the requirements of potential employment. During the interview, a variety of related questions may be used to investigate "social skills, interpersonal and communication skills, motivation, situational problem solving, dependability and trustworthiness, and attitudes toward appearance" (Colaprete, 2012). Such characteristics may not be easily discovered through asking questions that may be answered by simply responding affirmatively or negatively. Instead, they require open-ended responses from interviewees that require thoughtful reflection and analysis.

The period of questioning is not a one-way experience. Instead, it should facilitate mutual communication between both employers and job candidates. Both parties should ask questions and follow-up questions to learn about each other, and to gain information that may be used to influence decisions regarding employment suitability. Time should be allocated to ensure that both parties may respond sufficiently to the posed questions.

The closing step of the interview process represents the finality of the interview event. In some cases, a decision regarding employment suitability may be made immediately or deferred upon the closure of the interview (Narayan, 1999). Upon the closing of an interview, if an interviewer is empowered to either hire or reject a candidate immediately, then the appropriate decision should be exercised without hesitation (Narayan, 1999). However, in most cases, job candidates are generally told that the organization will inform them of a hiring decision at some future period.

Experiencing a job interview may be traumatic for both interviewers and interviewees. The tension of an interview experience may be mitigated by a variety of behaviors that may facilitate a congenial and bearable interview experience. Recommendations include the following (Narayan, 1999, pp. 458–459):

Body movement: Body movement should be controlled. Arms should not fling and should not be crossed. Gestures should not be excessive. Hands should not be placed inside of pockets. The head should be nodded appropriately to convey "agreement and interest" (Narayan, 1999, pp. 458–459).

Maintain posture: Good posture should be maintained by sitting upright while slightly leaning forward. Such positioning and posture exhibit "confidence and interest" (Narayan, 1999, pp. 458–459).

Maintain eye contact: Maintaining eye contact among each of the parties involved in the interview "suggests interest and trustworthiness" (Narayan, 1999, pp. 458–459).

Smile appropriately: Smiling conveys "a positive attitude" (Narayan, 1999, pp. 458–459). However, smiling should occur neither too little nor too much.

Listening: Attentive listening facilitates interest and also improves the ability to "answer questions appropriately" (Narayan, 1999, pp. 458–459).

Eliminate distractions: All "electronic devices" should be completely turned off to avoid the embarrassment of unexpected distractions (Narayan, 1999, pp. 458–459).

Vocal tone: Sincerity must permeate any enthusiasm. During interviews, one should avoid "sounding bored, frustrated, or sarcastic" (Narayan, 1999, pp. 458–459).

Avoid stalling: When speaking, one should avoid "verbal pauses" because they signal unpreparedness (Narayan, 1999, pp. 458–459). Examples include "ummm," "uhhhh," and so forth.

Exhibit confidence: Confidence should be exhibited throughout the interview process to convey "self assurance" (Narayan, 1999, pp. 458–459). Arrogance, condescension, and cockiness should be avoided.

During interviews, questions should be answered truthfully and sincerely without too much elucidation. Answers should directly relate to the questions posed without rambling or ignoring the subject of the intended question. When responding to questions, interviewees should relate the relevance of their qualifications and experience to the requirements of the potential job (Ober, 2008). Despite the best efforts to respond to questions, some feelings of nervousness and communications noise may permeate the interview event. No interview experience is absolutely perfect.

Imperfection permeates employment interviews in a variety of fashions. When interviewers speak too much and expend precious interview time, "little or no information" may be received from the job candidate (Rodriques, 2003, p. 233). In some cases, the interviewer may inaccurately transcribe or improperly evaluate information that is received from the interviewee. As a result, "several probable inferences" may be gleaned from the interview, and the "most probable" must be selected regarding the hiring decision (Rodriques, 2003, p. 233).

Other factors that influence the interview consist of the halo effect and the aesthetics of the interviewee (Rodriques, 2003, p. 233). In some cases, hiring managers may be influenced by mannerisms and appearances that unduly influence the hiring decision. Instead, interviewers should form a decision on the basis of the totality of the information gleaned, as well as the intangible characteristics of behaviors exhibited by interviewees. In some cases, interviewers may be unprepared or may have too casual an approach when interviewing (Rodriques, 2003, p. 233). These conditions may also contribute toward circumstances that impede the obtainment of information from interviewees and that influence the hiring decision adversely.

Extraneous conditions may also affect interviewing. Organizations that have a poor public perception or that exhibit poor goodwill may find it difficult to amalgamate an ample pool of job candidates. As a result, the judgment of the interviewer concerning the "comparative suitability of a candidate" may be impeded because of the "inadequate number of available candidates" (Rodriques, 2003, p. 235). In this case, bias may be interjected within the interview and hiring processes even before resumes and application packages are received by the hiring organization.

In Chapter 7, numerous discussions highlighted the need for practice as a measure of preparedness when performing communications orally. This notion is relevant for instances of employment interviews. Both interviewers and interviewees should practice and rehearse before experiencing an interview session. Certainly, many may feel that such preparation is basically more important for the interviewee than the interviewer.

From the perspective of an interviewee, preparing for a job interview involves more than merely practicing oral responses and nonverbal behaviors. Before one can experience an interview and give oral responses to questions, one must know where the interview is to occur. Therefore, an interviewee must determine the location of the interview and ensure an arrival of at least ten minutes before the interview occurs (Brounstein, Bell, Smith, Isbell, & Orr, 2010, p. 345). If possible, one should "drive by" the location a day before the scheduled interview and ensure that travel time includes allotment for "traffic and parking" (Brounstein et al., 2010, p. 345).

Interviewees also may prepare for actual interviews through the use of preparatory interviews. Two types of preparatory interviews may be leveraged before an actual interview occurs: mock and informational. When conducting mock interviews, a friend, relative, or colleague may act as the interviewer for such events. Various "career centers" also offer mock interview services (Brounstein et al., 2010, p. 346). Mock interviews may be recorded and reviewed to determine imperfections and shortcomings that may adversely influence communication. Such recording and reviewing contributes toward gaining performance feedback and improving self-confidence (Brounstein et al., 2010, p. 346). The use of "information interviews" is also a preparatory method through which one may improve interviewing acumen (Brounstein et al., 2010, p. 346). This type of interview involves meeting with an individual within one's "chosen field to discuss career information" (Brounstein et al., 2010, p. 346).

Attire also conveys silent messages during employment interviews. The choice of clothing for both males and females should be professional, not casual. Suits and dresses should be conservative, usually "navy or dark gray/black" (Dillon, 2009). Shoes should be dark and polished, shirts and blouses should be white (and pressed), and jewelry should be minimal (Dillon, 2009). A conservative portfolio is acceptable (Dillon, 2009). Neckties should neither be too long nor too short, and should leave a little space between the top of the belt and the point in the tie. The tie of a necktie should be tight and neat. Clothing should have no hanging threads. Hats should be removed when indoors, and worn only when outdoors (Advanced Etiquette, 2013).

Employment interviews are stressful events in which employers and potential employees examine each other to determine some choice of employment suitability. Preparedness is crucial for maximizing the effectiveness of the interview session, and may be embellished by adhering to the basic interview process described herein. No interview is perfect because any number of factors may impede communication, ranging from human nervousness to outright unpreparedness. Regardless, communicating in employment interviews is a reality that most everyone will experience during the course of a career.

Employment Follow-Up Letter

Experiencing an employment interview is not the termination of communicating with a potential employer. After completing an employment interview, one should immediately send a follow-up letter that expresses gratitude and that acts as an additional method of showing interest in the open position. Generally, a follow-up letter is less than a page in length, expresses gratitude for the interview, serves as a reminder of qualifications, and restates interest in the employment opportunity (Pfeiffer, 1993, p. 570). Figure 12.9 depicts a typical follow-up letter.

January 30, 2013

Chief Yuar Aperson
Big City Police Department
P.O. Box 2013
Big City, MS 55555

Chief Aperson,

I thoroughly enjoyed meeting you and interviewing with the Big City Police Department. I believe that your new community policing initiatives will be of great value to our local citizenry. Although your upcoming endeavors will be challenging, I believe that your organization is laying a foundation for success.

Per our interview, my experience and background qualify me to lead these new community policing initiatives. I have over 15 years of law enforcement administrative experience. I led community policing initiatives that received $75,000 in grant funding through which our department generated a 23% reduction in robbery rates. During this same period, I successfully achieved a 15% improvement in our police department's efficiency rating. I believe these experiences have seasoned my capacity to lead your community policing initiatives.

I am most interested in joining the force and serving the citizens of Big City. Again, I truly appreciate the opportunity to interview with the Big City Police Department.

Thank you for your time and attention.

Best Regards,

Ima Person

Ima Person

Figure 12.9 Sample follow-up letter.

Employment Offer Letters

Employers either hire or decline to hire a prospective employee. Simply, one is either accepted or rejected for potential employment. Informing interviewees of their hiring status after an interview involves communicating the outcomes of interviews verbally or through written language. These considerations of employment involve offer, acceptance, and rejection letters.

An offer letter is a "proposal by an employer to a prospective employee that specifies the terms of employment" (Hayes & Ninemeier, 2009). The use of offer letters may avert legal challenges arising that dispute the conditions and terms of employment and is appropriate for both exempt and nonexempt positions. Copies of offer letters should be retained among all personnel files. A robust offer letter should include the following attributes (Hayes & Ninemeier, 2009):

- Position offered
- Financial compensation

- Synopsis of any benefits
- Review schedules for evaluation and compensation
- Commencing date
- Employment location
- Conditions governing the offer
- References to employment and policy manuals
- Signatory lines for the employee and the employer
- Dates for each of the signature lines

Offer letters may represent "conditional or final" situations of employment (Hayes & Ninemeier, 2009). Conditional offer letters signify a tentative job offer that is subject to conditions that must be satisfied by the "applicant before the job offer is finalized" (Hayes & Ninemeier, 2009). Among law enforcement organizations, such a condition may be completing a background check, providing proof-of-training certifications, passing a drug test, or completing a polygraph examination. Only upon the satisfaction of any conditions and the accepting of the "terms of the offer letter" does a "legally binding employment agreement" occur (Hayes & Ninemeier, 2009). A final offer letter is unconditional, thereby imparting no terms that must be satisfied before its acceptance (Hayes & Ninemeier, 2009). Upon the acceptance of a final offer letter, an "enforceable employment contract" becomes effective (Hayes & Ninemeier, 2009).

Figure 12.10 shows an example offer letter that itemizes the conditions of employment. The example offer letter emphasizes the tentative and conditional attributes of the employment offer. Before employment commences, the conditions detailed within the offer letter must be satisfied by the job candidate. The offer letter also has specific deadlines regarding the completion of initial conditions, and for the returning of the offer letter indicating either an acceptance of the offer or its rejection by the candidate. Furthermore, the offer letter clarifies the attributes of financial compensation and personnel review periods. It also expresses the eligibility of the position regarding organizational benefits. By accession and reference, the offer letter also incorporates both policies of the Big City Police Department and of the municipality. Indicating a preference of either accepting or rejecting the offer is easily and clearly communicated through darkening the appropriate circle that is commensurate with the intent of the candidate.

Employment Rejection Letters

Rejection letters are the opposite of acceptance letters. Instead of extending an offer of employment, whether conditional or unconditional, rejection letters inform someone that they are unsuitable for employment with the interviewing organization. Rejection letters are generally succinct, and may or may not explain the reasoning for denying employment. Although rejection letters are dismissive, they should neither be insulting nor condescending. Many qualified candidates may be rejected in favor of someone whose skills, education, experience, and credentials were deemed to be superior to those of the other candidates. Rejection letters should be both amiable and formal, and should encourage applicants to be mindful of future opportunities with the organization. A sample rejection letter is presented in Figure 12.11.

February 3, 2013

Ima Person
P.O. Box 2929
Big City, MS 55555

Dear Officer Person,

Congratulations! You are hereby awarded tentatively the position of Patrol Supervisor with the Big City Police Department, Big City, MS commencing on April 1, 2013. This offer is tentatively extended to you with the understanding that the following conditions must be satisfied before April 1, 2013. The conditions of employment are as follows:

1. Satisfactory completion of a polygraph examination conducted at the Big City Police Department.
2. Completion of the physical fitness examination with a passing score per the state minimum.
3. Completion of marksmanship qualification with a passing score per the state minimum.
4. Satisfactory completion of the new employee orientation program.
5. Satisfactory completion of a background investigation.
6. Submission of State Police Academy transcripts and certificates.
7. Submission of college and university transcripts showing all schools attended and degrees awarded.
8. Employment may be terminated at any time either with or without notice by the employer.

The base salary for the Patrol Supervisor position is $52,000 per year. Bonuses may be awarded only if funding is available within the Big City budget each year and if the outcome of the annual performance review justifies a financial award above the base salary. Evaluations are conducted annually in December to determine employee performance and bonus pay qualification.

The Patrol Supervisor position qualifies for medical, dental, educational, and retirement benefits that are currently offered by the Big City Police Department. However, these benefits are subject to change at any time.

All employment is governed by the *Big City Police Department Policy Manual* and the *Big City Municipal Personnel Policy Manual*. Access and familiarize yourself with these policies before April 1, 2013.

Please darken the appropriate circle below to either accept or to reject this tentative, conditional offer of employment. Indicate whether you accept or reject this tentative offer of conditional employment, and return the signed document to me at the address below on or before March 1, 2013. If the signed copy of this document is not received before March 1, 2013, then this tentative offer of conditional employment will be null and void and considered withdrawn.

○ YES I accept this tentative offer of conditional employment and will satisfy the conditions expressed herein.

○ NO I reject this tentative offer of conditional employment and will not satisfy the conditions expressed herein.

Ima Person Date	Yuar Aperson, Chief Date
P.O. Box 2929	Big City Police Department
Big City, MS 55555	P.O. Box 2013
	Big City, MS 55555

Figure 12.10 Sample employment offer letter.

Employment Termination Letters

The termination of employment is stressful for both supervisors and subordinate personnel. The reactions and responses to termination differ among individuals. Some folks may shed tears and become emotional, whereas others may seem relieved. Thus, it may either be a shock or be anticipated (Davis, 2008). The act of firing someone is not easy, and may be traumatic for both supervisors and personnel. Communicating to someone that they are no longer employed represents the culmination of much observation, documentation, and consideration through time.

Generally, personnel counseling may occur one or more times before the termination of employment occurs. The pivotal act of communicating that someone is released from duty is the peak of a methodical process. This process involves six basic steps: (1) progress reviews and discussions, (2) "pinpoint" reasoning and concern, (3) determination of "legal and ethical obligations," (4) risk assessment and evaluation, (5) provision of "notification and pretermination counseling," and (6) "establish disposition and note in record" (Davis, 2008). It is imperative that written documentation of personnel counseling occur throughout this process when supervisors meet with subordinates. Such written documentation eventually leads to the crafting of the termination letter.

February 3, 2013

Ima Person
P.O. Box 2929
Big City, MS 55555

Dear Officer Person,

Thank you for interviewing for the position of Patrol Supervisor with the Big City Police Department. We enjoyed the interview, and hope your visit was both interesting and informative.

Unfortunately, we are only able to select one candidate from among the many candidates that applied for the position. Therefore, we regret to inform you that you were not selected as the leading candidate for the position of Patrol Supervisor. We are currently unable to offer you employment with the Big City Police Department.

We wish you the best of successes with your future endeavors. Please be mindful of any future opportunities that may exist with our department. We encourage you to apply for future jobs with our department.

Thank you for your interest in the Big City Police Department.

Regards,

Yuar Aperson

Yuar Aperson, Chief
Big City Police Department
P.O. Box 2013
Big City, MS 55555

Figure 12.11 Sample rejection letter.

The termination letter must unequivocally express and communicate the finality of the termination decision. The contents of the termination letter must be concise, factual, and straightforward. Its contents may be used as talking points for the termination meeting with the employee that is being discharged from duty.

A termination letter expresses the cause for termination or it may express the effects of "economic conditions" that adversely affect the employing organization that necessitate termination (Twomey, 2010). Figure 12.12 shows an example of a termination letter.

Other Employment Communication

The discussions herein are limited to the introductory concepts of employment communication. Readers desiring discussions of greater depth and scope may consult texts in advanced communications, management, or organizational communication and behavior. Employment communication is useful for a variety of other topics and functions. Letters and orders may be crafted to inform personnel that they are assigned to specific duty details or training regimens. Annual performance reviews and periodic employee counseling sessions may be documented and retained among personnel files.

Employment communication may be used to verify and confirm the receipt of materials or the contents of verbal conversations. Employment communications may express the clauses, tenets, and conditions of legally binding agreements through written contracts. Employment communication may involve the announcement of the hiring of new police chiefs or the outcomes of sheriff's elections, through press releases and other news media. Employment communication may be used to establish a historical record of events that

February 11, 2014

Ima Person
P.O. Box 2929
Big City, MS 55555

Dear Officer Person,

Your employment with the Big City Police Department will be terminated effective on February 12, 2014. We have issued three previous warning letters which you acknowledged the receipt of via certified mail return receipt. We conducted three previous counseling sessions to discuss your work performance and improvement measures which resulted in the issuing of these warning letters. Copies of these warning letters were also provided to you personally during these counseling meetings.

Fulfilling the requirements of these improvement measures was a condition of continued employment with the Big City Police Department. There has been no acceptable improvement in your work performance. I must inform you that the quality of your work does not satisfy the standards described within the *Big City Police Department Policy Manual* and the *Big City Municipal Personnel Policy Manual* with respect to your position as Patrol Supervisor.

Please return all issued departmental resources to the Personnel Department. The Personnel Department will facilitate separation and discharges processes and procedures in accordance with departmental and municipal policies. Please contact the Personnel Department regarding any issues that you may have regarding separation and transition.

Regards,

Yuar Aperson

Yuar Aperson, Chief
Big City Police Department
P.O. Box 2013
Big City, MS 55555

Figure 12.12 Sample termination letter.

transpire throughout the course of organizational pursuits and endeavors from the perspective of personnel.

Employment communication affects the recruiting, hiring, training, retaining, and discharging of personnel. It also affects the attrition of the organization and the perceptions of employees. In some cases, it may also affect public perceptions of the organization. Regardless, employment communication inescapably permeates all organizations within the justice domain.

Commentary Regarding Employment Communication

All facets of the justice domain are affected by employment communication. At some point, interest must be expressed and communicated regarding any interest of an individual when attempting to obtain employment within the justice system. Personnel records are maintained regarding all employees within the justice system, including records of various communications that occur during their tenure as employees. In most cases, it is assumed that the contents of such communications are truthful and accurate, and not intended for any misguided purposes.

However, in some cases, purposeful untruthfulness may be interjected within employment communication. Instances of such deceitfulness permeate all professional and vocational domains, including the justice system. One instance includes the Lewiston, Minnesota, case of Chief Dave Kleinschmidt. During 2010, Kleinschmidt was fired from his position because of allegations that he "had a criminal record" and "lied about his previous employment" (Christensen, 2010). It was also determined that he "was found guilty in 2000 of filing a false police report" (Christensen, 2010). Sadly, such incidents permeate the justice domain at all levels of operation. Some examples of other incidents are itemized as follows:

Massachusetts Supreme Court overturns an arbitration award reinstating an officer that falsely arrested a citizen and repeatedly lied in his reports about the event. "A police officer who … shrouds his own misconduct in an extended web of lies and perjured testimony, corrodes the public's confidence in its police force." *City of Boston v. Boston Police Assn.*, #SJC-09297, 443 Mass. 813, 824 N.E.2d 855, 2005 Mass. Lexis 151". (AELE Law Enforcement Legal Center, 2013)

Appellate court in California concludes that an investigator was lawfully terminated for making false statements on a workers' compensation claim form and was dishonest with his supervisor. *Holmes v. Dist. Atty.*, 81 Cal.Rptr.2d 174, 1998 Cal. App. Lexis 1094. [1999 FP 40]. (AELE Law Enforcement Legal Center, 2013)

Whistleblower law did not protect a North Carolina state trooper who was fired for omitting information about the use of force by another officer in his initial report, and then reported it in an amended report. *Newberne v. Crime Control and Public Safety*, #COA03-530, 606 S.E.2d 742, 2005 N.C. App. Lexis 176 (2005). (AELE Law Enforcement Legal Center, 2013)

Appellate court affirms termination of NYPD officer who omitted, on his employment application, any mention of his military service and the use of an alias. *Angelopoulos v. N. Y. Civil Serv.* Cmsn., 574 N.Y.S.2d 44 (A.D. 1991). [1992 FP 133-4]. (AELE Law Enforcement Legal Center, 2013)

These instances show varied deceptions within the context of communication that occurs among a variety of activities within the justice system. These instances affect the law enforcement organization, the employees, and society. They are representative of imperfections that exist among communications within the justice domain. Public announcement of trusted officials who betrayed their fiduciary obligations of honesty may incite feelings of disappointment, resentment, and distrust within the general public, thereby affecting the relationships between justice system entities and their served publics. Dishonesty within employment communications may adversely influence both the internal and external perceptions of the justice system.

Imperfection within employment communication also involves a consideration of resource allocation and financing. When someone is dismissed for causes and reasons associated with dishonest employment communication, an organization must endure the financial costs of recruiting, selecting, investigating, and training replacement personnel. Such activities require different amounts of time and resources given the qualifications and availability of an applicant pool. Because of such attrition, personnel replacement, and diminished public perceptions, the ability of law enforcement organizations to fulfill their missions may be impeded.

Given these notions, employment communication may be perceived as a factor that affects mission readiness and public service. Hampering the communication process through dishonesty or any other method diminishes the ability of law enforcement organizations and the justice system to render public service, and influences relationships with the general public. Regardless of the best efforts to ensure the integrity of employment communications, human fallibility and imperfection will always be interjected within the communications processes of the justice domain.

Chapter Comments and Summary

This chapter presented discussions regarding employment communication. This emphasis encompassed primarily written and verbal employment forms of communication that influence the justice domain. One perspective of written communication involves the posting of summaries of federal laws among work environments. Examples include posters that describe the primary points of the OSHA, FLSA, and other acts of federal legislation. These posters must be clear and prominently displayed in work settings.

A different perspective of written communications involves the crafting of resumes and letters that are associated with seeking and obtaining employment. Resumes are written methods of advocating the accomplishments of individuals who are seeking employment. Resumes may be tailored to reflect the skills, experience, and qualifications of individuals that are commensurate with the requirements expressed within job advertisements. In most cases, a cover letter accompanies a resume and serves as an introductory statement through which the initial contact with an organization is achieved.

However, before resumes and cover letters can be transmitted to an organization, someone must know about the job opening. Therefore, the crafting of advertisements and job announcements represents another consideration of written communication within the justice domain. Job postings and announcements may be advertised and marketed in just about any print venue ranging from newspapers to trade magazines. The primary purposes of job announcements are to inform and to elicit responses from the reading audience.

After employment is secured, there are times when personnel must be discharged from service for a variety of reasons. In some cases, the organization may be downsizing and other cases may be related to personnel performance. Terminating personnel is never a pleasant task. However, it is common within the justice domain. A process exists through which termination occurs, and involves the written documentation of personnel counseling sessions and other pertinent activities that are associated with termination. The ultimate phase of the process results in the issuance of a termination letter and the discharging of personnel.

Although communication permeates the justice domain, it involves considerations of imperfection. There are times when individuals may purposefully lie about their credentials or experiences. They may provide false documentation among departmental reports. In some cases, the provision of incorrect or untruthful information may not be purposeful, but accidental. Regardless, employment communication is subject to the fallibilities of human nature.

Terminology

Advertisement
Application
Attention
Business card
Chronological resume
Competition

Concise
Cover letter
Employee Polygraph Protection Act
Employment posting
Fair Labor and Standards Act
Family and Medical Leave Act
First impression
Functional resume
Hiring manager
Interview questions
Hybrid resume
Illegal questions
Job interview
Job posting
Occupational Safety and Health Act
Offer letter
Organization
Preparation
Professionalism
Readability
Rejection letter
Resume
Reviewer
Scan
Succinct
Termination letter

THOUGHT AND DISCUSSION QUESTIONS

1. Employment communication encompasses a variety of functions within the justice domain. One of these functions involves attempts to gain employment by job applicants. Do some research, and examine a typical application for employment that may be available from your local law enforcement agency. Write a brief essay that describes the type of information that is communicated between the job applicant and the hiring organization.
2. Employment communication may involve some aspects of public interaction. Do some research, and determine how your local justice system or law enforcement organization leverages public awareness within the context of employment communication. On the basis of your findings, write a brief essay that highlights the effects of public announcements regarding law enforcement personnel issues.
3. This chapter briefly introduced court cases and federal legislation that involve employment communication. These topics affect employment communication within the justice system and among law enforcement organizations. Do some research, and find some additional court cases or federal legislation that influences employment communication within the justice domain. Write a brief essay that details your findings.

4. Employment communication may often involve some aspects of confidentiality and nondisclosure. Do some research, and locate some court cases that have addressed these issues within the context of the justice domain. Write a brief essay that summarizes your findings.

References

Advanced Etiquette. (2013). The etiquette of wearing a hat. Retrieved from http://www.advancedetiquette.com/blog/life/hat-etiquette/ (accessed July 29, 2013).

AELE Law Enforcement Legal Center. (2013). AELE law library of case summaries: Employment & labor law for public safety agencies. Retrieved from http://www.aele.org/law/Digests/empl226.html#Lying%20to%20superiors%20or%20internal%20affairs (accessed January 20, 2013).

Bovee, C., & Thill, J. (2012). *Business Communication Today* (11th ed., p. 532). Upper Saddle River, NJ: Pearson Prentice Hall Publishing.

Brounstein, M., Bell, A., Smith, D., Isbell, C., & Orr, A. (2010). *Business communication: Communicate effectively in any business environment*. Hoboken, NJ: John Wiley & Sons Publishing.

Business Management Daily. (2007). Can you prove that you posted FMLA notice 'conspicuously'? Retrieved from http://www.businessmanagementdaily.com/3444/can-you-prove-that-you-posted-fmla-notice-conspicuously (accessed January 20, 2013).

Cazenovia College. (2013). Types of resumes. Retrieved from http://www.cazenovia.edu/default.aspx?tabid=1375 (accessed January 19, 2013).

Chiagouris, L. (2010). *The secret to getting a job after college: Marketing tactics to turn degrees into dollars* (p. 57). New York: Brand New World Publishing.

Christensen, M. (2010). Lewiston police chief had criminal record. *Winona Daily News*. Retrieved from http://www.winonadailynews.com/news/local/crime-and-courts/article_04b2d3e6-2d94-11df-a164-001cc4c002e0.html (accessed January 20, 2013).

City of Broken Arrow. (2013). Employment opportunities. Retrieved from http://www.brokenarrowok.gov/Jobs.aspx?UniqueId=97&From=All&CommunityJobs=False&JobID=Police-Reserve-Officers-64 (accessed January 18, 2013).

Colaprete, F. (2012). *Pre-employment background investigations for public safety professionals* (p. 288). Boca Raton, FL: CRC Press.

Coon, D., Mitterer, J., Brown, P., Malik, R., & McKenzie, S. (2010). *Psychology: A journey* (p. 85). Toronto, Canada: Nelson Education.

Davis, D. (2008). *Terminating therapy: A professional guide to ending on a positive note* (p. 182). Hoboken, NJ: John Wiley & Sons Publishing.

Debasish, S., & Das, B. (2009). *Business communication* (p. 295). New Delhi, India: PHI Learning Private Limited.

Dillon, L. (2009). *You're only perfect twice—At birth and on your resume: The insider's guide on changing jobs (A career survival book)* (p. 66). Durham, CT: Strategic Book Publishing.

Dlabay, L., Burrow, J., & Kleindl, B. (2009). *Intro to business* (7th ed., p. 222). Mason, OH: South-Western Cengage Publishing.

Everett, M. (2007). *Making a living while making a difference: Conscious careers for an era of interdependence* (p. 165). Gabriola Island, Canada: New Society Publishers.

Field, S. (n.d.). Fired quotes. Brainyquote.com. Retrieved from http://www.brainyquote.com/quotes/keywords/fired.html (accessed December 30, 2012).

Hayes, D., & Ninemeier, J. (2009). *Human resources management in the hospitality industry* (p. 128). Hoboken, NJ: John Wiley & Sons Publishing.

Lehman, C., & Dufrene, D. (2011). *Business communication* (16th ed.). Mason, OH: South-Western Cengage Publishing.

Maass, D. (2012). Wiretap translators allege DEA administered illegal polygraphs. *San Diego City Beat.* Retrieved from http://www.sdcitybeat.com/sandiego/blog-777-wiretap-translators-allege-dea-administered-illegal-polygraphs.html (accessed January 20, 2013).

Merriam-Webster Dictionary. (2013). s.v. "resume." Retrieved from http://www.merriam-webster.com/dictionary/resume (accessed January 19, 2013).

Narayan, B. (1999). *Communication management.* New Delhi, India: A.P.H. Publishing Corporation.

Ober, S. (2008). *Fundamentals of contemporary business communication* (p. 324). Boston: Houghton-Mifflin Publishing.

Pfeiffer, W. (1993). *Technical writing* (5th ed.). Upper Saddle River, NJ: Prentice-Hall Publishing.

Rodriques, M. (2003). *Effective business communication.* New Delhi, India: Concept Publishing Company.

Sethi, A., & Adhikari, B. (2010). *Business communication* (p. 150). New Delhi, India: Tata McGraw-Hill Publishing.

Silverglate, S., & Salner, C. (2011). Smartphones and the Fair Labor Standards Act. *For the Defense, 2011*(June).

Statsky, W. (2009). *Introduction to paralegalism: Perspectives, problems, and skills* (7th ed., p. 81). Clifton Park, NY: Delmar Cengage Publishing.

Twomey, D. (2010). *Labor and employment law: Text and cases* (14th ed., p. 465). Mason, OH: South-Western Cengage Publishing.

U.S. Department of Labor. (2013a). Employee Polygraph Protection Act (EPAA) poster. Retrieved from http://www.dol.gov/whd/regs/compliance/posters/eppa.htm#.UPjpgWffQbQ (accessed January 18, 2013).

U.S. Department of Labor. (2013b). Fair Labor and Standards Act. Retrieved from http://www.dol.gov/compliance/guide/minwage.htm (accessed January 18, 2013).

U.S. Department of Labor. (2013c). Family and Medical Leave Act (FMLA) poster. Retrieved from http://www.dol.gov/whd/regs/compliance/posters/fmla.htm#.UPjk22ffQbQ (accessed January 18, 2013).

U.S. Department of Labor. (2013d). Health benefits, retirement standards, and workers' compensation: Family and medical leave. Retrieved from http://www.dol.gov/compliance/guide/fmla.htm#RRN (accessed January 19, 2013).

U.S. Department of Labor. (2013e). Migrant and Seasonal Agricultural Worker Protection Act (MSPA) poster English/Spanish version. Retrieved from http://www.dol.gov/whd/regs/compliance/posters/mspaensp.htm#.UPjcy2ffQbQ (accessed January 17, 2013).

U.S. Department of Labor. (2013f). OSHA's free workplace poster. Retrieved from http://www.osha.gov/Publications/poster.html (accessed January 18, 2013).

U.S. Department of Labor. (2013g). Other workplace standards: Lie detector tests. Retrieved from http://www.dol.gov/compliance/guide/eppa.htm (accessed January 19, 2013).

U.S. Department of Labor. (2013h). Safety and health standards: Occupational safety and health. Retrieved from http://www.dol.gov/compliance/guide/osha.htm#who (accessed January 19, 2013).

U.S. Department of Labor. (2013i). Wage and hour division. Retrieved from http://www.dol.gov/whd/regs/compliance/posters/flsa.htm#.UPjUP2ffQbQ (accessed January 17, 2013).

U.S. Department of Labor. (2013j). Wages and hours worked: Worker protections in agriculture. Retrieved from http://www.dol.gov/compliance/guide/mspa.htm#RRN (accessed January 17, 2013).

Walker, R. (2011). *Strategic management communication for leaders* (2nd ed., p. 206). Mason, OH: South-Western Cengage Publishing.

Walter, L. (2009). OSHA orders southern air to withdraw lawsuit and pay $7.9 million to whistle-blowers. *EHS Today.* Retrieved from http://ehstoday.com/standards/news/osha-southern-lawsuit-pay-6734 (accessed January 20, 2013).

Leading the Way
Leadership Communication

13

There is a time to take counsel of your fears, and there is a time to never listen to any fear.
—General George S. Patton (Patton, n.d.)

Objectives

The objectives of this chapter are to

- Define the concept of leadership
- Discuss the relationship between communication and leadership
- Describe leadership styles
- Describe leadership techniques
- Describe communication styles
- Describe communication techniques

Introduction

Leadership represents both a "process" and a "property" (Griffin & Moorhead, 2012). The former perspective considers leadership as the "use of noncoercive influence to direct and coordinate the activities of group members to meet a goal" (Griffin & Moorhead, 2012). The latter perspective considers leadership as the array of "characteristics attributed to those who are perceived to use such influence successfully" (Griffin & Moorhead, 2012). Leadership may be considered from a process perspective. This perspective defines leadership as "the process of providing general direction and influencing individuals or groups to achieve goals" (Hitt, Miller, & Colella, 2009, p. 257). In any case, leadership involves a capacity to motivate and influence the behaviors of others toward the achievement of some desired outcome. Within organizations, leaders are those individuals who are "fitted by force of ideas, character, or genius or by strength of will or administrative ability to arouse, incite, and direct individuals in conduct and achievement" (Benton, 2005).

Effective and efficient leadership necessitates a strong capacity to communicate with others. Throughout history, many leaders have inspired and motivated others to pursue and accomplish a myriad of goals and objectives with respect to some aspect of visionary foresight. Leaders may affect only the life of a single individual or they may influence the existence and future of a nation. Through their words, writing, behavior, and physical cues, leaders affect others toward the achievement of some purpose. These same attributes of communication are used to praise others or to modify their behaviors, to provide critical analysis or to suggest new ideas, and to facilitate a mutual understanding of many different messages.

Leadership represents one of the strongest examined, but poorest understood, aspects of social interaction and phenomena (Bennis & Nanus, 1985). Commensurate with the dichotomy of communication, leadership is both an art and a science. It represents an art because it cannot be necessarily learned from books, and is honed through the experiences of time (Daft, 2008a, p. 25). It also involves a qualitative consideration of the intangible facets of humanity ranging from integrity to influence. Leadership is also a science because it may be quantitatively examined from the perspective of processes and "organizational goals" (Daft, 2008a, p. 25). One can consider the effectiveness of leadership with respect to whether the quantitative objectives of an organization were attained through time.

The successfulness of any organization is influenced by the successes and failures of its leadership through time. This same notion also is applicable to the successes of the "majority of nations" (Ghuman & Aswathappa, 2010). Organizations are no better than the people that comprise their ranks and components. Therefore, leaders must "set an example" through their actions, both tangibly and intangibly, to generate effectiveness in leadership and to influence others (Ghuman & Aswathappa, 2010). From the perspective of communication, effective leaders tend to "build commitment by affirming and communicating shared values that all can embrace and engaging others in achieving common goals" (Kouzes & Posner, 2011). Through such actions and the setting of examples, leaders contribute strategically toward the success of their respective organizations.

When one is influencing an organization, a group, or an individual, communication permeates every aspect of leadership. The leaders of law enforcement organizations often give speeches and participate in news or press releases to communicate various facets of their organizations. These leaders may also set an example that visibly communicates messages to their subordinates, peers, and colleagues. For instance, a sheriff or police chief may refrain from ingesting alcoholic beverages during duty hours, and visibly work extra hours to complete complex tasks. Judges may verbally reprimand someone within a courtroom forcefully or may exhibit a gentle demeanor when influencing others. Regardless of the situation, personnel within the justice system and among law enforcement organizations must acknowledge the scope and magnitude of communication within the context of leadership.

Leadership Theories and Paradigms

Leadership has been the subject of many different research studies throughout history. Many theories of leadership have emerged ranging from foundations of transforming organizations to the characteristics that are shared among individuals that exhibited strong leadership. Some theories involve the contrasting of the characteristics of leaders versus followers, whereas others involve facets of human behavior as a baseline principle. Regardless of the theoretical paradigm that is used to describe and model leadership, communication is an important aspect of leadership that must neither be ignored nor discounted. The succeeding sections provide an overview of leadership theories and paradigms that have emerged through time.

Great Man Theory

The great man theory emerged during the middle of the 1800s. Its basic premise is relatively easy to conceptualize and to understand: great leaders are born, not made. Essentially, this notion posits that leaders are destined to be born, and shall rise to meet the challenges of various situations through time. Thomas Carlyle, who in 1840 authored *On Heroes, Hero-Worship, and the Heroic in History*, advocated this simple premise. Within his writing, Carlyle expressed the following notions (Carlyle, 1840):

> For, as I take it, Universal History, the history of what man has accomplished in this world, is at bottom the History of the Great Men who have worked here. They were the leaders of men, these great ones; the modellers, patterns, and in a wide sense creators, of whatsoever the general mass of men contrived to do or to attain; all things that we see standing accomplished in the world are properly the outer material result, the practical realization and embodiment, of Thoughts that dwelt in the Great Men sent into the world: the soul of the whole world's history, it may justly be considered, were the history of these. (Carlyle, 1840)

Carlyle also described various facets of individuals who exhibited leadership in a variety of situations. His analysis and commentary examined both real and mythological figures, including Odin, Mahomet, Dante, Napoleon, Martin Luther, John Knox, Robert Burns, Jean-Jacques Rousseau, Samuel Johnson, and Oliver Cromwell (Carlyle, 1840). Carlyle summarized his observations of such leaders as follows (Carlyle, 1840):

> ...Great Men, taken up in any way, are profitable company. We cannot look, however imperfectly, upon a great man, without gaining something by him. He is the living light-fountain, which it is good and pleasant to be near. The light which enlightens, which has enlightened the darkness of the world; and this not as a kindled lamp only, but rather as a natural luminary shining by the gift of Heaven; a flowing light-fountain, as I say, of native original insight, of manhood and heroic nobleness;—in whose radiance all souls feel that it is well with them. (Carlyle, 1840)

These excerpts from Carlyle's writings provided a foundational basis for establishing the great man theory. The individuals who he examined certainly influenced human history, and each demonstrated various communicative potentials within the context of leadership. Napoleon used rudimentary semaphore communication systems to maintain contact between his field operations and Paris, France, even from distances "as far away as Russia" (Kassimeris & Buckley, 2010). Martin Luther, with the authoring and posting of his *Ninety-Five Theses*, became "much the mightiest spirit" that influenced both the "course and destiny" of the Reformation (Croll, 1884). The writings of Jean-Jacques Rousseau, including *On the Social Contract* and *Discourse on the Origin of Inequality*, continue to affect modern economic and political thought (Conklin, 1991). These individuals undoubtedly affected the course of human history. Although they each contributed vastly different achievements to history, they all leveraged communication and leadership strategically throughout their lifetimes.

Trait Theory

The trait theory arose during the 1930s, and involved the notion that "people are either born or are made with certain qualities that will make them excel in leadership roles" (Leadershipcentral.com, 2013). This theory indicates that people "possess certain physical or psychological" attributes that make them outstanding with respect to leadership potential (Kliem, 2004). Examples of these characteristics include physical prowess, height, or intelligence (Kliem, 2004). However, no empirical, scientific evidence exists to definitively support the trait theory; instead, many conflicting research studies exist (Montana & Charnov, 2008).

The trait theory represents an overgeneralization of leadership, and exhibits various shortcomings (Kansal & Rao, 2006). Examples include the following:

- Modes of thinking that are necessary for "effective and successful leadership" are not functions simply of traits; instead, leadership exhibits situational characteristics (Kansal & Rao, 2006, p. 237).
- Leaders are not born; instead, they may be made, "through training" (Kansal & Rao, 2006, p. 237).
- No specific traits have been identified that are absolutely necessary for exhibiting the attributes of "successful and effective leadership" (Kansal & Rao, 2006, p. 237).

Considerations of anxiety and argumentativeness show the difficulty of establishing definitively the basic premise of the trait theory. The trait theory has often been examined from the perspective of communication. Most notably, various research studies have approached this paradigm from the perspectives of speech anxiety and argumentativeness. Although some speech anxiety may be deemed normal, any amount of pathological speech anxiety is deemed as abnormal (Littlejohn & Foss, 2008). Such abnormality may spawn a range of personal issues, including an avoidance of communication that may inhibit any "productive and satisfying participation in society" (Littlejohn & Foss, 2008). Furthermore, such anxiety also produces physiological effects, such as changes in "heart rates" and causes "blushing" (Littlejohn & Foss, 2008). Such characteristics are incommensurate with the basic attributes of effective communicators.

Argumentativeness represents a "tendency to engage in conversations about controversial topics, to support your own point of view, and to refute opposing beliefs" (Littlejohn & Foss, 2008). Some potential associations between argumentativeness and leadership represent "logically firm" correlations (Mattina, 2009). Argumentativeness is deemed to be a positive trait within the context of effective communication (Swift, 2008). Although argumentativeness may be desirable in some cases, no guarantees exist that anyone possessing an argumentative demeanor has the capacity of being a good leader or is a good leader.

The basic premise of the trait theory eventually became disfavored as new theories and paradigms of leadership emerged through time. Despite the lack of a scientific foundation to support this paradigm of leadership, investigations of leadership traits have continued through the years. Over time, it was determined that leaders do possess different characteristics from others, and that such traits may be learned through training or experience (Hitt, Miller, & Colella, 2009). Most leaders possess the following traits: drive, motivation, integrity, self-confidence, cognitive ability, and domain knowledge (Hitt, Miller, & Colella, 2009).

Each of these traits may be considered from the perspective of communication. Drive considers the visionary aspects of leadership, and the attributes that contribute toward the crafting, expressing, and pursuing of vision. One example of leadership drive involves initiative (Hitt, Miller, & Colella, 2009). Assertive communicators take the initiative to "make constructive suggestions rather than attributing blame," possess self-confidence that is essential for "making proposals," tend to "actively solicit the opinions of others in order to try to accommodate them," and "actively listen to others" (Holding, 2012).

Motivation is certainly within the realm of communication. Through communication, leaders "motivate people to follow them" through words, actions, and mannerisms (Sciarra & Dorsey, 2002). Motivation through communication may be leveraged for the benefit of organizations and their personnel (Sciarra & Dorsey, 2002). Through communicating effectively and efficiently, leaders "can motivate an employee" to "work unusually hard" toward the reaping of "great rewards" in due time (Sciarra & Dorsey, 2002).

Integrity is an integral aspect of communication, especially within the justice domain. Among law enforcement organizations, the "integrity-enhancing objectives" of the organization include the ability of clearly communicating to personnel "the rules of conduct" that govern the organization (Klockars, Ivkovic, & Haberfeld, 2006). Reminders of acceptable and unacceptable conduct may be voiced during meetings or posted on bulletin boards. They may be contained within policy documents and employee handbooks. Additionally, they may be reinforced through continuing education and during annual performance reviews.

Self-confidence is essential for communicating efficiently and effectively. Individuals who lack self-confidence may be unable to "impress the message on the listener" when communicating (Rodriques, 2000). The receivers of messages may also be considered from the perspective of self-confidence. Individuals who have moderate levels of self-confidence tend to be more persuadable (Tyagi & Kumar, 2004). Therefore, communicators should assess the characteristics of their intended receiver(s) and leverage them for guiding "message and media development" (Tyagi & Kumar, 2004).

Understanding the subject matter embellishes the ability of individuals to convey and exchange information when communicating with respect to the successful accomplishment of mutual understandings between the senders and the receivers of messages. A primary example involves the researching, developing, and testing of technologies that are used within law enforcement settings (e.g., database systems or radio systems). When determining the specific needs and requirements of the users of such technologies, "both communication skills and industry domain knowledge" are relevant factors of "eliciting user requirements" (Tsui & Karam, 2011).

Although the basic premise of the trait theory is unfounded because no empirical evidence exists to support the notion that specific, human characteristics are innate toward the generation of leaders through time, there are certain traits that are exhibited by those who have become leaders. Leaders do possess various attributes that may not necessarily be possessed by others. Leaders are self-confident, truthful individuals who have a good knowledge of their respective subjects, and can communicate efficiently and effectively with others to motivate them toward fulfilling some goal or objective strategically. Despite such leadership characteristics, the trait theory failed to "account for behaviors in different types of situations" that necessitate different behaviors of leaders (Krumm, 2001). This shortcoming of the trait theory provided an opportunity for researchers to devote their attention to a different aspect of leadership—namely, the behavioral characteristics of leadership.

Behavioral Theory

The behavioral theory emerged during the 1940s and 1950s. Instead of focusing on physical or mental traits, it emphasized the characteristics of leadership behavior. This theory represents a drastic departure from the great man theory and the trait theory. Instead of suggesting that leaders are destined to be born in due time (i.e., great man theory) or that certain traits form a basis of leadership (i.e., trait theory), the primary premise of the behavioral theory introduced the notion that leaders are made, not born. Essentially, the behavioral theory focused on individuals instead of tasks, and emphasized the notion that "leadership can be studied and learned" (Bertocci, 2009).

Two research endeavors investigated the effectiveness of leadership with respect to the characteristics of individuals. One study was performed by the Ohio State University (OSU) and the other was performed by the University of Michigan (UM). These studies emphasized investigations of leadership style. Conceptually, leadership style represents the "combination of traits, skills, and behaviors" that is exercised by leaders when they "interact with followers" (Lussier & Achua, 2010, p. 70). Although a basis of both skills and traits is accommodated within this paradigm, behavior is the primary consideration because leaders are characterized by "relatively consistent" behavioral patterns (Lussier & Achua, 2010, p. 70).

The OSU research investigated how leadership behavior affected "work, group performance, and satisfaction" (Scutchfield & Keck, 2003). Two behavioral facets of leadership were identified from this research: consideration and initiating structure (Scutchfield & Keck, 2003). Consideration represented the extensiveness of exhibiting managerial concern for others (Scutchfield & Keck, 2003). It emphasized the significance of "job satisfaction," the expression of appreciativeness, and whether subordinates were involved in "major decisions" (Scutchfield & Keck, 2003). Initiating structure represented the extensiveness of defining and organizing work, and the extensiveness of devoting attention to "accomplishing objectives established by the manager" (Scutchfield & Keck, 2003). These two facets of leadership integrated to yield four categories of leadership styles. Figure 13.1 shows these relationships.

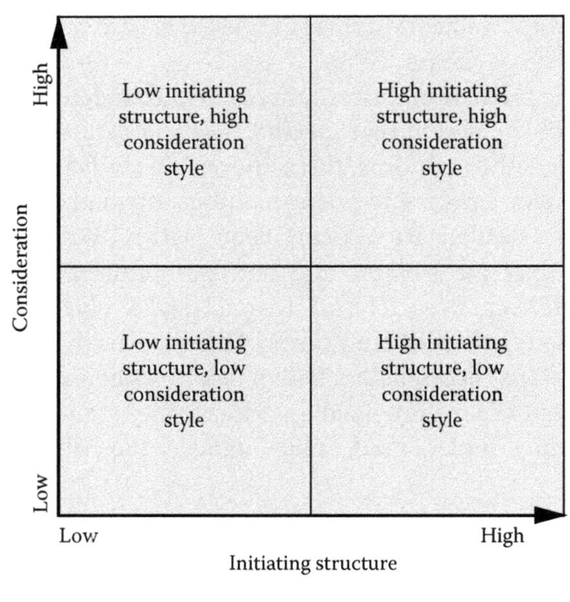

Figure 13.1 Leadership style. (From Scutchfield, D., & Keck, W. (2003). *Principles of public health practice* (2nd ed.). Clifton Park, NY: Thomson Delmar Learning, p. 147, Figure 9.6.)

The UM research examined the effectiveness of leadership from two perspectives: production-oriented and employee-oriented leaders (Callaway, 2006). The group representing production orientation expressed stringent standards for work, meticulously organized tasks, and "prescribed the work methods to be followed" (Saxena & Awasthi, 2010). The employee-oriented group advocated the participation of subordinate personnel when setting goals and in rendering "work decisions" (Saxena & Awasthi, 2010). Fostering respect and trust mutually also contributed to "high performance" (Saxena & Awasthi, 2010). Basically, this study showed that leadership effectiveness is highlighted by strong relationships with others and "high productivity" (Saxena & Awasthi, 2010).

These notions of the behavioral theory may be considered within the context of the justice domain. The problems associated with underage drinking often incorporate facets of the behavioral theory and communication strategically to diminish the potential impacts and incidents of underage drinking. Alcohol is the "most commonly used and abused drug among youth" within the United States, and it contributes to approximately 4700 deaths annually among minors (Centers for Disease Control, 2012). Despite the illegality of alcohol for anyone under the age of twenty-one years, the minor age group of twelve to twenty years represents approximately 11% of all alcohol consumption within the United States (Centers for Disease Control, 2012). During 2011, a thirty-day research study of high school youth revealed the following statistics (Centers for Disease Control, 2012):

- Thirty-nine percent drank some amount of alcohol
- Twenty-two percent binge drank
- Eight percent drove after drinking alcohol
- Twenty-four percent rode with a driver who had been drinking alcohol

The consumption and abuse of alcohol by minors is problematic and contributes to a greater risk of homicide and suicide, as well as the disruption of human development and growth (Centers for Disease Control, 2012). Developing strategic programs to diminish the use of alcohol by minors involves considerations of both the behavioral theory and communication (National Institute on Alcohol Abuse and Alcoholism, 2013). School strategies may incorporate various role-playing scenarios and discussions through which communicating effectively and efficiently contributes toward "successful criteria" (National Institute on Alcohol Abuse and Alcoholism, 2013). Within extracurricular strategies, the involvement of youth when "planning and implementing" various alternative courses of actions may improve participation rates (National Institute on Alcohol Abuse and Alcoholism, 2013). From the perspective of family strategies, relationships between parents and minors may be strengthened and embellished by communicating using "positive reinforcement" and "listening" (National Institute on Alcohol Abuse and Alcoholism, 2013).

The behavioral theory and communication have a wide scope of applications within the justice domain. One of the most obvious applications involves the leading and directing of law enforcement agencies strategically. Similarly, such notions are applicable to any type of organization within the justice domain, ranging from the leadership of correctional facilities and prisons to private security agencies. Within any organization, through the tenets of the behavioral theory, leaders and their communication skills may be developed and refined through training and experience.

Contingency Theory

The 1960s demonstrated the emergence of the contingency theory, which expresses the notion that there is no absolute, solitary best method or style of leadership. This notion contrasts with the trait theory and the behavioral theory that both sought to express a universal form of leadership. Instead, the contingency theory indicates that numerous forms of leadership styles may be exhibited depending on the circumstances of different situations. These different leadership styles may also be exhibited according to the nature of the followers. Essentially, the contingency theory represents a form of "leader-match theory" in which leaders are paired with "appropriate situations" (Northouse, 2010). Therefore, the effectiveness of leadership is viewed as being contingent upon "matching" leadership style with the "right setting" (Northouse, 2010). Within this approach, leadership style effectiveness is gauged by "the relationship between the characteristics of the leader, the followers, and the situation" (Gill, 2006). Essentially, synergy must be present regarding this combination of variables to produce effective leadership. If any one item is missing, then the "leadership process" is aborted (Manning & Curtis, 2003, p. 23).

The contingency theory may be considered from the perspective of leading police organizations. Within the United States, the contingency theory represents the "dominant theory" that is exercised to explore the "practices, behaviors, and structures of police organizations" (Archbold, 2013). Law enforcement entities often may necessitate alterations in the ways through which they conduct business, and may change their "goals in response to task environment" (Archbold, 2013). The structuring of law enforcement organizations also occurs with respect to the maximization of efficiency regarding specific endeavors (e.g., controlling crime) (Archbold, 2013). Therefore, the law enforcement organization adapts itself according to the circumstances of contingency.

Regardless of the mission, specific endeavor, or function of a law enforcement organization, communication permeates its personnel and components. Within the contingency theory, "all types of communication and feedback" are deemed to be essential organizational characteristics for crafting, developing, and maintaining the culture of the organization (Hamilton, 2011, p. 53). Organizational leaders may be "trained" to recognize and to adapt situational characteristics to fit their respective styles of leadership and communication (Hamilton, 2011, p. 52). Through such considerations of adaptive communication, the contingency theory represents a method of accommodating and dealing with uncertainties that may arise within the domains that are experienced by law enforcement organizations. Accomplishing this goal often necessitates the crafting, developing, and implementing of "internal lateral communication networks to cope with environmental uncertainty" (Jablin & Putnam, 2001).

Law enforcement organizations and their personnel are classified as first-responder entities during emergency situations. The dynamics of emergencies produce consistently and continuously changing situations to which personnel must adapt when deployed. Therefore, law enforcement personnel often participate in a variety of crisis communication efforts. Because of the dynamics associated with emergencies, the contingency theory is applicable regarding the communication methods and resources that are necessitated during emergencies (Coombs & Holladay, 2012). Facets of the contingency theory may vary with respect to "relevance" and use for "different public relations phenomena" (Coombs & Holladay, 2012).

Law enforcement organizations and their personnel grapple with change each day, thereby generating myriads of different situations that necessitate communication. Every service call is different, and has its own unique dynamics and characteristics. Service calls may be as simple as a pedestrian asking for directions or may be as complex as providing public leadership during responses to natural disasters. The specifics of communicating are different within these situations. However, in each different case, communication is necessary for accomplishing the changing goals of the law enforcement organization regarding each specific incident. Through the contingency theory, law enforcement personnel and organizations have a paradigm through which they may adapt to the dynamics of change.

Transactional Theory

The transactional theory arose during the 1970s. The transactional theory superseded theories involving situational leadership because they were viewed as being one-way expressions of the leadership in which leaders affected their respective followers but were not themselves affected by these same followers (Roeckelein, 1998). A primary purpose of this paradigm is to "maintain the stability within an organization through regular economic and social exchanges that achieve specific goals for both the leaders and their followers" (Lussier & Achua, 2010, p. 348). The transactional theory represents the notion of some form of exchange (i.e., transaction) of value between leaders and subordinates that highlights some type of mutual benefit between these parties. This exchange represents something "tangible," such as the exchanging of salary for production (Stroup, 2004, p. 11).

The notions of both rewards and punitive measures are affiliated with the transactional theory. Essentially, organizational leaders may offer to their followers some type of reward "in exchange for their desired efforts," and followers may attempt to procure the offered award (Foster, Goertzen, Nollette, & Nollette, 2013, p. 85). Within this paradigm, followers are deemed essential partners within the leadership relationship "because they are significantly involved in the negotiations" that are associated with the exchange or transaction (Rost, 1993). Similarly, the transactional theory also has punitive aspects (Riaz & Haider, 2010). If followers fail to accomplish tasks, goals, or objectives, then a variety of punitive measures may result from unsuccessful performance or compliance failures (Riaz & Haider, 2010). These aspects of rewards and punitive measures show that the transactional theory is strongly defined by exchanges—both positive and negative—between leaders and followers.

The transactional theory involves a consideration of communication. From the perspective of leadership, the transactional theory is synonymous with exchange approaches of communication (Wolvin, 2005). It also represents a form of dialogic communication involving exchanges of information between the senders and the receivers of messages within the communications process (Thomlinson, 2013). It facilitates a strong foundation of interpersonal relationships through exhibiting "genuine concern" when communicating (Thomlinson, 2013). Such communication is "characterized by trust, openness, spontaneity, caring, sensitivity, sincerity, and empathy" (Thomlinson, 2013).

These notions may be considered from the perspective of the justice domain. The leaders of law enforcement organizations may use annual performance reviews of their subordinates as methods of evaluating personnel performance through a specific period of time. Communication may occur as a method of facilitating negotiations between supervisors and subordinates during performance reviews regarding the negotiating of rewards and punitive measures (Benoliel, 2011). During annual performance reviews, supervisors and their subordinates may discuss openly the considered goals and objectives that are realistic and attainable, and any facets of mutual benefit for both the organization and law enforcement officer. Consensus may be achieved both verbally and expressed in writing regarding the outcome of performance review negotiations.

Transformational Theory

The transformational theory also emerged during the late 1970s and throughout the 1980s. Although this paradigm emerged during the late 1970s, many instantiations of contemporary leadership appear to be transformational (Burke & Friedman, 2011). A primary purpose of the transformational theory is to "change the status quo by articulating to followers the problems in the current system and a compelling vision of what a new organization could be" (Lussier & Achua, 2010, p. 348). Within transactional leadership, synergy and integration exist between leaders and followers toward the generation of "unity" and a "collective purpose" among organizations (Barker, 1992). Through transformational leadership, the relationships among people both empower and inspire them to have a sense of organizational commitment (Kelly, 2012). After its introduction in the 1970s, the transformational approach gained much interest during the 1980s and thereafter. It represents "the most widely researched form of leadership from the 1980s to 2011" (Coggins, 2013).

A fiduciary relationship exists between leaders and followers. This paradigm judges the effectiveness of leaders by determining whether the desired "social change" is accomplished that fulfills the motivations and needs of both leaders and followers (Coggins, 2013). Followers may experience change through experiencing periods of transformational leadership. Through time, as their needs are satisfied and as their "new needs, aspirations, and values emerge," they may "become leaders" as they mature personally and professionally (Coggins, 2013). Within the U.S. Army, the presence of transformational leadership is "is not designed merely to take soldiers from point A to point B, but to have produced an improved soldier in the course of the journey" (Stroup, 2004, p. 12).

Transformational leadership may be considered from the perspective of communication. Among small organizations that implement the transformational paradigm, effective communications may be achieved via engaging in various internal communications (Martinez, 2012). Transformational communication is characterized by the use of logical reasoning and argumentation, especially logos (Hunter, 2010). Communication within this paradigm also exhibits the Jungian characteristics of "thinking, sensing, intuiting, and feeling" (Sen, 2007). It also involves considerations of "empathic listening," "authentic expression," and an "unconditional acceptance of self and others" (Institute for Transformational Communication, 2013).

Transformational communication and leadership are pertinent aspects of the justice domain. From the perspective of mental health hearings, judicial reviews, involving dialogues between judges and defendants, incorporate some goals and facets of "change-oriented communication" (Kirkman, 2013). The dialogues among such hearings should exhibit "a functional, therapeutic, and persuasive framework so that the interaction between defendant and judge may be utilized constructively" (Kirkman, 2013). This communication involves "therapeutic interviewing, including solution-focused, language expectancy, motivational dialogues as well as transformational communication principles" (Kirkman, 2013). In such instances, the court system becomes a medium through which individuals are benefitted through the determination of solutions that actively incorporate effective communication between chancellors and their affected individuals.

Transformational communication and leadership may both be viewed as just that—transformational. The transformational paradigm is used by leaders to incite change through time organizationally and among personnel. Transformational leaders must be approachable, and open to the ideas, suggestions, and views of their subordinates toward the overall good of the organization. Transformational leaders must also be cognizant of the value of people within their ranks. Individual people are the building blocks of any organization, including the justice system and law enforcement organizations. By changing the characteristics of people (e.g., attitudes, beliefs, and credentials), organizations may change through time. Through such change, transformational leaders are better able to guide and direct organizations toward the fulfillment of their visions.

Participative Theory

The late 1960s and early 1970s exhibited the seeding of the participative theory by researchers Rensis Likert and Gary Yukl (Coggins, 2013). Since then until the current time, various and sundry researchers have explored this concept (Coggins, 2013). The participative theory represents the notion that better decisions are made within organizations by the mutual contributions of many within the decision process instead of rendering decisions according to the leeway of only one individual. Leaders invite the participation, comments, and feedback of other people when enacting the decision process. Examples of folks that may be incorporated within the participative regimen include stakeholders, subordinates, colleagues, peers, disaffected and neutral individuals, and superiors within the chain of command. Within this model, leaders may be free to accommodate a variety of sources of information regarding decisions, and may solicit feedback from a variety of individuals who the leader believes may have some bearing and influence regarding the rendering of a decision. The participative paradigm represents, in some aspects, a form of decentralization of decision authority organizationally.

This leadership paradigm may have various communications implications for organizations. Personnel may be more amenable to decisions that were rendered with respect to their inputs and feedbacks within the decision process, thereby showing that some consensus was achieved in which they actively participated and had some voice (Anderson, 2013). Personnel that have some opportunity to sound their thoughts may have a sense of ownership within the decision process. They may also have a sense of personal liability regarding the success of the organization through time (Anderson, 2013). These factors may have a positive bearing regarding the morale of the organization (Anderson, 2013).

Because leaders receive a variety of different forms and types of feedback from those involved within the participative paradigm, innovation and creativity may be embellished within the organization and among its personnel. Every individual is unique, and has different perceptions of the decision domain. The opinions, thoughts, and perspectives of one person may either be similar to or vastly different from those of others within the decision process. Some characteristics of the decision domain that may seem blatantly obvious to one person may be completely unobvious to someone else. In some cases, aspects of the decision domain may be conspicuous and observable by many individuals, but may be interpreted differently among individuals. Therefore, the participative model facilitates robustness within the decision domain.

Another aspect of the participative paradigm involves maintaining organizational personnel. Among some organizations, attrition exists for a variety of reasons ranging from salary dissatisfaction to a sense that the organization is uncaring and indifferent. Because of many reasons, personnel may choose to depart the organization. Thus, attrition exists among organizations. Through the participative model, leaders may attempt to quash various instances of attrition. By having a stake in the decision process and achieving a sense of consensus, personnel may "buy into" the beliefs of the organization and its approach to the decision domain (Borkowski, 2011). Therefore, personnel embellish their sense of organizational commitment that may alleviate instances of attrition and improve employee retention.

The notions of participative leadership and participative communication are foreign to many law enforcement organizations when communicating toward the rendering of organizational decisions. However, some law enforcement organizations do embrace the participative model in varying degrees and amounts. For instance, the Broken Arrow Police Department (BAPD) developed a "leadership team" whose membership consisted of the "police union, management, and most of the divisions, units, ranks, and functions in the department" (Dempsey & Forst, 2011). This Oklahoma law enforcement organization exhibited the capacity to render its decisions "democratically" involving "team interactions and communication" (Dempsey & Forst, 2011). Through using the participative model, the BAPD incorporates numerous perspectives, which may differ significantly, within the overall process of rendering decisions. Regardless, the decision domain becomes more robust and considers a greater variety of discussions that would be associated, in some cases, within traditional management environments of law enforcement organizations.

Charismatic Theory

Charisma is defined as "a personal magic of leadership arousing special popular loyalty or enthusiasm for a public figure (as a political leader)" or as "a special magnetic charm or appeal" (*Merriam-Webster*, 2013a). The charismatic theory emerged during the 1980s (Erasmus & Schneck, 2008). Its premise involves a notion that charisma may influence leadership. Within this paradigm, charismatic leaders often integrate various portions of the behavioral theory and the trait theory to profoundly affect and influence others (Foster et al., 2013, p. 52). The influence of this approach is generally "outside of formal authority," and involves various perceptions of "divine inspiration" that may be associated with leaders (Foster et al., 2013, p. 52). Essentially, followers attribute characteristics of heroics toward leaders (Buddhapriya, 1999).

Throughout history, numerous individuals were said to have charisma that influenced their leadership. Examples include Theodore Roosevelt, John F. Kennedy, Winston Churchill, and Ronald Reagan. Such charismatics leaders often possess and demonstrate an ability to exude self-confidence and conceptualize vision. They are able to communicate their conceptualized vision to others, including subordinates. They are firm in their beliefs and resolve to pursue their respective visions. Charismatic leaders influence and motivate others naturally regardless of chaos that may exist within their respective environments (Mauk, 2010). They are also facilitators of change among organizations (Mauk, 2010).

From the perspectives of followers and subordinates, three phases exist within this paradigm: assessing the environment and establishing vision, influencing and motivating followers, and unequivocal dedication to accomplishing a meaningful pursuit of vision in the hopes of it becoming reality in due time. During the initial stage, leaders evaluate and determine various "conditions that cause change" and identify others who are capable of managing change (Mauk, 2010). Next, followers are motivated and influenced to "partake in the vision" involving "clear details, direction, and an attitude of excitement toward change" (Mauk, 2010). The third stage consists of exhibiting performance that exceeds the expectations of what is necessary for achieving the established goals (Mauk, 2010).

Charismatic leadership also involves a consideration of communication. Within this paradigm, charismatic leaders leverage both verbal and nonverbal communications as complements to their physical characteristics toward the conveyance of "images of competence and success" (Awamleh, 2003). Certainly, these physical characteristics range from grooming to the wearing of specific types of clothing (e.g., police uniform). However, the verbal and nonverbal characteristics of communicating are equally as important as physical appearance.

Charismatic leaders use smile to facially express their reflections of "immediacy, intimacy, and warmth," and as a method of embellishing "interpersonal acceptance" (Awamleh, 2003). Smiling represents a communicative tool for motivating, moving, and inspiring followers (Awamleh, 2003). Through smiling, charismatic leaders communicate imagery of "happiness and reassurance" that usually invokes positive reactions among followers (Awamleh, 2003). This tool was leveraged frequently by President Ronald Reagan (Awamleh, 2003).

Charismatic leaders also leverage eye contact as a method of influencing others. Through the use of eye contact, charismatic leaders may "manipulate the feelings and influence the behavior of others" (Awamleh, 2003). Generally, people tend to make and hold eye contact with others with whom they "feel comfortable" (Awamleh, 2003). Through eye contact, points of interest may be emphasized during speeches or conversations, and it may be used as a method of soliciting feedback from listeners and viewers. Essentially, eye contact is a reinforcing mechanism to support verbal forms of communication (Awamleh, 2003).

Charisma may be attributed to leaders whose legacies have both positive and negative records. A primary example was Frank Rizzo, who was the Philadelphia police chief during the late 1960s and later mayor during the early 1970s. He was described as charismatic, and also as the "best friend of the police" (Treadwell, 1991). Although he had one of the lowest crime rates in the nation, his policing methods, tactics, and leadership were often questionable. For example, during a 1960s Philadelphia riot, he stated that "rioters should be stripped and forced to march naked through downtown Philadelphia" (Treadwell, 1991). While attending a formal dinner ceremony, he departed the "black-tie affair to go to a riot scene and arrived with a nightstick tucked into his tuxedo cummerbund" (Treadwell, 1991). However, despite his antics and flamboyance, his charismatic appeal was undaunted regarding various facets of public acceptance. He was described a "popular idol" whose "greeting and handshake" had a way of ennobling men, and by whose presence "women practically swooned at his near-approach" (Spector, 1999).

Servant Theory

Although the servant theory was fashioned during the 1970s, it did not gain a foothold until the 1990s. The basic premise of servant leadership is easily conceptualized and understood. Simply, it represents the following notions: "Servant leadership requires the leader to serve their followers first while placing themselves second ... this service is designed to develop the follower's potential, which enables them to achieve inner greatness" (Webb). Essentially, within this paradigm, leaders are perceived as servants from a variety of perspectives ranging from serving the needs of subordinates to serving the needs of organizational stakeholders. Ten characteristics generally highlight this type of leadership paradigm: (1) an ability to listen, (2) empathy, (3) healing, (4) awareness, (5) persuasion, (6) conceptualization, (7) foresight, (8) stewardship, (9) commitment to developing others, and (10) community building (Spears, 2004). Communication permeates each of these attributes within the servant theory.

Regardless of its application within the context of any leadership theory, listening ability is a salient consideration of the servant theory. Leaders who exhibit an ability to listen instead of speak primarily, then contemplate any gained information from listening, and who have little need for "external encouragement" may be classified as servant leaders (Waddell, 2006). Servant leaders also communicate with such frequency that they are consistently aware of the "challenges and problems of others," and also communicate outwardly to ensure that others are always knowledgeable of pertinent information (Manning & Curtis, 2003, p. 122).

Empathy is "the action of understanding, being aware of, being sensitive to, and vicariously experiencing the feelings, thoughts, and experience of another of either the past or present without having the feelings, thoughts, and experience fully communicated in an objectively explicit manner" (*Merriam-Webster*, 2013b). Communications within the servant leadership paradigm convey expression of empathy when leaders listen to others. From the perspective of the justice domain, empathy when communicating involves the experiencing of "a program or event from another participant's point of view" or attempting to visualize the combination of moments that "create the total experience" (Cortrite, 2007, p. 105).

Healing involves the "spiritual side" of leaders and leadership (Cortrite, 2007, p. 106). From the perspective of communications within the servant theory, healing involves both empathy and listening with respect to "understanding the importance of the healing process" (Cortrite, 2007, p. 106). Healing involves a sensitivity to the "personal concerns and well-being of others" within an organization, and taking time to address such issues (Northouse, 2013). Such interest may involve listening actively to the concerns of others, and collaboratively addressing the identified issues toward some type of resolution.

Awareness involves a consideration of not only the needs of others and of the organization, but also of self-awareness. From the communications perspective, awareness develops from "listening to, watching, and learning from others" (Flint, 2011). The perspectives of awareness strengthen leaders, and facilitate an understanding of "issues involving ethics and values" (Fennell, 2002). Becoming aware of such issues involves communication through which questioning and feedback occurs to inform leaders and followers of various situations and their circumstances. Awareness may incorporate periodic updates and communications to ensure that both leaders and followers consistently have relevant and timely information regarding issues that influence the organization.

Persuasion represents the communications concepts that have been introduced, explained, and reiterated within Chapter 3. Within the contexts of communication and the servant theory, persuasion represents the leveraging of "ideas, values, substance, and content" toward the defining of "purposes and core values" among organizations (Sergiovanni, 2007). Persuasion may involve convincing others to buy into the mission of the organization toward the fulfillment of vision through time. Persuasion may involve convincing others of the benefit that may be derived from working extra hours or performing tasks that might not necessarily be parts of one's typical duties. Essentially, within the servant theory, persuasion involves communicating to create some level of consensus among multiple parties (Ferch & Spears, 2011).

Conceptualization involves a visionary consideration of leadership with respect to broader concerns that affect organizations rather than concerns of daily operations (Ferch & Spears, 2011). This notion involves a realization that leaders must have a knowledge and understanding of "where an organization should be or what it should look like in the future" (Cortrite, 2007, p. 107). With respect to the strategic initiative, conceptualization also represents facets of "helping others through change" and reflects "commitment" (O'Brien, 2011). From the perspective of communication, leaders must effectively communicate organizational vision.

Foresight is a relevant factor of an organization becoming proactive and expressing an "incremental plan" (Spears & Lawrence, 2002). It also represents an ability to use past data and observations of the organization to project future events that may influence the organization both positively and negatively (Greenleaf, 2002). Obtaining the necessary historical information may occur through communication. One may review printed copies of annual reports, sales histories, cash flows, or any other written expression that details the historical performance of the organization. One may also review video resources or perform oral interviews with personnel to gain useful information.

Stewardship is a core attribute of the servant theory. Essentially, within this paradigm, stewardship represents a transcending of "self-interest to serve the needs of others, help others grow and develop, and provide opportunity for others to gain materially and emotionally" (Daft, 2008b, p. 176). Fulfilling these obligations involves communicating. Specifically, organizational leaders must continuously question "whom do you serve and for what purpose?" (Cortrite, 2007, p. 108). Gaining such information often necessitates polling a variety of sources, ranging from existing clients to public inquiries regarding public perceptions of the organization.

The servant theory is concerned with the well-being and benefit of others with whom organizational leaders may have relationships, either directly or indirectly. Such maturing of subordinates, peers, and other people has some implications for communications. From one perspective, organizations may provide opportunities for personnel to undergo various training courses through which they may improve their speaking, writing, listening, and presentation skills. In other cases, organizations may partner with professional organizations to sponsor professional workshops through which communication abilities are improved.

The notion of community building is also a central theme of the servant theory. Establishing and crafting a sense of community involves building and strengthening "relationships with other team members" and appreciating the "value and expertise and contribution of other disciplines in planning and provision of care…" (Hammick, Freeth, Copperman, & Goodsman, 2009). Communicating with others is essential when forging the relationships that are characteristic of a sense of community. Thus, communicating various facets of common values and goals is essential when establishing commonness as a foundation of community relationships.

The servant theory is certainly appropriate within the context of law enforcement organizations and the justice system because they are entities that render a variety of public services. From the perspective of police chaplaincy, servant leadership involves a variety of communications attributes. Police chaplains perform tasks for which typical field officers may be untrained or that may necessitate large amounts of time (Moosbrugger & Patterson, 2008). Such activities often involve varying amounts and types of communication. Examples include "counseling, performing visitation, providing death notification, filling the role of liaison, and providing crisis intervention" (Moosbrugger & Patterson, 2008). Throughout these roles, communication is necessary for addressing members of the public and peer law enforcement personnel.

In some cases, administrative factions of law enforcement organizations have voiced preferences and advocacies for servant leadership paradigms within the justice domain (Vito, Suresh, & Richards, 2011). Through the use of servant leadership paradigms, law enforcement organizations may embellish their capacities of exhibiting high ethical standards (Cortrite, 2007). Servant leadership is also a paradigm through which community-oriented policing initiatives may be embellished (Cortrite, 2007). Among these functions, communication is necessary for the functioning and operating of the law enforcement organization.

Law enforcement organizations that employ servant leadership exhibit a mindset that advocates service before self. Essentially, both organizational leadership and law enforcement personnel place the best interests of the general public and society ahead of their respective self-interests. In doing so, all communication employed by the law enforcement organization and its personnel must be both effective and efficient, and contribute toward the instantiation of the ten tenets of the servant theory. Thus, communication is a dominant consideration of successfully leveraging servant leadership within the justice domain.

Commentary Regarding Leadership Communication

Within his poem *Psalm of Life*, Henry Wadsworth Longfellow stated (Longfellow, 1839)

> Lives of great men all remind us
> We can make our lives sublime,
> And, departing, leave behind us
> Footprints on the sands of time;
> Footprints, that perhaps another,
> Sailing o'er life's solemn main,
> A forlorn and shipwrecked brother,
> Seeing, shall take heart again.

These few lines have great relevance for leadership communication. Great leaders forge and leave behind legacies that are reminders of their accomplishments, both positive and negative. History records these legacies through written words, audio snippets, and video resources. The lives of leaders are testaments to acts of motivation, inspiration, commitment, change, and the relentless pursuit of vision. Their legacies transcend generations and shape historical events that influence future generations. It is not uncommon for modern generations to examine various facets of historically notable leaders, ranging from President Ronald Reagan to Steve Jobs. Studying the lives, accomplishments, and characteristics of leaders provides a basis for understanding the domain of leadership. Any considerations of historically notable leaders and their exercised methods of leading also necessitate considerations of communication within the context of leadership.

Within the law enforcement domain, rising through the ranks to assume and maintain a leadership position entails much time, experience, and training (McElreath et al., 2013). New law enforcement personnel must complete some basic academy and initial entry qualifications ranging from physical fitness to marksmanship (McElreath et al., 2013). Their patrols familiarize them with the characteristics of their served communities (McElreath et al., 2013). After time, additional training, and experience, those officers who demonstrate leadership potential may be selected for leadership training, and may take advantage of periodic opportunities to advance within the supervisory and administrative ranks of their respective organizations (McElreath et al., 2013).

Throughout this progression, law enforcement officers develop and sharpen their communication skills. They must learn to actively and proactively communicate with others using written language, oral expressions and commands, and both video and audio resources. Regardless of the modality of communication, they must learn to be clear and succinct when communicating with others. Examples include the writing of incident reports, issuing of voice commands, and recording the activities of service calls for later review, analysis, and commentary.

Law enforcement personnel that ascend through the ranks into supervisory and administrative positions have ample opportunities to develop their leadership communications skills involving presentations and briefings, social gatherings, speaking opportunities among community events, and conducting press interviews. While rising through the ranks, law enforcement personnel may improve their leadership communications skills through a variety of methods. Three methods of improving leadership communication include storytelling, coaching, and planning.

Storytelling entails a "core competence of leadership," and it represents a cultural norm that is innate among all cultures (Denning, 2011, p. 9). It represents both persuasive and narrative forms of communication that are used to argue inductively toward influencing mindsets and behaviors (Denning, 2011, p. 9). Storytelling is used by organizational leaders to supplement and spark "analytical thinking" (Denning, 2011, p. 11). These goals are accomplished by embellishing the human ability to "imagine new perspectives" and also by "communicating change and stimulating innovation" within an organization (Denning, 2011, p. 11).

Using stories involves various aspects of analogies through which concepts are conveyed and expressed to personnel. Leaders must connect with their audiences. Often, doing so through the use of stories involves "symbolic convergence" (Burtis & Turman, 2010). This notion facilitates some commonness between the audience and the theme of the story presented, thereby providing some lesson as well as direction. By doing so, audiences are able to relate to the story. In many cases, this relationship is manifested through the swaying of emotions within the intended audience (Whitelaw & Wetzig, 2007). Through leveraging emotional appeals within stories, the audience tends to show a better remembrance of the communicated message conveyed within the story (Whitelaw & Wetzig, 2007).

Although storytelling may seem conspicuous as a communications method within the context of the justice domain, it has been leveraged effectively for some time. Within the law enforcement domain, one of the most recognizable uses of storytelling involves park rangers among U.S. national forests with respect to the Smokey Bear character. Through the use of storytelling, children are encouraged to observe fire safety and to report any incidents of fire. Figure 13.2a through d show an example of a typical context in which these concepts are communicated to children.

Another form of leadership communication involves coaching through which "open communication skills" may be developed and sharpened (Atwater & Waldman, 2008, p. 131). Coaching generally involves the following attributes (Atwater & Waldman, 2008, p. 55):

- Establishing rapport between the communicating parties involving trust and frankness with respect to a consideration of "best interests" (Atwater & Waldman, 2008, p. 55)
- Identification and incorporation of managerial "development needs" within the communications process
- Identification and expression of "specific goals and development plans" (Atwater & Waldman, 2008, p. 55)
- Evaluation of the progression toward the achievement of goals, and reassessing them as necessary

(a) (b)

Figure 13.2 (a, b) Storytelling with Smokey the Bear.

Figure 13.2 (Continued) (c, d) Storytelling with Smokey the Bear. (From http://www.smokeybear.com/resources/Smokey%20Activity.pdf.)

Coaching often focuses on the methods of communication that are present within organizations. By doing so, a goal of coaching is to "balance personal and leadership communication styles" with respect to the "larger imperatives of communication" that exist within the organization (Atwater & Waldman, 2008, p. 104). Successfully achieving this goal may diminish conflicts that exist among organizational communications and may "compensate" for anything that may be lacking among the "organizational communications processes" (Atwater & Waldman, 2008, p. 104). If coaching is leveraged effectively, leaders are able to contribute toward the openness of communications within an organization, and are able to provide direction regarding organizational "roles and responsibilities" (Gorrell & Hoover, 2009).

Planning is another important aspect of communication that must not be discounted or ignored. Planning failures often result in communications failures. Therefore, leaders must give consideration to every facet of communicating, and express the characteristics of who, what, when, where, how, and why communicating occurs. Additionally, planning also incurs some aspects of long-term versus short-term communications within an organization. Leaders must be mindful of whether their communications have strategic, long-term impacts and ramifications for the organization, and plan accordingly with respect to the goals and objectives that are pursued through time strategically (Matha & Boehm, 2008).

Rising through the ranks of any law enforcement organization takes much time, commitment, and experience. Regardless of the position held by or the responsibilities meted to personnel, one thing is certain: all law enforcement officers must communicate. From their very first contact with a hiring agency to the rigors of press conferences, law enforcement personnel must communicate succinctly, effectively, and efficiently. Through mastering the concepts of storytelling, coaching, and planning, personnel may improve and develop their communication skills throughout the course of a law enforcement career.

Once retired or departed from the practice of law enforcement, many leave notable legacies that transcend generations and inspire others through time. Although they eventually die, their oral statements and written communications may influence future generations. During the 1800s, Wyatt Earp served both as a U.S. Marshal and a deputy sheriff, and his exploits remain intriguing during modern times. He is famous for his participation in the O.K. Corral gunfight, and the town site of Earp, California, is named after him (Woog, 2010). From the perspective of marksmanship, one of his quotes still has relevance for modern law enforcement personnel: "fast is fine, but accuracy is everything" (Earp, n.d.).

Longfellow's poem has relevance for law enforcement leaders. They come and go through time, and leave behind legacies that influence their localities, regions, or the nation (in some cases). Regardless, they all had to communicate with others. Although the mastering of leadership communication may take time, it contributes toward establishing and defining the attributes of leaders. The words, behaviors, and deeds of law enforcement leaders provide a basis for communicating within existing periods, and have the capacity to influence future law enforcement officers.

Chapter Comments and Summary

This chapter introduced the basic concepts of leadership communications. Developing a reputation as a congenial, effective communicator may serve well the leaders of law enforcement organizations. Regardless of their roles and responsibilities across law enforcement organizations, all leaders must communicate effectively and efficiently. Leaders may communicate internally or externally regarding the organizational boundaries of law enforcement organizations. Through time, leaders must improve their leadership skills as they advance into higher levels of positions and authority.

The domain of leadership communications has matured greatly since its origins. Many of its earliest theories and tenets expressed the notion that leaders are born, but not made. This mindset incorporated some facets of providence with respect to situations through which leaders would emerge in due time. Later theories expressed opposite notions. These theories expressed notions that leadership can be learned through various facets of education and experience. Thus, leadership can be learned and applied among organizational settings.

Several leadership theories were voiced through the years: great man theory, trait theory, behavioral theory, contingency theory, transactional theory, transformation theory, participative theory, charismatic theory, and servant theory. These are only a few of the leadership theories that have emerged through the years; many more exist. Regardless of the leadership theory or style of a leader, communication is a paramount consideration of leadership.

Law enforcement personnel may advance through their respective ranks in due time to assume positions of leadership. Throughout this progression, law enforcement personnel must be mindful of developing and honing communications skills. By doing so, personnel improve their abilities of communicating with others either individually or involving groups. Three methods exist through which advancing personnel may improve their communication skills: storytelling, coaching, and planning.

Terminology

Adapt
Behavioral theory
Change
Charismatic theory
Circumstances
Coaching
Communication
Conflict
Contingency theory
Example setting
Follower
Goal
Great man theory
Influence
Leadership
Leadership style
Legacy
Management
Mission
Motivation
Objective
Participative theory
Planning
Relationship
Resolution
Servant theory
Situations
Smokey Bear
Storytelling
Strategy
Subordinate
Synergy
Trait theory
Transactional theory
Transformational theory
Vision

THOUGHT AND DISCUSSION QUESTIONS

1. This chapter presented only a few of the leadership theories that involve some aspect of leadership communication. Do some research in the literature of the management and leadership domains, and identify three other leadership theories and paradigms that are not included within this chapter. Write a brief essay that discusses the basic foundations of these three paradigms, and discuss how communication influences each theory.
2. This chapter identified a few individual leaders that exemplify their respective types of leadership and communication styles. Do some research, and identify other leaders within the justice domain whose leadership and communication attributes either are or were commensurate with the descriptions herein. Write a brief essay that highlights the leadership and communications attributes of these additional individuals.
3. Perform some research concerning the leadership versus management domains. Determine how leadership differs from management. Write a brief essay that compares and contrasts the basic concepts of leadership versus management. Within this essay, incorporate relevant facets of communication for each domain to show the primary aspects of similarities and differences between these concepts.
4. Leadership is concerned with the long-term, strategic perspectives of organizations through time with respect to the fulfillment of vision. Communicating vision downwardly and outwardly is often challenging for leaders and their respective organizations. Do some research in the domain of strategic management, and determine how organizational leaders may communicate vision effectively and efficiently both internally and externally regarding organizations within the justice domain. Write a brief essay that summarizes your findings.

References

Anderson, A. (2013). The advantages of participative leadership. *The Houston Chronicle*. Retrieved from http://smallbusiness.chron.com/advantages-participative-leadership-17629.html (accessed March 11, 2013).

Archbold, C. (2013). *Policing: A text/reader* (p. 213). Thousand Oaks, CA: Sage Publishing.

Atwater, L., & Waldman, D. (2008). *Leadership, feedback, and the open communication gap*. New York: Lawrence Erlbaum Associates.

Awamleh, R. (2003). Toward a model of charismatic non-verbal impression management. *International Business & Economics Research Journal, 2*(7), 27–38.

Barker, A. (1992). *Transformational nursing leadership: A vision for the future* (p. 42). New York: National League for Nursing Press.

Bennis, W., & Nanus, B. (1985). *Leadership: The strategies for taking charge*. New York: Harper and Row Publishing.

Benoliel, M. (2011). *Negotiation excellence: Successful deal making*. Hackensack: World Scientific Publishing Co., Ltd.

Benton, J. (2005). *Air force officer's guide* (34th ed., p. 21). Mechanicsburg, PA: Stackpole Books.

Bertocci, D. (2009). *Leadership in organizations: There is a difference between leaders and managers* (p. 28). Lanham, MD: University Press of America.

Borkowski, N. (2011). *Organizational behavior in health care* (p. 320). London: Jones and Bartlett Publishing.

Buddhapriya, S. (1999). *Women in management* (p. 37). New Delhi, India: APH Publishing Corporation.

Burke, R., & Friedman, L. (2011). *Essentials of management and leadership in public health*. Sudbury, MA: Jones and Bartlett Publishing.
Burtis, J., & Turman, P. (2010). *Leadership communication as citizenship* (p. 179). Thousand Oaks, CA: Sage Publishing.
Callaway, P. (2006). *The relationship between organizational trust and job satisfaction: An analysis in the U.S. federal work force* (p. 51). Boca Raton, FL: Dissertation.com.
Carlyle, T. (1840). *On heroes, hero-worship, and the heroic in history*. Retrieved from http://www.gutenberg.org/files/1091/1091-h/1091-h.htm (accessed March 7, 2013).
Centers for Disease Control. (2012). Fact sheets. Retrieved from http://www.cdc.gov/alcohol/fact-sheets/underage-drinking.htm (accessed March 9, 2013).
Coggins, E. (2013). The history of leadership studies and evolution of leadership theories. Retrieved from http://ecoggins.hubpages.com/hub/The-History-of-Leadership-Studies-and-Evolution-of-Leadership-Theories (accessed March 19, 2013).
Conklin, D. (1991). *Comparative economic systems*. New York: Cambridge University Press.
Coombs, T., & Holladay, S. (2012). *The handbook of crisis communication* (p. 44). Malden, MA: Blackwell Publishing.
Cortrite, M. (2007). *Servant leadership for law enforcement*. University of California, Los Angeles: Proquest.
Croll, P. (1884). *Tributes to the memory of Martin Luther* (p. 206). Philadelphia, PA: G.W. Frederick.
Daft, R. (2008a). *The leadership experience* (4th ed., p. 25). Mason, OH: Thomson Higher Education.
Daft, R. (2008b). *The leadership experience* (4th ed., p. 176). Mason, OH: Thomson Southwestern.
Dempsey, J., & Forst, L. (2011). *An introduction to policing* (6th ed., p. 75). Mason, OH: Cengage Publishing.
Denning, S. (2011). *The leader's guide to storytelling: Mastering the art and discipline of business narrative*. San Francisco: Jossey-Bass Publishing.
Earp, W. (n.d.). Wyatt Earp quotes. Brainyquote. Retrieved from http://www.brainyquote.com/quotes/authors/w/wyatt_earp.html (accessed March 16, 2013).
Erasmus, B., & Schneck, H. (2008). *South African human resource management: Theory and practice* (4th ed.). Cape Town, South Africa: Juta Publishing.
Fennell, D. (2002). *Ecotourism programme planning* (p. 164). New York: CABI Publishing.
Ferch, S., & Spears, L. (2011). *The spirit of servant leadership* (p. 12). Mahwah, NJ: The Paulist Press.
Flint, B. (2011). *The journey to competitive advantage through servant leadership: Building the company every person dreams of working for and every president has a vision of leading* (p. 70). Bloomington, IN: Westbow Press.
Foster, D., Goertzen, B., Nollette, C., & Nollette, F. (2013). *Emergency services leadership: A contemporary approach*. Burlington, MA: Jones and Bartlett Publishing.
Ghuman, K., & Aswathappa, K. (2010). *Management: Concepts, practice, and cases* (p. 381). New Delhi, India: Tata McGraw-Hill Publishing.
Gill, R. (2006). *Theory and practice of leadership* (p. 47). Thousand Oaks, CA: Sage Publishing.
Gorrell, P., & Hoover, J. (2009). *The coaching connection: A manager's guide to developing individual potential in the context of the organization* (p. 108). New York: American Management Association.
Greenleaf, R. (2002). *Servant leadership: A journey into the nature of legitimate power and greatness*. Mahwah, NJ: The Paulist Press.
Griffin, R., & Moorhead, G. (2012). *Organizational behavior: Managing people and organizations* (10th ed.). Mason, OH: South-Western Cengage Publishing.
Hamilton, C. (2011). *Communicating for results: A guide for business and the professions* (9th ed.). Boston: Wadsworth Cengage Publishing.
Hammick, M., Freeth, D., Copperman, J., & Goodsman, D. (2009). *Being interprofessional* (p. 55). Malden, MA: Polity Press.
Hitt, M., Miller, C. C., & Colella, A. (2009). *Organizational behavior: A strategic approach* (2nd ed.). Hoboken, NJ: John Wiley & Sons Publishing.

Holding, G. (2012). *Introducing mentoring: A guide for mentors and organisers of mentoring schemes* (p. 47). Bloomington, IN: Balboa Press.

Hunter, G. (2010). *The Celtic way of evangelism: How Christianity can reach the west ... again.* Nashville, TN: The Abingdon Press.

Institute for Transformational Communication. (2013). How it works. Retrieved from http://www.itranscomm.com/how_it_works.htm (accessed March 10, 2013).

Jablin, F., & Putnam, L. (2001). *The new handbook of organizational communication: Advances in theory, research, and methods* (p. 480). Thousand Oaks, CA: Sage Publishing.

Kansal, P. K., & Rao, P. C. (2006). *Preface to management.* New Delhi, India: Paragon Books.

Kassimeris, G., & Buckley, J. (2010). *The ashgate research companion to modern warfare* (p. 438). Burlington, VT: Ashgate Publishing.

Kelly, P. (2012). *Nursing leadership and management* (3rd ed.). Clifton Park, NY: Delmar Cengage Publishing.

Kirkman, D. (2013). Therapeutic dialogues: Interviewing strategies in mental health court status hearings and beyond. *Intermountain Mental Health Court Conference.* Retrieved from http://www.imhcc.org/schedule/sch_Details.cfm?pid=0&abid=74&ty=grid (accessed March 10, 2013).

Kliem, R. (2004). *Leading high performance projects* (p. 2). Plantation, FL: J. Ross Publishing.

Klockars, C., Ivkovic, S., & Haberfeld, M. (2006). *Enhancing police integrity* (p. 106). Dordrecht, The Netherlands: Springer Publishing.

Kouzes, J., & Posner, B. (2011). *The five practices of exemplary leadership: Nursing* (p. 2). San Francisco: Pfeiffer Publishing.

Krumm, D. (2001). *Psychology at work: An introduction to industrial/organizational psychology* (p. 241). New York: Worth Publishers.

Leadershipcentral.com. (2013). Leadership theories. Retrieved from http://www.leadership-central.com/leadership-theories.html#axzz2MutjnaLa (accessed March 7, 2013).

Littlejohn, S., & Foss, K. (2008). *Theories of human communication* (9th ed). Belmont, CA: Thomson Higher Education.

Longfellow, H. (1839). *Psalm of life.* Retrieved from http://www.bartleby.com/102/55.html (accessed March 14, 2013).

Lussier, R., & Achua, C. (2010). *Leadership: Theory, application, and skill development* (4th ed.). Mason, OH: South-Western Cengage Publishing.

Manning, G., & Curtis, K. (2003). *The art of leadership.* New York: McGraw-Hill Publishing.

Martinez, D. (2012). Organizational communication: Small organizations must transition into a communicative style that supports a culture of employee and organizational growth. Gonzaga University. Retrieved from http://web02.gonzaga.edu/comltheses/proquestftp/Martinez_gonzaga_0736M_10162.pdf (accessed March 7, 2013).

Matha, B., & Boehm, M. (2008). *Beyond the babble: Leadership communication that drives results.* San Francisco: Jossey-Bass Publishing.

Mattina, J. (2009). *The influence of verbal aggressiveness and verbal argumentativeness on college leadership styles* (p. 89). Ann Arbor, MI: Proquest.

Mauk, K. (2010). *Gerontological nursing: Competencies for care* (2nd ed., p. 733). Sudbury, MA: Jones and Bartlett Publishing.

McElreath, D., Doss, D., Jensen, C., Wigginton, M., Kennedy, R., Winter, K., ... Sumerel, J. M. (2013). *Introduction to law enforcement.* Boca Raton, FL: CRC Press.

Merriam-Webster Dictionary. (2013a). s.v. "charisma." Retrieved from http://www.merriam-webster.com/dictionary/charisma (accessed March 11, 2013).

Merriam-Webster Dictionary. (2013b). s.v. "empathy." Retrieved from http://www.merriam-webster.com/dictionary/empathy (accessed March 13, 2013).

Montana, P., & Charnov, B. (2008). *Barron's management* (4th ed.). Hauppage, NY: Barron's Educational Services, Inc.

Moosbrugger, D., & Patterson, K. (2008). The servant leadership of a law enforcement chaplain. Regent University. Retrieved from http://www.regent.edu/acad/global/publications/sl_proceedings/2008/moosbrugger-patterson.pdf (accessed March 13, 2013).
National Institute on Alcohol Abuse and Alcoholism. (2013). Strategies to prevent underage drinking. Retrieved from http://pubs.niaaa.nih.gov/publications/arh26-1/5-14.htm (accessed March 9, 2013).
Northouse, P. (2010). *Leadership: Theory and practice* (5th ed., p. 111). Thousand Oaks, CA: Sage Publishing.
Northouse, P. (2013). *Leadership: Theory and practice* (6th ed., p. 227). Thousand Oaks, CA: Sage Publishing.
O'Brien, M. (2011). *Spirituality in nursing: Standing on holy ground* (4th ed., p. 392). Sudbury, MA: Jones and Bartlett Publishing.
Patton, G. (n.d.). George S. Patton quotes. Brainyquote. Retrieved from http://www.brainyquote.com/quotes/authors/g/george_s_patton.html (accessed March 7, 2013).
Riaz, A., & Haider, M. (2010). Role of transformational and transactional leadership on job satisfaction and career satisfaction. *Business and Economic Horizons, 1*(1), 29–38.
Rodriques, M. V. (2000). *Perspectives of communication and communicative competence* (p. 80). New Delhi, India: Concept Publishing Company.
Roeckelein, J. (1998). *Dictionary of theories, laws, and concepts in psychology*. Westport, CT: Greenwood Publishing.
Rost, J. (1993). *Leadership for the twenty-first century* (p. 30). Westport, CT: Praeger Publishing.
Saxena, S., & Awasthi, P. (2010). *Leadership* (p. 52). New Delhi, India: PHI Learning Private, Ltd.
Sciarra, D., & Dorsey, A. (2002). *Leaders and supervisors in child care programs* (p. 8). Albany, NH: Delmar Cengage Publishing.
Scutchfield, D., & Keck, W. (2003). *Principles of public health practice* (2nd ed., p. 146). Clifton Park, NY: Thomson Delmar Learning.
Sen, L. (2007). *Communication skills* (p. 11). New Delhi, India: PHI Learning Private Limited.
Sergiovanni, T. (2007). *Rethinking leadership: A collection of articles* (2nd ed., p. 58). Thousand Oaks, CA: Corwin Press.
Spears, L. (2004). Practicing servant-leadership. *Leader to Leader, 34*(Fall), 7–11.
Spears, L., & Lawrence, M. (2002). *Focus on leadership: Servant-leadership for the twenty-first century* (p. 245). Hoboken, NJ: Wiley Publishing.
Spector, H. (1999). Limitation of statute. *Philadelphia City Paper*. Retrieved from http://archives.citypaper.net/articles/021899/slant.shtml?print=1 (accessed March 12, 2013).
Stroup, J. (2004). *Managing leadership: Toward a new and usable understanding of what leadership really is—and how to manage it*. Lincoln, NE: IUniverse.
Swift, C. (2008). *This house would ethically engage: A critical examination of competitor and coach leadership in a National Parliamentary Debate Association (NPDA) debate* (Doctoral dissertation). Baton Rouge, LA: Louisiana State University.
Thomlinson, T. D. (2013). Monologic and dialogic communication. University of Memphis. Retrieved from http://umdrive.memphis.edu/ggholson/public/Dialogue.html (accessed March 10, 2013).
Treadwell, D. (1991). Ex-Mayor Rizzo Dies at 70 amid campaign: Politics: The controversial former Philadelphia policeman suffers a heart attack. He switched to Republican in effort to win back office. *Los Angeles Times*. Retrieved from http://articles.latimes.com/1991-07-17/news/mn-2263_1_heart-attack (accessed March 13, 2013).
Tsui, F., & Karam, O. (2011). *Essentials of software engineering* (2nd ed., p. 144). Sudbury, MA: Jones and Bartlett Learning.
Tyagi, C. L., & Kumar, A. (2004). *Advertising management* (p. 74). New Delhi, India: Atlantic Publishers and Distributors.
Vito, G., Suresh, G., & Richards, G. (2011). Emphasizing the servant in public service: The opinions of police managers. *Policing: An International Journal of Police Strategies and Management, 34*(4), 674–686.

Waddell, J. (2006). Servant leadership (p. 6). Regent University. Retrieved from http://www.regent.edu/acad/global/publications/sl_proceedings/2006/waddell.pdf (accessed March 13, 2013).

Webb, M. A case study of Pennsylvania police leadership styles and training implications. Walden University (p. 45). Retrieved from http://www.ou.edu/ap/cohort5/materials/webb-dissertation.pdf (accessed March 12, 2013).

Whitelaw, G., & Wetzig, B. (2007). *Move to greatness: Focusing the four essential energies of a whole and balanced leader*. Boston: Nicholas Brealey Publishing.

Wolvin, A. (2005). Listening leadership: Hillary Clinton's listening tour. Retrieved from http://3rdyearwiki0809.pbworks.com/f/Listening%2BLeadership%2BHillary%2BClintons%2BListening%2BTour.pdf (accessed March 9, 2013).

Woog, A. (2010). *Wyatt Earp*. New York: Chelsea House Publishing.

High or Low? The Mathematics of Communication 14

> The media transforms the great silence of things into its opposite. Formerly constituting a secret, the real now talks constantly. News reports, information, statistics, and surveys are everywhere.
>
> **—Michel de Certeau (de Certeau, n.d.)**

Objectives

The objectives of this chapter are to

- Introduce quantitative methods in communication
- Introduce the quantitative characteristics of video communication
- Introduce the quantitative characteristics of audio communication
- Introduce the mathematics of network communication
- Introduce the mathematics of clandestine communication

Introduction

Mathematics is defined as the "science of numbers and their operations, interrelations, combinations, generalizations, and abstractions and of space configurations and their structure, measurement, transformations, and generalizations" (*Merriam-Webster*, 2013a). Most people do not generally associate mathematics with communication when conversing and interacting with others. Usually, people do not also ponder the mathematics that represent network communication models when sending or receiving faxes and electronic mail messages or when participating in video or audio conferences. Many people do not consider the mathematics of frame rates versus the biological functioning of the human eye when viewing videos. Many people do not consider the mathematics of sound traveling through the air when hearing a police siren. Most people do not contemplate the statistics that describe written communications markets. When securing confidential information electronically, many people do not think about the mathematics of encryption and decryption algorithms that are associated with cryptology. However, despite such absences of thought, mathematics pervades all aspects of communicating.

Practically everyone has heard a police siren at some point in their lives. From a distance, the sound of the siren seems diminished, whereas it becomes louder as it nears the listener. The pitch of the sound decreases suddenly when the police car passes the listener. This consideration of sound is known as the Doppler effect. This change in the listener's perception of sound is a classic example of mathematics to describe the human perceptions of sound waves relative to the position of the listener at any given point in time.

Many news programs frequently broadcast items involving law enforcement organizations or personnel. Video resources consist of many individual images that are perceived by humans as having the characteristics of movement when they are displayed very quickly. This concept of generating perceptions of movement is dependent on presenting each of the separate images sequentially "at an appropriate speed" (Strader, 2011). This specific speed is deemed to be the frame rate (Strader, 2011). If the sequential presentation of images is either too fast or too slow, then movement may appear to be abnormal.

Cryptography is defined as the study of methods to "convert information from its normal comprehensible form into an obscured guise, unreadable without special knowledge—the encryption" (Pachghare, 2009). Historically, cryptography has served a variety of purposes ranging from securing military communications to facilitating "digital signatures, digital cash, digital rights management for electronic commerce, and securing electronic commerce" (Pachghare, 2009). Cryptography is now common among digital communications architectures and digital communications algorithms (Pachghare, 2009). Although many people use a variety of digital communications devices each day (e.g., cellular phones and bank ATMs), they are typically unaware of the influences of cryptography that pervade their daily communications.

These examples are barely a thumbnail sketch of the vast array of mathematical principles that influence, govern, and describe communication. Certainly, many others exist within the domains of higher mathematics, physics, and computing. Audio communications are representative of sound waves that are generally examined within the domains of trigonometry and physics. Video communications are representative of the characteristics of light and motion that are generally examined in physics, higher mathematics, or media studies. The mathematical principles of cryptography are generally found within the domains of higher mathematics and computing. Regardless of their mathematical foundations, such concepts are foundationally important concepts that govern, influence, and describe communication throughout its various forms and modalities.

Wave Concepts

Sound is defined as the "sensation perceived by the sense of hearing," a "particular auditory impression," and the "mechanical radiant energy that is transmitted by longitudinal pressure waves in a material medium (as air) and is the objective cause of hearing" (*Merriam-Webster*, 2013b). The things that are heard by humans involve sound waves. All sound waves originate from a vibrating source and travel through some type of medium (e.g., air and water) (Giancoli, 2008). Basically, sound waves travel through anything that is composed of molecules (Giancoli, 2008). This traveling occurs because molecules collide with each other, thereby continuing the sound wave (Giancoli, 2008). However, sound waves are unable to travel through a vacuum because there are no molecules present through which the sound wave may be propagated (Giancoli, 2008).

Other waveforms that are a basis of modern communications can travel through a vacuum. For example, electromagnetic waves may travel through a vacuum despite the absence of molecules. Electromagnetic waves are originated when an "electric field couples with a magnetic field" (National Aeronautics and Space Administration, 2013). Electromagnetic waves represent a construct model in which "the magnetic and electric fields of an electromagnetic wave are perpendicular to each other and to the direction of the wave" (National

Aeronautics and Space Administration, 2013). A typical example of an electromagnetic wave is a radio wave used for radio communications.

Sound represents a type of pressure wave known as a longitudinal wave (University of Iowa, 2013). The longitudinal construct of sound waves represents "alternating areas of high and low pressure in whatever media it travels through" (University of Iowa, 2013). Two terms describe the molecular density of sound waves when they are traveling through some medium: compressions and rarefactions. Compressions represent denser areas of molecules, whereas rarefactions represent the least dense areas (University of Iowa, 2013). Figure 14.1 shows these concepts.

Sound waves also involve the notion of reflection in which they are "bounced back" toward their source after contacting a barrier (University of Iowa, 2013). When this situation occurs, the reflected wave represents an inverse of the "source wave" because it is upside down (University of Iowa, 2013). This situation is characteristic of the original compressions becoming rarefactions, and the original rarefactions becoming compressions (University of Iowa, 2013). Therefore, the reflected wave is deemed to be "out of phase" with respect to the attributes of the source wave (University of Iowa, 2013). Probably the most well known example of this situation is that of an echo. Sometimes, when a law enforcement officer discharges a weapon, the echoes of the gunshot may be heard for a few moments. These echoes represent the concept of sound reflection.

Refraction is another characteristic of sound waves. Refraction is defined as the "variation in the direction of sound transmission due to a spatial variation in the velocity of sound transmission in the medium" (Olson, 1967). The situation of refraction occurs when a "wave front hits the boundary" of another medium "at an angle" (Olson, 1967). When this event occurs, "one side of the wave will speed up or slow down before the other side, causing the wave to bend," thereby producing an instance of refraction (Olson, 1967). For example, sound waves may travel through air, and then travel through water. Figure 14.2 shows the concept of refraction.

Diffraction is another consideration of sound waves. The diffraction of sound occurs when a sound wave is bent or "spread out" after it "intersects an aperture, a solid object, a recess, or a surface protrusion" (Kang, 2002). Essentially, diffraction represents the bending of sound waves around objects or the "spreading out" of sound waves (Myers, 2006).

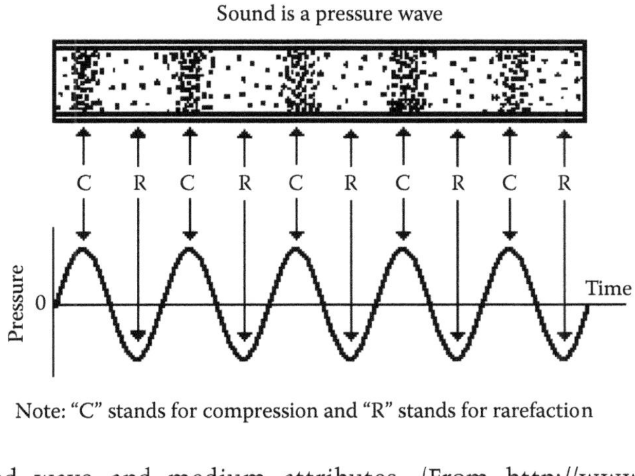

Figure 14.1 Sound wave and medium attributes. (From http://www.physics.uiowa.edu/~umallik/adventure/sound04.html.)

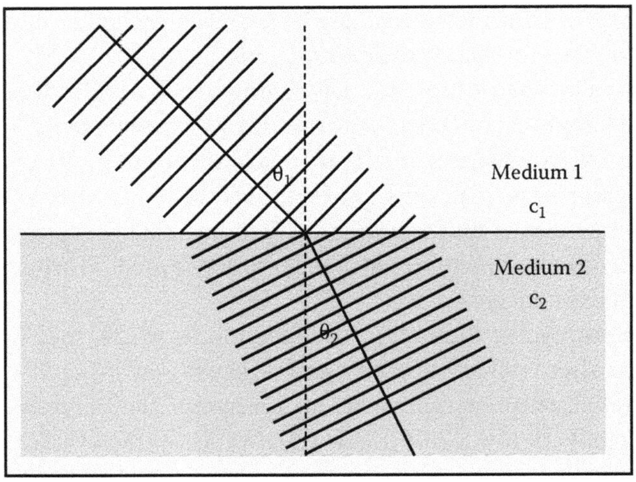

Figure 14.2 Sound wave refraction. (From http://www.physics.uiowa.edu/~umallik/adventure/sound04.html.)

A typical example of this concept involves the hearing of sound around corners (Myers, 2006). Additionally, police sirens are designed with "small openings" through which the diffraction of sound is enhanced (Myers, 2006). Figure 14.3 shows the concept of sound diffraction.

Sound waves are mathematically modeled and expressed through the concept of the sine wave. Sine waves represent periodic functions of mathematics involving waves.

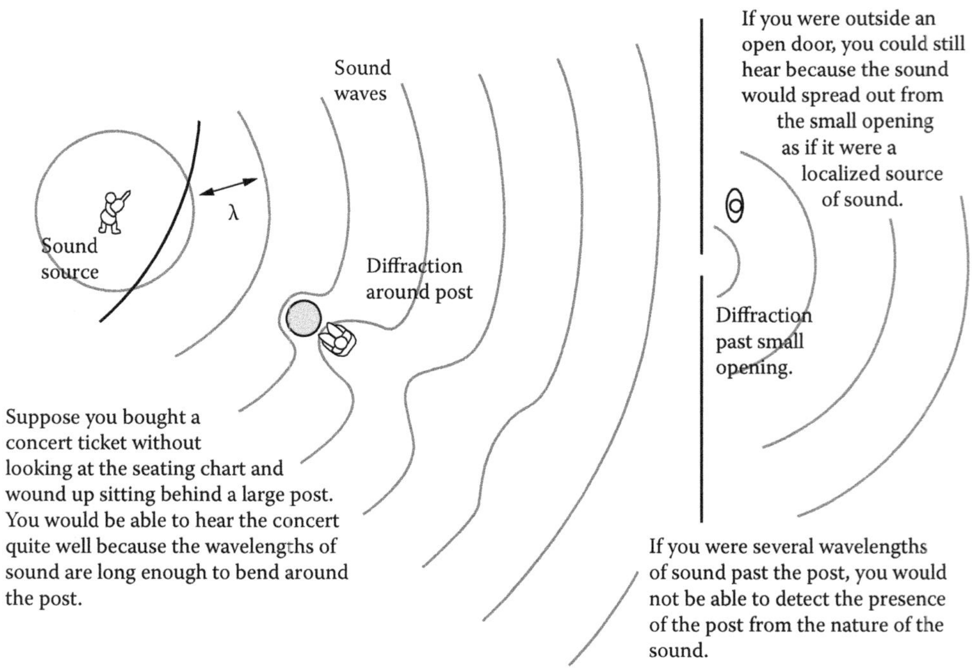

Figure 14.3 Concept of sound diffraction. (From http://www.physics.uiowa.edu/~umallik/adventure/sound04.html.)

The basic characteristics of sine waves include frequency, period, amplitude, and phase. Frequency refers to the quantity of times that sinusoidal patterns are repeated per unit time along the horizontal x-axis (Johnson, 2011). Frequency is generally measured in units of hertz (Hz) representing cycles per second. The repetitions of patterns are referred to as cycles. The length of time required for an individual cycle is known as period (Johnson, 2011). Amplitude involves the vertical y-axis with respect to deviations of pressure fluctuations from the attributes of normal, atmospheric pressure (Johnson, 2011). Phase refers to the timing of a given waveform with respect to a reference point (Johnson, 2011). Figure 14.4 shows the basic concept of a sine wave model.

This model may be considered from the perspective of a mathematical equation. The following equation represents the relationships of variables regarding a typical sine wave:

$$v(t) = A \sin \omega t \tag{14.1}$$

In English terms, this equation expresses the notion that any point along the sine wave, associated with an instantaneous value, $v(t)$, is equivalent to the "maximum value times the sine of the angular frequency at that point" (Sudhakar & Palli, 2010). The variable A represents amplitude, the variable ω represents angular frequency, and the variable t represents time. On the basis of the typical sine wave, other equations that govern and influence sound waves may be considered mathematically. Because the focus of this text is communications, the mathematical derivations of specific formulas are omitted within the discussions herein. Readers who desire to view the mathematical derivations of the following formulas are encouraged to consult other texts in advanced mathematics or physics.

The period of a wave represents the amount of time that exists between two successive compressions or two successive rarefactions. Mathematically, the notion of wave period is expressed within the following relationship:

$$\text{Period} = \frac{\text{wavelength}}{\text{velocity}} \tag{14.2}$$

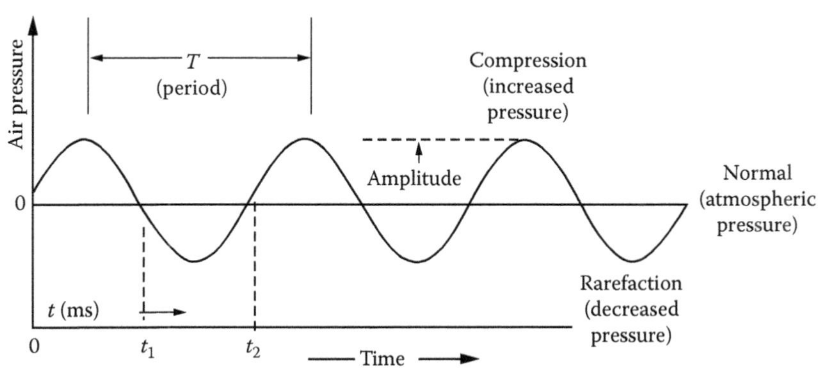

Figure 14.4 Sine wave concept. (From http://www.neurophys.wisc.edu/~ychen/figs/fig2.gif.)

These same variables may be used to determine the frequency of a wave. The frequency represents the quantity of oscillations that occur within a given period of time. Generally, frequency is measured in units of hertz (Hz). The following equation shows the frequency relationship mathematically.

$$\text{Frequency} = \frac{1}{\text{period}} = \frac{\text{velocity}}{\text{wavelength}} \tag{14.3}$$

Wavelength represents the distance between two corresponding, consecutive points along the wave with respect to phase. Wavelength may also be considered mathematically. The following formula represents the wavelength equation:

$$\text{Wavelength} = \frac{\text{velocity}}{\text{frequency}} \tag{14.4}$$

Various sample problems may be considered to show the functioning of these formulas mathematically. A sample problem to determine frequency and wavelength is presented as follows:

> With a given medium, the speed of a wave is 500 meters per second (m/s). If a total of 2000 waves pass along a certain point within one minute, calculate the frequency, the length of the wave, and the period of the wave.

EXAMPLE 14.1

Solving this problem is accomplished by exercising the aforementioned formulas appropriately. The solutions to these queries are shown as follows:

Step 1: Initialize the variables

The first step in solving this problem involves initializing the given variables. These values are expressed as follows:

Velocity: $v = 500$ m/s
Time: $t = 60$ seconds (1 minute)
Wave rate: 2000 waves per minute

Step 2: Implement the necessary formulas

This step involves expressing the pertinent formulas and substituting the given values appropriately. The sample problem necessitates a consideration of frequency. Determining the appropriate frequency is accomplished as follows:

$$\text{Frequency} = \frac{2000 \text{ waves}}{60 \text{ seconds}}$$

$$\text{Frequency} = 33.3 \text{ waves per second} = 33.3 \text{ Hz}$$

This frequency value may be substituted within the wavelength equation to determine the length of the wave. Determining the wavelength is accomplished as follows:

$$\text{Wavelength} = \frac{500 \text{ m/s}}{33.3 \text{ waves/s}}$$

$$\text{Wavelength} = 15.02 \text{ m/wave}$$

Using this data, the value for the variable associated with period may be calculated. The following formulas demonstrate this determination:

$$\text{Frequency} = \frac{1}{\text{period}}$$

$$\text{Period} = \frac{1}{\text{frequency}}$$

$$\text{Period} = \frac{1}{33.3\ \text{Hz}}$$

$$\text{Period} = 0.03$$

Presenting the formulas and exercising the equations to derive mathematical quantities also may need further contextualization. It is important to understand the potency of wave mathematics within the context of communication. Communication involves both sound and electromagnetic waves. Sound waves are incapable of traveling through a vacuum, whereas electromagnetic waves are capable of traveling through a vacuum. An obvious example of this notion is communication with the Mars rover. After all, space represents a vacuum in which sound waves are unable to be propagated. However, electromagnetic waves are used to facilitate communication, across the vacuum of space, between a base station on Earth and the vehicle on Mars.

Conceptually, the mathematical principles of waves are relatively easy to understand. Most folks have experienced ignorantly the concept of amplitude. The larger a wave is, the greater the amount of energy that is required to increase its amplitude (Study Physics, 2013). For example, within a sound system, the amplifier component increases the amplitude of waves "by using more electrical energy" (Study Physics, 2013). Given this notion, amplitude may be conceptualized as the "loudness" of a wave (Khan Academy, 2013).

Understanding wave theory is essential regarding communications concepts. The mathematics of waves governs all that humans perceive through the sense of hearing. The concepts of electromagnetic waves govern all radio communications within vacuums. During modern times, modern office environments are equipped with wireless networks. Law enforcement vehicles and many patrol officers are equipped with radio equipment. In both cases, the mathematics of wave theory governs the communications that occur through such devices. Waves are everywhere and exist in a variety of resources ranging from remote control devices to cellular communications. Understanding the concepts and mathematics of waves provides a solid foundation of conceptualizing the communications that occur among many devices within the justice domain.

Doppler Effect

The Doppler effect is defined scientifically as the "shift in the observed frequency of a wave as the result of relative motion of source and observer" (Elmore & Heald, 1969). Therefore, the Doppler effect necessitates a consideration of changing wavelengths with respect to the changes of relative positions of observers versus the sources of sounds. Most everyone has experienced the passing of a patrol car or an ambulance along a roadway, and heard the changing sound of a siren as the vehicle comes closer and then gets further away from the listener. This situation describes one of the most typical examples of the Doppler effect.

Although the concept is easily recognized and understood, the Doppler effect is governed by mathematics and formulas. Five scenarios must be considered within the context of Doppler effect mathematics: (1) a stationary listener versus an approaching source of sound, (2) a stationary listener versus a source of sound moving away, (3) a moving listener approaching a stationary source of sound, (4) a listener moving away from a stationary source of sound, and (5) conditions in which the listener and the source of sound are both moving simultaneously either closer together or further away from each other (Giancoli, 2008, pp. 440–441). All of these situations are described through mathematical formulas.

The formula that expresses the condition of a stationary listener versus an approaching source of sound is given as follows (Giancoli, 2008, pp. 440–441):

$$f' = \frac{f}{\left(1 - \dfrac{v_{\text{source}}}{v_{\text{snd}}}\right)} \tag{14.5}$$

The formula that expresses the condition of a stationary listener versus a source of sound that is moving away is given as follows (Giancoli, 2008, pp. 440–441):

$$f' = \frac{f}{\left(1 + \dfrac{v_{\text{source}}}{v_{\text{snd}}}\right)} \tag{14.6}$$

The formula that expresses the condition of a listener who is moving toward a stationary source of sound is given as follows (Giancoli, 2008, pp. 440–441):

$$f' = \left(1 + \frac{v_{\text{obs}}}{v_{\text{snd}}}\right) f \tag{14.7}$$

The equation that expresses the condition of a listener who is moving away from the source of sound is given as follows (Giancoli, 2008, pp. 440–441):

$$f' = \left(1 - \frac{v_{\text{obs}}}{v_{\text{snd}}}\right) f \tag{14.8}$$

The equation that expresses the relationship between a listener and a source of sound that are both moving simultaneously is given as follows (Giancoli, 2008, pp. 440–441):

$$f' = f\left(\frac{v_{\text{snd}} \pm v_{\text{obs}}}{v_{\text{snd}} \pm v_{\text{source}}}\right) \tag{14.9}$$

Within these equations, the following variables are pertinent:

f = frequency at rest of sound source
f' = Doppler effect frequency
v_{obs} = observer velocity
v_{snd} = sound velocity
v_{source} = source velocity

Straightforward examples may be considered to show the exercising of these formulas. The case of a stationary observer versus a moving source of sound is stated as follows:

> A police car is involved in a vehicular pursuit along a roadway and is traveling at 87 miles per hour. Listeners sitting in a restaurant watch the police car approach, pass, and depart their position. They also notice the changing sound of its siren. Typically, when the police car is at rest (i.e., not moving), the frequency of its siren is 2013 Hz. Determine the Doppler effect frequency change values that occur for both the approaching and departing conditions of the police car versus the stationary listeners. Traffic passes by the police car in the opposite lane of the roadway. These cars are traveling at 35 miles per hour. Determine the Doppler effect frequency change values that occur for both the moving police car and the moving, oncoming traffic. Assume that the speed of sound through air is approximately 340 m/s. (Pierce, 1989)

Solving this problem is accomplished easily via exercising the appropriate formulas. The solution is presented as follows:

Step 1: Initialize the variables

The first step necessary for solving this problem involves specifying the given data and showing the unknown quantities. Because most calculations involve the use of metric units, the measurements of miles per hour must be converted to meters per second. This conversion is necessary for standardization among the values used within the mathematical calculations. If standard values are not used, then an erroneous outcome will result from the mathematics. A conversion factor of 2.2369 is used to covert between the units appropriately (Havemeyer, 2013). This conversion is accomplished as follows:

$$\frac{87 \text{ mph}}{2.2369} = 38.89 \text{ m/s}$$

The next conversion is accomplished as follows:

$$\frac{35 \text{ mph}}{2.2369} = 15.64 \text{ m/s}$$

Now that standard units exist among the variables, all of the variables and their associated values are given as follows:

f = 2013 Hz
f' = ???

$v_{obs} = 15.64$ m/s
$v_{snd} = 340$ m/s
$v_{source} = 38.89$ m/s

Step 2: Exercise the formulas
This step involves exercising the appropriate formulas. This situation represents the condition in which the listeners are stationary, and the police car is moving toward them and then away from them. First, the case of the approaching police car is considered as follows:

$$f' = \frac{f}{\left(1 - \frac{v_{source}}{v_{snd}}\right)}$$

$$f' = \frac{2013\,\text{Hz}}{\left(1 - \frac{38.89\,\text{m/s}}{340\,\text{m/s}}\right)}$$

$$f' = \frac{2013\,\text{Hz}}{(1 - 0.1143)}$$

$$f' = \frac{2013\,\text{Hz}}{0.88}$$

$$f' = 2272.99\ \text{Hz}$$

Therefore, this outcome indicates that the patrol car siren is emitting approximately 2272.99 Hz as it approaches the listeners. Now, the case of the stationary listeners versus the patrol car moving away from them is considered. The appropriate solution is given as follows:

$$f' = \frac{f}{\left(1 + \frac{v_{source}}{v_{snd}}\right)}$$

$$f' = \frac{2013\,\text{Hz}}{\left(1 + \frac{38.89\,\text{m/s}}{340\,\text{m/s}}\right)}$$

$$f' = \frac{2013\,\text{Hz}}{(1 + 0.1143)}$$

$$f' = \frac{2013\ \text{Hz}}{1.1143}$$

$$f' = 1806.52\ \text{Hz}$$

The second half of the example problem considers the moving vehicles that are approaching, passing, and moving away from the traveling police car. The case of simultaneously approaching vehicles is solved through the following mathematics.

$$f' = f\left(\frac{v_{\text{snd}} \pm v_{\text{obs}}}{v_{\text{snd}} \pm v_{\text{source}}}\right)$$

$$f' = f\left(\frac{v_{\text{snd}} - v_{\text{obs}}}{v_{\text{snd}} - v_{\text{source}}}\right)$$

$$f' = 2013\ \text{Hz}\left(\frac{340\ \text{m/s} - 15.64\ \text{m/s}}{340\ \text{m/s} - 38.89\ \text{m/s}}\right)$$

$$f' = 2013\ \text{Hz}\left(\frac{324.36\ \text{m/s}}{301.11\ \text{m/s}}\right)$$

$$f' = 2013\ \text{Hz}\ (1.07)$$

$$f' = 2168.43\ \text{Hz}\ (1.07)$$

The outcome of these calculations shows that the approaching condition is approximately 2168.43 Hz. Similarly, the situation in which the vehicles are simultaneously moving away from each other may be investigated through the basic formula. The appropriate mathematics are given as follows:

$$f' = f\left(\frac{v_{\text{snd}} \pm v_{\text{obs}}}{v_{\text{snd}} \pm v_{\text{source}}}\right)$$

$$f' = f\left(\frac{v_{\text{snd}} + v_{\text{obs}}}{v_{\text{snd}} + v_{\text{source}}}\right)$$

$$f' = 2013\ \text{Hz}\left(\frac{340\ \text{m/s} + 15.64\ \text{m/s}}{340\ \text{m/s} + 38.89\ \text{m/s}}\right)$$

$$f' = 2013\,\text{Hz}\left(\frac{355.64\ \text{m/s}}{378.89\ \text{m/s}}\right)$$

$$f' = 2013\ \text{Hz}\ (0.9386)$$

$$f' = 1889.47\ \text{Hz}$$

The outcome of these calculations show a frequency of 1889 Hz to describe the situation in which the police car and passing vehicles are simultaneously moving away from each other.

Vehicle sirens are useful communication tools. Their wailing provides a high-pitched sound through which other motorists and pedestrians are warned regarding the approaching of any emergency vehicle, including law enforcement vehicles. On roadways and intersections, motorists yield the right-of-way to emergency vehicles whose sirens communicate the presence of an emergency vehicle. They also act as resources through which intersections may be cleared to facilitate the passing of emergency traffic. Not all sirens are completely mobile. Instead, some public warning systems use sirens during emergencies to warn people of inclement conditions that necessitate attention and that may endanger society. For example, many cities and towns use warning sirens to warn residents of impending storms, natural disasters, and their associated dangers. A classic example is the tornado siren. Regardless of their purposes and uses, the characteristics of the sounds emitted by both stationary and mobile sirens may be examined from the perspective of the Doppler effect.

These examples and mathematics are relatively straightforward and understandable. Within the domain of the justice system and public safety, many more instances of wave theory and Doppler applications are prevalent. Practically all law enforcement agencies have some type of radar system. The most blatant example involves a radar gun that is used to determine the speeds of passing vehicles. Not only can the speed of moving vehicles be detected, but distance can also be measured between the moving object and the observer (The University of Sydney, 2013). Aviation radar also involves these same principles of the Doppler effect, thereby facilitating an examination of aircraft distances (The University of Sydney, 2013). These concepts are not constrained to solely managing roadway or aviation traffic. Instead, they are applicable to objects emitting waves with respect to their relative positioning versus observers. Regardless of the type of scenario involving the emission of sound and the positioning relationships between emitting and observing entities, the mathematics of the Doppler effect are an essential aspect of communications.

Visual Resources

Video resources represent numerous platforms through which communications occur throughout the justice system. Evening news programs represent a strong method of communicating with audiences nationally. During 2011, "more than four times as many people watched the three network evening newscasts on ABC, CBS, and NBC during the dinner hour than watched the highest-rated shows on the three cable news channels (CNN, Fox News, and MSNBC) during prime time" (Network News, 2013). News media stories communicate to mass audiences the details of events that occur in the justice domain, ranging from the popular Casey Anthony trial to the reporting of local events among towns and cities.

Video resources are now accessible anywhere, anytime. People may view television programs or may download video materials via iPads, smartphones, or other cellular devices. Video resources are common and permeate nearly every facet of society. It is not uncommon for individuals to record visually a variety of events involving law enforcement officers and then upload them to video Internet sites. By doing so, the details of the recorded event are communicated to a mass audience.

Video resources are also used to record documentaries of events that occur within the justice system. They are also used to assist law enforcement organizations in the solving of crimes through the airing of such shows as *America's Most Wanted* or *Unsolved Mysteries*. For decades, video has been used to socialize various perspectives of policing and law enforcement entities through television shows such as *ADAM-12* and *NCIS*. Viewing such programs influences the mental models people have of law enforcement organizations and their personnel regardless of the accuracy of the shows.

Regardless of the video resource used to communicate some attributes of the justice domain, there are mathematical principles that govern and influence video resources. These mathematical principles also involve a consideration of the human mind and visual senses. Some research suggests that the "conscious perception" of humans involves the "global synchronization of neuronal assemblies in the β-frequency (15–25 Hertz)" (Vyshedskiy, 2013). Attention rhythm represents this wave involving the β-frequency. The premise of attention rhythm indicates that human consciousness is intermittent at a rate of "15 to 25 frames per second" (Vyshedskiy, 2013).

This concept of attention rhythm has long been leveraged by the producers of films. Silent films used frame rates between 16 and 23 frames per second (f/s); sound films used a frame rate of 24 f/s because of its slowness and low cost, and because it "allowed for sufficient sound quality"; and television also uses a rate of 24 f/s (Vyshedskiy, 2008, p. 118). Frame rates are important with respect to the ability of the human mind and visual sense to see and process information. From the biological perspective, regarding the rate of 15 f/s of the attention rhythm, the human eye uses the "least complicated" and slowest method of processing visual information that "serves the conscious mind" (Vyshedskiy, 2008, p. 119). Therefore, only by approximately the amount of 1 Hz, the 16 f/s rate exceeds the 15 Hz frequency minimum that is associated with the attention rhythm (Vyshedskiy, 2008, p. 119).

The notion of frames per second is pertinent within the context of ensuring that video images appear to exhibit normal movement when viewed by humans. Many law enforcement organizations may produce their own videos for training purposes (North Carolina Wesleyan College, 2013). Other films and videos may be produced by professional film companies (Emergency Film Group, 2013). In many cases, such videos may involve the use of models to simulate reality and are commonly associated with the notion of special effects.

When using models to generate special effects within video products, mathematical calculations are necessary to determine the "proper scale factor" that is necessary for increasing the speed of cameras for "any given angle" (Fielding, 2000). This speed represents the "rate of speed" at which "film passes through a motion-picture camera," thereby generating an expansion of "real time" to "restore the proper time-scale relationship to the moving miniature" (Fielding, 2000). For example, the effects of gravity may be expressed mathematically via the following formula (Fielding, 2000):

$$f = \sqrt{\frac{D}{d}} \tag{14.10}$$

Within this equation, the following variables are pertinent (Fielding, 2000):

f = factor increase of the operating speed of the camera
D = distance in feet regarding the real object
d = distance in feet regarding the miniature model

The derived factor increase may also be used to generate a new value that represents an increase in frames per second that is necessary to facilitate realism within the video imagery. The following formula may be used to calculate the new frame rate:

$$f_{\text{rate}} = (f)(\text{base rate}) \tag{14.11}$$

A relatively straightforward example problem may be considered to demonstrate this formula. Such a problem is stated as follows:

> A law enforcement training video is being produced that shows the wrecking of an automobile. A 1/8 scale model car is used to generate the required video scenes. If the distance fallen by a real car is 80 ft whereas the distance fallen by a model is 10 ft, calculate the factor increase for the operating of the camera. Assuming that the production involves a normal frame rate of 24 f/s, determine the new frame rate.

Solving this problem necessitates a consideration of the given data and the exercising of the formula appropriately. The solution is presented as follows:

Step 1: Initialize the data
Within the problem statement, the given data is expressed as follows:

$D = 80$ ft
$d = 10$ ft

Step 2: Determine the camera factor increase
This step necessitates the substitution of the given data into the formula appropriately, and then performing the necessary mathematics to derive the sought operating speed of the camera. These tasks are shown as follows:

$$f = \sqrt{\frac{D}{d}}$$

$$f = \sqrt{\frac{80 \text{ ft}}{10 \text{ ft}}}$$

$$f = \sqrt{8}$$

$$f = 2.82$$

Step 3: Determine the new frame rate

This step involves using the derived factor increase to calculate the new frame rate. Determining this value is accomplished by multiplying the factor increase by the base value of 24 f/s. The sought value is derived as follows:

$$f_{\text{rate}} = (f)(\text{base rate})$$

$$f_{\text{rate}} = (2.82)(24 \text{ f/s})$$

$$f_{\text{rate}} = 67.88 \text{ f/s}$$

The use of models is often less expensive and less dangerous than using real items when producing video scenes. Through mathematics, one may calculate the increases of camera factors and frame rates that are necessary for exhibiting realistic characteristics within video products. On the basis of the above formulas, Table 14.1 shows various model dimensions, camera factors, and frame rates that may be used to exhibit realism within video products.

Another consideration of visual imagery involves the shutter speed of cameras. Shutter speed is synonymous with the notion of exposure, which represents "the intensity of light that passes through the lens and the time each frame is exposed to the light"

Table 14.1 Model Dimensions, Camera Factors, and Frame Rates

Miniature Scale	Camera-Speed Increase Factor	Adjusted Operating Speed for Camera
1/2	1.4	33×/second
1/4	2	48×/second
1/8	2.8	67×/second
1/10	3.2	77×/second
1/12	3.5	84×/second
1/16	4	96×/second
1/20	4.5	108×/second
1/24	4.9	117×/second
1/36	6	144×/second
1/48	7	168×/second
1/64	8	192×/second
1/100	10	240×/second

Source: Fielding, Raymond. (2000). *The Technique of Special Effects Cinematography* (4th ed., p. 326). Woburn, MA: Focal Press.

(Ascher & Pincus, 2007). Shutter speed is measured in units of seconds. The shutter speed is calculated through the use of the following formula (Mamer, 2009):

$$S = \frac{1}{(2)(\text{frames per second})} \tag{14.12}$$

This formula is appropriate for a typical 180° shutter (Brown, 2002). Although this formula is relatively simple and basic, it does not accommodate varying shutter sizes. Most shutters use a half-moon construct, and other sizes and types are available. If a shutter of a different size is necessary, then a modified formula is necessary for calculating shutter speed. This modified formula is presented as follows (Brown, 2002):

$$S_m = \left(\frac{\text{degrees of shutter opening}}{(360)(\text{frames per second})}\right) \tag{14.13}$$

Determining the appropriate shutter size is relatively easy to accomplish regarding both formulas. For instance, using the typical 24 f/s and a 180° shutter, the appropriate shutter size would be $\frac{1}{48}$ second.

Understanding shutter size and exposure time is relevant within the context of the justice domain. Often, the scenes of various crimes are photographed either digitally or through the use of traditional film cameras. Such images may be released publically through news media or they may remain within the boundaries of the law enforcement organization to support the investigative process. They may also be used as evidence.

The importance of correctly calculating and judging the appropriate mathematical values for photography and visual resources cannot be understated. It is an imperative aspect of documenting various events within the justice domain. Portraying accurately and completely the details of a crime scene necessitates that "investigators and photographers thoughtfully and purposefully record true and accurate depictions of the location and evidence" (Duncan, 2010). Such meticulous attention to detail provides visual resources through which a relationship may be established "between evidence recovered at a crime scene and the identification of a defendant in a court of law" (Duncan, 2010).

The use of visual resources pervades the justice domain whether they involve disseminating information through news television programs or through newspaper photographs. Generating and producing these visual resources require a foundational knowledge of mathematical formulas that govern and influence a variety of products ranging from training films to news items. Only a few formulas are presented and discussed herein; many others exist, ranging from the calculation of photographic angles to various aspects of illumination. Readers desiring a greater understanding of such principles are encouraged to consult other texts in media production, cinematography, and photography. Regardless, mathematics is a salient consideration of visual communications within the justice domain.

Electronic Networks

The use of electronic networks is common within the justice system for a variety of purposes. Electronic networks provide a basis of communicating through electronic mail, computer networks, mobile and wireless devices (e.g., smartphones and iPads), fax machines, telephones, and a variety of other communication tools. Although people frequently use such devices, they may be ignorant of the mathematical principles that govern and influence the functioning of such devices and their associated communications. Much mathematics underlies the basics of electronic communications. Only a thumbnail sketch of such principles is discussed within this text. Readers desiring a greater understanding of these materials are encouraged to consult other texts in data communications, electronics technology, and computer science.

Within the corrections system, the use of radio frequency identification (RFID) serves a variety of purposes. Examples include improved monitoring and controlling of inmates and reducing of "staff time"; reducing both injuries and violence; reducing the potential of escapes; reducing the quantity of investigations and improving investigative capabilities; and reducing "inmate grievances, disciplinary actions, and lawsuits" (Hickman, Davis, Wells, & Eisman, 2010). Inmates may wear RFID devices as ankle or wrist bracelets (Hickman et al., 2010). One consideration of RFID communications involves transmission distance that represents the readable range at which readers are able to detect signals and at which RFID devices receive power that is sufficient for operating (Banks, Hannay, Pachano, & Thompson, 2007, p. 112).

Using RFID technologies necessitates a consideration of bandwidth and channel capacity within the communications environment. Regarding the issue of bandwidth, one may consider the channel capacity mathematically via the Nyquist method. The formula expressing the Nyquist method is stated as follows (Banks et al., 2007, p. 111):

$$C = 2B \log_2 L \tag{14.14}$$

Within the Nyquist method, the variable C represents the channel capacity (i.e., "the rate at which bits may be transmitted through the system"), the variable B represents the bandwidth, and the variable L represents the quantity of "logic levels used to encode bits" (Banks et al., 2007, p. 111). If a communications medium has between a 50 MHz and 100 MHz frequency spectrum and has two logic levels, its capacity is approximately 100 Mbps (Banks et al., 2007, p. 111).

Other facets of wireless communication involve the use of radio transmitters and receivers across some distance. Many mathematical principles govern and influence such communication technologies. For instance, known as the Friis equation, the mathematical formula that expresses the transmission distance is given as follows (Bakshi & Bakshi, 2008):

$$P_R = P_T G_T G_R \left(\frac{\lambda}{4\pi d} \right)^2 \tag{14.15}$$

The following variables are affiliated with this formula:

d = distance between antennae
G_R = directional gain of the receiving antenna
G_T = directional gain of the transmitting antenna
P_R = power received per unit area at the receiving antenna
P_T = power transmitted by the transmitting antenna
λ = wavelength

Demonstrating this concept is achieved through a sample problem. Such a sample problem is stated as follows (Bakshi & Bakshi, 2008):*

> Two antennae are separated from each other by a distance of approximately 30 miles, and the respective gains of each are 45 dB. Both are matched at 3 GHz, and are lossless. Determine what power is received if power is transmitted at 36.8115 W.

Solving this problem necessitates some intermediary conversions and preparatory calculations before the Friis equation may be exercised. The solution is given as follows:

Step 1: Initialize the data set
This step involves expressing the data that is contained within the problem statement. The instantiation of variables is shown as follows:

d = 30 miles
G_R = 45 dB
G_T = 45 dB
P_R = ??? (This value is sought.)
P_T = 36.8115 W
f = 3 GHz
λ = ??? (This value must be calculated.)

Step 2: Perform intermediary conversions and calculations
Distance must be converted into metric units. The distance of one mile is equivalent to approximately 1609.35 m. Therefore, the conversion is accomplished mathematically as follows:

$$(30 \text{ miles})\left(\frac{1609.35 \text{ m}}{1 \text{ mile}}\right) = 48,280.5 \text{ m}$$

The value of the wavelength was not stated within the given problem. Therefore, it must be calculated. Wavelength is equivalent to the speed of light divided by frequency. Therefore, wavelength is determined mathematically as follows:

$$\lambda = \frac{c}{f} = \frac{3\times10^8}{3\times10^9} = 0.1 \text{ m}$$

The values of G_T and G_R must also accommodate a common unit. Establishing this basis is accomplished as follows:

$$G_R = G_T = \text{Antilog}_{10}\left[\frac{45 \text{ dB}}{10}\right] = 31.622\times10^3$$

* Sample problem is a derivative of Bakshi and Bakshi.

Step 3: Exercise the Friis equation

This step involves the exercising of the Friis equation to determine the value of G_R. Determining the G_R value outcome is accomplished as follows:

$$P_R = P_T G_T G_R \left(\frac{\lambda}{4\pi d}\right)^2$$

$$P_R = (36.8115\text{ W})(31.622 \times 10^3)(31.622 \times 10^3)\left(\frac{0.1}{(4\pi)(48250.5)}\right)^2$$

$$P_R = 1 \times 10^{-3}$$

The outcome of the Friis equation indicates that a P_R value of 1×10^{-3} represents the power received. Algebraically, this formula may be manipulated to solve for any of its variables. When implementing the formula, readers must be mindful of the necessity of maintaining a consistent set of measurement units within the mathematical calculations to ensure correctness and accuracy. The Friis equation is only a sampling of the quantitative formulas that govern and influence communication networks.

Another consideration of network mathematics involves network attenuation that represents a "loss of signal strength" that originates from an array of sources, such as "cable type, cable length," or "poor terminations" (Jones & Jones, 1996). For networking involving copper cabling, the attenuation within a network may be examined quantitatively through the following formula (Anttalainen, 2003):

$$A_{dB} = k\sqrt{f}\,\text{dB} \tag{14.16}$$

Within this formula, the following variables are pertinent:

A_{dB} = attenuation measured in decibels
f = frequency
k = specific constant for each cable

The attenuation formula is rather straightforward and understandable, and involves few mathematical calculations. It is used to determine the "approximate attenuation at other frequencies if the attenuation at one frequency is known" (Anttalainen, 2003). Given this notion, one may examine the attenuation formula quantitatively. For instance, for an observed frequency of 250 kHz, the attenuation value is approximately 6 dB (Anttalainen, 2003). Using these values, it is determined that the "four times higher frequency of 1 MHz" exhibits an attenuation value of approximately 12 dB (Anttalainen, 2003).

Attenuation originates from a variety of sources thereby impeding communications. The magnitude of the effects of attenuation is dependent on the frequency of a wave and the characteristics of objects through which the wave passes (Wall, Kanclirz, Jing, Faircloth, & Barrett, 2004). Some objects may be impenetrable, whereas others impede communication in varying amounts. For instance, mountains are capable of attenuating 100% of a signal, thereby completely inhibiting the ability to communicate (Wall et al., 2004). Attenuation may worsen during circumstances involving natural or man-made conditions. Instances of rain or the presence of buildings may influence attenuation, thereby degrading the ability to communicate (Wall et al., 2004).

Many other formulas exist, ranging from methods of calculating bandwidth, FM demodulation, spectrum measurements, and a variety of other applications and measurements (Tretter, 2008). Regardless of the consideration, mathematical principles represent foundational aspects and descriptors of communications technologies within the justice domain, ranging from radio devices to computer networks. Although law enforcement personnel may be unaware of such mathematical premises, they are necessary for designing, developing, and exercising electronic communications systems within the justice domain.

Commentary Regarding Mathematics and Communication

Communicating occurs daily within the justice system throughout a variety of methods and serves a variety of purposes. People exchange information through personal conversations or through the various uses of communications technologies. Although this text presents various mathematical formulas and models that influence and govern such communications, many others exist. Because this text represents an introductory consideration of these concepts, it is beyond the scope of these writings to provide a deep exploration of higher mathematics within the communications domain. However, it is useful to mention such areas for readers that may wish to further explore these topics.

Among electronic settings, mathematics is prevalent within the context of data communications. From this perspective, mathematical formulas exist through which digital signal processing may be crafted and explored. Areas of analysis include error correction within data signals involving parity examinations, half-duplex and full-duplex transmissions, and numbering systems for communications devices (Horak, 2007). Such mathematics may involve simple algebraic formulas or may necessitate a higher knowledge of calculus and differential equations.

Discrete mathematics is a domain that involves an exploration of the foundations of computing mathematically. It provides mathematical techniques of logical proofs, network flows, graph theory, tree data structures, and probability and statistics that are used to influence the crafting of software and hardware systems (Ferland, 2009). Software and hardware systems represent relevant components of electronic communications networks, applications, and packages.

Communications technologies are composed of various electronic components. These resources involve much mathematics to describe their functioning. Examples include the use of formulas regarding AC and DC circuitry, band theory and diodes, field effect transistors, and digital circuits and devices (Eggleston, 2011). Other uses of mathematics within this realm include applications involving amplifiers, power supplies, opto-electric devices, and the design of circuit boards that are used within communication devices (Gates, 2012).

Mathematics is used to model, describe, and explore every facet of reality. Essentially, the use of mathematics is a form of communication that transmits messages regarding some facet of reality to observers who receive these messages. This concept is delineated within Figure 14.5 (Weaver, 2009).

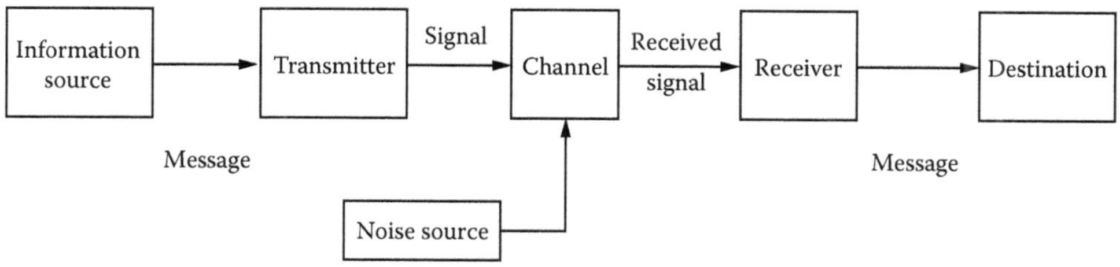

Figure 14.5 Communication system concepts. A communication system may be reduced to these fundamental elements. In telephony the signal is a varying electric current, and the channel is a wire. In speech the signal is varying sound pressure, and the channel the ear. Frequently things not intended by the information source are impressed on the signal. The static of radio is one example: distortion in telephony is another. All these additions may be called noise. (From Weaver, Warren (2009). The mathematics of communication. In C. David Mortensen (Ed.), *Communication Theory* (2nd ed., p. 29). New Brunswick, NJ: Transaction Publishers.)

Figure 14.5 shows the basic communication process and alludes to the mathematical principles that govern and influence human communication. Electric currents are governed by a range of mathematical principles representing Ohm's law in the domain of electronics (Brumbach & Clade, 2003). The wire channels involve notions of channel capacity and bandwidth that are discussed within this text. The concepts of sound pressure and the biological attributes of the human body are also introduced herein, and involve considerations of wave theory and the Doppler effect. Regarding the concept of noise, the discussion of attenuation within this chapter is pertinent.

The influence and governance of mathematics within the context of communicating are inescapable. All human communication is subjected to these tenets and theories. Understanding the intangible characteristics of communicating involves the use of mathematics to express the variables and their associated relationships that exist within communications domains. Therefore, mathematics itself represents a communicative resource through which ideas and concepts are exchanged among humans. Given such notions, mathematics itself may be perceived as a language through which mutual understandings may be achieved regarding the communications domain (Baber, 2011).

Chapter Comments and Summary

This chapter introduced the concepts of mathematics that influence and govern communications. All communications may be modeled and described mathematically. Within the justice system, people use daily electronic mail, fax machines, televisions, telephones (both landlines and mobile devices), global positioning systems, and an array of other communications devices. In most all cases, people are ignorant of the mathematical principles that govern and influence their communications.

Humans are capable of perceiving sound through the sense of hearing. Audio communication involves sound waves that travel through a medium. Usually, this medium is air. Sound waves may be considered from the perspective of the typical sine wave mathematics. Such waves exhibit the characteristics of period, frequency, and amplitude. Sound waves may also be considered from the perspective of the Doppler effect in which humans perceive changes in sound with respect to their relative position versus the source of the sound. The conditions that describe the Doppler effect involve situations in which the source of the sound is stationary and human observers are moving, stationary human observers versus a moving source of sound, and simultaneously moving human observers and sources of sound.

Humans are capable of perceiving a variety of physical events visually. This notion involves a consideration of the human capacity to process information mentally within the constraints of cognition and physically with respect to the biological characteristics of the human body. Video resources are used for a variety of purposes within the justice system, ranging from the production of training videos to the production of film documentaries. Mathematically, formulas exist through which scale-size models may be used within such visual resources or to determine appropriate frame rates that are necessary for mimicking realism when videos are viewed by observers.

Electronic networks permeate modern communication environments. People communicate through electronic mail, audio conferencing, and video conferencing through the use of electronic networks. Numerous mathematical constructs exist through which network models may be crafted, developed, and exercised to facilitate human communication. Mathematical models may be applied to explore network attenuation or to examine the characteristics of radio communication.

Mathematics permeates every facet of communications. The formulas presented herein represent only a few of the quantitative methods that exist within the communications domain that describe and explore the activities of communicating that occur within the justice domain. The entirety of the communications process involves different considerations of mathematical principles, ranging from theories of electric currents to wave theory. Regardless of the consideration, mathematics may be used to describe every facet of the communications process. Therefore, mathematics itself may be perceived as a communications resource and as a language through which mutual understandings may be facilitated within the communications domain.

Terminology

Amplitude
Attention rhythm
Attenuation
Biological constraint
Camera
Communications process
Compression
Cryptography
Diffraction
Doppler effect
Echo
Exposure
Frame rate
Frequency
Hertz

Language
Listener
Loudness
Mathematics
Model
Noise
Operating speed
Period
Rarefaction
Reflection
Refraction
Sequential
Shutter speed
Signal
Sinusoidal
Sound
Sound wave
Wave
Wavelength

THOUGHT AND DISCUSSION QUESTIONS

1. Mathematics permeates every facet of communicating that occurs within the justice system. This chapter introduces various mathematical principles that are associated with auditory and visual communications. However, many other formulas exist through which communication may be described mathematically. Do some research, and locate two additional formulas that describe auditory and visual communications that are not discussed within this chapter. Write a brief essay that discusses and demonstrates the functioning of your selected formulas.
2. This chapter introduces the concepts of electronic communications devices and some of their associated mathematical principles. In addition to the concepts discussed herein, two other formulas that involve a consideration of electronic components are Ohm's law and Kirchoff's law. Do some research regarding these theories, and write a brief essay that explains each theory. Within this essay, demonstrate sample problems that delineate the mathematics of both theories.
3. Discrete mathematics contains a variety of theories that influence the design and functioning of communications networks ranging from graph theory to tree structures. Do some research in the domain of discrete mathematics regarding each of these topics. Write a brief essay that discusses and explains how graph theory and tree structures may be leveraged to influence the designing and implementing of communications systems.
4. This chapter provides some considerations of mathematics with respect to the constraints and limitations of humans biologically regarding communications. Do some research concerning this issue, and identify two mathematical principles that influence humans biologically when communicating. Write a brief essay that details and discusses your findings.

References

Anttalainen, T. (2003). *Introduction to telecommunications network engineering* (2nd ed., p. 171). Norwood, MA: Artech House Publishing.

Ascher, S., & Pincus, E. (2007). *The filmmaker's handbook: A comprehensive guide for the digital age* (p. 233). London: Penguin Books.

Baber, R. (2011). *The language of mathematics: Utilizing math in practice*. Hoboken, NJ: John Wiley and Sons Publishing.

Bakshi, A., & Bakshi, U. (2008). *Antennas and wave propagation* (pp. 2–26). Pune, India: Technical Publications Pune.

Banks, J., Hannay, D., Pachano, M., & Thompson, L. (2007). *RFID applied*. Hoboken, NJ: Wiley Publishing.

Brown, B. (2002). *Cinematography theory and practice: Image making for cinematographers, directors, and videographers* (p. 125). Burlington, MA: Focal Press.

Brumbach, M., & Clade, J. (2003). *Industrial maintenance*. Clifton Park, NY: Delmar-Cengage Publishing.

de Certeau, M. (n.d.). Statistics quotes. Brainyquote.com. Retrieved from http://www.brainyquote.com/quotes/keywords/statistics_3.html (accessed February 17, 2013).

Duncan, C. (2010). *Advanced crime scene photography* (p. 1). Boca Raton, FL: CRC Press.

Eggleston, D. (2011). *Basic electronics for scientists and engineers*. New York: Cambridge University Press.

Elmore, W., & Heald, M. (1969). *Physics of waves* (p. 164). New York: McGraw-Hill.

Emergency Film Group. (2013). Frequently asked questions. Retrieved from http://www.efilmgroup.com/page.php/faq.htm (accessed February 22, 2013).

Ferland, K. (2009). *Discrete mathematics: An introduction to proofs and combinatorics*. Boston: Houghton-Mifflin Publishing.

Fielding, R. (2000). *The technique of special effects cinematography* (4th ed., p. 326). Woburn, MA: Focal Press.

Gates, E. (2012). *Introduction to electronics* (6th ed.). Clifton Park, NY: Delmar-Cengage Publishing.

Giancoli, D. (2008). *Physics for scientists and engineers with modern physics* (4th ed.). Upper Saddle River, NJ: Pearson Prentice Hall Publishing.

Havemeyer, H. (2013). How to convert meters per second to miles per hour. Retrieved from http://www.ehow.com/how_4821647_per-second-miles-per-hour.html (accessed February 21, 2013).

Hickman, L., Davis, L., Wells, E., & Eisman, M. (2010). *Tracking inmates and locating staff with active radio-frequency identification (RFID): Early lessons learned in one U.S. correctional facility* (p. x). Santa Monica, CA: RAND Corporation.

Horak, R. (2007). *Telecommunications and data communications handbook*. Hoboken, NJ: Wiley Publishing.

Johnson, K. (2011). *Acoustic and auditory phonetics* (3rd ed.). Hoboken, NJ: Wiley Publishing.

Jones, C., & Jones, S. P. (1996). *Patrick-Turner's industrial automation library* (p. 27). Garden Grove, CA: Patrick-Turner Publishing Company.

Kang, J. (2002). *Acoustics of long spaces: Theory and design practice* (p. 8). London: Thomas Telford Publishing.

Khan Academy. (2013). Amplitude, Period, Frequency and Wavelength of Periodic Waves. Retrieved from https://www.khanacademy.org/science/physics/waves-and-optics/v/amplitude–period–frequency-and-wavelength-of-periodic-waves (accessed February 20, 2013).

Mamer, B. (2009). *Film production technique: Creating the accomplished image* (5th ed., p. 268). Belmont, CA: Wadsworth Cengage Publishing.

Merriam-Webster Dictionary. (2013a). s.v. "mathematics." Retrieved from http://www.merriam-webster.com/dictionary/mathematics (accessed February 23, 2013).

Merriam-Webster Dictionary. (2013b). s.v. "sound." Retrieved from http://www.merriam-webster.com/dictionary/sound (accessed February 16, 2013).

Myers, R. (2006). *The basics of physics* (p. 143). Westport, CT: Greenwood Publishing Group.
National Aeronautics and Space Administration. (2013). What are electromagnetic waves? Retrieved from http://science.hq.nasa.gov/kids/imagers/ems/waves2.html (accessed February 15, 2013).
Network news: The pace of change accelerates. (2013). *The state of the news media 2012: An annual report of American Journalism.* Pew Research Center. Retrieved from http://stateofthemedia.org/2012/network-news-the-pace-of-change-accelerates/?src=prc-section (accessed February 22, 2012).
North Carolina Wesleyan College. (2013). Police gunfighting. Retrieved from http://faculty.ncwc.edu/mstevens/205/205lect02a.htm (accessed February 21, 2013).
Olson, H. (1967). *Music, physics, and engineering* (2nd ed., p. 14). Mineola, NY: Dover Publications.
Pachghare, V. K. (2009). *Cryptography and information security* (p. 6). New Delhi, India: PHI Private Learning, Ltd.
Pierce, A. (1989). *Acoustics: An introduction to its physical principles and applications* (p. 28). Melville, NY: Acoustical Society of America.
Strader, T. (2011). *Digital produce management, technology, and practice: Interdisciplinary perspectives* (p. 9). Hershey, PA: IGI Global Publishing.
Study Physics. (2013). Lesson 44: Frequency, wavelength, & amplitude. Retrieved from http://www.studyphysics.ca/newnotes/20/unit03_mechanicalwaves/chp141516_waves/lesson44.htm (accessed February 20, 2013).
Sudhakar, A., & Palli, S. (2010). *Circuits and networks: Analysis and synthesis* (4th ed., p. 168). New Delhi, India: Tata McGraw Hill Publishing.
The University of Sydney. (2013). Chapter 14: Doppler measurement. Retrieved from http://www.acfr.usyd.edu.au/pdfs/training/sensorSystems/14%20Doppler%20Measurement.pdf (accessed February 22, 2013).
Tretter, S. (2008). *Communication system design using DSP algorithms.* New York: Springer Publishing.
University of Iowa. (2013). Sound. Retrieved from http://www.physics.uiowa.edu/~umallik/adventure/sound04.html (accessed February 14, 2013).
Vyshedskiy, A. (2008). *On the origin of the human mind—Three theories: Uniqueness of human mind, evolution of the human mind, and the neurological basis of conscious experience.* Boston: Mobile Reference Publishing.
Vyshedskiy, A. (2013). On the origin of the human mind. Retrieved from http://www.mobilereference.com/mind/online/ch4p4.htm (accessed February 22, 2013).
Wall, D., Kanclirz, J., Jing, Y., Faircloth, J., & Barrett, J. (2004). *Managing and securing a cisco structured wireless-aware network* (p. 60). Rockland, MA: Syngress Publishing.
Weaver, W. (2009). The mathematics of communication. In C. D. Mortensen (Ed.), *Communication theory* (2nd ed., p. 29). New Brunswick, NJ: Transaction Publishers.

Communication Ethics and Professional Organizations

15

> Ethics is knowing the difference between what you have a right to do and what is right to do.
>
> **—Potter Stewart (Stewart, n.d.)**

Objectives

The objectives of this chapter are to

- Differentiate the concepts of values, ethics, and morals
- Introduce communication ethics from different cultural perspectives
- Introduce communication ethics from the perspective of decisions
- Introduce professional communications organizations and societies
- Introduce organizational and societal codes of ethics
- Demonstrate the scope of ethics within legal communications

Introduction

Communication permeates every society on Earth. Every society and nation communicates internally. Nations and societies also may exhibit some characteristics of external communication with different societies and nations. When the act of communicating occurs either within a single society or nation or between different societies or nations, the basic instantiations of the communications process are identical. Essentially, senders encode and transmit messages to receivers who decode them and who may generate feedback. Similarly, the basic concepts of noise within the communication domain are identical—human misunderstandings of messages occur, environmental factors affect communication, and so forth.

However, among nations and societies, there are differences that influence communications: morals, values, and ethics. Morals are the basic notions of right and wrong that permeate a society. A moral is defined as "relating to principles of right and wrong in behavior" and "capable of right or wrong action" (*Merriam-Webster*, 2013d). Morals represent the foundational beliefs of society, concerning the conceptualization of right versus wrong, that influence human behaviors through time. Values are "enduring beliefs" that are derived from "some early form of indoctrination and experience" that may be "learned from parents, the community, school, peers, professional organizations, and personal self-development" (Ledlow & Coppola, 2011). Morals and values are complementary, and affect the basic worldviews and beliefs of humans.

Ethics are derived from the complementation of morals and values. Ethics represents a fashion of mitigating the effects of uncertainty among situations "involving moral issues" (Banks, 2009). The rendering of decisions within the justice domain must exude professionalism, and is influenced by morals and values. Within the context of professionalism, the notion of ethics is perceived as "behaviors relating to a profession and is an analysis of behavior relevant to a certain profession" (Pollock, 2010). Ethics represents conceptually the "rightness or wrongness of an action or behavior" in which values are influential (West & Turner, 2009). Ethics are influenced by both external (e.g., "rules of society") and internal (e.g., personal character) factors that influence human decisions, thereby exhibiting both social and individual characteristics (Ward, 2010). Essentially, ethics represents "correct conduct, responsible practice, and fair human interactions according to certain principles and values," and involve both judgment and character (Ward, 2010). Ethics also represent a foundational aspect of "civilized society" (Fernando, 2009).

Societies worldwide are different and unique. Morals differ among societies, and change through time (Bunge, 2010). Therefore, no "universal rationality" exists globally regarding perceptions and beliefs of right versus wrong (Bentley, Earls, O'Brien, & Maeda, 2011). Ethics are derived from morals. Therefore, societal perceptions regarding ethical beliefs also differ globally. Such observations are also applicable to global values among societies. Given such notions, some actions and behaviors that are deemed moral and ethical in one society may be deemed as completely immoral and unacceptable within another society.

These observations have implications for communication within the justice domain. Law enforcement officers and agents within the justice system must communicate with a variety of different people representing an array of societal and cultural backgrounds. Within the communications process, messages that may be deemed appropriate for one audience may be somewhat or completely inappropriate for another audience. Other instances involve court proceedings concerning the First Amendment right of free speech in which judgments are rendered involving considerations of morality, values, and ethics. Another perspective involves the ethicality of decisions that are rendered by personnel within the justice system when communicating or by news media when reporting the facts of certain events (especially those of moral turpitude). Ethics represents a fashion of employing moral beliefs through reasoning, thereby exhibiting ethical conduct with respect to a "moral foundation" (Brown, 2011). Regardless of the situations or circumstances, the influences of morals, values, and ethics permeate communications within the justice domain.

Perspectives of Ethics

Ethics are an integral aspect of society and the justice domain. There is no one solitary perspective of ethics that encapsulates a thorough understanding of ethical concepts among societies. The discussions of this book provide an introductory synopsis of various perspectives that are applicable within the context of communication within the justice domain. Readers desiring to review discussions of additional depth are encouraged to consult other texts in philosophy or organizational ethics. Considerations of various perspectives of ethics exist through which one may gain an initial understanding of ethical concepts regarding communication in the justice domain.

One perspective of ethics involves the influences of religion. This perspective involves considerations of the influences that "religion makes about the relationship of the divine/eternal to humans and the world, and vice versa" within the context of human communication (Larson, 2010, p. 48). Police subculture may involve ethical situations of communication that involve tenets of religion (Kopko, 2011). For example, investigators may be tempted to alter reports to reduce paperwork (Kopko, 2011). Other instances involve officers lying to cover for each other to avoid the repercussions of misconduct or other unacceptable behaviors (Kopko, 2011). Some religious beliefs conflict such instances of deception. Officers whose religious beliefs are conflicting thereby must make a choice regarding truthfulness in communication that involves religious and personal ethics.

Another ethical perspective of communication may be considered from an organizational context (Seeger, 2001). Various situations necessitate the presence of organization policies and guidelines among workplaces. Organizations experience instances of communication involving "employee privacy and voice, free speech, persuasion and coercion," and facets of "advertising and public relations" (Seeger, 2001). Organizational policies serve as governing resources that define and express the acceptable and unacceptable behaviors that may be exhibited within work environments. Often, such policies accommodate a code of ethics that "sets the minimum standards for business owners, managers, and employees to follow when completing various business functions" (Vietz, 2013).

Another perspective of organizational communication involves the codes of ethics that are expressed by professional organizations. For example, the National Communication Association is a professional organization that exists to promote the "widespread appreciation of the importance of communication in public and private life, the application of competent communication to improve the quality of human life and relationships, and the use of knowledge about communication to solve human problems" (National Communication Association, 2013d). Its membership ascribes to a code of ethics that encompasses a variety of tenets, including "truthfulness, accuracy, honesty, and reason" when communicating (National Communication Association, 2013c).

Situational ethics also affect communication. The notion of relativism is synonymous with the basic premise of situational ethics (Pollock, 2012). Specifically, situational ethics involves the notion that "different situations call for different responses; some action can be right or wrong depending on the situational factors" (Pollock, 2012). Many scenarios involving "ethics and communication strategies" are influenced by the individual circumstances of the considered situation (Treadwell & Treadwell, 2005). Situational factors may be influenced by the desired intended audience that receives a communicated message (Treadwell & Treadwell, 2005). It may also involve attributes regarding the "what, when, where, how, and why" characteristics of the intended audience (Treadwell & Treadwell, 2005). Law enforcement organizations that craft news releases or public service messages must be concerned with these demographic characteristics. For example, communicating with the public along the U.S.–Mexican border may necessitate messages presented in both English and Spanish, and the content of the message must accommodate facets of societal culture.

Political perspectives of ethics involve the "implicit or explicit values and procedures" that are "accepted as crucial to the health and growth of a particular political system" (Larson, 2010, p. 50). Such notions involve considerations of public communication regarding the capacity of members of the public to "reach rational decisions, access to channels of public communication, and to relevant and accurate information about public issues, maximization of freedom of choice, tolerance of dissent, honesty in presenting motivations and consequences, and thoroughness and accuracy in presenting evidence and alternatives" (Larson, 2010, p. 50). These notions are highly relevant within the context of the justice system given the freedom of speech guaranteed within the U.S. Constitution. During elections for sheriffs, constables, or other law enforcement positions that are not appointed, communication with the general public is paramount to obtaining the votes of the citizenry. Communicating with the public may involve ethical arguments advocating a specific candidate or expressing the negative attributes of a candidate. The political parties that are affiliated with such candidates may sponsor advertising and marketing campaigns to influence public opinion and obtain votes.

Another perspective of communication and ethics involves legal communications. Within the justice system, attorneys communicate with clients, their peers, judges, juries, and a variety of other people. Such communication often involves ethical characteristics and influences. Within the justice system, instances of "withholding information" occur (Luizzi, 1993). Attorneys are entrusted with "defending those who have confessed to crimes" either verbally or in writing (Luizzi, 1993). During court proceedings, attorneys may also discredit and humiliate witnesses, "all to further the client's cause and all of which is beyond the purview or ordinary morality" (Luizzi, 1993). Certainly, within the context of ethics and legal communication also is the attorney–client privilege.

Other aspects of ethics and communication involve three paradigms: utilitarianism, altruism, and communitarianism. The basic premise of utilitarianism involves the notion that "good actions" are defined by the "consequences they bring" (Hendricks & Byers, 2006). Essentially, within utilitarianism, such actions are "judged by the extent to which they contribute to the good of the majority" (Hendricks & Byers, 2006). Within the utilitarian paradigm, actions are deemed ethical if they produce the "greatest good" for the largest quantity of people (West & Turner, 2011). From a communications perspective, reporting criminal activity to a law enforcement organization may result in the diminishment of crime within a locale. Therefore, the act of reporting the crime would be deemed ethical if its overall benefit was a societal reduction in crime.

Altruism involves the notion that "actions are moral if their primary purpose is to promote the best interests of others" (Northouse, 2010). Altruism is the foundational basis of numerous "movements and organizations" whose purposes and missions are benevolent (Johnson, 2012). Such organizations and movements leverage communications media to advance their causes and to inform the public of their beliefs and causes. Certainly, the issuance of public warnings by law enforcement organizations is an example of altruism. Another example that influences the justice domain is the Dads Against Drunk Driving (DADD) organization. It uses communications media to inform others of its purpose and beneficial programs through which instances of drunk driving may be reduced or averted. Figure 15.1 depicts the altruistic Internet presence of DADD (Dads Against Drunk Driving, 2013).

Figure 15.1 Altruistic communications of the DADD organization. (From http://www.dadd.org/.)

The foundational concept of communitarianism involves the community, instead of any individual, ethically as its "epicenter" (Lundy & Janes, 2009). Within the context of policing, the "radical communitarian agenda on crime prevention gives ethical priority to decisions over redistribution and reintegration," thereby allowing "all members to participate both in the decisions themselves, and, crucially, in the shared life of their communities" (McLaughlin & Muncie, 2006). The traditional goals of law enforcement organizations have been to maintain order and reduce crime within society. Accomplishing these goals often necessitates assistance from the community. Therefore, community involvement is imperative within the context of policing. Regarding the communitarianistic perspective, law enforcement organizations and their served publics must communicate mutually to effectively and efficiently generate the benefits of reduced crime within society. Through such communication, law enforcement assets may be coordinated toward the diminishment of crime.

These paradigms provide a basis for introducing some of the basic ethical paradigms that influence communications within the justice domain. Certainly, many others exist. On the basis of these introductory concepts, it is evident that these paradigms have various similarities and differences. Regardless, these foundational insights show that communication within the justice domain is complex, and involves considerations of morals, values, and ethics from different perspectives. Readers desiring a greater understanding of these concepts are encouraged to consult texts authored in the domain of philosophy or ethics.

Ethical Codes and Standards

The executive officers of for-profit prisons or for-profit security agencies may give formal or informal presentations regarding the annual performance of the organization. Among the states, the directors of public safety or state police organizations may need to address the public regarding issues ranging from inclement weather to notifications of escaped convicts. Local sheriffs and police chiefs may address school audiences or civic organizations. Such individuals represent the leadership of their respective organizations when communicating during the courses of their respective duties. Regardless of the scenario or organization, communicating with the public involves professionalism and a high degree of ethics.

Numerous ethical codes and standards govern and influence the communications endeavors of humans. They also affect the members of professional organizations and societies. Although numerous ethical codes and standards exist among professional entities, one specific example involving communications is the code of ethics that is advocated by the International Association of Business Communicators (IABC). One generally does not mentally associate the IABC with law enforcement organizations or the justice domain. However, such an association is relevant within the contexts of these entities. Leaders, managers, and administrations within both entities often have a need to communicate with the general public regarding a variety of issues. Such communications must be both professional and ethical. Figure 15.2 expresses the tenets that comprise the IABC code of ethics (International Association of Business Communicators, 2013).

Within the IABC ethics code, the first tenet states that "professional communicators uphold the credibility and dignity of their profession by practicing honest, candid, and timely communication and by fostering the free flow of essential information in accord with the

1. Professional communicators uphold the credibility and dignity of their profession by practicing honest, candid and timely communication and by fostering the free flow of essential information in accord with the public interest.
2. Professional communicators disseminate accurate information and promptly correct any erroneous communication for which they may be responsible.
3. Professional communicators understand and support the principles of free speech, freedom of assembly, and access to an open marketplace of ideas and act accordingly.
4. Professional communicators are sensitive to cultural values and beliefs and engage in fair and balanced communication activities that foster and encourage mutual understanding.
5. Professional communicators refrain from taking part in any undertaking which the communicator considers to be unethical.
6. Professional communicators obey laws and public policies governing their professional activities and are sensitive to the spirit of all laws and regulations and, should any law or public policy be violated, for whatever reason, act promptly to correct the situation.
7. Professional communicators give credit for unique expressions borrowed from others and identify the sources and purposes of all information disseminated to the public.
8. Professional communicators protect confidential information and, at the same time, comply with all legal requirements for the disclosure of information affecting the welfare of others.
9. Professional communicators do not use confidential information gained as a result of professional activities for personal benefit and do not represent conflicting or competing interests without written consent of those involved.
10. Professional communicators do not accept undisclosed gifts or payments for professional services from anyone other than a client or employer.
11. Professional communicators do not guarantee results that are beyond the power of the practitioner to deliver.
12. Professional communicators are honest not only with others but also, and most importantly, with themselves as individuals; for a professional communicator seeks the truth and speaks that truth first to the self.

Figure 15.2 IABC code of ethics. (From http://www.iabc.com/about/code.htm.)

public interest" (International Association of Business Communicators, 2013). This tenet may be applied within the justice domain. The public interest considerations are commensurate with public service communications functions. Law enforcement organizations are service entities that must maintain effective communication with the members of the general public. For example, in 2012, during press conferences emphasizing Hurricane Sandy, concern was expressed regarding approximately 12,000 prisoners who were incarcerated at Riker's Island, New York (Casella & Ridgeway, 2012). During press conference questioning, Mayor Bloomberg stated, "Rikers Island, the land is up where they are and jails are secured," and "don't worry about anybody getting out" (Casella & Ridgeway, 2012). During Hurricane Sandy, the New York City Department of Corrections also issued statements electronically regarding prisoner safety (Casella & Ridgeway, 2012). These statements are as follows:

> Given its elevation, Rikers Island can withstand any storm up to and including a Category 4 hurricane. Rikers Island facilities are NOT in low-lying areas, and therefore like nearby small islands Roosevelt Island and City Island, is not seriously threatened by severe flooding. The personal safety of New York City Department of Correction (NYCDOC) staff and the inmate population is clearly our top priority and in the highly unlikely event that an evacuation would become necessary, it would occur. The NYCDOC response to an unprecedented

> disaster of this magnitude would be integrated of course, into a city or region-wide strategy. The City has carefully reviewed Rikers Island, as it has done with the entire city, and no section of Rikers Island facilities are located in Hurricane Evacuation Zone A. Be assured that NYCDOC staff will remain on Rikers Island and the facility is a fully self-sustaining entity, prepared to operate and care for inmates in an emergency if such an emergency develops. (Casella & Ridgeway, 2012)

These examples are commensurate with the first and second tenets of the IABC ethics code. The information communicated during the press conferences served the best interests of the general public. Citizens were assured that prisoners were unable to escape during the storm by Mayor Bloomberg, thereby dispelling any fears of endangerments that may have been posed by escapees. The NYCDOC communicated assurances regarding the safety of its personnel and the safety of inmates housed at Rikers Island. In both cases, the information communicated to the general public was timely and relevant.

The third tenet involves a consideration of freedoms guaranteed within the U.S. Constitution. The activities of assembly and free speech are ensured constitutionally. Specifically, the First Amendment states, "Congress shall make no law respecting an establishment of religion, or prohibiting the free exercise thereof; or abridging the freedom of speech, or of the press; or the right of the people peaceably to assemble, and to petition the government for a redress of grievances" (American Library Association, 2013). Such an unrestricted communications environment facilitates the free exchange of ideas respectfully between the senders and receivers of messages.

The fourth tenet involves a consideration of societal cultures. Law enforcement officers and entities within the justice domain often interact with people of varying backgrounds whose primary language may not be English. Therefore, some personnel may be multilingual or may implement third-party interpreters when communicating with members of the public. Such activities are commensurate with cultural sensitivity to facilitate a mutual understanding among the communicating parties.

The fifth tenet of the IABC code directly references ethics and behavior within the context of communications. Any endeavor that may be considered unethical is disallowed. Both the verbal and nonverbal actions of justice system entities affect public perceptions regarding their ethical behaviors and integrity. During the 1990s, Chief Richard Pennington was tasked with rectifying gross corruption that existed within the New Orleans Police Department (NOPD) in Louisiana. The extensiveness of police corruption was unprecedented. The NOPD law enforcement personnel were "renting their radios to drug dealers and tow truck drivers," some had "substantiated Mafia connections," some were actively participating in and "running a cocaine ring," and some were involved in robbery and murder (Beech, n.d.). These involvements, relationships, and activities diminished public perceptions of the NOPD because they communicated a message of poor integrity regarding the law enforcement organization.

During his tenure as Chief of Police, Pennington discharged approximately 350 law enforcement personnel (Isenberg, 2010). He knew and understood that the corruption of the NOPD affected public perceptions of the organization. He also realized the value of good integrity and the message it presents to the citizenry. He also realized the importance of the message that was communicated through the observable conduct of law enforcement personnel. Pennington summarized these concepts via the following statements (Isenberg, 2010):

> I think integrity is number one. People have to view you as being of the highest integrity and that comes from the community and also from your own police personnel. Both have to trust what you're saying as being truthful and upfront. If they feel as though they cannot trust you by what you say or what you do, you won't be a very effective leader. I think your men and women need to be the same way in how the conduct themselves in the community and in the department. (Isenberg, 2010)

The sixth tenet of the IABC code involves a consideration of legal versus illegal activities and violations of public policy within the context of communicating. It also demonstrates a consideration of any appropriate remedies that are associated with such transgressions. The NOPD scenario also is commensurate with this sixth tenet. Many officers who betrayed the public's trust and confidence were appropriately incarcerated. Pennington instantiated a "public integrity unit" separate from the law enforcement organization through which citizens could report their complaints (Beech, n.d., p. 7). Although announcing publically the discharge of criminal personnel and demonstrating openly a positive effort to solicit public feedback may not improve a damaged public relationship immediately, it communicates and signals a willingness to change that may be perceived positively by the general public.

The seventh ethics tenet involves the adage of giving credit where credit is due and being accurate and truthful when communicating. The sources of information must be properly referenced in all manner of communicating. When using someone else's ideas and materials, the original source of these ideas and materials should be appropriately cited and credited. Willful and purposeful omissions and misrepresentations must be avoided. Violations of these basic principles constitute a variety of legal challenges within the justice system, ranging from copyright infringement to various cases of fraudulent documents. Various punitive measures are associated with the criminality aspects of this tenet ranging from financial fines to imprisonment.

A recent event highlights the relevance of truthfulness when communicating. During 2012, Ohio Attorney General Marc Dann had his law license suspended for a variety of charges that included "filing false financial disclosures" (Fields, 2012). Specifically, Dann "failed to disclose on his financial disclosure statement more than $17,000 he received as reimbursement from his campaign committee" (Fields, 2012). Regarding Dann's predicament, the Ohio Supreme Court stated that "Dann's criminal and ethical violations reflect poorly on his fitness to practice law and the legal profession as a whole, but also cause incalculable harm to the public perception of the attorney general's office" (Fields, 2012). This scenario shows the devastating effects of unethical communication and the impacts that exist regarding the potential of such situations to affect public perceptions. It also demonstrates the punitive aspects and negative consequences of unethical communication regarding the tarnishing of a career and a loss of professional respect.

The eighth tenet represents confidentiality and disclosure when communicating. Confidentiality represents notions of secrecy regarding a "willingness to confide," being "entrusted with confidences," or "containing information whose unauthorized disclosure could be prejudicial to the national interest" (*Merriam-Webster*, 2013b). Disclosure represents an "act or instant of disclosing" (*Merriam-Webster*, 2013d) or to "make known or public" (*Merriam-Webster*, 2013c). These concepts are essential characteristics of the justice domain.

Probably the most prominent examples of these issues involve the attorney–client privilege and communications between attorneys and clients. The attorney–client privilege is defined as the "rule of evidence that protects confidential communications between a lawyer and client made in the course of the professional relationship" (Cannon, 2008). This privilege pertains to both the "oral and written" communications that occur between attorneys and clients (Cannon, 2008). However, it is only applicable to legal advice, and not to any advice regarding "personal or business" issues (Cannon, 2008). Discussions that occur during "initial consultations" and activities in which the attorney "does not charge a fee" are also accommodated within the privilege despite whether the attorney agrees to represent the potential client (Cannon, 2008).

Any confidential aspects of communication between an attorney and client cannot be disclosed without the consent of the client (Edwards, Edwards, & Wells, 2009). Any undisclosed information that occurs when communicating between attorneys and clients is regarded as confidential (Edwards et al., 2009). The attorney–client privilege is not waived "if the person to whom the information is disclosed receives it for the purpose of furthering the client's interest or the disclosure is necessary for the communication of information" (Edwards et al., 2009). Within a law office, all personnel must adhere to the tenets governing the attorney–client privilege, and "must not disclose privileges information to spouses or anyone else" (Edwards et al., 2009).

Unimpeded communication is the cornerstone of establishing a strong, trustful relationship between attorneys and clients. Attorneys "cannot be compelled by statute or court order" to divulge information that is obtained when communicating directly with clients with the exception of "a few narrow circumstances" (Carper, McKinsey, & West, 2008). Although clients may waive the attorney–client privilege, attorneys are unable to waive this privilege (Carper et al., 2008). Clients must feel that they can tell anything to their attorney without fear of the information being revealed. Attorneys must have a full array of facts and accurate information to prepare the strongest cases for their clients. Therefore, the attorney–client privilege is an essential aspect of communications within the justice domain.

The ninth tenet of the ethics code furthers the duties regarding confidentiality to regarding the personal use of clandestine information and any conflicts of interest. These notions are also pertinent within the context of the justice domain. Within the attorney–client relationship, many issues of corporate functioning are confidential and often involve communicating information that could be financially beneficial for those who have an inside knowledge of such information. For example, some attorneys may have advance knowledge of corporate mergers, new products or services that are to be released within a market, corporate downsizing, corporate dissolution or bankruptcy, strategic partnerships, joint ventures, and so forth. Using such knowledge gained through the oral and written communications processes for personal benefit would be both illegal and unethical.

The tenth tenet within the IABC code indicates that compensation should be accepted only from clients or employers. This notion is certainly pertinent within the context of the justice system. For example, law enforcement officers are generally prohibited from accepting gratuities in exchange for their services, and receive payment only from their employer. As an example, a police chief should not accept a gratuity for giving a public performance or speech during the course of duty. A gratuity is defined as an item "of value received by someone because of his or her role or job rather than because of a personal relationship" (Dempsey & Forst, 2012). Among some localities, the accepting of gratuities by law enforcement personnel is deemed as a form of corruption (Dempsey & Forst, 2012).

The eleventh tenet of the ethical code deals with guarantees of results that exceed the capacity of an individual to provide. Within the justice domain, this tenet is especially prevalent regarding the testimony of expert witnesses. Any testimony or analysis provided by expert witnesses must be "objective and be an advocate of his or her opinion and the truth" (Tilstone, Savage, & Clark, 2006). Furthermore, expert witnesses must be capable of defending the "techniques and conclusions of any scientific analysis that he or she conducted pertaining to the case in question, and must be willing to discuss the shortcomings or limitations of a scientific technique, even though it may decrease the significance of a result, as well as any advantages" (Tilstone et al., 2006). Usually, expert witnesses express their services agreements through written contracts. The language within the contract generally expresses the notion that methods and results are objective, and that the expert will not provide any certain biased outcome or opinion.

The twelfth tenet involves a consideration of honesty in communications. This notion is a foundational principle of communicating within the justice domain. Attorneys must provide accurate and truthful advice for their clients. Law enforcement personnel must be honest and truthful when communicating. For example, when writing reports that must be submitted through the appropriate chain of command, law enforcement personnel must not alter or omit any details within the report, and the contents of the report must be truthful, objective, and accurate.

These tenets of the IABC represent a foundational approach to integrating ethical behaviors and conducts professionally and personally. Members of the justice domain must be mindful of the potential of their communications to affect not only the justice domain but also society, their served populaces, and public perceptions. Therefore, all communications within the justice domain must acknowledge ethical principles and incorporate them within the communications process. Embellishing communications within the justice domain ethically contributes toward establishing sound, trustful relationships, and improves perceptions of organizational integrity. Therefore, all personnel within the justice domain must be mindful of communications ethics when communicating with others.

Professional Organizations and Communication Ethics

Professional organizations represent a collection of individuals whose credentials, professions, and interests are similar, and may exhibit some mission or purpose. Professional organizations often host conferences and activities through which individuals may maintain their credentials, make personal and professional networking contacts, and may receive continuing education. Memberships among professional organizations may also provide a variety of benefits ranging from insurance programs to travel discounts. Professional organizations may have some political influence or have influence regarding the general public regarding a variety of issues. Regardless of the theme of a professional organization, some ethical principles are usually advocated by the entity to which its membership must adhere personally and professionally.

The ethical code of the IABC is not the only code of ethics that may influence communications within the justice domain. Many other professional organizations exist that have international, national, regional, local, and professional scopes of operations and memberships, and which also express their unique codes of ethics that influence communication.

Most notably, the American Bar Association, the International Association of Chiefs of Police, and state police chief associations are probably the most familiar professional organizations within the justice domain. Although these entities have codes of ethics that may influence the acts of communicating that may be undertaken by their members, their primary purpose for existence is unrelated to communication.

Within the context of communications, an example of a significant professional organization is the National Communications Association (NCA). A primary function of the NCA is to promote "the widespread appreciation of the importance of communication in public and private life, the application of competent communication to improve the quality of human life and relationships, and the use of knowledge about communication to solve human problems" (National Communication Association, 2013e). The ethical code of the NCA is presented in Figure 15.3 (National Communication Association, 2013a).

The NCA and the IABC codes of ethics have commonness. Both incorporate tenets that involve considerations of honesty, truthfulness, and accuracy, thereby bolstering the integrity of communication. Both pertain to freedom of expression and civility when communicating. Both also refer to confidentiality that affects the fiduciary obligations of relationships between people. Certainly, more commonalities are present within the two codes.

NCA Credo for Ethical Communication
(approved by the NCA Legislative Council, November 1999)

Questions of right and wrong arise whenever people communicate. Ethical communication is fundamental to responsible thinking, decision making, and the development of relationships and communities within and across contexts, cultures, channels, and media. Moreover, ethical communication enhances human worth and dignity by fostering truthfulness, fairness, responsibility, personal integrity, and respect for self and others. We believe that unethical communication threatens the quality of all communication and consequently the well-being of individuals and the society in which we live. Therefore we, the members of the National Communication Association, endorse and are committed to practicing the following principles of ethical communication:

We advocate truthfulness, accuracy, honesty, and reason as essential to the integrity of communication.

We endorse freedom of expression, diversity of perspective, and tolerance of dissent to achieve the informed and responsible decision making fundamental to a civil society.

We strive to understand and respect other communicators before evaluating and responding to their messages.

We promote access to communication resources and opportunities as necessary to fulfill human potential and contribute to the well-being of families, communities, and society.

We promote communication climates of caring and mutual understanding that respect the unique needs and characteristics of individual communicators.

We condemn communication that degrades individuals and humanity through distortion, intimidation, coercion, and violence, and through the expression of intolerance and hatred.

We are committed to the courageous expression of personal convictions in pursuit of fairness and justice.

We advocate sharing information, opinions, and feelings when facing significant choices while also respecting privacy and confidentiality.

We accept responsibility for the short- and long-term consequences for our own communication and expect the same of others.

Figure 15.3 NCA code of ethics. (From http://www.natcom.org/uploadedFiles/About_NCA/Leadership_and_Governance/Public_Policy_Platform/PDF-PolicyPlatform-NCA_Credo_for_Ethical_Communication.pdf.)

In any case, regardless of the organization, such ethical codes provide a foundational basis for influencing human behaviors when communicating with others.

The NCA exists as a professional organization whose ethical communications foundations are applicable within the context of the justice domain. Commensurate with the observations discussed regarding the ethical aspects of the IABC, the NCA ethical code may be used as a guideline for communications within the justice domain. Because the NCA is a professional organization, it has an interest group that is dedicated to issues that affect the justice domain. Specifically, one of its interest groups is the Law and Communication Division (National Communication Association, 2013b). The purpose and function of this group is summarized as follows (National Communication Association, 2013b):

> The Communication and Law Division membership reflects the diversity of study in communication and the law. Its primary goal is to advance the understanding of communication within the legal arena. Areas of membership interest include, but are not limited to, studies of jury decision-making, pre-trial processes, interaction within the courtroom and/or the law office, mass communication, interviewing, alternative dispute resolution, negotiation, and legal rhetoric. The division recognizes the diversity of methods used in research in the legal arena and embraces study from a variety of areas of communication study (e.g., argumentation, interpersonal, organizational, health, small group, etc.). It welcomes membership from academics, attorneys, trainers, consultants, and others with interest in the communication processes underlying law and litigation philosophy and practices. (National Communication Association, 2013b)

This description shows a robust array of communication attributes within the context of the justice domain. Through the NCA, practitioners and theoreticians may communicate and freely exchange information and ideas to improve their knowledge and network contacts. By doing so, one remains abreast of current concepts and applications of communication within the justice domain. Not only does this embellish personal and professional accomplishments, it also strengthens attributes of communications within the justice domain.

Another professional organization is the Public Relations Society of America (PRSA). The PRSA defines itself as "world's largest and foremost organization of public relations professionals," which "provides professional development, sets standards of excellence and upholds principles of ethics for its members and, more broadly, the multi-billion dollar global public relations profession" (Public Relations Society of America, 2013a). Similar to the NCA, the PRSA contains both an ethical code and interest divisions for its members. The ethical code of the PRSA is presented in Figure 15.4a through g (Public Relations Society of America, 2013d).

Examining the PRSA code of ethics yields some observations of commonness with the ethical codes of the NCA and the IABC. All three ethical codes provide guidelines that influence the communications activities of members and also of both personal and professional conducts and behaviors. All three incorporate facets of trustful relationships with society that influences public perception. All three ethical codes provide a basis for facilitating an open exchange of ideas, concepts, and information when communicating. These codes also embody confidentiality and disclosure concerns within the communications process.

Although there is much commonness among these ethical codes, the PRSA provides an additional consideration of ensuring ethical behavior. Its ethical code contains a written

(a)

Preamble

Public Relations Society of America Member Code of Ethics 2000

- Professional Values
- Principles of Conduct
- Commitment and Compliance

This Code applies to PRSA members. The Code is designed to be a useful guide for PRSA members as they carry out their ethical responsibilities. This document is designed to anticipate and accommodate, by precedent, ethical challenges that may arise. The scenarios outlined in the Code provision are actual examples of misconduct. More will be added as experience with the Code occurs.

The Public Relations Society of America (PRSA) is committed to ethical practices. The level of public trust PRSA members seek, as we serve the public good, means we have taken on a special obligation to operate ethically.

The value of member reputation depends upon the ethical conduct of everyone affiliated with the Public Relations Society of America. Each of us sets an example for each other - as well as other professionals - by our pursuit of excellence with powerful standards of performance, professionalism, and ethical conduct.

Emphasis on enforcement of the Code has been eliminated. But, the PRSA Board of Directors retains the right to bar from membership or expel from the Society any individual who has been or is sanctioned by a government agency or convicted in a court of law of an action that is not in compliance with the Code.

Ethical practice is the most important obligation of a PRSA member. We view the Member Code of Ethics as a model for other professions, organizations, and professionals.

PRSA Member Statement of Professional Values

This statement presents the core values of PRSA members and, more broadly, of the public relations profession. These values provide the foundation for the Member Code of Ethics and set the industry standard for the professional practice of public relations. These values are the fundamental beliefs that guide our behaviors and decision-making process. We believe our professional values are vital to the integrity of the profession as a whole.

ADVOCACY

Figure 15.4 PRSA code of ethics. (a) Page 1.

(b)

We serve the public interest by acting as responsible advocates for those we represent. We provide a voice in the marketplace of ideas, facts, and viewpoints to aid informed public debate.

HONESTY

We adhere to the highest standards of accuracy and truth in advancing the interests of those we represent and in communicating with the public.

EXPERTISE

We acquire and responsibly use specialized knowledge and experience. We advance the profession through continued professional development, research, and education. We build mutual understanding, credibility, and relationships among a wide array of institutions and audiences.

INDEPENDENCE

We provide objective counsel to those we represent. We are accountable for our actions.

LOYALTY

We are faithful to those we represent, while honoring our obligation to serve the public interest.

FAIRNESS

We deal fairly with clients, employers, competitors, peers, vendors, the media, and the general public. We respect all opinions and support the right of free expression.

PRSA Code Provisions

FREE FLOW OF INFORMATION

Core Principle Protecting and advancing the free flow of accurate and truthful information is essential to serving the public interest and contributing to informed decision making in a democratic society.

Intent:

To maintain the integrity of relationships with the media, government officials, and the public.

To aid informed decision-making.

Guidelines:

Figure 15.4 (Continued) PRSA code of ethics. (b) Page 2.

(c)

A member shall:

Preserve the integrity of the process of communication.

Be honest and accurate in all communications.

Act promptly to correct erroneous communications for which the practitioner is responsible.

Preserve the free flow of unprejudiced information when giving or receiving gifts by ensuring that gifts are nominal, legal, and infrequent.

Examples of Improper Conduct Under this Provision:

A member representing a ski manufacturer gives a pair of expensive racing skis to a sports magazine columnist, to influence the columnist to write favorable articles about the product.

A member entertains a government official beyond legal limits and/or in violation of government reporting requirements.

COMPETITION

Core Principle Promoting healthy and fair competition among professionals preserves an ethical climate while fostering a robust business environment.

Intent:

To promote respect and fair competition among public relations professionals.

To serve the public interest by providing the widest choice of practitioner options.

Guidelines:

A member shall:

Follow ethical hiring practices designed to respect free and open competition without deliberately undermining a competitor.

Preserve intellectual property rights in the marketplace.

Examples of Improper Conduct Under This Provision:

A member employed by a "client organization" shares helpful information with a counseling firm that is competing with others for the organization's business.

Figure 15.4 (Continued) PRSA code of ethics. (c) Page 3.

(d)

A member spreads malicious and unfounded rumors about a competitor in order to alienate the competitor's clients and employees in a ploy to recruit people and business.

DISCLOSURE OF INFORMATION

Core Principle Open communication fosters informed decision making in a democratic society.

Intent:

To build trust with the public by revealing all information needed for responsible decision making.

Guidelines:

A member shall:

Be honest and accurate in all communications.

Act promptly to correct erroneous communications for which the member is responsible.

Investigate the truthfulness and accuracy of information released on behalf of those represented.

Reveal the sponsors for causes and interests represented.

Disclose financial interest (such as stock ownership) in a client's organization.

Avoid deceptive practices.

Examples of Improper Conduct Under this Provision:

Front groups: A member implements "grass roots" campaigns or letter-writing campaigns to legislators on behalf of undisclosed interest groups.

Lying by omission: A practitioner for a corporation knowingly fails to release financial information, giving a misleading impression of the corporation's performance.

A member discovers inaccurate information disseminated via a website or media kit and does not correct the information.

A member deceives the public by employing people to pose as volunteers to speak at public hearings and participate in "grass roots" campaigns.

Figure 15.4 (Continued) PRSA code of ethics. (d) Page 4.

(e)

SAFEGUARDING CONFIDENCES

Core Principle Client trust requires appropriate protection of confidential and private information.

Intent:

To protect the privacy rights of clients, organizations, and individuals by safeguarding confidential information.

Guidelines:

A member shall: Safeguard the confidences and privacy rights of present, former, and prospective clients and employees.

Protect privileged, confidential, or insider information gained from a client or organization.

Immediately advise an appropriate authority if a member discovers that confidential information is being divulged by an employee of a client company or organization.

Examples of Improper Conduct Under This Provision:

A member changes jobs, takes confidential information, and uses that information in the new position to the detriment of the former employer.

A member intentionally leaks proprietary information to the detriment of some other party.

CONFLICTS OF INTEREST

Core Principle Avoiding real, potential or perceived conflicts of interest builds the trust of clients, employers, and the publics.

Intent:

To earn trust and mutual respect with clients or employers.

To build trust with the public by avoiding or ending situations that put one's personal or professional interests in conflict with society's interests.

Guidelines:

A member shall:

Figure 15.4 (Continued) PRSA code of ethics. (e) Page 5.

(f)

Act in the best interests of the client or employer, even subordinating the member's personal interests.

Avoid actions and circumstances that may appear to compromise good business judgment or create a conflict between personal and professional interests.

Disclose promptly any existing or potential conflict of interest to affected clients or organizations.

Encourage clients and customers to determine if a conflict exists after notifying all affected parties.

Examples of Improper Conduct Under This Provision:

The member fails to disclose that he or she has a strong financial interest in a client's chief competitor.

The member represents a "competitor company" or a "conflicting interest" without informing a prospective client.

ENHANCING THE PROFESSION

Core Principle Public relations professionals work constantly to strengthen the public's trust in the profession.

Intent:

To build respect and credibility with the public for the profession of public relations.

To improve, adapt and expand professional practices.

Guidelines:

A member shall: Acknowledge that there is an obligation to protect and enhance the profession.

Keep informed and educated about practices in the profession to ensure ethical conduct.

Actively pursue personal professional development.

Decline representation of clients or organizations that urge or require actions contrary to this Code.

Accurately define what public relations activities can accomplish.

Figure 15.4 (Continued) PRSA code of ethics. (f) Page 6.

(g)

Counsel subordinates in proper ethical decision making.

Require that subordinates adhere to the ethical requirements of the Code.

Report practices not in compliance with the Code, whether committed by PRSA members or not, to the appropriate authority.

Examples of Improper Conduct Under This Provision:

A PRSA member declares publicly that a product the client sells is safe, without disclosing evidence to the contrary.

A member initially assigns some questionable client work to a non-member practitioner to avoid the ethical obligation of PRSA membership.

PRSA Member Code of Ethics Pledge

I pledge:

To conduct myself professionally, with truth, accuracy, fairness, and responsibility to the public; To improve my individual competence and advance the knowledge and proficiency of the profession through continuing research and education; And to adhere to the articles of the Member Code of Ethics 2000 for the practice of public relations as adopted by the governing Assembly of the Public Relations Society of America.

I understand and accept that there is a consequence for misconduct, up to and including membership revocation.

And, I understand that those who have been or are sanctioned by a government agency or convicted in a court of law of an action that is not in compliance with the Code may be barred from membership or expelled from the Society.

____

Signature

____

Date

Figure 15.4 (Continued) PRSA code of ethics. (g) Page 7. (From http://www.prsa.org/AboutPRSA/Ethics/documents/Code%20of%20Ethics.pdf.)

pledge that binds members to an adherence of the tenets expressed within the PRSA ethical code. If one transgresses the ethical tenets expressed within the code, the pledge contains punitive measures that include expulsion or that prohibit membership within the PRSA. Among the three codes presented herein, the PRSA is unique because it is the only ethical code that necessitates a written pledge within its membership.

Public relations are certainly a concern of the justice domain. Law enforcement organizations often disseminate news releases regarding their performances or may provide personnel during community events. Maintaining a strong, trustful relationship with the public is a paramount consideration of community-oriented policing. The deeds and behaviors of law enforcement personnel communicate messages that influence public perceptions of the law enforcement entity and of the justice domain. Therefore, members of the justice domain must be ethical regarding any activity that may communicate messages to the general public.

The PRSA contains a public affairs and government interest section that pertains to public relations and the justice domain. Specifically, this entity "provides training and resources relevant to communicators in all levels of government and branches of the military, as well as those at counseling firms, corporations, and associations who are responsible for communicating with various audiences on public policy or public safety issues" (Public Relations Society of America, 2013c). For example, training sessions are available through PRSA interest sections that accommodate topics including the National Incident Management System (NIMS) (Public Relations Society of America, 2013b). Through this interest section, members have an opportunity to exchange information regarding a variety of topics that affect the justice domain.

The PRSA, NCA, and IABC serve different purposes and professional audiences, and have different missions and themes among their respective factions. Despite these differences, they all support the communications needs of their respective memberships through the provision of a variety of training programs, networking opportunities, and information exchanges. Throughout the entireties of their respective memberships, ethical principles are uncompromisingly integrated as foundational principles that guide the behaviors and conducts of humans. Emphasizing ethical communications provides a basis for ensuring not only the integrity of the professional organization but also of the individual members who comprise the organizations. Applying and practicing these ethical principles when communicating during the course of duty not only represents an adherence to the tenets of the respective organizations but also embellishes the integrity of law enforcement organizations whose personnel are members of such professional organizations and societies.

Communication Ethics and Decisions

Personnel within the justice system must render decisions daily when performing their duties. Such decisions must be ethical and legal. A primary example involves officer discretion when performing patrol duties. For example, when an officer is contemplating a decision about whether to cite someone for speeding, an amount of discretion is involved within the decision domain. An officer may contemplate whether a warning will suffice if the driver has no previous speeding ticket(s) or has just received a driver's license before deciding whether to issue a citation. The officer may ignore such considerations, and issue a citation that is commensurate with the letter of the law. After a decision is made, the officer must communicate the decision to the motorist.

The preceding codes of ethics exist as influences through which decisions may be contemplated from ethical perspectives. However, alone, they are insufficient to generate a decision. Instead, a decision methodology must be invoked through which a logical process occurs to generate a decision outcome, and that incorporates ethical considerations. Generally, such a decision method accommodates the following phases within the overall process of rendering decisions (Markkula Center for Applied Ethics, 2013a):

1. Recognize the ethical issue
2. Gather facts
3. Evaluate the alternatives
4. Make and test a decision
5. Reflect and act on the decision outcome

The first phase considers the decision within an ethical context. The ethical dimensions of the decision domain must be identified, examined, and accommodated within the initial stage of the decision process. Figure 15.5 highlights aspects of this phase (Markkula Center for Applied Ethics, 2013a).

The simple example of issuing a traffic citation and communicating the outcome of the decision involves ethical issues regarding the discretion of the officer. Within the decision process, the phase of recognizing ethical issues pertains to such scenarios. If a motorist is a single mother who is unemployed, then the increased costs of insurance and the cost of the traffic citation may be unaffordable financially. The issuance of a citation could generate cascading effects negatively for the motorist. The rate of speed and the attitude of the motorist are also influential factors. The officer must contemplate whether the issuance of a citation may be damaging or whether a citation is absolutely necessary. The officer may issue either a citation or a warning—both options are legal.

The second phase involves the gathering of facts regarding the decision. Such data must be timely and accurate. Figure 15.6 highlights the contemplations that occur during this phase of the decision process (Markkula Center for Applied Ethics, 2013a).

Again, the speeding citation scenario may be examined with respect to these queries. The law enforcement officer may determine the rate of speed, how much the observed rate of speed exceeds the posted speed limit, whether the driver has previous citations, whether the driver has outstanding warrants, whether a reason exists for the speeding incident (e.g.,

Recognize an Ethical Issue

1. Could this decision or situation be damaging to someone or to some group? Does this decision involve a choice between a good and bad alternative, or perhaps between two "goods" or between two "bads"?
2. Is this issue about more than what is legal or what is most efficient? If so, how?

Figure 15.5 Decision process phase 1. (From http://www.scu.edu/ethics/practicing/decision/framework.html.)

Get the Facts

3. What are the relevant facts of the case? What facts are not known? Can I learn more about the situation? Do I know enough to make a decision?
4. What individuals and groups have an important stake in the outcome? Are some concerns more important? Why?
5. What are the options for acting? Have all the relevant persons and groups been consulted? Have I identified creative options?

Figure 15.6 Decision process phase 2. (From http://www.scu.edu/ethics/practicing/decision/framework.html.)

medical emergency), the location of the speeding incident and traffic flow (e.g., rural area versus a municipal school zone), the experience of the driver (e.g., new driver versus someone with years of experience), whether the vehicle is stolen, and so forth. Such considerations also necessitate a consideration of the potential harm that could be inflicted against others. Perhaps the motorist was in a rural area at 1:00 A.M. with no other vehicles present, and exceeded the speed limit by only five miles per hours? Other factors may influence the decision ranging from zero-tolerance policing policies of municipalities to whether a speed limit sign was obscured. In an extreme case, perhaps the driver had no cellular phone, was bitten by a poisonous snake while hunting alone in the woods, and was a good distance from a medical facility? In any case, these contemplations show the complexity of even the smallest infraction, and demonstrate various facts that must be ascertained regarding the incident.

The third phase represents contemplations of ethical principles and values that permeate the decision domain within the context of evaluating decision alternatives. Regarding the speeding incident scenario, the decision rendered by the officer regarding the issuance of a citation or a warning must be both ethical and legal. Such decisions incorporate ethical paradigms and values. Figure 15.7 delineates these concepts (Markkula Center for Applied Ethics, 2013a).

The ethics of the decision domain represent various facets of the ethical paradigms that were introduced earlier within this chapter. Within Figure 15.3, the primary approach to

Evaluate Alternative Actions

6. Evaluate the options by asking the following questions:

   Which option will produce the most good and do the least harm? (The utilitarian approach)
   Which option best respects the rights of all who have a stake? (The rights approach)
   Which option treats people equally or proportionately? (The justice approach)
   Which option best serves the community as a whole, not just some members? (The common good approach)
   Which option leads me to act as the sort of person I want to be? (The virtue approach)

Figure 15.7 Decision process phase 3. (From http://www.scu.edu/ethics/practicing/decision/framework.html.)

ethical reasoning is represented by the queries associated with decision alternatives. In any case, the primary consideration is associated with the action that is to occur with respect to the rendering of a decision to either issue a citation or a warning. The law enforcement officer may ponder whether the issuance of a citation or a warning will modify the future behavior of the motorist so that it will conform to traffic laws, thereby averting future speeding incidents and producing societal good. The law enforcement officer may ponder earlier ticket versus warning decision outcomes regarding other motorists in the same location and similar circumstances with respect to treating the driver equally. Certainly, many more ethical considerations are accommodated within this phase of the decision process with respect to the different paradigms of ethical reasoning.

The fourth phase of the decision process accommodates the rendering of a decision. The speeding incident is unique to the particular situation. No two law enforcement service calls are identical; they are all unique. Therefore, the law enforcement officer must decide exactly what is to be done regarding the specific incident. The law enforcement officer may issue a citation or warning. In the event of a medical situation, the officer may summon assistance or provide assistance to ensure that the motorist arrives safely at a medical facility. Regardless of the decision, the law enforcement officer must communicate the decision outcome to the motorist. Figure 15.8 highlights the salient attributes of this phase in the decision process (Markkula Center for Applied Ethics, 2013a).

The final stage of the decision process involves the act of communicating the decision outcome and experiencing the aftermath of the decision. After communicating the outcome and acting accordingly, in some cases, cognitive dissonance may occur within the mind of the law enforcement officer, whereas other incidents may invoke a feeling of surety. Figure 15.9 depicts the considerations of this stage within the decision process.

Communicating the decision outcome to the motorist may incite a variety of different feedbacks. Some motorists may sulk and cry, whereas others may show rage and anger.

Make a Decision and Test It

7. Considering all these approaches, which option best addresses the situation?
8. If I told someone I respect—or told a television audience—which option I have chosen, what would they say?

Figure 15.8 Decision process phase 4. (From http://www.scu.edu/ethics/practicing/decision/framework.html.)

Act and Reflect on the Outcome

9. How can my decision be implemented with the greatest care and attention to the concerns of all stakeholders?
10. How did my decision turn out and what have I learned from this specific situation?

Figure 15.9 Decision process phase 5. (From http://www.scu.edu/ethics/practicing/decision/framework.html.)

Others may be congenial and exhibit a positive attitude. From the perspective of the communications process, such feedback is immediate. Other instances of feedback may occur through greater periods of time—perhaps a motorist wishes to challenge a traffic citation in court and must wait months before a court date is available? In any case, the act of communicating the decision and acting accordingly provides some form of feedback that represents a learning experience for both the motorist and the law enforcement officer.

The ability to render decisions ethically involves "a trained sensitivity to ethical issues and a practiced method for exploring the ethical aspects of a decision and weighing the considerations" that influence human courses of actions within a decision domain (Markkula Center for Applied Ethics, 2013b). A methodology that incorporates ethical principles is paramount to rendering human decisions (Markkula Center for Applied Ethics, 2013b). As the complexity of decisions incorporating ethics increases, so does the necessity of relying on "discussion and dialogue with others about the dilemma" (Markkula Center for Applied Ethics, 2013b). Therefore, communication is an absolutely indispensible characteristic of rendering many decisions ethically within the justice domain.

Commentary Regarding Ethics in the Justice Domain

Communication permeates every facet of the justice domain, ranging from the foot patrols of law enforcement officers to the verbal announcement of verdicts among courtrooms. Such communication must be both ethical and legal. Ethical codes are often used to express the acceptable and unacceptable communications behaviors and conducts that occur within the justice domain.

When considering the ethical paradigms discussed herein and their appropriateness within the justice domain when considering ethical codes that influence communicating and rendering decisions, one must be mindful of the various ethical influences that are derived from religion, politics, philosophy, scientific inquiry, culture, law, and personal subjectivity. However, these domains are not of themselves ethics despite their influences regarding ethical thought and principles. This notion is substantiated by the contents of Figure 15.10.

Ethics should guide the communications of justice system personnel and of professional associations within the justice domain. Notably, attorneys are bound by codes of ethics among the states that influence their communications. For example, within the state of New Jersey, an excerpt from the Rules of Professional Conduct indicates that the following rules govern legal communication (State of New Jersey, 2013):

1. A lawyer shall fully inform a prospective client of how, when, and where the client may communicate with the lawyer.
2. A lawyer shall keep a client reasonably informed about the status of a matter and promptly comply with reasonable requests for information.
3. A lawyer shall explain a matter to the extent reasonably necessary to permit the client to make informed decisions regarding the representation.
4. When a lawyer knows that a client expects assistance not permitted by the Rules of Professional Conduct or other law, the lawyer shall advise the client of the relevant limitations on the lawyer's conduct (State of New Jersey, 2013).

• Ethics is not the same as feelings. Feelings provide important information for our ethical choices. Some people have highly developed habits that make them feel bad when they do something wrong, but many people feel good even though they are doing something wrong. And often our feelings will tell us it is uncomfortable to do the right thing if it is hard.
• Ethics is not religion. Many people are not religious, but ethics applies to everyone. Most religions do advocate high ethical standards but sometimes do not address all the types of problems we face.
• Ethics is not following the law. A good system of law does incorporate many ethical standards, but law can deviate from what is ethical. Law can become ethically corrupt, as some totalitarian regimes have made it. Law can be a function of power alone and designed to serve the interests of narrow groups. Law may have a difficult time designing or enforcing standards in some important areas, and may be slow to address new problems.
• Ethics is not following culturally accepted norms. Some cultures are quite ethical, but others become corrupt -or blind to certain ethical concerns (as the United States was to slavery before the Civil War). "When in Rome, do as the Romans do" is not a satisfactory ethical standard.
• Ethics is not science. Social and natural science can provide important data to help us make better ethical choices. But science alone does not tell us what we ought to do. Science may provide an explanation for what humans are like. But ethics provides reasons for how humans ought to act. And just because something is scientifically or technologically possible, it may not be ethical to do it.

Figure 15.10 Considerations of ethics. (From http://www.scu.edu/ethics/practicing/decision/framework.html.)

These rules clearly incorporate ethical tenets regarding communications that may occur between clients and attorneys. They impose restrictions regarding the timing, location, and methods through which communication may occur between clients and attorneys. They also indicate that attorneys must elucidate any professional rules that may constrain any communications involving the advising of clients by attorneys. Communication between attorneys and clients is necessary to provide information that influences the decisions of clients.

Within the justice domain, another consideration of communications ethics involves the action of jury tampering that is deemed illegal among most justice systems. Jury tampering is defined as "communicating with a juror for the purpose of influencing the outcome of a case" (National Paralegal College, 2013). Jury tampering involves the notion that communicating with jurors may adversely influence their decisions regarding court cases. For instance, "a lawyer who reveals an adversary's history of committing domestic violence when the case is about trademark infringement, might prejudice the jury in a way that unfairly influences the outcome of the case" (National Paralegal College, 2013). In most states, jury tampering is "prohibited by criminal statutes" (National Paralegal College, 2013).

Regardless of the function of communication within the justice system, it must be ethical. All personnel within the justice system must be mindful of ethics when communicating. Ethics must be accommodated among all forms of justice system communication, ranging from press conferences to conversations between attorneys and clients. All personnel within the justice system should uncompromisingly incorporate ethical values and principles within their communication practices.

Chapter Comments and Summary

All societies on Earth communicate. Although the communications process is identical within these acts of communicating, differences exist regarding the influences of morals, ethics, and values that influence the communications process. Morals, ethics, and values differ among societies, and they affect various attributes of communicating domestically and internationally. The societal attributes of ethics affect communications within the justice domain. This chapter emphasized the foundational relationship between ethics and communication within the context of the justice domain. Communication permeates every facet of the justice domain, and is essential to ensure the efficient and effective functioning of the justice system. All communications within the justice domain must be both legal and ethical.

Various schools of thought exist regarding ethics and communication. This chapter introduced the concepts of utilitarianism, altruism, and communitarianism. Various factors influence the ethical dimensions of communication within the justice domain. Such influences include religion, organizational contexts, ethical codes, situational ethics, political perspectives, and legalities. The materials presented herein are introductory. Readers desiring a greater knowledge of these concepts should consult texts regarding philosophy or advanced communications ethics.

Numerous ethical codes and standards may affect communications within the justice domain. Ethical codes are found among numerous professional organizations and societies whose themes accommodate communication. Usually, these codes define and express the unacceptable and acceptable behaviors and conducts that govern organizational members. Most all codes of ethics accommodate tenets involving freedom of speech and information exchange, confidentiality and disclosure, compensation and gratuities, and mutual respect.

Within the justice domain, the outcomes of decisions may be communicated to any affected parties. Such decisions and the act of communicating them must both occur legally and ethically. Although there are ethical influences within the decision domain, a consideration of ethical influences is insufficient to render decisions. Instead, a methodical process must exist through which human decisions are facilitated. Such a process must incorporate ethical tenets throughout its phases.

Ethics affect all communications functions within the justice domain. Professional organizations host special-interest ethics groups through which like-minded individuals may exchange ideas and forge relationships. Ethics influence the communications that occur between attorneys and clients. Ethics influence the communications of judges and juries. Ethics influence communications of law enforcement officers. Given such notions, ethics represent an inescapable characteristic of communicating within the justice system.

Terminology

Altruism
Attorney–client privilege
Beliefs
Code of ethics
Communication ethics
Communitarianism
Confidential
Copyright
Corruption
Decision
Decision ethics
Decision process
Disclosure
Ethical system
Ethics
Gratuity
Infringement
Integrity
Jury tampering
Moral turpitude
Morals
Organizational ethics
Patent
Plagiarism
Policy
Political ethics
Religion
Right
Situational ethics
Societal differences
Trademark
Utilitarianism
Values
Wrong

THOUGHT AND DISCUSSION QUESTIONS

1. This chapter introduced three ethical paradigms: utilitarianism, altruism, and communitarianism. Texts in communication or philosophy often introduce additional ethical paradigms. Do some research, and locate some discussions regarding ethical paradigms that are not included within this text. Write a brief essay that describes the paradigms that you locate among other writings.
2. Morals, ethics, and values differ among societies globally. Do some research concerning how Asian perspectives of these concepts influence communications

ethically. Compare and contrast your findings with respect to communication ethics in the American justice system.
3. Morals, ethics, and values differ among societies globally. Do some research concerning how European perspectives of these concepts influence communications ethically. Compare and contrast your findings with respect to communication ethics in the American justice system.
4. This chapter introduced professional organizations whose codes of ethics influence communication. Perform some research that explores professional organizations that exist specifically within the justice domain, and examine their codes of ethics. On the basis of your findings, write a brief essay that describes how these ethical tenets influence the communications activities of organizational members.

References

American Library Association. (2013). First amendment of the Bill of Rights to the United States constitution. Retrieved from http://www.ala.org/offices/oif/firstamendment/firstamendment (accessed February 2, 2013).

Banks, C. (2009). *Criminal justice ethics: Theory and practice* (2nd ed., p. 3). Thousand Oaks, CA: Sage Publishing.

Beech, B. (n.d.). Ethics in policing: Not just shoulds, coulds, and ought to's. Florida Department of Law Enforcement. Retrieved from http://www.fdle.state.fl.us/Content/getdoc/84fec71c-556a-4827-946d-24db6d5cef93/Beech-bonnie-paper.aspx (accessed February 2, 2013).

Bentley, A., Earls, M., O'Brien, M. J., & Maeda, J. (2011). *I'll have what she's having: Mapping social behavior* (p. 13). Cambridge, MA: MIT Press.

Brown, F. (2011). *Journalism ethics: A casebook for professional conduct for news media* (p. 3). Portland, OR: Marion Street Press.

Bunge, M. (2010). *Matter and mind: A philosophical inquiry* (p. 115). New York: Springer Publishing.

Cannon, T. (2008). *Ethics and professional responsibility for paralegals* (5th ed., p. 110). New York: Aspen Publishers.

Carper, D., McKinsey, J., & West, B. (2008). *Understanding the law* (5th ed., p. 160). Mason, OH: Thomson Higher Education.

Casella, J., & Ridgeway, J. (2012). Prisoners to remain on Rikers island as hurricane Sandy heads for New York. *Solitary Watch*. Retrieved from http://solitarywatch.com/2012/10/28/prisoners-to-remain-on-rikers-island-as-hurricane-sandy-heads-for-new-york/ (accessed February 1, 2013).

Dads Against Drunk Driving. (2013). Retrieved from http://www.dadd.org/ (accessed January 26, 2013).

Dempsey, J., & Forst, L. (2012). *An introduction to policing* (6th ed., p. 219). Clifton Park, NY: Delmar Cengage Publishing.

Edwards, L., Edwards, J. S., & Wells, P. (2009). *Tort law for legal assistants* (4th ed., p. 262). Clifton Park, NY: Delmar Cengage Publishing.

Fernando, A. C. (2009). *Business ethics: An Indian perspective* (p. 10). New Delhi, India: Dorling Kindersley.

Fields, R. (2012). Former Ohio Attorney General Marc Dann loses law license for six months. Retrieved from http://www.cleveland.com/open/index.ssf/2012/11/former_ohio_attorney_general_m.html (accessed February 2, 2013).

Hendricks, J., & Byers, B. (2006). *Crisis intervention in criminal justice/social service* (4th ed., p. 48). Springfield, IL: Charles C. Thomas Publishers.

International Association of Business Communicators. (2013). IABC code of ethics for professional communicators. Retrieved from http://www.iabc.com/about/code.htm (accessed January 25, 2013).

Isenberg, J. (2010). *Police leadership in a democracy: Conversations with America's police chiefs* (p. 40). Boca Raton, FL: CRC Press.

Johnson, C. (2012). *Meeting the ethical challenges of leadership: Casting light or shadow* (4th ed., p. 171). Thousand Oaks, CA: Sage Publications.

Kopko, J. (2011). Facing ethics in criminal justice through a Christian worldview. Liberty University. Retrieved from http://www.google.com/url?sa=t&rct=j&q=religion%20ethics%20police&source=web&cd=26&cad=rja&ved=0CE4QFjAFOBQ&url=http%3A%2F%2Fdigitalcommons.liberty.edu%2Fcgi%2Fviewcontent.cgi%3Farticle%3D1224%26context%3Dhonors&ei=aNMAUZmoD4O88AT2joDoAg&usg=AFQjCNGJtT8YHlXLJqiljfY-HoDPnubWtg&bvm=bv.41248874,d.eWU (accessed January 26, 2013).

Larson, C. (2010). *Persuasion: Reception and responsibility* (12th ed.). Boston: Wadsworth Cengage Publishing.

Ledlow, G., & Coppola, M. N. (2011). *Leadership for health professionals: Theory, skills, and applications* (p. 243). Sudbury, MA: Jones and Bartlett Publishing.

Luizzi, V. (1993). *A case for legal ethics: Legal ethics as a source for universal ethic* (p. 4). Albany, NY: State University of New York Press.

Lundy, K., & Janes, S. (2009). *Community health nursing: Caring for the public's health* (p. 256). Sudbury, MA: Bartlett and Jones Publishing.

Markkula Center for Applied Ethics. (2013a). A framework for ethical decision making. Santa Clara University. Retrieved from http://www.scu.edu/ethics/practicing/decision/framework.html (accessed February 3, 2013).

Markkula Center for Applied Ethics. (2013b). A framework for thinking ethically. Santa Clara University. Retrieved from http://www.scu.edu/ethics/practicing/decision/framework.html (accessed February 3, 2013).

McLaughlin, E., & Muncie, J. (2006). *The SAGE dictionary of criminology* (2nd ed., p. 46). Thousand Oaks, CA: Sage Publications.

Merriam-Webster Dictionary. (2013a). s.v. "confidential." Retrieved from http://www.merriam-webster.com/dictionary/confidentiality (accessed February 2, 2013).

Merriam-Webster Dictionary. (2013b). s.v. "disclose." Retrieved from http://www.merriam-webster.com/dictionary/disclose (accessed February 2, 2013).

Merriam-Webster Dictionary. (2013c). s.v. "disclosure." Retrieved from http://www.merriam-webster.com/dictionary/disclosure?show=0&t=1359849612 (accessed January 2, 2013).

Merriam-Webster Dictionary. (2013d). s.v. "moral." Retrieved from http://www.merriam-webster.com/dictionary/moral (accessed January 21, 2013).

National Communication Association. (2013a). Credo for ethical communication. Retrieved from http://www.natcom.org/Tertiary.aspx?id=2119# (accessed February 2, 2013).

National Communication Association. (2013b). Interest group descriptions. Retrieved from http://www.natcom.org/interestgroups/#CAL (accessed February 2, 2013).

National Communication Association. (2013c). NCA credo for ethical communication. Retrieved from http://www.natcom.org/uploadedFiles/About_NCA/Leadership_and_Governance/Public_Policy_Platform/PDF-PolicyPlatform-NCA_Credo_for_Ethical_Communication.pdf (accessed January 26, 2013).

National Communication Association. (2013d). What is NCA? Retrieved from http://www.natcom.org/about/ (accessed January 16, 2013).

National Communication Association. (2013e). What is NCA? Retrieved from http://www.natcom.org/about/ (accessed February 2, 2013).

National Paralegal College. (2013). Communication with jurors. Retrieved from http://nationalparalegal.edu/public_documents/courseware_asp_files/Ethics/JudgesJurorsWitnesses/CommunicationWithJurors.asp (accessed February 4, 2013).

Northouse, P. (2010). *Leadership: Theory and practice* (p. 380). Thousand Oaks, CA: Sage Publishing.

Pollock, J. (2010). *Ethical dilemmas and decisions in criminal justice* (6th ed., p. 8). Belmont, CA: Wadsworth Cengage Publishing.

Pollock, J. (2012). *Ethical dilemmas and decisions in criminal justice* (7th ed., p. 44). Belmont, CA: Wadsworth Cengage Publishing.

Public Relations Society of America. (2013a). About PRSA: Advancing the profession and the professional. Retrieved from http://www.prsa.org/AboutPRSA/ (accessed February 3, 2013).

Public Relations Society of America. (2013b). Hear experts on the National Incident Management System (NIMS) training and strategic planning. Retrieved from http://podcast.prsa.org/pr/prsa/PAG-2010-Seminar.aspx (accessed February 3, 2013).

Public Relations Society of America. (2013c). Public affairs and government. Retrieved from http://www.prsa.org/Network/Communities/PAG/ (accessed February 3, 2013).

Public Relations Society of America. (2013d). Public Relations Society of America (PRSA) member code of ethics. Retrieved from http://www.prsa.org/AboutPRSA/Ethics/documents/Code%20of%20Ethics.pdf (accessed February 3, 2013).

Seeger, M. (2001). Ethics and communication in organizational contexts: Moving from the fringe to the center. Retrieved from http://ac-journal.org/journal/vol5/iss1/special/seeger.htm (accessed January 26, 2013).

State of New Jersey. (2013). Rules of professional conduct. New Jersey Courts. Retrieved from http://www.judiciary.state.nj.us/rules/apprpc.htm#x1dot4 (accessed January 4, 2013).

Stewart, P. (n.d.). Potter Stewart quotes. Brainyquote.com. Retrieved from http://www.brainyquote.com/quotes/authors/p/potter_stewart.html (accessed January 21, 2013).

Tilstone, W., Savage, K., & Clark, L. (2006). *Forensic science: An encyclopedia of history, methods, and techniques* (p. 136). Santa Barbara, CA: ABC-CLIO Publishing.

Treadwell, D., & Treadwell, J. (2005). *Public relations writing: Principles in practice* (2nd ed., p. 59). Thousand Oaks, CA: Sage Publications.

Vietz, O. (2013). Why do professional organizations have a code of ethics? *Houston Chronicle*. Retrieved from http://smallbusiness.chron.com/professional-organizations-code-ethics-1210.html (accessed January 16, 2013).

Ward, S. (2010). *Global journalism ethics* (p. 12). Quebec, Canada: McGill-Queen's University Press.

West, R., & Turner, L. (2009). *Understanding interpersonal communications: Managing choices in changing times* (2nd ed., p. 33). Boston: Wadsworth Cengage Publishing.

West, R., & Turner, L. (2011). *Understanding interpersonal communication: Making choices in changing times* (2nd ed., p. 35). Boston: Wadsworth Cengage Publishing.

Communications and the U.S. Constitution

16

The fact that we're protected under that Constitution in exercising the right of free speech, it's a wonderful thing. You've got to come from somewhere else to realize how valuable it is.

—Pat Oliphant (Oliphant, n.d.)

Objectives

The objectives of this chapter are to

- Introduce communications specificity within the justice domain
- Introduce basic concepts of the First Amendment
- Introduce court cases that have influenced communications
- Introduce constitutional issues affecting communication
- Discuss examples of communication practices in the justice domain

Introduction

Communication has existed within the American justice system since the founding and originating of the nation. Since its earliest court system, communication has pervaded the legal system of the United States. One of the earliest U.S. Supreme Court cases, *West vs. Barnes*, was argued on August 2, 1791 (U.S. Supreme Court, 2006). This case is significant because it represented the very first decision rendered by the U.S. Supreme Court (Miller, 2012). From the perspective of communication, this initial case is also significant because it was the first instance of oral argumentation that occurred before the U.S. Supreme Court (John Jay, 2013). Since then, numerous instances of oral communications have pervaded court environments across the nation.

The Supreme Court interprets the U.S. Constitution to effectively render its decisions and opinions regarding arguments and issues that it contemplates. The U.S. Constitution represents the highest law of the land, and its contents are expressed through the written word. Therefore, it represents a form of written communication. The U.S. Constitution expresses a variety of liberties and freedoms that influence communicating within American society. Throughout history, the Supreme Court has issued a variety of opinions and rendered numerous decisions that involve constitutional interpretation through which communicating is affected. Some of these opinions and decisions have changed through time, with varying instantiations of the court and its periodic interpretations of the Constitution.

Considerations of the First Amendment

The First Amendment of the U.S. Constitution guarantees the freedoms of religion, speech, press, assembly, and petition. Specifically, the First Amendment states the following:

> Congress shall make no law respecting an establishment of religion, or prohibiting the free exercise thereof; or abridging the freedom of speech, or of the press; or the right of the people peaceably to assemble, and to petition the government for a redress of grievances. (Cornell University—Legal Information Institute, 2013)

This amendment is significant regarding the characteristics of communication within American society and its justice system. It affects all communication that is printed, broadcasted, or voiced within society. Although the First Amendment guarantees the liberties of such communications modalities, it also affects the censoring of messages that may be written, broadcasted, or voiced within society. Throughout history, various interpretations of the U.S. Constitution have expressed with greater specificity the notions of religion, speech, press, assembly, and petition that affect communication.

The communications process involves the sending and receiving of messages. From the perspective of receiving messages, one court case was the 2006 event of *Beard v. Banks* involving prison settings. This case involved Banks claiming his rights involving the First Amendment were violated because of the inaccessibility of "nonreligious reading material" (Harr et al., 2012). This case determined that it was constitutional to "deny magazines, newspapers, and photographs to the most incorrigible inmates" as a method of promoting compliance with the rules of the prison environment and to enhance security (Cole & Smith, 2010).

One may consider the freedom of religion from the perspective of communication. One court case that has implications for religion and communication is the 1970 event of *Gittlemacker v. Prasse*. This case determined that the states must allow and permit inmates with the "opportunity to practice their religion," but are not "required to provide a member of the clergy" (Cole & Smith, 2010). Although prisoners may practice their religious faith, they may not always have the capability of orally communicating directly with a member of the clergy while incarcerated. Some arguments may consider such conditions to be a subduing of religion and communication. However, they are constitutional because such diminishments are "reasonably related to legitimate penological interests" (Hanser, 2013).

Communicating often involves video resources, especially when messaging with mass audiences. Throughout American history, opinions regarding the freedoms of the First Amendment have affected court decisions regarding video resources. During 1915, regarding the case of *Mutual Film Corp. v. Ohio Industrial Commission*, the U.S. Supreme Court rendered a decision involving films and motion pictures. The Court determined that the exhibition of films was a business, and it "defined film as commerce and not as a medium for the communication of ideas" (Romanowski, 2012). As a result, films and motion pictures were denied the protectiveness of free speech and were subjected to the tenets of "legal prior restraint" (Romanowski, 2012). However, in due time, this perspective and opinion changed regarding the scope of the First Amendment. During 1952, in the case of *Burstyn v. Wilson*, the Supreme Court determined that the scope of the First Amendment was applicable to films and motion pictures (Eastland, 2000, p. 133). This decision expressed the notion that films and motion pictures were modalities for communicating ideas, thereby affording them the protections of the First Amendment (Hendershot, 1998).

Communication also involves both television and radio modalities. Both mediums may also be considered from the perspectives of constitutionality and of the First Amendment. One court case that involved both television and radio is the 1973 event of *CBS v. Democratic National Committee*. This case determined that media broadcasters may refuse sales of "advertising time for discussion of controversial political issues" (Denniston, 1992). Therefore, both radio and television stations were allotted some amount of control regarding the messages that may be broadcasted and communicated (Curry et al., 1994). Although the ability to influence broadcast communications media was facilitated in this case, it also involved connotations and allusions regarding the First Amendment. Specifically, the ruling of the Supreme Court stated the following (Columbia Broadcasting v. Democratic Comm., 1973):

> My conclusion is that TV and radio stand in the same protected position under the First Amendment as do newspapers and magazines. The philosophy of the First Amendment requires that result, for the fear that Madison and Jefferson had of government intrusion is perhaps even more relevant to TV and radio than it is to newspapers and other like publications. That fear was founded not only on the spectre of a lawless government but of government under the control of a faction that desired to foist its views of the common good on the people. (Columbia Broadcasting v. Democratic Comm., 1973)

Other facets of communication may be considered from the perspective of the First Amendment. Communication occurs among cities and towns throughout the nation in which a variety of matters are petitioned and discussed. The right of the people to assemble themselves peaceably and to address the government regarding their grievances is guaranteed within the First Amendment. However, no guarantee exists that such assemblies will always exhibit and maintain a modicum of societal tranquility.

During 2011, the Occupy Wall Street event occurred in which grievances involved "bailouts of banks, auto companies, and major corporations including GM, Chrysler, and GE" (Kadlec, 2011). The premise of the movement also expressed opinions that are contrary to the foundations of liberty that are enjoyed by Americans, specifically the ownership of private property (Kadlec, 2011). This movement also exhibited incidents of theft, vandalism, littering, and "sexual assaults and rape" (Kadlec, 2011). Among the locations of the movement, approximately 3000 arrests were made by law enforcement entities (Brownfield, 2011). Figure 16.1 shows an arrest being made during the movement.

American society is diverse, and represents myriads of cultural, ethnic, religious, political, and economic characteristics and opinions within its cumulative populace. Ensuring that these segments of American society can openly communicate their respective messages is facilitated through the freedoms guaranteed within the First Amendment. Whether one is categorized as a member of a majority or minority group, the First Amendment provides a legal foundation through which ideas and information may be exchanged with others. Although one may not like, enjoy, or share the opinions and perspectives of others within society, the First Amendment provides a means through which all Americans have an opportunity to voice their respective beliefs openly and freely without the fear of government reprisal.

Figure 16.1 Arrest made during Occupy Wall Street movement. (From http://abcnews.go.com/US/occupy-wall-street-protesters-americans/story?id=14652698.)

Contexts of the First Amendment

The First Amendment of the U.S. Constitution may be perceived from a variety of perspectives. It may be perceived from a perspective of establishing a foundational paradigm of liberty within the United States versus a restrictive paradigm of oppression that may exist among foreign nations (and that existed within the British Empire, which spawned its American colonies). It influences the whole American society while simultaneously providing a mechanism for permitting and facilitating personal expression. Individuals, groups, and organizations may express rebuttals to refute opposing viewpoints or falsehoods. They may also complement and corroborate views with which they agree. The premise of the First Amendment provides a basis through which debate may occur, thereby contributing to both public and personal opinions.

The U.S. Constitution and the governmental systems of the United States represent cumulatively an antithesis conceptually regarding the characteristics of the governments from which the nation originated during the Colonial period. Within the First Amendment is the notion that the "Congress shall make no law respecting an establishment of religion, or prohibiting the free exercise thereof" (Cornell University—Legal Information Institute, 2013). During Colonial times, the Anglican Church was powerful in England, and represented the only church that was "supported by state taxation" (Blum et al., 1973). Only the members of this church were allowed to hold any form of "public office" (Blum et al., 1973). These members "voted on every act of Parliament" and were responsible for enforcement duties via the church through "jurisdiction over probate of wills and breaches of morality" (Blum et al., 1973). In contrast, Americans expected their "clergy to serve, not rule them" (Blum et al., 1973).

This initial mindset of the American colonists influenced the crafting of the First Amendment through its restraining and limiting the powers and abilities of government to establish and control religion. This paradigm continues to influence modern American society. From the perspective of communication, the First Amendment protects religious speech. During modern times, numerous court cases have involved considerations of public versus private speech within the context of religion and the Establishment Clause (Hellman et al., 2011). The Establishment Clause forbids any government speech that endorses religion, whereas private speech involving religion is protected by both the Free Exercise Clause and the Free Speech Clause (Hellman et al., 2011).

Another perspective of the First Amendment involves the value of discovering truth regarding the notion that "when truth and falsehood are allowed to freely grapple, truth will win out" (University of Missouri, 2013a). Truth may be viewed from two perspectives: its value may be embellished by "utilitarian considerations concerning progress and the development of society" or as "an autonomous and fundamental good" within society (Oxford University Press, 2013). If free speech is restricted, then the ascertainment and publication of "accurate facts and valuable opinion" within society are diminished or may be difficult (Oxford University Press, 2013). Because governmental legitimacy and purpose both necessitate the protection of "individual autonomy," the government is restrained from "interfering with freedom of speech" (Williams, 2004).

Through the First Amendment, many different viewpoints may be voiced within American society. Some may be questionable, whereas others may be quite accurate. Some viewpoints may be outright ludicrous. However, within the limits of the law, they all may be voiced openly and contemplated by the members of society. Theoretically, these different opinions and viewpoints may be voiced without government coercion regarding viewpoints that it deems must be accepted by the entirety of society. The First Amendment represents a mechanism through which many viewpoints are present within American society. Therefore, individuals may examine these different viewpoints, and perceive and discern what they deem to be truth. Figure 16.2 shows a debating of issues during the Washington Gubernatorial Debate.

This notion introduces the concept of debate and discussion within society. Because of the freedom guaranteed by the First Amendment, different opinions may be voiced, questioned, and debated openly and freely within society without government coercion. Opinions, viewpoints, and facts may be refuted through rebuttal. Debates may occur through which they are clarified and elucidated. Members of society may form their respective judgments of what they see, hear, read, or experience. Essentially, this scenario represents a marketplace of ideas. This notion represents the concept that the "same 'invisible

Figure 16.2 State of Washington 2012 Gubernatorial Debate. (From http://seattletimes.com/html/edcetera/2019413354_who_won_the_gubernatorial_deba.html.)

hand' that guides unregulated economic markets to maximum efficiency will guide unregulated markets in ideas to maximum discovery of truth" (Coplan, 2012a).

The U.S. justice system has "repeatedly" indicated that the "primary purpose" of the First Amendment is the protection of "an uninhibited marketplace where differing ideas can clash" (Oklahoma State University, 2013b). The Supreme Court has not acknowledged a solitary, "universal marketplace of ideas" (Oklahoma State University, 2013b). Instead, it has recognized numerous marketplaces of ideas representing different domains that exhibit unique "dynamics, parameters, regulatory schemes, and audiences" (Oklahoma State University, 2013b). Examples include "broadcasting, local communities, commercial speech, political speech, mail systems, school classrooms and libraries, state fairs, scholarly conferences and lectures, and picketing" (Oklahoma State University, 2013b). These subsets involve greater accessibility by audiences, "more common ground" among audiences, and an increased probability of "some resolution" regarding considered issues (Oklahoma State University, 2013b).

Conceptually, any marketplace of ideas must be taken with a grain of salt and examined with some suspicion. Biases may exist regarding the opinions, viewpoints, facts, and statements that are examined by the populace (Volokh, 2011). For instance, biases may be "self-serving," "inconsistent with existing beliefs" in which new ideas may be rejected by the audience, or involve manipulating statistics toward a certain viewpoint (Coplan, 2012b). Other forms of bias may include "power structures" and "ideology" (Ingber, 1984). Cumulatively, these considerations of biases represent impediments that may diminish the capacity of discerning truth.

Examining numerous concepts increases the ability of people to conclude some aspect of truth for themselves. This notion is relevant regarding the political decisions that are rendered by citizens within the context of the First Amendment, and may be considered from the perspectives of democracy and self-government. The First Amendment is a protective mechanism regarding self-governance within a free society (Oklahoma State University, 2013b). Alexander Meiklejohn advocated the protection of speech politically (Oklahoma State University, 2013b). Meiklejohn stated the following (Perry, 2011):

> The First Amendment is not, primarily, a device for the winning of new truth, though that is very important. It is a device for the sharing of whatever truth that has been won. Its purpose is to give every voting member of the body politic the fullest possible participation in the understanding of those problems with which the citizens of a self-governing society must deal.

Meiklejohn believed that citizens were the rulers within a democracy (Oklahoma State University, 2013b). Through discussions of politics, the citizenry is exposed to information that is necessary for rendering informed decisions (i.e., voting) upon "which a self-governing society is dependent" (Oklahoma State University, 2013b). Essentially, these concepts and Meiklejohn's statements represent the notion that free speech is necessary for the effective and proper functioning of government. It is posited that only through the communicating and exchanging of numerous, different ideas can the public be informed sufficiently to make decisions that influence society through time.

This notion of communicating with the public also has another implication for society and the general public. Because much information may be communicated to the public, the citizenry has opportunities to remain informed regarding the attributes of government. In this sense, the First Amendment provides a mechanism that embellishes the checks and balances of government performance with respect to the influences of an informed public and the citizenry. Therefore, the First Amendment and its guarantees of freedom of speech serve the interests of "political liberty" that avert and deter "tyranny" (Sullivan, 2010).

Maintaining this instantiation of political liberty occurs through skeptically viewing "all government efforts at speech suppression" that could possibly bias the "private ordering of ideas" (Sullivan, 2010). Therefore, the public is trusted sufficiently to evaluate speech and render decisions without any government intervention for the purposes of "paternalistic or redistributive reasons" (Sullivan, 2010). Although the intervention of government may be necessary to rectify certain instances of allocating "inefficiencies" regarding the modalities that "speech transactions" occur, the communication of ideas is "best left to a freely competitive ideological market" (Sullivan, 2010).

Overall, these considerations of free speech, provided through the First Amendment, show its continued and unceasing relevance within society both historically and during contemporary times. The First Amendment is a necessary and powerful resource through which the American populace embellishes its communications for both private and public functions. Through the First Amendment, American society possesses remarkable characteristics that are absent among many other nations—the freedom of expression, the exchange of ideas, and the embellishment of self-government.

Unprotected and Curtailed Communication

The word abridge is defined as "to reduce in scope," "to diminish," "to shorten in duration or extent," or to "shorten by omission of words without sacrifice of sense" (i.e., to "condense") (*Merriam-Webster*, 2013a). The First Amendment indicates that Congress shall not abridge the freedom of speech. However, there are times when the First Amendment must be considered from a variety of perspectives that may involve some aspects of curtailing the communicative modalities of speaking, writing, or broadcasting. Straightforward examples include situations and conditions involving considerations of personal injury, commercial speech, clear and present danger, incitement, national security and war, and obscenity and pornography.

The first consideration involves personal injury. These situations arise when the "body, mind, or emotions are hurt, usually due to someone else's negligence or carelessness" (Rottenstein Law Group, 2013). Personal injury law is synonymous with tort law (Rottenstein Law Group, 2013). Various examples of personal injury cases and disputes include accidents involving vehicles, liability involving consumer products (e.g., defectiveness that causes harm), injuries arising from animals (e.g., a dog biting someone), and so forth. From the perspective of communication, personal injury may be considered within the context of fighting words.

The fighting words concept and legal doctrine originated in 1942 regarding the court case of *Chaplinsky v. New Hampshire* (Silver et al., 2013). This original consideration of fighting words defined the concept broadly by including "words which are likely to incite an immediate fight and words which inflict injury" (Silver et al., 2013). However, through time and the experience of many succeeding court cases, the notion of fighting words has become limited in many fashions (Silver et al., 2013).

The notion of "fighting words" represents "a mode of communication, rather than a content-based category" (Eastland, 2000, p. 338). Prohibiting "fighting words" does not involve any specificity of "time, place, or manner restriction," and represents a prohibition against "a class of speech that conveys an overriding message of personal injury and imminent violence" (Eastland, 2000, p. 338). Fighting words may be spoken or written, generally are used to incite violence or hatred, and are unprotected by the First Amendment. Various definitions of fighting words exist among different jurisdictions. Fighting words generally involve some type of insults or language that is abusive (Gardner & Anderson, 2012). Fighting words must be addressed "face-to-face" between the communicating parties (Gardner & Anderson, 2012). Also, fighting words may cause the chance that the person being addressed will respond immediately with violence (Gardner & Anderson, 2012).

Commercial speech is another consideration of curtailed communication. During 1980, the U.S. Supreme Court considered commercial speech within the case of Central Hudson Gas and Electric Corp. v. Public Service Commission (1980). During the winter months of 1973 and 1974, there was a shortage of electricity in New York that necessitated the banning of advertising that promoted using electricity (Central Hudson Gas and Electric Corp. v. Public Service Commission, 1980). Although this shortage had subsided by 1976, the advertising ban was continued by the Public Service Commission (Central Hudson Gas and Electric Corp. v. Public Service Commission, 1980). The Central Hudson Gas and Electric Corp. filed a lawsuit claiming that both its First Amendment and Fourteenth Amendment rights were violated regarding commercial speech (Central Hudson Gas and Electric Corp. v. Public Service Commission, 1980).

The outcome of this case generated some interesting considerations of commercial speech. It provided an analytical method for the evaluation of commercial speech cases within the court system. Specifically, the analysis consists of (Central Hudson Gas and Electric Corp. v. Public Service Commission, 1980)

> (1) Whether the expression is protected by the First Amendment of the United States Constitution (Constitution). To be protected, it must concern lawful activity and not be misleading. (2) Whether the asserted governmental interest is substantial. If both part one and part two are satisfied then (3) a court must determine whether the regulation directly advances the governmental interest asserted. (4) Whether it is not more extensive than is necessary to serve that interest. (Central Hudson Gas and Electric Corp. v. Public Service Commission, 1980)

This analytical method is known as the Central Hudson test (Parkinson & Parkinson, 2008, pp. 30–31). Essentially, the outcome of this case showed that because the producers of "commercial communication are unlikely to accidentally misstate facts" and because producers are financially motivated to the extent that they are unmotivated by regulations, the "Court would permit greater regulation of commercial speech than noncommercial speech" (Parkinson & Parkinson, 2008, pp. 30–31). Therefore, commercial speech does not enjoy the full protections of the First Amendment.

Situations involving clear and present danger represent another consideration of curtailed speech. The concept of clear and present danger originated in 1919 regarding the Supreme Court case of *Schenck v. United States* (University of Missouri, 2013b). This case involved the event of a socialist who, during World War I, disseminated "15,000 leaflets to young men of draft age critical of the war effort and, especially, the draft" (University of Missouri, 2013b). Schenck was convicted of violating the Espionage Act of 1917 (University of Missouri, 2013b). Supreme Court Justice Oliver Wendell Holmes questioned whether the wording created "a clear and present danger" that it would "bring about substantive evils Congress has a right to prevent?" (University of Missouri, 2013b). This query represents the basic premise of the clear and present danger test.

This original query and consideration of the clear and present danger test showed that expression could be curtailed if evidence existed suggesting that "such expression would cause a dangerous condition, actual or imminent, that Congress has the power to prevent" (Bardes et al., 2012). Additional Supreme Court rulings further limited the protectiveness of the First Amendment regarding clear and present danger situations in 1925, 1951, and 1969 (Bardes et al., 2012).

Another consideration of curtailed communication involves incitement. The Brandenburg incitement standard indicates that speech must consist of "advocacy directed to inciting or producing imminent lawless action" and "speech that is likely to incite or produce such action" before the government may "punish advocacy of violence or other lawlessness:" (Harpaz, 2013) This consideration of incitement occurred as a result of the 1969 *Brandenburg v. Ohio* court case.

The law in Ohio prohibited the advocating or teaching of any "doctrines" related to "criminal syndicalism" (Brandenburg v. Ohio, 2013). Within the *Brandenburg v. Ohio* court case, Brandenburg was a leader within the Ku Klux Klan, and he "made a speech promoting the taking of vengeful actions against government and was therefore convicted under the Ohio law" (Brandenburg v. Ohio, 2013). The primary question considered by the court was whether the Ohio law that prohibited "public speech that advocated certain violent activities" violated his First Amendment and Fourteenth Amendment right of free speech? (Brandenburg v. Ohio, 2013) The outcome of this case showed that speech may be prohibited provided that it is directed toward producing or inciting "imminent lawless action," and if it is "likely to incite or produce such action" (Brandenburg v. Ohio, 2013).

From a practical perspective, liability may not have as its basis any speculation between harm and speech; the relationship must be "clear, direct, and immediate" (Lidsky, 2002). Therefore, this case expands the scope of protectiveness regarding the speech of "radical political dissidents" that may originate from "even the most despised groups in society" (Lidsky, 2002). These considerations also are applicable to "political dissidents" (Lidsky, 2002). Such considerations of the *Brandenburg* conditions are examined within the contexts of various "international human rights treaties" for ensuring that these tenets are applied to the U.S. "media" (Lidsky, 2002).

Communication may be curtailed during times of war and during situations involving national security. War is defined as a "state of usually open and declared armed hostile conflict between states or nations"; as a "period of such armed conflict"; as a "state of hostility, conflict, or antagonism"; or as a "struggle or competition between opposing forces or for a particular end" (*Merriam-Webster*, 2013g). The twentieth century exhibited various facets of armed hostilities among nations, involving the United States, during World War I, World War II, the Korean Conflict, the Vietnam War, and the Gulf War. Although the Cold War did not pit the United States against the Soviets in an open, armed conflict, it did involve much animosity and competition between the two nations globally until the demise of the Soviet Union. Although these categories of open, armed conflict and opposition politically and economically differ, they have commonness regarding the national security of the United States. During periods of war, maintaining the confidentiality of certain information and curtailing communication to prevent national harm are paramount to the outcomes and successfulness of war efforts.

One consideration of such conditions is the Totten doctrine. It originated during the War between the States as the result of the case involving *Totten v. the United States.* A Union spy was sent to infiltrate the Confederacy to gain intelligence regarding its assets and resources (Silverman, 2003). When the spy returned, he was compensated for his expenses but not for the wages that he was allegedly promised for performing the mission (Silverman, 2003). The U.S. Supreme Court dismissed this claim as a method of protecting "national security interests" (Silverman, 2003). Furthermore, the Totten doctrine did not permit "in camera review of allegedly secret evidence," thereby providing a foundational basis for dismissing "litigation brought by contractors for the development of military technology" and among other cases "involving classified information" (Silverman, 2003).

Another consideration of confidentiality and national security involves the State Secrets Act (SSA), which matured with the court case of *United States v. Reynolds.* This situation involved the crashing of a "military aircraft" that was performing a "secret surveillance mission," and which carried some civilians among its passengers (Silverman, 2003). Some widows of those killed sued the U.S. government, and attempted to gain information provided within "Air Force accident investigation reports" (Silverman, 2003). The government responded by making a claim of "privilege against revealing military secrets" (Silverman, 2003).

This court case also has implications for the justice system regarding a rather basic query: how do courts determine whether circumstances are proper for a claim of privilege without breaching the security of the information that the "privilege is designed to protect?" (Silverman, 2003) Judges must "sense whether" any claims of privilege are justified without understanding the foundational facts that comprise the basis of the claims (Silverman, 2003). Therefore, an implication of this case suggests that "even federal judges cannot be trusted with sensitive information" despite the existence of no absolute prohibition against the possibility of judges examining evidence "in camera" (Silverman, 2003).

During modern times, questions and debates continue to arise regarding the confidentiality and sensitivity of information versus the requirements of national security. During 2010, U.S. Army Private First Class Bradley Manning released a myriad of documents that contained classified information via the Wikileaks system of the Internet. Over the succeeding months, Wikileaks further distributed thousands more "classified documents," including many that revealed the locations of U.S. personnel and various "diplomatic cables" (Opper, 2011). Many of the resulting legal issues questioned whether national security was compromised, the impacts regarding "foreign relations," and whether violations of the Espionage Act of 1917 had occurred (Opper, 2011). During the period of this authorship, this case is ongoing and fuels much debate publically and privately. Only time will tell the outcomes, effects, and impacts of these issues and legal actions. Regardless, this case shows the importance of incidents that involve considerations of national security versus the curtailing of communication.

Obscenity and pornography are also consideration of curtailed speech within the context of the First Amendment. Obscenity is defined as the "quality or state of being obscene" (*Merriam-Webster,* 2013d). Anything that is obscene is defined as "disgusting to the senses," "abhorrent to morality or virtue," "containing or being language regarded as taboo in polite usage," "repulsive by reason of crass disregard of moral or ethical principles," or "so excessive as to be offensive" (*Merriam-Webster,* 2013c). Although people may immediately recognize connotations of sexuality with obscenity, many things may be deemed as being obscene because the basic concept of obscenity "deals with opinion and not objective facts" (White, 1997). Therefore, considerations of obscenity are subjective and may involve many different perceptions of indecency and community standards (White, 1997).

Regardless, obscenity is a unique form of speech that the Supreme Court denies the protections of the First Amendment without considering "whether it is harmful to individuals" (Cohen, 2009). During 1957, two Supreme Court cases reaffirmed this notion: *Roth v. United States* and *Alberts v. California*. Justice William Brennan stated the following:

> Implicit in the history of the First Amendment, it is the rejection of obscenity as utterly without redeeming social importance. This rejection for that reason is mirrored in the universal judgment that obscenity should be restrained, reflected in the international agreement of over 50 nations, in the obscenity laws of all the 48 states, and in the 20 obscenity laws enacted by the Congress from 1842 to 1956. We hold that obscenity is not within the area of constitutionally protected speech or press. (LaRue, 2005)

Defining obscenity is tedious given the subjective attributes of communities and individuals throughout the nation. During 1973, the U.S. Supreme Court case of *Miller v. California* provided a foundation for identifying and defining obscenity. This case involved the incident of Miller exercising a mass marketing campaign to "advertise the sale of illustrated adult material books" (Miller v. California, 1973). Because of these actions, a total of "five unsolicited advertising brochures" were mailed, thereby resulting in the conviction of Miller (Miller v. California, 1973). These mailings were sexually explicit, and involved various depictions graphically of men and women engaging in sexual intercourse (Miller v. California, 1973). As a result of this case, the Supreme Court indicated that each state is free to craft obscenity laws that are commensurate with the beliefs of individual communities throughout the nation.

The *Miller v. California* case also produced a legal test to examine whether certain materials may be deemed as obscene. The Miller Test is described as follows (LaRue, 2005):

- Whether the average person, applying contemporary adult community standards, would find that the material, taken as a whole, appeals to a prurient interest in sex (i.e., an erotic, lascivious, abnormal, unhealthy, degrading, shameful, or morbid interest in nudity, sex, or excretion)
- Whether the average person, applying contemporary adult community standards, would find that the work depicts or describes, in a patently offensive way, sexual conduct (i.e., ultimate sex acts, normal or perverted, actual or simulated; masturbation; excretory functions; lewd exhibition of the genitals; or sadomasochistic sexual abuse)
- Whether a reasonable person would find that the work, taken as a whole, lacks serious literary, artistic, political, or scientific value

The 1990s exhibited a national debate regarding obscenity with respect to the lyrics of Ice-T's *Cop Killer* song from the *Body Count* album by his band Body Count (1992). This music was "implicated in at least two shooting incidents" and heightened "racial tensions" throughout the United States (Martin, 1993). The lyrics of the song were laced with profanity, and they alluded to the murdering of police officers. The public response was sensational, and resulted in much backlash against both Time Warner and Ice-T. Specifically, executives of Time Warner received death threats, the band was released from its contract with Time Warner, and the *Cop Killer* song was "withdrawn from the album" (Woldu, 2008). During legal proceedings, the American Civil Liberties Union defended the album, citing that the situation represented the radical attitudes of residents among urban environments versus the universal imposition of political tastes upon all Americans (Etzioni, 2004).

During modern times, many incidents, which may be perceived as obscene, generate much debate within American society. For instance, during the 2004 Super bowl in which the entertainer Janet Jackson was performing, the broadcasting of the famous incident involving her "wardrobe malfunction" shocked many within American society (Kessler, 2013). Soon thereafter, a group consisting of the "four main networks and hundreds of affiliates" filed a lawsuit against the Federal Communications Commission in the hopes of "overturning rulings against broadcasts that contained myriads of "incidents of objectionable language or images" (Kessler, 2013). The next month, the U.S. Congress gave its approval of increases in fines involving such incidents, ranging from amounts of $32,500 to $325,000 (Kessler, 2013).

These notions of obscenity also introduce the concept of pornography, which is defined as the "depiction of erotic behavior (as in pictures or writing) intended to cause sexual excitement" or "material (as books or a photograph) that depicts erotic behavior and is intended to case sexual excitement" (*Merriam-Webster*, 2013e). A 1982 court case, *New York v. Ferber*, outlawed child pornography "even if the pictures are not obscene" when the Miller test is applied (Oklahoma State University, 2013a). This case confirmed and upheld the New York statutes that prohibited the "production, exhibition, or selling of any material that depicts any performance by a child under the age of 16 that includes 'actual or simulated sexual intercourse, deviate sexual intercourse, sexual bestiality, masturbation, sado-masochistic abuse or lewd exhibitions of the genitals'" (Oklahoma State University, 2013a). Commensurate with obscenity, child pornography does not have any of the protectiveness that is facilitated by the First Amendment. Therefore, the transmission and receipt of such items represents a form of curtailed communication in which the "government can restrict its availability to everyone" (National Academies Press, 2013).

The First Amendment is an instrument through which various principles and attributes of communication are protected broadly despite the fact that many people may disagree or be offended by the messages that are transmitted and received during the communications process. The communicative modalities of speaking, writing, or broadcasting have been examined and challenged legally through time with respect to a variety of issues ranging from obscenity to personal injury. However, there are times when communication must be curtailed as methods of protecting society, averting and deterring criminal activity, and maintaining societal order. Pursuing and achieving these goals encompass numerous facets and perspectives of communication, ranging from the interests of national security to subjective judgments regarding the morals of local communities.

In any case, the curtailing of communication is a serious issue, and must neither be discounted nor ignored given the freedoms allocated within the First Amendment. Any curtailing of communication must occur within the context of the overall benefit of society through time. It also must be considered with respect to the implications of affecting the whole of American society and succeeding generations. Given these notions, the legal system must be unceasingly vigilant when examining and reviewing incidents that have the potential of influencing societal communications within the United States.

Defamation, Libel, and Slander

Defamation, libel, and slander are concepts that have appeared many times among challenges and disputes within the legal system. Defamation is defined as "an act of communication that causes someone to be shamed, ridiculed, held in contempt, lowered in the estimation of the community, or to lose employment status or earnings or otherwise suffer a damaged reputation" (U.S. Legal, 2013). Establishing an instance of defamation generally involves identifying four characteristics of the communication: "a false statement purporting to be fact concerning another person or entity; publication or communication of that statement to a third person; fault on the part of the person making the statement amounting to intent or at least negligence; and some harm caused to the person or entity who is the subject of the statement" (Legal Information Institute, 2013a). From the perspective of communication, these notions represent false and inaccurate statements that are transmitted and received within the communications process. They may be communicated through a variety of means: printed, written materials, audio resources, electronic messages, social media involving the Internet, public statements made orally, or through video resources.

Libel is generally governed by state laws, and is a form of defamation that is expressed through "print, writing, pictures, signs, effigies, or any communication embodied in physical form that is injurious to a person's reputation, exposes a person to public hatred, contempt or ridicule, or injures a person in his/her business or profession" (Legal Information Institute, 2013b). Within the U.S. legal system, several cases have defined and matured the concept of libel:

1964—*New York Times Co. vs. Sullivan*
1974—*Gertz vs. Robert Welch Inc.*
1979—*Herbert vs. Lando*
1990—*Milkovich vs. Lorain Journal Co.*
1991—*Masson vs. New Yorker Magazine*
1997—*Zeran v. America Online*
2004—*Grace vs. Ebay Inc.*

During 1964, the *New York Times Co. vs. Sullivan* case established a foundational standard regarding malice within American society (University of Florida, 2013). During the tumultuous events of the civil rights period within the United States, the *New York Times* published advertising material that described oppressiveness that it alleged existed within Montgomery, Alabama (University of Florida, 2013). This material contained various "false statements, most of which were incidental" (University of Florida, 2013). Mr. L.B. Sullivan, who was the Commissioner of the Montgomery Police, filed a libel lawsuit claiming that the materials "damaged his reputation as a police official" and "demanded a retraction" from the *New York Times* (University of Florida, 2013). Essentially, this case showed that to "protect healthy public debate," with respect to the First Amendment, public officials must prove that any "defamatory language" was actually "published with knowing falsity or reckless disregard for the truth" (University of Florida, 2013).

The 1974 case involving *Gertz vs. Robert Welch Inc.* further refined and crafted the concepts of malice and libel. A family retained attorney Gertz for the purpose of suing a police officer that had killed their son (Gertz v. Robert Welch, Inc., 2013). Within the *American*

Opinion magazine, the John Birch Society labeled Gertz as a Leninist and Communist-fronter because of his representing a family that was "suing a law enforcement officer" (Gertz v. Robert Welch, Inc., 2013). Basically, the legal question involved whether a media resource may communicate "defamatory falsehoods about an individual who is neither a public official nor a public figure" (Gertz v. Robert Welch, Inc., 2013). The conclusion of this proceeding involved Gertz initially losing his libel case because it was determined that *American Opinion* had not transgressed the "malice test for libel" that had been established within the *New York Times Co. vs. Sullivan* case (Gertz v. Robert Welch, Inc., 2013). However, the U.S. Supreme Court reversed this decision, and indicated that Gertz's rights were violated on the basis that he was neither a public figure nor a public official (Gertz v. Robert Welch, Inc., 2013). As a result of this case, private individuals are afforded greater protections against libel than are experienced by public officials or public figures.

The 1979 *Herbert v. Lando* case involved considerations of editorial decisions involving mass communications media. Herbert was a former army officer who had served during the Vietnam War (Herbert v. Lando, 2013). During his military service, he accused his superior officers of concealing alleged atrocities that were supposedly committed by American forces (Herbert v. Lando, 2013). A documentary program was produced and broadcasted by the Columbia Broadcasting System (CBS) that detailed this story (Herbert v. Lando, 2013). Herbert filed a libel lawsuit claiming that the show caused him "financial loss" because it "falsely and maliciously portrayed his character" (Herbert v. Lando, 2013). As a method of attempting to prove libel and to "deduce the editorial decisions" that occurred when producing the program, depositions were taken from the editor, from the producer of the show, and from Lando (Herbert v. Lando, 2013). The primary legal question concerned whether the First Amendment and the Fourteenth Amendment "protect members of the press from inquiries into their thoughts, opinions, and conclusions" that are associated with editorial processes (Herbert v. Lando, 2013). The Supreme Court ruled that there is no absolute privilege regarding the answering of editorial inquiries (Herbert v. Lando, 2013).

The 1990 incident of *Milkovich vs. Lorain Journal Co.* showed that there is no guarantee that any opinions expressed within the media are completely safeguarded against libel. This case considered a situation in which a wrestling team became involved in a fight that necessitated "criminal investigation" (University of Florida, 2013). Within the *News-Herald* publication, an opinion labeled the coach as a liar, and which was determined by the court as having implied the coach "committed an act of perjury" (University of Florida, 2013). This case represents the reasoning that facilitates the use of "hyperbole, nuance, and figures of speech" among editorial and opinions published within the media because such methods are less susceptible to libel (University of Florida, 2013).

A year later, in 1991, the *Masson v. New Yorker Magazine* case involved the notion that "a deliberate alteration of words does not equate with knowledge of falsity, unless the alteration results in a material change in the meaning conveyed by the statement" (Masson v. New Yorker Magazine, 2013). The *New Yorker Magazine* published material that supposedly quoted Mr. Jeffrey Mason and others (Masson v. New Yorker Magazine, 2013). Instead of being exact words, the quotes were determined to be "interpretive summaries" of statements that had been made by Mason and others (Masson v. New Yorker Magazine, 2013). Because of the altering of words, a defamation lawsuit was filed.

The 1997 case of *Zeran v. America Online* introduced a consideration of communication within the virtual domain involving the Internet. Ken Zeran attempted to have

America Online (AOL) held responsible for defamatory comments that were made by an unknown AOL subscriber (Zeran v. America Online, 2013). Zeran lost his cases in trial and appeals courts, and the U.S. Supreme Court would not hear his appeal (Zeran v. America Online, 2013). Although Zeran failed to win his case against AOL for defamation, the basic premises of this dispute regarded "whether an online service, website, or other interactive computer service, can be held liable for defamation made by third parties, where the defamed party has been injured by defamatory speech made by persons who post in an interactive computer service" (Zeran v. America Online, 2013). The court found that AOL was immunized "from claims based on information posted by a third party" (Zeran v. America Online, 2013). This finding was also deemed as being applicable to other interactive and online providers of service within the virtual domain (Zeran v. America Online, 2013). This case was significant because its outcome prohibits any lawsuits that attempt to hold online service providers liable for "traditional editorial functions" ranging from the publication to the alteration of content (Zeran v. America Online, 2013).

During 2004, the *Grace v. Ebay Inc.* case involved considerations of liability within the virtual domain. In California, a court of appeals upheld a trial court decision that had dismissed the original complaint involving allegations that "eBay's refusal to remove what the plaintiff believed to be defamatory 'feedback' about plaintiff constituted defamation" (Barnett, 2011). Although Ebay claimed immunity regarding the Communications Decency Act of 1996, its claim was rejected by the court (Barnett, 2011). Despite this rejection, it was determined that the user agreement with Ebay, which had been accepted by Grace, included a clause that quashed any liability on behalf of Ebay (Barnett, 2011).

These examples provide a glimpse of how the legal system has matured regarding defamation among communications modalities from the perspective of libel. Another consideration of the maturing of the justice system involves the notion of slander within the context of communication. The reviewed literature for this chapter did not reveal a plethora of high-profile landmark cases involving defamation from the perspective of slander. However, one notable incident involved the 2000 election campaign of North Carolina Attorney General Roy Cooper that had future implications regarding "political advertising" (WFMY News, 2003). The opposing candidate, Dan Boyce, claimed that he was slandered by the campaign of Cooper because of television advertising that "accused Boyce of having overbilled in a class-action lawsuit against the state" (Roy Cooper, 2013). Boyce filed a lawsuit against Cooper a day before the election occurred (Roy Cooper, 2013). Although the advertisement indicated that Boyce sought a rate of $28,000 per hour for services, it did not state that he charged a rate of $28,000 per hour (Marshall, 2004). This nuance of language sparked a heated controversy legally. This case experienced many appeals, and appeared before the U.S. Supreme Court before being remanded to the Wake County Superior Court (WRAL News, 2009).

This issue concerns campaign communications and freedom of speech from a variety of perspectives. False speech is capable of distorting the "electoral process" (Marshall, 2004). It may also diminish the "quality of campaign discourse and debate" (Marshall, 2004). It also contributes to levels of "voter alienation" through inciting feelings of "cynicism" and causing some "distrust of the political process" (Marshall, 2004). Lying about someone's character may cause "reputational and emotional" injuries concerning the subject of the false statements (Marshall, 2004).

Because of the potential of false statements to influence the political process, influence voters, and to cause forms of injury, some arguments exist that may favor various forms and regulation concerning statements that are issued during campaigns. However, voters may be leery of campaign advertisements and the accuracy of any statements that they hear or see (Marshall, 2004). In some cases, the sanctioning of campaign speech may necessitate periods of time that exceed the length of the "election cycle" (Marshall, 2004). Certainly, a consideration of sanctioning and regulating campaign speech involves a consideration of the basic liberties and freedoms of speech that are guaranteed within the First Amendment (Marshall, 2004). Instances of "partisan abuse" may result from the sanctioning of speech involving its authorization by the government (Marshall, 2004). Furthermore, any regulating of political campaign speech may provide an opportunity to inflict "political damage" legally through the justice system during the campaign process (Marshall, 2004).

Regardless of the considerations, this incident shows the scope and magnitude of biased communications within the political process and its potential ramifications and implications for both the justice system and society. It also shows a different consideration of defamation involving the notion of slander within the communications process, and the resulting legal challenges that may be interjected within the justice system. In any case, slander represents a dangerous form of communication that often necessitates the attention of the justice system and that invokes considerations of the First Amendment.

Defamation involves aspects of both libel and slander that are exercised within the communications process. Both written and unwritten messages have the potential of harming others and their reputations both personally and professionally. Although the First Amendment facilitates a great freedom of speech, there are times when expressed messages may be outright incorrect or misleading. Regardless, in any case, such messaging within any form of media has the potential of spawning defamation lawsuits involving issues of slander and libel.

Intellectual Property

Within the justice system, many disputes arise regarding the issues of copyrights, patents, and trademarks. These tools are the methods through which individuals or organizations may establish and communicate a claim regarding the originality, rights, and ownership of some type of intellectual property. A copyright is defined as "the exclusive legal right to reproduce, publish, sell, or distribute the matter and form of something (as a literary, musical, or artistic work)" (*Merriam-Webster*, 2013b). A patent is the "exclusive right issued by the U.S. Patent Office that enables the recipient to manufacture, sell, or otherwise control an invention for a period of 20 years from the date of the grant" (Weygandt et al., 2010). Trademarks are "any word, name, symbol, or device, or any combination thereof—(1) used by a person, or (2) which a person has a bona fide intention to use in commerce and applies to register on the principal register established by this chapter, to identify and distinguish his or her goods, including a unique product, from those manufactured or sold by others and to indicate the source of the goods, even if that source is unknown" (U.S. Food and Drug Administration, 2013). Individuals and organizations are often presented with confirmation of any registration of their materials with the government. Figure 16.3 shows a patent certificate.

During modern times, technology facilitates the mass dissemination and communicating of information and materials quickly and easily between individuals and to mass audiences. In many cases, such communication involves the messaging of intellectual

THE UNITED STATES OF AMERICA

Whereas James Cording, Jr., of Philadelphia, and Miles J. Willard, Jr., of Glenside, Pennsylvania, assignors to the United States of America as represented by the Secretary of Agriculture,

Commissioner of Patents

Letters Patent

United States of America as represented by the Secretary of Agriculture

SEVENTEEN

In testimony whereof ... second ... April, ... fifty-seven, ... eighty-first.

Figure 16.3 Patent certificate. (From http://www.ars.usda.gov/is/pr/2007/070418.htm.)

property that may be the subject of copyright, patent, or trademark. Communicating the status of intellectual property is essential in maintaining the integrity of the copyright, patent, or trademark. Often such communication involves ensuring that "ownership and contact information stays permanently attached" wherever "it may travel and be accessed on the web or packaged media" (Digital Watermarking Alliance, 2013).

The justice system is no stranger to litigation involving intellectual property disputes and arguments. During recent years, Apple and Samsung became adversaries in an intellectual property lawsuit involving the characteristics of their technology products. The outcome of the initial court proceedings determined that "Samsung's devices infringed six Apple patents," and the resulting award of $1 billion represented "one of the largest patent awards on record" (Sherr, 2013). Although the initial outcome of this court case involved the awarding of approximately $1 billion to Apple, this award was reduced to the amount of approximately $598.9 million (Sherr, 2013).

This example highlights the importance and financial costs of high-profile lawsuits involving intellectual property. Establishing the rights and protections associated with intellectual property may be accomplished through the U.S. Copyright Office and the U.S.

Patent and Trademark Office. Communicating the status of works that have copyright, trademark, or patent is essential. Although communicating this status may be exercised, no guarantee exists that infringement shall not occur. In such cases, the legal system provides a mechanism through which dispute resolution occurs through time.

Privacy

Privacy is defined as the "quality or state of being apart from company or observation" or the "freedom from unauthorized intrusion" (*Merriam-Webster*, 2013f). Privacy issues abound in modern society ranging from simple conversations between individuals to vast amounts of data that are communicated electronically among computer networks. Within the communications domain, resulting from the advent and proliferation of modern technologies, numerous "privacy-enhancing technologies have been developed" (Horniak, 2004). Examples of such resources include sophisticated software algorithms for encrypting and decrypting messages and their associated electronic devices. Protecting the communications of American society is a paramount interest of law enforcement entities and the justice system.

Much legislation exists through which the privacy of communications is embellished and protected, and through which conditions are expressed that permit the breaching of communications privacy. Such acts also often detail the punitive measures that may be pursued when illegal breaches of privacy occur. Examples of such legislation include the Privacy Act of 1974, the National Security Act of 1947, the USA Patriot Act, the Intelligence Reform and Terrorism Prevention Act of 2004, the Electronic Communications Privacy Act, the Foreign Intelligence Surveillance Act of 1978, the Communications Act of 1934, and the Paperwork Reduction Act (U.S. Department of Justice, 2013).

The threats posed by both domestic and international entities that desire to harm American society are relevant considerations of the justice system and law enforcement organizations. Throughout time, legislation has adapted to the integration of technology in communications with respect to the persistent and continuous threats that endanger American society. This notion is reflected within the Electronic Communications Privacy Act (ECPA) of 1986 and its subsequent revisions through time.

The ECPA of 1986 represents a combination of the Stored Wire Electronic Communications Act and the Electronic Communications Privacy Act (U.S. Department of Justice, 2013). The ECPA represents a revision of the Federal Wiretap Act of 1968 (U.S. Department of Justice, 2013). The 1968 legislation occurred to "address interception of conversations using 'hard' telephone lines" (U.S. Department of Justice, 2013). The 1986 legislation resulted from the development and use of "computer and other digital and electronic communications" (U.S. Department of Justice, 2013). After the attack against the United States on September 11, 2001, federal legislation was again revised to reflect changes in communications technologies. For instance, the USA Patriot Act and its succeeding revisions and legislation have "clarified and updated the ECPA in light of the ongoing development of modern communications technologies and methods, including easing restrictions on law enforcement access to stored communications in some cases" (U.S. Department of Justice, 2013).

Maintaining the integrity and privacy of communication involves a consideration of legislation federally. Although federal legislation may address a variety of issues that delineate the conditions that are necessary for either ensuring privacy or breaching privacy, the legislation represents the needs of government and society during the period that it is crafted and enacted. Through time, technological changes and advancements occur that may make the breaching of privacy easier and harder to detect. When technology changes occur, various facets of privacy legislation also change in due time.

Commentary Regarding Communications in the Justice Domain

This chapter introduced a variety of court cases that either upheld or denied communication within the context of the First Amendment. Often, when such cases are actively being heard among court environments, judges may issue gag orders as protective measures to ensure the integrity of the court proceedings. A gag order is an order that prohibits "the attorneys and the parties to a pending lawsuit or criminal prosecution from talking to the media or the public about the case" (Law.com, 2013). Gag orders are imposed as a method of averting or diminishing the potential of bias from affecting ongoing court proceedings (Law.com, 2013). Gag orders also are resources through which attorneys are restrained from "trying the case in the press and on television," thereby possibly influencing public opinion (Law.com, 2013).

Essentially, gag orders are tools through which communication is quashed regarding various facets of court proceedings. Gag orders may be issued to restrict communications regarding evidence, records, testimony, and so forth. Despite the ability of judges to restrict communications through the use of gag orders, the First Amendment of the U.S. Constitution establishes and guarantees the freedom of the press. Therefore, theoretically, the media cannot be constitutionally restricted from "printing or broadcasting information about the case" (Law.com, 2013). However, judges may issue gag orders that prohibit participants in legal proceedings from any communications regarding the considered case or court proceedings (Law.com, 2013).

During 1976, the Supreme Court case of *Nebraska Press Association v. Stuart* involved considerations of a gag order that was issued against the press. This case involved the issuing of a "pretrial gag order" against the press regarding "all press coverage of a murder trial" (Nebraska Press Association v. Stuart, 2013). The press was prohibited from reporting "any of the accounts of confessions or facts" that had strong implications for the trial (Nebraska Press Association v. Stuart, 2013). The basic premise questioned whether the gag order violated the freedom of the press that was guaranteed within the U.S. Constitution (Nebraska Press Association v. Stuart, 2013). It was determined that such a violation had occurred through the instantiation of the gag order.

Although gag orders that bind the press are usually deemed unconstitutional, there are situations, circumstances, and times when they are apparently permissible (jrank.org, 2013). For instance, during the 1990 trial of Manuel Noreiga, involving the court case *United States v. Noriega*, the judge issued a gag order against the Cable News Network (CNN) (jrank.org, 2013). This gag order prohibited CNN from using "certain tapes of purportedly private conversations between Noriega and his lawyers that the network had obtained" (jrank.org, 2013). Noreiga was a former Panamanian dictator whose crimes included the trafficking of drugs between the nations of Panama and the United States (Archibold, 2011). Although CNN appealed the gag order to the Supreme Court, the court denied hearing the issue (Nieto & Schmitt, 2005). Afterward, the original judge reviewed his decision regarding

Figure 16.4 Inmate photograph of Manuel Noriega. (From http://www.npr.org/templates/story/story.php?storyId=9252490.)

the gag order, and abolished it because it was determined that the "tapes would not interfere with Noriega's right to a fair trial" (Nieto & Schmitt, 2005). Later, in 1994, charges of contempt of court were filed against CNN because it had broadcasted the contents of the tapes while the gag order was effective (Nieto & Schmitt, 2005). As a result, CNN was fined because of its violation of the gag order (Nieto & Schmitt, 2005). Figure 16.4 shows an inmate photograph of Noriega.

Considerations of gag orders represent a different perspective of communication within the legal system. The First Amendment widely and broadly allows and facilitates open communications, whereas instances of curtailed communications (e.g., transmissions of child pornography) are completely unacceptable and disallowed. These concepts show a dichotomy within communications that either permits or denies communication. However, gag orders may be considered as somewhere between these perspectives. Given the freedoms allocated by the First Amendment granting broad scopes of freedom of the press versus the illegalization of certain acts that completely disallow various types of communications, gag orders may be used in varying fashions and proportions to constrain communication. For example, they may be directed solely at individuals that participate in court proceedings or broadly against groups of people that participate in court proceedings. Regardless, in any case, gag orders are useful tools through which the integrity of court proceedings is maintained.

Chapter Comments and Summary

This chapter introduced various perspectives of communications within the legal domain, ranging from easily recognized forms of copyright to situations involving personal injury. Communication within the justice domain is multifaceted, and represents a variety of considerations that influence all Americans either directly or indirectly. Within the United States, a foundational premise establishing primarily free and open communications is the First Amendment of the U.S. Constitution.

The freedom of speech is guaranteed within the U.S. Constitution. Both individuals and organizations are able to express themselves as they deem necessary without any fears of government sanctions, regulations, or reprisals. Although this notion is usually and normally exercised daily without impediments, there are times and situations that necessitate the curtailing of communications. Any curtailing must occur within the limits of the law and with respect to the opinions of the court system. Generally, such curtailing occurs as a protective mechanism through which societal order is maintained and acts of crime are deterred.

American society involves much communication each day. Periodically, such communication necessitates the attention of the justice system. Throughout time, numerous lawsuits, legal challenges, and court opinions have affected communication within American society. Such impacts range from legal considerations regarding the definition and recognition of obscenity to espionage and the compromising of national security.

Modern society communicates frequently through the use of electronic technologies and software packages. These items provide the basis of networking through which social media and social networks are formed. During modern times, considerations of the First Amendment are applicable to communications that occur within the virtual domain. Although the First Amendment is applicable to the virtual domain, various pieces of legislation exist through which law enforcement organizations may observe communications that occur using technologies.

Terminology

Abridge
Bias
Brandenburg incitement standard
Censorship
Clear and present danger
Commercial speech
Confidentiality
Copyright
Defamation
Discovery of truth
Establishment clause
Fighting words
First Amendment
Free exercise clause
Free speech clause
Freedom of speech
Freedom of the press
Gag order
Incitement
Indecency
Intellectual property
Legislation
Libel

Malice
Marketplace of ideas
Miller test
National security
Obscene
Obscenity
Patent
Personal injury
Pornography
Privacy
Religious speech
Restrictive order
Self-governance
Slander
State Secrets Act
Technology
Totten doctrine
Trademark
Viewpoint
War

THOUGHT AND DISCUSSION QUESTIONS

1. Perform some legal research in your local law library regarding the issues of communication that have affected your locality or state. Write a brief essay that details the types of court cases and decisions that you find, that explains the outcomes and that discusses the communications implications of these court proceedings.
2. Perform some research concerning the marketplace of ideas. In addition to the items discussed within this chapter, identify other communications issues that are associated with the marketplace of ideas. Write a brief essay that details your findings.
3. This chapter introduced various and sundry considerations of free speech with respect to the tenets and guarantees of the First Amendment of the U.S. Constitution. In addition to the court cases presented within this chapter, identify some additional U.S. Supreme Court cases that have upheld instances of free speech. Write a brief essay that delineates your findings.
4. This chapter introduced various and sundry considerations of free speech with respect to the tenets and guarantees of the First Amendment of the U.S. Constitution. In addition to the court cases presented within this chapter, identify some additional U.S. Supreme Court cases that have denied instances of free speech. Write a brief essay that delineates your findings.
5. This chapter introduced the concept of communications within the virtual environment, and considered the cases of Ebay and AOL. Perform some research, and identify some court cases that have implications for the virtual domain with respect to the emergence of social media. Write a brief essay that discusses your findings.

References

Archibold, R. (2011). Noriega is sent to prison back in Panama, where the terror has turned to shrugs. *The New York Times*. Retrieved from http://www.nytimes.com/2011/12/12/world/americas/noriega-back-in-panama-for-more-prison-time.html?_r=0 (accessed March 6, 2013).

Bardes, B., Shelley, M., & Schmidt, S. (2012). *American government and politics today: The essentials* (p. 122). Boston: Wadsworth Cengage Publishing.

Barnett, C. (2011). When do internet ratings constitute business defamation? Retrieved from http://www.scottandscottllp.com/main/internet_ratings_business_defamation.aspx (accessed March 5, 2013).

Blum, J., Morgan, E., Rose, W., Schlesinger, A., Stamp, K., & Woodward, C. V. (1973). *The national experience* (3rd ed., p. 62). New York: Harcourt Brace Jovanovich Publishing.

Body Count. (1992). *Body Count*. Sire/Warner Bros. B000002MHE, Compact disc.

Brandenburg v. Ohio. (2013). Case Briefs. Retrieved from http://www.casebriefs.com/blog/law/constitutional-law/constitutional-law-keyed-to-stone/freedom-of-expression/brandenburg-v-ohio-2/ (accessed March 2, 2013).

Brownfield, M. (2011). Morning bell: Occupy Wall Street gets more violent. *The Foundry*. Retrieved from http://blog.heritage.org/2011/11/08/morning-bell-occupy-wall-street-gets-more-violent/ (accessed February 28, 2013).

Central Hudson Gas and Electric Corp. v. Public Service Commission. (1980). Case Briefs. Retrieved from http://www.casebriefs.com/blog/law/constitutional-law/constitutional-law-keyed-to-cohen/governmental-control-of-the-content-of-expression/central-hudson-gas-and-electric-corp-v-public-service-commission/ (accessed March 2, 2013).

Cohen, H. (2009). *Freedom of speech and press: Exceptions to the first amendment* (p. 1). Washington, DC: Congressional Research Service.

Cole, G., & Smith, C. (2010). *The American system of criminal justice* (12th ed., p. 489). Belmont, CA: Wadsworth Cengage Publishing.

Columbia Broadcasting v. Democratic Comm., 412 U.S. 94. (1973). FindLaw. Retrieved from http://caselaw.lp.findlaw.com/scripts/getcase.pl?court=us&vol=412&invol=94 (accessed February 28, 2013).

Coplan, K. (2012a). Climate change, political truth, and the marketplace of ideas. *Utah Law Review*, *2*(2012), 548.

Coplan, K. (2012b). Climate change, political truth, and the marketplace of ideas. *Utah Law Review*, *2*(2012), 556.

Cornell University—Legal Information Institute. (2013). First Amendment. Retrieved from http://www.law.cornell.edu/constitution/first_amendment (accessed February 28, 2013).

Curry, J., Riley, R., & Battistoni, R. (1994). *Constitutional government: The American experience* (5th ed., p. 492). Dubuque, IA: Kendall-Hunt Publishing.

Denniston, L. (1992). *The reporter and the law: Techniques of covering the courts* (p. 271). New York: Columbia University Press.

Digital Watermarking Alliance. (2013). Communication of ownership and copyrights. Retrieved from http://www.digitalwatermarkingalliance.org/app_comm.asp (accessed March 5, 2013).

Eastland, T. (2000). *Freedom of expression in the Supreme Court: The defining cases*. Lanham, MD: Rowman and Littlefield Publishing.

Etzioni, A. (2004). On protecting children from speech. *Chicago-Kent Law Review*, *79*(3), 3–53.

Gardner, T., & Anderson, T. (2012). *Criminal law* (11th ed., p. 225). Belmont, CA: Wadsworth Cengage Publishing.

Gertz v. Robert Welch, Inc. (2013). Oyez. Retrieved from http://www.oyez.org/cases/1970-1979/1973/1973_72_617/ (accessed March 5, 2013).

Hanser, R. (2013). *Introduction to corrections* (p. 82). Thousand Oaks, CA: Sage Publications.

Harpaz, L. (2013). First amendment rights review—Part one. Western New England University School of Law. Retrieved from http://www.wneclaw.com/firstamendment/reviewpartone.html (accessed March 3, 2013).

Harr, J. S., Hess, K., & Orthmann, C. (2012). *Constitutional law and the criminal justice system* (5th ed., p. 162). Belmont, CA: Wadworth Cengage Publishing.

Hellman, A., Araiza, W., & Baker, T. (2011). *First amendment law: Freedom of expression and freedom of religion*. Albany, NY: LexisNexis—Matthew Bender & Company, Inc.

Hendershot, H. (1998). *Saturday morning censors: Television regulation before the V-chip* (p. 227). Durham, NC: Duke University Press.

Herbert v. Lando. (2013). Oyez. Retrieved from http://www.oyez.org/cases/1970-1979/1978/1978_77_1105 (accessed March 5, 2013).

Horniak, V. (2004). Privacy of communication—Ethics and technology (p. 2). Retrieved from http://www.idt.mdh.se/utbildning/exjobb/files/TR0390.pdf (accessed March 3, 2013).

Ingber, S. (1984). The marketplace of ideas: A legitimizing myth. *Duke Law Journal*, *1*(1984), 1.

John Jay. (2013). Laws.com. Retrieved from http://supreme-court.laws.com/john-jay (accessed February 28, 2013).

jrank.org. (2013). Publicity in Criminal Cases—Preventing prejudicial publicity. Retrieved from http://law.jrank.org/pages/1891/Publicity-in-Criminal-Cases-Preventing-prejudicial-publicity.html (accessed March 4, 2013).

Kadlec, C. (2011). Social justice, greed, and the occupy Wall Street movement. *Forbes Magazine*. Retrieved from http://www.forbes.com/sites/charleskadlec/2011/11/21/social-justice-greed-and-the-occupy-wall-street-movement/ (accessed February 28, 2013).

Kessler, R. (2013). Obscenity, censorship, and the first amendment. *The Atlantic*. Retrieved from http://www.theatlantic.com/magazine/archive/2006/07/obscenity-censorship-and-the-first-amendment/305073/1/ (accessed March 4, 2013).

LaRue, J. (2005). Obscenity and the first amendment. *Concerned Women for America* (p. 1). Retrieved from http://www.cwfa.org/images/content/larue051905.pdf (accessed March 3, 2013).

Law.com. (2013). Gag Order. Retrieved from http://dictionary.law.com/default.aspx?selected=802 (accessed March 5, 2013).

Legal Information Institute. (2013a). Defamation. Cornell University. Retrieved from http://www.law.cornell.edu/wex/defamation (accessed March 4, 2013).

Legal Information Institute. (2013b). Libel. Cornell University. Retrieved from http://www.law.cornell.edu/wex/libel (accessed March 5, 2013).

Lidsky, L. (2002). Brandenburg and the United States' war on incitement abroad: Defending a double standard. *Wake Forest Law Review*, *37*(2002), 1009–1033.

Marshall, W. (2004). False campaign speech and the first amendment. *University of Pennsylvania Law Review*, *53*(283), 285–323.

Martin, D. (1993). The music of murder. *William and Mary Bill of Rights Journal*, *2*(1), 159–163.

Masson v. New Yorker Magazine. (2013). Case Briefs. Retrieved from http://www.casebriefs.com/blog/law/torts/torts-keyed-to-epstein/defamation/masson-v-new-yorker-magazine/ (accessed March 5, 2013).

Merriam-Webster Dictionary. (2013a). s.v. "abridge." Retrieved from http://www.merriam-webster.com/dictionary/abridge (accessed March 3, 2013).

Merriam-Webster Dictionary. (2013b). s.v. "copyright." Retrieved from http://www.merriam-webster.com/dictionary/copyright (accessed March 5, 2013).

Merriam-Webster Dictionary. (2013c). s.v. "obscene." Retrieved from http://www.merriam-webster.com/dictionary/obscene?show=0&t=1362534869 (accessed March 4, 2013).

Merriam-Webster Dictionary. (2013d). s.v. "obscenity." Retrieved from http://www.merriam-webster.com/dictionary/obscenity (accessed March 4, 2013).

Merriam-Webster Dictionary. (2013e). s.v. "pornography." Retrieved from http://www.merriam-webster.com/dictionary/pornography (accessed March 3, 2013).

Merriam-Webster Dictionary. (2013f). s.v. "privacy." Retrieved from http://www.merriam-webster.com/dictionary/privacy (accessed March 4, 2013).

Merriam-Webster Dictionary. (2013g). s.v. "war." Retrieved from http://www.merriam-webster.com/dictionary/war (accessed March 3, 2013).

Miller v. California. (1973). Case Briefs. Retrieved from http://www.casebriefs.com/blog/law/constitutional-law/constitutional-law-keyed-to-stone/freedom-of-expression/miller-v-california-3/ (accessed March 3, 2013).
Miller, W. (2012). *The social history of crime and punishment in America: An encyclopedia* (p. 1732). Thousand Oaks, CA: Sage Publishing.
National Academies Press. (2013). Pornography and the first amendment. Retrieved from http://www.nap.edu/netsafekids/pp_li_pfa.html (accessed March 3, 2013).
Nebraska Press Association v. Stuart. (2013). Case Briefs. Retrieved from http://www.casebriefs.com/blog/law/constitutional-law/constitutional-law-keyed-to-chemerinsky/first-amendment-freedom-of-expression/nebraska-press-association-v-stuart/ (accessed March 5, 2013).
Nieto, A., & Schmitt, J. (2005). *A student's guide to mass communication law* (p. 104). Lanham, MD: Rowman and Littlefield Publishing.
Oklahoma State University. (2013a). An Overview of How Courts Have Defined Obscenity. Retrieved from http://www.cas.okstate.edu/jb/faculty/senat/jb3163/obscenity.html (accessed March 3, 2013).
Oklahoma State University. (2013b). First Amendment Theories. Retrieved from http://www.cas.okstate.edu/jb/faculty/senat/jb3163/theorists.html (accessed March 3, 2013).
Oliphant, P. (n.d.). Free speech quotes. Brainyquote. Retrieved from http://www.brainyquote.com/quotes/keywords/free_speech.html (accessed February 28, 2013).
Opper, M. (2011). Wikileaks: Balancing first amendment rights with national security. *Loyola of Los Angeles Entertainment Law Review*, *31*(2), 237–267.
Oxford University Press. (2013). Why Protect Free Speech. p. 7. Retrieved from http://fds.oup.com/www.oup.com/pdf/13/9780199225811.pdf (accessed March 1, 2013).
Parkinson, M., & Parkinson, L. M. (2008). *Public relations law: A supplemental text* (pp. 30–31). New York: Taylor and Francis.
Perry, E. (2011). *A Socrates for all Seasons: Alexander Meiklejohn and deliberative democracy* (p. 239). Bloomington, IN: IUniverse.
Romanowski, W. (2012). *Reforming Hollywood: How American protestants fought for freedom at the movies* (p. 23). New York: Oxford University Press.
Rottenstein Law Group. (2013). What is personal injury? Retrieved from http://www.rotlaw.com/legal-library/what-is-personal-injury-law/ (accessed March 3, 2013).
Roy Cooper. (2013). Ballotpedia. Retrieved from http://ballotpedia.org/wiki/index.php/Roy_Cooper (accessed March 5, 2013).
Sherr, I. (2013). U.S. judge reduces Apple's patent award in Samsung case. *The Wall Street Journal*. Retrieved from http://online.wsj.com/article/SB10001424127887323478304578334540541100744.html (accessed March 5, 2013).
Silver, E., Stein, A., Surman, T., & Thompson, E. (2013). Fighting words. University of Maryland. Retrieved from http://www.bsos.umd.edu/gvpt/gvpt339/fightingwords.html (accessed March 2, 2013).
Silverman, M. (2003). National security and the first amendment: A judicial role in maximizing public access to information. *Indiana Law Journal*, *78*(3), 1101–1129.
Sullivan, K. (2010). Two concepts of freedom of speech. *Harvard Law Review*, *124*(1), 143–177.
University of Florida. (2013). Libel in the United States. Retrieved from http://plaza.ufl.edu/bshields/caselaw.html (accessed March 4, 2013).
University of Missouri. (2013a). Introduction to the free speech clause. Retrieved from http://law2.umkc.edu/faculty/projects/ftrials/zenger/freespeech.htm (accessed March 1, 2013).
University of Missouri. (2013b). The Clear and Present Danger Test. Retrieved from http://law2.umkc.edu/faculty/projects/ftrials/conlaw/clear&pdanger.htm (accessed March 2, 2013).
U.S. Department of Justice. (2013). Federal statutes. Retrieved from http://www.it.ojp.gov/default.aspx?area=privacy&page=1285 (accessed March 5, 2013).
U.S. Food and Drug Administration. (2013). Trademark Act of 1946. Retrieved from http://www.fda.gov/RegulatoryInformation/Legislation/ucm148719.htm (accessed March 5, 2013).

U.S. Legal. (2013). Defamation and libel law & legal definition. Retrieved from http://definitions.uslegal.com/d/defamation-and-libel/ (accessed March 3, 2013).

U.S. Supreme Court. (2006). Dates of Supreme Court decisions and arguments. Retrieved from http://www.supremecourt.gov/opinions/datesofdecisions.pdf (accessed February 28, 2013).

Volokh, E. (2011). In defense of the marketplace of ideas: Search for truth as a theory of free speech protection. *Virginia Law Review, 97*(3), 595–601.

Weygandt, J., Kimmel, P., & Kieso, D. (2010). *Financial accounting* (7th ed., p. 415). Hoboken, NJ: Wiley Publishing.

White, H. (1997). *Anatomy of censorship: Why the censors have it wrong* (p. 13). Lanham, MD: University Press of America.

Williams, S. (2004). *Truth, autonomy, and speech: Feminist theory and the first amendment* (p. 2). New York: New York University Press.

Woldu, G. (2008). *The words and music of ice cube* (p. 12). Westport, CT: Greenwood Publishing Group.

WFMY News. (2003). Officials: Donations to NC attorney general not a conflict. Retrieved from http://www.digtriad.com/news/local/story.aspx?storyid=18106 (accessed March 5, 2013).

WRAL News. (2009). Lawsuit against N.C. Attorney general will go forward. Retrieved from http://www.wral.com/news/local/politics/story/5111748/ (accessed March 5, 2013).

Zeran v. America Online. (2013). *Tech Law Journal.* Retrieved from http://www.techlawjournal.com/courts/zeran/Default.htm (accessed March 5, 2013).

Communication in the Justice System

17

This is the city. Los Angeles, California. I work here. I carry a badge. My name's Friday. The story you are about to see is true; the names have been changed to protect the innocent.

—Joe Webb as Sgt. Joe Friday, *Dragnet* TV series (Dictionary.com, n.d.)

Objectives

The objectives of this chapter are to

- Discuss the practices and applications of communication within the justice system
- Introduce procedural aspects of justice system communications
- Discuss courtroom and field interviewing practices and methods
- Discuss questioning practices, types, and styles
- Introduce the lawsuit process incorporating communication
- Discuss practical aspects of interviews and interrogations
- Discuss the communicative aspects of dispatching

Introduction

Communication affects every facet of the justice system. From the least of foot patrols to the highest echelon of the U.S. Supreme Court, communication affects every activity and outcome within the justice system. From the moment of detaining and arrest through the final stages of the justice system, communication pervades every phase of progressing of a case within the justice system. Figure 17.1 shows the methodical stages of the justice system among which communication is present.

In the field of criminal justice, understanding different communication styles and their strengths and weaknesses can help improve getting information during interviews and interrogations. Knowing the value of both verbal and nonverbal communication enhances a law enforcement officer's skill in getting to the truth of a matter (Stone, 2013). Having an understanding of questioning assists in knowing when, where, how, and why to pose specific and follow-up questions. Such notions were played out for a global audience during the 1990s court proceedings involving O.J. Simpson. Specifically, Johnny Cochran, the defense attorney representing Simpson, when referring to an attempt by Simpson to don a pair of gloves, famously stated: "If it doesn't fit, you must acquit" (CNN News, 1995). This statement was made to cast doubts on the argument of the prosecution and to show its inconsistencies.

Courtrooms are locations where disputes are heard and settled, and may involve emotional outbursts. For instance, unbridled emotional outcries may result in one being held in contempt of court. During 2013, in North Carolina, a law enforcement officer was held in contempt after exiting a courtroom following trial proceedings, and "loudly" confronting "a

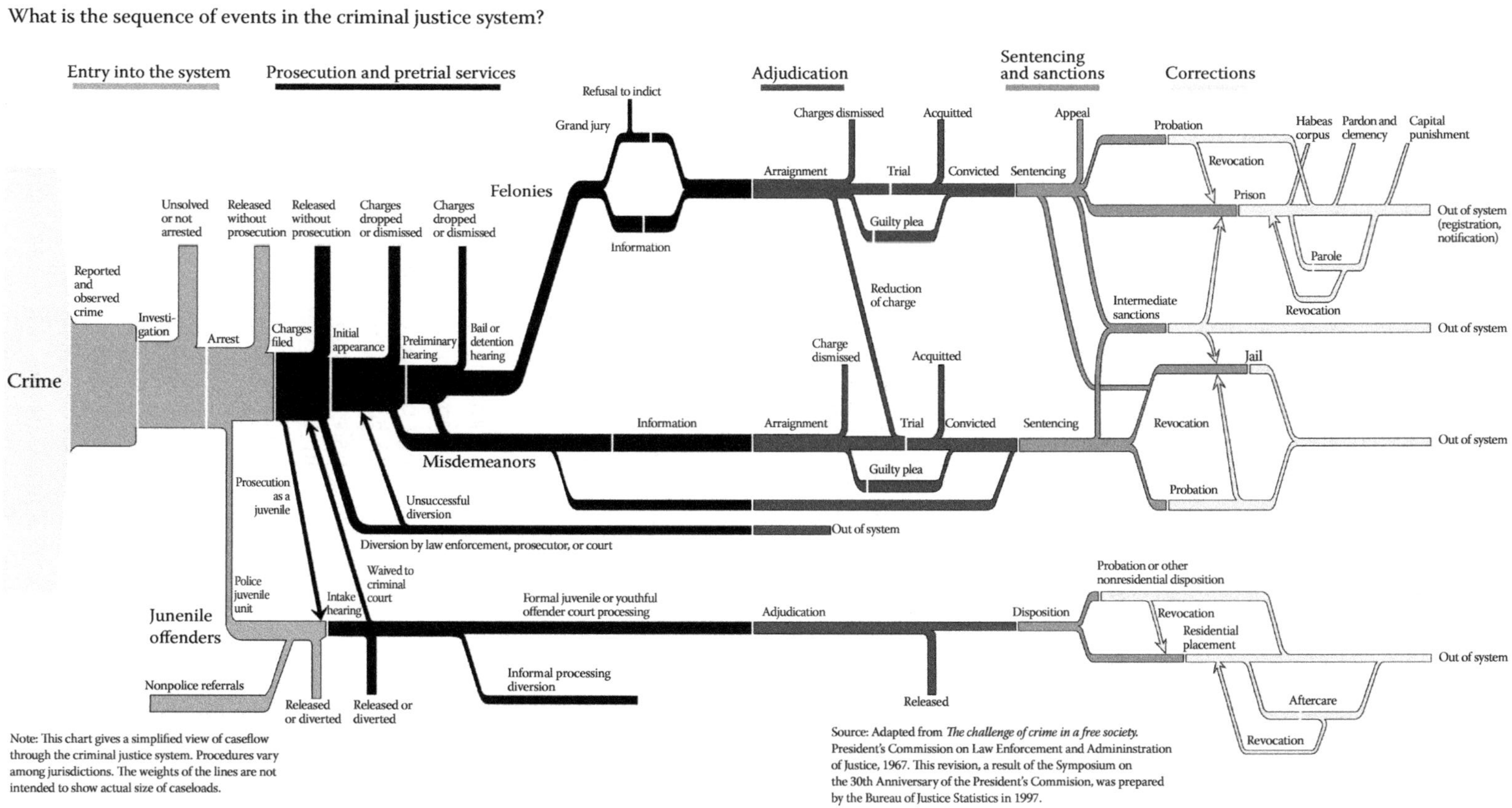

Figure 17.1 Event sequence of the criminal justice system. (From http://www.bjs.gov/content/largechart.cfm.)

defense attorney" (Hewlett, 2013). The law enforcement officer had to pay a fine in the amount of $100.00 (Hewlett, 2013). This outburst occurred because the defendant was found not guilty regarding a misdemeanor offense involving the possession of marijuana (Hewlett, 2013).

Such unexpected trial outcomes may incite furor within court settings. During 2013, in Los Angeles, California, a verdict of "not guilty" was rendered and announced concerning a murder trial in which the victim was a *Maxim* model (Kurzweil, 2013). The period of jury deliberation preceding this verdict and its announcement encompassed about one week (Kurzweil, 2013). After the verdict was announced, the courtroom erupted with an outcry (Kurzweil, 2013). Specifically, the event is described as: "Young women in the Redding row, which was the second row, began to cry very violently, shrieked 'You [*expletive*], you killed her, we know you killed her' " (Kurzweil, 2013).

The other end of this emotional spectrum may involve the expressing of joy and the physical showing of tears of elation. During 2011, in Valdosta, Georgia, the rendering and announcing of a "not guilty" verdict occurred after a trial involving charges of "burglary and aggravated assault" (Castro, 2011). This incident was described thusly: "The 27-year-old defendant who sat emotionless during the proceedings, other than slightly shaking his head in disagreement with the prosecutor, released a big smile and patted his attorney's back after the verdict was read. White's five family members and friends shed tears of joy and one was heard thanking God" (Castro, 2011).

Within these two instances, the announcement of the respective verdicts elicited different emotional responses. However, they both involved facets of communication. Certainly, Mr. Cochran leveraged communication during the O.J. Simpson trial to plant seeds of doubt within the minds of those who were viewing and hearing his defense comments. Regardless, the power of communication is undeniable among justice system environments.

Many other dimensions exist within communications regarding the justice system. When the general public requests 911 services via a telephone call, they expect to communicate with a dispatcher that is competent, efficient, and effective. When a suspect is interrogated by law enforcement personnel, communications must be robust to elicit truthful responses and to determine the characteristics of deception. Within a policing context, communication is a viable method of establishing levels of trustfulness between law enforcement entities and their served public. Communication skills are essential during interviews and interrogations. This chapter introduces some foundational aspects of communication within the justice system and among law enforcement organizations.

Types of Communication

Various types of communication exist within the justice system. Some people may be quite straightforward and direct, whereas others may be subdued and quiet when communicating. Some people may be evasive, whereas others may be genuinely confused when questioned. Regardless, described below are the primary classifications of communication types.

Passive communication: This style involves an indirect method of expressing both feelings and thoughts (Stone, 2013). Individuals within this category generally speak "weakly" or "softly" (Stone, 2013). Such individuals are usually liked by others and avoid confrontations (Stone, 2013).

Aggressive: This style involves communicating harshly and assertively (Stone, 2013). Within this category, individuals tend to be overpowering and intimidating via oral expressions (Stone, 2013). This style is useful among law enforcement officers when information must be elicited "quickly" or when situations necessitate immediate controlling for "safety reasons" (Stone, 2013). Although this type of communication may generate fast compliances with orders and commands, it may also "alienate the public from the officer" (Stone, 2013).

Passive–aggressive: This category involves risk aversion and the denying of feelings (Stone, 2013). Offenders often invoke this form of communicating as a method of avoiding incriminating themselves (Stone, 2013). Additionally, witnesses may invoke this form of communicating because they do not desire involvement in situations that they believe may become troublesome (Stone, 2013).

Assertive: This style of communicating represents a balancing of "aggressively pursuing understanding and truth" versus exhibiting a respect for other individuals (Stone, 2013). When communicating, law enforcement personnel may share their "thoughts and feelings" both honestly and directly, thereby contributing to stronger perceptions of "confidence and integrity" (Stone, 2013). Trustfulness may be established quickly through this type of communication (Stone, 2013).

Nonverbal: This form of communicating is generally silent and involves bodily communications cues. This type of communicating may result in quickly divulging the truthfulness of a situation. When someone is questioned, rapidly blinking the eyes may be representative of lying, and moving the "arms, legs, and feet" indicates deceptive behavior (Stone, 2013). When exercising this type of communication, the interviewing personnel should remember to maintain strong eye contact with the interviewee and to lean forward throughout the period of questioning (Stone, 2013). These actions establish a basis of assertiveness, interest, and confidence. Good interviewers learn to maintain good eye contact and lean forward during an interview to assertively communicate their interest and confidence (Stone, 2013).

Briefings and Roll Calls

During the changing of shifts and periodically, law enforcement organizations may exercise various briefings. These events consist of presentations by supervisory personnel through which pertinent information is conveyed to law enforcement officers before they commence patrols or other operations. Performing briefings ensures that all personnel have a mutual understanding of the pertinent issues that may be encountered during the shift or other operation. The information communicated and disseminated during briefings may include perpetrator descriptions, safety warnings, hazard warnings, community events, continuity of information from the preceding shift, crime reports, and so forth. During briefings, law enforcement officers may ask questions to clarify the information they receive, to expand on the topics discussed within the briefing, and to reiterate the communicated information.

Within the United States, law enforcement organizations exercise a shift roll call and perform inspections among uniformed officers. One purpose of such activities is to ensure that an accounting of personnel is obtained and communicated throughout the organization. Therefore, the law enforcement organization is aware of the officers that are available during the shift and is aware of absences (e.g., vacation or sick leave). The results of this accounting may be communicated through the appropriate chain of command and disseminated among shift personnel and administrators.

Dispatchers and Communication

The responsibilities and duties of dispatching are numerous. Dispatchers do not give direct orders to law enforcement personnel, and must communicate both quickly and objectively. Therefore, dispatchers much communicate both efficiently and effectively. Below are the salient functions of dispatchers:

Receiving and processing telephone calls: Dispatchers receive and process telephone calls involving both "911 and nonemergency numbers" (Barton, 2013). They must obtain and record information while simultaneously calming "panicked callers" (Barton, 2013). Generally, dispatchers must maintain the telephone call until the dispatched entities arrive at the scene of the reported incident (Barton, 2013).

Tracking resources: Dispatchers must constantly be aware of the locations and statuses of all dispatched resources (Barton, 2013). The responding entities may represent multiple organizations, such as police, fire, and ambulance services. Therefore, dispatchers are responsible for maintaining a constant awareness of the statuses and locations of resources involving multiple organizations and personnel (Barton, 2013).

Radios: Dispatchers must be trained and knowledgeable regarding a variety of radio communications devices and equipment. Dispatchers must concurrently "monitor several different radio frequencies and take calls for several agencies" (Barton, 2013). Additionally, dispatchers must "request mutual aid" among multiple agencies and organizations (Barton, 2013).

Paperwork and reporting: All dispatchers must complete and submit a variety of reports to ensure that information systems are updated and possess current information (Barton, 2013).

Dispatchers represent trained professionals that request and allocate a myriad of services involving law enforcement, fire departments, and medical resources. Most folks refer to dispatchers as "911 dispatchers" or 911 operators (Writing, 2013). Dispatchers receive and process telephone calls from individuals and organizations that require emergency service. Upon receiving such requests, dispatchers forward the telephone call to the appropriate organization depending on the type of emergency situation described (Writing, 2013). Figure 17.2 shows a typical dispatcher and communications equipment.

Dispatchers must possess strong communication skills and inquisitiveness. They must be able to verify and determine the genuineness of any received call for assistance (911 Dispatch, 2013). Dispatchers must possess strong decision skills regarding a determination of what agencies or organizations are appropriate for the given situation, what routes are optimal for the logistics of emergency service, and the necessary personnel quantities (911

Figure 17.2 Emergency dispatcher. (From http://www.mesaaz.gov/pdjobs/Communications.aspx.)

Dispatch, 2013). Dispatching duties are unceasing throughout the year. When someone calls 911, a dispatcher must be available to receive the telephone call and render assistance. Therefore, individuals and organizations are able to communicate with dispatchers at any hour of any day to request and to receive assistance (911 Dispatch, 2013).

When communicating, dispatchers must exhibit professionalism and objectivity. They should speak unemotionally, clearly, intelligibly, calmly, and slowly. Dispatchers should communicate using only a "minimum of words" without defensiveness, argumentation, or sarcasm (911 Dispatch, 2013). During dispatch communications, the use of personal names should be avoided and conversation must also be avoided (911 Dispatch, 2013). Instead, the use of "badge numbers" and "standard phrases" should be invoked (911 Dispatch, 2013).

Essentially, a primary function of dispatchers is informational when communicating. Therefore, dispatchers communicate information regarding a specific location, the happenings at the location, and any other pertinent information. Dispatchers do not order law enforcement personnel to perform a specific task (911 Dispatch, 2013). The following examples show both acceptable and unacceptable forms of dispatching:

Acceptable: "Echo 29, a 375 at 1312 Fake Lane."
Unacceptable: "Echo 29, report now to 1312 Fake Lane and stop a fight."

Within the context of communication, a significant portion of dispatching involves a consideration of prioritization. Law enforcement organizations generally have policies that delineate the methodology through which events are to be processed, especially regarding "critical incidents" (911 Dispatch, 2013). Such incidents are commonly associated with events "involving weapons or potential injury to a citizen or officer" (911 Dispatch, 2013). Other factors that affect prioritization include personnel availability, ongoing activities, personnel locations, data provided by the citizenry, and incident location (911 Dispatch, 2013). Commonly, dispatching priorities are classified as follows:

Top priority, dispatch immediately; emergencies, potential emergencies or urgent calls. (911 Dispatch, 2013)

Important, dispatch as soon as possible; cold reports of crimes, tows. (911 Dispatch, 2013)
Routine, dispatch when possible; parking matters with no tow, abandoned autos. (911 Dispatch, 2013)
Very routine; dispatch when possible. (911 Dispatch, 2013)

Dispatchers must always acknowledge and be mindful of this type of prioritization. Any mistake during dispatching may have the "gravest of consequences" regarding the allocation of resources and also for human life (911 Dispatch, 2013). Essentially, prioritization affects the general citizenry and emergency resources. Therefore, any crafted form of priorities must incorporate a consideration of the seriousness of the reported incident and whether human life is threatened.

During dispatch communications, clarity is absolutely essential to ensure the effectiveness and efficiency of messaging to facilitate a mutual understanding between the senders and receivers of messages. One method of bolstering this understanding is through the use of phonetic alphabets. A phonetic alphabet is a method of communicating in which words are substituted to represent individual characters of the English alphabet. These words begin with the first letter of the alphabetic symbol being communicated. For instance, the letter "A" may be expressed via the word "Alpha." Phonetic alphabets are used by both civilian and military police organizations. Tables 17.1 and 17.2 show both the civilian and military police phonetic alphabets.

Regardless of the setting, whether civilian or military, the use of these alphabets embellishes communication. For instance, when speaking with a dispatcher, a law enforcement officer may wish to spell individual words that may be hard to pronounce. Similarly, using these alphabets clarifies the messaging of tag numbers, vehicle identification numbers, and so forth, when communicating.

Dispatchers must have a sound understanding of the departmental communications policies, practices, processes, and procedures. They must remain calm and courteous at all times, and must avoid profanity and obscenity when communicating (as should all law enforcement personnel). Dispatchers must be trained and have a working knowledge of the communications equipment that is used when communicating.

Table 17.1 Civilian Phonetic Alphabet

Letter Symbol	English Word	Letter Symbol	English Word
A	Adam	N	Nora
B	Boy	O	Ocean
C	Charles	P	Paul
D	David	Q	Queen
E	Edward	R	Robert
F	Frank	S	Sam
G	George	T	Tom
H	Henry	U	Union
I	Ida	V	Victor
J	John	W	William
K	King	X	X-ray
L	Lincoln	Y	Young
M	Mary	Z	Zebra

Table 17.2 Military Police Phonetic Alphabet

Letter Symbol	English Word	Letter Symbol	English Word
A	Alpha	N	November
B	Bravo	O	Oscar
C	Charlie	P	Papa
D	Delta	Q	Quebec
E	Echo	R	Romeo
F	Foxtrot	S	Sierra
G	Golf	T	Tango
H	Hotel	U	Uniform
I	India	V	Victor
J	Juliet	W	Whiskey
K	Kilo	X	X-ray
L	Lima	Y	Yankee
M	Mike	Z	Zulu

When performing their duties, dispatchers have the potential to negatively or positively influence human lives via communication. Their ability to analyze a received telephone call and ensure that emergency resources are dispatched is a critical job. Dispatchers must be capable of multitasking while communicating, thereby demonstrating an ability to manage data and communicate with both emergency resources and the general public.

Policing Communication and Policy

From a policing context, some communications strategies and tactics should be considered when dealing with suspicious people. On the basis of some degree of suspicion regarding the circumstances of an incident or "upon information obtained from investigation," a law enforcement officer may instigate the stopping "of a suspect if he has reasonable suspicion to do so" (State of Georgia, 2013). According to the state of Georgia, policy excerpts regarding field interviews include the following itemization when performing an "authorized stop to conduct a field interview" (State of Georgia, 2013):

> When approaching the suspect, the officer shall clearly identify himself as a law enforcement officer, if not in uniform, by announcing his identity and displaying Agency identification.
>
> Officers shall be courteous at all times during the contact but maintain caution and vigilance for furtive movements to retrieve weapons, conceal or discard contraband, or other suspicious actions.
>
> Before approaching more than one suspect, individual officers should determine whether the circumstances warrant a request for backup assistance and whether the contact can and should be delayed until such assistance arrives.
>
> Officers shall confine their questions to those concerning the suspect's identity, place of residence, and other inquiries necessary to resolve the officer's suspicions. However, in no instance shall an officer detain a suspect longer than is reasonably necessary to make these limited inquiries.

Officers are not required to give suspects Miranda warnings in order to conduct field interviews unless and until additional information is available and sufficient to establish probable cause for arrest.

Suspects are not required, nor can they be compelled, to answer any questions posed during field interviews. Failure to respond to an officer's inquiries is not, in and of itself, sufficient grounds to make an arrest although it may provide sufficient justification for additional observation and investigation.

If after conducting a field interview there is no basis for making an arrest, the officer should record the facts of the interview and forward the documentation to the appropriate reporting authority as prescribed by Agency procedure.

Policing Communication and Arrests

During the course of policing, the arresting of individuals may be necessary. An arrest is defined as "to use the power of the law to take and keep (someone, such as a criminal)," "to stop the progress or movement of (something)," "to attract and hold the attention of (someone or something)," and "to take or keep in custody by authority of law" (*Merriam-Webster*, 2013b). Essentially, an arrest is the apprehension or detention of a person to answer for an alleged or suspected crime. The Fourth Amendment of the U.S. Constitution permits an arrest only if "probable cause" exists to "believe that a crime was committed" and that the suspected individual committed the crime (NOLO, 2013b). The question of whether the person is under arrest or not depends not on the legality of the arrest but on whether the person has been deprived of personal liberty of movement (NOLO, 2013b). An arrest also incorporates considerations of an intention to arrest by proper authorities, including the detaining or seizing of a person, that are also understood by the arrestee(s). Figure 17.3 shows an arrest.

Within the United States, in conjunction with an arrest and before any questioning of the arrestee occurs, the Miranda warning must also be administered. From a

Service special agents arrest a suspect wanted for wildlife crimes. Credit: Ryan Haggerty / USFWS

Figure 17.3 Wildlife agents conducting an arrest. (From http://www.fws.gov/le/careers.html.)

communications perspective, the Miranda warning may be administered orally. The Miranda warning (i.e., Miranda rights) represents a warning communicated by law enforcement entities to "criminal suspects in police custody or in a custodial interrogation before they are interrogated to preserve the admissibility of their statements against them in future criminal proceedings" (Komninos, 2013). The Miranda warning resulted from the 1966 U.S. Supreme Court case of *Miranda v. Arizona* (384 U.S. 436). Essentially, the Supreme Court ruled that any incriminating statement gained from a suspect who was uninformed of the contents of the Miranda warning violated both the Fifth and Sixth Amendments of the U.S. Constitution regarding the right to counsel. Basically, if law enforcement personnel declined the Miranda warning to any individual within their custody, they may act upon any information gained but may not use any statements made by the individual for the purpose of incrimination during criminal trial proceedings.

Policing Communication and Documentation Procedures

Many law enforcement organizations use an array of preprinted documents or forms for the purpose of recording certain characteristics of crime scene investigations (Allison, 2008). Although the design and formats of these documents may vary among individual agencies, commonness exists regarding their primary functions, purposes, and goals organizationally (Allison, 2008). There is generally a tendency to consider such documents as a method of covering "every possibility" that may be experienced by law enforcement personnel (Allison, 2008).

However, despite their differences, these documents tend to be viable reminders concerning a minimum of information that is necessary for completing tasks (Allison, 2008). All crime scenes and incidents are unique. Therefore, each separate instance necessitates various deviations from the basic template or format with respect to the complexity of the considered incident (Allison, 2008). Such documents are not alternatives for human thought; instead, they are "tools" through which law enforcement officers "fully exercise training and experience to meet the needs of a given situation" (Allison, 2008).

Policing Communication, Interviews, and Interrogations

Justice system communication involves the asking of questions. Interviewing and interrogating are neither identical nor synonymous. Interviews occur when a "person who is not a suspect is questioned to determine whether this person possesses information that is of value to the police investigator's case" (Kinnee, 1994, p. 341). Similarly, the purposes of interrogations are "essentially the same as that of interview," but the interviewee "is a suspect in the interviewing" (Kinnee, 1994, p. 341). Interviews may conceptually be envisioned as purposeful conversations between interviewers and interviewees (Kinnee, 1994, p. 342). In some cases, the information sought during the interview may not be damaging to the interviewee (Kinnee, 1994, p. 342). During the interview process, some rapport may be established between the interviewer and the interviewee (Kinnee, 1994, p. 342). However, during interrogations, some adversarial stances may exist between the interviewer and the interviewee.

Interviews involve three primary purposes. These purposes are described as follows:

- *Securing information*: Interview success is often "based on the interviewer's ability to solicit information with proper questions and to listen effectively" (Galle, 1996).
- *Giving information*: Interviewers may provide information during an interview. Interview success is often "determined by the interviewer's ability to choose and articulate the right information" (Galle, 1996).
- *Influencing behavior*: Some interviews may involve influencing the interviewee to alter behavior or to render a decision. Interview success is often "dependent upon the interviewer's ability to engender trust and credibility and to use persuasive tactics" (Galle, 1996).

Interviewing is not a random event. Instead, it involves thoughtful planning. Interviewing may facilitate relatively private conditions in which the interviewee feels at ease during the experience, thereby eliciting responses. Any communications noise is minimized throughout the interview process to ensure that the attention of the both the interviewer and the interviewee are focused on the matters at hand. The choice of questions are prepared and selected meticulously. Furthermore, experienced interviewers have a good sense of knowing how and when to ask questions appropriately and necessarily.

Interviewers must control the conversational aspects of the interview. Throughout the discourse with the interviewee, the interviewer often maintains a set of written notes, video recordings, or audio recordings to document the conversation. After all, human memory is imperfect. Furthermore, throughout the interview, the interviewer must be careful to avoid inundating the interviewee with a plethora of overwhelming questions. When the interviewee responds, the interviewer must exhibit good listening skills to record the response, show interest, and generate additional or follow-up questions. Maintaining some fashion of rapport is essential during the interview process, and the interview must terminate with positive feelings for both the interviewer and the interviewee.

Below are suggestions for improving communications during interviews:

- *Prepare carefully*: Preparation is an essential component of interview success (Kinnee, 1992).
- *Maintaining interview control*: Good interviewers maintain control personally and maintain control of the course that the interview is taking unceasingly (Kinnee, 1992). Regardless of how heinous an act of crime may be, the interviewer must remain objective and show no signs of judgment (Kinnee, 1992).
- *Listening ability*: Good listening skills are essential during interviews. The interviewer must be able to recognize and to interpret the verbal and nonverbal messages that that the interviewee shows to influence the tactics of attacking during the interview (Kinnee, 1992).
- *Behavior*: Effective interviewers are flexible, mentally sharp, patient, and are not pushy during the interview process (Kinnee, 1992).
- *Acting skills*: Effective interviewers must have strong listening skills. However, interviewers also must exhibit the characteristics of a fine actor. Therefore, some acting lessons may be appropriate for developing interviewing skills. Interviewers should exude self-confidence and professionalism during the course of the interview (Kinnee, 1992).

The physical environment selected for conducting an interview should be conducive to facilitating the communications process both efficiently and effectively. Communications noise, such as windows, ringing telephones, and so forth, should be eliminated from the interview environment as a method of bolstering attentiveness. The interview should conclude by offering an opportunity for further assistance, thereby embellishing the rapport between the interviewer and the interviewee. Such an opportunity contributes toward an interviewee feeling as though the information shared during the interview is beneficial and that a friend exists within the law enforcement organization.

Interviews may be conceptualized generally as congenial events. Contrastingly, interrogations may be viewed as adversarial events, depending on the situation and complexity of the offense. Interrogations are processes through which individuals are maneuvered and manipulated psychologically, carefully, and meticulously into a logical position of no retreat (Leo and Thomas, 1998). The dominant goal of interrogation is to solicit or acquire information that is generally not in the best legal interests of the individual who is being questioned by the law enforcement organization (Leo and Thomas, 1998). Essentially, through interrogation, the law enforcement entity hopes to elicit a confession from the individual being questioned (Leo and Thomas, 1998).

Interrogations usually involve an array of psychological manipulations as measures through which confessions may be elicited from suspects. Most interrogations commence with an interview session but become interrogations in due time through the course of questioning. As the emphasis of the conversation and dialogue narrows, the interview transforms from a congenial discourse to an accusation. After the interviewer has initiated the interrogation process, there exists no opportunity for returning to the pleasantness of the interview session. Instead, the interrogation becomes a structured event that may require several hours of unpleasant questioning and various amounts of resistance that may be exhibited by the suspect. Interrogations may involve the following characteristics:

- *Direct confrontation*: The suspect is informed by the interrogator that he or she is suspected of having some involvement with a criminal offense (Gordon and Fleisher, 2011). The interrogator presents the suspect with a synopsis of the events that transpired and then presents some evidence, which may or may not be factual, to substantiate the described crime scenario (Gordon and Fleisher, 2011). The interrogator observes the suspect to determine whether verbal and nonverbal cues suggest innocence or guilt, truthfulness or deception (Gordon and Fleisher, 2011).
- *Develop a theme*: The suspect is provided with some justification or excuses regarding the commission of the act of crime. For instance, some line of reasoning may be suggested regarding inappropriately touching a minor child associated with criminal charges of rape (Gordon and Fleisher, 2011). A question posed during the interrogation may involve "What is bad touching?" (Gordon and Fleisher, 2011) The respondent might say, "You know, like ripping her clothes, smacking her" (Gordon and Fleisher, 2011). Such questions may provide an explanatory opportunity regarding the response offered by the respondent.
- *Eliminate the potential of denials*: The interrogator attempts to eliminate any evasive opportunities for the suspect. The interrogator leverages factual attributes of the case to support the participation of the suspect in the criminal activity.
- *Overcoming any objections*: The interrogator may offer a line of reasoning to establish exactly why the suspect did not commit the criminal offense. Psychologically, this

activity represent an attempt to facilitate an understanding in the mind of the suspect that no other possible explanation exists that is commensurate with the known facts associated with the case. Therefore, the suspect begins to realize that the evidence cannot be neither immediately dismissed nor explained away regarding the "how" and "why" of the event (Gordon and Fleisher, 2011).
- *Gain the attention of the suspect*: The interrogator may attempt to project a sincere attitude as a method of gaining some level of trust from the suspect. By doing so, the suspect may be compelled to confess to the criminal offense as a method of attempting some absolution of psychological feelings of guilt. Success may be measured and perceived by the suspect accepting comfort and exhibiting silence.
- *Generating a confession*: The suspect may admit guiltiness and delineates any association and participation in the criminal activity. When this action occurs, the interrogator should immediately provide the suspect with comfort both emotionally and physically. The suspect may be encouraged to delineate and communicate his or her accounting of the event in writing, thereby further alleviating emotional feelings of guiltiness. Law enforcement personnel must remain supportive as a method of bolstering the absolving of feelings of guiltiness, and also to ensure the compliance of the suspect. The law enforcement personnel who are involved during interrogations must attempt to calm a suspect before the interrogation is concluded. Such calming occurs as a method of diminishing the possibility of the suspect inflicting self-harm after a confession is obtained.

Not all individuals experiencing an interrogation are guilty of the crimes for which they are accused. During the interrogation, the interrogator must be observant regarding the verbal and nonverbal cues exhibited by the respondent. These cues suggest truthfulness or deception during the course of questioning (Gordon and Fleisher, 2011). Suspects who are exhibiting truthfulness will "connect themselves to the issue" and are unafraid to "use harsh words such as rape, steal, and murder" (Gordon and Fleisher, 2011). Essentially, such individuals may talk about "moral values when describing" criminal activity, and may use "strong terminology" (Gordon and Fleisher, 2011). Furthermore, truthful suspects generally cooperate during the line of questioning, are "talkative," seem relaxed, and openly contribute toward the narrowing of questioning (Gordon and Fleisher, 2011).

However, some suspects are indeed guilty of committing the criminal offenses for which they are accused. In such instances, these individuals increasingly exhibit fear and nervousness throughout the line of questioning and passing of time (Gordon and Fleisher, 2011). Such individuals also attempt to "evade identifying the crime" and "distance themselves" from the issues of discussion (Gordon and Fleisher, 2011). Their use of language may not be overly condemning, may exhibit vagueness, and may be evasive (e.g., "It's about some money they think may be missing") (Gordon and Fleisher, 2011). Their responses may be "sweeping," thereby detracting from the narrowing of the line of questioning (Gordon and Fleisher, 2011).

The preceding discussions highlight the primary differences between interrogations and interviews. Despite their differences, they share some commonness within the context of communication. When experiencing a discourse of questioning, respondents will communicate both verbally and nonverbally, thereby suggesting their deceptiveness or truthfulness. Through time, training, and experience, law enforcement personnel may hone and sharpen their communication skills to incorporate planning, patience, listening ability,

Figure 17.4 Interrogation of former Arapaho County, Colorado, sheriff. (From http://kwgn.com/2012/04/27/interrogation-of-former-sheriff-raises-questions-about-more-charges/.)

timing, and observances of discourses to identify potential deceptiveness and truthfulness. Regardless, both interviewing and interrogating are practical forms of eliciting data and information from respondents via the communications process. Figure 17.4 shows a typical example of eliciting information from respondents.

Policing and Case Information

Case information represents the life's blood of any investigation. It involves a variety of communications concepts either separately or via some fashion of integration. Obtaining and amalgamating case information often necessitate inquiries via the questioning of individuals, collecting of photographs, developing of audio and video materials, searching of public records, and using of historical artifacts (e.g., a written statement made 30 years ago).

Gaining information to support a case file often occurs through communicating via oral interviews. Successful interviewers will already have answered several questions that they intend to pose during an interview period. Knowing the answers to specific questions, before they are asked, provides the interviewer with an advantageous position when communicating. Basically, because the interviewer already knows the answers to the specific questions, it is much easier to recognize and identify deceptiveness that may be exhibited by suspects.

Crafting case information is unconstrained regarding any notion that it consists of only contemporary findings. Instead, case information may also incorporate a variety of historical artifacts. When interviewing and investigating a suspect, questioning may accommodate whether the individual has any previous arrests or has any previous associations with criminality. These considerations are not limited solely to the suspect. Instead, they are also applicable to the suspect's associates, family, colleagues, friends, and so forth.

Case information may be gleaned from individuals that have some past experience with the suspect. For instance, if a suspect has a history of previous arrests or incarceration(s), information may be gained from communicating with the officer(s) who previously arrested the suspect. Similarly, if the suspect has a history of incarceration, then information may be gleaned by communicating with corrections personnel or cellmates who encountered the suspect. Examining any documents from the suspect's past (e.g., arrest records) may also be valuable sources of information. Certainly, information may also be obtained from former employers or organizations with whom the suspect had some association.

Having as much knowledge as possible about the suspect improves the ability of law enforcement personnel to conduct interviews and interrogations. Therefore, personal data regarding the suspect is useful when crafting a series of questions that may be posed during interviews and interrogations. Examples of topics within such questions include the following:

- Demographics: sex, age, height, weight, fitness, etc.
- Preferences: personal likes and dislikes, etc.
- Relationships: parental data; marital status; data regarding associates, friends, colleagues, lovers, etc.; names and sexes of children; and so forth.

Amalgamating, maintaining, and communicating case information requires varying amounts of time. It may encompass anywhere from weeks to years. Regardless, case information is a critical component of any investigation. In some instances, it may be communicated relative freely regarding information that may be publically available, whereas other facets of case information may involve strict confidentiality.

Policing Communication and Questioning Environments

The environmental characteristics of a questioning setting may be either formal or informal. Regardless of the setting, some expectations of privacy are necessary aspects of eliciting information from a respondent. Certainly, informing the suspect of Miranda rights must occur before questioning commences. Before any questioning of an individual occurs, law enforcement personnel must conduct some planning regarding the environment in which the questioning will occur. During the planning stages, law enforcement personnel must contemplate whether a formal or informal questioning environment is appropriate for the questioning session. The following points highlight the main ideas of the informal and formal modalities.

Informal setting: Interviews conducted within an informal setting may range from mere conversation to the presentation of outright accusations that are meant to narrow the focus of the questioning. If the latter approach occurs, then the interview becomes an interrogation. Information settings may range from questioning and conversation within a coffee shop to the conversation that occurs among street corners during community-oriented policing activities. Other informal communication settings may include work environments or personal residences.

Formal setting: Formal settings are less congenial than informal settings. Within this type of setting, law enforcement personnel tend to control the environment and situation. Law enforcement personnel have a good familiarity with the physical attributes of the location and its operational characteristics. For instance, within a police station, a police department interview room represents a formal setting.

> Wall adornments are reminders of police authority and presence, and the presence of uniformed, armed personnel also communicate authoritative characteristics to the suspect. When suspects are questioned within this environment, they may be more anxious and stressed.

Within the context of community-oriented policing, the informal setting facilitates good opportunities for law enforcement personnel to communicate with others in a relaxed fashion. Through this type of communication modality, law enforcement personnel both gain information and also establish some rapport with individuals and the citizenry. Through this type of communication setting, law enforcement officers may gain a better understanding of the social, professional, and personal relationships that exist within the community. When some rapport and trust exists between law enforcement personnel and the community, the gathering of information is easier because residents may be more apt to purposefully or inadvertently provide information during the course of a relaxed conversation.

Contrastingly, within a formal setting, questioning may become strained and antagonistic and involves a heightened level of seriousness. During this type of communication, law enforcement personnel attempt to eliminate all potential sources of communications noise that may impede the communications process. The congenial atmosphere of the informal setting does not exist within the formal setting. Instead, the formal setting is controlled by the law enforcement entity and involves specific, direct communication with the suspect.

When considering communication settings, some psychological and social effects may exist regarding the questioning session. For example, when speaking with someone during a traffic stop, depending on the attributes of the situation, a law enforcement officer may handcuff the individual and have him or her sit in the back seat of the police vehicle for the purposes of officer safety and suspect safety. During this time, the law enforcement officer may continue to speak with the individual while simultaneously performing a background investigation to determine whether the motorist has any outstanding warrants or is wanted by a law enforcement organization. Additionally, the events within the police car are constantly recorded both visually and audibly. During such instances, the anxiety of the individual may be increased, some embarrassment of the individual may occur, and passing motorists may view and perceive the event as some type of spectacle. Eliciting information from the individual may become more difficult. If no warrants are discovered, then the motorist may be released when the event is terminated.

Similarly, when questioning and conversation occur among work settings, the anxiety of the questioned individual may be increased. The presence of police personnel may arouse the curiosities of coworkers, clients, customers, and supervisors. Others may wonder whether the questioned individual is in some type of trouble, and rumors may abound within the organizational grapevine. Such questioning events may attract attention within the work setting and may detract from the performance of work functions. Eliciting responses from the questioned individual may be somewhat more difficult. In some instance, law enforcement personnel may arrange an appointment for a further conversation at some other location.

During communication sessions that occur within police facilities, the interviewee may be kept in an interview room. Such locations have few comforts, and they present few, if any, distractions that may inhibit the communications process. Discomfort

Figure 17.5 Interview room. (From http://www.boylston-ma.gov/Pages/BoylstonMA_Police/station.)

among such settings may be intentional by the law enforcement organization. The décor of such environments is sparse, thereby reducing the quantity of items that may be used as weapons against law enforcement personnel or others that may be present. The communication that occurs within this setting may be abrasive but may not be necessarily confrontational. Therefore, an instantiation of interrogation may not yet exist but may be necessary depending on the course of the questioning. Figure 17.5 shows a typical interview room.

Policing Communication and Question Types

When communicating with suspects, the initial questions posed are generally designed to put someone at ease and to establish the communication process. Such questions may consist of relatively simple concepts, such as name, telephone number, and so forth. After this introductory phase is completed, the act of communicating introduces questions of greater complexity. Generally, these types of questions represent the primary categories of open and closed questions. These types of questions are defined as follows:

Open question: This type of question consists of queries that require narrative responses (Inabu et al., 2013). Open questions necessitate some elaboration, description, and detail by the interviewee when responding to the query. Therefore, a simple yes or no response is unacceptable when responding to this type of questioning.

Closed question: This type of question consists of queries that require specific responses that may be constrained (Geldard and Geldard, 2010). In these instances, a simple yes or no response may be acceptable when responding to this type of questioning. Furthermore, responses to this type of questions may be categorical (e.g., red, green, or blue car).

Examples of open questions consist of the following statements:

- What do you think about prostitution?
- Please state your recollection of the robbery that you witnessed.
- Please state everything that happened to you Saturday night after 8:15 p.m.

Examples of closed questions consist of the following statements:

- Do you solicit prostitutes?
- Who do you believe stole the picture from the museum?
- Were you at work on Saturday night about 8:15 p.m.?

These types of questions provide opportunities for eliciting either elaborate or limited responses from suspects. Closed questions may be leveraged to exercise control during the questioning session, thereby constraining the potential responses that may be available to respondents. If a suspect exhibits some reluctance regarding an open question, then the use of an array of closed questions may be appropriate. Otherwise, the use of open questions necessitates some amount of thoughtfulness by the respondent. Open questions may also contribute toward the embellishment of rapport between the interviewer and the interviewee.

Closed questions represent a discrete set of responses. However, open questions involve a variety of approaches to inquiry and involve unconstrained responses. Given this notion, several classifications of leading questions exist. The basic types of open questions that may be used when communicating with respondents are summarized below.

Reflective question: This type of question represents a method of probing to motivate the respondent to elucidate upon the response given to an open question. Essentially, this type of question necessitates further expansion regarding the "subject while a probe question is used when an in-depth response is imperative" (Leeson, 1981). Reflective questions may be used when the interviewer believes that the response of the interviewee is "illogical or unrealistic," or may be confusing (Roelofse, 2006). For instance, an example of a reflective question is, "Let me get this straight, so you're saying you were at work about 9:00 p.m. Saturday night, right, and didn't leave until midnight?"

Pointed question: This type of question invokes specificity regarding the response to the initial open question, thereby diminishing the effects of ambiguity (Yeschke, 2004, p. 66). An example of a pointed question is, "You say your manager saw you; who else could have seen you at work the night when the museum picture was stolen?"

Directive question: This type of question alludes to cooperation between the interviewer and the interviewee. An example of this type of question is, "You do want to get to the bottom of this, don't you? I would think you'd want your side of the story in the report so that no one misunderstands what happened" (Tyska and Fennelly, 1999).

Indirect question: This type of question may alter the pace of communication during questioning between the interviewer and the interviewee. This type of question may assist the interviewee in saving face regarding sensitive topics, and allows the interviewee to interject personal opinion within the questioning session (Tyska and Fennelly, 1999). An example of this type of query is, "Everyone in the museum believes that … do you agree?"

Self-appraisal question: This type of query represents a catalyst for stimulating communication between the interviewer and the interviewee. Such questions increase the difficulty associated with deception attempts during responses, and may contribute toward revealing evasiveness by the respondent (Yeschke, 2004, p. 67). Maintaining the consistencies of untruthfulness and deception are difficult because respondents must continuously attempt to maintain, revise, and remember unfailingly the details of their falsehoods (Yeschke, 2004, p. 67). Additionally, this type of question is a tool through which an "investigative hypothesis" may be formulated (Yeschke, 2004, p. 67). An example of this type of query is, "Think about it … tell me what you have at stake in this situation."

Diversion question: This type of question represents a communications dichotomy conceptually regarding distracting the interviewee from the issues at hand versus establishing and embellishing some amount of rapport between the interviewer and interviewee (Tyska and Fennelly, 1999). Such questions are quite useful when querying interviewees who exhibit excessive emotions, because they facilitate an opportunity for someone to regain his or her composure (Tyska and Fennelly, 1999). An example of this type of question is, "What is your current occupation?"

Leading question: This type of question is not always abrasively designed provided that some contemplation occurs when they are designed and structured (Yeschke, 2004, p. 68). Leading questions incorporate some aspects of the assumptions that are made by the interviewer (Yeschke, 2004, p. 68). Although this type of question may have negative connotations associated with "invalid, unreliable" responses, leading questions may be leveraged to increase the level of compliance that is exhibited by the interviewee (Yeschke, 2004, p. 68). An example of this type of query is, "Based on what I've heard, you must have a hard time in your job at the museum?"

The use of questions represents intricate planning and detailing within the context of the communications process. When developing and structuring queries, they must be as simple as possible but of sufficient depth and scope to elicit information from the respondent. When communicating with interviewees, law enforcement personnel may pose a combination of question types that accommodate numerous queries. Law enforcement personnel must be fearless to unabashedly pose questions that may be deemed rude, difficult, or personal. A good investigator will ask any question. Questions may be repeated or phrased differently to elicit responses from interviewees. Only through asking an array of questions, incorporating various questioning modalities, can law enforcement personnel obtain information and determine whether indications of deception or evasiveness exist during the communications process.

Arraignment and Communication

An arraignment is defined as the stating of the "charges against someone who is accused of a crime in a formal procedure before a judge" (*Merriam-Webster*, 2013a). This event usually represents the initial appearance of a defendant before a judge regarding the stated charges (U.S. Legal Forms, 2013). Arraignments are components of both the federal and individual state court systems. During the arraignment proceedings, the defendant is asked whether he or she is aware of the charges levied; the charges against the defendant are read; and the defendant is asked how he or she wishes to plead to the charges (U.S. Legal Forms, 2013). Arraignments do not involve a consideration of innocence or guilt regarding the defendant (U.S. Legal Forms, 2013).

Normally, within a period encompassing twenty-four to forty-eight hours succeeding the arrest, the incarcerated defendant must appear before a judge for arraignment proceedings (U.S. Legal Forms, 2013). Within the United States, this period of time may vary depending on the laws of the individual states (U.S. Legal Forms, 2013). Furthermore, the U.S. Supreme Court decreed that any defendant that has no previous criminal record must appear before a judge within forty-eight hours to determine whether sufficient probable cause existed to instigate the arrest of the defendant (U.S. Legal Forms, 2013).

Communication and the Criminal Trial Process

Communicating is an essential aspect of all court proceedings. Among courtroom environments, a myriad of people must communicate effectively and efficiently with each other. Such communication exists throughout the duration of the trial processes of the justice system. Each stage of the trial process exhibits its unique communications attributes that contribute toward culminating in the rendering of a verdict and sentencing (if necessary provided that a guilty verdict is announced).

Rendering a decision regarding a trial by judge or jury represents the commencement of the trial process. Jurisdictional differences affect this decision. Although defenses may often have the right to determine if a "case will be tried to a judge or jury," some jurisdictions permit both defenses and prosecutions to "demand a jury trial" (NOLO, 2013).

In some cases, a jury trial is necessary. This phase of the trial process necessitates the selection of jurors via the act of "voir dire" (NOLO, 2013). This act represents the questioning of potential jurors to eliminate candidates that are deemed unfit for jury duty. Among federal settings and among some states, judges perform the voir dire process. During voir dire, judges may pose questions that are "suggested by attorneys" and may also pose their own original questions (NOLO, 2013).

A consideration of evidence occurs next. Before the trial occurs, the prosecution and defense may communicate a request that the court either exclude or admit "certain evidence" (NOLO, 2013). This type of request is referred to as a motion "in limine" (NOLO, 2013). Such motions are expressed in writing, and are often accompanied by a "memorandum of law" (Hart and Blanchard, 2007).

After evidence is considered, opening statements are made by both the prosecution and defense before a jury or judge (NOLO, 2013). The opening statements represent outlines of the case that both the prosecution and defense expect to prove during the trial (NOLO, 2013). Some reservations exist within both the defense and prosecution during this phase. Instead of appearing foolish, both factions only present those items they believe they are capable of proving (NOLO, 2013). Sometimes, the defense may wait until the "defense case" commences before presenting an opening argument (NOLO, 2013).

The next phase represents the presentation of the "main case" by the prosecution (NOLO, 2013). This action occurs through a "direct examination" of witnesses by the prosecutor (NOLO, 2013). These actions are referred to as the prosecution case-in-chief. Essentially, this phase comprises the "main body of a case, not including rebuttals or opening statements" (Welch and Fuller, 2014) Following the presentation of the prosecution, defense attorneys may cross-examine the prosecution's witnesses via questioning (NOLO, 2013). Redirection occurs when the prosecution reexamines "its witnesses" (NOLO, 2013). After this act of redirection, the prosecution rests its case via its finishing presentations (NOLO, 2013). At this time, an optional motion to dismiss may be instigated by the defense attorney. This motion represents the belief of the defense that an insufficient amount of prosecutorial evidence was produced to substantiate the rendering of a "guilty verdict" (NOLO, 2013). Generally, this motion to dismiss is denied by the judge (NOLO, 2013).

This juncture in the trial process represents the commencing of the arguments and presentations that are offered by the defense. This phase is referred to as the defense case-in-chief. Specifically, it involves the defense presenting its "main case" by directly examining its witnesses (NOLO, 2013). A cross-examination of these defense witnesses then occurs by the prosecutor and is followed by the redirection of the defense (NOLO, 2013). After this redirection is completed, the defense rests by finishing the presentations of its case (NOLO, 2013). The prosecutor is then able to offer a rebuttal in which the case of the defense is refuted (NOLO, 2013).

The next activity consists of communicating with the jury for instructional purposes. The judge performs this activity. Specifically, the judge informs the jury regarding applicable laws and how they jury should satisfy its duties (NOLO, 2013). After the appropriate instructions are communicated to jurors, the actions of jury deliberations commence (NOLO, 2013).

Deliberation occurs when the jurors are attempting to "reach a verdict" (NOLO, 2013). In cases that concern felony crimes of a serious nature, the jury must unanimously reach a verdict (NOLO, 2013). However, depending on the state, some verdicts do not have to be unanimous regarding misdemeanor trials involving less serious charges (NOLO, 2013). For instance, out of twelve jurors, ten may agree upon a verdict (NOLO, 2013). Regardless, depending on state laws, if the required minimum quantity of jurors is unable to agree upon a verdict, then the case may again be tried because a "hung jury" exists (NOLO, 2013).

Motions may be made following the announcement of the verdict. If a guilty verdict is rendered by the jury, then the defense may make a post-trial motion for the judge to "override the jury and either grant a new trial or acquit the defendant" (NOLO, 2013). Usually, these motions of the defense are denied by the judge (NOLO, 2013). Furthermore, if a guilty verdict is rendered, thereby necessitating a conviction, then the sentencing of the offender occurs. This event may be held immediately or it may be appointed for a future date (NOLO, 2013).

Other facets of communication also exist within the court setting regarding a post-trial status. Motions for a new trial may be expressed when the "jury misconstrued a jury instruction or the jury clearly should have found more damages" (Glover, 2013). A judge may grant a motion for a judgment notwithstanding the verdict (JNOV). This type of motion results when the "judge reverses the decision of the jury and enters judgment for the other side because, for example, the jury's verdict clearly did not conform to the evidence" (Glover, 2013). The granting of a JNOV is a rarity.

If the losing party is dissatisfied with the outcome of a trial, then an appeal may be communicated to a higher court regarding the issue. An appeal represents a "plea to a higher court to overturn all or part of decision of a lower court" (Stein, 2004). Generally, appeals have some limitations regarding filing and processing (Stein, 2004). The Courts of Appeals also exercise discretion when deciding which cases they desire to hear (Stein, 2004). For instance, the U.S. Supreme Court accepts roughly 5% of the 5000 appeals petitions that it receives annually (Stein, 2004).

These facets of communication are representative of criminal trials. However, they also exist similarly in civil litigation. Judges, juries, attorneys, plaintiffs, and defendants all exercise some form of communication when experiencing civil litigation. Regardless of whether a trial experience represents an instantiation of either civil or criminal proceedings, the communications process undeniably exists throughout its duration.

Communication and the Courtroom Setting

Certainly, communication affects the entirety of judicial processes and court proceedings throughout the justice system. Communication occurs both verbally and nonverbally among a variety of actors and agents within the justice setting. Within the justice environment, practically everything that is said or done by humans sends some type of message. The messages that are transmitted via body language are just as important as any message that may be expressed orally or through the written language.

Silent communication exists among trial proceedings. Body language is an observable form of communication that conveys messages silently and nonverbally. Behavioral profiling incorporates a consideration of body language (Ford, 2010). Personal and professional attire contribute toward signaling within the context of body language (Phipps, 2012). During trial proceedings, body language may convey symptoms of deception. This notion is summarized as follows:

> Liars have longer pauses, shorter answers, and longer times between a question and a response than someone who is merely nervous. It makes sense that liars need time to create the lie, recalling the truth takes less time. If you ask a clerk if they gave you back the correct change and there is a long pause before their response it may be an indication of deceit. This is not a cue you would take in isolation as fact. You might combine it with checking to see where their eyes go after you ask them the question. People tend to look up to the right to visualize or create a new response or down to the right to create the sounds of a new response. We recall information that occurred in the past by looking up to the left or down to the left. Spot a liar by listening for pauses and right eye movement. (Wood, 2013)

Other instantiations of communication exist during trial proceedings. Before a verdict is rendered, judges communicate instructions to the jury. Many types of jury instructions exist. Expressing an exhaustive listing is an impossible feat given the uniqueness of each individual instance of a trial process. However, Figure 17.6 shows some examples of the types of instructions that may be directed toward juries.

During court proceedings, whether criminal or civil events, witnesses can be used by both the prosecution and the defense. The statements made by witnesses are referred to as testimony. These statements may include accounts and opinions that are used to bolster concepts that they wish to be accepted by their audience(s). The perceived value of the testimony involves considerations of both the "listeners' opinion of its acceptability and to the speaker who presents it" (Sandmann, 1999).

Testimonies may involve either paraphrases or direct quotations. Paraphrasing of statements represents a robust way of reducing lengthy segments of text. It also contributes to the clarification of statements that may be confusing and not understandable by the intended audience. Furthermore, paraphrasing helps maintain the attention of the listening audience because listeners may ignore lengthy quotes or complex statements. However, when paraphrasing, the intent and meaning of the original message must be uncompromised. Therefore, the meaning and intent of the paraphrased statements versus the original statements must be unchanged and identical.

Courtroom communication also involves testimonies that may be oral or written. Court testimony involves the giving of an account during a live court session. Law enforcement

Instruction to jury as to the definition of conversion: You are instructed that conversion consists in the exercise of dominion and control over property inconsistent with, and in denial of, the rights of the true owner or the party having the right of possession. It is the exercise of a wrongful claim of right or dominion over the property which assumes that the converter is entitled to its possession. This taking to oneself of another person's property is a conversion.

Instruction to jury that refusal to deliver goods after demand and tender of freight and storage charges can constitute conversion: You are instructed that if you believe from the evidence that plaintiff was the owner of the property in question, and made proper demand and tender prior to this suit, but that defendant refused to deliver the property unless plaintiff paid freight and storage charges on other property not received or stored at the same time as the property in question, then such refusal of delivery by defendant constituted a conversion.

Instruction to jury that unauthorized sale of personal property can constitute conversion: You are instructed that any assertion of title to, or any act of dominion over, personal property inconsistent with the rights of the owner, such as a sale of the property of one person by another, is a conversion. Therefore, if you find that the plaintiff was the owner of the (*describe personal property*) at the time of the alleged taking, and that the defendant sold it without the plaintiff's consent you should find for the plaintiff.

Instruction to jury regarding compensatory damages for conversion: You are instructed that if, under the evidence and the instructions of the court, you find the defendant liable to the plaintiff for damages for conversion of the (*describe personal property*), then the measure of the plaintiff's damages will be the value of the property at the time and place of the conversion, with (*number*) percent interest since that date.

Figure 17.6 Sample jury instructions. (From http://williamhgloverjd.wordpress.com/2010/01/21/steps-in-a-lawsuit/.)

personnel are often witnesses during trial proceedings. They should be prepared to give a testimony and to experience questioning by both the prosecution and defense attorneys. When participating as a witness, law enforcement personnel should be mindful of the following items (Schroeder and Lombardo, 2010):

- Preparations should begin for testimony just as soon as a law enforcement officer "suspects that criminal activity may be occurring."
- The notes of a law enforcement officer are public records and may be subpoenaed.
- Any statements made to a law enforcement officer by a defendant should be recorded and "reported to the prosecutor."
- Juror perceptions and opinions may be influenced by the personal and professional appearances of law enforcement personnel.
- Before the court date occurs, a law enforcement officer should meet with the prosecutor to discuss the case.
- Any notes, evidence, and reports associated with the court case "should be brought to court."
- An accounting of "required witnesses" should be performed to determine presences and absences.
- The law enforcement officer should meet with the prosecutor to determine what to expect when on the witness stand.
- Simple yes and no responses are sufficient if a question does not require elaboration.
- Use the word "approximately" when describing quantities unless the precise quantity is known.
- It is permissible to ask to have questions repeated if the questions are not understood.
- Examine pieces of "physical evidence" before answering questions about these items.
- If one does not know the answer to a question, then it is fine to state that the law enforcement officer simply does not know the answer.

Another form of testimony involves depositions. This type of testimony represents the questioning and transcribing of witness accounts using written language. A deposition is an opportunity for discovering "new facts," obtaining "substantive information," and establishing "foundations for impeachment" (Sanger, 2011). During depositions, information from witnesses should be elicited with the assumption that it may be used during court proceedings (Sanger, 2011). However, before any statements are taken during the deposition, an oath is administered to the witness to be truthful, and it is identical to the oath that is administered during court testimonies. Therefore, the penalties associated with perjury are applicable regarding depositions.

Both the prosecution and defense may ask questions mutually of the opposing faction. The queries may be posed before and during trial proceedings regarding the characteristics of the case (e.g., facts and issues). When questioning witnesses, not only the oral or written responses are important but also the silent aspects of body language. These notions are indicative of the fact that communication permeates all facets of trial events. Communication may involve both oral and written statements. Regardless of its modality, silent, verbal, or written, communication exists throughout the trial process.

Commentary Regarding Communication in the Justice Domain

The justice domain incorporates a variety of silent, verbal, and written communications. Within the justice domain, communication affects everything from juror perceptions and opinions to the questions posed by defense and prosecution attorneys. From the perspective of body language, an example of silent communication involves the court case of Jodi Arias involving charges of first-degree murder and the associated guilty verdict (Figure 17.7). During a 2013 jury trial, Arias was found "guilty of murder in the first degree" (Melas, 2013). Arias admitted to stabbing Travis Alexander, her boyfriend, a total of 27 times, "slitting his throat, and shooting him in the head" (Melas, 2013). This account is given as follows:

> … instead of holding her head down in shame during the reading of the verdict, she stared into the eyes of each juror. This is another telling sign from Jodi that she thought she would be found innocent. "She shot daggers at each of the jurors," … "This is a sociopath that thinks she can fool the world. She was sure that she could have gotten this over on the jury … so this was shocking to her. That's when she looked at each juror instead of bowing her head and feeling remorse." (Melas, 2013)

Within this trial, the defense supported the notion that "Arias was the victim of a controlling, psychologically abusive relationship and that Alexander considered Arias 'his dirty little secret'" (McLaughlin, 2013). The defense also indicated that "Arias killed her ex in self-defense" (McLaughlin, 2013). The prosecution accused "Arias of playing the victim" and staging the scene of the crime so that it would appear "like self-defense" (McLaughlin, 2013).

The Arias trial is certainly an example of criminal proceedings. Its format and progression were commensurate with the communications facets of criminal trials described and discussed herein. It involved a combination of body language, written language, and oral testimony as forms and modalities of communication. It involved the presentation of arguments by both the defense and the prosecution, and it incorporated both testimony and questioning.

Figure 17.7 Jodi Arias. (From http://www.kjct8.com/news/jury-deliberations-start-in-jodi-arias-trial/-/163152/20014414/-/noadkp/-/index.html.)

Knowledge of the trial was neither limited to its affected locality nor region geographically. Instead, both domestic and international news resources broadcast various attributes of the Arias trial to mass audiences. Many viewers may have been shocked by her heinous deeds from the perspective of moral turpitude. Regardless, the details of the events were communicated among nations as they unfolded throughout the trial process.

Communication is ubiquitous. Through modern technologies, excerpts of the Arias trial were broadcast practically everywhere, thereby showing that communicating events of public interest is no longer constrained geographically to localities or nearby regions. Thus, events within the justice system may be communicated to wide and varied audiences. These notions allude to a dichotomy regarding communication within the justice system: (1) real-time observers and participants experience the communication process as it occurs within a locality, and (2) mass audiences, dispersed geographically, observe facets of the communications process after it has occurred.

Furthermore, these notions also show both internal and external perspectives of the justice system communications process. For instance, within the justice system, the internal perspective may involve communication among judges, attorneys, defendants, bailiffs, and so forth. Externally, communication may involve media resources and the general public. The former category consists of active participants in the communications process, whereas the latter category represents passive observers. Regardless, the mindsets and opinions of people within both categories are influenced via communication.

Communication pervades both civil and criminal divisions of the justice system. Although the primary examples contained herein delineate communication within the context of the criminal perspective, the appendix materials elucidate communication concepts from the perspective of civil litigation. Many subsets exist within these two divisions of the justice system, ranging from tax courts to chancery courts. Regardless of the faction or division, communication is an essential characteristic of the functioning of the justice system.

Chapter Comments and Summary

This chapter provides a foundation for understanding communication within a variety of applications and perspectives within the justice system. It considers communicating for the purposes of allocating and dispatching emergency resources through the necessity and application of communication among trial processes. Regardless of the scenario envisioned, the communications process pervades all aspects of the justice system from the entering of a case through its termination.

Various forms of communication exist, ranging from passive to aggressive. People may uniquely exhibit different communication attributes when questioned or interrogated. Some may be quite timid, whereas others may be extremely vocal. When presented with a communications catalyst, some people may exercise emotional control, whereas others may instigate emotional outbursts.

Within the justice system, communicating is absolutely essential for allocating, controlling, and monitoring emergency resources. Dispatchers are responsible for performing each of these activities. When dispatching, one must communicate unemotionally, calmly, succinctly, and clearly. Any mistakes that occur when dispatching may result in death or harm. Therefore, dispatchers must realize and acknowledge the seriousness of the duties.

Information is gained from suspects by asking questions. A good investigator will ask any question without reservation. Some questioning environments may be informal (e.g., coffee shops), whereas others may be formal (e.g., police station). Questioning suspects occurs through interviews and interrogations. These concepts are not synonymous. Interviews do not involve an accusation of the respondent, whereas interrogations do involve an accusation against the respondent.

Questioning involves planning, designing, and structuring. Some questions may be answered with a simple "yes" or "no" response, whereas others may require elaboration and elucidation. The former instance represents a closed question, whereas the latter instance represents an open question. When posing an array of questions, a combination of both closed and open questions may be necessary to obtain information from interviewees.

Communication pervades trial processes. From the point of entering the justice system to the culmination of a trial in which the verdict is announced, communication is an essential aspect of the trial process. Both civil and criminal trials incorporate communication.

Modern technologies are used to communicate the details of a myriad of happenings within the justice system. Because of the scope and magnitude of such technology, mass audiences, both domestically and internationally, may become aware of public events within the justice system.

Terminology

Account
Body language
Civil trial
Closed question
Communications policy
Court reporter
Criminal trial
Deception
Defense attorney
Deposition
Dispatcher
Evasive
Interrogation
Interview
Judge
Leading question
Mass audience
Open question
Phonetic alphabet
Prosecutor
Questioning
Testimony
Trial
Trial proceedings
Written language

THOUGHT AND DISCUSSION QUESTIONS

1. This chapter introduced allusions to silent communication using body language. Perform some research, and determine what other characteristics of body language are pertinent within the justice domain. Write a brief essay that highlights your findings.
2. This chapter introduced the concept of communications among criminal trials. Perform some research, and determine how communication affects and permeates civil litigation. Compare and contrast your findings with the attributes of communicating within the criminal context. Write a brief essay that delineates your findings.
3. This chapter introduced the notion of the phonetic alphabet within the context of law enforcement services. Perform some research, and determine what other organizations use a phonetic alphabet. Write a brief essay that discusses how these organizations find a phonetic alphabet to be beneficial when communicating.
4. This chapter introduced the concepts of witness testimony and offered several pointers for preparing and giving testimony. However, the listing within this chapter is not exhaustive and is merely introductory. Perform some research, and determine what other advice is pertinent regarding testimonies. Write a brief essay that highlights your findings.

References

911 Dispatch. (2013). Dispatcher Training Manual. Retrieved from http://www.911dispatch.com/training/train_police.html (accessed September 17, 2013).

Allison, R. (2008). *Investigation of crime scene* (p. 236). New Delhi, India: Global Vision Publishing House.

Barton, C. (2013). Police dispatcher duties. Retrieved from http://www.ehow.com/facts_5494914_police-dispatcher-duties.html (accessed September 17, 2013).

Castro, D. (2011). White found not guilty. *Valdosta Daily Times*. Retrieved from http://valdostadailytimes.com/top-local-news/x2023603397/White-found-not-guilty/print (accessed September 17, 2013).

CNN News. (1995). If it doesn't fit, you must acquit. Retrieved from http://www.cnn.com/US/OJ/daily/9-27/8pm/ (accessed September 17, 2013).

Dictionary.com. (n.d.). This is the city Los Angeles California I. Columbia World of Quotations. Columbia University Press, 1996. http://quotes.dictionary.com/This_is_the_city_Los_Angeles_California_I (accessed July 03, 2014).

Ford, M. (2010). *Body language and behavioral profiling* (p. 53). Bloomington, IN: AuthorHouse Publishing.

Galle, W. (1996). *Business communication: A technology-based approach* (p. 471). New York: Irwin Publishing.

Geldard, K., and Geldard, D. (2010). *Counselling adolescents: The proactive approach for young people* (3rd ed., p. 129). Thousand Oaks, CA: Sage Publishing.

Glover, W. (2013). Steps in a lawsuit. Retrieved from http://williamhgloverjd.wordpress.com/2010/01/21/steps-in-a-lawsuit/ (accessed September 19, 2013).

Gordon, N., and Fleisher, W. (2011). *Effective interviewing and interrogation techniques* (3rd ed., p. 98). Burlington, MA: Elsevier Publishing.

Hart, W., and Blanchard, R. (2007). *Litigation and trial practice* (6th ed., p. 469). Clifton Park, NY: Thomson Delmar Publishing.

Hewlett, M. (2013). Kernersville police officer found in contempt of court for outburst after trial. *Winston-Salem Journal*. Retrieved from http://www.journalnow.com/news/local/article_8fe7554a-de99-11e2-a7af-0019bb30f31a.html (accessed September 17, 2013).

Inabu, F., Reid, J., Buckley, J., and Jayne, B. (2013). *Criminal interrogation and confessions* (5th ed., p. 86). Burlington, MA: Jones and Bartlett Publishing.

Kinnee, K. (1992). *Practical gambling investigation techniques* (p. 164). New York: Elsevier Publishing.

Kinnee, K. (1994). *Practical investigation techniques*. Boca Raton, FL: CRC Press.

Komninos, J. (2013). Law office of Jason T. Komninos. Retrieved from http://www.jasonkomninos.com/miranda-rights-do-not-necessarily-apply-in-prison/ (accessed September 18, 2013).

Kurzweil, A. (2013). Courtroom erupts after not guilty verdict in model murder. *KTLA News*. Retrieved from http://ktla.com/2013/06/04/woman-not-guilty-of-first-degree-murder-in-model-murder-lesser-charge-possible/#axzz2fCLpcXGy (accessed September 17, 2013).

Leeson, M. (1981). *Systems analysis and design* (p. 91). Chicago: Science Research Associates.

Leo, R., and Thomas, G. (1998). *The Miranda debate: Law, justice, and policing* (p. 66). York, PA: Maple Press.

McLaughlin, E. (2013). Woman accused of stabbing ex-boyfriend, stuffing him into shower. Retrieved from http://www.kjct8.com/news/jury-deliberations-start-in-jodi-arias-trial/-/163152/20014414/-/noadkp/-/index.html (accessed September 19, 2013).

Melas, C. (2013). Jodi Arias: Shocked she was found guilty of first degree murder. Retrieved from http://hollywoodlife.com/2013/05/08/jodi-arias-first-degree-murder-conviction-shocked/ (accessed September 19, 2013).

Merriam-Webster Dictionary. (2013a). s.v. "arraignment." Retrieved from http://www.merriam-webster.com/dictionary/arraignment (accessed September 19, 2013).

Merriam-Webster Dictionary. (2013b). s.v. "arrest." Retrieved from http://www.merriam-webster.com/dictionary/arrest (accessed September 18, 2013).

NOLO (2013a). Criminal Trial Procedures: An Overview. Retrieved from http://www.nolo.com/legal-encyclopedia/criminal-trial-procedures-overview-29509.html (accessed September 19, 2013).

NOLO (2013b). What is an Arrest? Retrieved from http://www.nolo.com/legal-encyclopedia/justifies-arrest-probable-cause.html (accessed September 18, 2013).

Phipps, R. (2012). *Body language: It's what you don't say that matters* (p. 40). West Sussex, United Kingdom: John Wiley and Sons Publishing.

Roelofse, J. P. (2006). *From innovation to profit: An entrepreneur's guide*. Cape Town, South Africa: Juta and Co. Publishing.

Sandmann, W. (1999). *Speech 100: Fundamentals of communication* (p. 116). New York: Pearson.

Sanger, L. (2011). Preparing for and taking an effective deposition, part one. American Bar Association. Retrieved from http://apps.americanbar.org/litigation/committees/masstorts/articles/summer2011-effective-deposition.html (accessed September 19, 2013).

Schroeder, D., and Lombardo, F. (2010). *Police sergeant examination* (pp. 309–310). Hauppage, NY: Barron's Publishing.

State of Georgia. (2013). S.O.P. 9-4 Field interviews and pat-down searches. Retrieved from http://www.dca.state.ga.us/development/research/programs/downloads/law/Chap9-4.html (accessed September 17, 2013).

Stein, T. (2004). *The role of law in social work practice and administration* (p. 71). New York: Columbia University Press.

Stone, G. (2013). Styles of communication in criminal justice. Retrieved from http://www.ehow.com/list_7670987_styles-communication-criminal-justice.html (accessed September 17, 2013).

Tyska, L., and Fennelly, L. (1999). *Investigations: 150 things you should know* (p. 105). Burlington, MA: Butterworth-Heinemann Publishing.

U.S. Legal Forms. (2013). Arraignment Law and Legal Definition. Retrieved from http://definitions.uslegal.com/a/arraignment/ (accessed September 19, 2013).

Welch, C., and Fuller, J. (2014). *American criminal courts: Legal processes and social context* (p. 299). Waltham, MA: Elsevier Publishing.

Wood, P. (2013). How to spot a liar. Retrieved from http://www.pattiwood.net/article.asp?PageID=2314 (accessed September 19, 2013).

Writing, A. (2013). Dispatcher's duties in law enforcement. Retrieved from http://www.ehow.com/about_5522473_dispatchers-duties-law-enforcement.html (accessed September 17, 2013).

Yeschke, C. (2004). *Interrogation: Achieving confessions using permissible persuasion*. Springfield, IL: Charles C. Thomas Publishing.

Can You Hear Me Now? Physical Disability and Communication Challenges

18

All the world is full of suffering. It is also full of overcoming.

—Helen Keller (Keller, n.d.)

Objectives

The objectives of this chapter are to

- Introduce communication within the context of physical disability
- Discuss the Americans with Disabilities Act (ADA)
- Introduce communication regarding deafness
- Introduce communication regarding blindness
- Introduce communication regarding voice and speech impairments
- Discuss methods of embellishing the communications process to accommodate disabilities
- Discuss various court cases involving disabilities and communications

Disabilities

Personnel within the justice system must interact and communicate daily with a wide variety of people. Many of these individuals have physical disabilities that impede communication using physical senses. Two such disabilities are deafness and blindness. When communicating with such individuals, additional resources may be required to ensure that the communications process is both efficient and effective. For instance, when dealing with someone who is deaf, communication may occur through the use of an interpreter that is proficient in sign language or through written language. When communicating with someone who is blind, the use of braille and verbal communication may be necessary. When communicating with someone who is mute, then justice system personnel cannot expect to converse orally. Therefore, written language may serve as an acceptable communication modality.

According to the Centers for Disease Control and Prevention, regarding adult physical disabilities, American society exhibits a variety of statistics. Among noninstitutionalized adults, ages 18 years or older, the characteristics of American society are as follows:

- Quantity of adults with hearing difficulty: approximately 37.1 million (or approximately 16.0%) (Centers for Disease Control and Prevention, 2013a)
- Quantity of adults with vision difficulty: approximately 21.2 million (or approximately 9.2%) (Centers for Disease Control and Prevention, 2013a)
- Quantity of adults who are unable to walk at least a quarter of mile: approximately 17.6 million (or approximately 7.6%) (Centers for Disease Control and Prevention, 2013a)

- Quantity of adults who have any physical functioning difficulties: approximately 37.4 million (or approximately 16.2%) (Centers for Disease Control and Prevention, 2013a)
- Quantity of adults who have a minimum of one complex activity constraint or basic action difficulty: approximately 74.6 million (or approximately 32.9%) (Centers for Disease Control and Prevention, 2013a)

Data sets are available regarding physical disability and the sense of hearing. Deafness is defined as the inability to "hear" and "lacking or deficient in the sense of hearing" (*Merriam-Webster*, 2013b). Hearing impairment is defined as "decreased ability to hear and discriminate among sounds" (March of Dimes, 2013). Individuals who have hearing impairment may be completely deaf or may have varying amounts of hearing. According to the National Institute on Deafness and Other Communication Disorders, the following attributes are representative of hearing impairment within American society:

> About 2 to 3 out of every 1,000 children in the United States are born deaf or hard-of-hearing. Nine out of every 10 children who are born deaf are born to parents who can hear. (National Institute on Deafness and Other Communication Disorders, 2013b)
>
> Approximately 4,000 new cases of sudden deafness occur each year in the United States. Hearing loss affects only 1 ear in 9 out of 10 people who experience sudden deafness. Only 10 to 15 percent of patients with sudden deafness know what caused their loss. (National Institute on Deafness and Other Communication Disorders, 2013b)
>
> There is a strong relationship between age and reported hearing loss: 18 percent of American adults 45–64 years old, 30 percent of adults 65–74 years old, and 47 percent of adults 75 years old or older have a hearing loss. (National Institute on Deafness and Other Communication Disorders, 2013b)
>
> Men are more likely to experience hearing loss than women. (National Institute on Deafness and Other Communication Disorders, 2013b)
>
> Only 1 out of 5 people who could benefit from a hearing aid actually wears one. (National Institute on Deafness and Other Communication Disorders, 2013b)

Certainly, some of these individuals will experience an interaction with the justice system in some fashion, thereby necessitating communication. Some may be plaintiffs or defendants. Others may be employees or contractors within the justice system. Although written communication may be acceptable in some cases, many people communicate using sign language. Within the justice system, sign language interpreters may be used to communicate with individuals who have some form of hearing impairment. Figure 18.1 shows the symbols that comprise the alphabet using sign language.

Communicating with sign language is not constrained solely to fashioning individual, separate letters via hand signals. Instead, it also accommodates the use of entire words via hand signals to convey messages. Figure 18.2 shows the communicating of the Pledge of Allegiance using sign language.

Many people have vision impairments that influence the communications process. Blindness is defined as an inability "to see" and "of or relating to sightless persons" (*Merriam-Webster*, 2013a). Vision impairment is a condition in which "eyesight cannot be corrected to a 'normal' level" (Centers for Disease Control and Prevention, 2013b). Another definition is "the best-corrected visual acuity less than 6/12 (<20/40) in the better-seeing

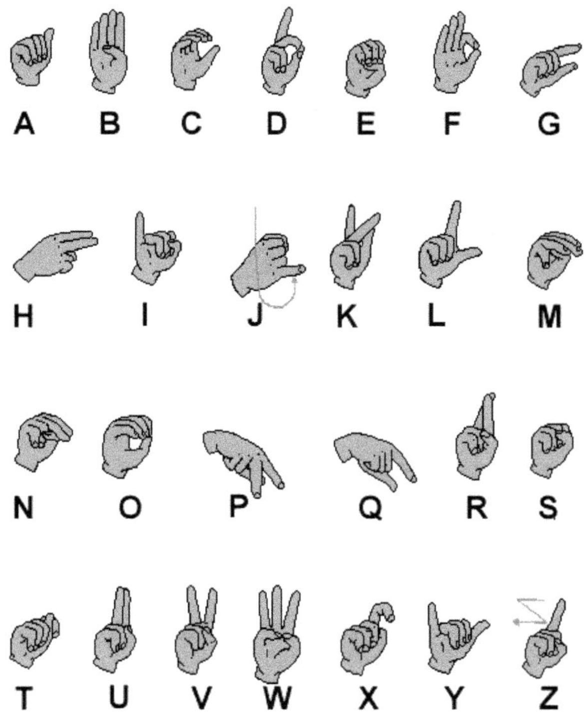

Figure 18.1 Sign language alphabet. (From http://www.iidc.indiana.edu/cedir/kidsweb/amachart.html.)

eye (excluding those who were categorized as being blind by the U.S. definition)" (National Eye Institute, 2013).

Although some people may experience surgery or necessitate glasses as remedies, some instances of visual impairment are incurable. Despite attempts to rectify visual impairment, others may experience limited vision or absolute blindness. Many individuals who have vision impairment may experience the justice system. Some may be its employees or contractors, whereas others may be plaintiffs and defendants. Certainly, some may be attorneys or employed as assistants.

Various demographics exist regarding vision impairment. During 2010, statistics were compiled by the National Eye Institute of the National Institute of Health. Regarding the United States, excerpts of these findings are given as follows (National Eye Institute, 2013):

- Among individuals with vision impairment, approximately 81% are white.
- Among individuals with vision impairment, approximately 8% are black.
- Among individuals with vision impairment, approximately 7% are Hispanic.
- Among individuals with vision impairment, approximately 4% represent a different ethnicity other than white, black, or Hispanic.
- Among individuals with vision impairment, approximately 36% are male.
- Among individuals with vision impairment, approximately 64% are female.

Various resources exist that embellish communicating with visually impaired people in the justice system. For instance, use of the braille code and text reading software

Figure 18.2 Pledge of Allegiance using sign language. (From http://flagetiquette.us/pledge-of-allegiance/american-sign-language-pledge-of-allegiance.)

within computing devices enhances the communications process. Braille code is defined as a "series of raised dots that can be read with the fingers by people who are blind or whose eyesight is not sufficient for reading printed material" (Iowa Department for the Blind, 2013). Braille code may be used within books as well as "on elevators, restrooms, and office numbers" (Iowa Department for the Blind, 2013). Figure 18.3 delineates the braille code.

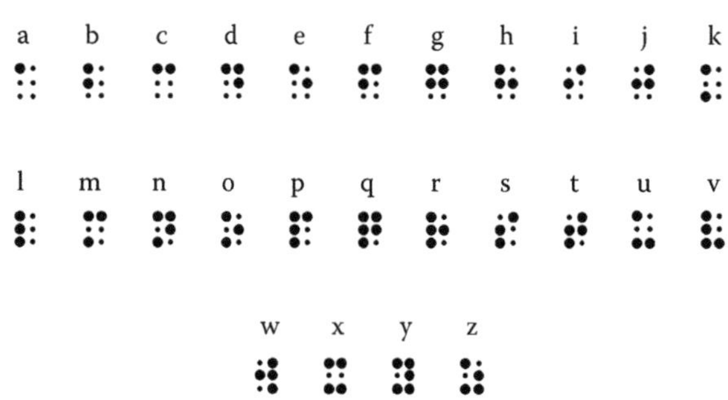

Figure 18.3 Braille code. (From http://www.blind.state.ia.us/publications/white-cane-magazine-spring-2010/departments.)

Voice and speech impairments are physical disabilities that impair communication. Examples include aphasia, muteness, stuttering, hoarseness, and so forth. Aphasia is a condition involving "a disorder that results from damage to portions of the brain that are responsible for language," and may result from strokes, head injuries, or tumors (National Institute on Deafness and Other Communication Disorders, 2013a). Aphasia affects approximately 100,000 individuals annually within the United States, and between 25% and 40% of stroke patients develop this condition (National Aphasia Association, 2013). Muteness is defined as "unable to speak" and as "lacking the power of speech" (*Merriam-Webster*, 2013d). Stuttering is speaking "with involuntary disruption or blocking of speech (as by spasmodic repetition or prolongation of vocal sounds)" (*Merriam-Webster*, 2013e). Hoarseness is speaking with roughness or harshness "in sound" (*Merriam-Webster*, 2013c). Below are some statistics regarding American voice and speech impairments:

- Within the United States, between 6 and 8 million individuals "have some form of language impairment" (National Institute on Deafness and Other Communication Disorders, 2013c).
- Within the United States, approximately "7.5 million people in the United States have trouble using their voices" (National Institute on Deafness and Other Communication Disorders, 2013c).
- At least approximately 3 million Americans have stuttering problems (National Institute on Deafness and Other Communication Disorders, 2013c).

Many individuals experience the workings of the justice system. Many may be defendants and plaintiffs, some may be officers of the court, and some may be employed in various other facets of the justice domain. Regardless, communicating with such individuals may necessitate a variety of methods, ranging from the use of written communication to auditory forms of communicating.

Americans with Disabilities Act of 1990

The Americans with Disabilities Act (ADA) of 1990 is also a consideration of the legal system. This legislation represented the initial civil rights laws through which the needs of disabled individuals were protected with respect to the prohibition of employment discrimination, public service, publically available accommodations, and telecommunications (U.S. Equal Employment Opportunity Commission, 2013a). The ADA legislation is described as follows:

> The Americans with Disabilities Act of 1990 (ADA) prohibits discrimination and ensures equal opportunity for persons with disabilities in employment, State and local government services, public accommodations, commercial facilities, and transportation. It also mandates the establishment of TDD/telephone relay services. The current text of the ADA includes changes made by the ADA Amendments Act of 2008 (P.L. 110-325), which became effective on January 1, 2009. The ADA was originally enacted in public law format and later rearranged and published in the United States Code. (U.S. Department of Justice, 2013b)

The ADA is composed of tenets that affect both public and private work settings. Enforcing this legislation is a function of the federal government. The governmental factions responsible for its enforcement are itemized as follows:

- *Equal Employment Opportunity Commission (EEOC)*: responsible for enforcing ADA components regarding employment issues (U.S. Department of Labor, 2013)
- *Department of Transportation (DOT)*: responsible for enforcing ADA components regarding transportation issues (U.S. Department of Labor, 2013)
- *Federal Communications Commission (FCC)*: responsible for enforcing ADA components regarding telecommunications (U.S. Department of Labor, 2013)
- *Department of Justice (DOJ)*: responsible for enforcing components regarding "public accommodations and state and local government services" (U.S. Department of Labor, 2013)

Since its origin, numerous lawsuits and disputes have occurred regarding disability issues within the context of the ADA. Examples range from a court case involving the discharging of an executive director from a security organization because of brain cancer to court cases involving the employment of individuals exhibiting mental retardation (U.S. Equal Employment Opportunity Commission, 2013a). The influence and governance of the ADA is unconstrained solely to civilian settings. Instead, it is also applicable among justice system entities.

The ADA affects the treatments of individuals within the justice system. Within the intermediary stages of the justice and court processes and among correctional settings, individuals exhibit a variety of disabilities that affect the communications process. For instance, with respect to individuals who experience hearing loss or deafness, among corrections settings, the ADA mandates the provision of "equal access" regarding "all services, programs, and activities" (McCay, 1995). Because this mandate exists, correctional facilities must craft and implement any organizational changes that are necessary for ADA compliance or be susceptible to the risks of "legal actions and substantial penalties" (McCay, 1995). Although this mandate exists, the ADA does not allocate funding to ensure that such equality exists (McCay, 1995).

The ADA also mandates that communication be effective. Basically, effectiveness is considered as "whatever is written or spoken must be as clear and understandable to people with disabilities as it is for people who do not have disabilities" (U.S. Department of Justice, 2013a). Therefore, the communication process must incorporate any attributes that are necessary to ensure that communication is effective. For instance, interpreters, translators, and so forth, may be used to embellish the basic communications process to accommodate the communication needs of disabled individuals. The use of translators and interpreters is considered to be the use of an auxiliary resource. Simply, an auxiliary aid or service is a resource that enables "effective communication for people with disabilities" (U.S. Department of Justice, 2013a).

Auxiliaries are used to embellish the written, oral, and visual forms of communicating (U.S. Department of Justice, 2013a). Figure 18.4 shows typical types of auxiliaries that are used to enhance communication (U.S. Department of Justice, 2013a).

Using these auxiliary items is dependent on a variety of factors with respect to the type of disability that one exhibits (U.S. Department of Justice, 2013a). Such use also

- Qualified interpreters
- Notetakers
- Screen readers
- Computer-aided real-time transcription (CART)
- Written materials
- Telephone handset amplifiers
- Assistive listening systems
- Hearing aid-compatible telephones
- Computer terminals
- Speech synthesizers
- Communication boards
- Text telephones (TTYs)
- Open or closed captioning
- Closed caption decoders
- Video interpreting services
- Videotext displays
- Description of visually presented materials
- Exchange of written notes
- TTY or video relay service
- E-mail
- Text messaging
- Instant messaging
- Qualified readers
- Assistance filling out forms
- Taped texts
- Audio recordings
- Brailed materials
- Large print materials
- Materials in electronic format (compact disc with materials in plain text or word processor format)

Figure 18.4 Auxiliary communication resources. (From http://www.ada.gov/pcatoolkit/chap3toolkit.htm.)

depends on the complexity and the length of the communication (U.S. Department of Justice, 2013a). Within the justice system, public service personnel must be familiar with the types and varieties of auxiliaries that may embellish communication (U.S. Department of Justice, 2013a). Therefore, organizations within the justice system may provide various training programs to familiarize personnel with auxiliary resources.Auxiliary resources are also categorized as either electronic or nonelectronic resources (National Black Disability Coalition, 2013). Some characteristics of electronic items are given as follows:

- Digital speech output (recorded human speech).
- Synthesized speech output (electronic speech).
- Prerecorded messages (hello, good morning, etc.).
- Ability to formulate messages spontaneously.
- Recording time depends on the memory of the device.
- Displays that can be changed to allow user to select more words.
- Tools to access communication devices: pointing devices, handheld, placed in mouth, or attached to a headband.
- Switch may be operated by a hand, foot, shoulder, face, or head.
- Eye gaze device. (National Black Disability Coalition, 2013)

Some characteristics of nonelectronic items are given as follows:

- Alphabet boards
- Picture and word boards
- Picture books

When using one of these devices, the person uses

- A series of letters to spell a word.
- A series of pictures to convey a thought or message.
- Spelling out every word can be time consuming.

- Pictures and symbols are limited by the amount that can fit on a page or board.
- Some words and ideas cannot be conveyed by a picture.
- Devices require a communication partner to assist the user and discern what he or she is trying to communicate. (National Black Disability Coalition, 2013)

Certain exclusions and organizational defenses exist regarding the ADA legislation. Reasonable accommodations are unnecessary if they "would impose an undue hardship on the employer" (Bagley & Savage, 2010). Employers may argue that discrimination is necessary if a condition of "business necessity" exists (Bagley & Savage, 2010). For instance, job-related criteria may be deemed as acceptable if they are job related and "consistent with business necessity" (Bagley & Savage, 2010). Examples include standards for qualification and employment testing (Bagley & Savage, 2010). Permissible exclusion occurs when a condition exists, involving the disability, regarding whether one (either "with or without reasonable accommodation") is incapable of performing the job-related functions and tasks or if employing the disabled individual endangers others significantly (Bagley & Savage, 2010).

During 2008, the ADA was amended via the Americans with Disabilities Act Amendments Act (ADAAA) (National Center for Learning Disabilities, 2013). This change emphasizes discrimination issues instead of an individual disability (Southeast ADA Center, 2013). The ADAAA also emphasizes a broad interpretation of disability, and also includes considerations of communications within its scope (Southeast ADA Center, 2013).

Regardless of the circumstance or situation, the ADA affects both the personnel of the justice system and the individuals who are subjected to the justice system. The ADA affects every correctional facility, both state and federal, within the United States (Miller, 2002). During 1998, regarding the case *Pennsylvania Department of Corrections vs. Yeskey*, 524 U.S. 206, the U.S. Supreme Court unanimously decided that the ADA applies to state prisons (Prison Law Office, 2013). It provides a basis for ensuring that communication occurs efficiently and effectively throughout the justice system, among corrections settings, and among law enforcement organizations. The ADA should not be merely viewed as a law with which conformance is mandated, but as a medium through which the needs and wants of disabled individuals are satisfied during the communications process.

Communicating in the Justice System

The justice system is rife with communication involving disabled individuals. Among corrections environments, accommodation plans must exist to satisfy the needs of disabled individuals. In the state of Washington, around 110 inmates exhibit hearing or visual impediments (Anderson & Hilliard, 2005). To accommodate the needs of such individuals, the corrections system created the position of "Deaf Offender Services Manager" to work in conjunction with deaf and blind inmates to accommodate their needs during periods of incarceration (Anderson & Hilliard, 2005). Most correctional facilities have a sufficient quantity of hearing-impaired inmates to justify the hiring of interpreters (Miller, 2002). Inmates should have a sufficient amount of time to meet individually with these supporting personnel so that familiarization occurs regarding the communications ability of the inmates (Miller, 2002).

Although such inmates may reside within the general population, they may be assigned to reside in "infirmaries" among facilities where personnel are unfamiliar or ignorant of special needs accommodations (Anderson & Hilliard, 2005). Accommodating the needs of these inmates requires contemplating various communications resources and embellishments. Blind inmates may necessitate the use of "tape recorders for listening to books and recording correspondence" (Anderson & Hilliard, 2005). Deaf inmates may require paging devices to notify them of announcements that are disseminated via the institution's public address system (Anderson & Hilliard, 2005).

Within the state of Texas, approximately 30% of inmates are either "deaf or hard of hearing" (Miller, 2002). Many more probably exist whose hearing impairments are unrealized and undiagnosed (Miller, 2002). Communicating with such inmates necessitates the use of alternative mediums or auxiliary resources. For instance, communicating anything involving "officers' directives, health care, education, legal proceedings, and all other communication" necessitates communications enhancements that incorporate the use of visual resources (Miller, 2002). Some inmates are capable of reading lips. In such instances, anyone attempting to communicate with such inmates should directly face the inmate, speak slowly, and eliminate "visual obstructions such as facial hair or chewing gum" (Miller, 2002). However, the typical deaf inmate may understand little oral communication via lip reading. On average, deaf individuals understand approximately 5% of "what is being said" through reading lips (McCay, 1995).

The use of written communication may be difficult and less effective when communicating with inmates that have hearing impairments. Such inmates often possess only a third-grade reading level, and qualify as being functionally illiterate (Miller, 2002). These inmates may also be inept regarding the "social norms of those who do not have hearing loss" (Miller, 2002). They may not withhold information in the same capacity that is exhibited by inmates that do not have hearing loss. For instance, regarding deaf inmates, information may be communicated much more readily, thereby earning them "snitch" titles within the correctional facility (Miller, 2002).

The provision of disability accommodations is often requested, in writing, by the disabled individual. Usually, paperwork specifies the characteristics of communications auxiliaries that are necessary for embellishing the communications process. Figure 18.5a through c shows an example of such a request.

Within the justice system, communications disabilities require some considerations of the ADA and any necessary accommodations that must be provided to ensure the efficiency and effectiveness of communication. Similarly, processing individuals throughout the various stages of processes within the justice system necessitates considerations of disabilities that may negatively affect the communications process. Each human is unique. Therefore, when contemplating the communications needs of disabled inmates, personnel within the justice system must be aware of the unique needs of each disabled person within the justice system.

Policy and Methods of Improving Communication

Accommodating the communication needs of people within the justice system may be considered strategically, tactically, and operationally. Each organization must craft policies

(a)

UNITED STATES DISTRICT COURT
CENTRAL DISTRICT OF CALIFORNIA

APPLICATION FOR ACCOMMODATIONS FOR TRIAL PARTICIPANTS WITH COMMUNICATION DISABILITIES, JURORS AND MEMBERS OF THE PUBLIC

(SUBMIT APPLICATION A MINIMUM OF TEN (10) COURT DAYS PRIOR TO A SCHEDULED COURT PROCEEDING; IF SUBMITTING BY U.S. MAIL SUBMIT A MINIMUM OF FIFTEEN (15) COURT DAYS PRIOR TO SCHEDULED COURT PROCEEDING)

CASE NAME: ______________________

CASE NO: ______________ **JUDGE:** ______________

APPLICANT'S NAME: ______________________

APPLICANT'S ROLE: ☐ **PARTY** ☐ **WITNESS** ☐ **ATTORNEY** ☐ **JUROR**
☐ **OTHER - SPECIFY:**

If applicant has checked "other" for applicant's role include a detailed explanation of the case-related interest in the court proceeding for which the accommodation is sought:

Applicant's Contact Information:

ADDRESS: ______________________

CITY: ______________ **STATE:** ________ **ZIP CODE:** ________

EMAIL: ______________ **PHONE NUMBER:** ______________

G-122 (01/18) APPLICATION FOR ACCOMMODATIONS FOR TRIAL PARTICIPANTS WITH COMMUNICATIONS DISABILITIES, JURORS, AND MEMBERS OF THE PUBLIC Page of

Figure 18.5 Accommodation request. (a) Page 1.

and procedures that accommodate the needs of its population. Such policies and procedures may be affected by both federal and state laws. They also may be affected by the characteristics of the organization. Regardless, all components of the justice system must contemplate policies and methods through which communicating with disabled individuals is accomplished efficiently and effectively. Some methods whereby communications may be improved are highlighted below.

Technology: Organizations may examine whether technological resources may be procured or obtained from vendor services (U.S. Department of Justice, 2013). If vendors are necessary, then determinations regarding the amount of advance notice for vendor services are advisable (U.S. Department of Justice, 2013).

(b)

In accordance with the local guidelines of this court, application is made for court provided sign language interpreters and/or other appropriate auxiliary aids as follows:

- ☐ Hearing impaired equipment
- ☐ CART (Communications Access Realtime Translation)
- ☐ Sign language interpreter
- ☐ Other communication/auxiliary aid or services, as specified:

Note: If specific auxiliary aids and services are requested, alternative auxiliary aids and services must be identified here by the requesting participant in case the primary auxiliary aids and services requested are unavailable, incompatible with the courtroom or too expensive.

Type of court proceeding or activity for which auxiliary aids and services are requested:

Proceeding Date/Time/Courtroom No.:

Note: Application should be made as far in advance of the requested implementation date as possible.

Description of the communication disability that necessitates the auxiliary aids and services (attach pages if necessary):

G-122 (01/13) APPLICATION FOR ACCOMMODATIONS FOR TRIAL PARTICIPANTS WITH COMMUNICATIONS DISABILITIES, JURORS, AND MEMBERS OF THE PUBLIC Page of

Figure 18.5 (Continued) Accommodation request. (b) Page 2.

Contracts: Contracts with vendors must also accommodate short-notice situations (U.S. Department of Justice, 2013). For instance, situations involving arrest, injury, hospitalization, or emergency circumstances may require communications embellishments (U.S. Department of Justice, 2013).

Training: Personnel within the justice system should experience some amounts of training and education regarding communications disabilities and the auxiliary resources that may be used to embellish the communications process (U.S. Department of Justice, 2013). All justice system personnel must be knowledgeable regarding their roles to ensure that communication occurs effectively (U.S. Department of Justice, 2013).

(c)

If physical accommodations are necessary this application will be forwarded to the ADA Officer designated by the General Services Administration to properly process and provide the necessary accommodations. Provide a description of the physical accommodations requested and a description of the disability that necessitates the accommodations:

If the communications disability is not obvious you may attach documentation from an appropriate health care or rehabilitation professional that is sufficient to substantiate the disability and the need for the auxiliary aids and services requested. Documentation is sufficient if it: (1) describes the nature, severity, and duration of the applicant's communication disability, the activity or activities that the disability limits, and the extent to which the disability limits the applicant's ability to perform the activity or activities; and (2) substantiates why the requested auxiliary aids and services are needed.

Check the applicable options below and sign and date application where indicated:

☐ I certify under penalty of perjury that I am deaf, hearing impaired, or have other communication disabilities that render me eligible for receipt of these auxiliary aids and services; and/or

☐ I certify under penalty of perjury that I require the physical accommodation(s) requested above.

Date: ____________ **Applicant's Signature:** ____________

Submit application by either:

(1) U.S. mail or personal delivery to: Virginia Wilson, Interpreter Services Manager/Access Coordinator, U.S. Courthouse, Western Division, 312 N. Spring Street, Room 541, Los Angeles, California 90012; or
(2) electronic mail to: Access_Coordinator@cacd.uscourts.gov; or
(3) facsimile transmission to: Access Coordinator at (213) 894-5483.

G-122 (01/13) APPLICATION FOR ACCOMMODATIONS FOR TRIAL PARTICIPANTS WITH COMMUNICATIONS DISABILITIES, JURORS, AND MEMBERS OF THE PUBLIC Page of

Figure 18.5 (Continued) Accommodation request. (c) Page 3. (From http://court.cacd.uscourts.gov/CACD/Forms.nsf/0b2b50f03ce1d589882567c80058610a/5cc1a55459547b3188257ae10066cdff/$FILE/G-122.pdf.)

Committees: Policies and programs may involve the use of committees. Members of these committees should include representatives of hearing-impaired individuals and "local professionals" who are familiar with hearing impairments (McCay, 1995).

Full-time personnel: Some components of the justice system may necessitate the hiring of full-time personnel to accommodate the communications needs of disabled individuals. For instance, prisons may hire full-time interpreters to provide communications services twenty-four hours per day (McCay, 1995).

Community: Inmates may be given a choice to live in communities that share their unique disability (McCay, 1995). For instance, a group of deaf inmates may choose to live together (McCay, 1995). This type of community may lower the costs of providing accommodations (McCay, 1995).

Tagging: Inmates with disabilities may be issued tags that identify their unique disability and needs. Such tags may be worn on their prison clothes or carried in a pocket (Miller, 2002). Use of tagging may avoid misunderstandings, altercations, and "disciplinary actions" that may occur within the prison setting (Miller, 2002).

Tracking: Tracking programs may be used to show the location of inmates at any point in time. Tracking facilitates the changing needs of accommodation through time (Miller, 2002).

Handcuffing: Although handcuffing is a consideration of officer safety, it is detrimental for inmates that communicate through sign language (Miller, 2002). For instance, hearing-impaired inmates may be handcuffed during transport but should be "released from handcuffs" during court proceedings (Miller, 2002). Releasing these offenders allows their participation during the "proceedings, in accordance with their due process rights under the U.S. Constitution and their right to effective communication under ADA" (Miller, 2002).

These methods are not an exhaustive delineation of the actions that organizations may pursue to embellish the communications process. Every organization within the justice system is unique. There exists no universal set of activities that may be pursued to accommodate the needs of all individuals and organizations within the justice system. Every organization within the justice system must craft its own unique policies and plans to accommodate the communications needs of disabled individuals.

Court Cases and Disability Communication

From the perspective of disability, numerous disputes occur within the justice system regarding communications or communications entities. Both federally and among the states, various issues have been decided regarding situations involving practically every form of communication involving disabled individuals. Some interesting court proceedings that involved disability issues in communications are described below.

EEOC vs. Verizon: During 2011, Verizon Communications was mandated to pay the amount of $20 million and to "provide significant equitable relief" as the result of a class-action lawsuit that was initiated by the EEOC (U.S. Equal Employment Opportunity Commission, 2013b). It included a total of twenty-four Verizon subsidiaries (U.S. Equal Employment Opportunity Commission, 2013b). The premise of the lawsuit involved allegations that Verizon "unlawfully denied reasonable accommodations" for many of its personnel, and that the company disciplined or terminated personnel in accordance with its "no fault" attendance policies (U.S. Equal Employment Opportunity Commission, 2013b). This case represented the "largest disability discrimination settlement in a single lawsuit in EEOC history" (U.S. Equal Employment Opportunity Commission, 2013b).

United States vs. Peroutka and Peroutka: During 2013, this settlement involved the allegation that Peroutka transgressed the ADA through refusing to accept "relay calls when the complainants called to resolve disputes involving alleged unpaid debts" (U.S. Department of Justice, 2013d). After a government investigation, the allegations were substantiated (U.S. Department of Justice, 2013d). Specifically, Peroutka admitted that it "directed its employees to refuse to accept calls made by individuals with disabilities through relay services and, instead, directed the callers to call back when a manager was available" (U.S. Department of Justice, 2013d). The remedies involved with this settlement included the mandate for Peroutka to establish and disseminate a communications policy among its personnel, to incorporate the use of auxiliary aids as necessary, to improve communications effectiveness during face-to-face communications, and to provide monetary compensation as a relief mechanism (U.S. Department of Justice, 2013d).

Holmes vs. Godinez: During 2011, in the state of Illinois, a lawsuit was filed that alleged violations of the ADA had occurred in the prison system (Johnson, 2011). The lawsuit claimed that access to interpreters for deaf inmates was limited, thereby eliminating them from religious activities and training regimens (Johnson, 2011). A component of the lawsuit also alleges that an inmate was denied food after being unable to communicate with a warden regarding accusations of theft (Johnson, 2011). During the period of this authorship, the outcome of this case was pending.

ADA Truths versus Myths

The tenets of the ADA are primarily common sense. Both private and public organizations have the responsibility of complying with its tenets. Certainly, compliance with the ADA is required within the justice system. When contemplating the ADA and various compliance aspects, many organizations and personnel may experience some confusion regarding the basic ADA concepts. Some basic truths regarding the ADA that affect the justice system are presented below.

Myth: ADA suits are flooding the courts.
Truth: The ADA has resulted in a surprisingly small number of lawsuits—only about 650 nationwide in five years. That's tiny compared to the 6 million businesses; 666,000 public and private employers; and 80,000 units of state and local government that must comply. (U.S. Department of Justice, 2013c)

Myth: The government thinks everything is readily achievable.
Truth: Not true. Often it may not be readily achievable to remove a barrier—especially in older structures. Let's say a small business is located above ground. Installing an elevator would not, most likely, be readily achievable—and there may not be enough room to build a ramp—or the business may not be profitable enough to build a ramp. In these circumstances, the ADA would allow a business to simply provide curbside service to persons with disabilities. (U.S. Department of Justice, 2013c)

Myth: Restaurants must provide menus in braille.
Truth: Not true. Waiters can read the menu to blind customers. (U.S. Department of Justice, 2013c)

Myth: Sign language interpreters are required everywhere.
Truth: The ADA only requires that effective communication not exclude people with disabilities—which in many situations means providing written materials or exchanging notes. The law does not require any measure that would cause an undue financial or administrative burden. (U.S. Department of Justice, 2013c)

Myth: The ADA forces business and government to spend lots of money hiring unqualified people.
Truth: No unqualified job applicant or employee with a disability can claim employment discrimination under the ADA. Employees must meet all the requirements of the job and perform the essential functions of the job with or without reasonable accommodation. No accommodation must be provided if it would result in an undue hardship on the employer. (U.S. Department of Justice, 2013c)

Myth: The government is no help when it comes to paying for accessibility.
Truth: Not so. Federal tax incentives are available to help meet the cost of ADA compliance. (U.S. Department of Justice, 2013c)

Myth: Businesses must pay large fines when they violate the ADA.
Truth: Courts may levy civil penalties only in cases brought by the Justice Department, not private litigants. The Department only seeks such penalties when the violation is substantial and the business has shown bad faith in failing to comply. Bad faith can take many forms, including hostile acts against people with disabilities, a long-term failure even to inquire into what the ADA requires, or sustained resistance to voluntary compliance. The Department also considers a business' size and resources in determining whether civil penalties are appropriate. Civil penalties may not be assessed in cases against state or local governments or employers. (U.S. Department of Justice, 2013c)

Myth: The Justice Department sues first and asks questions later.
Truth: The primary goal of the Department's enforcement program is to increase voluntary compliance through technical assistance and negotiation. Under existing rules, the Department may not file a lawsuit unless it has first tried to settle the dispute through negotiations—which is why most every complaint settles. (U.S. Department of Justice, 2013c)

Myth: The Justice Department never files suits.
Truth: The Department has been party to 20 suits under the ADA. Although it tries extensively to promote voluntary compliance, the Department will take legal action when entities continue to resist complying with the law. (U.S. Department of Justice, 2013c)

Myth: Many ADA cases involve frivolous issues.
Truth: The Justice Department's enforcement of the ADA has been fair and rooted in common sense. The overwhelming majority of the complaints received by the Justice Department have merit. Our focus is on fundamental issues related to access to goods and services that are basic to people's lives. We have avoided pursuing fringe and frivolous issues and will continue to do so. (U.S. Department of Justice, 2013c)

Myth: Everyone claims to be covered under the ADA.
Truth: The definition of 'individual with a disability' is fraught with conditions and must be applied on a case-by-case basis. (U.S. Department of Justice, 2013c)

Myth: The ADA is being misused by people with 'bad backs' and 'emotional problems.'
Truth: Trivial complaints do not make it through the system. And many claims filed by individuals with such conditions are not trivial. There are people with severe depression or people with a history of alcoholism who are judged by their employers, not on the basis of their abilities, but rather upon stereotypes and fears that employers associate with their conditions. (U.S. Department of Justice, 2013c)

Commentary Regarding Disability Communication

Thus far, this chapter has considered the communications needs of disabled individuals within the justice system and facets of the justice system that affect communication regarding disabilities. However, another perspective exists regarding this facet of communication: the individual. Communicating with disabled individuals, regardless of the disability, is a necessary action undertaken by justice system personnel daily.

Some individuals may be sensitive or insensitive regarding disability issues when communicating. Therefore, it may be advisable to avoid certain words or phrases that may be perceived as derogatory, derisive, or offensive. Furthermore, some considerations of protocol, courtesy, and etiquette must be considered when communicating with disabled individuals. Figures 18.6 through 18.12 show basic principles that are associated with these characteristics of communication.

The principles delineated within Figures 18.6 through 18.12 provide guidance for communications within the contexts of auditory, visual, oral, and physical disabilities. Personnel within the justice system must be mindful of these tenets when communicating with disabled individuals. Every human is unique; some communications may be amiable, whereas others may be tedious. Regardless, personnel within the justice system must communicate respectfully, and attempt to communicate both efficiently and effectively.

Words

Positive language empowers. When writing or speaking about people with disabilites, it is important to put the person first. Group designations such as "the blind", "the retarded" or "the disabled" are inappropriate because they do not reflect the individuality, equality or dignity of people with disabilities. Further, words like "normal person" imply that the person with a disability isn't normal, whereas "person without a disability" is descriptive but not negative. The accompanying chart shows examples of positive and negative phrases.

Affirmative phrases	Negative phrases
Person with an intellectual, cognitive, developmental disability	Retarded; mentally defective
Person who is blind, person who is visually impaired	The blind
Person with a disability	The disabled; handicapped
Person who is deaf	The deaf; deaf and dumb
Person who is hard of hearing	Suffers a hearing loss
Person who hasmultiple sclerosis	Afflicted by MS
Person with cerebral palsy	CP victim
Person with epilepsy, person with seizure disorder	Epileptic
Person who uses a wheelchair	Confined or restricted to a wheelchair
Person who has a mascular dystrophy	Stricken by MD
Person with a physical disability, physically disabled	Crippled; lame; deformed
Unable to speak, uses synthetic speech	Dumb; mute
Person with psychiatric disability	Crazy; nuts
Person who is successful, productive	Has overcome his/her disability; is courageous (when it implies the person has courage because of having a disability)

Figure 18.6 Word listing. (From U.S. Department of Labor, http://www.dol.gov/odep/pubs/fact/comucate.htm.)

General Tips for Communicating with People with Disabilities

- When introduced to a person with a disability, it is appropriate to offer to shake hands. People with limited hand use or who wear an artificial limb can usually shake hands. (Shaking hands with the left hand is an acceptable greeting.)
- If you offer assistance, wait until the offer is accepted. Then listen to or ask for instructions.
- Treat adults as adults. Address people who have disabilities by their first names only when extending the same familiarity to all others.
- Relax. Don't be embarrassed if you happen to use common expressions such as "See you later," or "Did you hear about that?" that seem to relate to a person's disability.
- Don't be afraid to ask questions when you're unsure of what to do.

Figure 18.7 General communication tips. (From U.S. Department of Labor, http://www.dol.gov/odep/pubs/fact/comucate.htm.)

Tips for Communicating with Individuals Who are Blind or Visually Impaired

- Speak to the individual when you approach him or her.
- State clearly who you are; speak in a normal tone of voice.
- When conversing in a group, remember to identify yourself and the person to whom you are speaking.
- Never touch or distract a service dog without first asking the owner.
- Tell the individual when you are leaving.
- Do not attempt to lead the individual without first asking; allow the person to hold your arm and control her or his own movements.
- Be descriptive when giving directions; verbally give the person information that is visually obvious to individuals who can see. For example, if you are approaching steps, mention how many steps.
- If you are offering a seat, gently place the individual's hand on the back or arm of the chair so that the person can locate the seat.

Figure 18.8 Visual communication principles. (From U.S. Department of Labor, http://www.dol.gov/odep/pubs/fact/comucate.htm.)

Tips for Communicating with Individuals Who are Deaf or Hard of Hearing

- Gain the person's attention before starting a conversation (i.e., tap the person gently on the shoulder or arm).
- Look directly at the individual, face the light, speak clearly, in a normal tone of voice, and keep your hands away from your face. Use short, simple sentences. Avoid smoking or chewing gum.
- If the individual uses a sign language interpreter, speak directly to the person, not the interpreter.
- If you telephone an individual who is hard of hearing, let the phone ring longer than usual. Speak clearly and be prepared to repeat the reason for the call and who you are.
- If you do not have a Text Telephone (TTY), dial 711 to reach the national telecommunications relay service, which facilitates the call between you and an individual who uses a TTY.

Figure 18.9 Auditory communication principles. (From U.S. Department of Labor, http://www.dol.gov/odep/pubs/fact/comucate.htm.)

Tips for Communicating with Individuals with Mobility Impairments

- If possible, put yourself at the wheelchair user's eye level.
- Do not lean on a wheelchair or any other assistive device.
- Never patronize people who use wheelchairs by patting them on the head or shoulder.
- Do not assume the individual wants to be pushed —ask first.
- Offer assistance if the individual appears to be having difficulty opening a door.
- If you telephone the individual, allow the phone to ring longer than usual to allow extra time for the person to reach the telephone.

Figure 18.10 Physical communication principles. (From U.S. Department of Labor, http://www.dol.gov/odep/pubs/fact/comucate.htm.)

Tips for Communicating with Individuals with Speech Impairments

- If you do not understand something the individual says, do not pretend that you do. Ask the individual to repeat what he or she said and then repeat it back.
- Be patient. Take as much time as necessary.
- Try to ask questions which require only short answers or a nod of the head.
- Concentrate on what the individual is saying.
- Do not speak for the individual or attempt to finish her or his sentences.
- If you are having difficulty understanding the individual, consider writing as an alternative means of communicating, but first ask the individual if this is acceptable.

Figure 18.11 Oral communication principles. (From U.S. Department of Labor, http://www.dol.gov/odep/pubs/fact/comucate.htm.)

Tips for Communicating with Individuals with Cognitive Disabilities

- If you are in a public area with many distractions, consider moving to a quiet or private location.
- Be prepared to repeat what you say, orally or in writing.
- Offer assistance completing forms or understanding written instructions and provide extra time for decision-making. Wait for the individual to accept the offer of assistance; do not "over-assist" or be patronizing.
- Be patient, flexible and supportive. Take time to understand the individual and make sure the individual understands you.

Figure 18.12 Cognitive communication principles. (From U.S. Department of Labor, http://www.dol.gov/odep/pubs/fact/comucate.htm.)

Chapter Comments and Summary

Disabled individuals are processed within the justice system daily. Throughout their individual experiences and journeys within the justice system, they must communicate efficiently and effectively. Although attempts are made to satisfy the communications needs and wants of disabled persons within the justice system, no guarantee exists that these needs and wants are satisfied. Certainly, numerous cases are disputed, heard, and remedied within the justice system regarding a number of communications issues involving disabilities.

Disabilities are manifested in many forms that affect the communications process. Common examples include oral, auditory, and visual impediments. Often, the uses of interpreters, braille, computer equipment, and so forth, are used to ensure that communication occurs efficiently and effectively within the justice system. Such items are referred to as auxiliary resources.

The ADA exists as a legal resource through which disabled individuals are protected from a variety of forms of discrimination and alienation. It ensures that the communications needs and wants of disabled individuals are satisfied within the context of reasonable accommodations. Although the ADA provides various protections, certain exclusions and circumstances exist that allow organizations to refuse compliance.

Among organizations within the justice system, policies, processes, and procedures should exist to ensure ADA compliance and to ensure the effectiveness and efficiency of communications. Improving communications within the justice system may incorporate a variety of activities ranging from the use of committees to the tagging and tracking of inmates among corrections environments.

Since its origin, the justice system has processed a variety of complaints and disputes regarding the ADA and communication involving disabilities. Some lawsuits are filed against private organizations, whereas other lawsuits involve complaints and disputes against various components of the justice system. Regardless, both private and public entities must comply with the ADA. Although organizations may make their best effort to comply with the ADA, there are often times when confusion exists regarding its basic principles. Failing to comply with tenets of the ADA results in a variety of penalties. This chapter highlighted various truths and myths regarding the ADA.

Communicating with disabled individuals involves respect and dignity. Some folks may be amiable regarding such communication, whereas others may be uncomfortable. Regardless, personnel within the justice system must attempt to communicate effectively and efficiently with disabled individuals. This chapter provided some communications principles through which communicating with disabled individuals may be facilitated.

Terminology

Americans with Disabilities Act
Aphasia
Auxiliary resource
Blind
Braille
Deaf
Disability
Communication impairment
Head injury
Hearing impairment
Impairment
Mute
Penalty
Speech impairment
Stroke
Stutter
Translation
Vision impairment
Voice impairment

THOUGHT AND DISCUSSION QUESTIONS

1. This chapter introduced briefly a variety of impairments and disabilities that affect the communications process. Perform some research, and determine what other physical ailments may affect the communications process. Write a brief essay that highlights your findings. Within your response, incorporate discussion of how communications difficulties may be diminished or alleviated.
2. This chapter introduced some auxiliary resources that are used to embellish disability communications within the justice system. Perform some research regarding your local or state justice systems with respect to the types of auxiliary resources that are used to enhance disability communication. Write a brief essay

that highlights your findings. Within your response, provide some conclusions and recommendations regarding the disability communications of your chosen entity.

3. Perform some research regarding your local court system. Determine how it complies with the tenets of the ADA. Write a brief essay that highlights your findings.
4. Perform some research regarding your local law enforcement organization. Determine how it complies with the tenets of the ADA. Write a brief essay that highlights your findings.

References

Anderson, E., & Hilliard, T. (2005). Managing offenders with special health needs: Highest and best use strategies. *Corrections Today*, *67*(1), 58–61.

Bagley, C., & Savage, D. (2010). *Managers and the legal environment: Strategies for the 21st century* (p. 493). Mason, OH: Cengage Publishing.

Centers for Disease Control and Prevention. (2013a). Disability and functioning. Retrieved from http://www.cdc.gov/nchs/fastats/disable.htm (accessed September 20, 2013).

Centers for Disease Control and Prevention. (2013b). What is it like to not be able to see? Retrieved from http://www.cdc.gov/ncbddd/kids/vision.html (accessed September 21, 2013).

Iowa Department for the Blind. (2013). Independent living. Retrieved from http://www.blind.state.ia.us/publications/white-cane-magazine-spring-2010/departments (accessed September 21, 2013).

Johnson, C. (2011). Deaf Illinois inmates sue for access to interpreters. *Peoria Journal Star*. Retrieved from http://www.pjstar.com/free/x1067127716/Deaf-Illinois-inmates-sue-for-access-to-interpreters?zc_p=0 (accessed November 1, 2013).

Keller, H. (n.d.). Helen Keller quotes. Brainyquote. Retrieved from http://www.brainyquote.com/quotes/authors/h/helen_keller.html (accessed September 20, 2013).

March of Dimes. (2013). Hearing impairment. Retrieved from http://www.marchofdimes.com/baby/hearing-impairment.aspx (accessed September 21, 2013).

McCay, V. (1995). New rights for inmates with hearing loss. *Corrections Today*, *57*(2), 140.

Merriam-Webster Dictionary. (2013a). s.v. "blind." Retrieved from http://www.merriam-webster.com/dictionary/blindness (accessed September 21, 2013).

Merriam-Webster Dictionary. (2013b). s.v. "deaf." Retrieved from http://www.merriam-webster.com/dictionary/deafness (accessed September 20, 2013).

Merriam-Webster Dictionary. (2013c). s.v. "hoarse." Retrieved from http://www.merriam-webster.com/dictionary/hoarseness?show=0&t=1379820205 (accessed September 22, 2013).

Merriam-Webster Dictionary. (2013d). s.v. "mute." Retrieved from http://www.merriam-webster.com/dictionary/muteness (accessed September 23, 2013).

Merriam-Webster Dictionary. (2013e). s.v. "stutter." Retrieved from http://www.merriam-webster.com/dictionary/stutter (accessed September 22, 2013).

Miller, K. (2002). Population management strategies for deaf and hard-of-hearing offenders. *Corrections Today*, *64*(7), 90–93.

National Aphasia Association. (2013). Aphasia FAQ. Retrieved from http://www.aphasia.org/content/aphasia-faq (accessed September 22, 2013).

National Black Disability Coalition. (2013). Communication assistance device. Retrieved from http://www.blackdisability.org/content/communication-assistance-device (accessed November 1, 2013).

National Center for Learning Disabilities. (2013). Americans with Disabilities Act Amendments Act. Retrieved from http://www.ncld.org/disability-advocacy/learn-ld-laws/adaaa-section-504/americans-disabilities-act-amendments-act-adaaa (accessed November 1, 2013).

National Eye Institute. (2013). All vision impairment. National Institute of Health. Retrieved from http://www.nei.nih.gov/eyedata/vision_impaired.asp (accessed September 21, 2013).

National Institute on Deafness and Other Communication Disorders. (2013a). Aphasia. Retrieved from http://www.nidcd.nih.gov/health/voice/pages/aphasia.aspx (accessed September 22, 2013).

National Institute on Deafness and Other Communication Disorders. (2013b). Quick statistics. Retrieved from http://www.nidcd.nih.gov/health/statistics/Pages/quick.aspx (accessed September 21, 2013).

National Institute on Deafness and Other Communication Disorders. (2013c). Voice, speech, and language: Quick statistics. Retrieved from http://www.nidcd.nih.gov/health/statistics/vsl/Pages/stats.aspx (accessed September 22, 2013).

Prison Law Office. (2013). Major cases and achievements. Retrieved from http://www.prisonlaw.com/cases.php (accessed November 1, 2013).

Southeast ADA Center. (2013). ADA Amendments Act of 2008: Summary and resources. Retrieved from http://www.adasoutheast.org/ada/publications/adaaa_resources.doc (accessed November 1, 2013).

U.S. Department of Justice. (2013a). ADA best practices tool kit for state and local governments. Retrieved from http://www.ada.gov/pcatoolkit/chap3toolkit.htm (accessed October 31, 2013).

U.S. Department of Justice. (2013b). The Americans with Disabilities Act of 1990 and Revised ADA Regulations Implementing Title II and Title III. Retrieved from http://www.ada.gov/2010_regs.htm (accessed October 28, 2013).

U.S. Department of Justice. (2013c). Myths and facts about the Americans with Disabilities Act. Retrieved from http://www.ada.gov/archive/mythfact.htm (accessed November 2, 2013).

U.S. Department of Justice. (2013d). Settlement Agreement between the United States of America and Peroutka and Peroutka, P.A., under the Americans with Disabilities Act, DJ #202-35-207 and DJ #202-35-236. Retrieved from http://www.ada.gov/peroutka_sa.htm (accessed November 1, 2013).

U.S. Department of Labor. (2013). Americans with Disabilities Act. Retrieved from http://www.dol.gov/dol/topic/disability/ada.htm (accessed October 30, 2013).

U.S. Equal Employment Opportunity Commission. (2013a). The Americans with Disabilities Act of 1990. Retrieved from http://www.eeoc.gov/eeoc/history/35th/1990s/ada.html (accessed October 28, 2013).

U.S. Equal Employment Opportunity Commission. (2013b). Verizon to pay $20 million to settle nationwide EEOC disability suit. Retrieved from http://www.eeoc.gov/eeoc/newsroom/release/7-6-11a.cfm (accessed November 1, 2013).

Back to the Future
Communications Innovation and Emerging Concepts 19

> Of all of our inventions for mass communication, pictures still speak the most universally understood language.
>
> **—Walt Disney (Disney, n.d.)**

Objectives

The objectives of this chapter are to

- Introduce the concept of innovation
- Introduce the concept of cryptography
- Introduce the concept of steganography
- Introduce the concept of holography
- Introduce the concept of human connectivity
- Discuss communications innovation and emerging concepts

Introduction

The history of communication is diverse, and represents numerous inventions that have increased both the efficiency and effectiveness of communicating. Regardless of the invention or derivative thereof, the basic principles associated with the foundational communications process are unchanged. Basically, someone encodes and transmits a message to someone who receives and decodes the message. The receiver may supply some type of feedback regarding the received message. Communication is deemed successful if both the sender and the receiver have a mutual comprehension and understanding of concepts that are associated with the intended message. These notions permeate any fashion of communicating between humans regardless of the communications modality.

Numerous inventions and human cleverness have embellished communication modalities through the ages. The emergence of European cave art more than 30,000 years ago represents some of the earliest human capacities of "symbolization and communication" (Humphrey, 1999). The ancient Greeks used statues of notable individuals to express "a particular individual's exemplary embodiment of civic virtue" (Rutter & Sparkes, 2000). During modern times, statues are also used to express and convey messages. For example, in New York, the Statue of Liberty silently represents and communicates the "cultural attitudes and values of the United States regarding personal freedom and opportunity" (Samovar, Porter, & McDaniel, 2010). Throughout history, various optical signals were used to communicate. Examples include light and "smoke signals" (Coe, 1993).

Throughout history, humans have improved upon their inventions to yield a variety of innovative items that facilitate and embellish communication. The periods of communicating that necessitated months of ocean travel using wooden ships were reduced to the instantaneousness of the modern wonders of real-time cellular telephone conversations. Such innovativeness contributed toward the improvement of efficiency and effectiveness when communicating.

Innovation continues to herald new advances within the communications domain. The uses of electronic technology and information processing have greatly enhanced communication both openly and clandestinely. The applications of cryptography and steganography provide resources through which messages exist within other messages. Although the concepts of hidden communications are not new, the technologies used to instantiate clandestine communications now provide a plethora of methods through which messaging may be secretive.

Innovation has embellished the portability and convenience of communicating. Twenty years ago, most folks were dependent on their immobile, landline telephones as a primary method of conducting voice communication. Interactive smartphones now facilitate communication from anywhere and provide a variety of applications that users may access when communicating. These observations of mobility and portability show the magnitude of technological advancement through time.

Such notions highlight the relevance of innovation within the context of communicating. Although the basic concepts describing the communications process are unchanged throughout history, human innovation has improved the technologies and resources through which communication occurs. In any case, such innovation has improved the efficiency and effectiveness of communicating between factions. Although no one can foretell the future with certainty and accuracy, modern communications attributes will continue to experience innovation through which future communications improvements are generated. The purpose of this chapter is to explore such innovation.

Holography

The term holography is a derivative of the Greek roots "holos" and "graphos" that mean "whole message" (Massachusetts Institute of Technology, 2013). They may also be interpreted to mean "entire picture" (Ohio State University, 2013). Holography involves using the diffraction and interference properties of light to totally "reconstruct" an "object wave" (Ackermann & Eichlier, 2007). Holography represents a "process by which three-dimensional images can be stored and reproduced using laser light" (Massachusetts Institute of Technology, 2013). Essentially, holography represents "a technique which allows the recording and playback of three-dimensional images that offer the viewer the advantages of perspective, parallax, form and content" (Ohio State University, 2013). The basic concepts of holography are summarized as follows:

> A hologram is created when information about a scene is recorded in a very special way; holograms do not store visual images like ordinary photographs. Without the proper illumination, a hologram appears blank. However, when illuminated properly, the scene can be recreated in three dimensions. What is observed is not a psychological effect; this means that the light arriving from the hologram into the viewer's eyes is physically the same as the light that was emitted from the original scene. (Ohio State University, 2013)

A holographic image is presented in Figure 19.1.

Figure 19.1 Holographic image and image materials. (From Figure 5 from http://www.nature.com/nature/journal/v468/n7320/full/nature09521.html?pagewanted=al.)

The concept of holography is nothing new. During 1947, while attempting to "improve the resolution of an electron microscope," Dennis Gabor originated the holographic theory (Bellis, 2013). Gabor immersed himself in researching holography during the coming decades. As a result of his holography research, Gabor was awarded the Nobel Prize in physics during 1971 (Bellis, 2013). Gabor's experiments heralded research that may now be poised to affect an array of communications applications.

Holography has various implications for the communications domain via the notion of holographic communication in which real-time, three-dimensional imagery is used to embellish the communications process. Holographic communication is a relatively new field of research and development and is in its beginning stages. Eventually, it is hoped that communication may occur through the use of three-dimensional images of senders and receivers interacting mutually within the communications process.

Holography has matured greatly within a brief period. Initially, only static images were generated as holograms. Generating dynamic imagery that mimics video is much more challenging. A few years ago, researchers at the University of Arizona introduced a machine that was capable of refreshing a "holographic image once every few minutes—it took around three minutes to produce a single-colour image, followed by a minute to erase that image before a new one could be written into its place" (Jha, 2010). Later experimentation yielded technological improvements that significantly reduced the timing of refreshing holographic images. Instead of many minutes, the refresh rate was reduced to a period of "two seconds," including the use of "full color" (Jha, 2010). The improvements also included the instantiation of "parallax, whereby people looking at the image from different angles will see different views of the image, just as if they were looking at the original object" (Jha, 2010).

Canadian researchers also have generated promising results regarding technological advancements within the domain of holography. Researchers at Queen's University have developed video conferencing pods that allow "people in different locations to video conference as if they are standing in front of each other" (Queen's University, 2013). This holographic communication system involves multiple "life-size, cylindrical pods" that are used to project holographic images (Queen's University, 2013). The generated holographic image is visible for a full 360 degrees, and one can walk around the communications pod to see any view of the other person (Queen's University, 2013).

Much time will be required to refine and improve such devices and systems to facilitate communications affordably, practically, and conveniently. However, limited amounts of holographic imagery are currently used to communicate the authenticity of documents. Many credit cards contain holographic images as a method of deterring crime. Such holograms implement a "specially processed three-dimensional appearance that is extremely expensive and difficult to counterfeit" (City of Minneapolis, 2013). The authenticity of the credit card may be verified by tilting it among various angles, and viewing the holographic image (City of Minneapolis, 2013). Similarly, holograms may be embedded among police identification cards as a method of ensuring authenticity (Easy Id Card, 2013).

Dennis Gabor stated, "You can't predict the future but you can invent it" (Woodford, 2013). Certainly, the applications of holography will improve through the passing of time and continued research and development. Future applications may involve the generation of three-dimensional maps that may embellish the functions of crime mapping and evacuation route planning. Other future applications may involve the use of holographic images to verbally communicate portions of Park Ranger tours among national parks or to embellish training functions. Regardless, the future applications of holography are only limited by the human imagination.

Communication Technologies

Communication often necessitates forging the communications process across multiple cultures, boundaries, and languages to facilitate real-time conversations and messaging. Similarly, within a homogenous society, the communications process also exists to facilitate real-time communications. Given the advent and proliferation of globalism, communication across vast distances has also increased through time. In most all cases involving some consideration of physical distance, such communication involves the use of electronic computer networks.

Computer networking and communications technologies are the foundational backbones of modern communication. Landline telephone systems and mobile cell phones and smart phones all involve electronic communications involving switching, routing, encoding, decoding, and a myriad of other functions. Certainly, multimedia devices incorporate several electronic considerations associated with supporting verbal and visual data processing to support communication.

The modern instantiations of communications technology resulted from the historically cascading innovations and achievements of various generations of computing technologies. These generations are itemized as follows:

First generation: This generation encompassed approximately 1940 until 1956 (Goel, 2010, p. 4). Its primary technological foundation was vacuum tubes (Goel, 2010, p. 4). Examples include the Universal Automatic Computer (UNIVAC), Electronic Numerical Integrator and Calculator (ENIAC), and the Electronic Discrete Variable Automatic Computer (EDVAC) (Goel, 2010, p. 4). These machines were very large, and encompassed the space of entire rooms (Goel, 2010, p. 4). Their input mechanisms consisted of "punched cards and paper tapes" (Goel, 2010, p. 4).

Second generation: This generation encompassed approximately 1956 until 1963 (Goel, 2010, p. 5). Transistors were the foundational basis of this technology (Goel, 2010, p. 5). Examples of this generation include the PDP-8 and the IBM 1401 (Goel, 2010, p. 5). Because transistors were smaller than vacuum tubes, the physical size of the computing machines was greatly reduced (Goel, 2010, p. 5). These machines were programmed using assembly language (Goel, 2010, p. 5).

Third generation: This generation encompassed the period between 1964 and 1971 (Goel, 2010, p. 5). Integrated circuitry was the technological foundation of this generation of computing (Goel, 2010, p. 5). The overall size of these computing devices was again greatly reduced because of miniaturization (Goel, 2010, p. 5). Examples of this generation included the PDP 11. Input and output devices consisted of keyboards and monitors (Goel, 2010, p. 5). Again, the computational speed of these devices was greatly improved when compared with the computational speeds of predecessors.

Fourth generation: This generational period of computing began in 1971 and represents the characteristics of modern computing (Goel, 2010, p. 5). The technological foundation of this generation involves the use of microprocessors (Goel, 2010, p. 5). Some arguments persist about whether it has matured into a fifth generation. During 1981, Japanese researchers announced a development program to explore fifth-generation computing involving artificial intelligence, database management, human–computer interaction, and very-large-scale integration (Gaines, 1984).

These advancements in computer potential occurred over approximately seventy years of research and development. They occurred in conformance to Moore's law, which expresses the notion that "the density of silicon chips doubles every eighteen months" (Null & Nabor, 2012). Another perspective of Moore's law expresses the notion that performance of computing power has the potential of doubling every eighteen months (*The Economist*, 2011). However, there may be limitations to the traditional concepts of Moore's law. The economic and financial costs associated with producing such technological advancements also increase accordingly. This notion is expressed by Rock's law, which states, "the cost of capital equipment to build semiconductors will double every four years" (Null & Nabor, 2012). Furthermore, physical limitations may constrain future patterns of miniaturization that are normally associated with Moore's law. Given these notions, future advancements in the electronics that comprise modern digital communications systems may be constrained through time.

Given the tenets posed by both Moore's law and Rock's law, much speculation exists regarding the characteristics of future communications technologies that will improve the ability to communicate. Computing devices are now found in practically every facet of modern communications technologies. Microprocessors are found everywhere, ranging from smart phones to satellite communication systems. Computing devices represent the basis of future communications technologies. Only time will divulge the attributes of future communications technologies.

The power of smart phone technology is expected to increase through time. Personal characteristics of the owner of the smart phone may store "credit card, debit card, identification and membership information" within the memory of the personal communications device (Marsan, 2011). Furthermore, smart phones are expected "to instantaneously over a next-generation network" interact with databases that both interpret and react to queries in the native language of the user (Marsan, 2011).

These potential advancements have implications for policing. Currently, law enforcement personnel and members of the justice system access a variety of databases and interact with people using multiple languages. Although many law enforcement vehicles are now equipped with computer terminals through which numerous database queries are made, they are stationary within the vehicle. Smart phones are highly mobile and portable, and may be carried anywhere. Therefore, law enforcement personnel may someday have the capability of accessing information quickly and instantly from any location through such communication devices. Furthermore, because of improved language abilities, it is not infeasible that such devices could be used as portable language translators. Such devices would be useful both among court environments and among field patrol settings.

Future advancements in communications technology will undoubtedly be incorporated within the law enforcement domain. During the early twentieth century, August Vollmer had a visionary perspective of communications technology in the law enforcement domain and introduced radio communications systems to embellish law enforcement operations. Vollmer's original vision now is common among all law enforcement agencies. Similarly, modern visions of communications technologies have the potential of affecting future law enforcement operations and organizations commensurately. As new communications technologies are developed, refined, and made available publically, they will be adapted and integrated among law enforcement settings in due time.

Natural Language Processing

Natural language processing (NLP) is defined as "a theoretically motivated range of computational techniques for analyzing and representing naturally occurring texts at one or more levels of linguistic analysis for the purpose of achieving human-like language processing for a range of tasks or applications" (Liddy, 2001). Essentially, in simple terms, this definition indicates that NLP is a research field that is devoted to facilitating communication via computing devices using natural languages (e.g., English or Spanish) to perform a variety of tasks. Therefore, as well as typing on a keyboard to enter data into a computing device using written language, one would interact with the device using spoken language. NLP also has connotations associated with similarly processing written communication.

The use of NLP has the potential of affecting communication within the law enforcement domain. Law enforcement organizations process a vast quantity of written reports daily that contain information regarding a variety of incidents (e.g., facts of the incident) and that contain administrative data (e.g., time of day, reporting officer, and contact information). Creating these reports often involves a combination of written and verbal communication. Orally questioning victims is an essential method of gaining data regarding the incident. This data is generally transcribed within a police report.

Within such contexts, NLP is used as a method of extracting information from law enforcement incident reports. The extraction of information serves the purpose of obtaining "specific, predefined entities from texts" (Ku, Iriberri, & Leroy, 2008). Using electronic and computer technologies, extraction methods consist of leveraging artificial intelligence and neural networks, lexical analysis, statistical analysis, Markov models, and machine learning (Ku, Iriberri, & Leroy, 2008).

Although a report may be taken, it may have a variety of defects. The handwriting of the reporting officer may be illegible. Law enforcement officers may incorrectly transcribe data, may accidently interject spelling or grammatical errors, or may accidentally mark an incorrect checkbox within report forms. Basically, humans are imperfect creations, and may reflect such imperfection within the communications process. Additionally, ambiguity may exist within the incident report. The use of NLP may be influenced by communications errors that result from such imperfection. Therefore, NLP is not a perfect method of parsing and processing natural language communications within the justice domain.

Regardless, the collection of data via NLP methods is useful within the justice domain. Data and information obtained through the NLP parsing of incident reports may be used for a variety of purposes, ranging from database construction and queries to establishing a case history that may be accessed immediately during future periods. It is used to create charts and graphs, and provide inputs for statistical analysis. It may also be used to support crime mapping activities and to enhance presentations and briefings regarding crime issues that influence communities. Figure 19.2 shows a typical NLP process through which such resulting uses are facilitated.

Figure 19.2 shows a method through which information is extracted using the NLP paradigm. Information from incident reports is parsed to eventually generate output that may be used within spreadsheets, presentations, and written forms of communication. In essence, it may be viewed conceptually as a form of paraphrasing in which selected excerpts and words are taken from input received from incident reports. Throughout this process of

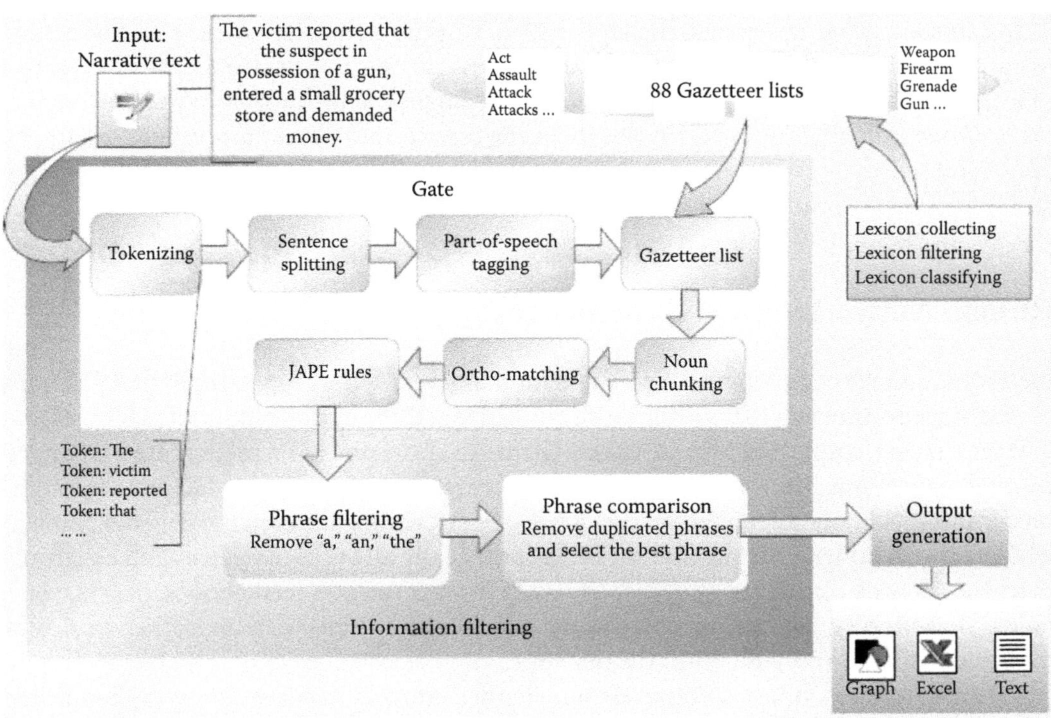

Figure 19.2 Natural language processing. (From http://www.academia.edu/334638/Natural_Language_Processing_and_E- Government_Crime_Information_Extraction_From_Heterogeneous_Data_Sources.)

extracting information, it must be noted that a goal of processing language exists instead of a goal of understanding language. Machines are incapable of understanding; it is only something that is accomplishable currently only by sentient, living beings.

These notions are expressed within the primary goal of NLP: "to accomplish human-like language processing" (Liddy, 2001). Although machines are currently unable to understand natural language, achieving such a goal is being pursued within the domain of artificial intelligence and NLP research and development. Achieving this goal involves a consideration of the following: (1) paraphrasing an input text, (2) translating the "text into another language," (3) answering "questions about the contents of the text," and (4) drawing inferences regarding the text (Liddy, 2001). Much progress has been made regarding the first three items. However, the fourth item, inference, is complex. Currently, "NLP systems cannot, of themselves, draw inferences from text" (Liddy, 2001). Certainly, much more research and development is necessary before NLP systems can boast of inference and understanding of language.

Despite the advances in NLP research and development, a "full understanding" of text is desirable within future NLP systems (Liddy, 2001, p. 4). Regarding such future attributes, knowledge about the "real world" is essential concerning the ability to "understand the participant's goals and beliefs" when communicating via NLP systems (Liddy, 2001, p. 4). The characteristics of "speech acts, conversation, and discourse structure" are also necessary (Liddy, 2001, p. 4). Such an understanding is essential in establishing a contextual awareness regarding the communication activity and the communication domain.

The potential future applications of NLP within the justice domain may be varied. Law enforcement personnel may be able to query databases through the use of speech. Translators may be developed through which language translation may occur almost instantaneously. Such devices may be very useful during the field operations of patrol officers when encountering individuals who lack English skills or that have poor English skills. Other potential uses may involve dictating reports into transcription systems. In any case, NLP represents a technological avenue that may have promise for improving future law enforcement communications activities.

Human Networking and Cybernetics

Electronic computer networks have existed for many years. They represent both collections of machines and devices that are physically linked together and collections of machines and devices that are connected by wireless mechanisms. Data and information are exchanged through communications technology infrastructures. These constructs facilitate the communications of law enforcement officers whether performing duties in the field or stationed within office settings. During modern times, practically all types of devices and electronic machines may be connected to or disconnected from networks—cell phones, pagers, computers, monitoring devices, cameras—and may communicate with any other device or machine that is connected within the network.

During modern times, some question whether humans may eventually be connected via some type of futuristic network paraphernalia. Although some may consider such a question to be haughty and laughable, it is not meritless. Near the end of the 1990s, some research investigated the potential of linking together humans, via the surgical implantation of electronic chips, to facilitate network connectivity.

The most notable experiments of such endeavors involved Dr. Kevin Warwick of the University of Reading. During 1998, his initial research involved "the neuro-surgical implantation of a device (Utah Array/BrainGate) into the median nerves of his left arm in order to link his nervous system directly to a computer to assess the latest technology for use with the disabled" (Warwick, 2013). As a result of this experiment, Warwick gained the ability of operating "doors, lights, heaters, and other computers without lifting a finger" (Warwick, 2013). The primary purpose of this experiment was to "determine whether information could be transmitted to and from an implant" (Wired, 2000). The outcomes of this initial experiment showed success.

Warwick attempted a second experiment involving surgically implanted electronic devices that were linked directly with his nervous system. During 2002, he experienced the implantation of an array of one hundred electrodes within his left arm (The University of Reading, 2013). This implant allowed him to control "an electric wheelchair and an intelligent artificial hand" (The University of Reading, 2013). His wife also voiced a desire to have a similar device implanted within her body (The University of Reading, 2013). A purpose of this experiment also involved examining the characteristics of communications between these implanted devices (The University of Reading, 2013).

Cybernetics is defined as the "science of communication and control theory that is concerned especially with the comparative study of automatic control systems (as the nervous system and brain and mechanical–electrical communication systems)" (*Merriam-Webster*, 2013a). Within the cybernetics domain, the experiments of Warwick further various facets of communications knowledge. Such experiments showed that communication may occur to and from electronic devices that are implanted within humans. Warwick's experiments were revolutionary because they represented the first integration of electronic implants with the human nervous system in which facets of communication were investigated.

Only time will tell the future of such research and any developments that may occur and result from the investigative processes of inquiry. However, these initial experiments are interesting because they may eventually lead to new breakthroughs and products that may improve the quality of life for many individuals. Warwick's first experiment successfully showed that information could be communicated to and from an implanted device. This observation of communication may form the basis for initiating research that investigates the uses of such devices among people with disabilities.

Within the United States, approximately 189 law enforcement officers are assaulted daily when performing their duties (American Police Hall of Fame, 2013). A study of law enforcement personnel, which investigated law enforcement retirements in the years 2003 and 2005, showed that approximately 13% of these retirements were because of disabilities cumulatively (Morrison, 2013). Many of these personnel experience injuries that may result in different amounts of paralysis.

By examining whether information may be transmitted to and from an implanted electronic device, Warwick's research may open new avenues of restoring some personal freedom and independence for such individuals. Through the implantation of such electronic devices, disabled individuals could possibly perform a variety of tasks unaided, ranging from controlling the environmental features of their homes (e.g., lighting or heating) to manipulating robotic arms or legs. Certainly, only the passing of time will tell whether such visionary devices become common realities. Figure 19.3 shows Dr. Warwick and a robotic arm that was controlled through such implants.

Figure 19.3 Dr. Kevin Warwick and a robotic arm. (From http://www.kevinwarwick.com/.)

Demonstrating the ability to communicate to and from an implanted electronic device also has other implications, one of which involves the notion that humans may eventually be connected together as networked nodes. Such a construct would facilitate the communication of information directly between humans effortlessly. Warwick describes such a scenario as follows (BBC News, 2013):

> What is commonly thought of as telepathy will, I have no doubt, be achieved this century. Instead of communicating by speech as we do presently, we'll be able to think to each other, simply by implants connected to our nervous system linking our brains electronically together, possibly even over the Internet. That will completely change what it means to be human. We won't need the languages that we presently do, we'll need a new language of ideas and concepts in order to communicate thoughts from brain to brain.

These comments may be considered from the perspective of law enforcement organizations and personnel. Instead of relying on radios or telephone systems, personnel could communicate among themselves through mere thoughts. If an officer needed assistance, then someone could be summoned practically instantaneously. During shift meetings or administrative briefings, information could be disseminated to a mass audience efficiently and effectively.

Many officers are either killed or harmed in the line of duty annually. For those whose bodies are maimed and result in disabilities, the use of such communication devices may facilitate medical advancements through which paralysis may be abated. For instance, during future periods, signals from the human brain may be transmitted to electronic devices that may be implanted within arms, legs, or digits (Rodriguez, Weissberg, & Loeb, 2007). These transmissions of data may facilitate the animation of human appendages (Rodriguez, Weissberg, & Loeb, 2007).

The integration of humans and machines in such a fashion would usher an initial generation of cyborgs that communicate through the use of implanted electronic devices. However, some may have moral or ethical reservations regarding the implantation and use of such devices. Regardless, the research of Warwick provides a foundational basis from which such networked communication may eventually become feasible and practical between humans.

Public Safety and Awareness

Street lights are common across the nation. They provide lighting at night unceasingly and during periods when lighting conditions are poor (e.g., storms), and may be underappreciated by most citizens. Within the United States, street lamps were introduced by Benjamin Franklin (Isaacson, 2003). The street lamps of Franklin's time were relatively simple constructs that used only candles for illumination (Franklin, 1790). Through the years, street lamp constructs and designs improved to accommodate gas, kerosene, and electric means of illumination. Regardless of the historical period, street lamps have served a valuable public service function of providing illumination to improve public safety.

Modern times exhibit a myriad of street lamps across the nation. Although some may be simple constructs in which lighting is the sole function of the lamp, many newer versions of street lamps provide a range of tools, including communication devices. One of the most robust street lamp designs is that of Intellistreets. This street lamp mechanism not only provides street lighting but also facilitates communication for public awareness and public warning functions. The Intellistreet construct is presented within Figure 19.4.

The Intellistreets system is unique and is the only street lamp system of its type globally (Intellistreets, 2013). The system is controlled via Internet communications across computer networks (Intellistreets, 2013). It provides a means of communicating quickly with pedestrians in public areas (Intellistreets, 2013). The Intellistreets system facilitates communication during periods of both emergencies and daily, routine conditions. Specifically, it contains "amber strobe lights that can guide people along detour or evacuation routes during emergencies" (Intellistreets, 2013). Additionally, if a pedestrian needs assistance, interactive communication is facilitated by a "two-way connection to a 9-1-1 dispatcher, the person's location is mapped for the dispatcher and responding law enforcement, and activates a camera that will record any potential criminal activity in the vicinity of the pole" (Intellistreets, 2013). Therefore, communication may be unidirectional or bidirectional depending on the situation.

These communication abilities embellish public safety. Although the digital signage contained within the Intellistreets system may be used for advertising or artistic purposes, it may be converted to display public service announcements when necessary (Pittman, 2013). Similarly, Intellistreets contains an audio system that may normally broadcast news or music. However, during any period of emergency, the audio system may also be converted to broadcast audibly and communicate public safety messages (Pittman, 2013).

The financial cost of the Intellistreets system may be expensive for many municipalities. Although street lamps may be funded through taxation, various grant programs are available through which intelligent lighting systems may be purchased. Examples of such programs include grant funds that may be obtained from the Department of Homeland Security, grant funding from the National Science Foundation, and Community Development Block Grants (Intellistreets, 2013). In some cases, funding may be available from "local energy commissions" (Intellistreets, 2013).

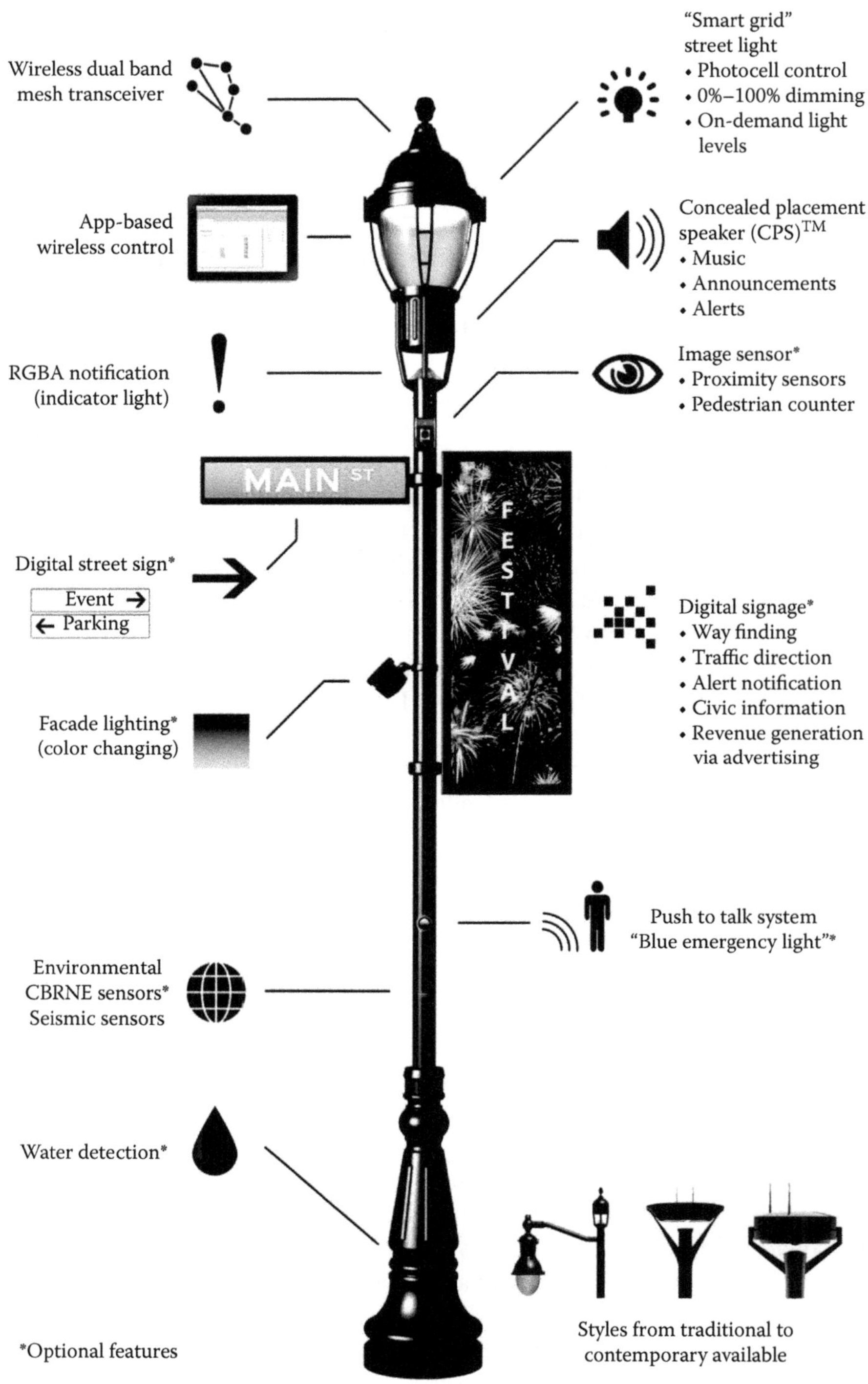

Figure 19.4 Intellistreets device. (From http://intellistreets.com/.)

The Intellistreet system bolsters the ability of municipalities to reduce crime and to maintain societal order. These goals are both traditional goals of policing. Pedestrians may summon assistance and invoke bidirectional communication when the presence of law enforcement is required at or near the scene of an incident. Law enforcement entities may monitor the scene of an incident through the camera and audio components of the Intellistreet system.

The Intellistreets system represents a method of embellishing public safety through the ability to communicate between pedestrians and law enforcement entities. It also represents an attempt to reduce or avert crime through the lighting of public areas. Some research studies show that crime may be reduced by the implementation of "improved street lighting" (Farrington & Welsh, 2002). However, other studies show that criminal activity may adapt to the improved lighting conditions and may exhibit different levels of crime displacement (Clarke, 2008). Regardless, the Intellistreets system represents a mechanism through which not only illumination is provided for public areas but also public safety communication occurs.

Steganography

Steganography is the "art or practice of concealing a message, image, or file within another message, image, or file" (*Merriam-Webster*, 2013b). It is derived from the Greek language, and means "covered writing" (Berry, 2008, p. 23). Essentially, steganography represents a method of hiding messages within communications without the concealed message being conspicuously or blatantly obvious to observers. This method of concealment has been used avidly for approximately 2500 years within communications environments representing "military, diplomatic, personal, and intellectual property applications" (Judge, 2001). One of the most famous and recognizable instances of steganography occurred during World War II when Navajo code talkers were used to communicate militarily using their native language (Berry, 2008, p. 24).

Within modern digital environments, steganography may be incorporated in two methods: least significant bit method and the frequency domain encoding method. The least significant bit method involves changing the lowest level of data within computer image files, and is the "most popular" method of concealment regarding "encoded images" (Rice University, 2013). Using this method, the least significant bits of image files are changed, but not so much as to alter the physical viewing of the image to indicate that a secret message is present within the file. For example, within a "24-bit image, 3 bytes are used for each pixel, so each pixel could encode 3 bits of a secret message" (Rice University, 2013). In this case, "the altered image would look identical to the human eye, even when compared to the original" (Rice University, 2013).

The frequency domain encoding method involves the use of advanced mathematics to facilitate the encoding of concealed items. It uses a two-dimensional (2-D) fast Fourier transform (FFT) "of the container image" (Rice University, 2013). This method is summarized as follows:

> The 2-D FFT separates the frequencies of the image into rings centered around an axis. Those rings closest to the axis represent the low frequencies of the image, and those furthest away represent the high frequencies. In the frequency domain encoding method, the secret message is encoded in the middle frequencies of the image. This is done by converting the message text to bits and overlaying these bits in a ring shape in the desired frequency band on the 2-D FFT. (Rice University, 2013)

Visual, oral, and written communications methods are not the only forms of steganography. Auditory methods also exist. Because digital audio communications are composed of bits, the least significant bit method may also be employed to conceal messages within audio transmissions (Jayaram, Ranganatha, & Anupama, 2011). Examples of other audio concealment steganographic processes include parity coding and phase coding. Within parity coding, messages are hidden within the parity bits of audio files. Within phase coding, "the phase of an initial audio segment" is replaced "with a reference phase that represents the secret information" (Jayaram, Ranganatha, & Anupama, 2011). Regardless of the concealment process, the goal of auditory steganography involves generating audio communication in which the hidden message is imperceptible when sounds are heard by human listeners.

This text represents an introductory discourse in communications. Therefore, it is beyond the scope of the discussions herein to explain the foundational concepts of advanced mathematics from which the least significant bit, parity bit, and FFT paradigms are derived. Readers desiring a greater knowledge of these foundations are encouraged to peruse other texts in calculus, differential equations, and electronic data communications.

Regardless of the method employed to conceal data and information among audio, visual, or digital media, the basic concept of steganograpy involves hiding a message imperceptibly within a seemingly innocuous entity. Messages to be concealed are integrated with an original cover message, via some steganographic process involving an encryption key, to generate a stego file representing an entity that seems normal when viewed or heard (Jayaram, Ranganatha, & Anupama, 2011). Figure 19.5 shows this concept (Meghanathan, 2013).

The stego file represents an entity in which a message is hidden via the process of steganography. Upon initial inspection or a cursory examination, the stego file may appear to be normal. Essentially, images and sounds may appear to be normal when viewed or heard. Similarly, when applying steganography to written communications, a seemingly innocuous message may be observed that conceals a hidden message.

The extraction of concealed messages may be accomplished through an algorithmic process. Implementing this process "should be possible without the cover," and "can be applied on any cover, whether or not it contains a secret message" (Meghanathan, 2013). The messages contained within stego files may be read by conducting this algorithmic process. Figure 19.6 shows this concept (Meghanathan, 2013).

During modern times, steganography exists in various fashions and is used for a variety of purposes. Contemporary uses of steganography are usually associated with digital

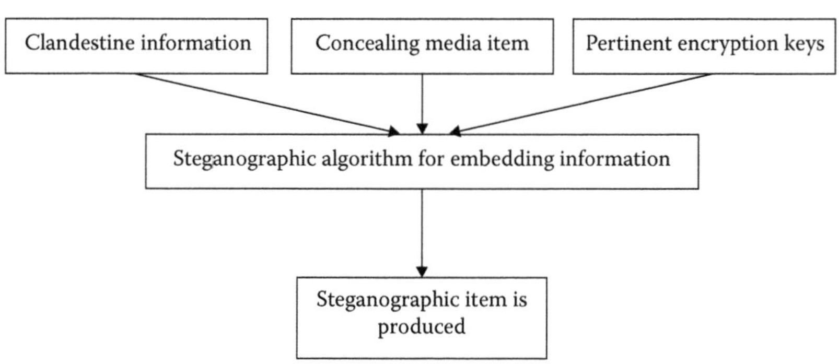

Figure 19.5 Steganography.

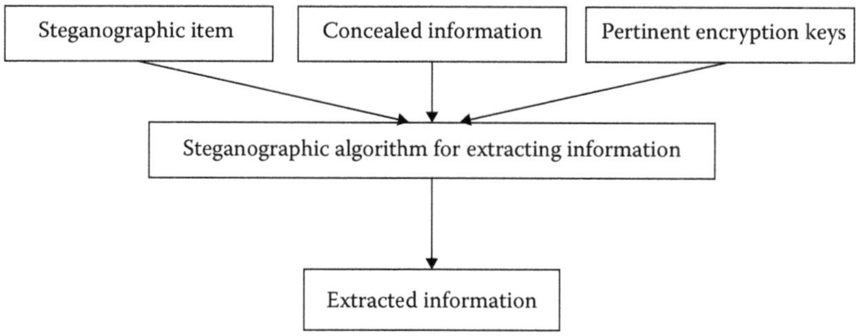

Figure 19.6 Steganography extraction.

and electronic forms of media and communication (Bennett, 2004). Certainly, legal uses of steganography are most appropriate to accommodate numerous products and services. The use of steganography may diminish instances of digital piracy and counterfeiting through the embellishment of copyright markings (Research and Markets, 2009). Legitimate, future uses of steganography may include the following:

> In the future, digital camera manufacturers could implement steganographic features as a part of camera firmware to annotate pictures with the photographer's copyright information. Camcorder manufacturers could also follow suit and implement steganography and watermarking techniques for protecting video content captured on camcorders and video cameras. Going forward, legitimate applications such as tagging of multimedia content with hidden information could become an important application area for steganography. (Research and Markets, 2009)

Steganography also is used for illicit purposes ranging from transmitting messages among criminal factions to facilitating the communications of international espionage. During the course of its activities, al Qaeda was discovered to have used steganography to facilitate clandestinely its organizational communications. During 2011, in Berlin, Germany, hidden messages were found within a pornographic video that was possessed by a member of the terrorist organization (Gallagher, 2012). A total of "141 separate text files" were discovered within the video that discussed the operations of the terrorist organization, including materials discussing some of its planned future operations (Gallagher, 2012).

Steganography was also used by Anna Chapman and her group of Russian spies. They partially evaded the National Security Agency (NSA) by encoding "secret text messages in image files, which they then placed on websites" (Stokes, 2010). When communicating across computer networks involving the Internet, the network messaging appeared as though it were "normal HTTP traffic" (Stokes, 2010). Because of steganography, it was difficult for methods of data mining to detect and "extract truly reliable signals from even a relatively high-quality, carefully curated dataset" (Stokes, 2010). Despite the efforts of the NSA to parse communications to investigate language patterns for potential threats, this use of steganography concealed messages within what appeared to be innocuous communication.

The basic concept of communicating via steganography represents the old adage of hiding in plain sight. Simply, secret messages are concealed and communicated within surface messages that appear to be nonchalant and innocuous. Both legal and illegal uses of steganography permeate communications globally, internationally, and nationally. Regardless of its use, steganography represents a powerful form of communicating clandestinely, and has implications for national security as well as for ensuring the legitimacy of products and services within an economy.

Innovators

Resources and technologies do not magically appear from thin air. After all, there is no such thing as spontaneous generation. Modern communications technologies are the result of many years of researching, developing, testing, and improving them through time. Although necessity is deemed to be the mother of invention, many visionary people often are enlightened to explore an existing product or resource, and find ways of making it better. Thus far, other than the consideration of Dr. Kevin Warwick, the discussions of this chapter have focused on products and services, and have not emphasized people. However, it is people that contrive the various and sundry innovations through which acts of communicating may be improved. Historically, within the domain of policing, two such individuals were August Vollmer and John Edgar Hoover.

August Vollmer

Any consideration of innovation in policing would be incomplete without introducing the visionary accomplishments of August Vollmer. This individual is often acknowledged as the father of modern American policing because of his foresight and innovation that greatly improved the efficiency and effectiveness of law enforcement organizations. Vollmer served as the Berkeley, California, Chief of Police between 1905 and 1932 (Dempsey & Forst, 2010). He crafted and implemented numerous programs and resources that changed and improved policing during the twentieth century, many of which continue to influence modern law enforcement organizations. From the perspective of communication, examples of Vollmer's contributions to policing communications are itemized below:

- 1906—Developed a "centralized police records system, one of the first in the United States" (Dinkelspiel, 2010).
- 1914—Vollmer mandated the use of "radio communications between officers" (Dinkelspiel, 2010).
- 1921—Became the "first chief to use the lie detector in investigations" (Dinkelspiel, 2010).
- 1928—First chief to develop and implement a radio system for patrol cars (Petherick, Turvey, & Ferguson, 2010).

The historical accomplishments of Vollmer influenced policing during the twentieth century. Through time, his innovations were integrated among law enforcement organizations throughout the nation, and they remain vital characteristics of modern policing. For example, the Hagerstown (Maryland) Police Department uses a centralized records system that facilitates "police records maintenance, control, and retrieval" (City of Hagerstown,

2013). The use of such a system contributes toward the payroll, personnel, reporting, arrest, and budgeting function of the organization (City of Hagerstown, 2013).

During modern times, radio communication is an integral component of policing. Vollmer's experiment with radio communication provided a foundation for communicating quickly, efficiently, and effectively that is now both a common and indispensable police capability. Law enforcement vehicles are equipped with radio systems through which personnel may communicate with dispatchers and other personnel. Additionally, law enforcement officers often wear portable radio systems that provide communication. Such uses of radio communications within the policing domain are attributable to the innovativeness of Vollmer.

Vollmer also introduced polygraphs within policing. During modern times, polygraphs are often used during the questioning of suspects and are generally used as a tool during the personnel hiring process of law enforcement organizations. Although polygraph examination outcomes are not admissible in court, a confession is most certainly admissible within court settings (Iacono, 2008). Generally, polygraph examinations are constructed to elicit some form of a confession from individuals who are truly guilty of a crime (Iacono, 2008). However, because of validity concerns and a lack of empirical evidence to support polygraphs, it must be noted that polygraphs do not represent "the ultimate arbiter of truthfulness" (Iacono, 2008). Despite such concerns and imperfections, the use of polygraphs continues to increase within the justice domain (Iacono, 2008).

Vollmer's insight and vision were outstanding for his time. Few, if any, fellow officers probably could conceptualize and realize the potential of communications devices within the context of policing. Because of Vollmer, future generations of law enforcement were affected by communication technologies. Although technology has changed with time, the basic concepts introduced by Vollmer (e.g., radio communication) are an integral aspect of modern policing.

Through time, technologies will change. However, the basic notion of the communication process is unchanging. Vollmer successfully leveraged the technology of his time to facilitate law enforcement communications. In due time, when technology changes and new devices are invented, the justice domain will adapt them to satisfy its communications needs just as Vollmer did most innovatively.

John Edgar Hoover

Regarding the domain of communications, another individual that influenced the justice system was John Edgar Hoover. During 1917, he entered government service and became an assistant to the attorney general in 1918 (Federal Bureau of Investigation, 2013b). During 1919, he became the chief of the General Intelligence Division, which later was a component of the Bureau of Investigation (The J. Edgar Hoover Foundation, 2013). He was appointed to the position of acting director of the Bureau of Investigation in 1924 (The J. Edgar Hoover Foundation, 2013). For approximately 48 years, Hoover maintained his leadership position until his death in 1972 (The J. Edgar Hoover Foundation, 2013). During this tenure, Hoover leveraged a variety of media communications to build the public images of himself and the FBI, and to influence public opinions and perceptions.

Communicating through media resources is a method of behavioral adjustment and influencing public perceptions. Media communications were leveraged as a method of influencing public mindsets and projecting Hoover's image as a lawman nationally. Beginning in 1935, an array of *G-MAN* movies were produced that heralded J. Edgar Hoover as "Public Hero Number One" and that portrayed the bureau as an independent, capable organization (Bardsley, 2013a). Such communications were designed to positively influence public perceptions of the bureau and Hoover, and to cast criminality negatively.

Other media communications outlets were advantageously leveraged by Hoover and the bureau. Hoover leveraged newspaper photograph opportunities to show the potency of the bureau and to further strengthen his public image. For example, he "rushed to New York for the photo opportunity when the New York City Police Commissioner announced the arrest of Bruno Hauptmann" despite the fact that the "bureau had done almost nothing on the case" (Bardsley, 2013a). However, the American public was swayed to "believe that master detective J. Edgar Hoover had triumphed once again" (Bardsley, 2013a).

His leveraging of other media communications outlets included a failed *G-MAN* radio show, and both a "comic strip and pulp magazines glorifying the FBI" (Bardsley, 2013a). By leveraging the media and capitalizing on various law enforcement successes, Hoover was perceived as "a national hero and a force to be reckoned with" (Bardsley, 2013a). During his leadership of the bureau, numerous wanted posters were also disseminated to communicate the characteristics of wanted individuals. For example, wanted posters were disseminated regarding many gangsters, including John Dillinger. Figure 19.7 shows Dillinger's poster (Federal Bureau of Investigation, 2013a).

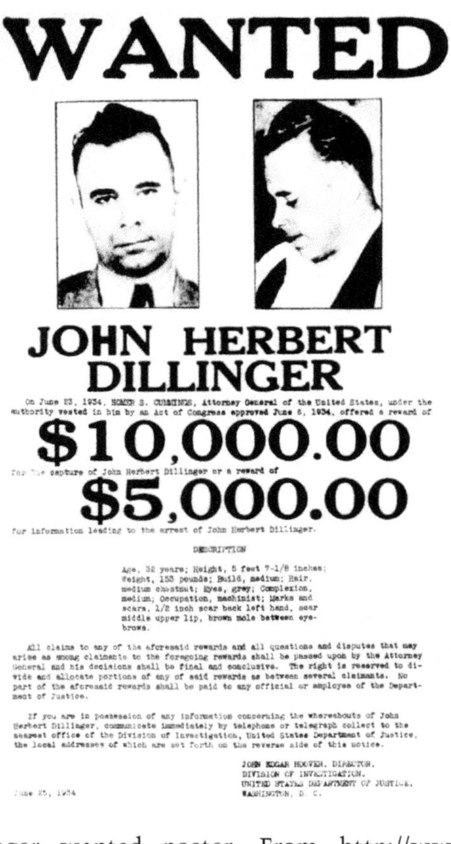

Figure 19.7 John Dillinger wanted poster. From http://www.fbi.gov/about-us/history/famous-cases/john-dillinger.)

Often, for security purposes, it is necessary to not release information publically through media communication outlets. Instead, public ignorance and communications silence are necessary to accomplish the goals and objective of criminal investigations and law enforcement operations. Hoover also implemented news blackouts and communications silence when necessary. An account of such actions, during World War II, is stated as follows (Bardsley, 2013b):

> A stroke of luck gave the Bureau a terrific publicity opportunity to create a myth of invincibility. In June of 1942, a Coast Guard patrolman saw four men struggling in a raft near Amagansett, Long Island. The men called themselves fishermen, but the patrolman was suspicious and reported the incident to his superiors. When the FBI got wind of it the next day, the Coast Guard had already found explosives, as well as German uniforms and cigarettes. The four men and the submarine that landed them were gone. Hoover was worried about sabotage and even the beginning of a military invasion, so with FDR's concurrence, he ordered a news blackout of the story and the largest manhunt in FBI history. The four men had split up and obtained hotel rooms in New York City. At that point, the leader of the four, George J. Dasch, told his partner Ernst P. Berger that he had no intention of carrying out his sabotage mission because he really preferred the American cause. Berger agreed with him and wanted to take off with the $84,000 the German military had given them. Instead Dasch took the money and eventually got in to see Hoover. Not only did he turn over the funds to the FBI, but also he was an excellent source of information on the sabotage training he and his colleagues received and the sabotage targets they were given. Also, he identified seven other colleagues that were in on the venture, who were eventually arrested. Hoover refused to give out the details of this sensational story, preferring to let the Germans think that their intelligence networks were compromised by FBI agents instead of George Dasch's voluntary betrayal of his mission. (Bardsley, 2013b)

Hoover also used media communication in other ways. Before the commencement of the 1919 Red Scare and the 1920 Palmer Raids, Hoover and the bureau attempted to sway public opinions and perceptions "against the radical supporters (whether aliens or citizens) of the Bolshevik Revolution" and regarding the threat of communism (Theoharis, Poveda, Rosenfeld, & Powers, 1999). Such media communications efforts included propaganda representing "news releases to the mass media," the dissemination of a *General Intelligence Bulletin*, and "sensational government-sponsored films that used silent movie melodramas to dramatize the heroism of the Bureau of Investigation operatives who foiled the plots of bomb-throwing radicals" (Theoharis et al., 1999). Hoover issued numerous media releases that predicted a "communist uprising in the United States" before the Palmer Raids occurred (Cunningham, 2006). These actions left a lasting impression within the minds of Americans (Theoharis et al., 1999).

Hoover successfully leveraged the communications technologies, resources, and media of his time. His actions influenced the practice of enforcing law and accomplished the swaying public opinion. During future time, law enforcement leaders will also leverage their available technologies to achieve similar results. The primary goals of law enforcement are unchanging: maintaining societal order and diminishing criminality. However, the communications resources through which these goals are accomplished will change in the future. Regardless of the technological advancements that may be manifested, the leaders of law enforcement organizations will adapt them to accomplish their goals and objectives.

Commentary Regarding Innovation and Emerging Concepts

This chapter introduced only a few of the products, services, and people that are associated with the concepts of communications innovation and emerging concepts. Certainly, there are many, many more that influence the civilian and law enforcement domains of communication. Although the examples and discussions contained within this chapter span an array of different concepts, there is some commonness therein: knowledge, networking, opportunity, innovation, and humans. Such commonness represents the foundational aspects of entrepreneurship and innovation with respect to the emergence of technologies, products, and services (Desai, Nijkamp, & Stough, 2011).

At some point in time, someone had an idea that they desired to bring to fruition. One may have had an epiphany regarding either an existing product or service or had an idea for something entirely new. Regardless, making the intangible vision into a realistic product or service required much effort, many resources, and various amounts of time. In any case, communication is a necessary aspect of such transference of messages between the mind of an individual and others in the physical world.

Anyone exhibiting an entrepreneurial vision should possess some amount of communication skills. The ability to communicate is the foundation of expressing concepts and ideas succinctly and clearly. This ability enhances the communication prowess of someone to create service and product requirements, blueprints and design documents, technical documents, and business plans. It underlies the creation of legal documents that pertain to new products and services, and is useful when drafting copyright and patent documentation. Communication "brings together" multiple parties toward achieving a common goal and facilitates "interdisciplinary cooperation" that is necessary for achieving success (Krueger, 2002). Essentially, communication permeates all facets of entrepreneurship regarding both new and emerging services and products.

Innovative concepts, ideas, and emerging services and products all are the subjects of much critical analysis. At times, one may examine condescendingly such entities and bluntly question whether they are the best that can be derived, or call into question various defects, imperfections, and limitations. In some cases, such a line of questioning may involve reasons to discard the concepts, ideas, services, or products. Such queries may diminish the motivation of the entrepreneur. Instead, one may view such characteristics differently—perhaps by asking how one could "do better?" (Shread, 2012). Such a method may improve entrepreneurial motivation, and act "to turn negative statements and questions into positive ones" (Shread, 2012). Through this communications approach, improvements may be made to the original entity or new perspectives may be obtained.

Communication is essential when solving problems and addressing issues that may arise regarding new and emerging services and products. Generating solutions and discussing issues involves human interaction and the exchanging of information. These actions are facilitated by communicating both "clearly and confidently," and may involve requests for information (Greene, 2012).

Visionaries and entrepreneurs must communicate externally. Both Vollmer and Hoover are prime examples of this notion. Any exploitation of opportunity necessitates "external communications mechanisms because the exploitation of the opportunity requires the acquisition of information from customers, suppliers, and investors" (Shane, 2003). Communicating externally also embellishes the social relationships that are necessary for stakeholder supportiveness and "economic action" (Shane, 2003). Furthermore, the "frequency and quality" of such communications are "associated with the creation of new ventures" (Shane, 2003).

Because concepts and ideas may be new, others generally have no understanding of them. Communicating is the tool through which the salient characteristics of new and emerging concepts and ideas are exchanged. Communicating is essential when countering the "liabilities of newness" because activities necessary for legitimizing; creating a "positive perception or reputation"; and establishing "reliable production, delivery, and accountability systems" involve informational exchanges between different parties (Carsrud & Brännback, 2009). Humans must interact with each other, via communication, to facilitate this exchanging of information.

Any aspect of entrepreneurship is heavily dependent on communication regarding the attributes of new and emerging services and products. The relevance and saliency of "effective communication" must neither be discounted nor ignored within the context of entrepreneurship regarding new services and products (Kam & Jong, 1993). The ability to communicate contributes toward "narrowing the gap" that exists "between the intention of the entrepreneur and the performance that actually results from his or her efforts" (Kam & Jong, 1993).

Cumulatively, communication is essential regarding every facet of innovation concerning new and emerging services and products. Any such entities within the justice system are subject to the wiles of communication from the earliest stages of concept through the stages of implementation and feedback. The ideas of Vollmer were revolutionary, and were communicated through the use of journals and news items to inform both justice system entities and the public regarding his innovations. During modern times, the importance and use of communication is unchanged. All visionaries within the justice domain must be able to effectively and efficiently communicate with others to advocate, explain, and herald new and emerging services and products that may improve policing and the functioning of law enforcement organizations.

Chapter Comments and Summary

This chapter introduced communications innovation and emerging concepts. Regardless of the period in history, organizations have integrated the technologies of the time to improve the efficiency and effectiveness of communicating. Within the justice domain, this notion also is true. For example, August Vollmer, often referred to as the father of modern policing, was heralded as a visionary innovator because of his foresight regarding the use of radio communications devices among law enforcement organizations and operations (Bumgarner, 2004).

Innovation continues to influence communications for both legal and illegal purposes. A primary example of this concept involves a consideration of steganography as a method of concealing secret messages within communications that may otherwise appear quite innocuous. Steganography may be used to embed copyright information legitimately as a method of protecting intellectual property. It may also be used to hide numerous types of information when communicating, ranging from lessons learned to operations plans of terrorist organizations (Gallagher, 2012).

The justice domain involves interactions between different peoples. Often, differences in language may impede communication. Although human translators may be used to facilitate communication, NLP represents a promising domain through which language translation may eventually occur through the use of technology. Currently, the domain of processing natural language is a growing field, and involves a parsing of language without understanding of human language by technology. Therefore, much more research and development is necessary before NLP systems can be judged as having any understanding of human language.

Innovation and technology go hand in hand. This notion is especially true within the domain of communications. Research and development endeavors unceasingly investigate the crafting of new technologies to improve the act of communication between humans. A primary example involves the explorations and investigations of Dr. Kevin Warwick involving the implantation of electronic chips within his body and connecting them to his nervous system. These experiments represented the first of their kind, and may open avenues of developing future technologies that may facilitate human networking and connectivity.

Such future considerations of communicating may exist only as visionary concepts during the present time, and may eventually become reality. However, such visions are within the imaginations of humans. Only human ingenuity and creativity can innovatively make an intangible concept become a tangible reality. Within the justice domain, two such visionaries were August Vollmer and John Edgar Hoover.

New ideas and emerging concepts are considerations of the justice domain. Communication is a key aspect of taking an intangible concept and turning it into a viable service or product within the physical world. The ability to communicate is an invaluable characteristics of visionaries such as August Vollmer and Kevin Warwick. Purposefully and actively pursuing the ideas of such visionaries may lead to the crafting of products and services that benefit not only the justice domain but also the entirety of society. Essentially, communicating is an essential aspect of entrepreneurship within the justice domain.

Terminology

August Vollmer
Clandestine messaging
Communication
Computer network
Connectivity
Cryptogram
Cryptography
Cyborg
Entrepreneurship
Extraction
Hologram
Holography
Human networking

Hype cycle
Implant
Information extraction
Innovation
Intellistreets
John Edgar Hoover
Kevin Warwick
Life cycle
Moore's law
Natural language processing
Neural connection
News blackout
Rock's law
Steganography
Universal language translator

THOUGHT AND DISCUSSION QUESTIONS

1. This chapter introduced the research and experiments of Dr. Kevin Warwick. Given his initial explorations of communications involving the implantation of chips within the human body, do some research regarding the potential use of such technologies concerning the restoration of independence for disabled individuals. Other than the examples discussed herein, how do you believe such technology could improve the quality of life for disabled law enforcement officers and other disabled individuals? Write a brief essay that discusses your findings.
2. This chapter introduced the concept of natural language processing. Law enforcement officers are often first responders to any emergency incident. Given the discussions of natural language processing contained within this chapter, do some additional research concerning this topic. On the basis of your findings, how do you believe natural language processing could be used to support law enforcement operations during emergency incident responses? Write a brief essay that discusses your findings.
3. This chapter introduced the concept of steganography as a method of concealing messages within open communications. Detecting such clandestine messaging requires effort, and is not necessarily an easy task. Steganalysis involves the examination of messaging to investigate potential instances of steganography. Do some research, and identify three forms of steganalysis that are used to investigate potentially concealed communications. Write a brief essay that discusses your findings.
4. This chapter primarily discussed communications innovation and the potential future of communication. Do some research on emerging technologies in communication, and consider how three of these items may influence the communications of law enforcement organizations. Write a brief essay that expresses your opinions and that describes your findings.

References

Ackermann, G., & Eichlier, J. (2007). *Holography: A practical approach* (p. 4). Weinheim, Germany: Wiley-Verlag Publishing.

American Police Hall of Fame. (2013). Family fund for paralyzed and disabled police officers. Retrieved from http://www.aphf.org/disabled.html (accessed February 9, 2013).

Bardsley, M. (2013a). The life and career of J. Edgar Hoover: The gangster era. Retrieved from http://www.trutv.com/library/crime/gangsters_outlaws/cops_others/hoover/7.html (accessed February 16, 2013).

Bardsley, M. (2013b). The life and career of J. Edgar Hoover: Roosevelt years. Retrieved from http://www.trutv.com/library/crime/gangsters_outlaws/cops_others/hoover/8.html (accessed February 16, 2013).

BBC News. (2013). Kevin Warwick, Professor of Cybernetics. Retrieved from http://news.bbc.co.uk/hi/english/static/special_report/1999/12/99/back_to_the_future/kevin_warwick.stm (accessed February 9, 2013).

Bellis, M. (2013). History of holography. Retrieved from http://inventors.about.com/od/hstartinventions/a/Holography.htm (accessed February 8, 2013).

Bennett, K. (2004). Linguistic steganography: Survey, analysis, and robustness concerns for hiding information in text. Center for Education and Research in Information Assurance and Security, Purdue University. Retrieved from http://www.cerias.purdue.edu/tools_and_resources/bibtex_archive/archive/2004-13.pdf (accessed February 14, 2013).

Berry, J. (2008). *What we see from afar.* Maintland, FL: Xulon Press.

Bumgarner, J. (2004). *Profiling and criminal justice in America.* Santa Barbara, CA: ABC-CLIO Publishing.

Carsrud, A., & Brännback, M. (2009). *Understanding the entrepreneurial mind: Opening the black box* (p. 342). New York: Springer Publishing.

City of Hagerstown. (2013). Records. Retrieved from http://www.hagerstownmd.org/index.aspx?NID=492 (accessed February 16, 2013).

City of Minneapolis. (2013). Forgery and fraud. Retrieved from http://www.minneapolismn.gov/police/report/police_crime-reporting_forgery-fraud (accessed February 9, 2013).

Clarke, R. (2008). *Improving street lighting to reduce crime in residential areas.* Washington, DC: U.S. Department of Justice.

Coe, L. (1993). *The telegraph: A history of Morse's invention and its predecessors in the United States* (p. 2). Jefferson, NC: McFarland & Company.

Cunningham, K. (2006). *J. Edgar Hoover: Controversial FBI director* (p. 35). Minneapolis, MN: Compass Point Books.

Dempsey, J., & Forst, L. (2010). *An introduction to policing* (5th ed., p. 20). Clifton Park, NY: Delmar Cengage Publishing.

Desai, S., Nijkamp, P., & Stough, R. (2011). *New directions in regional economic development: The role of entrepreneurship theory and methods, practice, and policy.* Cheltenham, UK: Edward Elgar Publishing, Ltd.

Dinkelspiel, F. (2010). Remembering August Vollmer, the Berkeley police chief who created modern policing. *Berkeleyside.* Retrieved from http://www.berkeleyside.com/2010/01/27/remembering-august-vollmer-the-berkeley-police-chief-who-created-modern-policing/ (accessed February 15, 2013).

Disney, W. (n.d.). Communication quotes. Brainyquote.com. Retrieved from http://www.brainyquote.com/quotes/topics/topic_communication.html (accessed February 4, 2013).

Easy Id Card. (2013). Greentea Solutions. Police identification cards. Retrieved from http://www.easyidcard.com/police-id-cards.asp (accessed February 9, 2013).

The Economist. (2011). A deeper law than Moore's? Retrieved from http://www.economist.com/blogs/dailychart/2011/10/computing-power (accessed February 9, 2013).

Farrington, D., & Welsh, B. (2002). *Effects of improved street lighting on crime: A systematic review* (p. 39). Retrieved from http://cops.usdoj.gov/Publications/e1208-StreetLighting.pdf (accessed February 14, 2013).

Federal Bureau of Investigation. (2013a). John Dillinger. Retrieved from http://www.fbi.gov/about-us/history/famous-cases/john-dillinger (accessed February 16, 2013).

Federal Bureau of Investigation. (2013b). John Edgar Hoover. Retrieved from http://www.fbi.gov/about-us/history/directors/hoover (accessed February 16, 2013).

Franklin, B. (1790). *The autobiography of Benjamin Franklin*. Carlisle, MA: Applewood Books.

Gaines, B. (1984). Perspectives of fifth generation computing. University of Calgary. Retrieved from http://pages.cpsc.ucalgary.ca/~gaines/reports/MFIT/OSIT84/OSIT84.pdf (accessed February 9, 2013).

Gallagher, S. (2012). Steganography: How al-Qaeda hid secret documents in a porn video. Retrieved from http://arstechnica.com/business/2012/05/steganography-how-al-qaeda-hid-secret-documents-in-a-porn-video/ (accessed February 14, 2013).

Goel, A. (2010). *Computer fundamentals*. New Delhi, India: Dorling Kindersley.

Greene, C. (2012). *Entrepreneurship: Ideas in action* (5th ed., p. 26). Mason, OH: South-Western Cengage Publishing.

Humphrey, N. (1999). Cave art, autism, and the evolution of the human mind. *Journal of Consciousness Studies: Controversies in Science and the Humanities*, *6*, 116–125. Thorverton, UK: Imprint Academic.

Iacono, W. (2008). Effective policing: Understanding how polygraph tests work and are used. *Criminal Justice and Behavior*, *35*(10), 1295–1308.

Intellistreets. (2013). New technology provides all-in-one lighting, sound and public safety applications. Retrieved from http://intellistreets.com/pressHealper.php?id=2012-02-01-01 (accessed February 14, 2013).

Isaacson, W. (2003). *Benjamin Franklin: An American life*. New York, NY: Simon and Schuster Publishing.

The J. Edgar Hoover Foundation. (2013). Biography of John Edgar Hoover. Retrieved from http://www.jehooverfoundation.org/hoover-bio.asp (accessed February 16, 2013).

Jayaram, P., Ranganatha, H., & Anupama, H. (2011). Information hiding using audio steganography—A survey. *The International Journal of Multimedia & Its Applications*, *3*(3), 86–97.

Jha, A. (2010). Holographic communication flickers into life in Arizona. *The Guardian*. Retrieved from http://www.guardian.co.uk/science/2010/nov/03/holographic-communication-telepresence (accessed February 8, 2013).

Judge, J. (2001). Steganography: Past, present, and future. SANS Institute. Retrieved from http://www.sans.org/reading_room/whitepapers/stenganography/steganography-past-present-future_552 (accessed February 14, 2013).

Kam, C., & Jong, R. (1993). A communicative analysis of innovations and entrepreneurship. *Journal of Small Business and Entrepreneurship*, *11*(1), 18–34.

Krueger, N. (2002). *Entrepreneurship: Critical perspectives on business and management* (Vol. 3, p. 201). New York: Routledge Publishing.

Ku, C., Iriberri, A., & Leroy, G. (2008). Natural language processing e-government: Crime information extraction from heterogeneous data sources. Proceedings of the 9th Annual International Digital Government Research Conference (p. 163). Retrieved from http://www.academia.edu/334638/Natural_Language_Processing_and_E-Government_Crime_Information_Extraction_From_Heterogeneous_Data_Sources (accessed February 9, 2013).

Liddy, E. (2001). Natural language processing. Retrieved from http://surface.syr.edu/cgi/viewcontent.cgi?article=1043&context=istpub (accessed February 9, 2013).

Marsan, C. (2011). 25 ways IT will morph in the next 25 Years. *Network World*. Retrieved from http://www.networkworld.com/supp/2011/25thanniversary/050911-anniversary-future.html (accessed February 9, 2013).

Massachusetts Institute of Technology. (2013). The holograms. Retrieved from http://web.mit.edu/museum/lightforest/holograms.html (accessed February 8, 2013).

Meghanathan, N. (2013). Basics of steganography and security of steganographic systems. Jackson State University. Retrieved from http://www.jsums.edu/cms/tues/docs/Steganography/Basics-Steganography-Security.pdf&sa=U&ei=ih8fUYKKB43I9gT3q4CIDA&ved=0CAcQFjAA&client=internal-uds-cse&usg=AFQjCNGQ4f1V-38nWJXuOH38Y7IV8i2u4A (accessed February 15, 2013).

Merriam-Webster Dictionary. (2013a). s.v. "cybernetics." Retrieved from http://www.merriam-webster.com/dictionary/cybernetics (accessed February 9, 2013).

Merriam-Webster Dictionary. (2013b). s.v. "steganography." Retrieved from http://www.merriam-webster.com/dictionary/steganography (accessed February 14, 2013).

Morrison, T. (2013). The Disabled Police Officers Counseling Center, Inc. (DPOCC) and the Disabled Police Officers of America, Inc.(DPOA) Joint Report on a National Police Disability Study. Disabled Police Officers of America. Retrieved from http://www.drpoef.com/study/disabilityStudy.html (accessed February 9, 2013).

Nature. Retrieved from http://www.nature.com/nature/journal/v468/n7320/full/nature09521.html?pagewanted=all.

Null, L., & Nabor, J. (2012). *The essentials of computer organization and architecture* (3rd ed., p. 30). Sudbury, MA: Jones and Bartlett Publishing.

The Ohio State University. (2013). Holography. Retrieved from http://www.physics.ohio-state.edu/~kagan/holography/ (accessed February 8, 2013).

Petherick, W., Turvey, B., & Ferguson, C. (2010). *Forensic criminology* (p. 31). Burlington, MA: Elsevier Academic Publishing.

Pittman, E. (2013). Emerging technology could positively impact all phases of emergency management. *Intellistreets*. Retrieved from http://intellistreets.com/pressHealper.php?id=2012-12-01-02 (accessed February 14, 2013).

Queen's University. (2013). Beam me up Scotty: Life-size hologram-like telepods revolutionize videoconferencing. Retrieved from http://www.hml.queensu.ca/telehuman (accessed February 8, 2013).

Research and Markets. (2009). Steganography: Future of information hiding. Retrieved from http://www.researchandmarkets.com/reports/1207270/steganography_future_of_information_hiding (accessed February 14, 2013).

Rice University. (2013). What is steganography? Retrieved from http://www.clear.rice.edu/elec301/Projects01/steganosaurus/background.html (accessed February 15, 2013).

Rodriguez, N., Weissberg, J., & Loeb, G. (2007). Communication and control for reanimating paralyzed limbs via a network of wireless micro-implants. 4th International Workshop on Wearable and Implantable Body Sensor Networks (BSN 2007), March 26–28, Aachen University, Germany. *IFMBE Proceedings, 13*(2007), 278–283.

Rutter, K., & Sparkes, B. (2000). *Word and image in ancient Greece* (p. 196). Edinburgh, UK: Edinburgh University Press, Ltd.

Samovar, L., Porter, R., & McDaniel, E. (2010). *Communication between cultures* (7th ed., p. 13). Boston, MA: Wadsworth Publishing.

Shane, S. (2003). *A general theory of entrepreneurship: The individual-opportunity nexus* (p. 244). Cheltenham, UK: Edward Elgar Publishing, Ltd.

Shread, P. (2012). Effective communication for entrepreneurs. *Time Magazine*. Retrieved from http://business.time.com/2012/06/05/effective-communication-for-entrepreneurs/ (accessed February 16, 2013).

Stokes, J. (2010). How even the dumbest Russian spies can outwit the NSA. Retrieved from http://arstechnica.com/tech-policy/2010/07/how-even-the-dumbest-russian-spies-outwit-the-nsa/ (accessed February 14, 2013).

Theoharis, A., Poveda, T., Rosenfeld, S., & Powers, R. (1999). *The FBI: A comprehensive reference guide* (p. 265). Phoenix, AZ: Oryx Press.

The University of Reading. (2013). The next step towards true cyborgs? Retrieved from http://www.kevinwarwick.com/Cyborg2.htm (accessed February 9, 2013).

Warwick, K. (2013). What happens when a man is merged with a computer? The University of Reading. Retrieved from http://www.kevinwarwick.com/Cyborg1.htm (accessed February 9, 2013).
Wired. (2000). Kevin Warwick outlines his plan to become one with his computer. Retrieved from http://www.wired.com/wired/archive/8.02/warwick.html (accessed February 9, 2013).
Woodford, C. (2013). *Light: Investigating visible and invisible electromagnetic radiation* (p. 36). New York: The Rosen Publishing Group.

Appendix A: The Declaration of Independence

> Our founders got it right when they wrote in the Declaration of Independence that our rights come from nature and nature's God, not from government.
>
> **—Paul Ryan (Ryan, n.d.)**

The original version of the Declaration of Independence was engrossed using "animal skin" parchment (U.S. National Archives and Records Administration, 2013). This material was "treated with lime and stretched to create a strong, long-lasting writing support" (U.S. National Archives and Records Administration, 2013). Paper copies were "read aloud" among the colonies, generally at town squares, as a method of communicating to people the intention to separate from England (U.S. National Archives and Records Administration, 2013).

The Declaration of Independence

In Congress, July 4, 1776

The Unanimous Declaration of the Thirteen United States of America

When in the Course of human events, it becomes necessary for one people to dissolve the political bands which have connected them with another, and to assume among the powers of the earth, the separate and equal station to which the Laws of Nature and of Nature's God entitle them, a decent respect to the opinions of mankind requires that they should declare the causes which impel them to the separation.

We hold these truths to be self-evident, that all men are created equal, that they are endowed by their Creator with certain unalienable Rights, that among these are Life, Liberty and the pursuit of Happiness.—That to secure these rights, Governments are instituted among Men, deriving their just powers from the consent of the governed,—That whenever any Form of Government becomes destructive of these ends, it is the Right of the People to alter or to abolish it, and to institute new Government, laying its foundation on such principles and organizing its powers in such form, as to them shall seem most likely to effect their Safety and Happiness. Prudence, indeed, will dictate that Governments long established should not be changed for light and transient causes; and accordingly all experience hath shewn, that mankind are more disposed to suffer, while evils are sufferable, than to right themselves by abolishing the forms to which they are accustomed. But when a long train of abuses and usurpations, pursuing invariably the same Object evinces a design to reduce them under absolute Despotism, it is their right, it is their duty, to throw off such Government, and to provide new Guards for their future security.—Such has been the patient sufferance of these Colonies; and such is now the necessity which constrains them to alter their former Systems of Government. The history of the present King of Great Britain is a history of repeated injuries and usurpations, all having in direct object the establishment of an absolute Tyranny over these States. To prove this, let Facts be submitted to a candid world.

He has refused his Assent to Laws, the most wholesome and necessary for the public good.

He has forbidden his Governors to pass Laws of immediate and pressing importance, unless suspended in their operation till his Assent should be obtained; and when so suspended, he has utterly neglected to attend to them.

He has refused to pass other Laws for the accommodation of large districts of people, unless those people would relinquish the right of Representation in the Legislature, a right inestimable to them and formidable to tyrants only.

He has called together legislative bodies at places unusual, uncomfortable, and distant from the depository of their public Records, for the sole purpose of fatiguing them into compliance with his measures.

He has dissolved Representative Houses repeatedly, for opposing with manly firmness his invasions on the rights of the people.

He has refused for a long time, after such dissolutions, to cause others to be elected; whereby the Legislative powers, incapable of Annihilation, have returned to the People at large for their exercise; the State remaining in the mean time exposed to all the dangers of invasion from without, and convulsions within.

He has endeavoured to prevent the population of these States; for that purpose obstructing the Laws for Naturalization of Foreigners; refusing to pass others to encourage their migrations hither, and raising the conditions of new Appropriations of Lands.

He has obstructed the Administration of Justice, by refusing his Assent to Laws for establishing Judiciary powers.

He has made Judges dependent on his Will alone, for the tenure of their offices, and the amount and payment of their salaries.

He has erected a multitude of New Offices, and sent hither swarms of Officers to harrass our people, and eat out their substance.

He has kept among us, in times of peace, Standing Armies without the Consent of our legislatures.

He has affected to render the Military independent of and superior to the Civil power.

He has combined with others to subject us to a jurisdiction foreign to our constitution, and unacknowledged by our laws; giving his Assent to their Acts of pretended Legislation:

For Quartering large bodies of armed troops among us:

For protecting them, by a mock Trial, from punishment for any Murders which they should commit on the Inhabitants of these States:

For cutting off our Trade with all parts of the world:

For imposing Taxes on us without our Consent:

For depriving us in many cases, of the benefits of Trial by Jury:

For transporting us beyond Seas to be tried for pretended offences

For abolishing the free System of English Laws in a neighbouring Province, establishing therein an Arbitrary government, and enlarging its Boundaries so as to render it at once an example and fit instrument for introducing the same absolute rule into these Colonies:

For taking away our Charters, abolishing our most valuable Laws, and altering fundamentally the Forms of our Governments:

For suspending our own Legislatures, and declaring themselves invested with power to legislate for us in all cases whatsoever.

He has abdicated Government here, by declaring us out of his Protection and waging War against us.

He has plundered our seas, ravaged our Coasts, burnt our towns, and destroyed the lives of our people.

He is at this time transporting large Armies of foreign Mercenaries to compleat the works of death, desolation and tyranny, already begun with circumstances of Cruelty & perfidy scarcely paralleled in the most barbarous ages, and totally unworthy the Head of a civilized nation.

He has constrained our fellow Citizens taken Captive on the high Seas to bear Arms against their Country, to become the executioners of their friends and Brethren, or to fall themselves by their Hands.

He has excited domestic insurrections amongst us, and has endeavoured to bring on the inhabitants of our frontiers, the merciless Indian Savages, whose known rule of warfare, is an undistinguished destruction of all ages, sexes and conditions.

In every stage of these Oppressions We have Petitioned for Redress in the most humble terms: Our repeated Petitions have been answered only by repeated injury. A Prince whose character is thus marked by every act which may define a Tyrant, is unfit to be the ruler of a free people.

Nor have We been wanting in attentions to our Brittish brethren. We have warned them from time to time of attempts by their legislature to extend an unwarrantable jurisdiction over us. We have reminded them of the circumstances of our emigration and settlement here. We have appealed to their native justice and magnanimity, and we have conjured them by the ties of our common kindred to disavow these usurpations, which, would inevitably interrupt our connections and correspondence. They too have been deaf to the voice of justice and of consanguinity. We must, therefore, acquiesce in the necessity, which denounces our Separation, and hold them, as we hold the rest of mankind, Enemies in War, in Peace Friends.

We, therefore, the Representatives of the united States of America, in General Congress, Assembled, appealing to the Supreme Judge of the world for the rectitude of our intentions, do, in the Name, and by Authority of the good People of these Colonies, solemnly publish and declare, That these United Colonies are, and of Right ought to be Free and Independent States; that they are Absolved from all Allegiance to the British Crown, and that all political connection between them and the State of Great Britain, is and ought to be totally dissolved; and that as Free and Independent States, they have full Power to levy War, conclude Peace, contract Alliances, establish Commerce, and to do all other Acts and Things which Independent States may of right do. And for the support of this Declaration, with a firm reliance on the protection of divine Providence, we mutually pledge to each other our Lives, our Fortunes and our sacred Honor.

The 56 signatures on the Declaration appear in the positions indicated:

Column 1

Georgia:

Button Gwinnett
Lyman Hall
George Walton

Column 2

North Carolina:

William Hooper
Joseph Hewes
John Penn

South Carolina:

Edward Rutledge
Thomas Heyward, Jr.
Thomas Lynch, Jr.
Arthur Middleton

Column 3

Massachusetts:

John Hancock

Maryland:

Samuel Chase
William Paca
Thomas Stone
Charles Carroll of Carrollton

Virginia:

George Wythe
Richard Henry Lee
Thomas Jefferson
Benjamin Harrison
Thomas Nelson, Jr.
Francis Lightfoot Lee
Carter Braxton

Column 4

Pennsylvania:

Robert Morris
Benjamin Rush
Benjamin Franklin
John Morton
George Clymer
James Smith
George Taylor
James Wilson
George Ross

Delaware:

Caesar Rodney
George Read
Thomas McKean

Column 5

New York:

William Floyd
Philip Livingston
Francis Lewis
Lewis Morris

New Jersey:

Richard Stockton
John Witherspoon
Francis Hopkinson
John Hart
Abraham Clark

Column 6

New Hampshire:

Josiah Bartlett
William Whipple

Massachusetts:
Samuel Adams
John Adams
Robert Treat Paine
Elbridge Gerry
Rhode Island:
Stephen Hopkins
William Ellery
Connecticut:
Roger Sherman
Samuel Huntington
William Williams
Oliver Wolcott
New Hampshire:
Matthew Thornton

Obtained from Library of Congress Archives, Figure A.1 shows a print of the Declaration of Independence (U.S. National Archives and Records Administration, 2013b).

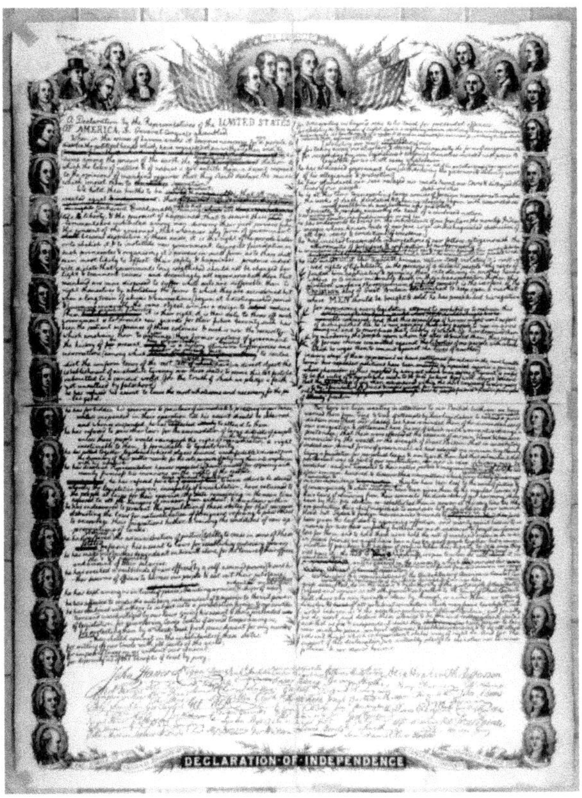

Figure A.1 Copy of the Declaration of Independence. (From http://www.loc.gov/pictures/item/2003656533/.)

References

Ryan, P. (n.d.). Declaration quotes. Brainyquote.com. Retrieved from http://www.brainyquote.com/quotes/keywords/declaration.html (accessed December 17, 2012).

The National Archives. (1776). The declaration of independence: A transcription. Retrieved from http://www.archives.gov/exhibits/charters/declaration_transcript.html (accessed December 17, 2012).

U.S. National Archives and Records Administration. (2013a). Declaration of independence facts. Retrieved from http://www.archives.gov/exhibits/charters/treasure/declaration_facts.html (accessed September 20, 2013).

U.S. National Archives and Records Administration. (2013b). The declaration of independence: A transcription. Retrieved from http://www.archives.gov/exhibits/charters/declaration_transcript.html (accessed December 17, 2012).

Appendix B: Press Conference of President Gerald Ford

An American tragedy in which we all have played a part.

—President Gerald R. Ford (Ford, n.d.)

The following transcription records the first press conference of President Gerald R. Ford (Ford, 1974). This event occurred on September 16, 1974.

Text of the Press Conference

THE PRESIDENT. Ladies and gentlemen, this press conference is being held at a time when many Americans are observing the Jewish religious New Year. It begins a period of self-examination and reconciliation. In opening this press conference, I am mindful that the spirit of this holy day has a meaning for all Americans. In examining one's deeds of the last year and in assuming responsibility for past actions and personal decisions, one can reach a point of growth and change. The purpose of looking back is to go forward with a new and enlightened dedication to our highest values. The record of the past year does not have to be endlessly relived, but can be transformed by commitment to new insights and new actions in the year to come. Ladies and gentlemen, I am ready for your questions.

Mr. Cormier [Frank Cormier, Associated Press].

QUESTIONS PARDON FOR FORMER PRESIDENT NIXON [1.]:

Q: Mr. President, some Congressional Republicans who have talked to you have hinted that you may have had a secret reason for granting President Nixon a pardon sooner than you indicated you would at the last news conference, and I wonder if you could tell us what that reason was?

THE PRESIDENT: At the outset, let me say I had no secret reason, and I don't recall telling any Republican that I had such a reason. Let me review quickly, if I might, the things that transpired following the last news conference. As many of you know, I answered two, maybe three, questions concerning a pardon at that time. On return to the office, I felt that I had to have my counsel undertake a thorough examination as to what my right of pardon was under the Constitution. I also felt that it was very important that I find out what legal actions, if any, were contemplated by the Special Prosecutor. That information was found out, and it was indicated to me that the possibility exists, the very real possibility, that the [former] President would be charged with obstructing justice and 10 other possible criminal actions. In addition, I asked my general counsel to find out, if he could, how long such criminal proceedings would take, from the indictment, the carrying on of the trial, et cetera. And I was informed that this would take a year, maybe somewhat longer, for the whole process to go through. I also asked my counsel to find out whether or not, under decisions of the judicial system, a fair trial could be given to the former President. After I got that information, which took 2 or 3 days,

I then began to evaluate, in my own mind, whether or not I should take the action which I subsequently did.

Miss Thomas [Helen Thomas, United Press International].

Q: Throughout your Vice Presidency, you said that you didn't believe that former President Nixon had ever committed an impeachable offense. Is that still your belief, or do you believe that his acceptance of a pardon implies his guilt or is an admission of guilt?

THE PRESIDENT: The fact that 38 members of the House Committee on the Judiciary, Democrat and Republican, have unanimously agreed in the report that was filed that the former President was guilty of an impeachable offense, I think, is very persuasive evidence. And the second question, I don't—

Q: Was it an admission of guilt?

THE PRESIDENT: Was the acceptance of the pardon by the President an admission of guilt? The acceptance of a pardon, I think. can be construed by many, if not all, as an admission of guilt.

Yes, Mr. Nessen [Ron Nessen, NBC News].

Q: What reports have you received on Mr. Nixon's health, and what effect, if any, did this have on your decision to pardon him now?

THE PRESIDENT: I have asked Dr. Lukash, who is the head physician in the White House, to keep me posted in proper channels as to the former President's health. I have been informed on a routine day-to-day basis, but I don't think I am at liberty to give any information as to those reports that I have received. You also asked what impact did the President's health have on my decision. I think it is well known that just before I gave my statement, at the time that I gave the pardon, I personally wrote in a phrase "the threat to the President's health." The main concern that I had at the time I made the decision was to heal the wounds throughout the United States. For a period of 18 months or longer, we had had turmoil and divisiveness in the American society. At the same time, the United States had major problems, both at home and abroad, that needed the maximum personal attention of the President and many others in the Government. It seemed to me that as long as this divisiveness continued, this turmoil existed, caused by the charges and countercharges, the responsible people in the Government could not give their total attention to the problems that we had to solve at home and abroad. And the net result was I was more anxious to heal the Nation—that was the top priority. And I felt then, and I feel now, that the action I took will do that. I couldn't be oblivious, however, to news accounts that I had concerning the President's health, but the major reason for the action I took related to the effort to reconcile divisions in our country and to heal the wounds that had festered far too long.

Q: Mr. President, after you had told us that you were going to allow the legal process to go on before you decided whether to pardon him, why did you decide on Sunday morning, abruptly, to pardon President Nixon?

THE PRESIDENT: I didn't decide abruptly. I explained a moment ago the process that I went through subsequent to the last press conference. And when I had assembled all of that information that came to me through my counsel, I then most carefully analyzed the situation in the country, and I decided that we could not afford in America an extended period of continued turmoil. And the fact that the trial and all of the parts thereof would have lasted a year, perhaps more, with the continuation of the divisions in America, I felt that I should take the action that I did promptly and effectively.

FORMER PRESIDENT'S TAPES AND DOCUMENTS [2.]

Q: Mr. President, I would like to ask you a question about the decision relating to custody of the Nixon tapes and documents. Considering the enormous interest that the Special Prosecutor's office had in those documents for further investigation, I am wondering why the negotiations with Mr. Nixon's representatives were conducted strictly between the counsel in your office without bringing in discussions with either Mr. Jaworski's representatives or those from the Justice Department?

THE PRESIDENT: In the first place, I did receive a memorandum, or legal opinion, from the Department of Justice which indicated that in the opinion of the Department of Justice, the documents, tapes—the ownership of them—were in the hands of the former President. And historically, that has been the case for all Presidents. In a news briefing held on September 8, 1974, Counsel to the President Philip W. Buchen announced, in regard to the status of the Presidential materials of Richard Nixon, that Attorney General William B. Saxbe had determined that "such materials are the present property of Mr. Nixon; however, it is also concluded that during the time the materials remain in the custody of the United States, they are subject to subpoenas and court orders directed to any official who controls that custody." The texts of the Attorney General's legal opinion, dated September 6, 1974, and a September 6 letter of agreement between Mr. Nixon and Administrator of General Services Arthur F. Sampson concerning control of and access to Mr. Nixon's Presidential materials, were released by the White House September 8. They are printed in the Weekly Compilation of Presidential Documents (vol. 10, pp. 1104 and 1105). Now, the negotiations for the handling of the tapes and documents were undertaken and consummated by my staff and the staff of the former President. I believe that they have been properly preserved, and they will be available under subpoena for any criminal proceeding. Now, the Special Prosecutor's staff has indicated some concern. I am saying tonight that my staff is working with the Special Prosecutor's staff to try and alleviate any concerns that they have. I hope a satisfactory arrangement can be worked out.

PREVIOUS STATEMENTS ON PARDON [3.]

Q: Mr. President, during your confirmation hearings as Vice President, you said that you did not think that the country would stand for a President to pardon his predecessor. Has your mind changed about such public opinion?

THE PRESIDENT: In those hearings before the Senate Committee on Rules and Administration, I was asked a hypothetical question. And in answer to that hypothetical question, I responded by saying that I did not think the American people would stand for such an action. Now that I am in the White House and don't have to answer hypothetical questions but have to deal with reality, it was my judgment, after analyzing all of the facts, that it was in the best interest of the United States for me to take the action that I did. I think if you will reread what I said in answer to that hypothetical question, I did not say I wouldn't. I simply said that under the way the question was phrased, the American people would object. But I am absolutely convinced, when dealing with reality in this very, very difficult situation, that I made the right decision in an effort—an honest, conscientious effort—to end the divisions and the turmoil in the United States.

Mr. Lisagor [Peter Lisagor, Chicago Daily News].

SAFEGUARDING OF TAPES AND DOCUMENTS [4.]

Q: Mr. President, is there any safeguard in the tapes agreement that was made with Mr. Nixon, first, with their destruction in the event anything happens to him, because under the agreement they will be destroyed, and secondly, should not the tapes be kept in the White House until the Special Prosecutor has finished dealing with them?

THE PRESIDENT: The tapes and the documents are still in our possession, and we are, as I said a moment ago, working with the Special Prosecutor's office to alleviate any concerns they have as to their disposition and their availability. The agreement as to destruction is quite clear-cut. As long as Mr. Nixon is alive and during the period of time that is set forth, they are available for subpoena by a court involving any criminal proceedings. I think this is a necessary requirement for the protection of evidence for any such action.

THE CIA AND CHILE [5.]

Q: Mr. President, recent Congressional testimony has indicated that the CIA, under the direction of a committee headed by Dr. Kissinger, attempted to destabilize the Government of Chile under former President Allende.

Is it the policy of your Administration to attempt to destabilize the governments of other democracies?

THE PRESIDENT: Let me answer in general. I think this is a very important question.

Our Government, like other governments, does take certain actions in the intelligence field to help implement foreign policy and protect national security. I am informed reliably that Communist nations spend vastly more money than we do for the same kind of purposes. Now, in this particular case, as I understand it—and there is no doubt in my mind—our Government had no involvement whatsoever in the Allende coup. To my knowledge, nobody has charged that. The facts are we had no involvement in any way whatsoever in the coup itself. In a period of time, 3 or 4 years ago, there was an effort being made by the Allende government to destroy opposition news media, both the writing press as well as the electronic press, and to destroy opposition political parties.

The effort that was made in this case was to help and assist the preservation of opposition newspapers and electronic media and to preserve opposition political parties.

I think this is in the best interest of the people in Chile and, certainly, in our best interest.

Now, may I add one further comment. The 40 Committee was established in 1948. It has been in existence under Presidents since that time. That Committee reviews every covert operation undertaken by our Government, and that information is relayed to the responsible Congressional committees where it is reviewed by House and Senate committees. It seems to me that the 40 Committee should continue in existence, and I am going to meet with the responsible Congressional committees to see whether or not they want any changes in the review process so that the Congress, as well as the President, are fully informed and are fully included in the operations for any such action.

Mr. Sperling [Godfrey Sperling, Jr., Christian Science Monitor].

FURTHER QUESTIONS ON PARDON DECISION [6.]

Q: In view of public reaction, do you think that the Nixon pardon really served to bind up the Nation's wounds? I wonder if you would assess public reaction to that move.

THE PRESIDENT: I must say that the decision has created more antagonism than I anticipated. But as I look over the long haul with a trial, or several trials, of a former President, criminal trials, the possibility of a former President being in the dock, so to speak, and the divisions that would have existed not just for a limited period of time but for a long period of time, it seems to me that when I had the choice between that possibility and the possibility of taking direct action hoping to conclude it, I am still convinced, despite the public reaction so far, that the decision I made was the right one.

Q: Mr. President, in regard to the pardon, you talk about the realities of the situation. Now those realities, rightly or wrongly, include a good many people who speculate about whether or not there is some sort of arrangement-they even, some of them, call it a deal—between you and the former President, or between your staff and his staff—resignation in exchange for a full pardon. The question is: Is there or was there, to your knowledge, any kind of understanding about this?

THE PRESIDENT: There was no understanding, no deal between me and the former President, nor between my staff and the staff of the former President, none whatsoever.

ACCESS TO INCOME TAX RETURNS [7.]

Q: Mr. President, sir, there is a bill that the Treasury Department has put forward, I think it is about 38 pages. Under this bill, which deals with getting hold of the returns, Internal Revenue returns, of citizens of the country, you could take action to get those returns whenever you wanted to. I wonder if you are aware of this and if you feel that you need to get those returns of citizens?

THE PRESIDENT: It is my understanding that a President has, by tradition and practice and by law, the right to have access to income tax returns. I personally think that is something that should be kept very closely held. A person's income tax return is a very precious thing to that individual, and therefore, I am about to issue an Executive order [11805] that makes it even more restrictive as to how those returns can be handled. And I do think that a proposed piece of legislation that is coming to me and subsequently will be submitted, as I recollect, to the Congress would also greatly tighten up the availability or accessibility of income tax returns. I think they should be closely held, and I can assure you that they will be most judiciously handled as far as I am concerned.

OWNERSHIP OF PRESIDENTIAL PAPERS [8.]

Q: Mr. President, looking beyond the Nixon papers and in view of some criticism in Congress, do you believe we may have now reached the point where Presidential White House papers should remain in the Government's hands as the property of the Government?

THE PRESIDENT: As far as I am personally concerned, I can see a legitimate reason for Presidential papers remaining the property of the Government. In my own case, I made a decision some years ago to turn over all of my Congressional papers, all of my Vice Presidential papers, to the University of Michigan archives.

As far as I am concerned, whether they go to the archives for use or whether they stay the possession of the Government, I don't think it makes too much difference. I have no desire, personally, to retain whatever papers come out of my Administration.

Mr. Mollenhoff [Clark R. Mollenhoff, Des Moines Register and Tribune].

THE PARDON DECISION [9.]

Q: Mr. President, at the last press conference you said, "The code of ethics that will be followed will be the example that I set." Do you find any conflicts of interest in the decision to grant a sweeping pardon to your life-long friend and your financial benefactor with no consultation for advice and judgment for the legal fallout?

THE PRESIDENT: The decision to grant a pardon to Mr. Nixon was made primarily, as I have expressed, for the purpose of trying to heal the wounds throughout the country between Americans on one side of the issue or the other. Mr. Nixon nominated me for the office of Vice President. I was confirmed overwhelmingly in the House as well as in the Senate. Every action I have taken, Mr. Mollenhoff, is predicated on my conscience without any concern or consideration as to favor as far as I am concerned.

CONDITIONAL AMNESTY AND THE PARDON DECISION [10.]

Q: If your intention was to heal the wounds of the Nation, sir, why did you grant only a conditional amnesty to the Vietnam war draft evaders while granting a full pardon to President Nixon?

THE PRESIDENT: The only connection between those two cases is the effort that I made in the one to heal the wounds involving the charges against Mr. Nixon and my honest and conscientious effort to heal the wounds for those who had deserted military service or dodged the draft. That is the only connection between the two. In one case, you have a President who was forced to resign because of circumstances involving his Administration, and he has been shamed and disgraced by that resignation. In the case of the draft dodgers and Army and military deserters, we are trying to heal the wounds by the action that I took with the signing of the proclamation this morning.

REPORTS ON WATERGATE INVESTIGATION [11.]

Q: Mr. President, another concern that has been voiced around the country since the pardon is that the judicial process as it finally unwinds may not write the definitive chapter on Watergate and perhaps with particular regard to Mr. Nixon's particular involvement, however total, however it may have been in truth. My question is, would you consider appointing a special commission with extraordinary powers to look into all of the evidentiary material and to write that chapter and not leave it to later history?

THE PRESIDENT: Well, it seems to me as I look at what has been done, I think you find a mass of evidence that has been accumulated. In the first instance, you have the very intensive investigation conducted by the House Committee on the Judiciary. It was a very well-conducted investigation. It came up with volumes of information. In addition, the Special Prosecutor's office under Mr. Jaworski has conducted an intensive investigation and the Special Prosecutor's office will issue a report at the conclusion of their responsibilities that I think will probably make additional information available to the American people. And thirdly, as the various criminal trials proceed in the months ahead, there obviously will be additional information made available to the American people. So, when you see what has been done and what undoubtedly will be done, I think the full story will be made available to the American people.

SUCCESSORS TO GENERAL HAIG AND PRESS SECRETARY TER HORST [12.]

Q: Mr. President, could you give us an idea who will succeed General Haig, and how are you coming on your search for a Press Secretary?

THE PRESIDENT: Do I have a lot of candidates here? [Laughter] No shows. [Laughter]

I have several people in mind to replace General Haig, but I have made no decision on that. It was just announced today that the NATO countries have accepted him as the officer handling those responsibilities. The President's nomination of Gen. Alexander M. Haig, Jr., to be Supreme Allied Commander, Europe, was approved by the NATO Defense Planning Committee. I think he is to take office succeeding General Goodpaster on December 15. He assumes his responsibilities as the head of U.S. military forces November 1. In the next few days undoubtedly

I will make the decision as to the individual to succeed him. As far as the Press Secretary is concerned, we are actively working on that, and we hope to have an announcement in a relatively short period of time.

THE FORMER PRESIDENT'S HEALTH [13.]

Q: Mr. President, prior to your deciding to pardon Mr. Nixon, did you have, apart from those reports, any information either from associates of the President or from his family or from any other source about his health, about his medical condition?

THE PRESIDENT: Prior to the decision that I made granting a pardon to Mr. Nixon, I had no other specific information concerning his health other than what I had read in the news media or heard in the news media. I had not gotten any information from any of the Nixon family. The sole source was what I had read in the news media plus one other fact. On Saturday, before the Sunday, a member of my staff was working with me on the several decisions I had to make. He was, from my staff, the one who had been in negotiations on Friday with the President and his staff. At the conclusion of some decisions that were made, I asked him, how did the President look, and he reported to me his observations. But other than what I had read or heard and this particular incident, I had no precise information concerning the President's health.

Yes, Mr. Joyce [Thomas H. Joyce, Newsweek Magazine].

POSSIBILITY OF A DEPRESSION [14.]

Q: Mr. President, your own economic advisers are suggesting—say the economy is very bad and they're very pessimistic—we are hearing the word "depression" used now. I wonder how you feel about whether we are heading for a depression?

THE PRESIDENT: Let me say very strongly that the United States is not going to have a depression. The overall economy of the United States is strong. Employment is still high. We do have the problem of inflation. We do have related problems, and we are going to come up with some answers that I hope will solve those problems.

We are not going to have a depression. We are going to work to make sure that our economy improves in the months ahead.

FOOD AID POLICY [15.]

Q: Mr. President, in the face of massive food shortages and the prospects of significant starvation, will the United States be able to significantly increase its food aid to foreign countries, and what is our position going to be at the Rome conference on participation in the world grain reserves?

THE PRESIDENT: Within the next few days a very major decision in this area will be made. I am not at liberty to tell you what the answer will be because it has not been decided.

But it is my hope that the United States for humanitarian purposes will be able to increase its contribution to those nations that have suffered because of drought or any of the other problems related to human needs.

INTELLIGENCE ACTIVITIES AND INTERNATIONAL LAW [16.]

Q: Back to the CIA. Under what international law do we have a right to attempt to destabilize the constitutionally elected government of another country, and does the Soviet Union have a similar right to try to destabilize the Government of Canada, for example, or the United States?

THE PRESIDENT: I am not going to pass judgment on whether it is permitted or authorized under international law. It is a recognized fact that historically, as well as presently, such actions are taken in the best interest of the countries involved.

ADMINISTRATION OPENNESS AND CANDOR [17.]

Q: Mr. President, last month when you assumed the Presidency, you pledged openness and candor. Last week you decided on the ex-President's pardon in virtually total secrecy. Despite all you have said tonight, there would still seem to be some confusion, some contradiction.

My question is this: Are your watchwords of your Administration still openness and candor?

THE PRESIDENT: Without any question, without any reservation. And I think in the one instance that you cite, it was a sole decision, and, believe me, it wasn't easy. And since I was the only one who could make that decision, I thought I had to search my own soul after consulting with a limited number of people. And I did it. And I think in the long run it was the right decision.

MR. CORMIER: Thank you, Mr. President.

Commentary

The decision to pardon President Nixon riveted the nation. Some viewed this action positively, whereas others viewed it negatively. Regardless, the Watergate scandal resulted in the first resignation of a president. Figure B.1 shows the front page of *The Washington Post* (1974) in which the announcement of the pardon was communicated to its readers. Figure B.2 shows the announcement in the *New York Times* (1974).

Figure B.3a and b shows page 1 and page 2 of the pardon, respectively.

The Weather

The Washington Post

FINAL

97th Year No. 278 MONDAY, SEPTEMBER 9, 1974

Ford Grants Nixon Full Pardon, Says He Has 'Suffered Enough'

TerHorst Quits in Protest

Nixon To Control His Papers

Not Consulted About Pardon, Jaworski Says

Figure B.1 Pardoning of President Nixon announced in the *Washington Post*. (From http://mitchellarchives.com/richard-nixon-pardoned-for-watergate.htm.)

"All the News That's Fit to Print"

The New York Times

LATE CITY EDITION

NEW YORK, MONDAY, SEPTEMBER 9, 1974

20 CENTS

FORD GIVES PARDON TO NIXON, WHO REGRETS 'MY MISTAKES'

U.S.-Bound Plane With 88 Crashes in Sea Off Greece

All on T.W.A. Flight From Tel Aviv Are Believed Dead—Wreckage Is Sighted

'PAIN' EXPRESSED

Ex-President Cites His Sorrow at the Way He Handled Watergate

NO CONDITIONS SET

Action Taken to Spare Nation and Ex-Chief, President Asserts

The Statement by Nixon

Proclamation of Pardon

State Panel Charges City Fails to Pursue Fugitives

Jaworski Won't Challenge Pardon, Spokesman Says

CANDIDATES SKIRT LAWS ON FINANCING

Knievel Safe as Rocket Falls Into Snake Canyon

Nixon Tapes Must Be Kept 3 Years for Use in Court

Some Mixed Reactions in Foley Square

terHorst Quits Post To Protest Pardon

Figure B.2 Announcement of the pardon by the *New York Times*. (From http://www.nytimes.com/learning/general/onthisday/big/0908.html.)

(a)

GRANTING PARDON TO RICHARD NIXON

BY THE PRESIDENT OF THE UNITED STATES OF AMERICA

A PROCLAMATION

Richard Nixon became the thirty-seventh President of the United States on January 20, 1969 and was reelected in 1972 for a second term by the electors of forty-nine of the fifty states. His term in office continued until his resignation on August 9, 1974.

Pursuant to resolutions of the House of Representatives, its Committee on the Judiciary conducted an inquiry and investigation on the impeachment of the President extending over more than eight months. The hearings of the Committee and its deliberations, which received wide national publicity over television, radio, and in printed media, resulted in votes adverse to Richard Nixon on recommended Articles of Impeachment.

As a result of certain acts or omissions occurring before his resignation from the Office of President, Richard Nixon has become liable to possible indictment and trial for offenses against the United States. Whether or not he shall be so prosecuted depends on findings of the appropriate grand jury and on the discretion of the authorized prosecutor. Should an indictment ensue, the accused shall then be entitled to a fair trial by an impartial jury, as guaranteed to every individual by the Constitution.

It is believed that a trial of Richard Nixon, if it became necessary, could not fairly begin until a year or more has elapsed. In the meantime, the tranquility to which this nation has been restored by the events of recent weeks could be irreparably lost by the prospects of bringing to trial a former President of the United States. The prospects of such

Figure B.3 President Ford's pardon. (a) Page 1.

(b)

2

trial will cause prolonged and divisive debate over the propriety of exposing to further punishment and degradation a man who has already paid the unprecedented penalty of relinquishing the highest elective office of the United States.

NOW, THEREFORE, I, Gerald R. Ford, President of the United States, pursuant to the pardon power conferred upon me by Article II, Section 2, of the Constitution, have granted and by these presents do grant a full, free, and absolute pardon unto Richard Nixon for all offenses against the United States which he, Richard Nixon, has committed or may have committed or taken part in during the period from January 20, 1969 through August 9, 1974.

IN WITNESS WHEREOF, I have hereunto set my hand this eighth day of September, in the year of our Lord nineteen hundred and seventy-four, and of the Independence of the United States of America the one hundred and ninety-ninth.

Gerald R. Ford

4311

Figure B.3 (Continued) President Ford's pardon. (b) Page 2. (From http://www.fordlibrarymuseum.gov/museum/exhibits/watergate_files/content.php?section=5&pa ge=c&doc=2.)

The pardoning of President Nixon was unpopular and disliked by some individuals within American society, including the administrative White House staff of President Ford. Figure B.4 shows the resignation of Press Secretary Jerald TerHorst, which was tendered in conjunction with the decision to pardon President Nixon.

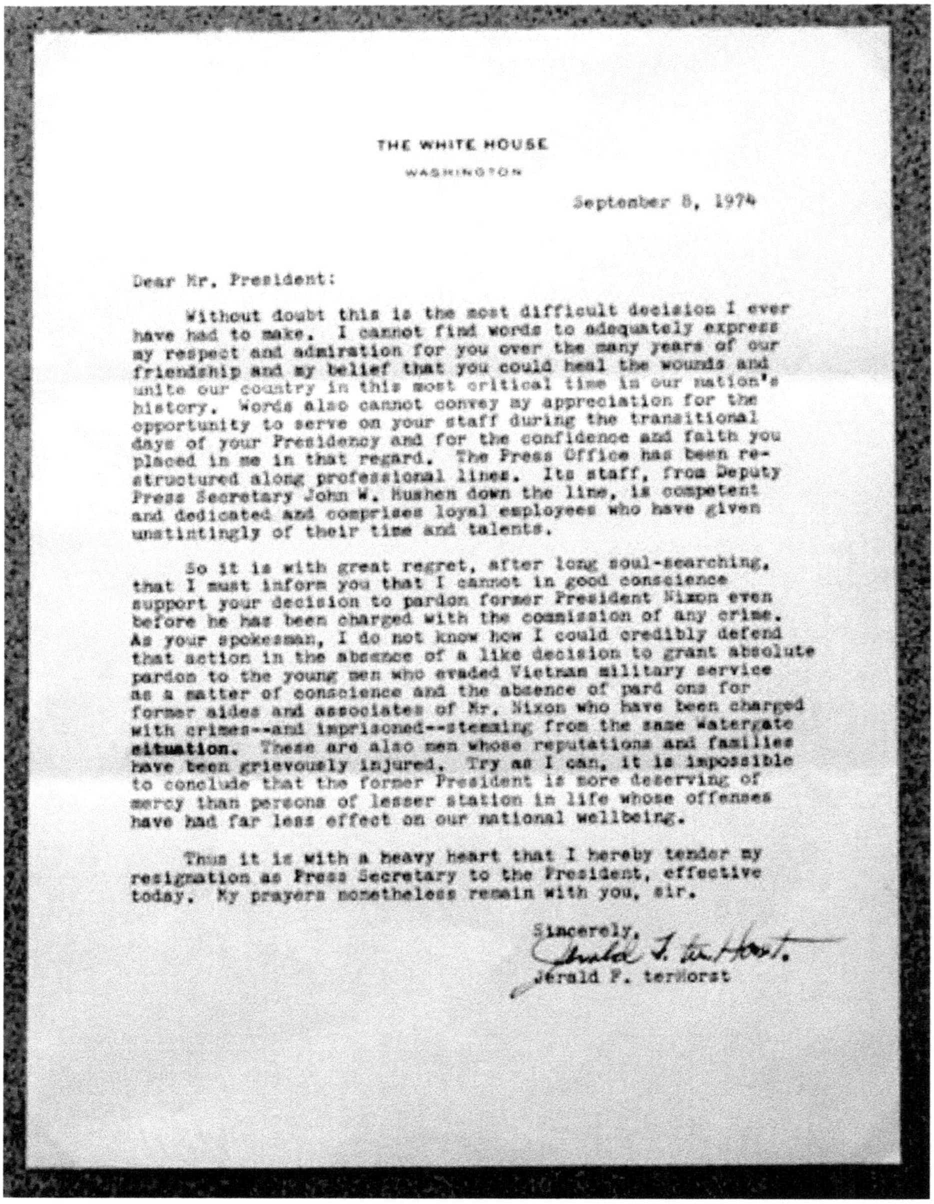

THE WHITE HOUSE
WASHINGTON

September 8, 1974

Dear Mr. President:

Without doubt this is the most difficult decision I ever have had to make. I cannot find words to adequately express my respect and admiration for you over the many years of our friendship and my belief that you could heal the wounds and unite our country in this most critical time in our nation's history. Words also cannot convey my appreciation for the opportunity to serve on your staff during the transitional days of your Presidency and for the confidence and faith you placed in me in that regard. The Press Office has been restructured along professional lines. Its staff, from Deputy Press Secretary John W. Hushen down the line, is competent and dedicated and comprises loyal employees who have given unstintingly of their time and talents.

So it is with great regret, after long soul-searching, that I must inform you that I cannot in good conscience support your decision to pardon former President Nixon even before he has been charged with the commission of any crime. As your spokesman, I do not know how I could credibly defend that action in the absence of a like decision to grant absolute pardon to the young men who evaded Vietnam military service as a matter of conscience and the absence of pard ons for former aides and associates of Mr. Nixon who have been charged with crimes--and imprisoned--stemming from the same Watergate situation. These are also men whose reputations and families have been grievously injured. Try as I can, it is impossible to conclude that the former President is more deserving of mercy than persons of lesser station in life whose offenses have had far less effect on our national wellbeing.

Thus it is with a heavy heart that I hereby tender my resignation as Press Secretary to the President, effective today. My prayers nonetheless remain with you, sir.

Sincerely,
Jerald F. terHorst

Figure B.4 Resignation of Press Secretary Jerald terHorst. (From http://www.fordlibrarymuseum.gov/museum/EduCenter09/images/gallery_pardon/terHorstletter.jpg.)

References

Ford, G. (n.d.). Gerald R. Ford quotes. Brainyquote.com. Retrieved from http://www.brainyquote.com/quotes/authors/g/gerald_r_ford.html (accessed December 19, 2012).

Ford, G. (1974). The president's news conference. Retrieved from http://www.presidency.ucsb.edu/ws/index.php?pid=4717 (accessed December 19, 2012).

New York Times. (1974). Retrieved from http://www.nytimes.com/learning/general/onthisday/big/0908.html.

The Washington Post. (1974). "Ford Grants Nixon Full Pardon, Says 'He Has Suffered Enough,'" September 9, 1974.

Appendix C: Steps in a Lawsuit

> I supported Arizona's immigration law by joining in that lawsuit to defend it. Every day I have Texans on that border that are doing their job.
>
> **—Governor Rick Perry (Fox News, 2011)**

Instigating a lawsuit necessitates a methodical, systematic process within the justice system. Lawsuits incorporate a variety of communication attributes ranging from the initiating of a complaint through the rendering of a verdict. This appendix delineates the primary steps of a lawsuit.

Step 1: Filing a Complaint or Petition

Any complaint or petition for relief in a court must be filed within the statutory time limit (Statute of Limitations). These statutes vary from state to state. These statutes also vary depending on what your cause of action is. For example, in many states, the statute of limitations regarding a cause of action for breach of contract is three years, while the cause of action for an intentional tort, like slander, is one year.

A complaint is a general statement of the plaintiff's claim. The complaint must describe the actions that led to the claim of a violation (i.e., violation of rights). The claim can be for money damages. It could also be a claim for equitable remedies like specific performance (e.g., court forcing a party to abide by a contract) or an injunction (e.g., stopping a person from doing something). The complaint must establish jurisdiction of the court in which it is filed. For example, if the complaint is filed in federal court, it must show diversity of citizenship or that a federal statutory or constitutional question is involved.

Class actions are sometimes filed against large companies. A class action can occur when a group of plaintiffs have same cause of action against one defendant. For example, a group of consumers might sue a lender for failure to pay abide by federal truth-in-lending disclosures on their loan forms. One advantage in a class action is that legal expenses can be shared by a large group of plaintiffs. Class actions have been the subject of abuse. Oftentimes individual plaintiffs get a small amount, while their lawyers get a fee based on the total amount paid to all members of the class. This amount can be huge. This practice has led to some frivolous class action suits.

Step 2: Service of Process

This generally involves attaching a copy of the complaint to a summons which is served on the defendant. The summons explains to the defendant what is going on and certain rights that that the defendant has. The summons explains:

1. That the defendant is being sued
2. The name of the Court in which he is being sued
3. When he must file an answer
4. The fact that a default judgment will be entered if no answer is filed

The summons (or process) is delivered by an officer of the court. In many state courts, this can be a deputy sheriff or a professional process server. Deputy marshals or process servers are used in federal court. Constables are used in justice court of some states. In exceptional circumstances, when the defendant cannot be found, service may be made by publication in a newspaper.

The summons must normally be served on the individual defendant. Some states allow service on a member of defendant's household if the defendant is not available. A plaintiff must serve a corporate defendant by serving the registered agent or an appropriate officer of the corporation.

Step 3: The Answer

In the answer, the defendant tells his side of the story. He is supposed to admit facts that are true and deny allegations that are not true. This answer must be filed within a certain period of time which is usually stated on the summons. Failure to file an answer can result in a default judgment against the defendant. This is a judgment for failure to defend that is entered against the defendant just like there had been a trial.

The defendant can file a counterclaim against the plaintiff as part of his answer. The effect of the counterclaim is that the defendant is suing the plaintiff in the same action. The plaintiff must file an answer to the counterclaim or a default judgment will be taken against him.

Step 4: Ending a Suit through Motions

Motions are formal requests for the court to take some sort of action. The pleadings generally will consist of the complaint, the answer, any counterclaim, and all motions. In a motion for judgment on the pleadings, the defendant is arguing that even if everything said in the complaint were true, plaintiff would still have no cause of action against defendant. For example, suppose you have a business partner who calls you a liar in a room where only you and your partner were present. You sue you partner for slander. He would be entitled to a judgment on the pleadings since there was no publication (verbally or in writing) of your slanderous remark. Only he heard it. If the court grants this motion, the case is over unless you appeal the judgment.

Another type of motion that is often filed is a motion to dismiss. Two common grounds for this motion are expiration of the appropriate statute of limitations or that the court lacks jurisdiction over the case. For example, courts of equity in some states have jurisdiction over disputes involving land. If such a dispute were filed in a circuit court, a motion to dismiss for lack of jurisdiction would be appropriate.

A motion for summary judgment is appropriate in situations where there are no important facts in dispute and the only dispute is how the law should be applied to the facts. If there is no dispute over the important facts of the case, there is nothing for a jury to determine since that is their job, to decide what the facts are based on the evidence presented at trial. The judge will therefore apply the law to the facts and render a judgment. That will be the end of the case unless there is an appeal. Generally, this motion is not made unless all discovery has been completed.

Step 5: Discovery

The period allowed for discovery is when the plaintiff and defendant get information from each other and other people to use as evidence at trial. Discovery pleadings generally consist of the following:

1. Requests for production of documents: These are written requests served on the opposing party's attorney requesting that documents relevant to the case be produced for inspection and copying.
2. Requests for admission: These are requests from one party to another to admit facts that are not in dispute so that the evidence produced at trial will basically include matters that are in dispute. Honest and complete responses can shorten the trial.
3. Depositions: These are statements of the parties or potential witnesses taken under oath by a court reporter. Depositions are usually taken by a private court reporter (i.e., one not employed by a court) in the office of one of the lawyers. Depositions are used to pin down the testimony of witnesses and to find out what witnesses are going to say at trial.

Courts are generally very liberal regarding what information is subject to discovery. It must be generally relevant in some way although, technically, courts will allow the parties to ask for anything that is reasonably calculated to lead to discoverable evidence. Attorneys do not have to disclose work product. Work product consists of the thoughts, strategies, and theories of the attorneys of the parties, whether it is in the form of memos, notes, letters, or any similar document.

Pretrial conferences always are required in Federal Courts and are being required more and more in some state courts. The following usually occur in pretrial conferences:

1. The parties agree on the facts not in dispute.
2. They tell each other whom their witnesses will be.
3. They identify what their evidence will be and provide copies of documents that will be offered into evidence.

Each party will submit in writing the facts they intend to prove and the law or jury instructions that should be applied to the facts. The judge will generally act somewhat as a mediator, at least in federal court, and try to get the parties to settle case.

Step 6: The Trial

Facts have to be in dispute to make a trial necessary. The trier of fact can either be a jury or a judge alone, unless a jury is required by law. A jury trial is generally required by

Constitution if the amount in controversy exceeds $20. However, a jury trial is generally not required if it is an equitable issue like an injunction action. The right to a jury can be waived. There is an absolute right to a jury trial in criminal cases.

Prospective jurors are drawn at random from voting lists or other lists (like licensed drivers) and make up the pool from which the juries are picked. Some prospective jurors are excused, like mothers of small children or someone on whom serving would be a hardship like an accountant during tax season.

Voir dire is used to weed out jurors that may be biased in some way. The judge and the attorneys ask questions about a prospective juror's knowledge of the case, occupation, relationship to the attorneys or parties, and similar questions. Most states have jurors fill out a questionnaire on general topics to save time. Jurors can be challenged for cause. The argument would be that they were incapable of making an impartial decision. For example, they might be friends of one of the parties or one of the attorneys.

Attorneys can also use a limited number of peremptory challenges to remove potential jurors with whom they are uncomfortable. A peremptory challenge is a right to strike a juror with or without cause. However, the challenge can't be based on race or sex. In a personal injury action involving a big company, plaintiff attorneys sometimes will want jurors of limited education rather than business people. People with limited education are sometimes more likely to rule on emotion against a big rich insurance company, for example.

In the opening statement, each party's attorney gives a summary of what he intends to prove and the evidence that will be used. Next, the plaintiff presents his evidence, which will primarily consist of the testimony of witnesses. The plaintiff has the burden of proof. The standard of proof is the preponderance of evidence in most civil cases. The standard in criminal cases is beyond a reasonable doubt. The standard in some civil cases, like in a suit charging fraud, is clear and convincing evidence. This standard is somewhere in between beyond a reasonable doubt and preponderance of evidence.

In direct examination of a witness, the attorney calling the witness will ask the questions. In the cross-examination of the witness, the opposing counsel asks questions. He will often try to discredit the witness. For example, if accident that is the subject of the suit occurred at night, the questioning might go something like this:

- You testified that you were 60 ft. from the accident, is that correct?
- The accident happened on August 15, is that correct?
- It was cloudy that night, wasn't it?
- It was dark, wasn't it?
- You couldn't see very well, could you?

A good cross-examiner will only ask questions that he knows the answer to and which will yield a yes or no answer. However, a witness has the right to explain his answer. In redirect examination, the attorney who called the witness will try to undo any damage caused by the cross-examination. The opposing counsel will then have the right to re-cross. This is similar to cross-examination.

The witness must have personal knowledge of what he is testifying about. He must have direct or indirect contact with facts of case, *e.g.*, actually witnessed the accident in question or overheard the contract in dispute being negotiated. A witness must testify based on his personal knowledge. He generally cannot give his opinion unless it is based on his five senses. Examples:

- Looked dark
- Smelled smoke
- Saw the defendant take the item from the store
- Felt pain
- Heard the misrepresentations made by the salesman

An expert witness can give opinions. For example, in a medical malpractice case involving a doctor, an expert witness (usually another doctor) will have to give an opinion that the defendant doctor's actions were negligent in that they were not in accordance with the standard of care of the medical community. In an eminent domain suit a main issue will be the fair market value of the real property that is to be condemned. Both parties will need to call an appraiser as an expert witness to give his opinion as to the fair market value of the property.

After the plaintiff presents all his evidence, he *rests* his case. In a jury trial, the plaintiff will ordinarily make a motion for a directed verdict. This motion is to be granted by the judge if the plaintiff has not made a prima facie case. The plaintiff must offer proof of each legal element of his claim. This is called making a prima facie case. For example, to prove fraud, you would normally have to prove

- That a false statement had been made
- That defendant knew it was false
- That defendant made statement to deceive plaintiff
- That plaintiff was deceived
- Resulting in damages to plaintiff

Failure to offer proof on one of these elements could cause a motion for directed verdict to be sustained. That would be the end of the trial.

Next, the defendant (i.e., the defendant's attorney) calls his witnesses and introduces his evidence. Evidence, other than testimony, that either party could introduce would be documents, like a contracts or a letter, or tangible items like a defective piece of equipment.

Hearsay evidence is testimony that is offered by a witness who does not have personal knowledge of the information being given but just heard it from someone else. This type of evidence is generally inadmissible. In a suit where the issue is whether or not a contract was breached, suppose that testimony is offered by a witness to the effect that the witness heard the defendant say that he had no intention of strictly abiding by the terms of the contract. Such evidence would be hearsay and generally not admissible. There are several exceptions to the hearsay rule.

In the closing argument each attorney summarizes what he has proven. Hopefully, each attorney will have proven what he promised to prove during his opening statement. Attorneys for each party will also try to point out defects in the case of the opposition.

In a jury trial jury instructions are given to the jury at the end of the case. These instructions are prepared by the attorneys of both parties and presented to the judge for approval. The instructions tell the jurors what the law is and how to apply the law to the facts that have been proven.

During jury deliberations, the jurors will decide on a verdict. A unanimous verdict is ordinarily not required in civil cases. In some states, only nine out of twelve of the jury must agree on a verdict. A hung jury occurs when the jury cannot agree on a verdict. The case must be tried over again or dismissed.

Post trial motions generally consist of the following:

- *Motion for a new trial.* Sample grounds would be if the jury misconstrued a jury instruction or the jury clearly should have found more damages.
- *Motion for a judgment notwithstanding the verdict (JNOV).* If the judge grants a JNOV, the judge reverses the decision of the jury and enters judgment for the other side because, for example, the jury's verdict clearly did not conform to the evidence. It is rare for a judge to grant a JNOV.

An *appeal* to a higher court can be made by the party who lost the case or if the party who won believes that damages do not conform to the evidence. There are time limits on appeal. The time in which a party has to file a notice of appeal depends on the court. The appellate court makes its decision on selected portions to the transcript of the trial, legal briefs of the attorneys, and oral arguments of the attorneys, if permitted by court. No witnesses are heard or evidence is presented.

Although this process seems quite simple, especially since it only consists of six primary components, it can be quite complex from the perspective of communications. It incorporates multiple instantiations of just about every type of communication modality possible (e.g., sight, sound, speech, or writing). Both the participants (e.g., judges, attorneys, plaintiffs, and defendants) and observers (e.g., the general public attending a court session) are affected by these instantiations of communication. These elements of communication

Table C.1 Communication and the Lawsuit Process

Event	Communication Example
Filing a complaint or petition	Written complaint or petition
Service of process	Delivery of written summons documents
The answer	Written response to complaint or petition
Ending a suit through motions	Oral and written motions
Discovery	Administering of oaths for deposition
	Oral and written communication between defenders and prosecutors
	Written statements of facts
The trial	Oral testimony
	Oral questioning of witnesses
	Nonverbal cues during questioning
	Use of auditory, visual, or written evidence
	Use of motions
	Court transcription
	Consideration of hearsay
	Jury instructions
	Announcing of verdict
Post-trial	Written appeal
	Post-trial motions

affect not only the internal workings of the justice system and its participants but also of society. For instance, notable lawsuits are newsworthy items thereby influencing public opinion regarding a variety of topics. Regardless, communication undeniably permeates the lawsuit process. Table C.1 shows the basic lawsuit process and examples of the types of communication that are pertinent within each stage of the process.

Reference

Fox News. (2011). *Transcript: Fox News-Google GOP Debate*. Retrieved from http://www.foxnews.com/politics/2011/09/22/fox-news-google-gop-2012-presidential-debate/ (accessed July 31, 2014).

Appendix D: Communication and the Chain of Custody

> In 1994, the U.S. Court of Appeals decided in the case of Oliver North to permit the release of grand jury evidence, because it had already been so thoroughly leaked.
> **—Donella Meadows (Meadows, n.d.)**

Objectives

The objectives of this appendix are to

- Explain the chain-of-custody concept
- Explain the importance of chain of custody
- Discuss the relationship between the chain of custody and communication

Introduction

A chain of custody is defined as follows (Turvey, 2008):

> … the record of everyone who has controlled, taken custody of, or had contact with a particular item of evidence from its discovery to the present day. It has tremendous importance with respect to providing context for, and a record of, any scientific examinations. It also has considerable value with respect to establishing the origins of, and influences on, evidence presented in court. (Turvey, 2008)

A chain of custody is synonymous with the concept of a transfer log that records transactions of materials between parties. The chain of custody is absolutely an essential mechanism for preserving the integrity of evidence that may be observed and accumulated during the courses of law enforcement and justice system activities. All evidence and materials must be appropriately handled and transferred among various parties using a chain of custody to describe each individual event that represents the transference of materials from one party to another party. The chain of custody is used for an array of types of evidence ranging from computer and electronic evidence to physical evidence such as weapons and clothing.

Communication is an essential characteristic of the chain of custody. All chains of custody must communicate the characteristics of "when, how, and by whom" evidence may have been discovered, "secured, collected, transported, preserved, and tested" (Philbin, 2012). Each transaction within the chain of custody is recorded via written expression. Generally, most chain-of-custody logs may indicate a time, date, location, item being transferred, and the parties involved within the transaction. The written records of such transactions communicate the characteristics of the various transactions that occur between parties. A typical chain-of-custody form is presented in Figure D.1.

Figure D.1 shows the federal drug testing custody and control form. Within this document, the individual fields are used to record and communicate pertinent data regarding the exchange transaction. It contains separate sections to preserve the integrity of the transaction by expressing the recorded characteristics of the donor, collector, laboratory, and reviewer. Through the expression of such transaction characteristics, this form effectively and efficiently communicates the relevant attributes associated with a chain of custody.

Not all chain-of-custody forms adhere exactly to this format. Individual departments and organizations may craft their own unique forms through which the attributes of the chain of custody are communicated. Some may have many details, whereas others may have fewer details. Regardless, in any case, the purpose of such forms is to establish a chain

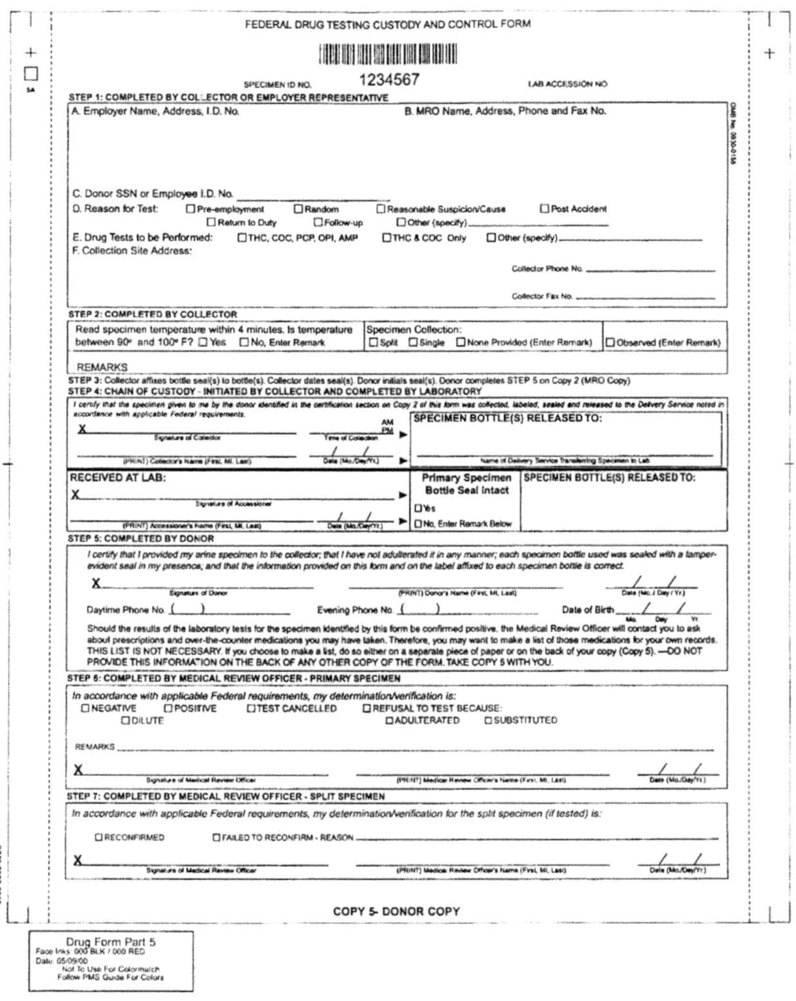

FEDERAL DRUG TESTING CUSTODY AND CONTROL FORM

SPECIMEN ID NO. 1234567 LAB ACCESSION NO.

STEP 1: COMPLETED BY COLLECTOR OR EMPLOYER REPRESENTATIVE

A. Employer Name, Address, I.D. No.

B. MRO Name, Address, Phone and Fax No.

C. Donor SSN or Employee I.D. No. ______

D. Reason for Test: ☐ Pre-employment ☐ Random ☐ Reasonable Suspicion/Cause ☐ Post Accident ☐ Return to Duty ☐ Follow-up ☐ Other (specify) ______

E. Drug Tests to be Performed: ☐ THC, COC, PCP, OPI, AMP ☐ THC & COC Only ☐ Other (specify) ______

F. Collection Site Address:

Collector Phone No. ______

Collector Fax No. ______

OMB No. 0930-0158

STEP 2: COMPLETED BY COLLECTOR

Read specimen temperature within 4 minutes. Is temperature between 90° and 100° F? ☐ Yes ☐ No, Enter Remark

Specimen Collection: ☐ Split ☐ Single ☐ None Provided (Enter Remark) ☐ Observed (Enter Remark)

REMARKS

STEP 3: Collector affixes bottle seal(s) to bottle(s). Collector dates seal(s). Donor initials seal(s). Donor completes STEP 5 on Copy 2 (MRO Copy)

STEP 4: CHAIN OF CUSTODY - INITIATED BY COLLECTOR AND COMPLETED BY LABORATORY

I certify that the specimen given to me by the donor identified in the certification section on Copy 2 of this form was collected, labeled, sealed and released to the Delivery Service noted in accordance with applicable Federal requirements.

X ______ Signature of Collector | ______ AM PM Time of Collection

______ (PRINT) Collector's Name (First, MI, Last) | / / Date (Mo./Day/Yr.)

SPECIMEN BOTTLE(S) RELEASED TO:

______ Name of Delivery Service Transferring Specimen to Lab

RECEIVED AT LAB:

X ______ Signature of Accessioner

______ (PRINT) Accessioner's Name (First, MI, Last) | / / Date (Mo./Day/Yr.)

Primary Specimen Bottle Seal Intact ☐ Yes ☐ No, Enter Remark Below

SPECIMEN BOTTLE(S) RELEASED TO:

STEP 5: COMPLETED BY DONOR

I certify that I provided my urine specimen to the collector; that I have not adulterated it in any manner; each specimen bottle used was sealed with a tamper-evident seal in my presence; and that the information provided on this form and on the label affixed to each specimen bottle is correct.

X ______ Signature of Donor | ______ (PRINT) Donor's Name (First, MI, Last) | / / Date (Mo. / Day / Yr.)

Daytime Phone No. ( ) ______ Evening Phone No. ( ) ______ Date of Birth / / Mo. Day Yr.

Should the results of the laboratory tests for the specimen identified by this form be confirmed positive, the Medical Review Officer will contact you to ask about prescriptions and over-the-counter medications you may have taken. Therefore, you may want to make a list of those medications for your own records. THIS LIST IS NOT NECESSARY. If you choose to make a list, do so either on a separate piece of paper or on the back of your copy (Copy 5). —DO NOT PROVIDE THIS INFORMATION ON THE BACK OF ANY OTHER COPY OF THE FORM. TAKE COPY 5 WITH YOU.

STEP 6: COMPLETED BY MEDICAL REVIEW OFFICER - PRIMARY SPECIMEN

In accordance with applicable Federal requirements, my determination/verification is:

☐ NEGATIVE ☐ POSITIVE ☐ TEST CANCELLED ☐ REFUSAL TO TEST BECAUSE: ☐ DILUTE ☐ ADULTERATED ☐ SUBSTITUTED

REMARKS ______

X ______ Signature of Medical Review Officer | ______ (PRINT) Medical Review Officer's Name (First, MI, Last) | / / Date (Mo./Day/Yr.)

STEP 7: COMPLETED BY MEDICAL REVIEW OFFICER - SPLIT SPECIMEN

In accordance with applicable Federal requirements, my determination/verification for the split specimen (if tested) is:

☐ RECONFIRMED ☐ FAILED TO RECONFIRM - REASON ______

X ______ Signature of Medical Review Officer | ______ (PRINT) Medical Review Officer's Name (First, MI, Last) | / / Date (Mo./Day/Yr.)

COPY 5- DONOR COPY

0000-0000-0225

Drug Form Part 5
Face Inks: 000 BLK / 000 RED
Date: 05/09/00
Not To Use For Colormatch
Follow PMS Guide For Colors

Figure D.1 Chain-of-custody form. (From https://www.federalregister.gov/articles/2000/06/23/00-15889/federal-drug-testing-custody-and-control-form.)

of custody, protect and ensure the integrity of the chain of custody, and communicate the details of each transaction that comprises the chain of custody through time.

Chain of Custody

The chain of custody is especially important regarding court proceedings and the processing of cases within the justice system. A chain of custody is generally the "only thing" that links "defendants to the evidence that brought them to trial" (Philbin, 2012). Maintaining the integrity of the chain of custody is imperative when considering the success of court cases. If a chain of custody is broken or questionable, then various disputes may arise regarding the evidence, its handling, and transference. A familiar incident involving a chain-of-custody dispute was the O.J. Simpson trial. This issue is described as follows:

> … LAPD criminalist Collin Yamauchi confirmed that at one time during testing, he inadvertently transferred blood from the Simpson vial onto his plastic gloves. The defense tried to infer that this blood might, in fact, have then been transferred onto the leather glove found at Simpson's home (as part of a police conspiracy). (Philbin, 2012)

This admission contributed toward undermining the "credibility of the prosecution" (Philbin, 2012). Usually, as a method of maintaining the credibility and validity of evidence, a chain of custody may be used to "reasonable certainty that the evidence is the same as that seized and that there has been no tampering or substitution" (Cook v. State, 2007). A chain of custody is preserved when "a reasonable assurance of the identity of the evidence" is established and communicated via some recording process (Cook v. State, 2007). This recording process is necessary for communicating the salient points of exchange regarding the collection of evidence, its intermediary exchanges, and current location. Defense attorneys may "challenge" any aspect of evidence if the chain of custody "is broken at any point in time" (Haglund & Sorg, 1997). If a break occurs within the chain of custody or if documentation is incomplete, then courts may rule that evidence may be deemed as inadmissible.

Among court proceedings, considerations of admissibility are critical from the perspectives of chains of custody. During 2002, a Florida Supreme Court case, *Floyd v. State*, 27 FLW S697, considered the chain of custody of a bullet within the context of murder proceedings in which the defendant was convicted. Specifically, this case questioned "whether a complete chain of custody had to be established before a bullet removed from a murder victim could be introduced at trial" (State of Florida, 2013). Regarding the chain of custody, an excerpt from the ruling of the Florida Supreme Court is given as follows (State of Florida, 2013):

> … ruled that a gap in the chain of custody will only result in the exclusion of the evidence if the defense can show a probability that it was tampered with. Since agent Leary testified that the bullet was in the same condition at trial as it was when he last saw it, there was no indication of tampering. Therefore, it was not necessary for the prosecution to establish a continuous chain of custody. (State of Florida, 2013)

Thus far, the considerations of chains of custody have considered the tracking and communicating of attributes that are associated with tangible forms of evidence. Often, intangible entities are subjected to the chain of custody regarding the processing of digital and electronic materials. This perspective involves a consideration of electronic and computer forensics. Specifically, this notion is defined as the "science of locating, extracting, analyzing, and protecting types of data from different devices, which specialists then interpret to serve as legal evidence" (Marcella & Menendez, 2008). Communicating the exchanges of such evidence also occurs through the chain of custody.

Within this context, the chain of custody involves the documentation of "serial numbers" associated with the examined systems and devices, the personnel that both had custody and handled these items, the length of time these items were in the possession of such personnel, the shipping method of the examined system, and "any other steps in the process" (Ciampa, 2009). Communicating this information accurately and completely is crucial to court proceedings. If any imperfection exists within the chain of custody, arguments may arise stating that improper handling of evidence occurred, and that it could have been changed or tainted (Casey, 2011). Furthermore, such imperfection may cause the evidence to be lost or misplaced, or contaminated (Casey, 2011). In some instances, court cases have been dismissed because of issues associated with imperfections within the chain of custody.

Figure D.2 shows a typical chain-of-custody form that communicates the salient characteristics of electronic and computer items. Its initial section contains unique identifiers that communicate specifically and exactly what item is being maintained within the chain of custody. Producers of electronic and computer equipment include both serial and model numbers among their products.

The serial and model numbers uniquely identify a specific unit of production, and may be used to specifically identify an item throughout the chain of custody. In some cases, law enforcement organizations or entities within the justice system may assign a separate identifier to uniquely identify the item. The example form also includes specificity for the manufacturer. Communicating this information also helps further identify uniquely the considered item because it shows that the serial and product numbers are associated with a specific manufacturer, thereby eliminating the possibility that serial or model numbers may be questionable because they may be repeated among different manufacturers. Therefore, the identification of an item is greatly enhanced through the communicating of the combination of the manufacturer, serial number, and model number.

Some electronic or computer equipment may be considered as peripheral devices. Peripheral devices include keyboards, scanners, printers, USB drives, and so forth. Although these items are electronic devices that may be used with computer equipment, they are supplemental items that may be attached to laptop or desktop computers. In some cases, multiple components may be associated with the functioning of the peripheral (e.g., adapters and cables). As a method of ensuring that equipment cases are unopened, thereby reducing the chance of tampering, tamper seals may be applied that must remain intact until such time it is deemed necessary for the item to be opened. The sample form contains data fields communicating whether the considered item is a peripheral device, whether multiple components exist, and whether a tamper seal is present.

The second section provides a description of the item being maintained within the chain of custody. Personnel may describe the item physically. For instance, one may indicate that the item is a portable laptop computer, has a certain size screen, has a certain type of processor, and has various physical characteristics (e.g., black case, any scratches or scars, or someone's name written on the item). This section communicates the physical

Electronic Device and Computer Equipment
Chain of Custody Form

Serial Number: ____________ Peripheral Device: ___ Yes ___ No
Model Number: ____________ Multiple Components: ___ Yes ___ No
Manufacturer: ____________ Tamper Seal: ___ Yes ___ No

Description:

Transaction Record			
Chronology	From	To	Describe Transaction
Date:	Name:	Name:	
Time:	Signature:	Signature:	
Transaction No:	Department:	Department:	
Date:	Name:	Name:	
Time:	Signature:	Signature:	
Transaction No:	Department:	Department:	
Date:	Name:	Name:	
Time:	Signature:	Signature:	
Transaction No:	Department:	Department:	

Page 1 of ____

Figure D.2 Electronic device and computer equipment chain of custody form.

attributes of the considered item. When coupled with the data recorded within the first section of the form, a basic understanding of what (i.e., the item) is subject to the chain of custody is established.

The third section communicates the salient characteristics of transactions that occur chronologically within the chain of custody. The form communicates the date and time of the transaction, and provides a field for assigning a unique transaction number for each individual exchange that occurs throughout the chain of custody. By doing so, each instance of changed possession may be recorded and expressed through written language to show the flow of the item throughout the chain of custody. If properly completed when transactions occur, credence is given chronologically to the integrity of the chain of custody. Basically, this information communicates when items are exchanged within the chain of custody.

The form also denotes the individual parties that are subject to each specific transaction that occurs within the chain of custody. The entity possessing the item and the entity receiving the item are both expressed within the form. The form communicates this information twice—once that may involve a printed or typed name and another instance requiring a hand signature for both parties. These data fields identify the persons between whom the item is exchanged through time. Therefore, this section communicates who is associated with the chain of custody at all points through time.

Each transaction within the chain of custody is unique. The form communicates this uniqueness by specifying a description of the exchange. For example, personnel may communicate that the item is being transferred from a law enforcement agency to a forensics laboratory for a specific type of examination. Basically, this data field communicates why and where a transaction is occurring within the chain of custody.

Examining the sample form provides multiple perspectives regarding communications and the chain of custody. Essentially, these perspectives are commensurate with the basic questions of communication that were introduced within the opening discussions of the textbook regarding the following queries: who, what, when, where, and why? The question "how" remains, and may be considered from the completeness of the form. Throughout the entirety of the chain of custody, opportunity is provided to communicate the salient aspects of how an item is transferred. For instance, identifiers within the form describing a transaction show the people, places, times, and item that was transferred thereby providing some insight regarding "how" an item moved within the chain of custody through time.

The chain of custody is a necessary component of the justice system. Communicating the details associated with the conveyance of items throughout the chain of custody strengthens the integrity of maintaining evidence and reduces arguments that may arise regarding transactions of items through time. Whether tangible or intangible (e.g., software), all evidence is subject to the chain of custody and must be handled appropriately within the justice system. Through the use of various chain-of-custody forms, the characteristics of evidence and its transactions are communicated within the justice system.

Commentary Regarding Chain of Custody and Communication

Using a chain-of-custody form to communicate the characteristics of evidence transference and handling embellishes the integrity of the justice system and interjects accountability among its processes and procedures involving evidence. Accountability exists through the specifying of individuals between whom evidence is transferred and passed, and is embellished by the provision of original signatures indicating the receipt of evidence within a chain-of-custody form.

The chain-of-custody form may be used to track the progress of both tangible and intangible forms of evidence within the justice system. Within the chain-of-custody form, personnel may enter a variety of data attributes that reflect the primary questions of communication introduced during the opening discussions of this text: who, what, when, where, why, and how? Although the formats of chain-of-custody forms may vary among organizations, they all must communicate the characteristics of these issues regarding the maintaining, handling, and transferring of evidence.

Chains of custody are often disputed with respect to arguments involving considerations of tampering, accidental spoiling of evidence, or improper handling procedures when processing evidence (Hassell & Steen, 2005). A notable court case involving such concepts was *Gates Rubber Company v. Bando Chemical Industries Ltd.*, 167 F.R.D. 90, 112 (D. Colo. 1996) (Hassell & Steen, 2005). This case involved "forensically invalid" reproductions of computer hard disks for the purpose of collecting and analyzing computer-based evidence (Hassell & Steen, 2005). Because of these hard disks and the "forensically unsound procedure utilized to copy the drives," electronic date information was changed, thereby destroying the chain of custody (Hassell & Steen, 2005). Therefore, a failure to "preserve evidence in the most appropriate manner" occurred, which resulted in sanctioning. (*The Gates Rubber Company v. Bando*, 1996)

More recently, during 2008, another court case that disputed its associated chain of custody occurred in Newport, Tennessee. This case involved allegations of driving under the influence (DUI) charges (Soesbee, 2008). The following excerpts describe inconsistencies within the chain of custody (Soesbee, 2008):

> … the jury did not learn about the results of the test because Judge Hooper ruled that the results were inadmissible on a motion by defense attorney Bill Leibrock. The reason was that the state had failed to show a solid "chain of custody" of that evidence, specifically who had possession of the blood sample at each step in the investigative process. One problem was that the sample was sent to the crime laboratory by UPS instead of being directly delivered by an officer, which is the standard procedure in such cases. So, Agent Massengill was unable to positively testify concerning who had possession of the blood sample at specific times and what might have happened to it … Judge Hooper told the jury that "the chain of custody was broken in this case," adding that "every drug [Cruz] had in her system she had a valid prescription for." (Soesbee, 2008)

Such events highlight the importance of policies that govern the processes and the procedures that are used to handle evidence and to communicate the attributes of evidentiary transactions that occur within a chain of custody. Within the justice system and among law enforcement entities, policies must exist that delineate methods of handling evidence and expressing the characteristics of transactions involving evidence. An example of such a policy is the *Chain-of-Custody Manual* (State of Oregon, 2010), of the Oregon State Public Health Laboratory and the Oregon Health Authority.

This policy delineates various controls regarding exchange transactions that exist within the chain of custody. The Oregon policy ensures that an "accurate written record" must exist that shows the historical events that occur regarding the possessing and "handling" of materials commencing with the evidentiary collection to the period of "analysis and/or disposal" (State of Oregon, 2010). Every facet of communicating the characteristics of exchange is expressed and defined within the policy manual. Within the policy, clauses exist that affect the following chain-of-custody elements: specimens and materials, handling, supplies and equipment, safety, engineering controls, procedures, limitations constraining procedures, and chain-of-custody forms. Further, the Oregon policy document itself represents a written form of communication through which controls affecting the chain of custody are expressed and delineated.

The crafting and dissemination of policy among entities within the justice system embellishes accountability. When exercised appropriately and correctly, no gaps should exist within the chain of custody because the attributes of each separate exchange and possession are communicated within chain-of-custody forms. Policy guides the actions that occur throughout the chain of custody to ensure that an adherence to handling rules and procedures occurs without incident. However, if a shortcoming occurs, then policy should influence the corrective or punitive actions that may be necessary.

The importance of communication throughout the chain of custody must not be understated. Without efficient communication, the recording of information regarding the exchanging of items within the chain of custody may be absent, thereby yielding a failed understanding of events that transpired when evidence was handled or exchanged. As a result, such an absence of communicated details may facilitate disputes and questions regarding the integrity of the chain of custody and of the considered evidence or materials. Regardless, all law enforcement organizations and entities within the justice system must strive to maintain proper documentation toward effectively and efficiently communicating chain-of-custody attributes and events.

Appendix Comments and Summary

This appendix introduced the chain-of-custody concept and the methods of communicating that are essential regarding the handling and transferring of evidence. Maintaining and communicating the details of transactions regarding evidence are critical aspects of processing court cases within the justice system. Prosecutors, defense attorneys, law enforcement organizations, and society have a vested interest in ensuring that chains of custody exhibit integrity. Facets of integrity may be strengthened through the meticulous recording and expressing of attributes that describe the conveyance and transference of evidence within the justice system through the use of various chain-of-custody forms.

Despite the best efforts of an organization to embellish the integrity of its chain of custody, disputes regarding evidence and its handling may arise within the justice system. Some chains of evidence may be completely destroyed, whereas others may be very questionable because of inconsistencies, accidents, or omissions regarding the recording and expressing of attributes describing evidentiary transactions. These errors often result in the dismissal of court cases. Therefore, meticulousness is necessary when communicating the attributes of change that occur throughout the entirety of the chain of custody.

The chain of custody is a pertinent consideration of both large and small cases within the justice system. In some cases, disputes involving the chain of custody may generate national noteworthiness. For example, during the heralded case of O.J Simpson, laboratory mistakes within the chain of custody weakened the credibility of the prosecution (Philbin, 2012). Another notable incident involved mistakes made within a crime scene involving a murder that was perpetrated by the Mason family. In this instance, a bloody fingerprint discovered on a doorbell was actually the fingerprint of a detective who had pressed the bloodied doorbell to gain entry into the examined house (Philbin, 2012).

Communication is of paramount importance throughout each link within the chain of custody. Extreme care must be taken to ensure that a written record exists that details every exchange of items and every attribute of handling items. Crafting this type of historical document greatly enhances accountability and integrity within chains of custody. Such historical records are established via chain-of-custody forms. Essentially, these forms exist as resources through which chain-of-custody attributes are documented and communicated via written language.

Terminology

Accountability
Admissible
Break

Chain of custody
Contamination
Dismissed case
Documentation
Evidence
Form documentation
Inadmissible
Integrity
Manufacturer
Model number
Policy
Sanction
Serial number
Tainted
Tamper seal
Tampering

THOUGHT AND DISCUSSION QUESTION

1. If you own a laptop or desktop computer, locate the manufacturer identification, the serial number, and the model number. On the basis of this information, complete the sample form presented in Figure D.2. Assume that your device completes several transactions. Provide a commentary regarding your opinion of whether the completed form is sufficient to identify your specific device if it were subject to a chain of custody. Within your response, provide a commentary regarding your opinion of whether the integrity of the chain of custody could be maintained with respect to the completed form presented in Figure D.2.

References

Casey, E. (2011). *Digital evidence and computer crime: Forensic science, computers, and the internet* (p. 22). Boston: Academic Press.

Ciampa, M. (2009). *Security plus guide to network security fundamentals* (3rd ed., p. 13). Boston: Course Technology.

Cook v. State. (2007). Findlaw.com. Retrieved from http://caselaw.findlaw.com/ga-court-of-appeals/1396659.html (accessed April 3, 2013).

The Gates Rubber Company, a Colorado corporation, Plaintiff, vs. Bando Chemical Industries, Limited, a Japanese company; Bando American, Inc., an Illinois corporation; Bando Manufacturing of America, Inc., a Kentucky corporation; Bando U.S.A., Inc., a Delaware corporation; Allen Hanano, an individual; Steven R. Piderit, an individual; Ron Newman, an individual; Denise Hanano, an individual; and John Does 1–93, Defendants. (1996). Harvard University. Retrieved from http://cyber.law.harvard.edu/digitaldiscovery/library/preservation/gates.html (accessed April 17, 2013).

Haglund, W., & Sorg, M. (1997). *Forensic taphonomy: The postmortem fate of human remains* (p. 65). Boca Raton, FL: CRC Press.

Hassell, J., & Steen, S. (2005). Preserving and protecting computer evidence. Electronic Evidence Retrieval. Retrieved from http://www.electronicevidenceretrieval.com/preserving_protecting_evidence.htm (accessed April 17, 2013).

Marcella, A., & Menendez, D. (2008). *Cyber forensics: A field manual for collecting, examining, and preserving evidence of computer crimes* (p. 5). Boca Raton, FL: Auerbach Publications.

Meadows, D. (n.d.). Leaked quotations. Retrieved from http://www.brainyquote.com/words/le/leaked184087.html (accessed April 2, 2013).

Philbin, T. (2012). *The killer book of cold cases: Incredible stories, facts, and trivia from the most baffling true crime cases of all time* (p. 200). Naperville, IL: Sourcebooks, Inc.

Soesbee, G. (2008). Plea, mistrial come from DUI trials. *The Newport Plain Talk*. Retrieved from http://newportplaintalk.com/story/25536 (accessed April 17, 2013).

State of Florida. (2013). 02-13: Chain of custody. Retrieved from http://www.fdle.state.fl.us/Content/getdoc/9de70859-0791-4811-a0e8-191d3d15d700/02-13----Chain-of-Custody.aspx (accessed April 5, 2013).

State of Oregon. (2010). *Chain of custody* (p. 1). Retrieved from http://public.health.oregon.gov/laboratoryservices/laboratoryresponsenetwork/documents/cofcprocedure.pdf (accessed April 18, 2013).

Turvey, B. (2008). *Criminal profiling: An introduction to behavioral evidence analysis* (3rd ed., p. 178). San Diego, CA: Elsevier Publishing.

Appendix E: The Constitution of the United States of America*

> Don't interfere with anything in the Constitution. That must be maintained, for it is the only safeguard of our liberties.
>
> **—President Abraham Lincoln (Lincoln, n.d.)**

Commentary

The U.S. Constitution is a robust document that has survived and endured over two centuries of national change. The Constitution is the foundational document from which all U.S. law is derived and constrained. Its emergence necessitated approximately eight years of experience, change, debate, and discussion encompassing the years between 1781 and 1789 (McFerran, 2005). The U.S. Constitution succeeded the Articles of Confederation as the basis of American government and law. Since its origin, the Constitution has been amended formally more than "two dozen times" (Smith, 2011). Through time, its interpretation has changed in conjunction with events of national duress. For instance, its interpretation changed during the War between the States, the "Great Depression, and the Civil Rights Movement" (Smith, 2011). Regardless, the U.S. Constitution is a testament of longevity and affects American society during modern times. Figure E.1 shows the room of Independence Hall in which the U.S. Constitution was debated.

Constitution of the United States of America

Preamble to the Constitution of the United States of America

We the People of the United States, in Order to form a more perfect Union, establish Justice, insure domestic Tranquility, provide for the common defence, promote the general Welfare, and secure the Blessings of Liberty to ourselves and our Posterity, do ordain and establish this Constitution for the United States of America.

Articles of the Constitution of the United States of America

Article I

Section 1
All legislative Powers herein granted shall be vested in a Congress of the United States, which shall consist of a Senate and House of Representatives.

* This version represents the original form of the U.S. Constitution. It is taken from the National Archives, and the source materials, including additional commentaries, are available via National Archives (2012).

Figure E.1 Independence hall. (From http://law2.umkc.edu/faculty/projects/ftrials/conlaw/convention1787.html.)

Section 2

The House of Representatives shall be composed of Members chosen every second Year by the People of the several States, and the Electors in each State shall have the Qualifications requisite for Electors of the most numerous Branch of the State Legislature.

No Person shall be a Representative who shall not have attained to the Age of twenty five Years, and been seven Years a Citizen of the United States, and who shall not, when elected, be an Inhabitant of that State in which he shall be chosen.

Representatives and direct Taxes shall be apportioned among the several States which may be included within this Union, according to their respective Numbers, which shall be determined by adding to the whole Number of free Persons, including those bound to Service for a Term of Years, and excluding Indians not taxed, three fifths of all other Persons. The actual Enumeration shall be made within three Years after the first Meeting of the Congress of the United States, and within every subsequent Term of ten Years, in such Manner as they shall by Law direct. The Number of Representatives shall not exceed one for every thirty Thousand, but each State shall have at Least one Representative; and until such enumeration shall be made, the State of New Hampshire shall be entitled to chuse three, Massachusetts eight, Rhode-Island and Providence Plantations one, Connecticut five, New-York six, New Jersey four, Pennsylvania eight, Delaware one, Maryland six, Virginia ten, North Carolina five, South Carolina five, and Georgia three.

When vacancies happen in the Representation from any State, the Executive Authority thereof shall issue Writs of Election to fill such Vacancies.

The House of Representatives shall chuse their Speaker and other Officers; and shall have the sole Power of Impeachment.

Section 3

The Senate of the United States shall be composed of two Senators from each State, chosen by the Legislature thereof for six Years; and each Senator shall have one Vote.

Immediately after they shall be assembled in Consequence of the first Election, they shall be divided as equally as may be into three Classes. The Seats of the Senators of the first Class shall be vacated at the Expiration of the second Year, of the second Class at the Expiration of the fourth Year, and of the third Class at the Expiration of the sixth Year, so that one third may be chosen every second Year; and if Vacancies happen by Resignation, or otherwise, during the Recess of the Legislature of any State, the Executive thereof may make temporary Appointments until the next Meeting of the Legislature, which shall then fill such Vacancies.

No Person shall be a Senator who shall not have attained to the Age of thirty Years, and been nine Years a Citizen of the United States, and who shall not, when elected, be an Inhabitant of that State for which he shall be chosen.

The Vice President of the United States shall be President of the Senate, but shall have no Vote, unless they be equally divided.

The Senate shall chuse their other Officers, and also a President pro tempore, in the Absence of the Vice President, or when he shall exercise the Office of President of the United States.

The Senate shall have the sole Power to try all Impeachments. When sitting for that Purpose, they shall be on Oath or Affirmation. When the President of the United States is tried, the Chief Justice shall preside: And no Person shall be convicted without the Concurrence of two thirds of the Members present.

Judgment in Cases of Impeachment shall not extend further than to removal from Office, and disqualification to hold and enjoy any Office of honor, Trust or Profit under the United States: but the Party convicted shall nevertheless be liable and subject to Indictment, Trial, Judgment and Punishment, according to Law.

Section 4

The Times, Places and Manner of holding Elections for Senators and Representatives, shall be prescribed in each State by the Legislature thereof; but the Congress may at any time by Law make or alter such Regulations, except as to the Places of chusing Senators.

The Congress shall assemble at least once in every Year, and such Meeting shall be on the first Monday in December, unless they shall by Law appoint a different Day.

Section 5

Each House shall be the Judge of the Elections, Returns and Qualifications of its own Members, and a Majority of each shall constitute a Quorum to do Business; but a smaller Number may adjourn from day to day, and may be authorized to compel the Attendance of absent Members, in such Manner, and under such Penalties as each House may provide.

Each House may determine the Rules of its Proceedings, punish its Members for disorderly Behaviour, and, with the Concurrence of two thirds, expel a Member.

Each House shall keep a Journal of its Proceedings, and from time to time publish the same, excepting such Parts as may in their Judgment require Secrecy; and the Yeas and Nays of the Members of either House on any question shall, at the Desire of one fifth of those Present, be entered on the Journal.

Neither House, during the Session of Congress, shall, without the Consent of the other, adjourn for more than three days, nor to any other Place than that in which the two Houses shall be sitting.

Section 6

The Senators and Representatives shall receive a Compensation for their Services, to be ascertained by Law, and paid out of the Treasury of the United States. They shall in all Cases, except Treason, Felony and Breach of the Peace, be privileged from Arrest during their Attendance at the Session of their respective Houses, and in going to and returning from the same; and for any Speech or Debate in either House, they shall not be questioned in any other Place.

No Senator or Representative shall, during the Time for which he was elected, be appointed to any civil Office under the Authority of the United States, which shall have been created, or the Emoluments whereof shall have been encreased during such time; and no Person holding any Office under the United States, shall be a Member of either House during his Continuance in Office.

Section 7
All Bills for raising Revenue shall originate in the House of Representatives; but the Senate may propose or concur with Amendments as on other Bills.

Every Bill which shall have passed the House of Representatives and the Senate, shall, before it become a Law, be presented to the President of the United States: If he approve he shall sign it, but if not he shall return it, with his Objections to that House in which it shall have originated, who shall enter the Objections at large on their Journal, and proceed to reconsider it. If after such Reconsideration two thirds of that House shall agree to pass the Bill, it shall be sent, together with the Objections, to the other House, by which it shall likewise be reconsidered, and if approved by two thirds of that House, it shall become a Law. But in all such Cases the Votes of both Houses shall be determined by yeas and Nays, and the Names of the Persons voting for and against the Bill shall be entered on the Journal of each House respectively. If any Bill shall not be returned by the President within ten Days (Sundays excepted) after it shall have been presented to him, the Same shall be a Law, in like Manner as if he had signed it, unless the Congress by their Adjournment prevent its Return, in which Case it shall not be a Law.

Every Order, Resolution, or Vote to which the Concurrence of the Senate and House of Representatives may be necessary (except on a question of Adjournment) shall be presented to the President of the United States; and before the Same shall take Effect, shall be approved by him, or being disapproved by him, shall be repassed by two thirds of the Senate and House of Representatives, according to the Rules and Limitations prescribed in the Case of a Bill.

Section 8
The Congress shall have Power To lay and collect Taxes, Duties, Imposts and Excises, to pay the Debts and provide for the common Defence and general Welfare of the United States; but all Duties, Imposts and Excises shall be uniform throughout the United States;

To borrow Money on the credit of the United States;

To regulate Commerce with foreign Nations, and among the several States, and with the Indian Tribes;

To establish an uniform Rule of Naturalization, and uniform Laws on the subject of Bankruptcies throughout the United States;

To coin Money, regulate the Value thereof, and of foreign Coin, and fix the Standard of Weights and Measures;

To provide for the Punishment of counterfeiting the Securities and current Coin of the United States;

To establish Post Offices and post Roads;

To promote the Progress of Science and useful Arts, by securing for limited Times to Authors and Inventors the exclusive Right to their respective Writings and Discoveries;

To constitute Tribunals inferior to the supreme Court;

To define and punish Piracies and Felonies committed on the high Seas, and Offences against the Law of Nations;

To declare War, grant Letters of Marque and Reprisal, and make Rules concerning Captures on Land and Water;

To raise and support Armies, but no Appropriation of Money to that Use shall be for a longer Term than two Years;

To provide and maintain a Navy;

To make Rules for the Government and Regulation of the land and naval Forces;

To provide for calling forth the Militia to execute the Laws of the Union, suppress Insurrections and repel Invasions;

To provide for organizing, arming, and disciplining, the Militia, and for governing such Part of them as may be employed in the Service of the United States, reserving to the States respectively, the Appointment of the Officers, and the Authority of training the Militia according to the discipline prescribed by Congress;

To exercise exclusive Legislation in all Cases whatsoever, over such District (not exceeding ten Miles square) as may, by Cession of particular States, and the Acceptance of Congress, become the Seat of the Government of the United States, and to exercise like Authority over all Places purchased by the Consent of the Legislature of the State in which the Same shall be, for the Erection of Forts, Magazines, Arsenals, dock-Yards, and other needful Buildings;—And

To make all Laws which shall be necessary and proper for carrying into Execution the foregoing Powers, and all other Powers vested by this Constitution in the Government of the United States, or in any Department or Officer thereof.

Section 9

The Migration or Importation of such Persons as any of the States now existing shall think proper to admit, shall not be prohibited by the Congress prior to the Year one thousand eight hundred and eight, but a Tax or duty may be imposed on such Importation, not exceeding ten dollars for each Person.

The Privilege of the Writ of Habeas Corpus shall not be suspended, unless when in Cases of Rebellion or Invasion the public Safety may require it.

No Bill of Attainder or ex post facto Law shall be passed.

No Capitation, or other direct, Tax shall be laid, unless in Proportion to the Census or enumeration herein before directed to be taken.

No Tax or Duty shall be laid on Articles exported from any State.

No Preference shall be given by any Regulation of Commerce or Revenue to the Ports of one State over those of another; nor shall Vessels bound to, or from, one State, be obliged to enter, clear, or pay Duties in another.

No Money shall be drawn from the Treasury, but in Consequence of Appropriations made by Law; and a regular Statement and Account of the Receipts and Expenditures of all public Money shall be published from time to time.

No Title of Nobility shall be granted by the United States: And no Person holding any Office of Profit or Trust under them, shall, without the Consent of the Congress, accept of any present, Emolument, Office, or Title, of any kind whatever, from any King, Prince, or foreign State.

Section 10

No State shall enter into any Treaty, Alliance, or Confederation; grant Letters of Marque and Reprisal; coin Money; emit Bills of Credit; make any Thing but gold and silver Coin a Tender in Payment of Debts; pass any Bill of Attainder, ex post facto Law, or Law impairing the Obligation of Contracts, or grant any Title of Nobility.

No State shall, without the Consent of the Congress, lay any Imposts or Duties on Imports or Exports, except what may be absolutely necessary for executing it's inspection Laws: and the net Produce of all Duties and Imposts, laid by any State on Imports or Exports, shall be for the Use of the Treasury of the United States; and all such Laws shall be subject to the Revision and Controul of the Congress.

No State shall, without the Consent of Congress, lay any Duty of Tonnage, keep Troops, or Ships of War in time of Peace, enter into any Agreement or Compact with another State, or with a foreign Power, or engage in War, unless actually invaded, or in such imminent Danger as will not admit of delay.

Article II

Section 1

The executive Power shall be vested in a President of the United States of America. He shall hold his Office during the Term of four Years, and, together with the Vice President, chosen for the same Term, be elected, as follows:

Each State shall appoint, in such Manner as the Legislature thereof may direct, a Number of Electors, equal to the whole Number of Senators and Representatives to which the State may be entitled in the Congress: but no Senator or Representative, or Person holding an Office of Trust or Profit under the United States, shall be appointed an Elector.

The Electors shall meet in their respective States, and vote by Ballot for two Persons, of whom one at least shall not be an Inhabitant of the same State with themselves. And they shall make a List of all the Persons voted for, and of the Number of Votes for each; which List they shall sign and certify, and transmit sealed to the Seat of the Government of the United States, directed to the President of the Senate. The President of the Senate shall, in the Presence of the Senate and House of Representatives, open all the Certificates, and the Votes shall then be counted. The Person having the greatest Number of Votes shall be the President, if such Number be a Majority of the whole Number of Electors appointed; and if there be more than one who have such Majority, and have an equal Number of Votes, then the House of Representatives shall immediately chuse by Ballot one of them for President; and if no Person have a Majority, then from the five highest on the List the said House shall in like Manner chuse the President. But in chusing the President, the Votes shall be taken by States, the Representation from each State having one Vote; A quorum for this purpose shall consist of a Member or Members from two thirds of the States, and a Majority of all the States shall be necessary to a Choice. In every Case, after the Choice of the President, the Person having the greatest Number of Votes of the Electors shall be the Vice President. But if there should remain two or more who have equal Votes, the Senate shall chuse from them by Ballot the Vice President.

The Congress may determine the Time of chusing the Electors, and the Day on which they shall give their Votes; which Day shall be the same throughout the United States.

No Person except a natural born Citizen, or a Citizen of the United States, at the time of the Adoption of this Constitution, shall be eligible to the Office of President; neither shall any Person be eligible to that Office who shall not have attained to the Age of thirty five Years, and been fourteen Years a Resident within the United States.

In Case of the Removal of the President from Office, or of his Death, Resignation, or Inability to discharge the Powers and Duties of the said Office, the Same shall devolve on the Vice President, and the Congress may by Law provide for the Case of Removal, Death, Resignation or Inability, both of the President and Vice President, declaring what Officer shall then act as President, and such Officer shall act accordingly, until the Disability be removed, or a President shall be elected.

The President shall, at stated Times, receive for his Services, a Compensation, which shall neither be increased nor diminished during the Period for which he shall have been elected, and he shall not receive within that Period any other Emolument from the United States, or any of them.

Before he enter on the Execution of his Office, he shall take the following Oath or Affirmation:—"I do solemnly swear (or affirm) that I will faithfully execute the Office of President of the United States, and will to the best of my Ability, preserve, protect and defend the Constitution of the United States."

Section 2

The President shall be Commander in Chief of the Army and Navy of the United States, and of the Militia of the several States, when called into the actual Service of the United States; he may require the Opinion, in writing, of the principal Officer in each of the executive Departments, upon any Subject relating to the Duties of their respective Offices, and he shall have Power to grant Reprieves and Pardons for Offences against the United States, except in Cases of Impeachment.

He shall have Power, by and with the Advice and Consent of the Senate, to make Treaties, provided two thirds of the Senators present concur; and he shall nominate, and by and with the Advice and Consent of the Senate, shall appoint Ambassadors, other public Ministers and Consuls, Judges of the supreme Court, and all other Officers of the United States, whose Appointments are not herein otherwise provided for, and which shall be established by Law: but the Congress may by Law vest the Appointment of such inferior Officers, as they think proper, in the President alone, in the Courts of Law, or in the Heads of Departments.

The President shall have Power to fill up all Vacancies that may happen during the Recess of the Senate, by granting Commissions which shall expire at the End of their next Session.

Section 3

He shall from time to time give to the Congress Information of the State of the Union, and recommend to their Consideration such Measures as he shall judge necessary and expedient; he may, on extraordinary Occasions, convene both Houses, or either of them, and in Case of Disagreement between them, with Respect to the Time of Adjournment, he may adjourn them to such Time as he shall think proper; he shall receive Ambassadors and other public Ministers; he shall take Care that the Laws be faithfully executed, and shall Commission all the Officers of the United States.

Section 4

The President, Vice President and all civil Officers of the United States, shall be removed from Office on Impeachment for, and Conviction of, Treason, Bribery, or other high Crimes and Misdemeanors.

Article III

Section 1

The judicial Power of the United States shall be vested in one supreme Court, and in such inferior Courts as the Congress may from time to time ordain and establish. The Judges, both of the supreme and inferior Courts, shall hold their Offices during good Behaviour, and shall, at stated Times, receive for their Services a Compensation, which shall not be diminished during their Continuance in Office.

Section 2

The judicial Power shall extend to all Cases, in Law and Equity, arising under this Constitution, the Laws of the United States, and Treaties made, or which shall be made, under their Authority;—to all Cases affecting Ambassadors, other public Ministers and Consuls;—to all Cases of admiralty and maritime Jurisdiction;—to Controversies to which the United States shall be a Party;—to Controversies between two or more States;—between a State and Citizens of another State,—between Citizens of different States,—between Citizens of the same State claiming Lands under Grants of different States, and between a State, or the Citizens thereof, and foreign States, Citizens or Subjects.

In all Cases affecting Ambassadors, other public Ministers and Consuls, and those in which a State shall be Party, the supreme Court shall have original Jurisdiction. In all the other Cases before mentioned, the supreme Court shall have appellate Jurisdiction, both as to Law and Fact, with such Exceptions, and under such Regulations as the Congress shall make.

The Trial of all Crimes, except in Cases of Impeachment, shall be by Jury; and such Trial shall be held in the State where the said Crimes shall have been committed; but when not committed within any State, the Trial shall be at such Place or Places as the Congress may by Law have directed.

Section 3
Treason against the United States, shall consist only in levying War against them, or in adhering to their Enemies, giving them Aid and Comfort. No Person shall be convicted of Treason unless on the Testimony of two Witnesses to the same overt Act, or on Confession in open Court.

The Congress shall have Power to declare the Punishment of Treason, but no Attainder of Treason shall work Corruption of Blood, or Forfeiture except during the Life of the Person attainted.

Article IV

Section 1
Full Faith and Credit shall be given in each State to the public Acts, Records, and judicial Proceedings of every other State. And the Congress may by general Laws prescribe the Manner in which such Acts, Records and Proceedings shall be proved, and the Effect thereof.

Section 2
The Citizens of each State shall be entitled to all Privileges and Immunities of Citizens in the several States.

A Person charged in any State with Treason, Felony, or other Crime, who shall flee from Justice, and be found in another State, shall on Demand of the executive Authority of the State from which he fled, be delivered up, to be removed to the State having Jurisdiction of the Crime.

No Person held to Service or Labour in one State, under the Laws thereof, escaping into another, shall, in Consequence of any Law or Regulation therein, be discharged from such Service or Labour, but shall be delivered up on Claim of the Party to whom such Service or Labour may be due.

Section 3
New States may be admitted by the Congress into this Union; but no new State shall be formed or erected within the Jurisdiction of any other State; nor any State be formed by the Junction of two or more States, or Parts of States, without the Consent of the Legislatures of the States concerned as well as of the Congress.

The Congress shall have Power to dispose of and make all needful Rules and Regulations respecting the Territory or other Property belonging to the United States; and nothing in this Constitution shall be so construed as to Prejudice any Claims of the United States, or of any particular State.

Section 4
The United States shall guarantee to every State in this Union a Republican Form of Government, and shall protect each of them against Invasion; and on Application of the Legislature, or of the Executive (when the Legislature cannot be convened), against domestic Violence.

Article V

The Congress, whenever two thirds of both Houses shall deem it necessary, shall propose Amendments to this Constitution, or, on the Application of the Legislatures of two thirds of the several States, shall call a Convention for proposing Amendments, which, in either Case, shall be valid to all Intents and Purposes, as Part of this Constitution, when ratified by the Legislatures of three fourths of the several States, or by Conventions in three fourths thereof, as the one or the other Mode of Ratification may be proposed by the Congress; Provided that no Amendment which may be made prior to the Year One thousand eight hundred and eight shall in any Manner affect the first and fourth Clauses in the Ninth Section of the first Article; and that no State, without its Consent, shall be deprived of its equal Suffrage in the Senate.

Article VI

All Debts contracted and Engagements entered into, before the Adoption of this Constitution, shall be as valid against the United States under this Constitution, as under the Confederation.

This Constitution, and the Laws of the United States which shall be made in Pursuance thereof; and all Treaties made, or which shall be made, under the Authority of the United States, shall be the supreme Law of the Land; and the Judges in every State shall be bound thereby, any Thing in the Constitution or Laws of any State to the Contrary notwithstanding.

The Senators and Representatives before mentioned, and the Members of the several State Legislatures, and all executive and judicial Officers, both of the United States and of the several States, shall be bound by Oath or Affirmation, to support this Constitution; but no religious Test shall ever be required as a Qualification to any Office or public Trust under the United States.

Article VII

The Ratification of the Conventions of nine States, shall be sufficient for the Establishment of this Constitution between the States so ratifying the Same.

The Word, "the," being interlined between the seventh and eighth Lines of the first Page, the Word "Thirty" being partly written on an Erazure in the fifteenth Line of the first Page, The Words "is tried" being interlined between the thirty second and thirty third Lines of the first Page and the Word "the" being interlined between the forty third and forty fourth Lines of the second Page.

Attest William Jackson Secretary

Done in Convention by the Unanimous Consent of the States present the Seventeenth Day of September in the Year of our Lord one thousand seven hundred and Eighty seven and of the Independence of the United States of America the Twelfth. In witness whereof We have hereunto subscribed our Names,

Go. Washington
President and deputy from Virginia
Delaware
Geo: Read
Gunning Bedford jun
John Dickinson
Richard Bassett
Jaco: Broom
Maryland
James McHenry
Dan of St Thos. Jenifer
Danl. Carroll
Virginia
John Blair
James Madison Jr.
North Carolina
Wm. Blount
Richd. Dobbs Spaight
Hu Williamson

South Carolina
J. Rutledge
Charles Cotesworth Pinckney
Charles Pinckney
Pierce Butler
Georgia
William Few
Abr Baldwin
New Hampshire
John Langdon
Nicholas Gilman
Massachusetts
Nathaniel Gorham
Rufus King
Connecticut
Wm. Saml. Johnson
Roger Sherman
New York
Alexander Hamilton
New Jersey
Wil: Livingston
David Brearley
Wm. Paterson
Jona: Dayton
Pennsylvania
B Franklin
Thomas Mifflin
Robt. Morris
Geo. Clymer
Thos. FitzSimons
Jared Ingersoll
James Wilson
Gouv Morris

Preamble to the Bill of Rights

Congress of the United States begun and held at the City of New-York, on Wednesday the fourth of March, one thousand seven hundred and eighty nine.

THE Conventions of a number of the States, having at the time of their adopting the Constitution, expressed a desire, in order to prevent misconstruction or abuse of its powers, that further declaratory and restrictive clauses should be added: And as extending the ground of public confidence in the Government, will best ensure the beneficent ends of its institution.

RESOLVED by the Senate and House of Representatives of the United States of America, in Congress assembled, two thirds of both Houses concurring, that the following Articles be proposed to the Legislatures of the several States, as amendments to the Constitution of the United States, all, or any of which Articles, when ratified by three fourths of the said Legislatures, to be valid to all intents and purposes, as part of the said Constitution; viz.

ARTICLES in addition to, and Amendment of the Constitution of the United States of America, proposed by Congress, and ratified by the Legislatures of the several States, pursuant to the fifth Article of the original Constitution.

Amendments to the Constitution of the United States of America*

Amendment I

Congress shall make no law respecting an establishment of religion, or prohibiting the free exercise thereof; or abridging the freedom of speech, or of the press; or the right of the people peaceably to assemble, and to petition the Government for a redress of grievances.

Amendment II

A well regulated Militia, being necessary to the security of a free State, the right of the people to keep and bear Arms, shall not be infringed.

Amendment III

No Soldier shall, in time of peace be quartered in any house, without the consent of the Owner, nor in time of war, but in a manner to be prescribed by law.

Amendment IV

The right of the people to be secure in their persons, houses, papers, and effects, against unreasonable searches and seizures, shall not be violated, and no Warrants shall issue, but upon probable cause, supported by Oath or affirmation, and particularly describing the place to be searched, and the persons or things to be seized.

Amendment V

No person shall be held to answer for a capital, or otherwise infamous crime, unless on a presentment or indictment of a Grand Jury, except in cases arising in the land or naval forces, or in the Militia, when in actual service in time of War or public danger; nor shall any person be subject for the same offence to be twice put in jeopardy of life or limb; nor shall be compelled in any criminal case to be a witness against himself, nor be deprived of life, liberty, or property, without due process of law; nor shall private property be taken for public use, without just compensation.

Amendment VI

In all criminal prosecutions, the accused shall enjoy the right to a speedy and public trial, by an impartial jury of the State and district wherein the crime shall have been committed, which district shall have been previously ascertained by law, and to be informed of the nature and cause of the accusation; to be confronted with the witnesses against him; to have compulsory process for obtaining witnesses in his favor, and to have the Assistance of Counsel for his defence.

Amendment VII

In Suits at common law, where the value in controversy shall exceed twenty dollars, the right of trial by jury shall be preserved, and no fact tried by a jury, shall be otherwise re-examined in any Court of the United States, than according to the rules of the common law.

Amendment VIII

Excessive bail shall not be required, nor excessive fines imposed, nor cruel and unusual punishments inflicted.

* The text is a transcription of the first ten amendments to the Constitution in their original form. These amendments were ratified December 15, 1791, and form what is known as the "Bill of Rights."

Amendment IX

The enumeration in the Constitution, of certain rights, shall not be construed to deny or disparage others retained by the people.

Amendment X

The powers not delegated to the United States by the Constitution, nor prohibited by it to the States, are reserved to the States respectively, or to the people.

Amendment XI

Passed by Congress March 4, 1794. Ratified February 7, 1795.

Note: Article III, section 2, of the Constitution was modified by amendment 11.

The Judicial power of the United States shall not be construed to extend to any suit in law or equity, commenced or prosecuted against one of the United States by Citizens of another State, or by Citizens or Subjects of any Foreign State.

Amendment XII

Passed by Congress December 9, 1803. Ratified June 15, 1804.

Note: A portion of Article II, section 1 of the Constitution was superseded by the 12th amendment.

The Electors shall meet in their respective states and vote by ballot for President and Vice-President, one of whom, at least, shall not be an inhabitant of the same state with themselves; they shall name in their ballots the person voted for as President, and in distinct ballots the person voted for as Vice-President, and they shall make distinct lists of all persons voted for as President, and of all persons voted for as Vice-President, and of the number of votes for each, which lists they shall sign and certify, and transmit sealed to the seat of the government of the United States, directed to the President of the Senate;—the President of the Senate shall, in the presence of the Senate and House of Representatives, open all the certificates and the votes shall then be counted;—The person having the greatest number of votes for President, shall be the President, if such number be a majority of the whole number of Electors appointed; and if no person have such majority, then from the persons having the highest numbers not exceeding three on the list of those voted for as President, the House of Representatives shall choose immediately, by ballot, the President. But in choosing the President, the votes shall be taken by states, the representation from each state having one vote; a quorum for this purpose shall consist of a member or members from two-thirds of the states, and a majority of all the states shall be necessary to a choice. [And if the House of Representatives shall not choose a President whenever the right of choice shall devolve upon them, before the fourth day of March next following, then the Vice-President shall act as President, as in case of the death or other constitutional disability of the President.—]* The person having the greatest number of votes as Vice-President, shall be the Vice-President, if such number be a majority of the whole number of Electors appointed, and if no person have a majority, then from the two highest numbers on the list, the Senate shall choose the Vice-President; a quorum for the purpose shall consist of two-thirds of the whole number of Senators, and a majority of the whole number shall be necessary to a choice. But no person constitutionally ineligible to the office of President shall be eligible to that of Vice-President of the United States.

**Superseded by section 3 of the 20th amendment.*

Amendment XIII

Passed by Congress January 31, 1865. Ratified December 6, 1865.

Note: A portion of Article IV, section 2, of the Constitution was superseded by the 13th amendment.

Section 1
Neither slavery nor involuntary servitude, except as a punishment for crime whereof the party shall have been duly convicted, shall exist within the United States, or any place subject to their jurisdiction.

Section 2
Congress shall have power to enforce this article by appropriate legislation.

Amendment XIV

Passed by Congress June 13, 1866. Ratified July 9, 1868.

Note: Article I, section 2, of the Constitution was modified by section 2 of the 14th amendment.

Section 1
All persons born or naturalized in the United States, and subject to the jurisdiction thereof, are citizens of the United States and of the State wherein they reside. No State shall make or enforce any law which shall abridge the privileges or immunities of citizens of the United States; nor shall any State deprive any person of life, liberty, or property, without due process of law; nor deny to any person within its jurisdiction the equal protection of the laws.

Section 2
Representatives shall be apportioned among the several States according to their respective numbers, counting the whole number of persons in each State, excluding Indians not taxed. But when the right to vote at any election for the choice of electors for President and Vice-President of the United States, Representatives in Congress, the Executive and Judicial officers of a State, or the members of the Legislature thereof, is denied to any of the male inhabitants of such State, being twenty-one years of age,* and citizens of the United States, or in any way abridged, except for participation in rebellion, or other crime, the basis of representation therein shall be reduced in the proportion which the number of such male citizens shall bear to the whole number of male citizens twenty-one years of age in such State.

Section 3
No person shall be a Senator or Representative in Congress, or elector of President and Vice-President, or hold any office, civil or military, under the United States, or under any State, who, having previously taken an oath, as a member of Congress, or as an officer of the United States, or as a member of any State legislature, or as an executive or judicial officer of any State, to support the Constitution of the United States, shall have engaged in insurrection or rebellion against the same, or given aid or comfort to the enemies thereof. But Congress may by a vote of two-thirds of each House, remove such disability.

Section 4
The validity of the public debt of the United States, authorized by law, including debts incurred for payment of pensions and bounties for services in suppressing insurrection or rebellion, shall not be questioned. But neither the United States nor any State shall assume or pay any debt or obligation incurred in aid of insurrection or rebellion against the United

States, or any claim for the loss or emancipation of any slave; but all such debts, obligations and claims shall be held illegal and void.

Section 5
The Congress shall have the power to enforce, by appropriate legislation, the provisions of this article.

**Changed by section 1 of the 26th amendment.*

Amendment XV

Passed by Congress February 26, 1869. Ratified February 3, 1870.

Section 1
The right of citizens of the United States to vote shall not be denied or abridged by the United States or by any State on account of race, color, or previous condition of servitude—

Section 2
The Congress shall have the power to enforce this article by appropriate legislation.

Amendment XVI

Passed by Congress July 2, 1909. Ratified February 3, 1913.

Note: Article I, section 9, of the Constitution was modified by amendment 16.

The Congress shall have power to lay and collect taxes on incomes, from whatever source derived, without apportionment among the several States, and without regard to any census or enumeration.

Amendment XVII

Passed by Congress May 13, 1912. Ratified April 8, 1913.

Note: Article I, section 3, of the Constitution was modified by the 17th amendment.

The Senate of the United States shall be composed of two Senators from each State, elected by the people thereof, for six years; and each Senator shall have one vote. The electors in each State shall have the qualifications requisite for electors of the most numerous branch of the State legislatures.

When vacancies happen in the representation of any State in the Senate, the executive authority of such State shall issue writs of election to fill such vacancies: *Provided*, That the legislature of any State may empower the executive thereof to make temporary appointments until the people fill the vacancies by election as the legislature may direct.

This amendment shall not be so construed as to affect the election or term of any Senator chosen before it becomes valid as part of the Constitution.

Amendment XVIII

Passed by Congress December 18, 1917. Ratified January 16, 1919. Repealed by amendment 21.

Section 1
After one year from the ratification of this article the manufacture, sale, or transportation of intoxicating liquors within, the importation thereof into, or the exportation thereof from the United States and all territory subject to the jurisdiction thereof for beverage purposes is hereby prohibited.

Section 2
The Congress and the several States shall have concurrent power to enforce this article by appropriate legislation.

Section 3
This article shall be inoperative unless it shall have been ratified as an amendment to the Constitution by the legislatures of the several States, as provided in the Constitution, within seven years from the date of the submission hereof to the States by the Congress.

Amendment XIX

Passed by Congress June 4, 1919. Ratified August 18, 1920.

The right of citizens of the United States to vote shall not be denied or abridged by the United States or by any State on account of sex.

Congress shall have power to enforce this article by appropriate legislation.

Amendment XX

Passed by Congress March 2, 1932. Ratified January 23, 1933.

Note: Article I, section 4, of the Constitution was modified by section 2 of this amendment. In addition, a portion of the 12th amendment was superseded by section 3.

Section 1
The terms of the President and the Vice President shall end at noon on the 20th day of January, and the terms of Senators and Representatives at noon on the 3rd day of January, of the years in which such terms would have ended if this article had not been ratified; and the terms of their successors shall then begin.

Section 2
The Congress shall assemble at least once in every year, and such meeting shall begin at noon on the 3rd day of January, unless they shall by law appoint a different day.

Section 3
If, at the time fixed for the beginning of the term of the President, the President elect shall have died, the Vice President elect shall become President. If a President shall not have been chosen before the time fixed for the beginning of his term, or if the President elect shall have failed to qualify, then the Vice President elect shall act as President until a President shall have qualified; and the Congress may by law provide for the case wherein neither a President elect nor a Vice President shall have qualified, declaring who shall then act as President, or the manner in which one who is to act shall be selected, and such person shall act accordingly until a President or Vice President shall have qualified.

Section 4
The Congress may by law provide for the case of the death of any of the persons from whom the House of Representatives may choose a President whenever the right of choice shall have devolved upon them, and for the case of the death of any of the persons from whom the Senate may choose a Vice President whenever the right of choice shall have devolved upon them.

Section 5
Sections 1 and 2 shall take effect on the 15th day of October following the ratification of this article.

Section 6
This article shall be inoperative unless it shall have been ratified as an amendment to the Constitution by the legislatures of three-fourths of the several States within seven years from the date of its submission.

Amendment XXI

Passed by Congress February 20, 1933. Ratified December 5, 1933.

Section 1
The eighteenth article of amendment to the Constitution of the United States is hereby repealed.

Section 2
The transportation or importation into any State, Territory, or Possession of the United States for delivery or use therein of intoxicating liquors, in violation of the laws thereof, is hereby prohibited.

Section 3
This article shall be inoperative unless it shall have been ratified as an amendment to the Constitution by conventions in the several States, as provided in the Constitution, within seven years from the date of the submission hereof to the States by the Congress.

Amendment XXII

Passed by Congress March 21, 1947. Ratified February 27, 1951.

Section 1
No person shall be elected to the office of the President more than twice, and no person who has held the office of President, or acted as President, for more than two years of a term to which some other person was elected President shall be elected to the office of President more than once. But this Article shall not apply to any person holding the office of President when this Article was proposed by Congress, and shall not prevent any person who may be holding the office of President, or acting as President, during the term within which this Article becomes operative from holding the office of President or acting as President during the remainder of such term.

Section 2
This article shall be inoperative unless it shall have been ratified as an amendment to the Constitution by the legislatures of three-fourths of the several States within seven years from the date of its submission to the States by the Congress.

Amendment XXIII

Passed by Congress June 16, 1960. Ratified March 29, 1961.

Section 1
The District constituting the seat of Government of the United States shall appoint in such manner as Congress may direct:

A number of electors of President and Vice President equal to the whole number of Senators and Representatives in Congress to which the District would be entitled if it were a State, but in no event more than the least populous State; they shall be in addition to those appointed by the States, but they shall be considered, for the purposes of the election of President and Vice President, to be electors appointed by a State; and they shall meet in the District and perform such duties as provided by the twelfth article of amendment.

Section 2
The Congress shall have power to enforce this article by appropriate legislation.

Amendment XXIV

Passed by Congress August 27, 1962. Ratified January 23, 1964.

Section 1
The right of citizens of the United States to vote in any primary or other election for President or Vice President, for electors for President or Vice President, or for Senator or Representative in Congress, shall not be denied or abridged by the United States or any State by reason of failure to pay poll tax or other tax.

Section 2
The Congress shall have power to enforce this article by appropriate legislation.

Amendment XXV

Passed by Congress July 6, 1965. Ratified February 10, 1967.

Note: Article II, section 1, of the Constitution was affected by the 25th amendment.

Section 1
In case of the removal of the President from office or of his death or resignation, the Vice President shall become President.

Section 2
Whenever there is a vacancy in the office of the Vice President, the President shall nominate a Vice President who shall take office upon confirmation by a majority vote of both Houses of Congress.

Section 3
Whenever the President transmits to the President pro tempore of the Senate and the Speaker of the House of Representatives his written declaration that he is unable to discharge the powers and duties of his office, and until he transmits to them a written declaration to the contrary, such powers and duties shall be discharged by the Vice President as Acting President.

Section 4
Whenever the Vice President and a majority of either the principal officers of the executive departments or of such other body as Congress may by law provide, transmit to the President pro tempore of the Senate and the Speaker of the House of Representatives their written declaration that the President is unable to discharge the powers and duties of his office, the Vice President shall immediately assume the powers and duties of the office as Acting President.

Thereafter, when the President transmits to the President pro tempore of the Senate and the Speaker of the House of Representatives his written declaration that no inability exists, he shall resume the powers and duties of his office unless the Vice President and a majority of either the principal officers of the executive department or of such other body as Congress may by law provide, transmit within four days to the President pro tempore of the Senate and the Speaker of the House of Representatives their written declaration that the President is unable to discharge the powers and duties of his office. Thereupon Congress shall decide the issue, assembling within forty-eight hours for that purpose if not in session. If the Congress, within twenty-one days after receipt of the latter written declaration, or, if Congress is not in session, within twenty-one days after Congress is required to assemble, determines by two-thirds vote of both Houses that the President is unable to discharge the powers and duties of his office, the Vice President shall continue to discharge the same as Acting President; otherwise, the President shall resume the powers and duties of his office.

Amendment XXVI

Passed by Congress March 23, 1971. Ratified July 1, 1971.

Note: Amendment 14, section 2, of the Constitution was modified by section 1 of the 26th amendment.

Section 1

The right of citizens of the United States, who are eighteen years of age or older, to vote shall not be denied or abridged by the United States or by any State on account of age.

Section 2

The Congress shall have power to enforce this article by appropriate legislation.

Amendment XXVII

Originally proposed September 25, 1789. Ratified May 7, 1992.

No law, varying the compensation for the services of the Senators and Representatives, shall take effect, until an election of representatives shall have intervened.

References

Lincoln, A. (n.d.). Abraham Lincoln quotes. Brainyquote.com. Retrieved from http://www.brainyquote.com/quotes/authors/a/abraham_lincoln.html (accessed July 29, 2013).

McFerran, W. (2005). *Birth of the republic: The origin of the United States* (p. 127). Gretna, LA: Pelican Publishing.

National Archives. (2012). Constitution of the United States. *Charters of Freedom*. Retrieved from http://archives.gov/exhibits/charters/constitution_transcript.html (accessed December 19, 2012).

Smith, R. (2011). *The American anomaly: U.S. politics and government in comparative perspective* (2nd ed., p. 10). New York: Routledge Publishing.

Appendix F: Hand Signals and Body Signals

If you saw a heat wave, would you wave back?
—**Steven Wright (Wright, 2013)**

Objectives

The objectives of this appendix are to

- Introduce communication for marshalling aircraft
- Introduce communication for traffic control

Commentary

Many law enforcement and emergency service organizations incorporate some aspects of aviation when performing their duties and satisfying their tenets of mission. The types of aircraft often vary, and range from helicopters to light airplanes. These resources may be used for search and rescue and traffic monitoring along roadways. When performing their duties, aviation resources communicate with ground entities through the use of radio communications.

However, when aviation resources are not flying, they are on the ground. Moving an airplane or helicopter across an airfield necessitates communication. Aircraft marshalling is a communications method of using the hands and body to communicate with aircrew personnel to move aircraft within airfield settings. Figure F.1 shows a typical action of aircraft marshalling.

Aircraft marshalling occurs within both civilian and military environments. If one is observant when flying with commercial airlines, one may view marshalling when the airplane is departing the terminal and moving toward the runway area. Similarly, one may see someone communicating with a helicopter using marshalling messages. Aircraft marshalling incorporates a variety of signals. When marshalling, one normally uses bright, handheld batons. Figure F.2a through F.2g show the typical signals that are used for marshalling.

Aircraft marshalling is not the only form of communication that exists involving ground entities. Both civilian law enforcement personnel and military police often operate traffic control points (TCPs) for a variety of reasons. If stop signs do not exist or electric stoplights are malfunctioning (or absent) at an intersection, then the use of someone to direct traffic occurs. In some cases, TCPs may be used in conjunction with security checkpoints that necessitate the directing of traffic flows. Regardless of the event, the use of someone to direct traffic is not uncommon within society.

Figure F.1 Aircraft marshalling. (From http://www.afcent.af.mil/news/story.asp?id=123303743.)

(a)

	**1. Wingwalker/guide** Raise right hand above head level with wand pointing up; move left-hand wand pointing down toward body. Note.— This signal provides an indication by a person positioned at the aircraft wing tip to the pilot/ marshaller/ push-back operatorthat the aircraft movement on/off a parking position would b e unobstructed.
	**2. Identify gate** Raise fully extended arms straight above head with wands pointing up.
	**3. Proceed to next signalman or as directed by tower/ground control** Point both arms upward; move and extend arms outward to sides of body and point with wands to direction of next signalman or taxi area.
	**4. Straight ahead** Bend extended arms at elbows and move wands up and down from chest height to head.

Figure F.2 Marshalling signals. (a) Part 1.

(b)

5 a). Turn left (from pilot's point of view)

With right arm and wand extended at a 90-degree angle to body, make "come ahead" signal with left hand. The rate of signal motion indicates to pilot the rate of aircraft turn.

5 b). Turn right (from pilot's point of view)

With left arm and wand extended at a 90-degree angle to body, make "come ahead" signal with right hand. The rate of signal motion indicates to pilot the rate of aircraft turn.

6 a). Normal stop

Fully extend arms and wands at a 90-degree angle to sides and slowly move to above head until wands cross.

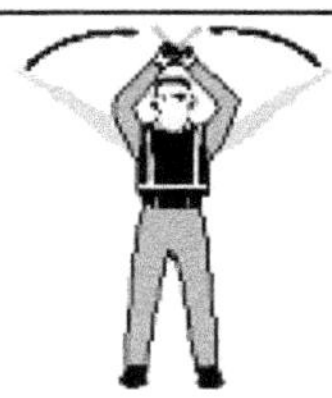

6 b). Emergency stop

Abruptly extend arms and wands to top of head, crossing wands.

7 a). Set brakes

Raise hand just above shoulder height with open palm. Ensuring eye contact with flight crew, close hand into a fist. Do not move until receipt of "thumbs up" acknowledgement from flight crew.

7 b). Release brakes

Raise hand just above shoulder height with hand closed in a fist. Ensuring eye contact with flight crew, open palm. Do not move until receipt of "thumbs up" acknowledgement from flight crew.

Figure F.2 (Continued) Marshalling signals. (b) Part 2.

(c)

	**8 a). Chocks inserted** With arms and wands fully extended above head, move wands inward in a "jabbing" motion until wands touch. Ensure acknowledgement is received from flight crew.
	**8 b). Chocks removed** With arms and wands fully extended above head, move wands outward in a "jabbing" motion. Do not remove chocks until authorized by flight crew.
	**9. Start engine(s)** Raise right arm to head level with wand pointing up and start a circular motion with hand; at the same time, with left arm raised above head level, point to engine to be started.
	**10. Cut engines** Extend arm with wand forward of body at shoulder level; move hand and wand to top of left shoulder and draw wand to top of right shoulder in a slicing motion across throat.
	**11. Slow down** Move extended arms downwards in a "patting" gesture, moving wands up and down from waist to knees.

Figure F.2 (Continued) Marshalling signals. (c) Part 3.

(d)

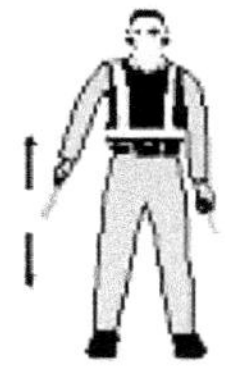	**12. Slow down engine(s) on indicated side** With arms down and wands toward ground, wave either *right* or *left* wand up and down indicating engine(s) on *left* or *right* side respectively should be slowed down.
	**13. Move back** With arms in front of body at waist height, rotate arms in a forward motion. To stop rearward movement, use signal 6 a) or 6 b).
	**14 a). Turns while backing (for tail to starboard)** Point left arm with wand down and bring right arm from overhead vertical position to horizontal forward position, repeating right-arm movement.
	**14 b). Turns while backing (for tail to port)** Point right arm with wand down and bring left arm from overhead vertical position to horizontal forward position, repeating left-arm movement.
	**15. Affirmative/all clear** Raise right arm to head level with wand pointing up or display hand with "thumbs up"; left arm remains at side by knee.

Figure F.2 (Continued) Marshalling signals. (d) Part 4.

(e)

16. Hover

Fully extend arms and wands at a 90-degree angle to sides.

17. Move upwards

Fully extend arms and wands at a 90-degree angle to sides and, with palms turned up, move hands upwards. Speed of movement indicates rate of ascent.

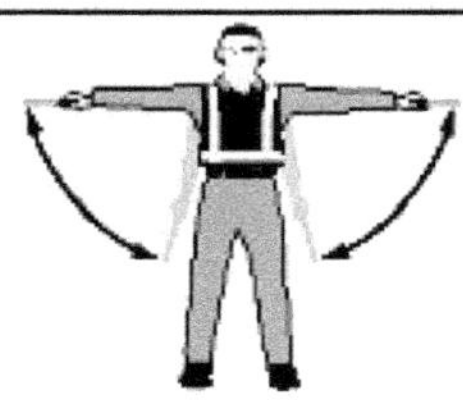

18. Move downwards

Fully extend arms and wands at a 90-degree angle to sides and, with palms turned down, move hands downwards. Speed of movement indicates rate of descent.

19 a). Move horizontally left (from pilot's point of view)

Extend arm horizontally at a 90-degree angle to right side of body. Move other arm in same direction in a sweeping motion.

19 b). Move horizontally right (from pilot's point of view)

Extend arm horizontally at a 90-degree angle to left side of body. Move other arm in same direction in a sweeping motion.

Figure F.2 (Continued) Marshalling signals. (e) Part 5.

(f)

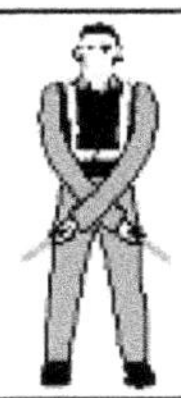	**20. Land** Cross arms with wands downwards and in front of body.
	**21. Fire** Move right-hand wand in a "fanning" motion from shoulder to knee, while at the same time pointing with left-hand wand to area of fire.
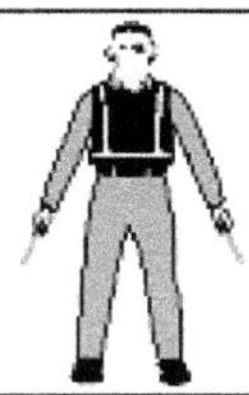	**22. Hold position/stand by** Fully extend arms and wands downwards at a 45-degree angle to sides. Hold position until aircraft is clear for next manoeuvre.
	**23. Dispatch aircraft** Perform a standard salute with right hand and/or wand to dispatch the aircraft. Maintain eye contact with flight crew until aircraft has begun to taxi.
	**24. Do not touch controls (technical/servicing communication signal)** Extend right arm fully above head and close fist or hold wand in horizontal position; left arm remains at side by knee.

Figure F.2 (Continued) Marshalling signals. (f) Part 6.

(g)

25. Connect ground power (technical/servicing communication signal)

Hold arms fully extended above head; open left hand horizontally and move finger tips of right hand into and touch open palm of left hand (forming a "T"). At night, illuminated wands can also be used to form the "T" above head.

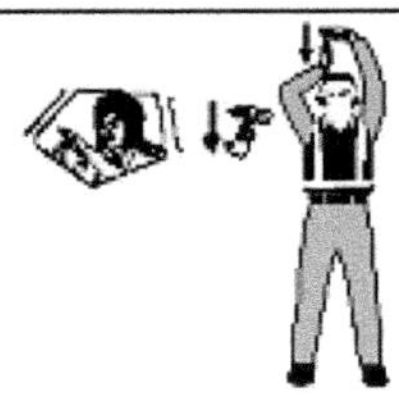

26. Disconnect power (technical/servicing communication signal)

Hold arms fully extended above head with finger tips of right hand touching open horizontal palm of left hand (forming a "T"); then move right hand away from the left. Do not disconnect power until authorized by flight crew. At night, illuminated wands can also be used to form the "T" above head.

27. Negative (technical/servicing communication signal)

Hold right arm straight out at 90 degrees from shoulder and point wand down to ground or display hand with "thumbs down"; left hand remains at side by knee.

28. Establish communication via interphone (technical/servicing communication signal)

Extend both arms at 90 degrees from body and move hands to cup both ears.

29. Open/close stairs (technical/servicing communication signal)

With right arm at side and left arm raised above head at a 45-degree angle, move right arm in a sweeping motion towards top of left shoulder.
Note.— This signal is intended mainly for aircraft with the set of integral stairs at the front.

Figure F.2 (Continued) Marshalling signals. (g) Part 7. (From www.faa.gov/about/initiatives/iasa/model_aviation/media/PART08is.doc.)

Directing traffic involves the use of a law enforcement officer who communicates with drivers via bodily motions and signals. Some personnel may use batons and whistles to embellish the directing of traffic. With respect to both civilian and military police entities, Figure F.3a and F.3b show examples of common hand and body signs that are necessary for directing traffic.

(a)

Stand facing traffic with the arms raised, palms open, in the same plane as the shoulders.

Stand facing traffic with the arm raised, palm open.

Figure F.3 (a) Traffic control signals.

(b)

Stand with the back to traffic, the arm raised, palm open. Rotate the upper body so the palm faces traffic.

Stand with the right side facing traffic, left arm extended, palm open. The right arm is parallel to the ground and bent with the palm at shoulder level.

Stand with the left side facing traffic. right arm extended, palm open. The left arm is parallel to the ground with the palm at shoulder level.

Figure F.3 (Continued) (b) Traffic control signals. (From http://library.enlisted.info/field-manuals/series-2/FM21_60/2CH.PDF.)

Terminology

Aircraft marshalling
Hand signal
Intersection
Marshalling signal
Signal
Traffic control point
Traffic direction

THOUGHT AND DISCUSSION QUESTION

1. This appendix introduced the basic hand signals that are necessary for marshalling aircraft and for directing traffic. Perform some research, and determine what other hand signals are available for communicating messages by both civilian law enforcement officers and military police entities.

Reference

Wright, S. (2013). Steven Wright quotes. Retrieved from http://www.brainyquote.com/quotes/authors/s/steven_wright_2.html (accessed September 22, 2013).

Index

Page numbers followed by f and t indicate figures and tables, respectively.

F

G

H

I

O

T

Y

Z

For Product Safety Concerns and Information please contact our EU
representative GPSR@taylorandfrancis.com
Taylor & Francis Verlag GmbH, Kaufingerstraße 24, 80331 München, Germany

www.ingramcontent.com/pod-product-compliance
Ingram Content Group UK Ltd.
Pitfield, Milton Keynes, MK11 3LW, UK
UKHW050801180926
475701UK00008B/1166
9780367669188